Starke's
International Law

Starke's International Law

Eleventh Edition

I A Shearer

Challis Professor of International Law, University of Sydney

Butterworths

London, Boston, Dublin, Durban, Edinburgh, Kuala Lumpur, San Juan, Singapore, Sydney, Toronto, Wellington

1994

United Kingdom	Butterworth & Co (Publishers) Ltd, Halsbury House, 35 Chancery Lane, LONDON WC2A 1EL and 4 Hill Street, EDINBURGH EH2 3JZ
Australia	Butterworths, SYDNEY, MELBOURNE, BRISBANE, ADELAIDE, PERTH, CANBERRA and HOBART
Canada	Butterworths Canada Ltd, TORONTO and VANCOUVER
Ireland	Butterworth (Ireland) Ltd, DUBLIN
Malaysia	Malayan Law Journal Sdn Bhd, KUALA LUMPUR
New Zealand	Butterworths of New Zealand Ltd, WELLINGTON and AUCKLAND
Puerto Rico	Butterworth of Puerto Rico, Inc, SAN JUAN
Singapore	Butterworths Asia, SINGAPORE
South Africa	Butterworths Publishers (Pty) Ltd, DURBAN
USA	Butterworth Legal Publishers, CARLSBAD, California and SALEM, New Hampshire

A CIP Catalogue record for this book is available from the British Library.

First edition	1947
Second edition	May 1950
Third edition	September 1954
Fourth edition	June 1958
Fifth edition	July 1963
Sixth edition	May 1967
Seventh edition	February 1972
Eighth edition	June 1977
Ninth edition	April 1984
Tenth edition	May 1989
Eleventh edition	September 1994

ISBN   0 406 01623 2 (Original Edition)
          0 406 05098 8 (Butterworth International Edition)

Printed by Mackays of Chatham plc, Chatham, Kent.

Preface

This eleventh edition of *Starke's International Law* is the first that has not been prepared by Professor Starke himself. Happily Professor Starke is still actively engaged in scholarship but, having passed his 80th year, he has decided to hand over the preparation of this edition to the present writer.

The first edition of this book, under the title *Introduction to International Law*, appeared in 1947; the last in 1989. It need hardly be said that the landscape of international law has changed greatly during those years, and markedly so in the wake of the collapse of the Soviet Union, which occurred just after the publication of the 10th edition of this book. The early euphoria which followed the apparent liberation of the powers of the United Nations Security Council from the crippling exercise of the veto during the Cold War era has lessened, but not entirely evaporated, in the face of the economic and political realities which impede the full realisation of the potential of the United Nations. A flow-on effect from the more active engagement of the United Nations with problems of the world has been evident throughout the entire body of international law. Respect for human rights and for the environment are especially important examples of areas of concern in which great advances have been made in recent years.

Professor Starke generously gave me a free hand with this edition. I wanted, however, to maintain the structure and flavour of the existing book which has secured a wide and loyal following since its first appearance. I have therefore made only those excisions, additions, and revisions which I thought necessary in order to take account of recent developments.

I desire to record my thanks to the staff of Butterworths for their helpfulness and care.

The effective date of completion of this edition was May 1994.

IA Shearer

Preface

Contents

Chapter 9

The law of the sea and maritime highways 218

Chapter 10

State responsibility 264

Chapter 11

Succession to rights and obligations 290

Chapter 12

The state and the individual 307

Chapter 13

The state and economic interests—international economic and monetary law 339

Chapter 14

Development and the environment 357

PART 4

INTERNATIONAL TRANSACTIONS 381

Chapter 15

The agents of international business: diplomatic envoys, consuls, and other representatives 383

Chapter 16

The law and practice as to treaties 397

PART 5

DISPUTES AND HOSTILE RELATIONS (INCLUDING WAR, ARMED CONFLICTS AND NEUTRALITY) 439

Chapter 17

International disputes 441

Table of cases

PAGE

C

of these early jurists reveal significantly that one major preoccupation of sixteenth century international law was the law of warfare between states, and in this connection it may be noted that by the fifteenth century the European Powers had begun to maintain standing armies, a practice which naturally caused uniform usages and practices of war to evolve.

By general acknowledgment the greatest of the early writers on international law was the Dutch scholar, jurist, and diplomat, Grotius (1583–1645), whose systematic treatise on the subject *De Jure Belli ac Pacis* (The Law of War and Peace) first appeared in 1625. On account of this treatise, Grotius has sometimes been described as the 'father of the law of nations', although it is maintained by some that such a description is incorrect on the grounds that his debt to the writings of Gentilis is all too evident[4] and that in point of time he followed writers such as Belli, Ayala and others mentioned above. Indeed both Gentilis and Grotius owed much to their precursors.

Nor is it exact to affirm that in *De Jure Belli ac Pacis* will be found all the international law that existed in 1625. It cannot, for example, be maintained that Grotius dealt fully with the law and practice of his day as to treaties, or that his coverage of the rules and usages of warfare was entirely comprehensive.[5] Besides, *De Jure Belli ac Pacis* was not primarily or exclusively a treatise on international law, as it embraced numerous topics of legal science, and touched on problems of theological or philosophic interest. Grotius's historical pre-eminence rests rather on his continued inspirational appeal as the creator of the first adequate comprehensive framework of the modern science of international law.

In his book, as befitted a diplomat of practical experience, and a lawyer who had practised, Grotius dealt repeatedly with the actual customs followed by the states of his day. At the same time Grotius was a theorist who espoused certain doctrines. One central doctrine in his treatise was the acceptance of the 'law of nature' as an independent source of rules of the law of nations, apart from custom and treaties. The Grotian 'law of nature' was to some extent a secularised version, being founded primarily on the dictates of reason, on the rational nature of men as social human beings, and in that form it was to become a potent source of inspiration to later jurists.

Grotius has had an abiding influence upon international law and international lawyers, although the extent of this influence has fluctuated at different periods, and his actual impact upon the practice of states was never so considerable as is traditionally represented. While it would be wrong to say that his views were

---

in Eastern Europe such as Paulus Vladimiri (1371– 1435) of the University of Cracow, should also not be overlooked. For discussion of the writings of Vittoria and Suarez, see Bernice Hamilton *Political Thought in Sixteenth Century Spain* (1963).

4.   As to the influence of Gentilis on Grotius, see Fujio Ito *Rivista Internazionale di Filosofia del Diritto* July–October 1964, pp 621–627. See also Lord McNair 'The Practitioners' Contribution to International Law' (1963) III Ind JIL 271 at 272–273. For a biography of Grotius see Liesje van Someren *Umpire to the Nations* (Dobson Books Ltd, London, 1965). The quatercentenary of his birth was celebrated in 1983.

5.   For a modern treatment for the laws and usages of war in the later Middle Ages, see M. H. Keen *The Laws of War in the Late Middle Ages* (1965); this may be usefully read in the light of what Grotius wrote.

always treated as being of compelling authority—frequently they were the object of criticism—nevertheless his principal work, *De Jure Belli ac Pacis*, was continually relied upon as a work of reference and authority in the decisions of courts, and in the textbooks of later writers of standing. Also several Grotian doctrines have left their mark on, and are implicit in the character of modern international law, namely, the distinction between just and unjust war,[6] the recognition of the rights and freedoms of the individual, the doctrine of qualified neutrality, the idea of peace, and the value of periodic conferences between the rulers of states. Nor should it be forgotten that for over three centuries Grotius was regarded as the historic standard-bearer of the doctrine of the freedom of the seas by reason of his authorship of the work, *Mare Liberum*, published in 1609.

The history of the law of nations during the two centuries after Grotius was marked by the final evolution of the modern state-system in Europe, a process greatly influenced by the Treaty of Westphalia of 1648 marking the end of the Thirty Years' War, and by the development from usage and practice of a substantial body of new customary rules. Even relations and intercourse by treaty or otherwise between European and Asian governments or communities contributed to the formation of these rules. Moreover the science of international law was further enriched by the writings and studies of a number of great jurists. Side by side there proceeded naturally a kind of action and reaction between the customary rules and the works of these great writers; not only did their systematic treatment of the subject provide the best evidence of the rules, but they suggested new rules or principles where none had yet emerged from the practice of states. The influence of these great jurists on the development of international law was considerable, as can be seen from their frequent citation by national courts during the nineteenth century and even up to the present time.

The most outstanding writers of the seventeenth and eighteenth centuries following the appearance of Grotius's treatise were Zouche (1590–1660), Professor of Civil Law at Oxford, as had been Gentilis (see above), and an Admiralty Judge, Pufendorf (1632–1694), Professor at the University of Heidelberg, Bynkershoek (1673–1743), a Dutch jurist, Wolff (1679–1754), a German jurist and philosopher, who constructed an original, systematic methodology of international law and the law of nature, Moser (1701–1795), a German Professor of Law, von Martens (1756–1821), also a German Professor of Law, and Vattel (1714–1767), a Swiss jurist and diplomat, who was greatly influenced by the writings of Wolff, and who perhaps of these seven men proved to have the greatest influence, and found the widest acceptance, wider even than that extended to Grotius. In the eighteenth century, there was a growing tendency among jurists to seek the rules of international law mainly in custom and treaties, and to relegate to a minor position the 'law of nature', or reason, as a source of principles. This tendency was extremely marked, for instance, in the case of Bynkershoek's writings and found expression particularly also in the works of Moser, and von Martens. There were, however, jurists who at the same time clung to the traditions of the law of nature, either almost wholly, or coupled with a lesser degree of emphasis upon custom and treaties as components of

6. Cf Joan D. Tooke *The Just War in Aquinas and Grotius* (1965).

international law. As contrasted with these adherents to the law of nature, writers such as Bynkershoek who attached primary or major weight to customary and treaty rules were known as 'positivists'.

In the nineteenth century international law further expanded. This was due to a number of factors which fall more properly within the scope of historical studies, for instance, the further rise of powerful new states both within and outside Europe, the expansion of European civilisation overseas, the modernisation of world transport, the greater destructiveness of modern warfare, and the influence of new inventions. All these made it urgent for the international society of states to acquire a system of rules which would regulate in an ordered manner the conduct of international affairs. There was a remarkable development during the century in the law of war and neutrality, and the great increase in adjudications by international arbitral tribunals following the *Alabama Claims Award* of 1872 provided an important new source of rules and principles. Besides, states commenced to acquire the habit of negotiating general treaties in order to regulate affairs of mutual concern. Nor was the nineteenth century without its great writers on international law. The works of jurists belonging to a number of different nations contributed significantly to the scientific treatment of the subject; among them were Kent (American), Wheaton (American), De Martens (Russian), Klüber (German), Phillimore (British), Calvo (Argentinian), Fiore (Italian), Pradier-Fodéré (French), Bluntschli (German), and Hall (British). The general tendency of these writers was to concentrate on existing practice, and to discard the concept of the 'law of nature', although not abandoning recourse to reason and justice where, in the absence of custom or treaty rules, they were called upon to speculate as to what should be the law.

Other important developments have taken place in the twentieth century. The Permanent Court of Arbitration was established by the Hague Conferences of 1899 and 1907. The Permanent Court of International Justice was set up in 1921 as an authoritative international judicial tribunal, and was succeeded in 1946 by the present International Court of Justice. Then there has been the creation of permanent international organisations whose functions are in effect those of world government in the interests of peace and human welfare, such as the League of Nations and its present successor, the United Nations, the International Labour Organisation, the International Civil Aviation Organisation, and others referred to in Chapter 20 of this book. And perhaps most remarkable of all has been the widening scope of international law to cover by multilateral treaty or convention not only every kind of economic or social interest affecting states (eg, patents and copyright), but also the fundamental rights and freedoms of individual human beings.

It is characteristic of the latter-day evolution of international law that the influence of writers has tended to decline, and that modern international lawyers have come to pay far more regard to practice and to decisions of tribunals. Yet the spelling out of rules of international law from assumed trends of past and current practice cannot be carried too far. This was shown at the Geneva Conference of 1958 on the Law of the Sea, at the Vienna Conferences of 1961, 1963, and 1968–1969 on, respectively, Diplomatic Relations, Consular Relations, and the Law of Treaties, and in the sessions 1973–1982 of the Third United Nations Conference on the Law of the Sea (UNCLOS III), when in a number of instances an apparent weight of practice in favour of a proposed rule of international law did not necessarily result in its general acceptance by the states represented at the Conferences. Nevertheless, 'natural law' writers have ceased to command the same degree of influence as formerly, perhaps because of the emergence of a number of states outside Europe which did not inherit doctrines of Christian civilisation such as that of 'natural law', or which possessed traditional cultures impelling them towards differing perceptions with respect to law and legal procedure. These new states (in particular the Afro-Asian group) have challenged certain of the basic principles of international law, stemming from its early European evolution in the seventeenth and eighteenth centuries, albeit they have to some extent recognised natural law in regard to certain concepts, eg, self-determination.[7] Moreover, many long-standing rules and concepts of international law have been subjected to severe strains and stresses under the impact of modern developments in technology, of modern economic exigencies, and—not least—the more enlightened sociological views and attitudes which prevail today.

Above all, there is the rapidly changing world situation to which the traditional system of international law must adapt itself. The era of East-West rivalry between blocs led by the two superpowers has given way to a more natural—in a sense—order of things in which states are asserting their individual self-interest. This development has its ugly side when it is impelled by ethnic or religious intolerance or by authoritarian ideologies. The notion of the Third World—a term coined at the Bandung Conference in 1955 to indicate states not aligned with either the Western or the Communist blocs—has given way to a category of 'developing states', within which exists a subcategory of desperately poor 'least developed states'. Trade has become the major concern of the developed states as they vie for markets and self advancement, not only in traditional goods and commodities but also in technology, in which intellectual and industrial property rights play an important role. Of particular concern to developing states is the increasing degree to which trade, development assistance, respect for human rights, and the protection of the natural environment have become linked, not always to their immediate advantage. New hope is emerging for the effective end of the threat of use of nuclear arms. Another positive sign is the more co-operative spirit demonstrated in the United Nations Security Council since the end of the Cold War which may enable the Charter provisions for collective world security to be realised more effectively. But structural and political problems remain to be solved within the United Nations system. Apart from this, international law is now called upon to find new rules or guidelines to govern the fields of nuclear and thermonuclear energy (indeed of all forms of energy, having regard to events since 1973, and the depletion of oil reserves), and

7. Reference should be made in this connection to the important activities in the field of study of international law, of the Asian-African Legal Consultative Committee, representing the Afro-Asian group of states. Certain sessions of this Committee have been attended by an observer from the International Law Commission, which has a standing invitation to send an observer. For the impact upon international law of the new Asian and other states, see Syatauw *Some Newly Established Asian States and the Development of International Law* (1961), S. P. Sinha *New Nations and the Law of Nations* (1967), R. P. Anand *New States and International Law* (1972), and F. C. Okoye *International Law and the New African States* (1972).

scientific research generally, to provide special régimes for various areas of international trade (eg the international sale and international sea-carriage of goods), to regulate state activities in the upper atmosphere and in the cosmos, to protect and control the natural environment,[8] to control the growth of world population (cf the 'Action Plan' adopted at Bucharest in August 1974, by the United Nations World Population Conference), to deal with the trans-border flow of computer data so as, inter alia, to protect privacy, to develop a general universal system to regulate key aspects of communication and dissemination of information, and to establish a new legal régime for the exploration and exploitation of the resources of the seabed beyond the limits of national sovereignty.

Present-day status of international law

International law, as we know it today, is that indispensable body of rules regulating for the most part the relations between states, without which it would be virtually impossible for them to have steady and frequent intercourse. It is in fact an expression of the necessity of their mutual relationships. In the absence of some system of international law, the international society of states could not enjoy the benefits of trade and commerce, of exchange of ideas, and of normal routine communication.

The present century has witnessed a greater impetus to the development of international law than at any previous stage of its history. This was a natural result of the growing interdependence of states, and of the vastly increased intercourse between them due to all kinds of inventions that overcame the difficulties of time, space, and intellectual communication. New rules had to be found or devised to meet innumerable new situations. Whereas previously the international society of states could rely on the relatively slow process of custom[9] for the formation of rules of international law, modern exigencies called for a speedier method of law-making. As a result, there came into being the great number of multilateral treaties of the last 80 years laying down rules to be observed by the majority of states—'law-making treaties' or 'international legislation', as they have been called. Apart from these 'law-making treaties' there was a remarkable development in the use of arbitration to settle international disputes, and at the same time the Permanent Court of International Justice came by its decisions to make an important contribution to the growth of international law. The mantle of the Permanent Court then descended upon its successor, the International Court of Justice. Nor should there be forgotten the work of codifying and progressively developing international law at present being sponsored by the United Nations with the expert aid of a body known as the International Law Commission, created in 1947.[10]

8.   Cf Richard A. Falk 'New Trends in International Law: The Challenges of the Ecological Age' (1980) 61 US Naval War College International Studies 122, especially at pp 128–129.
9.   Although treaties had nevertheless played an important role in the medieval law of nations and, also, in the relations between European states and nations or entities in Asia during the seventeenth, eighteenth and nineteenth centuries.
10. The Statute of the Commission was adopted by the United Nations General Assembly on 21 November 1947; for text of Statute, see *UN Year Book* 1947–1948 211, or the handbook, *The Work of the International Law Commission* (3rd edn, 1980) pp 103–108. The Commission, consisting originally of 15 members, appointed in their individual capacity as experts, first met in 1949. Subjects dealt with by the Commission since 1949 have included the basic rights and

It is true that in some quarters there is a tendency to disparage international law, even to the extent of questioning its existence and value. There are two main reasons for this:

a. the generally held view that the rules of international law are designed only to maintain peace; and
b. ignorance of the vast number of rules which, unlike the rules dealing with 'high policy', that is, issues of peace or war, receive little publicity.

Actually, however, a considerable part of international law is not concerned at all with issues of peace or war. In practice, legal advisers to Foreign Offices and practising international lawyers daily apply and consider settled rules of international law dealing with an immense variety of matters. Some of these important matters which arise over and over again in practice are claims for injuries to citizens abroad, the reception or deportation of aliens, extradition, questions of nationality, the extra-territorial operation of certain national legislation, and the interpretation of the numerous complicated treaties or arrangements now entered into by most states with reference to commerce, finance, transport, civil aviation, nuclear energy, and many other subjects.

Breaches of international law resulting in wars or conflicts of aggression and the inability of international law to cope with such endemic problems as disarmament, international terrorism and trafficking in conventional arms tend to receive adverse attention, and from them the public incorrectly deduces the complete breakdown of international law. The answer to this criticism is that even, for example, in time of war or armed conflict there is no absolute breakdown of international law, as many rules affecting the relations of belligerents inter se or with neutrals are of vital importance and to a large extent are strictly observed. Another consideration is worth mentioning, namely that in the case of war or armed conflict, the states involved seek to justify their position by reference to international law. This applies also in 'crisis' situations, short of war; for example, during the Cuban missile crisis of 1962, the United States relied to some extent on the Inter-American Treaty of Reciprocal Assistance of 1947 as a legal basis for its 'selective' blockade or 'quarantine' of Cuba.

It is possible to argue further that in municipal law (that is, state law), breaches, disturbances and crimes take place, but no one denies the existence of law to which all citizens are subject. Similarly, the recurrence of war and armed conflicts between states does not necessarily involve the conclusion that international law is non-existent.

---

duties of states, offences against the peace and security of mankind (the Nuremberg principles), reservations to conventions, the regime of the high seas, the law of treaties, arbitral procedure, nationality, statelessness, international criminal jurisdiction, the definition of aggression, state responsibility, diplomatic and consular practice, succession of states and governments, relations between states and inter-governmental organisations, the most-favoured-nation clause, jurisdictional immunities of states and state property, and the non-navigational uses of international watercourses. The Commission now consists of 34 members following an enlargement in 1981 of its composition (it had been previously enlarged in 1956 to 21, and then in 1961 to 25). As to the methods and procedures followed by the Commission in discharging its functions of the 'codification' and 'progressive development' of international law, see *The Work of the International Law Commission* (3rd edn, 1980) pp 11–21. For the records of its work see the *Yearbook of the International Law Commission* (1949-).

Finally, it is incorrect to regard the maintenance of peace as the entire purpose of international law. As one authority well said half a century ago,[11] its raison d'être is rather to:

'form a framework within which international relations can be conducted and to provide a system of rules facilitating international intercourse; and as a matter of practical necessity it has, and will, operate as a legal system even when wars are frequent.'

The same authority went on to say:

'It is, of course, true that the ideal of international law must be a perfectly legal system in which war will be entirely eliminated, just as the ideal of municipal law is a Constitution and legal system so perfect, that revolution, revolt, strikes, etc can never take place and every man's rights are speedily, cheaply, and infallibly enforced.'

Lapses from such ideals are as inevitable as the existence of law itself.

2. THEORIES AS TO THE BASIS OF INTERNATIONAL LAW

Much theoretical controversy has been waged over the nature and basis of international law.

Some discussion of the theories should help to throw light on many important aspects of the subject.

Is international law true law?

One theory which has enjoyed wide acceptance is that international law is not true law, but a code of rules of conduct of moral force only.[12] The English writer on jurisprudence, John Austin (1790–1859), must be regarded as foremost among the protagonists of this theory. Others who have questioned the true legal character of international law have been Hobbes, Pufendorf, and Bentham.

Austin's attitude towards international law was coloured by his theory of law in general. According to the Austinian theory, law stricto sensu was the result of edicts issuing from a determinate sovereign legislative authority. Logically, if the rules concerned did not in ultimate analysis issue from a sovereign authority, which was politically superior, or if there were no sovereign authority, then the rules could not be legal rules, but rules of moral or ethical validity only. Applying this general theory to international law, as there was no visible authority with legislative power or indeed with any determinate power over the society of States, and as in his time the rules of international law were almost exclusively customary, Austin concluded that international law was not true law but 'positive international morality' only, analogous to the rules binding a club or society. He further described it as consisting of 'opinions or sentiments current among

---

11. W. E. (Sir Eric) Beckett in (1939) 55 LQR 265.
12. For an excellent authoritative treatment of the problems concerning the legality of international law, see Dennis Lloyd *The Idea of Law* (Penguin revised edn, 1970) pp 37–40, 186–90, 224–5, and 238–9. Cf also passim L. Henkin *How Nations Behave* (2nd edn, 1979) and J. G. Merrills *Anatomy of International Law* (2nd edn, 1981). For a challenging analysis of international law and international society see P. Allott *Eunomia: New Order for a New World* (1990). See also A. Carty *The Decay of International Law?* (1986).

nations generally'.[13] This was in accordance with his classification of three categories, divine law, positive law and positive morality.

The reply to Austin's view is as follows:

a. Modern historical jurisprudence has discounted the force of his general theory of law. It has been shown that in many communities without a formal legislative authority, a system of law was in force and being observed, and that such law did not differ in its binding operation from the law of any state with a true legislative authority.

b. Austin's views, however right for his time, are not true of present-day international law. In the present century a great mass of 'international legislation' has come into existence as a result of law-making treaties and conventions, and the proportion of customary rules of international law has correspondingly diminished.[14] Even if it be true that there is no determinate sovereign legislative authority in the international field, the procedure for formulating these rules of 'international legislation' by means of international conferences or through existing international organs is practically as settled, if not as efficient, as any state legislative procedure.

c. Questions of international law are always treated as legal questions by those who conduct international business in the various Foreign Offices, or through the various existing international administrative bodies. In other words, the authoritative agencies responsible for the maintenance of international intercourse do not consider international law as merely a moral code. As, nearly a century ago, Sir Frederick Pollock well said:

> 'If international law were only a kind of morality, the framers of State papers concerning foreign policy would throw all their strength on moral argument. But, as a matter of fact, this is not what they do. They appeal not to the general feeling of moral rightness, *but to precedents, to treaties, and to opinions of specialists*. They assume the existence among statesmen and publicists of a series of legal as distinguished from moral obligations in the affairs of nations.'[15]

Certain countries indeed in practice expressly treat international law as possessing the same force as the ordinary law binding their citizens. Under the Constitution of the United States of America, for example, treaties are 'the supreme law of the land' (art VI, para 2). Judges of the United States Supreme Court—the highest Court of the land—have repeatedly recognised the constitutional validity of international law. In one case,[16] Marshall CJ declared that an Act of Congress 'ought never to be construed to violate the law of nations

---

13. See *Lectures on Jurisprudence* (4th edn, revised and edited by R. Campbell, 1873) Vol I, pp 187–188, 222, and also now W. L. Morison *John Austin* (1982) pp 64, 73, 78 and 99–100.
14. Indeed a significant number of customary rules of international law have now been formulated as rules in multilateral conventions; as, eg, in the case of the three Vienna Conventions of 18 April 1961, on Diplomatic Relations, of 24 April 1963, on Consular Relations, and of 22 May 1969, on the Law of Treaties, codifying respectively the customary rules as to diplomatic and consular privileges and immunities, and as to the law and practice of treaties, and in a number of provisions of the United Nations Convention on the Law of the Sea, opened for signature at Montego Bay, Jamaica, on 10 December 1982.
15. Pollock *Oxford Lectures* (1890) p 18.
16. *Murray v The Schooner Charming Betsy* 6 US (2Cranch) 64 (1804) at 118.

if any other possible construction remains'. In another case,[17] Gray J made the following remarks:

> '*International law is part of our law*, and must be ascertained and administered by the Courts of Justice of appropriate jurisdiction, as often as questions of right depending upon it are duly presented for their determination.'

Moreover, the legally binding force of international law has been asserted again and again by the nations of the world in international conference. To take one illustration, the Charter creating the United Nations Organisation, drawn up at San Francisco in 1945, is both explicitly and implicitly based on the true legality of international law. This is also clearly expressed in the terms of the Statute of the International Court of Justice, annexed to the Charter, where the court's function is stated as being 'to decide *in accordance with international law* such disputes as are submitted to it' (see art 38). One of the latest such multipartite manifestations supportive of the legality of international law was the Helsinki Declaration of 1 August 1975, whereby over 30 European states, the Holy See, the United States of America, and Canada subscribed to the following pledges: 'The participating states will fulfil in good faith their obligations under international law [including] those obligations arising from the generally recognized principles and rules of international law. . . . In exercising their sovereign rights, including the right to determine their laws and regulations, they will conform with their legal obligations under international law.'

In connection with the Austinian theory, it is useful to bear in mind the difference between rules of international law proper, and the rules of 'international comity'. The former are legally binding, while the latter are for the most part rules of goodwill and civility, founded on the moral right of each state to receive courtesy from others. The essence of these usages of 'comity' is thus precisely what Austin attributed to international law proper, namely a purely moral quality.[18] Non-observance of a rule of international law may give rise to a claim by one state against another for some kind of satisfaction, whether it be diplomatic in character or whether it takes the concrete form of indemnity or reparation. Non-observance of a usage of 'comity' on the other hand produces no strict legal consequences as regards the state withholding the courtesy; the state affected by the withdrawal of the concession may reply in the same kind and retract its own courtesy practices, but beyond this narrow reciprocity, there is no other legal action open to it.[19]

17. *The Paquete Habana* 175 US 677 (1900) at 700.
18. An illustration of such a usage of courtesy was the privilege accorded, within certain limits, to diplomatic envoys to import, free of customs dues, goods intended for their own private use. This courtesy privilege has now become a matter of legal duty upon the state of accreditation under art 36 (1) (b) of the Vienna Convention on Diplomatic Relations of 18 April 1961.
19. In this connection, reference should be made to judicial 'comity'. For example, British courts apply 'comity' when giving recognition to the legislative, executive, and judicial acts of other states. See *Foster v Driscoll* [1929] 1 KB 470. This application of judicial 'comity' is illustrated also by the recent trend of British courts to give effect to the principle of *forum non conveniens*, ie abstention from the exercise of local jurisdiction where a foreign court is the more appropriate forum for the relevant proceedings; cf *Spiliada Maritime Corpn v Cansulex Ltd* [1987] AC 460 (but not followed by the High Court of Australia in *Voth v Manildra Flour Mills Pty Ltd* (1990) 171 CLR 538). 'Comity', in its general sense, cannot, however, be invoked to prevent the United Kingdom, as a sovereign state, from taking steps to protect its own revenue laws from gross

This cumulative evidence against the position taken by Austin and his followers should not blind us to the fact that necessarily international law is *weak law*. Existing international legislative machinery, operating mainly through law-making conventions, is not comparable in efficiency to state legislative machinery. Frequently the rules expressed in such conventions are formulated in such a way as to give wide options or areas of choice to the states parties (see, eg, the Convention on the Settlement of Investment Disputes between States and Nationals of Other States, 18 March 1965). In spite of the achievement of the United Nations in re-establishing a World Court under the name of the International Court of Justice, there still is no universal compulsory jurisdiction for settling legal disputes between states. Finally, many of the rules of international law can only be formulated with difficulty, and, to say the least, are quite uncertain, being often incapable of presentation except as a collection of inconsistent state practices, while there are, in different areas of the subject, fundamental disagreements as to what the rules should be. In 1960, the second Geneva United Nations Conference on the Law of the Sea, with 87 states participating, failed to agree on a general rule fixing the width of the territorial sea, thus repeating the experience of the Hague Conference of 1930, while the Vienna Conference on the Law of Treaties of 1968–1969 revealed basic differences over the rules as to invalidity of treaties, and over the doctrine of jus cogens[20] (superior principles or norms governing the legality of treaty provisions). Deep-seated differences also emerged throughout the course of the sessions, extending from 1973 to 1982, of the Third United Nations Conference on the Law of the Sea (UNCLOS III), and even on the occasion at Montego Bay, Jamaica, on 10 December 1982, when the United Nations Convention on the Law of the Sea, adopted by the Conference, was opened for signature, with a number of states, including the United States of America, declining to sign the Convention (see Chapter 9 below).

Theories as to 'law of nature'

From earliest times,[1] as we have seen, the concept of the 'law of nature' exercised a signal influence on international law. Several theories of the character and binding force of international law were founded upon it.

At first the 'law of nature' had semi-theological associations, but Grotius to some extent secularised the concept, and as his followers later applied it, it denoted the ideal law founded on the nature of man as a reasonable being, the body of rules which Nature dictates to human reason. On this basic conception, theorists erected various structures, some writers adopting the view that international law derived its binding force from the fact that it was a mere

---

abuse; see decision of House of Lords in *Collco Dealing Ltd v IRC* [1962] AC 1 at 19, [1961] 1 All ER 762 at 765. Likewise, a charge of conspiracy to commit the offence of importing dangerous drugs into the United Kingdom, based on an alleged agreement made outside British jurisdiction, is not in violation of 'international comity' (*DPP v Doot* [1973] AC 807 at 834–835).

20. See pp 48–50 below.

1. The concept of a 'law of nature' goes back to the Greeks, and its history can be traced through the Roman jurists up to medieval times when it found expression in the philosophy of St Thomas Aquinas (1226–1274). See Barker, Introduction to Gierke *Natural Law and the Theory of Society* (transl 1934) Vol I, xxxiv–xliii.

application to particular circumstances of the 'law of nature'. In other words, states submitted to international law because their relations were regulated by the higher law—the 'law of nature', of which international law was but a part. The concept of the 'law of nature' underwent further specialisation in the eighteenth century. The later refinements can be seen in the following passage from Vattel's *Droit des Gens* (1758)[2]:

'We use the term necessary Law of Nations for that law which results from applying the natural law to nations. It is necessary, because nations are absolutely bound to observe it. It contains those precepts which the natural law dictates to States, and it is no less binding upon them than it is upon individuals. For States are composed of men, their policies are determined by men, and these men are subject to the natural law under whatever capacity they act. This same law is called by Grotius and his followers the internal Law of Nations, inasmuch as it is binding upon the conscience of nations. Several writers call it the natural Law of Nations.'

Vattel's views in this connection led him to hold that the assumption that one or more states could overview and control the conduct of another state would be contrary to the law of nature.

The general objection to theories based on the 'law of nature' is that each theorist uses it as a metaphor for some more concrete conception such as reason, justice, utility, the general interests of the international community, necessity, or religious dictates. This leads to a great deal of confusion, particularly as these interpretations of the 'law of nature' may differ so widely.

Traces of the 'natural law' theories survive today, albeit in a much less dogmatic form. Kelsen has said:[3] 'The theory of natural law, which was dominant throughout the 17th and 18th centuries, after relapsing during the 19th, has again in the 20th re-entered the foreground of social and legal philosophy, in company with religious and metaphysical speculation'. An approach kindred to that of 'natural law' colours the current movement to bind states by international Covenants to observe human rights and fundamental freedoms,[4] while to some extent a 'natural law' philosophy underlies the Draft Declaration on the Rights and Duties of States of 1949 prepared by the International Law Commission of the United Nations.[5] 'Natural law' was invoked also in order to justify the punishment of offenders, guilty of the grosser and more brutal kind of war crimes. Besides, there are the writers who adopt an international sociological standpoint, who treat the conception of 'natural law' as identical with reason and justice applied to the international community, and who look upon it as thereby elucidating the lines of the future development of international law.[6]

Because of its rational and idealistic character, the conception of the 'law of nature' has had a tremendous influence—a beneficent influence—on the

2. *Préliminaires*, para 7.
3. See his study, 'The Foundation of the Theory of Natural Law' in *Essays in Legal and Moral Philosophy* (1973) ch VI, 114 at 141; and cf ch II, 'The Idea of Natural Law', ibid, pp 27–60.
4. The United Nations General Assembly, on 16 December 1966, unanimously approved a Covenant on Economic, Social and Cultural Rights, and a Covenant on Civil and Political Rights. The two Covenants were opened for signature on 19 December 1966, and came into force in 1976.
5. See below, pp 89–90.
6. Cf Le Fur (1927) 18 Hague Recueil 263–442.

development of international law. If it has lacked precision, if it has tended to be a subjective rather than an objective doctrine, it has at least generated respect for international law, and provided, and still provides, moral and ethical foundations that are not to be despised. As against this, its main defect has been its aloofness from the realities of international intercourse shown in the lack of emphasis on the actual practice followed by states in their mutual relations, although the majority of rules of international law originally sprang from this practice.

Positivism

The theory known as 'positivism' commands a wide support, and has been adopted by a number of influential writers. We have already seen that Bynkershoek was an eighteenth-century 'positivist', but the modern 'positivist' theories have refinements and are expressed in generalisations not to be found in Bynkershoek's writings.

The 'positivists' hold that the rules of international law are in final analysis of the same character as 'positive' municipal law (ie state law) inasmuch as they also issue from the will of the state. They believe that international law can *in logic* be reduced to a system of rules depending for their validity only on the fact that states have consented to them.[7]

Positivism begins from certain premises, that the state is a metaphysical reality with a value and significance of its own, and that endowed with such reality the state may also be regarded as having a will. This psychological notion of a state-will is derived from the great German philosopher Hegel. To the state-will the positivists attribute complete sovereignty and authority.

Pursuant to their initial assumptions, the positivists regard international law as consisting of those rules which the various state-wills have accepted by a process of voluntary self-restriction (*Selbstbeschränkung*).[8] Without such manifestation of consent, international law would not be binding on the society of states. Zorn, one of the most characteristic of the positivists, indeed regarded international law as a branch of state law, as external public law (*äusseres Staatsrecht*), and only for that reason binding on the state.[9]

The positivists concede that the difficulty in the application of their theory relates to customary international law. They admit that sometimes it is impossible to find an express consent in treaties, state papers, public documents, diplomatic notes, or the like, to being bound by particular customary rules. They therefore, consistently with their consensual theory, argue that in such exceptional cases

7. This is the more specialised meaning of the term 'positivist'. In its broader sense, the term 'positivist' denotes a writer, such as Bynkershoek and others, who maintains that the practice of states (custom and treaties) constitutes the primary source of international law. Also, some 'positivists' held that the only true law, 'positive' law, must be the result of some externally recognisable procedure; see Ago 'Positive Law and International Law', 51 AJIL (1957) 691–733.

8. The *Selbstbeschränkung* theory was adopted by Jellinek in his work, *Die rechtliche Natur der Staatenverträge* (1880).

9. Another refinement of positivist theory is Triepel's view that the obligatory force of international law stems from the *Vereinbarung*, or agreement of states to become bound by common consent; this agreement is an expression of a 'common will' of states, and states cannot unilaterally withdraw consent.

principles of the Charter so far as may be necessary for the maintenance of international peace and security.

These objections to positivism are by no means exhaustive,[16] but they sufficiently illustrate the main defect of the theory—the fallacy of the premise that some consensual manifestation is necessary before international law can operate.

In spite of its many weaknesses, positivist theory has had one valuable influence on the science of international law. It has concentrated attention on the actual practice of states by emphasising, perhaps unduly, that only those rules which states do in fact observe can be rules of international law. This has led to a more realistic outlook in works on international law, and to the elimination of much that was academic, sterile, and doctrinal.

Sanctions of observance of international law

A controversial question is the extent to which sanctions, including sanctions by way of external force, are available under international law, to secure observance of its rules. At one extreme there is the view that international law is a system without sanctions. However, it is not quite true that there are no forcible means of compelling a state to comply with international law. The United Nations Security Council may, pursuant to Chapter VII of the United Nations Charter, in the event of a threat to the peace, breach of the peace, or act of aggression, institute enforcement action against a particular state to maintain or restore international peace and security, and to the extent that the state concerned is in breach of international law, this is in effect a form of collective sanction to enforce international law. Also, under article 94, paragraph 2 of the Charter, if any state, party to a case before the International Court of Justice, fails to perform the obligations incumbent upon it under a judgment rendered by the Court, the Security Council may upon application by the other state, party to the same case, make recommendations or decide upon measures to be taken to give effect to the judgment. It must be acknowledged, however, that the United Nations Charter does not otherwise allow the use of force, collectively or individually, for the enforcement of international law in general.[17] Under article 2, paragraph 4 of the Charter, member states are to refrain from the threat or use of force against the territorial integrity or political independence of any state, or in any other manner inconsistent with the Purposes of the United Nations. The right of self-defence permitted to member states by article 51 of the Charter

---

16. Other criticisms of the positivists are that they rely almost entirely on the state practice, including treaties, of European and American states, inter se, to the neglect of practice and treaties in the relations, prior to the twentieth century, between Western states and Afro-Asian countries, and, as well, that they would exclude any recourse by international tribunals to intangible sources of law, such as equitable principles and persuasive analogies derivable from state domestic laws.
17. See Kunz 'Sanctions in International Law' 54 AJIL (1960) 324–347; O. Schachter, *International Law in Theory and Practice* (1991), ch xi. United Nations 'peacekeeping' operations cannot, strictly speaking, be regarded as a category of sanctions for the observance of international law, although sometimes serving to prevent the occurrence of breaches of international law. The primary purpose of United Nations peacekeeping forces or peacekeeping missions is to restore or maintain peace, or to mitigate deteriorating situations, or to facilitate a settlement of a dispute likely to constitute a threat to the peace: see pp 590–592 below.

is only against an actual armed attack.[18] These provisions have restricted the liberty formerly enjoyed by states to use forcible measures, short of war, such as retorsion and reprisals (see Chapter 17, below), or to go further and resort to war in order to induce other states to fulfil their international obligations. Historically, war used to be, in a sense, the ultimate sanction by which international law was enforced, but upon its strict interpretation the Charter prohibits the unilateral application, without the authority or licence of the Security Council, of sanctions to enforce international law, and permits only sanctions, of the nature of enforcement or preventative action, duly authorised by the Security Council, in order to maintain or restore international peace and security. These may include, not only the actual use of force, but also economic sanctions (eg, the imposition of a collective embargo upon trade with a particular state or entity), as has occurred in such cases as South Africa, Rhodesia, Iraq, and Libya.[19] Moreover, since the critical point is the need for the Security Council's authority, it is not required that force be applied collectively by a number of states, for a single individual member of the United Nations,[20] or a group of particular members, may be authorised to take unilateral forcible action.

If the word 'sanctions' be taken in the larger sense of measures, procedures, and expedients for exerting pressure upon a state to comply with its international legal obligations, then the above-mentioned provisions of the United Nations Charter are not exhaustive of the sanctions which may become operative in different areas of international law. By way of illustration, reference may be made to the following instances:

a. Under the Constitution of the International Labour Organisation (see articles 24–34), a procedure is laid down for dealing with complaints regarding a failure by a member state to secure the effective observance of an International Labour Convention binding it; this can lead to a reference to a Commission of Enquiry, or if necessary to the International Court of Justice, and in the event of a member state failing to carry out the recommendations in the Commission's report or in the decision of the International Court of Justice, the Governing Body of the Organisation may recommend *'action'* to the International Labour Conference in order to secure compliance with the recommendations.[1]

b. Under the Single Convention on Narcotic Drugs of 30 March 1961 (see article 14), if any country or territory fails to carry out the provisions of the Convention, the aim of which is to limit the quantity of narcotic drugs in use to the amount needed for legitimate purposes, a body known as the International Narcotics Control Board is entitled to call for explanations

18. Or, it may be argued, against a clear and imminent threat of armed attack; see further below, ch 18.
19. These cases, and others, are described below, pp 586–590.
20. As in the case of the oil embargo against Rhodesia in 1966 when the United Kingdom was authorised by the Security Council to prevent ships from carrying oil destined for land-locked Rhodesia to ports in the neighbouring Portuguese colony of Mozambique, by force if necessary. In 1990 the United States, the United Kingdom, and other states co-operating with Kuwait in its self-defence against Iraq were authorised by the Security Council to use 'all necessary means' to expel Iraq from the territory of Kuwait: see further below, p 588.
1. Quaere whether 'action' could include economic sanctions; see Landy *The Effectiveness of International Supervision* (1966) p 178.

from the country or territory; should the explanations be unsatisfactory, the Board may call the attention of other competent United Nations organs to the position, and may go to the length of recommending a stoppage of drug imports or exports or both to and from the country or territory in default.

c.   The constituent instruments of certain international organisations provide that member states not complying with the basic principles laid down in these instruments may be suspended or expelled, or otherwise denied the benefits and privileges of participation[2] (see eg, article 6 of the United Nations Charter).

d.   An international legal obligation is sometimes enforceable through the procedures of domestic legal systems, subject to the appropriate sanctions applying under these systems; for example, under articles 54–55 of the Convention of 1965 on the Settlement of Investment Disputes between States and Nationals of Other States, each contracting state is to recognise an arbitral award made pursuant to the Convention as binding, and is to enforce the pecuniary obligations imposed by the award as if it were a final judgment of a court in that state.

e.   Acts by a particular state, in breach of international law, may sometimes be treated by other states as invalid and inoperative. In its Advisory Opinion of 21 June 1971, on the *Legal Consequences for States of the Continued Presence of South Africa in Namibia (South West Africa)*, the International Court of Justice ruled that South Africa's continued presence in Namibia (South West Africa) was illegal, and that member states of the United Nations were obliged to recognise the invalidity of South Africa's acts as to Namibia, and to refrain from acts and dealings with South Africa implying acceptance of the legality of its presence in, and administration of Namibia, or lending support or assistance to these.[3]

Notwithstanding the sanctions possible under the United Nations Charter, together with the range of pressures which may be applied to compel a state to comply with international law, it still remains true that the international community does not have available to it a permanent organised force for securing obedience to the law, similar to that which exists in a modern state. The question then is whether this complete absence of an organised external force necessarily derogates from the legal character of international law. In this connection, there is a helpful comparison to be made between international law and the canon law, the law of the Catholic Church. The comparison is the more striking in the early history of the law of nations when the binding force of both systems was founded to some extent upon the concept of the 'law of nature'. The canon law is like international law unsupported by organised external force, although there are certain punishments for breach of its rules, for example, excommunication

2.   See Joseph Gold in 66 AJIL (1972) 744–751, as to denials of benefits and declarations of ineligibility in the case of the International Monetary Fund where a member of the Fund fails to comply with its obligations. Note also the compulsory jurisdiction conferred on the European Court of Justice by arts 170 and 173 of the Treaty of Rome of 25 March 1957 (establishing the European Economic Community), enabling the Court to review the legality of acts of member states and of the Council and Commission, where it is alleged that there have been infringements of provisions of the Treaty.

3.   ICJ 1971, 16 at 54, 56.

and the refusal of the sacraments. But generally the canon law is obeyed because as a practical matter, the Catholic society is agreeable to abide by its rules. This indicates that international law is not exceptional in its lack of organised external force.

Nor should it be forgotten that there are tangible sanctions for those rules of international law, at least, which impose duties upon individuals. For example, persons who, contrary to international law, commit war crimes, are no less subject to punishment than those who are guilty of criminal offences under municipal law. Another illustration is that of the international law crime of piracy jure gentium; every state is entitled to apprehend, try, and punish (if convicted) persons guilty of this crime (see Geneva Convention on the High Seas of 29 April 1958, arts 19 and 21, the United Nations Convention on the Law of the Sea of 10 December 1982, arts 101–107, and Chapter 9 below). Similarly, under the Hague Convention of 16 December 1970 for the Suppression of Unlawful Seizure of Aircraft, hijacking and like acts endangering the safety of aircraft, and persons and property on aircraft, are made punishable by contracting States who are entitled to place offenders in custody and take other appropriate measures.[4]

It is clear from the above analysis of theories as to the basis of international law, that a complete explanation of its binding force, embracing all cases and conditions, is hardly practicable. Indeed, there is something pedantic in the very notion that such a comprehensive explanation is necessary or desirable.

Apart from the sanctions and pressures mentioned above, the main elements reinforcing the obligatory character of the rules of international law are the empirical facts that states will insist on their rights under such rules against states which they consider should observe them, and that states recognise international law as binding upon them.[5] Obviously, if states did not insist on respect for these rules, international law would not exist. The ultimate reasons that impel states to uphold the observance of international law belong to the domain of political science, and cannot be explained by a strictly legal analysis. These reasons include a wish to maintain a reputation for reliability, to play an influential role as a responsible member of the international community, and a desire to foster beneficial reciprocal links in trade, development assistance, investment, communications and tourism. In other words, to some extent at least, the problem of the binding force of international law ultimately resolves itself into a problem no different from that of the obligatory character of law in general.

4. See below, pp 213–217.
5. Cf Sir Gerald Fitzmaurice in (1956) 19 MLR 8–9.

or popularised maxims of law are not of themselves 'general principles', in this sense. The revised American Law Institute Restatement of the Foreign Relations Law of the United States (1986) has categorised these 'general principles' as a 'secondary source of international law' (see § 102).

On several occasions the former Permanent Court of International Justice found it necessary to apply or refer to such 'general principles'. Thus in the *Chorzów Factory (Indemnity) Case*, it applied the principle of res judicata and it referred to the 'general conception of law', that 'any breach of an engagement involves an obligation to make reparation'.[6] In the *Mavrommatis Palestine Concessions Case*, the Court referred to the 'general principle of subrogation',[7] and in the *Case of the Diversion of Water from the Meuse*, Judge Manley O. Hudson expressed the view that the Court might apply Anglo-American equitable doctrines as being 'general principles'.[8] But on at least one occasion, the Court refused to apply an alleged 'general principle'—in the *Serbian Loans Case* where it held that the principle in English law known as 'estoppel' was inapplicable.[9] On the other hand, the private law doctrine of trusts was considered as helpful in order to deal with certain questions relating to the Mandates and Trusteeship systems.[10] 'General principles' include procedural[11] and evidentiary[12] principles, as well as principles of substantive law, provided that these do possess some character of generality over and above the context of each particular legal system to which they belong in common. However, these 'general principles' are less a material 'source' of international law than a particular instance of judicial reason and logic which the most authoritative international tribunal of the day is specially enjoined to employ.[13]

Public: *Problèmes Théoriques* (Paris, 1965, tr from Russian) p 127. The principle of freedom of association for trade union purposes has been considered by some writers (eg Jenks) to have become a general principle of law by a process of 'emancipation' from its original treaty basis, through the impact of persistent action by the International Labour Organisation (ILO), penetrating the world's major legal systems; Alexandrowicz *The Law-Making Functions of the Specialised Agencies of the United Nations* (1973) pp 38, 156.

6.   (1928) PCIJ, Series A, No 17, p 29.
7.   (1924) PCIJ, Series A, No 2, p 28.
8.   (1937) PCIJ, Series A/B, Fasc No 70 pp 76 et seq.
9.   (1929) PCIJ, Series A, Nos 20–21, pp 38–9. Yet the International Court of Justice applied the principle of estoppel or preclusion in the *Case Concerning the Temple of Preah Vihear* ICJ 1962, 6, and also dealt with that principle in the *Barcelona Traction Case, Preliminary Objections* ICJ 1964, 6, where however the principle was held not to debar Belgium from proceeding. Note also the references to estoppel: (a) in the *North Sea Continental Shelf Cases* ICJ 1969, 3 at 26 in respect to the question whether a non-party had accepted a treaty provision; and (b) in the *Argentina-Chile Boundary Arbitration Award* (1966) 38 ILR 10, as to alleged estoppels by reason of representations regarding the course of boundary lines.
10.   See *Advisory Opinion on the Status of South West Africa* ICJ 1950, 146–150.
11.   In the *South West Africa Cases, 2nd Phase* ICJ 1966, 6 at 39, 47, the International Court of Justice applied the 'universal and necessary' principle of procedural law that there was a distinction between: (a) a plaintiff's legal right appertaining to the subject-matter of his claim; and (b) his right to activate a Court and the Court's right to examine the merits; and at the same time, it refused to allow anything like an actio popularis, ie a right in a member of a community to vindicate a point of public interest, albeit such action was known to certain domestic legal systems.
12.   See the *Corfu Channel Case* ICJ 1949, 4 at 18.
13.   For a discussion of the whole subject of 'general principles', see Bin Cheng *General Principles of Law as Applied by International Courts and Tribunals* (1953), and Schlesinger 51 AJIL (1957) 734–753.

From the theoretical standpoint, the provision for applying the 'general principles' has been regarded as 'sounding the death-knell' of positivism, inasmuch as it explicitly rejects the broad positivist view that custom and treaties are to be considered the exclusive sources of international law. It has also been said to resolve the problem of non liquet, ie the powerlessness of an international court to decide a case legally because of inability to find any rules of law that are applicable.[14] Finally, the provision may fairly be considered as not laying down a new rule, but as being merely declaratory of the long-established practice of international courts.

Each of the material 'sources' will now be discussed in turn.

1. CUSTOM[15]

Until recent times, international law consisted for the most part of customary rules. These rules had generally evolved after a long historical process culminating in their recognition by the international community. The preponderance of traditional customary rules was diminished as a result of the large number of 'law-making' treaties concluded since the middle of the last century, and must progressively decline in measure as the work of the International Law Commission in codifying and restating customary rules produces results in treaties such as the Vienna Conventions of 18 April 1961, of 24 April 1963, and of 22 May 1969, on Diplomatic Relations, Consular Relations, and the Law of Treaties respectively.[16] Yet according to views recently expressed by some writers, international custom may still have a significant role to play as a dynamic source of fresh rules of international law where the international community undergoes change in new areas untouched by treaties, judicial decisions or the writings of jurists.

The terms 'custom' and 'usage' are often used interchangeably. Strictly speaking, there is a clear technical distinction between the two. Usage represents the initial stage of custom. Custom begins where usage becomes general. Usage is an international habit of action that has not yet received full legal attestation. Usages may be conflicting, custom must be unified and self-consistent. *Viner's Abridgement*, referring to custom in English law, has the matter in a nutshell.[17]

---

14. Art 11 of the model Draft Articles on Arbitral Procedure drawn up by the International Law Commission of the United Nations in 1958 provides that an arbitral tribunal is not to bring in a finding of non liquet 'on the ground of the silence or obscurity of the law to be applied'.
15. See passim Wolfke *Custom in Present International Law* (1964); D'Amato *The Concept of Custom in International Law* (1971); Bin Cheng 'Custom: The Future of General State Practice in a Divided World' in Macdonald and Johnston (eds) *The Structure and Process of International Law* (1983) 513 et seq; M. E. Villiger *Customary International Law and Treaties* (1985). For a radical reassessment see M. Koskiennemi *From Apology to Utopia: The Structure of International Legal Argument* (1989).
16. In the *Gulf of Maine Boundary (United States/Canada) Case* ICJ 1984, 246, a special chamber of the International Court of Justice distinguished customary international law and treaties, declaring that the former could not be expected to provide equitable criteria and guidelines for practical methods to be followed in the delimitation of maritime boundaries to the same degree as treaty law.
17. Viner *Abridgement* vii, 164, citing *Tanistry Case* (1608) Dav Ir 28.

'A custom, in the intendment of law, is such a usage as hath obtained the force of a law.'

A customary element has, as we have seen, been a feature of the rules of international law from antiquity to modern times. In ancient Greece, the rules of war and peace sprang from the common usages observed by the Greek City States. These customary rules crystallised by a process of generalisation and unification of the various usages separately observed by each city republic. A similar process was observable among the small Italian states of the Middle Ages. When in the sixteenth and seventeenth centuries Europe became a complex of highly nationalistic, independent territorial states, the process was translated to a higher and more extensive plane. From the usages developed in the intercourse of modern European states there emerged the earliest rules of international law.

Customary rules crystallise from usages or practices which have evolved in approximately three sets of circumstances:

(a)   Diplomatic relations between states.
Acts or declarations by representatives of states, opinions of legal advisers to state governments, bilateral treaties,[18] and press releases or official statements by governments may all constitute evidence of usages followed by states. In this regard, both conduct and statements (written and oral) are on the same footing.

(b)   Practice of international organs.
The practice of international organs, again whether by conduct or declarations, may lead to the development of customary rules of international law concerning their status, or their powers and responsibilities. Thus in its Advisory Opinion holding that the International Labour Organisation had power to regulate internationally the conditions of labour of persons employed in agriculture, the Permanent Court of International Justice founded its views to a certain extent on the practice of the Organisation.[19] In a noted Advisory Opinion, the International Court of Justice based its opinion that the United Nations had international legal personality partly on the practice of the United Nations in concluding conventions.[20]

(c)   State laws, decisions of state courts, and state military or administrative practices.
A concurrence, although not a mere parallelism, of state laws or of judicial decisions of state courts or of state practices may indicate so wide an adoption of similar rules as to suggest the general recognition of a broad principle of law. This is particularly well illustrated by a decision of the United States Supreme Court, *The Scotia.*[1] The facts were as follows: In 1863 the British Government adopted a series of regulations for preventing collisions at sea. In 1864 the American Congress adopted practically the same regulations, as did within a

18. See also below, pp 39–41.
19. (1922) PCIJ, Series B, No 2, especially at pp 40–41.
20. *Advisory Opinion on Reparation for Injuries Suffered in the Service of the United Nations* ICJ 1949, 174 et seq.
1. (1871) 14 Wallace 170 at 188.

short time after, the governments of nearly all the maritime countries. Under these circumstances the *Scotia* (British) collided in mid-ocean with the *Berkshire* (American), which was not carrying the lights required by the new regulations. As a result, the *Berkshire* sank. The question was whether the respective rights and duties of the two vessels were determined by the general maritime law before the British regulations of 1863. It was held that these rights and duties must be determined by the new customary rules of international law that had evolved through the widespread adoption of the British regulations, and that therefore the fault lay with the *Berkshire*:

> 'This is not giving to the Statutes of any nation extra-territorial effect. It is not treating them as general maritime laws, but it is recognition of the historical fact that, by common consent of mankind, these rules have been acquiesced in as of general obligation. Of that fact we think we may take judicial notice. Foreign municipal laws must indeed be proved as facts, but it is not so with the law of nations.'

For evidence of state practices, it may be necessary to refer to official books or documents, such as military, naval, and air force manuals, or the internal regulations of each state's diplomatic and consular services. Comparison of these may indicate the existence of a practice uniformly followed by all states.

A general, although not inflexible, working guide is that before a usage may be considered as amounting to a customary rule of international law, two tests must be satisfied. These tests relate to: (i) the material, and (ii) the psychological aspects involved in the formation of the customary rule.

As regards the material aspect, there must in general be a recurrence or repetition of the acts which give birth to the customary rule. A German court held in the case of *Lübeck v Mecklenburg-Schwerin* [2] that a single act of a state agency or authority could not create any rights of custom in favour of another state which had benefited by the act; conduct to be creative of customary law must be regular and repeated.[3] Material departures from a practice may negative the existence of a customary rule, but minor deviations may not necessarily have this negative consequence.[4] Apart from recurrence, the antiquity of the acts may be also a pertinent consideration. Yet even a short time may be enough where the state practice has been extensive and for all practical purposes uniform (eg, as with evolution of the principle that a coastal state has the rights of exploitation, etc, with respect to its continental shelf; see below, pp 242–244).

The psychological aspect is better known as the *opinio juris sive necessitatis*, or as one authority[5] has termed it 'the mutual conviction that the recurrence . . . is the result of a compulsory rule'. This needs further explanation. Recurrence of the usage or practice tends to develop an expectation that, in similar future situations, the same conduct or the abstention therefrom will be repeated. When

2. See Annual Digest of Public International Law Cases 1927–8, No 3.
3. There are none the less certain instances of a single act creating a custom; eg, in the practice of international organisations, when a Resolution or decision may suffice to create a precedent for future action. In the *Asylum Case* ICJ 1950, 276–277, the International Court of Justice stressed the necessity for constancy and uniformity of usages or practices, before they can be recognised as custom. See also Kunz in 47 AJIL (1953) 662 et seq.
4. Cf *Anglo-Norwegian Fisheries Case* ICJ 1951, 116 at 138.
5. Judge Negulesco of the Permanent Court of International Justice, PCIJ (1927), Series B, No 14, at p 105. Cf Briggs 45 AJIL (1951) 728–731.

this expectation evolves further into a general acknowledgment by states that the conduct or the abstention therefrom is a matter both of right and of obligation,[6] the transition from usage to custom may be regarded as consummated. In this process, there is involved, to some extent, an element of acceptance or assent on the part of states generally. This conviction, this opinio juris, is a convenient if not invariable test that a usage or practice has crystallised into custom; there is, for example, an absence of opinio juris when states conform to a usage for motives of comity or courtesy only.[7] At the same time, the opinio juris is not an essential element of custom, but if it is present, it is helpful as distinguishing custom from a course of action followed as a matter of arbitrary choice or for other reasons.[8]

It would follow from the judgments of the Permanent Court of International Justice in the *Lotus Case*[9] that the opinio juris is a matter of inference from all the circumstances, not merely the detailed acts which constitute the material element of the alleged customary rule. One test for the existence of opinio juris is that set out in *West Rand Central Gold Mining Co v R.*[10] There the Court laid down that it must be proved by satisfactory evidence that the alleged rule 'is of such a nature, and has been so widely and generally accepted, that it can hardly be supposed that any civilised State would repudiate it'. This amounts to a test of 'general recognition' by the international society of states.

Such test of 'general recognition' underlies the provision[11] in the Statute of the International Court of Justice, under which the Court is directed to apply international custom 'as evidence of a general practice accepted as law', and is to be found also in art 53 of the Vienna Convention of 1969 on the Law of Treaties providing that a norm of jus cogens must be one 'accepted and recognised by the international community of States *as a whole*'.

The International Court of Justice has held, however, in the *Right of Passage over Indian Territory Case* (Portugal-India),[12] that a *particular* practice between two states only, which is accepted by them as law, may give rise to a binding customary rule between the two.

6. The necessity for customary rules to have binding quality was stressed by the International Court of Justice in the *Case Concerning Rights of Nationals of the United States of America in Morocco* ICJ 1952, 199–200. See also dicta of the Court in the *Asylum Case* ICJ 1950, 276–277. In the *North Sea Continental Shelf Cases* ICJ 1969, at 44, the Court stressed that opinio juris involved a feeling by states that they were conforming to what amounted to a legal obligation; habitual action in itself was not enough. In the *Nicaragua v The United States (Merits) Case* ICJ 1986, 14, the Court took the view that the general consent of member states of the United Nations to the adoption of resolutions of the United Nations General Assembly could be enough to serve to establish an *opinio juris* (in this instance the recognition of a customary rule prohibiting the use of force per se).
7. See p 18 above. In this connection, it is relevant to consider the acquiescence of other states, and the matter of protest or absence of protest by such states; cf Oppenheim *International Law* (9th edn, 1992) Vol I, pp 1194–1195. Bin Cheng, op cit, (n 15 above, in this chapter) p 548 takes the view, however, that *opinio juris* is in fact 'the essence' of general international law.
8. See Kelsen *General Theory of Law and State* (1961 edn) p 114.
9. (1927) PCIJ , Series A, No 10.
10. [1905] 2 KB 391 at 407.
11. See art 38 of the Statute.
12. ICJ 1960, 6. On 'regional customary law' see also the *Asylum Case* (Colombia/Peru) ICJ 1950, 266.

Judicial application of custom

Both national and international courts play an important role in the application of custom. Often it is claimed by one of the parties before the court that a certain rule of customary international law exists. The court must then investigate whether or not the rule invoked before it is a validly established rule of international custom, and in the course of this inquiry it examines all possible materials, such as treaties, the practice of states, diplomatic correspondence, decisions of state courts, and juristic writings. In certain cases, the court's function may be more than purely declaratory; while not actually creating new customary rules, the court may feel constrained to carry to a final stage the process of evolution of usages so generally recognised as to suggest that by an inevitable course of development they will crystallise into custom. To use Mr Justice Cardozo's words, by its *imprimatur* the Court will attest the 'jural quality' of the custom.[13]

Two instructive cases illustrating the judicial methods in the application of custom are *The Paquete Habana*,[14] a decision of the United States Supreme Court, and the *Lotus Case*,[15] a decision of the Permanent Court of International Justice.[16] In the former case, the Supreme Court, after a detailed investigation of the materials mentioned above, namely state laws and practices, treaties, writings of publicists evidencing usage, and decisions of courts, found that they uniformly proved the existence of a valid customary rule giving immunity to small fishing vessels, honestly pursuing their calling, from belligerent capture in time of war; in the latter case, the Permanent Court, following the same method, decided that there was no customary rule conferring exclusive penal jurisdiction in maritime collision cases (on the high seas) on the country of the ship's flag, as regards all incidents on the ship, because, of the relevant materials considered, state laws were not consistent, decisions of state courts conflicted, no uniform trend could be deduced from treaties, and publicists were divided in their views. Although the same method of detailed consideration of all materials was followed in both cases, weightier proof of the customary rule was required by the Permanent Court than by the Supreme Court, and owing to the absence of such proof the Permanent Court decided against the existence of the rule.

13. See *New Jersey v Delaware* 291 US 361 (1934), at 383–384.
14. 175 US 677 (1900).
15. (1927) PCIJ Series A, No 10.
16. These two cases should, however, be used with caution, as the customary rule found to exist according to *The Paquete Habana*, viz, the immunity of small fishing vessels from belligerent action in time of war is, semble, now obsolete, while the alleged customary rule of exclusive penal jurisdiction of the flag state in maritime collision cases (on the high seas) negatived in the *Lotus Case*, was adopted by the Geneva Conference of 1958 on the Law of the Sea, and formulated as art 11 para 1 of the Convention on the High Seas of 29 April 1958 (subject to the concurrent jurisdiction of the state of nationality over the persons responsible for the collision, etc), and a similar provision is now contained in art 97 of the United Nations Convention on the Law of the Sea of 10 December 1982. A more recent illustration of judicial investigation of the problem whether the practice of states conclusively reflects the existence of a customary rule of international law is the *North Sea Continental Shelf Cases* ICJ 1969, 3 where the International Court of Justice ruled against the existence of a customary rule that the division of a common continental shelf of adjacent countries must be effected according to the equidistance principle.

Multilateral law-making conventions may also be the means through which rules of customary international law crystallise and thus become binding even on states not bound contractually by the convention in question. For this very reason a conclusion that a convention, or other international instrument, has passed into customary international law is not lightly to be drawn. The conditions under which a principle or rule may thus be transformed in character from a purely conventional norm binding only the parties, to a generally binding norm were declared by the International Court of Justice in the *North Sea Continental Shelf Cases* as follows:

i.   the provision concerned should, at all events potentially, be of a fundamentally norm-creating character such as could be regarded as forming the basis of a general rule of law;
ii   there should be widespread and representative participation in the convention, including that of states whose interests are especially affected.
iii. within the period since the adoption of the convention, short or long as that may be, state practice, including that of states especially affected, should be both extensive and virtually uniform in the sense of the provision invoked, and demonstrate also a general recognition that a rule of law or legal obligation is involved (*opinio juris sive necessitatis*).[17]

An emerging rule of customary international law, which does not yet fully satisfy the above conditions but is regarded as likely to do so in time, is called *lex ferenda*, and described adverbially as being a rule *de lege ferenda*.[18]

The difficulties involved in extracting a customary rule or principle of international law from the mass of heterogeneous documentation of state practice, state judicial decisions, diplomatic history, etc, are not to be minimised, as the two cases just mentioned, amply illustrate. Not only, also, is the documentation itself frequently defective or incomplete, but the practice of some states is documented less adequately than that of other states. Moreover, the experience of the International Law Commission, and of the conferences called from 1958 onwards to consider the Commission's drafts, revealing as it did so much disagreement in areas where there were customary rules assumed to be generally recognised, should induce the utmost caution in drawing inferences as to the existence of such general recognition.

17. ICJ 1969, 3, at paras 71–81. In the *Nicaragua Case*, ICJ 1986, 14, at 98, the International Court stressed that it was not to be expected that state practice should be in rigorous conformity with the posited rule; it was sufficient that it be, in general, consistent with the rule, and that instances of conduct inconsistent with the rule should have been regarded at the time as breaches of it, not as indications of the recognition of a new rule. Moreover, where a state defends itself against criticism by appealing to exceptions or justifications contained within the posited rule, 'then whether or not the State's conduct is in fact justifiable on that basis, the significance of that attitude is to confirm rather than to weaken the rule.'
18. See the *Fisheries Jurisdiction Case* (Merits), ICJ 1974, 3, and note that the majority of the court considered that at that time preferential rights to living marine resources to 200 miles were of the character of *lex ferenda* only, whereas for Judges Forster, Bengzon, Jiménez de Aréchaga, Singh and Ruda, in their joint opinion, the expressions of delegates in favour of marine resource zones at UNCLOS III, then in progress, had already unsettled the earlier law, depriving it of opposability to Iceland.

By article 24 of its Statute of 21 November 1947, the International Law Commission of the United Nations was specifically directed to 'consider ways and means for making the evidence of customary international law more readily available',[19] and the Commission subsequently reported to the General Assembly of the United Nations on the matter.[20]

2. TREATIES

Treaties represent a second important material source of international law. That importance is increasing.

The effect of any treaty in leading to the formation of rules of international law depends on the nature of the treaty concerned. In this connection there is a useful, although not rigid, distinction between:

a. 'law-making' treaties, which lay down rules of universal or general application;

b. 'treaty-contracts' for example, a treaty between two or only a few states,[1] dealing with a special matter concerning these states exclusively. This corresponds to some extent to the distinction made by continental jurists between *Vereinbarungen* and *Verträge*.

a. 'Law-making' treaties

The provisions of a 'law-making' treaty are directly a source of international law. This is not so with the 'treaty-contracts', which simply purport to lay down special obligations between the parties only.

There has been an astonishing development of 'law-making' treaties since the middle of the nineteenth century. One authority[2] enumerated 257 such instruments concluded in the period 1864–1914. This rapid expansion of what

19. See Memorandum submitted by the Secretary-General of the United Nations 1949, 'Ways and Means of Making the Evidence of Customary International Law more readily Available'.

20. Among the Commission's recommendations was one that the General Assembly should call the attention of governments to the desirability of their publishing Digests of their diplomatic correspondence. The matter has also occupied the General Assembly at its sessions in 1950 and subsequent years. For the Commission's recommendations, see *Report* on the work of its second session (1950) and also *The Work of the International Law Commission* (3rd edn, 1980) pp 23–24. Since the time when the Commission's recommendations were made, the Secretary-General of the United Nations has been authorised by the General Assembly to issue most of the publications so recommended, as well as certain other publications pertinent to the recommendations. A number of countries have also commenced publishing or working on Digests or *Répertoires* of their practice, materials, etc relating to international law. In 1958 the General Conference of the United Nations Educational Scientific and Cultural Organisation (UNESCO) adopted two conventions with relevance to the subject, viz the Convention concerning the Exchange of Official Publications and Government Documents between States, and the Convention concerning the International Exchange of Publications.

1. In certain cases, a bilateral treaty may have a 'law-making' effect; eg, the now historic Hay-Pauncefote Treaty of 1901 between the United States and Great Britain, providing that the Panama Canal should be free and open to the vessels of all nations on terms of entire equality. See below, pp 261–263, as to the Panama Canal Treaties concluded in 1977, superseding the former treaties. See generally M. Villiger *Customary International Law and Treaties* (1985).

2. Hudson *International Legislation* (1931) Vol I, pp xix et seq.

has been called 'international legislation' was due to the inadequacy of custom in meeting the urgent demands of the international society of states for the regulation of its common interests. The urgency of these demands arose from the deep-rooted changes which were transforming the whole structure of international life. Industrial and economic developments were bringing states into closer intercourse with each other, and as international communications thus became more intimate, the range of interests springing from the relationships between states grew in size and complexity. In some regulation of these complex international activities every state had a direct interest which rose superior to considerations of national autonomy and independence.

A rapid glance at the principal 'law-making' treaties and conventions concluded before and after the Second World War amply confirms this trend. These instruments deal, for example, with Red Cross work, weights and measures, the protection of industrial property, the protection of submarine cables, the suppression of the slave trade, aerial navigation, international waterways, the pacific settlement of international disputes, international economic and monetary questions, control of narcotics, and nationality and statelessness, all subjects which called urgently for international statute law, and where to rely on the growth over several years of customary rules would have been impolitic.

A 'law-making' treaty cannot in the nature of things be one containing rules of international law always of universal application. We are forced to admit that 'law-making' treaties may be of two kinds:

a. enunciating rules of universal international law, eg, the United Nations Charter;
b. laying down general or fairly general rules.[3]

Then, even to the extent that a 'law-making' treaty is universal or general, it may be really a 'framework Convention', imposing duties to enact legislation, or offering areas of choice, within the ambit of which states are to apply the principles laid down therein; see, eg, articles 35–37 (provisions for co-operation in the penal repression of the illicit drug traffic) of the Single Narcotic Drugs Convention signed at New York, 30 March 1961. Besides, some multilateral treaties are to a large extent either confirmatory of, or represent a codification of customary rules, as for example the Vienna Convention on Diplomatic Relations of 18 April 1961.

The use of the term 'law-making' applied to treaties has been criticised by some writers on the ground that these treaties do not so much lay down rules of law as set out the contractual obligations which the states parties are to respect. In making such a criticism these writers overlook the number of conventions and international legislative instruments that are now *adopted* by the organs of international institutions, such as the General Assembly of the United Nations and the Conference of the International Labour Organisation, instead as before of being signed by the plenipotentiaries at diplomatic conferences. True it is that some of these conventions and instruments need to be ratified or accepted by

---

3. Cf distinction made by Quintana *Tratado de Derecho Internacional* (1963) Vol I, p 78. Cf also E. Vitta in *Annuaire Français de Droit International* (1960) pp 225–238.

states in order to come into force, but certain of them are not even expressed in the consensual form.

It may be that the designation 'normative treaties' is the more appropriate one. This would be capable of embracing:

1. Treaties operating as general standard-setting instuments, or which states apply either on a de facto or on a provisional basis; eg, the General Agreement on Tariffs and Trade of 30 October 1947, which conditions the trading relations of so many non-party states;
2. Unratified conventions, significant as agreed statements of principles to which a large number of states have subscribed;
3. 'Closed' or 'limited participation' treaties opened for signature by a restricted number of countries;
4. Treaties formulating regional or community rules;
5. Treaties creating an internationally recognised status or régime, operative, to some extent, erga omnes; eg, the Twelve-Power Treaty on Antarctica signed at Washington, 1 December 1959;
6. Instruments such as Final Acts, to which are annexed International Regulations intended to be applied by states parties as general rules inter se; eg, the International Regulations of 1960 for preventing collisions at sea, formulated by the London Conference of the same year on the Safety of Life at Sea, and being an annex to the Conference's Final Act.[4]

Inter-agency agreements, ie those between international organisations, and in addition, even agreements between an international organisation and a state, can also be 'normative' in the sense that they may lay down norms of general application in certain areas.

The mere fact that there are a large number of parties to a multilateral convention does not mean that its provisions are of the nature of international law, binding non-parties. Generally speaking, non-parties must by their conduct distinctly evidence an intention to accept such provisions as general rules of international law. This is shown by the decision of the International Court of Justice in 1969 in the *North Sea Continental Shelf Cases*,[5] holding on the facts that article 6 of the Geneva Convention of 1958 on the Continental Shelf, laying down the equidistance rule for apportionment of a common continental shelf, had not been subsequently accepted by the German Federal Republic—a non-party—in the necessary manifest manner.

b. Treaty-contracts

In contrast to 'law-making' treaties, treaty-contracts are not directly a 'source' of international law. They may, however, as between the parties or signatories thereto, constitute particular law; hence the use of the expression 'particular' conventions in article 38, paragraph 1a of the Statute of the International Court

---

4. These Regulations were superseded as a consequence of the effect of a convention adopted in 1972, upon the entry into force of that instrument. This convention was subsequently amended in 1981; see below, p 260.
5. ICJ 1969, 3 at 25–26.

of Justice.[6] Such treaties lead also to the formation of international law through the operation of the principles governing the development of customary rules. There are three cases to be considered:

i　A series or a recurrence of treaties laying down a similar rule may produce a principle of customary international law to the same effect. Such treaties are thus a step in the process whereby a rule of international custom emerges. This function treaties share with, for example, diplomatic acts, state laws, state judicial decisions, and the practice of international organs. An illustration is the series of bilateral extradition treaties concluded during the nineteenth century from which such general rules as those that persons accused or convicted of political offences are not extraditable, were deduced and were considered by some writers as being of general application. A further illustration is the number of identical provisions concerning consular privileges and immunities to be found in the numerous recent bilateral consular conventions and treaties, and which were used by the International Law Commission in 1960–1961 in drawing up its Draft Articles on Consular Relations,[7] which formed the basis of the later concluded convention of 24 April 1963.

ii.　It may happen with a treaty originally concluded between a limited number of parties only that a rule in it be generalised by subsequent independent acceptance or imitation. In this case, the treaty represents the initial stage in the process of recurrence of usage by which customary rules of international law have evolved. Thus, for instance, the rule 'free ships, free goods', ie that enemy goods carried on a neutral vessel are in general immune from belligerent action, first appeared in a treaty of 1650 between Spain and the United Provinces, and became established only at a much later period after a long process of generalisation and recognition.[8] In the *North Sea Continental Shelf Cases*,[9] the International Court of Justice expressed the view that before a treaty provision could generate such a process of evolution into custom, it should potentially be of a norm-creating character so as to be capable of maturing into a general rule of law. Apart from this, a widespread and representative participation in a treaty rule, inclusive of the states whose interests were specially affected, might be sufficient to mark completion of the process.

iii.　A treaty may be of considerable *evidentiary* value as to the existence of a rule which has crystallised into law by an independent process of development. Such effect is due to the special authority and solemnity

6.　*'Bilateralisation' of multilateral conventions:* There is also the case of the novel technique of laying down general rules in a multilateral convention, with provision for states parties to enter into bilateral agreements confirming inter se and/or amplifying the rules in the convention; cf arts 21–23 of the Convention on the Recognition and Enforcement of Foreign Judgments in Civil and Commercial Matters, adopted 26 April 1966, by the Hague Conference on Private International Law.
7.　See *Report* on the work of the Commission's 13th Session (1961) ch II.
8.　See Hall *International Law* (8th edn, 1924) pp 837 et seq, for an account of the development of the rule.
9.　ICJ 1969, 3 at 42.

possessed by this type of instrument. One authority[10] has pointed out that it is 'a sound maxim that a principle of international law acquires additional force from having been solemnly acknowledged as such in the provisions of a Public Treaty'. It may also happen that a treaty is so framed as to contain a provision or provisions that may be expressly or impliedly declaratory of a rule of international law; the evidentiary value of such provision or provisions is then, a fortiori, more compelling. It is of course true that if the treaty concerned provides in absolute or general terms for a right of withdrawal or the making of reservations, or even, in cases, for revision, this may tend to diminish the evidentiary value of the provision or provisions concerned.

3. DECISIONS OF JUDICIAL OR ARBITRAL TRIBUNALS

International judicial decisions

The only existing permanent international judicial tribunal with a general jurisdiction is the International Court of Justice, which in 1946 succeeded the former Permanent Court of International Justice, itself first created in 1921. The International Court of Justice functions under a Statute containing virtually the same organic regulations as the Statute of the former Permanent Court. During the period 1923–1940, the Permanent Court gave a large number of judgments and advisory opinions on matters of international import, thereby contributing, as was intended by the founders of the Court, to the development of international jurisprudence. The work of its successor has been of equal importance.

It would be misleading to say that any decision of the former Permanent Court created a binding rule of international law. Under article 59 of its Statute (now article 59 of the Statute of the new International Court of Justice) the Court's decisions were to have 'no binding force except between the parties and in respect of that particular case'. Pursuant to its Statute, the Permanent Court did not treat its own prior decisions as per se binding, and such decisions could therefore hardly be regarded by the international society of states as binding legal precedents. The Court, however, did use its prior decisions for guidance as to the law, for example, for purposes of illustrating or distinguishing the application of particular rules; also, it had regard to the principles of international law and to the reasoning on which previous decisions were based, since the expression 'decision' in article 59 connoted only the operative portion of the Court's judgment, as distinct from the grounds given for such judgment; and as a general practice it followed a line or series of its prior decisions and opinions which were consistently of a similar trend, although it did not at any time purport to bind itself by any expressed doctrine of judicial precedent. The present International Court of Justice has in its turn followed a practice consistent with that of its

---

10. Phillimore *Commentaries upon International Law* (2nd edn, 1871) Vol I, p 52. Declarations adopted by international diplomatic conferences may also be of evidentiary value as to rules of international law, although not purporting to state or affirm norms of international law; eg, the Helsinki Declaration adopted on 1 August 1975 by the Conference on Security and Co-operation in Europe. See comment by Harold S. Russell 70 AJIL (1976) 248.

predecessor.[11] Moreover, the International Court has shown that it regards itself as free to 'develop' international law, without being tied by the weight of prior practice and authority, as witness its judgment in 1951 in the *Fisheries Case* (United Kingdom-Norway)[12] upholding the legitimacy of the baselines method for delimiting the territorial sea in certain coastal waters. Clearly, to the extent that a decision by the Court, or a particular principle laid down by it becomes accepted by states generally, as occurred with this baselines method (see now article 4 of the Geneva Convention of 29 April 1958, on the Territorial Sea and the Contiguous Zone, and articles 3–7 of the United Nations Convention on the Law of the Sea of 10 December 1982), the Court would be justified in regarding itself as bound by its former pronouncements.

Quite apart from the attitude of both Courts towards their own prior decisions, the judgments and advisory opinions delivered by them are considered by international lawyers generally as elucidating the law, as being the expression of what the most authoritative international judicial body holds to be the international law on a given point, having regard to a given set of circumstances.

An example of a temporary—as distinct from a permanent—international judicial body contributing substantially towards the development of international law is that of the judgment of the International Military Tribunal at Nuremberg in 1946 which laid down important principles relating to crimes against the peace and security of mankind.[13]

Not to be overlooked in this connection is the contribution to the development of international law in particular areas due to decisions of regional international courts such as, for example, the Court of Justice of the European Communities (referred to in Chapter 1, above) and the two regional courts concerned with human rights, namely, the European Court of Human Rights and the Inter-American Court of Human Rights (referred to in Chapter 12, below).

State judicial decisions

There are two ways in which the decisions of state courts may lead to the formation of rules of international law:

(a)　The decisions may be treated as weighty precedents, or even as binding authorities. According to Marshall CJ of the United States Supreme Court:[14]

> 'The decisions of the Courts of every country show how the law of nations, in the given case, is understood in that country, and will be considered in adopting the rule which is to prevail in this.'

A notable example is furnished by the decisions of the great British Prize Court judge, Lord Stowell (1745–1836), who presided over the court during the Napoleonic Wars. Lord Stowell's judgments received universal acknowledgment as authoritative declarations of the law, and he became particularly identified

---

11. In the *South West Africa Case, 2nd Phase* ICJ 1966, 6 at 36–37, the Court ruled that an earlier decision by it upon a preliminary objection could not conclusively bind the Court in deciding a matter appertaining to the merits of the case.
12. See ICJ 1951, 116 and below, p 225.
13. See below, pp 54–55.
14. *Thirty Hogsheads of Sugar, Bentzon v Boyle* (1815) 9 Cranch 191 at 198.

with the establishment of important doctrines, such as: that blockade to be binding must be effective, that contraband of war is to be determined by probable destination, and the doctrine of continuous voyage. Similarly, both as exponent and as agent for the development of international law, the Supreme Court of the United States has played an important role; for example, its judgments in the *Paquete Habana* [15] and the *Scotia* [16] did much to clarify the nature of international custom.

(b)　The decisions of state courts may, under the same principles as dictate the formation of custom, lead directly to the growth of customary rules of international law. Thus, for example, certain rules of extradition law and of state recognition were in the first instance derived from the uniform decisions of state courts. A concurrence of such decisions is usually necessary for this purpose, for if there be no uniformity, a customary rule of international law will not be inferred. Thus, in the *Lotus Case* [17] the Permanent Court of International Justice refused to deduce a customary rule where, to use the Court's expression, state judicial decisions on the point were 'divided'.

Decisions of international arbitral tribunals

Decisions of international arbitral tribunals such as the Permanent Court of Arbitration, the British-American Mixed Claims Tribunal, and others, have contributed to the development of international law. In the following branches, arbitral decision has either added to or clarified the law: territorial sovereignty, neutrality, state jurisdiction, state servitudes, and state responsibility. Many notable arbitrations, for example, the *Alabama Claims Arbitration* (1872), the *Behring Sea Fisheries Arbitration* (1893), the *Pious Fund Case* (1902), and the *North Atlantic Fisheries Case* (1910) are regarded as landmarks in the history of international law.

Some writers have refused to acknowledge this contribution on the ground of an alleged fundamental distinction between arbitral and judicial decisions. According to these writers, arbitrators have as a general practice tended to act as negotiators or diplomatic agents rather than as judges on questions of fact and law. They insist that arbitrators have been influenced to an unreasonable extent by the necessity of reaching a compromise. There is naturally an element of truth in this conception of arbitral decision, and arbitrators are less strictly bound by necessary technicalities than judges working within the ambit of established rules of procedure, but the distinction from judicial decision is by no means so fundamental as pictured. In the great majority of cases arbitrators have regarded themselves as acting to some extent judicially, rather than as *aimables compositeurs*. Moreover, if arbitral awards were merely quasi-diplomatic compromises, it would be difficult to explain how notable awards like *The Alabama Claims*, the *Behring Sea Fisheries*, and so on, have contributed to the growth of international law.

The 'compromise' element in arbitral adjudications has been unduly exaggerated because under so many treaties arbitrators were authorised to act

15. See above, p 35.
16. See above, pp 32–33.
17. See above, p 35.

'ex æquo et bono', but even in such cases arbitrators commonly acted according to judicial principles. By far the great majority of arbitral awards have been based on strictly legal considerations in form and substance. Judge J. B. Moore, with unrivalled knowledge of arbitral adjudications, declared:[18]

'I have failed to discover support for the supposition that international arbitrators have shown a special tendency to compromise, or that they have failed to apply legal principles or to give weight to legal precedents. Indeed, even in the abridged form in which many of the decisions cited in my *History and Digest of International Arbitrations*, published in 1898, were necessarily given in that work, nothing is more striking than the consistent effort to ascertain and apply principles of law approved by the best authorities, and to follow pertinent prior adjudications where any existed.'

The main distinction between arbitration and judicial decision lies not in the principles which they respectively apply, but in the manner of selection of the judges, their security of tenure, their independence of the parties, and the fact that the judicial tribunal is governed by a fixed body of rules of procedure instead of by ad hoc rules for each case. It must also be stressed that while the functions of an international judicial tribunal involve predominantly the adjudication of conduct alleged not to conform with international law, this is not necessarily always the preoccupation of an arbitral tribunal, which may frequently be concerned to make a determination in settlement of a dispute regardless of whether or not the matters in issue involve compliance or non-compliance with international law.

4. JURISTIC WORKS

It is perhaps needless to insist on the important role played by jurists in the development of international law.

Juristic works are not an independent 'source' of law, although sometimes juristic opinion does lead to the formation of international law. According to the report of one expert body to the League of Nations,[19] juristic opinion is only important as a means of throwing light on the rules of international law and rendering their formation easier. It is of no authority in itself, although it may become so if subsequently embodied in customary rules of international law; this is due to the action of states or other agencies for the formation of custom, and not to any force which juristic opinion possesses.

Article 38 of the Statute of the International Court of Justice directs the Court to apply 'the teachings of the most highly qualified publicists of the various nations, as *subsidiary* means for the determination of rules of law'. This provision emphasises the evidentiary value of juristic works. No doubt the principal function of juristic works is to furnish reliable evidence of the law. Jurists have been largely responsible for deducing customary rules from a coincidence or cumulation of similar usages or practices, and to this extent, they perform an

18. Moore *International Adjudications Ancient and Modern* (1929–1936) Vol I, pp xxxix–xc. See also Wetter *The International Arbitral Process* (1979) Vol I, pp 3–5, 19–26.
19. The Sub-Committee on State responsibility of the Committee of Experts for the Progressive Codification of International Law, League of Nations Document, C.196. M.70. 1927. V, p 94.

indispensable service. The evidentiary function of juristic works has been well described by Gray J[20] of the United States Supreme Court:

'. . . Where there is no treaty, and no controlling executive or legislative act or judicial decision, resort must be had to the customs and usages of civilised nations, and as evidence of these, to the works of jurists and commentators who by years of labour, research, and experience have made themselves peculiarly well acquainted with the subjects of which they treat. Such works are resorted to by judicial tribunals, not for the speculations of their authors concerning what the law ought to be, but for trustworthy evidence of what the law really is.'

Although there are several authorities which deny that the opinions or speculations of jurists whether a certain rule ought to be recognised are of any force,[1] it is an undoubted fact that juristic opinion may be evidence not merely of established customary rules, but of customary rules which are bound in course of time to become established. The reaction of juristic opinion may be of great importance in assisting the transition from usage to custom.

In view of this evidentiary function, the passage of time will add weight to the authority of juristic opinion, particularly if generally relied upon, or if no principles contrary to such opinion become established.[2] To this extent, juristic works may acquire a kind of prescriptive authority. However, the labours of the International Law Commission and the various multilateral conventions adopted as a consequence of such labours since its inception have shown how cautious one must be in accepting as conclusive evidence of a generally recognised customary rule, even an established consensus omnium among jurists.

In one exceptional case, juristic opinion does assume importance. Where there are no established customary or treaty rules in regard to a particular matter, recourse may be had to juristic opinion as an independent 'source', in addition to the views expressed in decided cases or in diplomatic exchanges. Thus in the Privy Council case of *Re Piracy Jure Gentium*,[3] the question arose whether actual robbery was an essential element in the crime of piracy at international law.[4] On this point, the Privy Council found itself mainly dependent on juristic opinion, and ruled that it could not only seek a *consensus* of views, but select what appeared to be the better views. It finally decided that robbery was not an essential element in piracy jure gentium, and that a frustrated attempt to commit piratical robbery was equally piracy jure gentium.

5. DECISIONS OR DETERMINATIONS OF THE ORGANS OF INTERNATIONAL INSTITUTIONS, OR OF INTERNATIONAL CONFERENCES

Decisions or determinations of the organs of international institutions, or of international conferences, may lead to the formation of rules of international law in a number of different ways:

20. *The Paquete Habana* 175 US 677 (1900) at 700.
1. *West Rand Central Gold Mining Co v R* [1905] 2 KB 391 at 407.
2. Cf Wheaton *International Law* (Dana edn, 1866) pp 23–24.
3. [1934] AC 586 at 588–9.
4. See also below, pp 212–213, 247–250.

1. They may represent intermediate or final steps in the evolution of customary rules, particularly those governing the constitutional functioning of these institutions. The decisive criterion is the extent to which the decision, determination or recommendation has been adhered to in practice;[5] of itself it is not of normative effect.[6] Thus from the practice of the United Nations Security Council (cf similarly the League of Nations Council), there has developed the rule that an abstention by a member state from voting is not to be deemed a non- concurring vote for the purpose of determining whether a decision on a non-procedural question has been validly taken by the Security Council according to the voting requirements of article 27 of the United Nations Charter.[7] As regards international law in general, the Resolutions since 1952 of the United Nations General Assembly have gone far towards confirming a rule that dependent peoples are entitled to self-determination.[8]

    A significant number of such General Assembly Resolutions have been framed in the form of a Declaration or of a Charter (eg, the Charter of Economic Rights and Duties of 1974), and these have contributed in due course to the adoption of conventions on the same subject matter; eg, the Declaration of 1963 on the Elimination of All Forms of Racial Discrimination which paved the way for the Convention of 1965 on the Elimination of All Forms of Racial Discrimination. It is also suggested that these Resolutions in the form of Declarations may be relevant as serving to contain authentic interpretations of the United Nations Charter, or as being declaratory of, or as authentic evidence of, existing customary law.[9] Certain writers have treated these collective pronouncements, even if not binding in

5. Cf also Professor G. I. Tunkin's *Droit International Public: Problèmes Théoriques* (Paris, 1965, tr from Russian) pp 109–110, and Alexandrowicz *The Law-Making Functions of the Specialised Agencies of the United Nations* (1973) pp 152–161.
6. *Decisions by way of consensus:* Note in this connection the practice of adopting a *consensus*, without formal vote; eg the consensus on hijacking adopted by the United Nations Security Council on 20 June 1972, whereby it called for co-operation by states against hijacking and hijackers, and the consensus adopted in June 1976 by the Special Committee of Twenty-Four of the United Nations on Decolonisation denouncing South Africa's continued administration of Namibia (South-West Africa). A consensus is sometimes referred to as a 'quasi-resolution', and can be a first-step in the evolution of a customary rule of international law. There can, on the other hand, be a consensus, coupled with the declared adoption of a corresponding resolution. In the course of the sessions, 1973–1982, of the Third United Nations Conference on the Law of the Sea, the provisions of the draft text of the Convention eventually opened for signature on 10 December 1982, were adopted by consensus.
7. See below pp 577–579.
8. As to Resolutions of the United Nations General Assembly, see Asamoah *The Legal Significance of the Declarations of the General Assembly of the United Nations* (1966) p v, and passim; Castaneda *Legal Effects of United Nations Resolutions* (1969); and Sloan in (1987) 58 BYIL 93.
9. But cf the arbitral award in *Texaco Overseas Petroleum v Libyan Arab Republic* (1978) 17 ILM 1–37, where the view was taken that a resolution, not confirming existing law, but purporting to enunciate new precepts should be regarded not as evidence of the law, but as laying down, de lege ferenda, what the law ought to be. According to some writers, certain Resolutions may serve negatively to demonstrate the absence of established rules. One argument against the legislative effect of General Assembly Resolutions is that under articles 10 and 13 of the United Nations Charter the General Assembly is empowered only to discuss, initiate studies and make recommendations so that its Resolutions are not intended to have binding force.

any absolute legal sense, as containing a kind of tertium quid, ie 'soft law', or as some French-speaking writers have put it, *'normes sauvages'* or *'para-droit'*. According to the weight of opinion, the legal value of these Resolutions must vary in the light of their subject-matter and the surrounding circumstances, including the voting pattern in respect of their adoption.

2. A Resolution of the organ of an international institution which validly formulates principles or regulations for the internal working of the institution may have full legal effect as laying down rules which are binding on the members and organs of the institution.

3. Inasmuch as an organ of an international institution has inherent power, in doubtful cases not precisely covered by its Constitution, to determine the limits of its own competence, such decisions by it on questions of its jurisdiction may have a law-making effect.

4. Sometimes, organs of international institutions are authorised to give binding determinations concerning the interpretation of their constituent instruments (for example, the Executive Directors and the Board of Governors of the International Monetary Fund have such power under article XVIII of the Articles of Agreement of the Fund, of 22 July 1944).[10] These interpretative decisions will form part of the law of the international institution in question.

5. Some organs of international institutions are empowered to give general decisions or directives of quasi-legislative effect, binding on all the members to whom they are addressed; for example, the Council and Commission of the European Economic Community (Common Market) under article 189 of the Treaty of Rome of 25 March 1957, establishing the Community.

6. A special case is that of the determinations or opinions of Committees of Jurists, specifically instructed by the organ of an international institution to investigate a legal problem.[11] These necessarily bear some weight and authority.

Reference should also be made to the discussion in Chapter 20, below, of the legislative and regulatory powers of international institutions.[12]

Order of use of material 'sources'

The final question is in what *order* should these material 'sources'— custom, treaties, arbitral and judicial decisions bearing on legal matters, juristic works, and decisions or determinations of the organs of international institutions—be used for ascertaining the law on a given matter. It will be remembered that the

10. See Hexner 'Interpretation by Public International Organisations of their Basic Instruments' 53 AJIL (1959) 341–370, and Gold (1954) 3 ICLQ 271–272. Semble, for an analogous reason, a General Assembly Resolution may be of legal significance if it should purport to specify with greater precision the obligations of member states under the United Nations Charter, eg, a duty not to torture an individual under colour of law; see *Filartiga v Pena-Irala* 630 F 2d 876 (1980).

11. See, eg, the opinion of the Committee of Jurists appointed in 1920 by the League of Nations Council to advise on the question of the Aaland Islands. The Committee's view that a Convention of 1856, whereby Russia agreed not to fortify the Aaland Islands, created a special military status, conferring rights on interested adjoining states although not parties to the Convention, has been cited with express or implied approval in leading textbooks.

12. See below pp 562–563, and Alexandrowicz *The Law-Making Functions of the Specialised Agencies of the United Nations* (1973) passim.

order in which the material 'sources' were set out in paragraph 1 of article 38 of the Statute of the International Court of Justice was:

1. Treaties and conventions.
2. Custom.
3. 'General principles of law recognised by civilised nations'.
4. Judicial decisions and juristic opinion, 'as subsidiary means for the determination of rules of law'.

This order is generally followed in practice. Treaties and conventions, custom, and general principles of law recognised by civilised nations are deemed to prevail over judicial decisions and juristic opinion, which are expressly declared by paragraph 1 of article 38 of the Statute of the International Court of Justice to be 'subsidiary means for the determination of rules of law'. So far as the first three categories are concerned, priority would normally be attributed to treaties and conventions expressly recognised by the states concerned provided that the treaty or convention was not in conflict with jus cogens, ie applicable peremptory norms of international law (see below, pp 48–50); if there were no treaties or conventions applicable, preference would be accorded to established customary rules, while if there were no such rules, recourse could be had to general principles of law recognised by civilised nations. If none of these three categories furnished clear rules applicable to the matter, judicial and arbitral decisions, and juristic opinion could be resorted to, with more weight being given usually to decisions of courts than to expressions of opinion by jurists and textbook writers. The weight to be given to a decision or determination of an international institution would depend upon its nature and content, and upon the provisions of the constituent instrument of the organisation. There may also be duplication of applicability, as for example when a convention contains a provision declaratory of customary international law, or when a general principle of law recognised by civilised nations is at the same time confirmatory of a treaty or customary rule.[13]

Peremptory principles or norms of international law; jus cogens
Lastly, mention should be made of the concept of jus cogens,[14] that is to say the body of peremptory principles or norms from which no derogation is permitted,

---

13. *'Intertemporal law'*: In his arbitral award in the *Island of Palmas Case* (see Wetter *The International Arbitral Process* (1979) Vol I, p 213), Dr Max Huber introduced the concept of 'intertemporal law' by way of dealing with the problem of which rules of international law prevailing at different periods of time are to be applied in a particular case. In certain respects, the expression 'intertemporal law', as such, is objectionable, as also is the distinction drawn by Dr Huber, which may not apply in an absolute manner, between the creation, on the one hand, and the existence or evolution, on the other hand, of rights. The concept of 'intertemporal' international law cannot be regarded as exactly analogous to the concept in English law of ambulatory and non-ambulatory statutory provisions. It seems that the issue normally is not really one of choice of law (as in private international law), but whether or not, in the absence of some question of historical applicability, a right or obligation, operative at a particular point of time, has been eliminated or modified by some subsequently created new rule or rules of international law, coming into effect as the result of the evolution of new customary rules or the general adoption of a new 'law-making' multilateral convention.
14. See generally on the subject, E. Suy and Others *The Concept of Jus Cogens in International Law* (1967); J. Sztucki *Jus Cogens and the Vienna Convention on the Law of Treaties; A Critical Appraisal* (1974); R. Ago (1971) III Hague Recueil des Cours 320 et seq.

and which may therefore operate to invalidate a treaty or agreement between states to the extent of the inconsistency with any of such principles or norms.[15] According to article 53 of the Vienna Convention on the Law of Treaties of 23 May 1969, it is an additional characteristic of a norm of jus cogens that it 'can be modified only by a subsequent norm of general international law having the same character', although in this article jus cogens is defined merely 'for the purposes' of the Convention. There is undoubtedly some analogy between jus cogens and the principles of public policy which at common law render a contract void if it offends against these, such as the principle that parties cannot by agreement between themselves oust the ordinary courts from their jurisdiction.[16] For example, in the international field, a treaty for the purpose of carrying out operations of piracy jure gentium would be void and would not be enforced by an international tribunal. Assuming that this analogy holds good, one must correspondingly bear in mind some of the metaphors used by harassed common law judges to describe the doctrine of public policy, such as 'a very unruly horse', 'treacherous ground', and 'slippery ground'.[17] Critics of the concept of jus cogens in international law have also urged that it may be resorted to as a means of avoiding onerous treaty obligations, or even to justify interference in matters otherwise falling within the domestic jurisdiction of states.

One major difficulty is related to the identification of norms of jus cogens. First, should this function of identification be performed solely by multilateral law-making conventions, or may a norm of jus cogens evolve through the same process as in the case of customary rules of international law? Article 64 of the Vienna Convention on the Law of Treaties provides that 'if a new peremptory norm of general international law emerges, any existing treaty which is in conflict with that norm becomes void and terminates'. The word 'emerges' shows that it was contemplated that a norm of jus cogens could be one of customary international law. Whether a rule of jus cogens can be derived from sources other than treaties or custom is a moot question on which there continues to be a division of opinion. Second, there is a lack of consensus as to what, at the present time, are norms of jus cogens. Two such generally acceptable norms seem to be the prohibition against the threat or use of force in the terms laid down in article 2, paragraph 4 of the United Nations Charter, and the principle of pacta sunt servanda, as defined in article 26 of the Vienna Convention on the Law of Treaties. Other suggested norms, for example the principle of sovereign equality of states, and the principle of peaceful settlement of disputes, while acceptable as propositions of law have not found general favour as being of the nature of jus cogens. According to one learned writer,[18] the rules of jus cogens include:

'the *fundamental* rules concerning the safeguarding of peace . . . *fundamental* rules of a humanitarian nature (prohibition of genocide, slavery and racial discrimination,

---

15. It may be, of course, that the treaty as a whole must be treated as void, because of the inseverability of its content, or because the treaty's operations is dependent upon a condition precedent which offends against a norm of jus cogens.
16 See *Lee v Showmen's Guild of Great Britain* [1952] 2 QB 329 at 342.
17. For the various metaphors used, see *Newcastle Diocese Trustees v Ebbeck* (1960) 104 CLR 394 at 415 (High Court of Australia).
18. Ago, op cit, p 324.

protection of essential rights of the human person in time of peace and war), the rules prohibiting any infringement of the independence and sovereign equality of States, the rules which ensure to all the members of the international community the enjoyment of certain common resources (high seas, outer space, etc).'

A general provision as to jus cogens is contained in article 53 (mentioned above) of the Vienna Convention on the Law of Treaties;[19] this reads:

'A treaty is void if, at the time of its conclusion, it conflicts with a peremptory norm of general international law. For the purposes of the present Convention, a peremptory norm of general international law is a norm accepted and recognised by the international community of States as a whole as a norm from which no derogation is permitted and which can be modified only by a subsequent norm of general international law having the same character.'

The article reflects the underlying notion in jus cogens that its component norms are conditioned by the interests of the international community *as a whole*. The drafting of the first sentence is open to objection. If it means that the whole of a treaty is void when a single provision offends against jus cogens, this is an untenable proposition, for in many cases the provision may be severable. The sentence would be more acceptable if the word 'provision' were added after the word 'treaty'. Inasmuch as a norm of jus cogens must be one accepted by the international community as a whole, and may only be modified by a subsequently emerging norm of the same character, it follows that a regional association cannot modify or derogate from it in the absence of any decision to that effect by the international community as a whole.

It remains to say that the concept of jus cogens, if applicable to treaties, must also, a fortiori, render inoperative usages or practices conflicting with peremptory norms.

19. As to its drafting history at the Vienna Conference, see R. D. Kearney and R. E. Dalton 64 AJIL (1970) 535–538.

CHAPTER 3

The subjects of international law

International law is primarily concerned with the rights, duties, and interests of *states*. Normally the rules of conduct that it prescribes are rules which states are to observe, and in the same way treaties may impose obligations which the signatory states alone agree to perform. But this does not necessarily imply that no other entities or persons, whether natural or legal, can come within the dominion or bounty of international law.[1]

However, certain authorities assert that states are the only subjects[2] with which international law is concerned. A natural stumbling block for so wide a theory has always been the case of slaves and pirates. As a result of general treaties,[3] certain rights of protection, etc, have been bestowed on slaves by the society of states. Also under customary rules of international law, individuals who commit the offence of piracy jure gentium on the high seas are liable as enemies of mankind to punishment by any apprehending state.[4] These two apparent exceptions to the general rule have been reconciled by treating slaves and pirates jure gentium as *objects*, and in no sense as subjects of international law. Moreover it has been said by the same authorities that on a proper analysis, it would be

1. See Oppenheim *International Law* Vol I (9th edn, 1992) pp 16–22; W. Paul Gormley *The Procedural Status of the Individual before International and Supranational Tribunals* (1966); Nørgaard *The Position of the Individual in International Law* (1962); Rousseau *Droit International Public* Vol II (1974), *Les Sujets de Droit*; H. Mosler 'Subjects of International Law' in *Encyclopaedia of Public International Law* Vol 7 (1984) pp 442–459.
2. The term 'subject of international law' is capable of meaning: (a) an incumbent of rights and duties under international law; (b) the holder of a procedural privilege of prosecuting a claim before an international tribunal; (c) the possessor of interests for which provision is made by international law; and (d) the capacity to conclude treaties with states and international organisations. These four meanings are not always kept distinct in the literature on the question whether individuals and non-state entities may be subjects of international law.
3. See, eg, art 13 of the Geneva Convention on the High Seas of 29 April 1958, providing that any slave taking refuge on board any ship, whatever its flag, shall ipso facto be free, and see now the similar provision in art 99 of the United Nations Convention on the Law of the Sea of 10 December 1982. See also below at p 247. Another case of individuals possessing rights under international law is, semble, that of astronauts under the provisions of the Agreement of 1968 on the Rescue of Astronauts, the Return of Astronauts, and the Return of Objects Launched into Outer Space; see below, pp 168–169.
4. See below, pp 212–213, 247–250.

found that the so-called rights or duties of slaves and pirates jure gentium are technically those of states and states only. Thus, in the case of slaves, it is argued, the international conventions under which slaves enjoy protection really cast duties on the states parties; without such duties on the states to recognise and protect their interests, slaves would not possess any rights at international law.

As against this theory that individuals are only incumbents of rights and duties at international law insofar as they are objects and not subjects, there is a theory which goes to the limit in the opposite direction. This theory which is held by the noted jurist Kelsen (1881–1973) and his followers maintains that in the ultimate analysis, individuals alone are the subjects of international law. A faint version of this theory had already appeared in the following passage in Westlake:[5]

'The duties and rights of States are only the duties and rights of the men who compose them.'

Kelsen analyses the notion of a state, and affirms that it is purely a technical legal concept serving to embrace the totality of legal rules applying to a group of persons within a defined territorial area; the state and the law may almost be described as synonymous. The concept of the state is used to express in technical language legal situations in which individuals alone are bound to do certain acts or receive certain benefits in the name of the collectivity of human beings to which they belong.[6] For instance, when we say that the United Kingdom is responsible at international law for some wrong committed against another state by one of its officials or a member of its armed forces, this is only a technical method of expressing the fact that the British people as a whole, ie the individuals subject to British law, are bound through the persons who constitute its government to give redress for the wrong imputed to the United Kingdom as a state. The duties resting on a state at international law are thus ultimately duties binding on individuals.

In this respect, according to Kelsen, there is no real distinction between state law and international law. Both systems bind individuals, although international law as a matter of technique does so only *mediately* and through the concept of the state.

From the purely theoretical standpoint, and in logic, Kelsen's views are undoubtedly correct. But as a matter of practice, international lawyers and the state leaders they advise, work on the realistic basis that their primary concern is with the rights and duties of states. It is true that from time to time treaties do provide that individuals may have rights, a remarkable illustration of this being the 1965 Convention on the Settlement of Investment Disputes between States and Nationals of other States, enabling private foreign investors to have access to international machinery for the settlement of their disputes with investment-receiving states.[7] But otherwise it will generally be found that treaty provisions are couched in the form of rules of conduct binding upon, or conferring rights

5.   *Collected Papers* (1914) Vol I, p 78. To much the same effect is a passage in Professor Scelle's study in Lipsky (ed) *Law and Politics in the World Community* (1953) p 56.
6.   See Kelsen (1926) 14 Hague Recueil 231 at pp 239 et seq.
7.   Note also that art 7 of the Geneva Prisoners of War Convention of 1949 provides that prisoners of war may in no circumstances renounce 'the rights' secured to them by the Convention.

on states. This is also consistent with the long-standing British practice of treaty negotiation. The Crown when negotiating treaties does not do so as trustee or agent for private citizens. As Lord Atkin said in an important judgment:[8]

'When the Crown is negotiating with another sovereign a treaty, it is inconsistent with its sovereign position that it should be acting as agent for the nationals of the sovereign State, unless indeed the Crown chooses expressly to declare that it is acting as agent.'

At the same time, it serves no purpose to gloss over the exceptions to the general working rule. There are cases where international law binds individuals *immediately* and not merely mediately in Kelsen's sense. It is a pure play on words to say that slaves and pirates jure gentium are not subjects, but objects of international law. For example, the rule of international law by which states are authorised to attack, seize, and punish pirates jure gentium, is a rule 'imposing a legal duty directly upon individuals and establishing individual responsibility'.[9] It would be straining the facts to interpret the rule as casting a duty not on individuals but on states, for no state is bound to punish pirates if it chooses to abstain from doing so, while the power to apprehend pirates is scarcely a right in its proper connotation.

It is maintained by the protagonists of the traditional theory that, in any event, such alleged exceptional cases are only in fact apparent exceptions, for in essence the liability to punishment of pirates jure gentium and the right of slaves to their freedom derives from municipal law, and not from international law. They claim that generally no rule of international law can operate directly or indirectly upon individuals without some municipal legislative implementation of the rule.[10] However, as to pirates jure gentium Kelsen cogently says:[11]

'The fact that the specification of the punishment is left to national law, and the trial of the pirate to national courts, does not deprive the delict and the sanction of their international character.'

That is a consideration applicable to all the exceptional cases.

Irrespective of municipal legislative implementation of the rules therein contained, there is no question that, however exceptionally, many modern treaties do bestow rights or impose duties upon individuals. It was authoritatively decided by the Permanent Court of International Justice in the *Danzig Railway Officials' Case* that if by a particular treaty the parties intended to confer rights on individuals, then these rights should receive recognition and effect at international law, that is to say from an international court.[12] In that case, Poland contended that the agreement between itself and Danzig fixing the conditions of employment of Danzig railway officials, which it had taken over, conferred no right of action on these officials. Poland maintained that the agreement being an international treaty, and not having been incorporated into Polish law, created rights and obligations only between the contracting parties, and that failure to carry out such obligations would involve it in responsibility only to Danzig and not to

---

8. *Civilian War Claimants Association Ltd v R* [1932] AC 14 at 26–27.
9. Kelsen *Peace Through Law* (1944) p 76.
10. See generally as to this question below, pp 66–67.
11. Kelsen, op cit, p 76.
12. See *Advisory Opinion on the Jurisdiction of the Courts of Danzig*, (1928) PCIJ Series B No 15.

private individuals. While the Permanent Court was ready to admit this as a general rule, it declared that in the particular case the intention of the parties was to create rights enforceable by private citizens, and therefore the Danzig officials had their cause of action against the Polish administration as under the agreement. It may well be said that insofar as it purports to confer rights upon individuals, the Geneva Prisoners of War Convention of 1949 (as supplemented by the two Protocols, I and II, adopted in 1977 by the Geneva Diplomatic Conference on the Reaffirmation and Development of International Law Applicable in Armed Conflicts[13]) is such a treaty, within the meaning of the Permanent Court's decision.

This controversy as to whether international law binds individuals is by no means of theoretical significance only. Towards the end of the Second World War when the Allies were concerting measures to prosecute war criminals, there was some hesitation whether international law could indeed reach out to punish heads of state, ministers, and high military and administrative functionaries responsible for initiating the war and authorising the perpetration of atrocities. In the event, the theoretical objections to such a course were disregarded, and pursuant to agreements to this effect which were without precedent in international law,[14] international trial tribunals were set up at Nuremberg and Tokyo. Among the offences for which charges were laid were crimes against peace (for example, beginning a war of aggression or in violation of treaties), crimes against humanity (for example, murder or persecution of racial or religious groups), crimes under the laws of war, and the conspiracy to commit these crimes. The judgment of the Nuremberg International Tribunal in 1946 (followed later by the judgment in 1948 of the Tokyo International Tribunal) establishing the guilt of certain of the defendants in respect of these charges, and affirming their individual responsibility under international law, is of historic significance. The principles of international law recognised in the Agreement or Charter setting up the Tribunal of 8 August 1945,[15] and in the Tribunal's judgment were subsequently formulated by the International Law Commission of the United Nations as a Draft Code of Principles Recognized in the Tribunal's judgment (see *Report* concerning the work of its second session presented to the General Assembly in 1950). In these principles, as formulated, the references are to 'persons' as being guilty of crimes against the peace and security of mankind. In the light of these principles, too, one point has been clarified, namely that international law can reach over and beyond traditional technicalities, and

13. See pp 512–515 below.
14. The Agreement for setting up the Nuremberg Tribunal, dated 8 August 1945, between Great Britain, the United States, France, and Russia provided in art 7 of the Charter annexed thereto that: '. . . The official position of the defendants, whether as Heads of State or responsible officials in Government Departments, shall not be considered as freeing them from responsibility or mitigating punishment'. Cf the Charter of 19 January 1946, concerning the constitution of the Tokyo Tribunal.
15. Some writers questioned the validity and propriety of the Tribunal, as well as the legality of conferring upon it by Agreement of the Four Powers (ie Great Britain, the United States, France, and Russia), jurisdiction to deal with certain offences against the law of nations, formulated for the first time in such Agreement, eg, crimes against the peace, and crimes against humanity. Cf Kelsen (1947) I ILQ 153.

prevent guilty individuals sheltering behind the abstract concept of the state.[16] According to the Nuremberg Tribunal:[17]

'Crimes against international law are committed by men, not by abstract entities, and only by punishing individuals who commit such crimes can the provisions of international law be enforced.'

This trend of international law towards attaching direct responsibility to individuals was reaffirmed in the Genocide Convention adopted by the United Nations General Assembly on 9 December 1948, which is somewhat in advance of the Nuremberg principles.[18] Under the Convention, the states parties agreed that genocide (ie acts committed with intent to destroy in whole or in part national, ethnical, racial, or religious groups) and the conspiracy or incitement to commit genocide, attempts, and complicity therein, should be punishable on trial by national courts or by an international criminal tribunal. Article IV of the Convention emphasised the aspect of individual responsibility by providing that *persons* committing the acts should be punished 'whether they are constitutionally responsible rulers, public officials or private individuals'.

These developments lay in the direction of imposing duties on individuals under international law.

But parallel thereto, there has been also a movement for conferring rights on individuals, even as against states of which such individuals are nationals or citizens. This is implicit in the Nuremberg judgment of 1946, inasmuch as it recognises that the victims of crimes against humanity committed even by their own governments, are entitled to the protection of international criminal law. So also does the Genocide Convention of 1948 purport to protect the very right of human groups to exist as groups. In this connection reference must be made to the movement to protect human rights and fundamental freedoms sponsored by the United Nations under the powers given in article 1 and other provisions of the United Nations Charter, a subject which is discussed in a later chapter.[19] In Europe the human rights movement has been advanced as a result of the European Convention for the Protection of Human Rights and Fundamental Freedoms signed at Rome on 4 November 1950.[20] Under the Convention, there were established a European Commission of Human Rights with administrative

16. The Nuremberg Tribunal rejected the argument urged on behalf of the defendants that they were being prosecuted for international crimes under rules of law ex post facto inasmuch as prior to 1939–40, such crimes as crimes against the peace had not been defined or made punishable under existing international law. It pointed out that the defendants must have known that their actions were illegal and wrong, and in defiance of international law (see Official Record of Trials, Vol I, *Official Documents*, at p 219). This ruling has been widely criticised; for typical criticism and discussion, see Finch 41 AJIL (1947) 33.

17. See Official Record, Vol I, *Official Documents*, at p 223. The Tribunal also pointed out that it had long been recognised that 'international law imposes duties and liabilities upon individuals as well as upon States'.

18. Note that in respect of the crimes against humanity as charged before the Nuremberg Tribunal, the Tribunal limited its jurisdiction over these to such as were committed in connection with or in execution of crimes against peace, or war crimes proper. See as to the Genocide Convention, L. J. Le Blanc 'The Intent to Destroy Groups in the Genocide Convention' (1984) 78 AJIL 369.

19. See below, ch 12.

20. See below, pp 330–333.

power to investigate and report on violations of human rights, and a European Court of Human Rights, which commenced to function in 1959, and in numerous cases already,[1] both the Commission and the Court have inquired into a violation of human rights alleged by an individual against his or her own government.

In regard to individuals in general, it should be noted that there is a widely recognised rule of international practice that before an international tribunal, the rights of, or the obligations binding individuals at international law, are respectively enforceable at the instance of or against those states only whose nationality such individuals possess.[2] In other words individuals cannot generally assert their own rights against a state before an international tribunal or be answerable to a state in the same jurisdiction for failing in their obligations, but only through the state of which they are nationals.

The European Court of Human Rights does not represent an exception to the rule, as the parties to the European Convention for the Protection of Human Rights and Fundamental Freedoms, and the European Commission of Human Rights have alone the right to bring a case before the Court. Individuals cannot of their own motion invoke the Court's jurisdiction. The First Optional Protocol to the United Nations International Covenant on Civil and Political Rights, 1966, allows the Committee on Human Rights to receive communications from individuals who claim to be victims of a violation of a right set forth in Covenant by a State Party to the Protocol. The Committee's functions are essentially conciliatory and recommendatory in nature; unlike the European Court of Human Rights it has no powers of binding decision.[3]

Certain points require emphasis in this connection. In the first place, the rule precluding an individual from approaching an international tribunal is one of a general nature only, and already certain exceptions to it have appeared. Thus, by treaties concluded after the First World War (see articles 297 and 304 of the Treaty of Versailles 1919, and the Polish-German Convention of 15 May 1922, relating to Upper Silesia[4]) individual claimants were allowed access to the various Mixed Arbitral Tribunals set up pursuant to the provisions of these instruments, although as it turned out governments intervened in some of the more important cases in support of their nationals. Again, under the Treaty creating the European

1. See pp 332–333.
2. See per Judge Hackworth in ICJ Reports, 1949, at pp 202 et seq. Note also art 34 of the Statute of the International Court of Justice, providing that 'only States may be parties in cases before the Court'. In regard to United Nations officials, making complaints to the United Nations Administrative Tribunal against the employing international organisation for non-observance of the terms of their employment, the International Court of Justice may have power however in its advisory jurisdiction, on an application to review the Tribunal's award, to deal with a claim by an aggrieved individual, who may be, *in substance*, if not in form, the litigating party; see, inter alia, *Advisory Opinion on Review of Judgment No 158 of the United Nations Administrative Tribunal (Fasla Case)* ICJ 1973, 166; *Advisory Opinion on Review of Judgment No 273 of the United Nations Administrative Tribunal* (the *Mortished Case*) ICJ 1982, 325; and *Application for Review of Judgment No 333 of the United Nations Administrative Tribunal, Advisory Opinion* ICJ 1987, 18.
3. As at the end of 1993 there were 71 States Parties to the Protocol. On the protection of human rights see further below, ch 12.
4. Under this Convention, the independent procedural capacity of individuals as claimants before an international tribunal was recognised even as against the state of which they were nationals; see *Steiner and Gross v Polish State* (1928) Annual Digest of Public International Law Cases, 1927–1928, Case No 188.

Coal and Steel Community of 18 April 1951, under the Treaty establishing the European Economic Community (Common Market) of 25 March 1957, and under the Treaty establishing the European Atomic Energy Community (EURATOM) of 25 March 1957, individuals, private enterprises, and corporate entities have been given certain rights of direct appeal to the Court of Justice of the Communities against decisions of organs of the Communities.[5] Mention may also be made of the right of United Nations officials to take proceedings before the United Nations Administrative Tribunal for alleged non-observance of their contracts of employment or the terms of their appointment. Moreover, the opinion of many international lawyers is that, in certain limited cases, access by individuals or corporations to international tribunals is necessary and should be allowed, and it may be expected that in the future changes in this direction will come about.[6] Second, the fact that individuals have such procedural incapacities before international tribunals is not necessarily inconsistent with their status as subjects of international law. There are similar instances of persons with procedural incapacities before municipal courts (for example, infants, who under English law can only bring an action by a next friend or defend it by a guardian ad litem), who are nevertheless regarded as subjects of municipal law. Third, the International Court of Justice has held that an international institution, as distinct from a state, is entitled to espouse the claim of one of its officials against a state for damage or injury suffered, thus recognising that, at all events, this function of protection does not belong exclusively to states.[7]

International practice has in recent years extended the range of subjects far beyond that of states only:[8]

a.   International institutions and organs, such as the United Nations and the International Labour Organisation (ILO) were established under international

---

5. Cf the decision of the Court of Justice of the European Communities in 1974, holding that the provisions concerning freedom of movement in art 48 of the Treaty of Rome of 1957 creating the European Economic Community (EEC), and art 3 of an EEC Directive as to the movement and residence of foreign nationals, conferred rights directly on individuals which they could enforce in the courts of member States of the EEC; Case 41/74: *Van Duyn v Home Office* (No 2) [1975] Ch 358, [1975] 3 All ER 190. For the authorities generally on this subject, see D. Wyatt and A. Dashwood *The Substantive Law of the EEC* (1980) pp 26 et seq.
6. An early precedent also is that of the Central American Court of Justice (1908–1918), which did have jurisdiction to deal with disputes between states and private individuals, although no significant conclusions can be drawn from its meagre record of activity over a period of ten years, when only five cases were brought by individuals, but in each instance without success.
7. See *Advisory Opinion on Reparation for Injuries Suffered in the Service of the United Nations*, 1949 ICJ, at 182 et seq.
8. A special illustration of such a non-state entity is the Bank for International Settlements (BIS), which has its seat at Basle, Switzerland. In 1980, the BIS celebrated its 50th anniversary, and the BIS handbook, *The Bank for International Settlement and the Basle Meetings* (1980), published for the occasion, contained the following passage (pp 103–104): 'Founded as a result of State treaties, endowed with significant immunities, exempt from the legislation of the country in which it has its seat, the BIS is clearly an international organisation in the true sense of the term. *It is a subject of international law*'. Two other instances of non-state entities that, as subjects of international law, play a significant part in the actitivities of the international community, may be mentioned; namely, the Intergovernmental Oceanographic Commission, and the South Pacific Forum, comprising the Heads of Government of the independent and self-governing territories of the South Pacific.

conventions containing constitutional provisions regulating their duties and functions, for example, the United Nations Charter 1945, and the Constitution of the International Labour Organisation.

In its Advisory Opinion just mentioned the International Court of Justice expressly held, in terms which are applicable to other international organisations, that the United Nations is, under international law, an international person. According to the Court:[9]

> 'That is not the same thing as saying that it is a State, which it certainly is not, or that its legal personality and rights and duties are the same as those of a State . . . What it does mean is that it is a *subject of international law* and capable of possessing international rights and duties, and that it has capacity to maintain its rights by bringing international claims.'

Moreover within the United Nations and the International Labour Organisation, for example, are other organs, and even individuals,[10] whose activities are regulated by rules set out in these constitutional instruments.

Even regional international organisations and communities may by the terms of their constituent instruments be endowed with international personality, as, for example, the North Atlantic Treaty Organisation (NATO), which possesses 'juridical personality' under article 4 of the Agreement of 20 September 1951 on the Status of the North Atlantic Treaty Organisation, National Representatives, and International Staff. Perhaps the most outstanding current example is that of the European Union (or Community) which has become in the fullest sense an international entity with all the rights, duties and capabilities of a subject of international law—a position reinforced in a formal manner by the *Single European Act* (which entered into force in 1987) and by the Maastricht Treaty on European Union and Economic and Monetary Union (which entered into force in 1993), amending the Treaty of Rome of 25 March 1957. In particular, the European Community commonly participates in international conferences, enters into conventions or agreements with other states and conducts diplomatic relations with them through permanent missions.

It should be mentioned, however, that some positivist writers oppose the attribution of international personality to international institutions, and maintain what is known as a theory of 'common organs'. Under this theory international organisations are regarded as domestic institutions common to the participating states, and whose activities are in essence the activities of these states, and not as true international agencies. It is difficult to reconcile such a conception of the status of international institutions with all the facts, and in the *South West Africa Cases, 2nd Phase* (1966)[11] the International Court of Justice, dealing with the League of Nations, ruled that individual member states had, with reference to mandates, no separate, self-contained right they could assert before a court, over and above the League's collective, institutional activity.

9.   See *Advisory Opinion*, op cit, p 179.
10. Eg, the Secretary-General of the United Nations. See Schwebel *The Secretary-General of the United Nations: His Political Powers and Practice* (1952), and E. McWhinney *United Nations Law Making* (1984) pp 145–150.
11. ICJ 1966, 6 at 29, 63.

b.   Several 'law-making' conventions have been concluded in regard to matters of international criminal law, for example, the Geneva Convention dealing with the Suppression of Counterfeiting Currency (1929), the Single Narcotic Drugs Convention adopted at New York in 1961, the Tokyo Convention on Offences and Other Acts Committed on board Aircraft (1963), the Hague Convention for the Suppression of the Unlawful Seizure of Aircraft (1970), the Montreal Convention for the Suppression of Unlawful Acts against the Safety of Civil Aviation (1971) the Convention on the Prevention and Punishment of Crimes against Internationally Protected Persons, including Diplomats (1973), the International Convention against the Taking of Hostages (1979), the Torture Covention (1984), and the IMO Convention on the Suppression of Unlawful Acts against the Safety of Maritime Navigation (1988). Under these conventions, states have concerted or may concert their action for the punishment of certain international offences or crimes in which individuals alone were concerned. Thereby, delinquents such as international drug traffickers and counterfeiters, and persons 'hijacking' an aircraft, have become subjects of conventional rules of international criminal law in much the same way, although not to the same extent, as pirates jure gentium under customary rules.

c.   Under treaties concerning national minorities, individuals, as already mentioned, were given the right of securing redress by application to an international Court (see, for example, articles 297 and 304 of the Treaty of Versailles 1919).

d.   Subdivisions of states,[12] dependencies, protectorates, and territories were brought within the scope of several 'law-making' conventions, in order better to secure the working of the provisions of these conventions which required application by all administrative units throughout the world, whether states, colonies, protectorates, or territories. An appropriate example is the provision in article 8 of the Constitution of the World Health Organisation of 1946 that territories or groups of territories 'not responsible for the conduct of their international relations' may be admitted as associate members of that Organisation.

e.   Insurgents as a group may be granted belligerent rights in a contest with the legitimate government, although not in any sense organised as a state.[13]

12. Under the Convention of 18 March 1965, on the Settlement of Investment Disputes between States and Nationals of other States, a constituent subdivision of a state party (eg, a province or state of a federation) may, with the approval of that state, go to arbitration or conciliation with an investor of another state party (see art 8).
13. Cf Protocol I (1977) Additional to the Geneva Conventions, 1949, relating to the Protection of the Victims of Armed Conflict, article 96(3). For the special case of governments in exile, as during the Second World War, see F. E. Oppenheim 'Governments and Authorities in Exile' 36 AJIL (1942) 568 et seq. A further case of a non-state entity, which is possibly a subject of international law, is that of the International Committee of the Red Cross (ICRC); see Kunz 53 AJIL (1959) 132. More controversial is the case of national liberation movements, which have participated in, or been granted observer status in recent conferences, or meetings of bodies of the United Nations or of the United Nations 'family' organisations.

A further significant point, often lost sight of, is the fact that international law is not solely concerned with advancing the political interests of states, but to a large extent also with the interests and needs of individuals and non-state entities. So it is that a primary aim of many notable 'law-making' Conventions of the past eighty years, including such instruments as the Geneva Prisoners of War Convention of 1949 and the Geneva Convention of 1949 for the Protection of Civilian Persons in Time of War (as supplemented by the two Protocols, I and II, adopted in 1977 by the Geneva Diplomatic Conference on the Reaffirmation and Development of International Humanitarian Law Applicable in Armed Conflicts[14]), and the large number of conventions adopted by the Conferences of the International Labour Organisation, has been the welfare and health of the individual. Moreover, a number of international organisations are specifically devoted to advancing and ensuring respect for the rights and interests of individuals, in effect taking over, to some extent, internationally, the functions of diplomatic protection formerly performed by states. It would not therefore be a very revolutionary step if one further step were to be taken, and international law were to confer rights on individuals directly and ex proprio vigore without necessarily operating for this purpose through the medium and under the cover of the state. So far, it is only in exceptional cases that such an advance has been made.

Then there is the fact that a considerable weight of contemporary opinion, represented particularly by the newly emerged states, favours the view that *peoples as such*[15] have certain inalienable rights under international law, among which are the right to self-determination, the right freely to choose their political, economic and social systems, the right to dispose of the natural wealth and resources of the territory occupied by them, the right to development, the right to peace and security and the right to protection of their physical and social environment. In 1984–1985 the United Nations Educational, Scientific and Cultural Organisation (UNESCO) sponsored studies and discussions designed, inter alia, to clarify the nature and scope of peoples' rights, and the precise coverage of the term 'people'. This involved examination of the extent of the rights of indigenous minority peoples and tribes in countries and territories the subject of settlement by Europeans. Obviously this conception of the inalienable rights of peoples as such conflicts with the traditional doctrine that states are the exclusive subjects of international law. These rights of peoples as such were recognised in the Declaration on Principles of International Law Concerning Friendly Relations and Co-operation Among States in Accordance with the United Nations Charter, adopted by the General Assembly in 1970, where the Declaration elaborates in detail the principle of equal rights and self-determination of peoples, and, as well, in the Universal Declaration of the Rights

14. See pp 512–515 below.
15. It may even be claimed that ethnic, religious and linguistic groups have rights under international law; cf art 27 of the International Covenant on Civil and Political Rights of 1966: 'In those States in which ethnic, religious or linguistic minorities exist, persons belonging to such minorities shall not be denied the right, in community with other members of their group, to enjoy their own culture, to profess and practise their own religion, or to use their own language'. See Y. Dinstein 'Collective Human Rights of Peoples and Minorities' (1976) 25 ICLQ 102–120; E. Fischer *Minorities and Minority Problems* (1980); and G. Nettheim 'Justice and Indigenous Minorities: A New Province for International and National Law' in Blackshield (ed) *Legal Change* (1983) pp 251–263.

of Peoples, adopted at Algiers in July 1976. In its Advisory Opinion of 21 June 1971, on the *Legal Consequences for States of the Continued Presence of South Africa in South West Africa (Namibia)*, the International Court of Justice treated the people of the Mandated Territory of South West Africa as having, in effect, rights at international law, including a right of progress towards independence, which had been violated by South Africa's failure as Mandatory Power to comply with its obligations to submit to the supervision of United Nations organs (see ICJ 1971, 16 at 56 where the Court referred to the people of the Territory as a 'jural entity' and as an 'injured entity'[16]).

Finally, reference may be made to two categories of non-state entities, in respect of which it is controversial whether they should be regarded as subjects of international law, namely: (a) intergovernmental or quasi-intergovernmental associations concerned with the production and price stability of particular kinds of commodities, irrespective of whether these have been established by an international treaty or otherwise formed, eg, the International Tin Council (ITC) and the Organisation of Petroleum Exporting Countries (OPEC); (b) the many regional or international corporations, formed under national law, but operating in practice largely on an intergovernmental basis, eg, certain multipartite transport corporations. One tenable solution is to characterise these entities as subjects of transnational law, that is to say, a legal order of the nature of a tertium quid intermediate between international law, on the one hand, and domestic national law, on the other.

To sum up, it may be said:

a. That under modern practice, the number of exceptional instances of individuals or non-state entities enjoying rights or becoming subject to duties directly under international law, has grown.
b. That the doctrinaire rigidity of the procedural convention precluding individuals from prosecuting a claim under international law except through the state of which they are nationals, has been to some extent tempered.
c. That the interests of individuals, their fundamental rights and freedoms, have become a primary concern of international law.

These and other developments of recent years[17] appear to show that the theory that states are the exclusive subjects of international law cannot be accepted today

16. Cf in addition the International Court's *Advisory Opinion on Western Sahara* ICJ 1975, 12 at 31–35. The Helsinki Accord of 1975 also contained in Principle VIII a reference to 'the principle of equal rights and self-determination of *peoples*'.
17. One interesting development was the conclusion in February and November 1965 of educational and cultural agreements between France and the Canadian Province of Quebec, with provision for a supervisory France-Quebec Co-operation Commission. True, this was with the concurrence of the Canadian Government, but in the result a component of a federation was brought within the range of international law. See Fitzgerald 60 AJIL (1966) 529–531 and T. A. Levy 'Provincial International Status Revisited' 3 Dalhousie LJ (1976) 70 at 99–103. A later development was the conclusion in September 1969 of a Quebec-Louisiana Cultural Co-operation Agreement, ie between subdivisions of different federations. Further instances of agreements made by Canadian provinces with states are referred to in Marzo 'The Legal Status of Agreements Concluded by Component Units of Federal States with Foreign Entities', *Canadian Yearbook of International Law* (1978) p 197 at 206 et seq. These have been described as 'transnational agreements' (ibid, at 222). As to the extent to which the Soviet Union Republics were subjects of international law, see *Soviet Year Book of International Law* (1963) pp 105 et seq.

as accurate in all respects, although it may be a good working generalisation for the practical international lawyer. The use of the state as a medium and screen for the application of international law cannot now do justice to all the far-reaching aims of the modern system.

Yet it is as wrong to minimise this traditional theory as artificially to explain away the developments that have subjected the theory to such strain. The bulk of international law consists of rules which bind states, and it is only in the minority of cases, although it is a substantial minority, that lawyers have to concern themselves with individuals and non-state entities or associations as subjects of international law.

CHAPTER 4

The relation between international law and state law

1. GENERAL

Nothing is more essential to a proper grasp of the subject of international law than a clear understanding of its relation to state law. A thorough acquaintance with this topic is of the utmost practical importance. Particularly is it of value in clarifying the law of treaties—perhaps the most important branch of international law, and one which impinges so frequently on the domain of state law.

Although this book aims only at stating the fundamentals of modern international law, it is desirable to give more than a merely elementary account of the relation between international law and state law. For this purpose, it is necessary to include some treatment of the theoretical aspects before dealing briefly with the practice observed by states at the present time. The importance of such theoretical analysis cannot be overrated, for numerous are the questions which come for opinion before an international lawyer, involving a nice consideration of the limits between international law and state law. Apart from the aspect of theory, there is the important practical problem of more immediate concern to municipal courts, namely, to what extent may such courts give effect within the municipal sphere to rules of international law, both where such rules are, and where they are not in conflict with municipal law. It is this problem which requires a consideration of the practice of states. Besides, in the international sphere, international tribunals may be called upon to determine the precise status and effect of a rule of municipal law, which is relied upon by one party to a case.

2. THEORIES AS TO THE RELATION BETWEEN INTERNATIONAL LAW AND STATE LAW[1]

The two principal theories are known as *monism* and *dualism*. According to monism, international law and state law are concomitant aspects of the one

---

1. See generally on the subject, Kelsen *Principles of International Law* (2nd edn, 1966, revised and edited by R. W. Tucker) pp 553–588, and G. Tunkin and R. Wolfrum (eds) *International Law and Municipal Law* (1988).

system—law in general; according to dualism, they represent two entirely distinct legal systems, international law having an *intrinsically* different character from that of state law. Because a large number of domestic legal systems are involved, the dualist theory is sometimes known as the 'pluralistic' theory, but it is believed that the term 'dualism' is more exact and less confusing.

Dualism

Probably it is true to say that it would not have occurred to the earliest writers on international law (for example, Suarez) to doubt that a monistic construction of the two legal systems was alone correct, believing as they did that natural law conditioned the law of nations and the very existence of states. But in the nineteenth and twentieth centuries, partly as a result of philosophic doctrines (for example, of Hegel) emphasising the sovereignty of the state-will, and partly as a result of the rise in modern states of legislatures with complete internal legal sovereignty, there developed a strong trend towards the dualist view.

The chief exponents of dualism have been the positivist writers, Triepel[2] and Anzilotti.[3] For the positivists, with their consensual conception of international law, it was natural to regard state law as a distinct system. Thus, according to Triepel, there were two fundamental differences between the two systems:

a.   The subjects of state law are individuals, while the subjects of international law are states solely and exclusively.
b.   Their juridical origins are different; the source of state law is the will of the state itself, the source of international law is the common will (*Gemeinwille*) of states.

As to point a, we have already shown in Chapter 3 above that it is now far from correct, and that international law binds individuals and entities other than states. As to b, the statement is somehow misleading; it begs the question to say that the alleged *Gemeinwille* is a source of international law, because the really important question is under what circumstances an expression of the *Gemeinwille* can become decisive. The natural inference is that over and above the *Gemeinwille* there are fundamental principles of international law, superior to it and indeed regulating its exercise or expression.

Anzilotti adopted a different approach; he distinguished international law and state law according to the fundamental principles by which each system is conditioned. In his view, state law is conditioned by the fundamental principle or norm that state legislation is to be obeyed, while international law is conditioned by the principle pacta sunt servanda, ie agreements between states are to be respected. Thus the two systems are entirely separate, and Anzilotti maintained further that they are so distinct that no conflicts between them are possible; there may be references (*renvois*) from one to the other, but nothing more. As to Anzilotti's theory, it is enough to say that for reasons already given,[4] it is incorrect to regard pacta sunt servanda as the underlying norm of

2.   See his *Völkerrecht und Landesrecht* (1899).
3.   See his *Corso di Diritto Internazionale* (3rd edn, 1928) Vol I, pp 43 et seq. See also above, p 22.
4.   See above, pp 22–23.

international law; it is a partial illustration of a much wider principle lying at the root of international law.

Apart from the positivist writers, the theory of dualism has received support from certain non-positivist writers and jurists, and implicitly too from a number of judges of municipal courts.[5] The reasoning of this class of dualists differs from that of the positivist writers, since they look primarily to the empirical differences in the formal sources of the two systems, namely, that on the one hand, international law consists for the most part of customary and treaty rules, whereas municipal law, on the other hand, consists mainly of judge-made law and of statutes passed by municipal legislatures. In recent writings on international law another ground relied upon in support of dualism is the difference reflected in the fact that since 1945 international law has expanded to so great an extent into many different areas, while domestic national laws have continued to be concerned with a more limited range of subject matters.

Monism

Modern writers who favour the monistic construction endeavour for the most part to found their views upon a strictly scientific analysis of the internal structure of legal systems as such.

By contrast with the writers adopting dualism, the followers of monism regard all law as a single unity composed of binding legal rules, whether those rules are obligatory on states, on individuals, or on entities other than states. In their view, the science of law is a unified field of knowledge, and the decisive point is therefore whether or not international law is true law. Once it be accepted as a hypothesis that international law is a system of rules of a truly legal character, it was impossible according to Kelsen (1881–1973)[6] and other monist writers to deny that the two systems constitute part of that unity corresponding to the unity of legal science. Thus any construction other than monism, and in particular dualism, is bound to amount to a denial of the true legal character of international law. There cannot in the view of the monist writers be any escape from the position that the two systems, because they are both systems of legal rules, are interrelated parts of the one legal structure.

There are, however, other writers who have favoured monism for less abstract reasons, and who maintain, as a matter purely of practical appraisal, that international law and state law are both part of a universal body of legal rules binding all human beings collectively or singly. In other words, it is the individual who really lies at the root of the unity of all law.

The harmonisation approach

'A radical view of the whole subject may be propounded to the effect that the entire monist-dualist controversy is unreal, artificial, and strictly beside the point, because

5. See, eg, the passage in *Commercial and Estates Co of Egypt v Board of Trade* [1925] 1 KB 271 at 295.
6. Kelsen's monistic theory is founded on a philosophic approach towards knowledge in general. According to Kelsen, the unity of the science of law is a necessary deduction from human cognition and its unity. Cf Luigi 'International Law and Municipal Law: the Complementarity of Legal Systems' in Macdonald and Johnston (eds) *The Structure and Process of International Law* (1983) 715, and Rubanov 'International Law and the Co-existence of National Legal Systems' in *Soviet Law and Government* Vol 24 (1986) 52.

it assumes something that has to exist for there to be any controversy at all — and which in fact does not exist — namely a common field in which the two legal orders under discussion both simultaneously have their spheres of activity.'

So wrote Judge Sir Gerald Fitzmaurice in his Hague Academy lectures in 1957.[7] Since only international law applies on the inter-governmental plane, and national law is supreme in the national domain (subject to national constitutions and laws which may in particular instances give equal or superior force to international law) the two systems cannot collide as such. What may happen, of course, is a conflict of obligations, where national law says one thing and international law another. Such a conflict must be resolved: internally in such ways as may be found by the organs of the state, and externally by the rules of international law. To resolve conflicts of obligation by adhering to a theory that asserts the automatic superiority of the one legal order over the other does not reflect the reality, on the one hand, of legal rules that compel national judges to follow the law commanded by national authority, and on the other hand the leeways of judicial choice[8] open to judges in some circumstances to apply international law as part of national law. What should rather be the approach is to harmonise wherever possible the two competing legal prescriptions so as to avoid a conflict of obligations.[9] National legislatures certainly, and the courts to some extent as we shall see, have competence to bring about this harmonisation. Except in the rare clear cases of direct conflict, attention is increasingly coming to be focused on the infusion of international legal standards, couched in general terms, into national legal orders by processes of adaptation to local laws, institutions and cultures. This is especially marked in the field of human rights.

'Transformation' and 'specific adoption' theories

The above discussion would be incomplete without briefly referring to certain theories concerning the application of international law within the municipal sphere.

On the one hand, the positivists have put forward the view that the rules of international law cannot directly and ex proprio vigore be applied within the municipal sphere by state courts or otherwise; in order to be so applied such rules must undergo a process of *specific adoption* by, or specific incorporation into, municipal law. Since, according to positivist theory, international law and state law constitute two strictly separate and structurally different systems, the former cannot impinge upon state law unless the latter, a logically complete system, allows its constitutional machinery to be used for that purpose. In the case of treaty rules, it is claimed that there must be a *transformation* of the treaty, and this transformation of the treaty into state law,[10] which is not merely a formal but a *substantive* requirement, *alone* validates the extension to individuals of the rules laid down in treaties.

---

7. 92 *Recueil des Cours* (1957-II), 5 at 70-80.
8. A phrase coined by Professor Julius Stone *The Province and Function of Law* (1946).
9. O'Connell *International Law* (2nd edn, 1970), Vol 1, 50-54.
10. Eg, by legislation approving the treaty, or implementing its provisions.

These theories rest on the supposed consensual character of international law as contrasted with the non-consensual nature of state law. In particular, the *transformation* theory is based on an alleged difference between treaties on the one hand, and state laws or regulations on the other; according to the theory, there is a difference between treaties which are of the nature of *promises*, and municipal statutes which are of the nature of *commands*. It follows from this basic difference that a transformation from one type to the other is *formally* and *substantively* indispensable. Critics of the transformation theory have objected that this point is somewhat artificial. They maintain that if due regard be paid to the real function of provisions in treaties or in statutes it will be seen that the one no more 'promises' than the other 'commands'. The real object of treaties and of statutes—indeed their common ground—is to stipulate that certain situations of fact will involve certain determinate legal consequences. The distinction between promise and command is relevant to *form* and *procedure* but not to the true legal character of these instruments. It is therefore incorrect to consider that the transformation from one to the other is *materially* essential.

In answer to the transformation theory, the critics have put forward a theory of their own—*the delegation theory*. According to this theory there is *delegated* to each state constitution by constitutional rules of international law, the right to determine when the provisions of a treaty or convention are to come into force and the manner in which they are to be embodied in state law. The procedure and methods to be adopted for this purpose by the state are a continuation of the process begun with the conclusion of the treaty or convention. There is no transformation, there is no fresh creation of rules or municipal law, but merely a prolongation of one single act of creation. The constitutional requirements of state law are thus merely part of a unitary mechanism for the creation of law.

Whatever be the ultimate merits of this theoretical controversy over the alleged necessity for a transformation or specific adoption of international law by municipal law, the actual practice of states concerning the application of international law within the municipal sphere must remain of critical importance. It is therefore proposed to pass to a consideration of such state practice, and then to derive therefrom any necessary conclusions relative to the matter.

3. STATE PRACTICE AS TO THE OPERATION OF INTERNATIONAL LAW WITHIN THE MUNICIPAL SPHERE

The object of the present discussion is to ascertain in what manner and to what extent municipal courts do apply a rule of international law. How far do they give effect to it automatically, and how far is some specific municipal measure of statutory or judicial incorporation required before that rule can be recognised as binding within the municipal sphere? A further question is, how far a rule of international law will be applied by a municipal court if it actually conflicts with a rule of municipal law judge-made or statutory rule. The answers to these questions will be found to require distinctions to be made, on the one hand, between customary and treaty rules of international law; and on the other between statutory and judge-made municipal law.

British practice

British practice draws a distinction between: (i) customary rules of international law; (ii) rules laid down by treaties.

(i)   The rule as to customary international law according to the current of modern judicial authority is that customary rules of international law are deemed to be part of the law of the land, and will be applied as such by British municipal courts, subject to two important qualifications:

a.   That such rules are not inconsistent with British statutes,[11] whether the statute be earlier or later in date than the particular customary rule concerned.
b.   That once the scope of such customary rules has been determined by British courts of final authority, all British courts are thereafter bound by that determination, even though a divergent customary rule of international law later develops.[12]

These qualifications must be respected by British municipal courts, notwithstanding that the result may be to override a rule of international law; the breach of such a rule is not a matter for the courts, but concerns the executive in the domain of its relations with foreign Powers.[13]

The rule as stated above is somewhat narrower than that which was formerly applicable. In the eighteenth century, by a doctrine known sometimes as the 'Blackstonian' doctrine (because so affirmed by Sir William Blackstone (1723–1780) but more generally as the 'incorporation' doctrine, customary international law was deemed automatically to be part of the common law, and the two above-mentioned qualifications were not expressly formulated.[14] Thus Blackstone's statement of the doctrine was in these terms:[15]

'The law of nations, wherever any question arises which is properly the object of its jurisdiction is here adopted in its full extent by the common law, *and it is held to be a part of the law of the land.*'

This doctrine was favoured not only by Blackstone but also by Lord Mansfield and other judges in the eighteenth century.[16]

During the nineteenth century it was reaffirmed in a succession of decisions by distinguished common law and equity Judges; in *Dolder v Huntingfield* (1805) by Lord Eldon,[17] in *Wolff v Oxholm* (1817) by Lord Ellenborough,[18] in *Novello*

---

11. See *Mortensen v Peters* (1906) decision of the High Court of Justiciary of Scotland, 8 F 93, and *Polites v The Commonwealth* (1945) decision of the High Court of Australia, 70 CLR 60.
12. See *Chung Chi Cheung v R* [1939] AC 160 at 168, noting, however, *The Berlin* [1914] P 265 at 272. This principle was not however accepted by Lord Denning MR in *Trendtex Trading Corpn v Central Bank of Nigeria* [1977] QB 529, [1977] 1 All ER 881.
13. See *Polites v The Commonwealth* note 11 above.
14. These qualifications emerged presumably because of two nineteenth-century developments: a. The crystallisation after 1830 of a rigid doctrine of the binding character of British judicial precedents. b. The growth of the modern doctrine of parliamentary sovereignty in Great Britain.
15. *Commentaries* Vol IV, p 55.
16. For eighteenth-century cases supporting the doctrine, see *Barbuit's Case* (1737) Cas temp Talb 281; *Triquet v Bath* (1764) 3 Burr 1478, and *Heathfield v Chilton* (1767) 4 Burr 2015.
17. 11 Ves 283.
18. 6 M & S 92 at 100–106.

v Toogood (1823) by Abbott CJ,[19] in *De Wutz v Hendricks* (1824) by Best CJ,[20] and in *Emperor of Austria v Day and Kossuth* (1861) by Stuart V-C.[1] In terms the courts of law and equity stated that they would give effect to settled rules of international law as part of English law. This did not mean, however, that they would enforce international law if it conflicted with an English statute or judicial decision.

In 1876, in *R v Keyn (The Franconia)*,[2] the Court for Crown Cases Reserved held by a majority that English courts had no jurisdiction over crimes committed by foreigners within the maritime belt extending to three miles from the English coast, although it was claimed that such jurisdiction belonged to them under international law. This decision was nullified by Parliament passing the Territorial Waters Jurisdiction Act of 1878 to give English courts jurisdiction in such circumstances, but the judicial opinions expressed in the case seemed to throw doubts on the scope of the incorporation doctrine. According to these, an English court could not give any effect to rules of international law unless such rules were proved to have been adopted by Great Britain, in common with other nations, in a positive manner. Moreover, if such rules conflicted with established principles of the English common law, an English court was bound not to apply them. But in 1905, in the decision of *West Rand Central Gold Mining Co v R*,[3] there was a partial return to the traditional 'incorporation' doctrine, albeit the Court of Appeal in that case reaffirmed it in none too positive terms.

In a number of later pronouncements, the doctrine again received recognition, though in somewhat hesitant language, and with certain qualifications. Thus Lord Atkin declared in *Chung Chi Cheung v R*:[4]

'The Courts acknowledge the existence of a body of rules which nations accept among themselves. On any judicial issue they seek to ascertain what the relevant rule is, and, having found it, they will treat it as incorporated into the domestic law, *so far as it is not inconsistent with rules enacted by Statutes or finally declared by their tribunals*.'

In addition to the qualifications stated by Lord Atkin, that a customary rule must not be inconsistent with statutes or prior judicial decisions of final authority, it is also a condition precedent that the rule is one generally accepted by the international community.

'It is a recognised prerequisite of the adoption in our municipal law of a doctrine of public international law that it shall have attained the position of general acceptance by civilised nations as a rule of international conduct, evidenced by international treaties and conventions, authoritative textbooks, practice, and judicial decisions.'[5]

19. 1 B & C 554.
20. 2 Bing 314.
1. 30 LJ Ch 690 at 700.
2. 2 Ex D 63 at 202 et seq and 270.
3. [1905] 2 KB 391.
4. [1939] AC 160 at 168. Cf however the dicta of Lord Denning MR in *Trendtex Trading Corpn v Central Bank of Nigeria* [1977] QB 529 at 554–557, [1977] 1 All ER 881 at 889–890. See also on the binding operation of statutes, even if in contravention of international law, *Croft v Dunphy* [1933] AC 156 at 163–4.
5. *Compania Naviera Vascongado v SS Cristina* [1938] AC 485 at 497 per Lord MacMillan.

Despite the more far-reaching endorsement of the automatic incorporation doctrine by Lord Denning in *Trendtex Trading Corpn v Central Bank of Nigeria*[6], Lord Atkin's view seems closer to the one judicially accepted today. That view may best be expressed, as by Sir Owen Dixon of the High Court of Australia, in the form that international law is not automatically part of the common law but is one of the sources of rules applied by British courts.[7] A clear rule of a prescriptive or proscriptive nature[8], such as the immunity of diplomats or the existence of genocide as a crime, will always be applied. However, a merely permissive rule[9], or a rule not clearly established as such in international law[10], may not be applied, unless the court, exercising its power within the permitted leeways of judicial choice, chooses to change or develop the common law in the direction of harmonising it with what it perceives to be, or likely to be, a rule of international law.[11]

Apart from the two qualifications to the rule as stated above, there are two important exceptions to the automatic applicability of customary international law by British municipal courts:

1. Acts of state by the executive, for example a declaration of war, or an annexation of territory, may not be questioned by British municipal courts, notwithstanding that a breach of international law may have been involved.[12]
2. British municipal courts regard themselves as bound by a certificate or authoritative statement on behalf of the executive (that is to say, the Crown) in regard to certain matters falling peculiarly within the Crown's prerogative powers, such as the de jure or de facto recognition of states, the sovereign nature of governments, and the diplomatic status of persons claiming jurisdictional immunity on the grounds of diplomatic privilege, although such certificate or statement may be difficult to reconcile with existing rules of international law.[13]

Notwithstanding judicial doubts as to its scope, the incorporation doctrine has left its definite mark in two established rules recognised by British courts:

6. [1977] QB 529, [1977] 1 All ER 881.
7. *Chow Hung Ching v R* (1949) 77 CLR 449, 477.
8. A helpful description by the editors of *Oppenheim's International Law* (9th edn, 1992), 57.
9. Such as the rule permitting jurisdiction to be exercised over foreign citizens in the territorial sea, considered in *R v Keyn*, supra.
10. Eg the juridical personality of international organisations: *JH Rayner (Mincing Lane) Ltd v Board of Trade; Maclaine Watson v Board of Trade* (The International Tin Council Case) [1990] 2 AC 418. Contrast *Arab Monetary Fund v Hashim (No 3)* [1991] 2 AC 114, where the entity had legal status under foreign law.
11. Thus Lord Denning succeeded, by virtue of the later cases following *Trendtex* (eg *I Congreso del Partido* [1983] 1 AC 244), in changing the common law relating to sovereign immunity in actions in personam. In *Dietrich v R* (1992) 177 CLR 292 the High Court of Australia markedly ignored submissions based on the provisions of art 14(d) of the International Covenant on Civil and Political Rights, which was argued to have crystallised as a binding rule of general law a right to legal counsel for accused in serious criminal cases. Nevertheless the court overtly changed the common law in the same direction as this international law standard.
12. See *Cook v Sprigg* [1899] AC 572, and W. Harrison Moore *Act of State in English Law* (1906) pp 78, 82, and pp 132 et seq.
13. See, eg, *The Arantzazu Mendi* [1939] AC 256, and *Engelke v Musmann* [1928] AC 433. See also pp 135–137 below. Section 21 of the United Kingdom State Immunity Act 1978 renders

a. *A rule of construction.* Acts of Parliament and statutory instruments are to be interpreted so as not to conflict with international law. There is indeed a presumption that Parliament did not intend to commit a breach of international law.[14] But this rule of construction does not apply if the statute is otherwise clear and unambiguous,[15] in which case it must be applied.
b. *A rule of evidence.* International law need not, like foreign law, be proved as a fact by expert evidence or otherwise. The British courts will take judicial notice of its rules, and may of their own volition refer to textbooks and other sources for evidence thereof.[16]

In the matter of giving effect to international law, the position of British Prize Courts is different from that of the courts of common law and equity. Prize Courts are specifically appointed to apply international law, and according to the leading case of *The Zamora*[17] are not bound by an executive Order-in-Council which contravenes or purports to alter a rule of international law, although presumably they would be obliged to follow an Act of Parliament in breach of international law.

(ii) The British practice as to treaties, as distinct from customary international law, is conditioned primarily by the constitutional principles governing the relations between the executive (that is to say, the Crown) and Parliament. The negotiation, signature, and ratification of treaties are matters belonging to the prerogative powers of the Crown. If, however, the provisions of a treaty made by the Crown were to become operative within Great Britain automatically and without any specific act of incorporation, this might lead to the result that the Crown could alter the British municipal law or otherwise take some important step without consulting Parliament or obtaining Parliament's approval.

---

conclusive a certificate by or on behalf of the Secretary of State as to a number of material questions for the purposes of the privileges and immunities conferred by the first Part of the Act, namely, whether a country is a state, whether any territory is a constituent part of a federal state and whether a person or persons may be regarded as the head of a government or of a state.

14. *The Le Louis* (1817) 2 Dods 210 at 251 and 254; *Corocraft Ltd v Pan American Airways Inc* [1969] 1 QB 616, [1969] 1 All ER 82; *R v Chief Immigration Officer, Heathrow Airport, ex p Bibi* [1976] 3 All ER 843 at 847; and cf *James Buchanan & Co Ltd v Babco Forwarding and Shipping (UK) Ltd* [1978] AC 141; *Fothergill v Monarch Airlines Ltd* [1981] AC 251; *Vervaeke v Smith* [1981] Fam 77, [1981] 1 All ER 55; and *The Alastor* [1981] 1 Lloyd's Rep 581.
15. See decision of House of Lords in *Collco Dealings Ltd v IRC* [1962] AC 1 at 19, [1961] 1 All ER 762 at 765; decision of High Court of Australia in *Polites v Commonwealth* (1945) 70 CLR 60; and the judgments of the Court of Appeal in *Salomon v Customs and Excise Comrs* [1967] 2 QB 116, [1966] 3 All ER 871. The court may look at the relevant multilateral convention implemented by the statute in order to resolve ambiguities in the statute, even though the statute does not mention the convention, or does not exactly correspond with the convention in wording or in effect, or even if the statute is enacted before the ratification of the convention; see *The Banco* [1971] P 137 at 145, 151, 157 and *D and R Henderson (MFG) Pty Ltd v Collector of Customs (NSW)* (1974) 48 ALJR 132 at 135. Cf also *Mohammad Mohy-ud-Din v King Emperor (India)* (1946) 8 FCR 94; *Theophile v Solicitor-General* [1950] AC 186 at 195; and *Cheney v Conn (Inspector of Taxes)* [1968] 1 All ER 779 at 781A.
16. *Re Piracy Jure Gentium* [1934] AC 586.
17. [1916] 2 AC 77 at 91–94.

Hence it has become established that:[18]

a.   Treaties which: (1) affect the private rights of British subjects, or (2) involve any modification of the common or statute law[19] by virtue of their provisions or otherwise,[20] or (3) require the vesting of additional powers in the Crown, or (4) impose additional financial obligations, direct or contingent, upon the government of Great Britain, must receive parliamentary assent through an enabling Act of Parliament, and, if necessary, any legislation to effect the requisite changes in the law must be passed.[1]

b.   Treaties made expressly subject to the approval of Parliament require its approval, which is usually given in the form of a statute, though sometimes by Resolution.

c.   Treaties involving the cession of British territory require the approval of Parliament given by a statute.

d.   No legislation is required for certain specific classes of treaties, namely, treaties modifying the belligerent rights of the Crown when engaged in maritime warfare[2] (presumably because such treaties involve no major intrusion on the legislative domain of Parliament), and administrative agreements of an informal character needing only signature, but not ratification, provided they do not involve any alteration of municipal law.

Where under the above-mentioned rules, a British treaty is required to be implemented by legislation, a mere general or vague allusion to the treaty in a statute is not sufficient to constitute the necessary legislative implementation.[3]

---

18. Note the constitutional convention known as the 'Ponsonby Rule', whereby treaties, subject to ratification, are tabled in both Houses of Parliament for a period of 21 days before the government proceeds to ratification.

19. Exceptions to (1) and (2) are:

   a.   An agreement to admit a foreign armed force, conceding certain immunities from local jurisdiction to the members of that force; see *Chow Hung Ching v R* (1949) 77 CLR 449, and below, pp 207–210.

   b.   A treaty of peace to which the United Kingdom is a party, terminating a war; this will, semble, put an end to the situation under which persons voluntarily resident in, or carrying on business in, enemy territory, are treated as enemy aliens, who are not entitled to bring proceedings in the courts without the licence of the Crown (cf *Porter v Freudenberg* [1915] 1 KB 857).

   c.   A treaty conceding special immunities and privileges to the diplomatic and consular officers of a particular state and a treaty regulating the conduct of war (cf McNair *The Law of Treaties* (1961) pp 89–91).

20. Eg, a treaty or convention signed by Great Britain binding it to pass certain legislation.

1.   See *Walker v Baird* [1892] AC 491 at 497; *The Parlement Belge* (1879) 4 PD 129; *A-G for Canada v A-G for Ontario* [1937] AC 326 at 347; *Blackburn v A-G* [1971] 1 WLR 1037, CA; *Laker Airways Ltd v Department of Trade* [1977] QB 643; *Simsek v Macphee* (1982) 148 CLR 636; and *Maclaine Watson & Co Ltd v International Tin Council* ([1990] 2 AC 418: inapplicability of 6th International Tin Agreement which entered into force in July 1982). Cf *Francis v R* (1956) 3 DLR (2d) 641, and Mann *Studies in International Law* (1973) p 328.

2.   But not treaties increasing the rights of the Crown in that connection; cf *The Zamora* [1916] 2 AC 77.

3.   See *Republic of Italy v Hambros Bank Ltd* [1950] Ch 314. See also, as to the necessity for *specific* legislative implementation, the Australian case *Bradley v Commonwealth of Australia* (1973) 128 CLR 447 (United Nations Charter not specifically implemented by any appropriate legislation).

It follows also that, where a statute contains provisions which are unambiguously[4] inconsistent with those of an earlier treaty, a British municipal court must apply the statute in preference to the treaty. However, where the statute is ambiguous, a presumption arises that Parliament did not intend to legislate contrary to the Crown's international obligations under a treaty, and the court may look at the treaty for the purpose of interpreting the ambiguous statutory language, notwithstanding that the statute does not specifically incorporate or refer to the treaty.[5]

A qualified exception is the European Convention on Human Rights, 1950, which has not been made part of the statute law of the United Kingdom. Strictly speaking, its constitutional position is no different from that of other treaties, but in practice British courts tend to be more ready to find gaps or ambiguities in the common or statute law in order to permit its application.[6] In *Derbyshire County Council v Times Newspapers Ltd* the Court of Appeal held that whether or not a statutory authority could pursue a suit in defamation for attacks made on its reputation was not clearly settled in the common law, and looked to the Convention for guidance in holding that no such right should exist, having regard to the principle of freedom of speech as applied to public authorities. The House of Lords on appeal held that the common law unambiguously excluded such a right of action at the suit of public authorities; thus it was unnecessary to consider the Convention (which, if applied, would have led to the same result).[7] In *R v Secretary of State for the Home Department, ex p Brind* it was held by the House of Lords that the European Convention on Human Rights had not been incorporated into domestic law 'through the back door' so as to govern the exercise of executive discretion created by statute without reference to the Convention. Lord Bridge stated that:

> 'Where Parliament has conferred on the executive an administrative discretion without indicating the precise limits within which it must be exercised, to presume that it must be exercised within Convention limits would be to go far beyond the resolution of an ambiguity. It would be to impute to Parliament an intention not only that the executive should exercise the discretion in conformity with the Convention, but also that the domestic courts should enforce that conformity by the importation into domestic administrative law of the text of the Convention and the jurisprudence of the European Court of Human Rights in the interpretation and application of it.'[8]

In view of the binding effect of decisions of the European Court of Human Rights in cases to which the United Kingdom is a party[9] the pressure towards direct statutory implementation of the Convention in United Kingdom law is gaining strength.

---

4. See decision of House of Lords in *Collco Dealings Ltd v IRC* [1962] AC 1, [1961] 1 All ER 762, and *The Banco* [1971] P 137 at 145, 151, 157.
5. *Salomon v Customs and Excise Comrs* [1967] 2 QB 116, [1966] 3 All ER 871; *R v Secretary of State for the Home Dept, ex p Brind* [1991] 1 AC 696.
6. Eg *A-G v Guardian Newspapers Ltd (No 2)* [1990] 1 AC 109, per Lord Goff at 283. But cf *Malone v Metropolitan Police Comr* [1979] Ch 344.
7. [1992] QB 770, CA; [1993] AC 534, HL.
8. [1991] 1 AC 696 at 748.
9. See eg *Malone v United Kingdom* (1984) 7 EHRR 14, E Ct HR.

The above-mentioned rules concerning British practice as to the applicability of treaties are subject to the special exception of European Community law which, where given direct effect in accordance with Community treaties, have direct effect in United Kingdom law and have primacy over past or future statute law.[10] For this purpose 'Community law' does not include the European Convention on Human Rights, 1950, which antedated the establishment of the Community and is open to participation by a wider group of states.

American practice

In the matter of customary rules of international law, the American practice is very similar to the British practice. Such rules are administered as part of the law of the land,[11] and Acts of the United States Congress are construed so as not to conflict therewith,[12] although a later clear statute will prevail over earlier customary international law.[13] Also, an American court is entitled to ascertain the rules of international law on a particular point by referring to textbooks, state practice, and other sources.[14] Deference is, however, paid to the views of the executive, as in the case of British courts, to the extent that American courts normally regard themselves as bound by the certificates or 'suggestions' of the executive regarding such matters as the recognition of foreign states, the territorial limits of a foreign country, and the immunity of governments, persons, corporations, or vessels from jurisdiction.[15]

But so far as treaties are concerned, there is a radical difference from the British practice. The American practice does not depend like the British practice upon any reconciliation between the prerogative powers of the executive and the legislative domain of Parliament, but upon the provisions of the United States Constitution stipulating that 'all Treaties made, or which shall be made under the Authority of the United States', shall be 'the supreme Law of the Land' (see article VI, para 2), and upon a distinction drawn by American courts between 'self-executing' and 'non-self-executing' treaties.[16] A self-executing treaty is one

10. European Communities Act 1972, s 2; *R v HM Treasury, ex p Smedley* [1985] QB 657, CA; *The Siskina* [1979] AC 210; *Factortame Ltd v Secretary of State for Transport* [1990] 2 AC 85, HL; sub nom C–219/89 *R v Secretary of State for Transport, ex p Factortame Ltd (No 2)* [1991] 1 AC 603, ECJ.
11. *The Paquete Habana* 175 US 677 (1900) at 700, and *United States v Melekh* 190 F Supp 67 (1960). However, in *Pauling v McElroy* 164 F Supp 390 (1958), a federal court refused to give effect to the principle of the freedom of the high seas in a suit brought by individuals to restrain the government from detonating nuclear weapons in the Marshall Islands. Moreover, customary rules of international law not accepted or disputed by the United States, will not be applied in American courts; see Buergenthal and Maier *Public International Law* (1985) p 204.
12. *Murray v Schooner Charming Betsy* 6 US (2 Cranch) 64 (1804) at 118.
13. *The Over the Top* 5 F 2d at 842 (1925). An American federal statute will not be treated as superseded by customary international law; see *Banco Nacional de Cuba v Sabbatino* 376 US 398 (1964) at 423. A fortiori the courts will not give effect to a rule of international law which conflicts with the United States Constitution; see *Tag v Rogers* 267 F 2d 664 (1959).
14. *The Paquete Habana*, note 11 above.
15. In *Spacil v Crowe* 489 F 2d 614 (1974) at 619–20, a Circuit Court of Appeals declined to treat, as open to judicial review, a Department of State 'suggestion' allowing the immunity of a Cuban vessel from arrest or attachment, and held that the judiciary was bound by the executive's decision. The executive may also appear as *amicus curiae*.
16. See *Foster v Neilson* 27 US (2 Pet) 253 (1829) at 314, and cf *Dreyfus v Von Finck* 534 F 2d 24 (1976).

which does not in the view of American courts expressly or by its nature require legislation to make it operative within the municipal field, and that is to be determined by regard to the intention of the signatory parties and to the surrounding circumstances.[17] If a treaty is within the terms of the Constitution, and it is self-executing within the meaning just referred to, then under the Constitution it is deemed to be operative as part of the law of the United States, and will prevail, also, over a customary rule of international law.[18] On the other hand, treaties which are not self-executing, but require legislation, are not binding upon American courts until the necessary legislation is enacted.[19] Moreover, if the relevant treaty purports to deal with a particular subject matter in respect of which the United States Congress has exclusive legislative powers, the treaty will be considered as prima facie non-self-executing irrespective of what the intention of the parties is claimed to be. The distinction between the two kinds of treaties involves some anomalies, and in 1952, Senator Bricker's proposed amendment to the Constitution included a provision to make all treaties, in effect, non-self-executing.

Self-executing treaties or conventions ratified by the United States, are binding on American courts, even if in conflict with previous American statutes,[20] provided that there is no conflict with the United States Constitution.[1] But a statute passed by Congress overrules previous treaties that have become the law of the land,[2] although there is a presumption that Congress did not intend to overrule such treaties, and unless the purpose of Congress to overrule

17. *Sei Fujii v The State of California* 38 Cal 2d 718 (1952) (Cal Sup Ct). In this case, the question was to what extent certain provisions of the United Nations Charter were self-executing. It was held that the human rights provisions of the Charter (arts 55–56) were not self-executing, but that, semble, the provisions relative to the privileges and immunities of the United Nations (arts 104–5) were. Note also *Pauling v McElroy* 164 F Supp 390 (1958), where it was held that the Charter, and the Trusteeship Agreement for the Trust Territory of the Pacific Islands were not self-executing treaties. But see *People of Saipan ex rel Guerrero v United States Department of Interior* 502 F 2d 90 (1974) where, on the one hand, Judge Goodwin held that the Trusteeship Agreement created judicially enforceable rights, for which relief could be obtained in the Trust Territory local Court, while, on the other hand, Judge Trask was of opinion that the Agreement was not self-executing, but had been sufficiently implemented by legislation (and see note in (1975) Texas ILJ 138–149).
18. See *Tag v Rogers* 267 F 2d 664 (1959), and Reiff 'The Enforcement of Multipartite Administrative Treaties in the United States' 34 AJIL (1940) 661–679. A self-executing treaty will prevail also over the contrary law of an American state: *Clark v Allen* 331 US 503 (1947).
19. Note also the constitutional distinction between 'treaties' and 'executive agreements' made by the President of the United States, the latter instruments not being subject to the requirement under art II, s 2 of the Constitution, of concurrence of two-thirds of the Senate; see the United Nations publications, *Laws and Practices concerning the Conclusion of Treaties* (1953) pp 129–130, Buergenthal and Maier *Public International Law* (1985) pp 199–200, and cf the Opinion (delivered by Mr Justice Sutherland) of the United States Supreme Court in *United States v Belmont* 301 US 324 (1937).
20. *Whitney v Robertson* 124 US 190 (1888) at 194. Cf also *Iannone v Radory Construction Corpn* 141 NYS 2d 311 (1955). This rule does not apply to 'executive agreements', which are invalid if they conflict with a substantive federal enactment: see *Seery v United States* 127 F Supp 601 (1955). See, however, *Territory v HO* (1957) 41 Hawaii Reports 565. As to the constitutional validity of legislation giving effect to an executive agreement, note *Kinsella v Krueger* 354 US 1 (1957). A treaty will prevail over an earlier statute only if it contains a substantive inconsistency with the statute; see *Bank Voor Handel en Scheepvaart NV v Kennedy* 288 F 2d 375 (1961).
1. *Cherokee Tobacco Co v United States* 11 Wall 616 (1870).
2. See *Tag v Rogers* 267 F 2d 664 (1959), and *Mercado v Feliciano* 260 F 2d 500 (1958).

international law has been clearly expressed, such abrogation or modification will not be deemed to have been carried out.[3]

Practice of states other than Great Britain and the United States
The practice of states other than Great Britain and the United States reveals wide variations both in the requirements of constitutional law, and in the attitudes of municipal courts concerning the application therein of customary international law and of treaties.

So far as one can sum up this practice, and despite the hazard of generalisation on so complex a matter, the following propositions may be ventured:

1. In a large number of states, customary rules of international law are applied as part of internal law by municipal courts, without the necessity for any specific act of incorporation, provided that there is no conflict with existing municipal law.
2. Only a minority of states follow a practice whereby, without the necessity for any specific act of incorporation, their municipal courts apply customary rules of international law to the extent of allowing these to prevail in case of conflict with a municipal statute or municipal judge-made law.
3. There is no uniform practice concerning the application of treaties within the municipal sphere. Each country has its own particularities as regards promulgation or publication of treaties, legislative approval of treaty provisions, and so on.[4] Moreover, certain treaties, such as informal administrative arrangements, are never submitted to the legislature. Also the courts in some countries, for example the German Federal Republic, will, like American courts, give effect to self-executing treaties, that is to say, those capable of application without the necessity of legislative implementation. In other countries, for example, Belgium, legislative enactment or legislative approval is necessary for almost all treaties, particularly those which affect the status of private citizens.[5] As to conflicts between the provisions of treaties and earlier or later statutes, it is only in relatively few countries that the superiority of the treaty in this regard is established. France is a case in point, for if a treaty has been duly ratified in accordance with law, French tribunals, both judicial and administrative, will give effect to it, notwithstanding a conflict with internal legislation. But in most countries, for example, Norway, treaties do not per se operate to supersede state legislation or judge-made law. Exceptionally, however, there are some countries the courts of which go so far as to give full force to treaties, even if contrary to the provisions of the constitution of the country concerned.
4. In general, there is discernible a considerable weight of state practice requiring that in a municipal court, primary regard be paid to municipal law, irrespective of the applicability of rules of international law, and hence

3. *Cook v United States* 288 US 102 (1933) at 120.
4. Note the curious case of Austria; treaties automatically bind the Administration without publication, but need to be gazetted in order to affect rights of the public in general. At the same time, purely departmental and administrative agreements are not usually published.
5. See as to India, decision in *Biswambhar v State of Orissa* A 1957, Orissa 247, and Basu *Commentaries on the Constitution of India* (1962) Vol II, p 323.

relegating the question of any breach of international law to the diplomatic domain.

Reference should be made in this connection to certain modern constitutions, containing far-reaching provisions to the effect that international law shall be treated as an integral part of municipal law. A current example is article 25 of the Basic Law for the Federal Republic of Germany which lays down that the general rules of public international law shall form part of federal law, and shall take precedence over the laws of and create rights and duties directly for the inhabitants of the federal territory.[6] It has been claimed that this and similar constitutional provisions reflect a growing tendency among states to acknowledge the supremacy of international law within the municipal sphere. Be that as it may, it is none the less curious that these constitutional provisions appear to support the positivist thesis that before international law can be applicable by municipal courts some specific adoption by municipal law is required, since it is only in virtue of these provisions of municipal constitutional law that the rules of international law are valid and applicable within the municipal sphere. This reasoning may well be carried a stage further; even the Anglo-American judge-made doctrine that customary international law, subject to certain qualifications, forms part of the law of the land,[7] appears to be a doctrine of municipal law on the same plane as express municipal constitutional provisions of similar effect and to support the view that a specific municipal adoption of international law is required. Yet, admitting this, it must still be added that it is unlikely that when the British 'incorporation' doctrine was first enunciated by British courts in the eighteenth century, those courts were purporting to declare a principle of municipal constitutional law rather than to acknowledge the validity as such of the law of nations.

In regard, however, to the application of treaties within the municipal sphere, the above survey of state practice does not support the thesis that some municipal *transformation* is required in every case before treaties become operative in the municipal field. The necessity for some formal municipal change appears to depend upon two matters principally:

1.   The nature and provisions of the particular treaty concerned. Thus some treaties are self-operating or self-executing,[8] and do not require any legislative implementation, as appears from the state practice considered above.

---

6.   Cf art 4 of the German Republican Constitution of 1919, which provided that 'the universally recognised rules of international law are valid as binding constituent parts of German Federal law'. Art 25 of the Basic Law does not operate to confer supremacy on treaties concluded by the Federal Republic over municipal law, or to enable international law to prevail over fundamental provisions of the Basic Law; cf Case 11/70: *Internationale Handelsgesellschaft mbH v Einführ-und Vorratsstelle für Gertreide und Futtermittel* [1972] CMLR 255, and Ulrich Scheuner 'Fundamental Rights in European Community Law and in National Constitutional Law' (1975) 12 CML Rev 171 at 177 et seq.

7.   See above, pp 68–71 and 74 in this chapter.

8.   The Court of Justice of the European Communities held in *International Fruit Co NV v Productschap Voor Groenten en Fruit* 67 AJIL (1972) 559–563 that art XI of the General Agreement on Tariffs and Trade (GATT) of 30 October 1947, prohibiting, subject to qualifications and restrictions, quantitative restrictions was not, in effect, self-executing in countries within the framework of the European Economic Community.

2. The constitutional or administrative practice of each particular state (see above). Also, it frequently happens that certain states (an outstanding illustration is Austria) allow the execution of a treaty to proceed by administrative practice alone without enacting laws or issuing regulations. In such a case, there is no structural transformation of the rules laid down in the treaty.

4. INTERNATIONAL TRIBUNALS AND THE OPERATION OF MUNICIPAL LAW

The fact that municipal courts must pay primary regard to municipal law in the event of a conflict with international law, in no way affects the obligations of the state concerned to perform its international obligations. A municipal court which defers to municipal law, notwithstanding an inconsistent rule of international law, itself acts in breach of international law, and will, as an organ of the state, engage the international responsibility of that state. Hence, before an international tribunal, a respondent state cannot plead that its municipal law (not even its constitution[9]) contains rules which conflict with international law, nor can it plead the *absence* of any legislative provision or of a rule of internal law as a defence to a charge that it has broken international law. This point was well put in the course of proceedings in the *Finnish Ships Arbitration:*[10]

> 'As to the manner in which its municipal law is framed, the State has under international law, a complete liberty of action, and its municipal law is a domestic matter in which no other State is entitled to concern itself, *provided that the municipal law is such as to give effect to all the international obligations of the State.*'

This may even import a duty upon a state, in an appropriate case, to pass the necessary legislation to fulfil its international obligations.[11] To this extent, the primacy of international law is preserved.

The same rule applies with regard to treaties. A state cannot plead that its domestic law exonerated it from performing obligations imposed by an international treaty, unless in giving its consent to the treaty, a fundamental rule of municipal law concerning constitutional competence to conclude the treaty

---

9. See the *United Nations Headquarters Agreement Case*, ICJ 1988, 12, concerning the closure of the Palestine Liberation Organization's Mission to the United Nations pursuant to United States legislation in conflict with its treaty obligations to the UN; *Advisory Opinion on the Treatment of Polish Nationals in Danzig*, (1932) PCIJ , Series A/B, No 44 at 24, and also *Case of the Free Zones of Upper Savoy and Gex*, (1932) PCIJ, Series A/B No 46 at 167. Art 7 of the Constitution of El Salvador of 1950, laying down that the territory of the Republic included the adjacent waters to a distance of two hundred sea-miles from low water-line, was alleged by the United States in 1950 to be in breach of international law.

10. See *United Nations Reports of International Arbitral Awards* Vol 3, p 1484. Art 13 of the Draft Declaration of Rights and Duties of States adopted by the International Law Commission in 1949 also provides: 'Every State has the duty to carry out in good faith its obligations arising from treaties and other sources of international law, and it may not invoke provisions in *its constitution or its laws* as an excuse for failure to perform this duty'.

11. *Advisory Opinion on the Exchange of Greek and Turkish Populations* (1925) PCIJ Series B, No 10 p 20.

concerned was broken, and this breach of municipal constitutional law was manifest.[12]

The effect of article 25 of the United Nations Charter is to give binding force to decisions of the Security Council, notwithstanding municipal law to the contrary. Article 103 also gives superior force to obligations under the Charter over conflicting treaties.[13]

This overriding regard for international law before international tribunals does not mean that the rules of municipal law are irrelevant in cases before international tribunals. Frequently, on the threshold of the determination of some international claim, it is necessary for an international tribunal to ascertain or interpret or apply municipal law, for example, where it is claimed that a denial of justice by a municipal tribunal has taken place, or where a treaty provision, calling for interpretation, refers to municipal law,[14] or sometimes merely for the purpose of elucidating the facts. Again, international tribunals are often constrained to consider the municipal laws of states generally, to ascertain whether cumulatively they lead to the inference that a customary rule of international law has evolved.[15] Or it may be that for the purpose of assisting in the determination of a difficult point of international law, an international tribunal will have regard to municipal law or to the special characteristics of municipal legal institutions,[16] or in an appropriate case may have recourse to analogies drawn from municipal law.

In this connection, a close study of the pleadings and arguments in the cases decided by the Permanent Court of International Justice and its present successor, the International Court of Justice, shows how important a role municipal law played in each instance. Indeed, few were the cases in which these courts reached a solution without the most minute examination of the municipal law relevant to the questions calling for determination, while one of the most striking aspects of the process by which both courts arrived at their decisions was the manner in which, almost spontaneously, the issues of international law emerged and became disengaged from the mass of municipal legal material relied upon by the parties in the pleadings and in the oral proceedings.

12. Vienna Convention of 23 May 1969 on the Law of Treaties, arts 27 and 46; and cf *Advisory Opinion on the Jurisdiction of the Courts of Danzig,* (1928) PCIJ Series B, No 15, pp 26–27.
13. *Case concerning Questions of Interpretation and Application of the 1971 Montreal Convention Arising from the Aerial Incident at Lockerbie* (Libya v USA, Libya v UK): Request for Provisional Measures, ICJ 1992, 3, 114.
14. The so-called 'reference without reception' to municipal law.
15. As in the *Lotus Case* (1927) Pub PCIJ Series A, No 10.
16. See *Case Concerning the Barcelona Traction, Light and Power Co Ltd (Second Phase)* ICJ 1970, 3, where the International Court of Justice, in reaching the conclusion that, as a general rule, the national state of shareholders of a company was not entitled to espouse their claim for loss suffered as a result of an international wrong done to the company itself, had regard to the general position at municipal law that an infringement of a company's rights by outsiders did not involve liability towards the shareholders. See para 50 of the judgment, where the Court said: 'If the Court were to decide the case in disregard of the relevant institutions of municipal law it would, without justification, invite serious legal difficulties. It would lose touch with reality, for there are no corresponding institutions of international law to which the Court could resort.'

5.   CONCEPT OF OPPOSABILITY

The concept of opposability (French, *opposabilité*), which has come into current use in the field of international law,[17] is of some value where the relationship between international law and municipal law is concerned.

In a dispute before an international tribunal between two states, A and B, where state A relies upon some ground in support of its claim, state B may seek to invoke as against, ie 'oppose' to state A some rule, institution, or régime under state B's domestic law in order to defeat the ground of claim set up by state A. As a general principle, if the domestic rule, institution, or régime is in accordance with international law, this may be legitimately 'opposed' to state A in order to negate its ground of claim,[18] but if not in accordance with international law, the domestic rule, institution, or régime may not be so 'opposed'.[19]

The convenience of the concept of opposability lies in the fact that if a rule of domestic law is held to be non-opposable, this does not necessarily mean that the rule ceases to be valid in the domestic domain; and, in any event, as Kelsen has pointed out,[20] international law provides no procedure of invalidation, within the domestic framework, of a rule of municipal law. If the position be that the rule of domestic law, held to be non-opposable, is itself invalid by reference to the provisions of domestic constitutional law, then the rule is not opposable also to states other than the claimant state, unless perhaps such other states have expressly waived the constitutional invalidity of the rule.

Of course, a treaty rule may be opposable by one state to another state, in respect of the latter's ground of claim, in the same way as with a rule of domestic law, and similarly if the treaty rule is deemed to be non-opposable, it may none the less be validly opposable to certain states other than the claimant state.[1]

According to the Advisory Opinion of 21 June 1971, of the International Court of Justice on the *Legal Consequences for States of the Continued Presence*

17. See *North Sea Continental Shelf Cases, Pleadings, Oral Arguments, Documents* ICJ 1968, 1, Counter-Memorial of Denmark, pp 176–177, and judgment of the International Court of Justice in the same Cases, ICJ 1969, 3 at 41 and cf Bin Cheng *Year Book of World Affairs* (1966) p 247.
18. Eg the baselines method of delimitation of the territorial sea was successfully opposed by Norway to the United Kingdom's claim of free fishery rights in the waters concerned, in the *Fisheries Case* ICJ 1951, 116, and see pp 224, 235 below.
19. Eg in the *Nottebohm Case (second phase)* ICJ 1955, 4, Liechtenstein's grant of nationality to a German, resident for many years in Guatemala, was not held to be invalid for all purposes but was held, in effect, to be non-opposable to Guatemala for the purpose of asserting a right of espousal by Liechtenstein of Nottebohm's complaint against his former state of habitual residence. Also in 1974 in the *Fisheries Jurisdiction Cases (United Kingdom and Federal German Republic v Iceland)* ICJ 1974, 3, 175, the International Court of Justice held that the Icelandic Regulations of 14 July 1972, representing a unilateral extension of the Iceland coastal fisheries limit to 50 miles, were not 'opposable' either to the United Kingdom or to the Federal Republic of Germany by reason of their established historic fishing rights in the affected areas.
20. Kelsen *Pure Theory of Law* (2nd edn, translated by Max Knight, 1967) p 331.
1. Eg in the *North Sea Continental Shelf Cases* ICJ 1969, 3, art 6 of the Geneva Convention on the Continental Shelf of 29 April 1958, containing the equidistance rule for the delimitation of a continental shelf common to adjacent countries, was held not opposable to the German Federal Republic (ibid at 41), which had not ratified the Convention, but in the event of a subsequent case involving a state which had ratified the Convention without reservation as to art 6, this article would be opposable to such a state.

of South Africa in South West Africa (Namibia),[2] a determination of the United Nations Security Council, which declares that a certain situation is illegal, may be opposable to all states, whether members or non-members, that may seek to rely upon the legality of the situation. Thus, in the Court's opinion, the termination of South Africa's mandate over South West Africa, by reason of its refusal to submit to the supervision of United Nations organs, and the consequence that its presence in the territory was illegal, according to the terms of a Security Council Resolution of 1970, were opposable to all states in the sense of barring erga omnes the legality of South Africa's continued administration of the mandate.

2.   ICJ 1971, 16 at 56.

PART 2

States as subjects of international law

CHAPTER 5

States in general

1. NATURE OF A STATE AT INTERNATIONAL LAW

As we have seen, states are the principal subjects of international law. Of the term 'state' no exact definition is possible, but so far as modern conditions go, the essential characteristics of a state are well settled.

Article 1 of the Montevideo Convention of 1933 on the Rights and Duties of States (signed by the United States and certain Latin American countries) enumerates these characteristics:

'The State as a person of international law should possess the following qualifications:—(a) a permanent population; (b) a defined territory; (c) a Government;[1] and (d) a capacity to enter into relations with other States.'

As to (b), a fixed territory is not essential to the existence of a state provided that there is an acceptable degree of what is characterised as 'consistency' in the nature of the territory in question and of its population,[2] although in fact all modern states are contained within territorial limits. Accordingly, alterations, whether by increase or decrease, in the extent of a particular state's territory, do not of themselves change the identity of that state.[3] Nor need the territory

1. Ie a government to which the population renders habitual obedience. The temporary exile of the government while an aggressor state is in military occupation does not result in the disappearance of the state; cf the cases of governments-in-exile (eg Norway) during the Second World War 1939–45, which issued decrees, took part in international conferences, and signed agreements on behalf of their states; see *Netherlands v Federal Reserve Bank of New York* 201 F 2d 455 (1953).
2. Thus, Israel was admitted as a member state of the United Nations in May 1949, notwithstanding that its boundaries were not then defined with precision, pending negotiations regarding demarcation. Professor Jessup (later a judge of the International Court of Justice), speaking as United States representative on the Security Council, said on 2 December 1948, with regard to Israel's qualifications to be admitted to the United Nations: 'The formulae in the classic treatises somewhat vary, one from the other, but both reason and history demonstrate that the concept of territory [of a state] does not necessarily include precise delimitation of the boundaries of that territory'.
3. In August 1990 the German Democratic Republic (established in 1949 in the Soviet Occupation Zone) and the Federal Republic of Germany (established in 1949 in the occupation zone of the western powers) agreed to merge by way of accession of the former to the Federal Republic under provisions of the latter's constitution: Treaty on the Establishment of German Unity, 31

possess geographical unity; it may consist of territorial areas, lacking connection, or distant from each other.

So far as international law is concerned, the qualification (d) is the most important. A state must have recognised capacity to maintain external relations with other states. This distinguishes states proper from lesser units such as members of a federation, or protectorates, which do not manage their own foreign affairs, and are not recognised by other states as fully-fledged members of the international community.

The state is by no means necessarily identical with a particular race or nation, although such identity may exist.[4]

As we have already pointed out,[5] Kelsen's conception of the state emphasises that it is purely a technical notion expressing the fact that a certain body of legal rules binds a certain group of individuals living within a defined territorial area; in other words, the state and the law are synonymous terms.[6] On closer analysis, it will be seen that this theory is a condensation of the four characteristics of a state, set out above, and, in particular, the existence of a legal system is involved in the very requirement of a government as a component of statehood, for as Locke said:

> 'a government without laws is . . . a mystery in politics, inconceivable to human capacity and inconsistent with human society.'[7]

Kelsen's conception has not found favour with a number of more recent writers, particularly in Germany, who maintain that Kelsen, in stressing the identity of the state and the law, failed to do justice to the aspects of political power and sociological consequences involved in the establishment and continuance in being of a state. However, it is not to be denied that the existence of a legal system is a primal condition of statehood.

August 1990, (1991) 30 ILM 498. The merger took place at midnight on 2/3 October 1990. Thus there was an extinction of the German Democratic Republic, but no change of statehood of the Federal Republic of Germany: merely an enlargement of its territory. On 12 September 1990 France, the Soviet Union, the United Kingdom, and the United States signed a Treaty on the Final Settlement with Germany which brought to an end their responsibilities as victors over the German Reich, to which the Federal Republic of Germany can now be seen clearly as the successor, albeit within reduced territory. The post-1945 borders with Poland were confirmed by Germany in the treaty signed at Warsaw on 14 November 1990: see Piotrowicz in (1992) 63 BYIL 367-414. By contrast, the Federal Republic of Yugoslavia (Serbia and Montenegro) has not been accepted by the European Community or by the United Nations as the same state as the former Socialist Federal Republic of Yugoslavia: UN General Assembly Res 47/1, 22 September 1992, and see further below, p 292. For books on the subject of the identity and continuity of states in general, see K. Marek *Identity and Continuity of States in Public International Law* (1954), and Crawford *The Creation of States in International Law* (1979).

4.   Nor is the term 'state' necessarily or always equivalent to the expression 'country', more particularly where the latter expression is used in the constituent instrument of an international non-governmental association; see *Reel v Holder* [1981] 3 All ER 321 at 325, 326.

5.   See above, p 52.

6.   See Kelsen 55 Harv LR (1942) 65, where he trenchantly criticised the traditional notion of the 'dualism' of the state and the law.

7.   Quoted by Lord Wilberforce in *Carl-Zeiss-Stiftung v Rayner and Keeler Ltd (No 2)* [1967] 1 AC 853 at 954, [1966] 2 All ER 536 at 577.

In this connection, an important point is whether the statehood of an entity depends upon that entity being itself legal, and as well possessing a legal system which is juridically valid. Is an illegal state a contradiction in terms? In *Madzimbamuto v Lardner-Burke*,[8] the Judicial Committee of the Privy Council ruled that the Rhodesian régime created as a result of the unilateral declaration of independence of 11 November 1965, and of subsequent Rhodesian legislation, was illegal, and that, notwithstanding the de facto authority exercised by the régime, the laws of that régime were illegal and void by virtue of nullifying legislation in the United Kingdom.[9]

A state may exhibit all the hallmarks of statehood yet be denied recognition by other states by reason of the circumstances of its creation offending fundamental norms of the international legal order. The United Nations has come to play a crucial role in influencing recognition of statehood, either by way of ruling on an application for membership in the organisation or by way of resolutions condemning a declaration of statehood. The latter may be accompanied by a direction to UN Member States not to extend recognition to the illegal entity.[10] A claimant new state emerging as a result of aggression[11], the application of a system of racial discrimination[12], or the denial of the right of self-determination[13], will be condemned by the United Nations. When territory is acquired by the use of force contrary to the United Nations Charter, this too will normally be condemned.[14] The United Nations also declared illegal South Africa's continued presence in Namibia, a former mandated territory which remained subject to supervision by the United Nations, until South Africa granted it independence in 1990.

The United Nations, the European Community, and the Conference on Security and Cooperation in Europe have all played vital roles in assisting at the birth of the new states of Bosnia-Herzegovina, Croatia, Macedonia[15], and Slovenia in the face of opposition from Yugoslavia of which they were formerly

8. [1969] 1 AC 645 at 722–728.
9. See, however, the dissenting judgment of Lord Pearce at 731–745. The Appellate Division of the High Court of Rhodesia also decided contra in *R v Ndhlovu* 1968 (4) SA 515 at 532–535, holding, inter alia, that the government in Rhodesia was the only lawful government, and that effect should be given to the laws and constitution adopted in Rhodesia, pursuant to which that government was functioning.
10. See generally J Dugard *Recognition and the United Nations* (1987).
11. The League of Nations called on all its members not to recognise the State of Manchukuo, established by Japan as a result of aggression against China, in 1932. The Turkish Republic of Northern Cyprus was the subject of similar condemnatory resolutions of the UN Security Council in 1983 and 1984, as was Iraq's purported annexation of Kuwait in 1990.
12. The creation of the so-called 'black homelands' of South Africa—Transkei, Bophuthatswana, Venda, and Ciskei—were condemned by the Security Council between 1976 and 1981. See J Dugard *International Law—A South African Perspective* (1994) ch 5.
13. The cases of Rhodesia and the South African black homelands overlap with this category.
14. The United Nations condemned and called for non-recognition of Israel's annexation of East Jerusalem and of the Golan Heights. By contrast, Indonesia's acquisition of the Portuguese colony of East Timor by force in 1975 was 'deplored' in a series of UN resolutions from 1975 to 1982, but no call for non-recognition was included.
15. Admitted to the United Nations in April 1993 under the provisional name 'Former Yugoslav Republic of Macedonia' (FYROM) in order to take account of objections by Greece to the use of a name and symbols regarded by it as historically Greek. Greece has continued to withhold recognition of the FYROM.

part.[16] The Republic of Yugoslavia (Serbia and Montenegro) has been denied the right to occupy the Yugoslav seat in the United Nations on the ground that it is not the same legal entity as the former Socialist Federal Republic of Yugoslavia.[17].

States may also re-emerge after their sovereignty has been suppressed. Such are the cases of Estonia, Latvia, and Lithuania, which were forcibly incorporated into the Soviet Union in 1940. Most other states (including the United Kingdom) recognised that incorporation de facto but not de jure. In 1990-91 the three states successfully reclaimed their independence, which was acknowledged by most other states as a resumption of full statehood, but not as the creation of new states. The other constituent republics of the Soviet Union became recognised as independent states in 1991-92, exercising a right of secession contained in the Soviet Constitution but previously denied in practice. Belarus (formerly the Byelorussian SSR) and Ukraine retained their seats as original members of the United Nations which had been granted in 1945, despite their lack of true independence, as a strategic East-West compromise.[18] The other successor states to the Soviet Union (except the Russian Federation, which retained the permanent seat in the Security Council) were required to apply for United Nations membership as new states.[19]

'Micro-states'

A 'micro-state' was defined by the Secretary-General of the United Nations in his Introduction to his Annual Report of the work of the Organisation 1966–1967[20] as an entity, 'exceptionally small in area, population and human and economic resources', but which has emerged as an independent state.[1] The corresponding term in the pre-war days of the League of Nations was a 'Lilliputian state' (another term used currently is 'mini-state'). As the Secretary-General pointed out, even the smallest territories are entitled through the exercise of the right of self-determination to attain independence. However, there is necessarily a difference between independence, on the one hand, and the right of full membership of international organisations, such as the United Nations,

---

16. The Conference on Yugoslavia was established by the European Community and its Member States on 27 August 1991. It created an Arbitration Commission to consider the legal aspects of the break-up of the former Yugoslavia. The Commission delivered opinions in 1991-92 on the qualifications and conditions of statehood meriting recognition: 92 ILR 162-208, and see further below, p 571.
17. See M Weller in (1992) 86 AJIL 569; (1993) 42 ICLQ 433.
18. Stalin had argued for separate membership of each of the 15 constituent Soviet republics as a counterweight to the presumed influence Great Britain had over the independent members of the British Commonwealth.
19. See Rich in (1993) 4 Europ Jl Int Law 36-65.
20. See Report, p 20. See also, passim, *Small States and Territories: Status and Problems* (United Nations Institute for Training and Research, UNITAR, 1971), and Crawford *The Creation of States in International Law* (1979) pp 139–141.
1. An illustration is Nauru, which attained independence on 31 January 1968; the area of the island is 8.25 square miles, and the indigenous population about 3,000 persons. For a valuable, insightful book on micro-states, with particular reference to the Pacific area, see S. A. de Smith *Microstates and Micronesia* (1970), and for a general monograph on the subject, see Dieter Ehrhardt *Der Begriff des Mikrostaats im Völkerrecht und in der Internationalen Ordnung* (Aalen, 1970).

on the other. The obligations of membership of the United Nations may be too onerous for micro-states with their limited resources and population, while this might also weaken the United Nations itself.

There can be forms of association with the United Nations, short of full membership, conferring certain benefits without the burdens, and in the interests both of micro-states and of full member states, such as:

a. a right of access to the International Court of Justice;
b. participation in an appropriate United Nations regional economic commission;
c. participation in certain of the specialised agencies, and in diplomatic conferences summoned to adopt international conventions.

Nor is there any valid objection to a micro-state maintaining a permanent observer mission to the United Nations, as distinct from a permanent mission proper. This does not exhaust the possibilities of involvement in the work of the United Nations and its specialised agencies, open to micro-states.[2] It has been proposed (by the United States, among others) that micro-states should be catered for by a special form of 'associate membership' of the United Nations as such, not merely in relation to particular organs; semble, this would require an amendment of article 4 of the Charter, and related provisions.

Apart from the relationship of micro-states to international organisations, it seems that they may legitimately join with other states in forming regional groupings or associations, or in the establishment of a 'Community' of a functional nature.

Is a micro-state none the less a state within the meaning of the definition considered at the beginning of the present chapter? In principle, minuteness of territory and population, imposing practical limitations upon capacity to conduct external relations, does not constitute a bar to statehood.[3] The non-participation of a micro-state in the United Nations as a full member is conditioned by the express terms of article 4 of the Charter, under which one requirement of admission is ability to carry out the obligations contained in the Charter, and inability for other reasons to meet this condition might be an obstacle to the admission of a state of normal magnitude.

Doctrine of basic rights and duties of states

Numerous writers have purported to formulate lists of so-called 'basic' or 'fundamental' rights and duties of states. Such formulations have also been a persistent preoccupation of international Conferences or international bodies; among them may be mentioned those of the American Institute of International

2. As to these possibilities of participation, see S. A. de Smith, op cit, pp 10–14. Note also the status accorded to Nauru in 1968 of 'special member' of the Commonwealth, giving it a right of participation in functional activities, and attendance at ministerial or official meetings on educational, health, and technical questions, but not Heads of Government Conferences. Another example of this kind of participation is the fact that over twenty small *independent* island territories, each having less than one million people, are members of the International Monetary Fund (IMF); see *Finance and Development* June 1984 pp 42–43.
3. See Alain Coret 'L'Indépendence de l'Ile Nauru', *Annuaire Français de Droit International* (1968) pp 178–188.

Law in 1916, the Montevideo Convention of 1933 on the Rights and Duties of States, and the Draft Declaration on the Rights and Duties of States drawn up by the International Law Commission of the United Nations in 1949.[4] This latter draft Declaration still remains a draft under study by governments, and has failed to command general adoption.

The doctrine of basic rights and duties was favoured by certain of the naturalist writers,[5] being derived by them from the notion of the state as a creature of natural law; twentieth century formulations of the doctrine, especially those made in the Latin-American states, appear on the other hand to be directed towards the establishment of universal standards of law and justice in international relations, and this indeed seems to be the object of the Draft Declaration of 1949 (above).

The basic *rights* most frequently stressed have been those of the independence and equality of states, of territorial jurisdiction, and of self-defence or self-preservation. The basic *duties* emphasised have been, among others, those of not resorting to war, of carrying out in good faith treaty obligations, and of not intervening in the affairs of other states.[6]

There are grounds for scepticism as to the utility of the doctrine. Certain of the rights and duties declared to be 'basic' seem no more fundamental than other rights and duties not so formulated, or to be no more than restatements of truisms or axioms of international law (for example, the alleged basic duty to observe international law itself), or to be too sweepingly general to be accurate. Yet sometimes international tribunals have invoked a certain basic right or duty in determining the rules governing the case before them,[7] a recent illustration being the decision in 1986 of the International Court of Justice in *Nicaragua v United States*, where the Court expressly upheld the freedom of every state to choose which political, social, economic or cultural system it should adopt, and declared, inter alia, that the adherence by a particular state to any special political doctrine did not constitute a violation of any rule of customary international law.[8]

Sovereignty and independence of states

Normally a state is deemed to possess independence and 'sovereignty' over its subjects and its affairs, and within its territorial limits. 'Sovereignty' has a much more restricted meaning today than in the eighteenth and nineteenth centuries when, with the emergence of powerful highly nationalised states, few limits on

4. The rights listed by the Commission in the Draft Declaration included the rights of states to independence, to territorial jurisdiction, to equality in law with other states, and to self-defence against armed attack. The duties included those of not intervening in the affairs of other states, of not fomenting civil strife in other states, of observing human rights, of settling disputes peacefully, of not resorting to war as an instrument of national policy, and of carrying out in good faith obligations under treaties.
5. See above, pp 9, 19–21.
6. For a treatment of the question of basic rights and duties by a distinguished Russian jurist, see V. M. Koretsky *Soviet Year Book of International Law* (1958) pp 74–92.
7. See, eg, the *Advisory Opinion relating to the Status of Eastern Carelia* (1923) PCIJ Series B, No 5, p 27, where the Permanent Court of International Justice relied on the basic rights of states to independence and equality.
8. [1986] ICJ 1986, 14 at 133. For general critical discussion of the Draft Declaration of 1949, above, see Kelsen 44 AJIL (1950) 259–276. As to jus cogens, see above, pp 48–50.

state autonomy were acknowledged. At the present time there is hardly a state which, in the interests of the international community, has not accepted restrictions on its liberty of action. Thus most states are members of the United Nations and the International Labour Organisation (ILO), in relation to which they have undertaken obligations limiting their unfettered discretion in matters of international policy. Therefore, it is probably more accurate today to say that the sovereignty of a state means the *residuum* of power which it possesses within the confines laid down by international law. It is of interest to note that this conception resembles the doctrine of early writers on international law, who treated the state as subordinate to the law of nations, then identified as part of the wider 'law of nature'.

In a practical sense, sovereignty is also largely a matter of degree. Some states enjoy more power and independence than other states. This leads to the familiar distinction between independent or sovereign states, and non-independent or non-sovereign states or entities, for example, protectorates and dependent territories. Even here it is difficult to draw the line, for although a state may have accepted important restrictions on its liberty of action, in other respects it may enjoy the widest possible freedom. 'Sovereignty' is therefore a term of art rather than a legal expression capable of precise definition.

When we say that a particular state is independent, in a concrete way we attribute to that state a number of rights, powers, and privileges at international law. Correlative to these rights, etc, there are duties and obligations binding other states who enter into relations with it. These rights, etc, and the correlative duties are the very substance of state independence.

Examples of the rights, etc, associated with a state's independence are:

a. the power exclusively to control its own domestic affairs;
b. the power to admit and expel aliens;
c. the privileges of its diplomatic envoys in other countries;
d. the exclusive jurisdiction over crimes committed within its territory.

Examples of the correlative duties or obligations binding states are:

i. the duty not to perform acts of sovereignty on the territory of another state;
ii. the duty to abstain and prevent agents and subjects from committing acts constituting a violation of another state's independence or territorial supremacy;
iii. the duty not to intervene in the affairs of another state.

As to (i), it is, for instance, a breach of international law for a state to send its agents to the territory of another state to apprehend there persons accused of criminal offences against its laws. The same principle has been considered to apply even if the person irregularly arrested is charged with crimes against international law, such as crimes against the peace or crimes against humanity. Thus in June 1960 the United Nations Security Council adopted the view that the clandestine abduction from Argentina to Israel of Adolf Eichmann, a Nazi war criminal, to be tried by Israeli courts, was an infringement of Argentina's sovereignty, and requested Israel to proceed to more adequate reparation.[9] In

9. By a subsequent settlement, the two countries regarded the incident as closed.

the case of the affair of the sinking in July 1986 of the Greenpeace vessel, the *Rainbow Warrior*, in New Zealand internal waters as a result of the acts of French agents (an affair known in France as 'l'Affaire Greenpeace'), it was accepted that the French Government, by authorising such acts, had committed a breach of international law, and that apart from the responsibility of France itself, the individual agents could not be exonerated by the so-called 'immunity of attribution' doctrine as committing state-like acts, these acts having been committed in time of peace. In the event, the persons responsible were duly tried and convicted, and received sentences imposed by a New Zealand court.[10]

It is not clear whether international law goes so far as to impose a duty on states to refrain from exercising jurisdiction over persons apprehended in violation of the territorial sovereignty of another state, or in breach of international law. State practice is conflicting in this regard, but in the *Savarkar Case* (1911),[11] the Permanent Court of Arbitration held that a country irregularly receiving back a fugitive is under no obligation to return the prisoner to the country where he had been apprehended. In the *Eichmann Case* (1961), the Jerusalem District Court held, in a decision affirmed on appeal, that it had jurisdiction to try Eichmann for crimes against humanity and other crimes, notwithstanding his irregular abduction to Israel from Argentina.[12]

The principle of respect for a state's territorial sovereignty is illustrated by the decision of the International Court of Justice in the *Corfu Channel Case (Merits)* (1949).[13] There the Court held that the British protective minesweeping operations in Albanian territorial waters in the Corfu Channel in November 1946, three weeks after the damage to British destroyers and loss of life through mines in the Channel, were a violation of Albanian sovereignty, notwithstanding Albania's negligence or dilatoriness subsequent to the explosions.

An illustration of (ii) is the duty on a state to prevent within its borders political terrorist activities directed against foreign states. Such a duty was expressed in article 4 of the Draft Declaration on the Rights and Duties of States, prepared by the International Law Commission in 1949, and in wider and more general terms in the Declaration on Principles of International Law Concerning Friendly Relations and Co-operation Among States, in Accordance with the United

---

10. For the subsequent ruling by the United Nations Secretary-General, see 74 ILR 241; (1987) 26 ILM 1346.
11. Scott *Hague Court Reports* (1916) 275. So far as practice in municipal law is concerned, the courts of states are increasingly holding that the seizure of a person in violation of international law, or custody obtained without legal process, to which their own authorities are a knowing party, either vitiates jurisdiction or constitutes a discretionary ground for the court to refuse to exercise jurisdiction by reason of abuse of process: *R v Horseferry Road Magistrates Court, ex p Bennett* [1994] AC 42, overruling previous British authorities to the contrary. See also *S v Ebrahim* (1992) 31 ILM 888 (South Africa); *S v Beahan* [1992] 1 SALR 307 (Zimbabwe); *R v Hartley* [1978] 2 NZLR 199, 213-217 (New Zealand); *Levinge v Director of Custodial Services* (1987) 9 NSWLR 546 (Australia). Against this trend, the old maxim *male captus bene detentus* is still followed by the United States Supreme Court: *United States v Alvarez-Machain* 119 L Ed 2d 441 (1992). For that case see Rayfuse in (1993) 42 ICLQ 882. Where no complicity on the part of the authorities of the receiving state is shown, the European Court of Human Rights has held that the state may accept such 'windfall' jurisdiction: *Stocké v Germany* (1991) 13 EHRR 839.
12. (1961) 36 ILR 5; (1962) 36 ILR 277.
13. ICJ 1949, 4 et seq.

Nations Charter, adopted by the General Assembly in 1970. On 2 February 1971, the duty was affirmed in article 8 of the Convention to Prevent and Punish Acts of Terrorism approved by the General Assembly of the Organisation of American States (OAS), and in s VI of the Helsinki Declaration adopted on 1 August 1975, by 30 European states, the Holy See, the United States, and Canada, the declaring states pledged themselves to 'refrain from direct or indirect assistance to terrorist activities'. The subject had been raised as long ago as the year 1934 in connection with the assassination at Marseilles by certain terrorists of the Yugoslav monarch—King Alexander. Yugoslavia formally accused the Hungarian Government before the League of Nations of tacitly conniving in the assassination inasmuch as it had knowingly allowed the major preparations for the deed to be carried out on Hungarian territory. In the course of the settlement of this dispute between the two nations, the League of Nations Council affirmed that two duties rested on every state:

1. neither to encourage nor to tolerate on its territory any terrorist activity with a political purpose;
2. to do all in its power to prevent and repress terrorist acts of a political character, and for this purpose to lend its assistance to governments which request it.[14]

The duty not to intervene in the affairs[15] of another state (see (iii), above) requires some comment. International law generally forbids such intervention,

14. Arising out of this dispute, the League ultimately promoted the conclusion in November 1937, of a Convention for the Repression of International Terrorism. This Convention did not, however, come into force. Cf also in a similar connection the convention adopted in July 1936, under League auspices, concerning the Use of Broadcasting in the Cause of Peace, under which the parties undertook to prohibit radio transmissions calculated to provoke the commission of acts affecting public safety in the territory of other states parties. The subject of measures to prevent international terrorism came before the United Nations General Assembly in December 1972, when an Ad Hoc 35-member committee on terrorism was established by the Assembly. This Committee considered various drafts and proposals, and the subject has since come before the General Assembly which in December 1985 condemned as criminal 'all acts, methods, and practices of terrorism'. One major difficulty, inter alia, concerns the search for a formula or formulae to define or describe the concept of 'terrorism'. See T. M. Franck and B. B. Lockwood Jr 'Preliminary Thoughts towards an International Convention on Terrorism' 68 AJIL (1974) 69–90, and Sofaer in *Dialogue* (US Information Service) No 2 of 1987 at 1 et seq. The Council of Europe opened for signature in January 1977 a European Convention on the Suppression of Terrorism, and in January 1982 the Council of Ministers adopted a recommendation concerning International Co-operation in the Prosecution and Punishment of Terrorism. Cf also the International Convention against the Taking of Hostages adopted by the United Nations General Assembly in December 1979, and the Convention of 1973 on the Prevention and Punishment of Crimes against Internationally Protected Persons, including Diplomatic Agents, below, pp 387–389. Recent moves within the International Civil Aviation Organisation (ICAO) and the International Maritime Organisation (IMO) to extend anti-terrorist measures to situations not previously dealt with have led, inter alia, to the adoption at Montreal in 1988 of the Protocol for the Suppression of Unlawful Acts of Violence at Airports, and at Rome in 1988 of the Convention on the Suppression of Unlawful Acts Against the Safety of Maritime Navigation, and for the Safety of Platforms on the Continental Shelf.
15. The duty extends both to internal and external affairs. This is recognised in arts 1 and 3 of the Draft Declaration on the Rights and Duties of States adopted in 1949 by the United Nations International Law Commission, and by the Declaration on Principles of International Law Concerning Friendly Relations and Co-operation among States in Accordance with the United Nations Charter, adopted by the United Nations General Assembly in 1970, which proclaims

which in this particular connection means something less than aggression (see below, p 485) but more than mere interference and much stronger than mediation or diplomatic suggestion. To fall within the terms of the prohibition, it must generally speaking be in opposition to the will of the particular state affected, and almost always, as Hyde points out and as has now been made clear by the International Court of Justice in 1986 in *Nicaragua v United States of America*,[16] serving by design or implication to impair the political independence of that state. According to the International Court of Justice, an intervention is prohibited by international law if: (a) it impinges on matters as to which each state is permitted to make decisions by itself freely (eg, choice of its own political or economic system or adoption of its own foreign policy); and (b) it involves interference in regard to this freedom by methods of coercion, especially force (eg, provision of indirect forms of support for subversive activities against the state subject of the alleged intervention). Anything which falls short of this is strictly speaking not intervention within the meaning of the prohibition under international law. A notable historical example of dictatorial intervention—for which there was ostensible justification—was the joint *démarche* in 1895 by Russia, France and Germany, to force Japan to return to China the territory of Liaotung which she had extorted from the Chinese by the Treaty of Shimonoseki. As a result of this intervention, Japan was obliged to retrocede Liaotung to China, a fateful step which led ultimately to the Russo-Japanese War of 1904–5.

The imperious type of diplomatic intervention just described differs fundamentally from other more active kinds of interference in the internal or external affairs of another state, which are commonly grouped under the expression 'intervention', and which may go so far as to include military measures. It is possible to distinguish[17] three kinds of active, material intervention, which unlike the type first mentioned, do not have the character of a diplomatic *démarche*:

1. *'Internal' intervention.* An example is state A interfering between the disputing sections of state B, in favour either of the legitimate government or of the insurgents.

---

certain principles as to non-intervention. This Declaration also treats as intervention an interference with a state's 'inalienable right to choose its political, economic, social and cultural systems'. Cf the Declaration on the Inadmissibility of Intervention in the Domestic Affairs of States, and the Protection of their Independence and Sovereignty, adopted by the UN General Assembly, 21 December 1965. For the whole of Europe (not merely the Member States of the European Union) see the Declaration on the Principles Guiding Relations between Participating States, adopted at Helsinki in 1975 by the Conference on Security and Cooperation in Europe (CSCE): 14 ILM 1292. In 1990 the CSCE adopted the Charter of Paris for a New Europe: 30 ILM 190. New states emerging in Europe have been required to subscribe, inter alia, to the Charter of Paris as a condition of recognition. See further below, p 125.

16. Hyde *International Law* (2nd edn, 1947) Vol I, para 69 and ICJ 1986, 14. It follows logically that where a state consents by treaty to another state exercising a right to intervene, this is not inconsistent with international law, as a general rule, but see p 96 below. So far as concerns the claim that intervention is permissible in order to protect human rights, see generally *Nicaragua v United States* above, and N. Ronzitti *Rescuing Nationals Abroad through Military Coercion and Intervention on Grounds of Humanity* (1985) ch 4.

17. Winfield *The Foundations and the Future of International Law* (1941) pp 32–33.

2. '*External*' *intervention*. An example is state A interfering in the relations—generally the hostile relations—of other states, as when Italy entered the Second World War on the side of Germany, and against Great Britain.
3. '*Punitive*' *intervention*. This is the case of a reprisal, short of war, for an injury suffered at the hands of another state; for example, a pacific blockade instituted against this state in retaliation for a gross breach of treaty.

The term 'intervention' has also been used by some writers in the expression 'subversive intervention', to denote propaganda or other activity by one state with the intention of fomenting, for its own purposes, revolt or civil strife in another state. International law prohibits such subversive intervention.[18]

The following are, broadly expressed, the principal exceptional cases in which it is claimed that a state has at international law a legitimate right of intervention:

a. collective intervention[19] pursuant to the Charter of the United Nations;
b. to protect the rights and interests, and the personal safety of its citizens abroad, being one of the grounds relied upon by the United States Government as justifying the landing of a multinational force on the island of Grenada in October 1983;
c. self-defence,[20] if intervention is necessary to meet a danger of an actual armed attack;
d. in the affairs of a protectorate under its dominion;
e. if the state subject of the intervention has been guilty of a gross breach of international law in regard to the intervening state, for example, if it has itself unlawfully intervened.

States must subordinate the exercise of any such exceptional rights of intervention to their primary obligations under the United Nations Charter, so that except where the Charter permits it, intervention must not go so far as the threat or use of force against the territorial integrity or political independence of any state (see article 2 paragraph 4).

18. See the Resolutions of the United Nations General Assembly on this subject, of 3 November 1947, of 1 December 1949, and of 17 November 1950, and note art 2 (5) of the International Law Commission's 1954 Draft Code of Offences against the Peace and Security of Mankind, condemning 'organised activities calculated to foment civil strife in another State'. The Declaration on Principles of International Law Concerning Friendly Relations and Co-operation among States in Accordance with the United Nations Charter, adopted by the General Assembly in 1970, proclaims that 'no State shall organise, assist, foment, finance, incite or tolerate subversive, terrorist or armed activities directed towards the violent overthrow of the régime of another State, or interfere in civil strife in another State'.
19. This would be by enforcement action under the authority of the United Nations Security Council, pursuant to Chapter VII of the Charter, or any action sanctioned by the General Assembly under the Uniting for Peace Resolution of 3 November 1950 (see below, p 574). For these actions, such as in Kuwait, Somalia, and Bosnia-Herzegovina see below, p 588. Otherwise, the United Nations is prevented by art 2, para 7, of the Charter from intervening in matters 'essentially within the domestic jurisdiction' of any state. The mere discussion by a United Nations organ of a matter on its agenda affecting the internal jurisdiction of any state is not an 'intervention' in breach of this article. The Security Council may even, in a serious case, directly call upon a State to carry out its international obligations, such as in 1994 when it called upon the Democratic Peoples Republic of Korea to allow full inspection by the International Atomic Energy Agency of its nuclear facilities.
20. As to which, see below, pp 488–489. This would include collective self-defence by the parties to a mutual security treaty such as the North Atlantic Pacific of 4 April 1949.

Before the Spanish Civil War of 1936–1938, the principle was generally approved that revolution or civil war or other grave emergency in another state might be cause for intervention if the safety of the state desiring to intervene were affected by the conflict, or emergency, or if there were serious interference with the exercise by it of some rights which should be respected.[1]

How far this principle remains valid today, particularly in the light of a state's obligations under the United Nations Charter, is open to question. In 1936, the European Great Powers departed from the principle by agreeing not to intervene in the Spanish Civil War under any circumstances (even by certain kinds of trading with the contestants).

However, since then, and certainly since the coming into force of the United Nations Charter, it can no longer be asserted that there is such a general right of intervention. Nor is it any longer the case that in a civil war there is a right of intervention in support, and at the invitation, of the established government, unless forces opposed to that government are being supported by another state, contrary to international law. In the latter event the established government has the right to seek support in collective self-defence under article 51 of the United Nations Charter, provided that the support received by rebels from outside the state is sufficiently large-scale to amount to an armed attack.[2]

These principles are not always easy to apply in practice, when there may be a dispute as to the facts, or a genuine difference of opinion in the appreciation of the facts. For example, was the participation of the United States in the Vietnam War, beginning in a substantial way in 1964 and ending in 1974, an unlawful intervention in a civil war, or a lawful exercise of the right of self-defence of the Republic of (South) Vietnam against support given to the Viet Cong by the Democratic Republic of (North) Vietnam?[3] Was the intervention of the Soviet Union in Afghanistan in 1979 in support of a government battling insurgents justified by the level of support those insurgents were receiving from outside Afghanistan?

It may be wiser to ascribe these and the more or less plausible justifications for other cases of intervention occurring during the era of the Cold War to the intensity of East-West fears, each side having its 'client' states and spheres of influence, and to the virtual paralysis of the Security Council by reason of the frequent exercise of the power of veto from 1946 until 1990. These cases cannot be regarded as offering a principled guide to state practice. There was a tendency too, for the same reasons, for the major powers to stretch the principle of self-defence beyond legitimate limits, or to invoke the umbrella of regional organisations (such as the Organisation of American States in the case of the 'quarantine' of Cuba in 1962, and of the Organisation of Eastern Caribbean

1. Hyde, op cit, paras 69 et seq.
2. This was the principal holding of the International Court of Justice in the *Case Concerning Military and Paramilitary Activities in and against Nicaragua*, ICJ 1986, 14. See generally J. N. Moore (ed) *Law and Civil War in the Modern World* (1974).
3. See the *Memorandum on the Legality of United States Participation in the Defense of Vietnam*, prepared by the Legal Adviser to the US State Department, and other writings, both in support of and against those arguments, collected in R. A. Falk (ed) *The Vietnam War and International Law*, 4 vols (1968-76).

States in the intervention in Grenada in 1983)[4] in circumstances not entirely conforming with articles 52 and 53 of the UN Charter.

Since 1990, when an effective response was made to Iraq's invasion of Kuwait, and when the Soviet Union began to dissolve, it has not been so predictable that the veto will be used as it had been in the past. In cases where in the past one or other of the major powers might have intervened unilaterally, such as in Iraq, Somalia, Liberia, Haiti, and Bosnia-Herzegovina, collective endorsement by the Security Council has been sought and obtained for various measures.[5] A further positive aspect of the tendency towards collective measures endorsed by the Security Council in place of unilateral measures is the possible emergence of new justifications for intervention in the internal affairs of states: that law and order has broken down completely, or that human rights are being systematically and seriously violated, or even that the people of a state are being denied the right to choose a democratic form of government.[6] Failing an amendement of the Charter, it seems that such justifications would rest on a notion that a 'threat to the peace' (article 39)—the necessary trigger to the operation of chapter VII of the Charter—can be constituted also by purely internal events that have the potential to affect neighbouring or regional states through violent acts in those states in sympathy, or through massive refugee outflows, or by the resonance that violations of human rights—especially racial or religious persecution—tend to cause among related peoples outside, or indeed generally in the international community.

Co-operation in peace-enforcement, peace-keeping, and humanitarian relief is not always either prompt or adequate, as experience in the above and other instances since 1990 has shown. The present structures of the United Nations require reform if the new possibilities of collective action are to be realised.[7] In the meantime there remains the problem of the kind of emergency which occurred in 1976 when Jewish passengers aboard an Air France aircraft bound for Israel were taken hostage by hijackers who diverted the aircraft to Uganda. When it appeared that Uganda was taking no steps to deal with the situation an Israeli task force carried out a successful rescue mission. The Security Council later considered the issue of the violation of Ugandan sovereignty by Israel but came to no conclusion. The United States delegate recognised that the rescue mission necessarily involved a 'temporary breach' of the territorial integrity of Uganda but argued in justification of Israel's action that 'there is a well-established right to use limited force for the protection of one's own nationals from any imminent threat of injury or death in a situation where the state in whose territory they are located is either unwilling or unable to protect them.'[8] The United States itself attempted (but unsuccessfully) a rescue mission of its embassy and consular officials, held hostage in Iran, in 1980. Shortly afterwards the International Court

4. A. Chayes *The Cuban Missile Crisis* (1974); W. C. Gilmore *The Grenada Intervention* (1984).
5. On these operations see further below, p 590.
6. On the last of these see Franck in (1989) 86 AJIL 46.
7. The United Nations Secretary-General, Dr Boutros-Ghali, published in 1992 *An Agenda for Peace* raising many of these issues. For a detailed supportive response by the Australian Foreign Minister see G. Evans *Co-operating for Peace: The Global Agenda for the 1990's and Beyond* (1993).
8. The proceedings are reprinted in (1976) 15 ILM 1224.

of Justice handed down its judgment in the *US Diplomatic and Consular Staff in Tehran Case*, which it was in the course of preparing when the rescue mission took place. The Court expressed its 'concern' at the action which was 'of a kind calculated to undermine respect for the judicial process' and breached the interim measures of protection ordered earlier by the Court (which had also included an unsatisfied order for the immediate release of the hostages). The Court refrained, however, from condemning the action on any wider ground; nor did it consider the general issue of 'humanitarian intervention'. This suggested exception to the rule of non-intervention must therefore remain of cloudy legality. It is evident that it is open to abuse in circumstances which do not urgently require its application; moreover, relatively few states have the capacity to carry out such operations with the necessary combination of skill, surprise, speed, and sufficient force to accomplish the aim with minimum collateral damage. Collective measures are therefore preferred in principle by most states.

Monroe Doctrine

The history of the American Monroe Doctrine throws some light on the political, as distinct from the legal aspects of intervention. As originally announced by President Monroe in a Message to Congress in 1823, it contained three branches:

1. a declaration that the American continent would no longer be a subject for future colonisation by a European Power;
2. a declaration of absence of interest in European wars or European affairs;
3. a declaration that any attempt by the European Powers 'to extend their system' to any portion of the American continent would be regarded as 'dangerous' to the 'peace and safety' of the United States.[9]

The third branch was the most important, and by a paradoxical development it came by the end of the nineteenth century to attract a claim by the United States, enforced on several occasions, to intervene in any part of the American continent subject to a threat of interference from a European Power, or wherever in such continent vital interests of the United States were endangered. Thus a doctrine originally directed against intervention was converted into a theory justifying intervention by the state which had first sponsored the doctrine. After the First World War, however, America's 'good neighbour' policy towards other American states brought the Monroe Doctrine closer to its former objectives of 1823. And now by reason of recent inter-American regional security arrangements, it might seem as if the Monroe Doctrine, regarded as an affirmation of the solidarity of the American continent, has been transformed from a unilateral declaration[10] into a collective understanding of the American

9. Branch (1) of the Monroe Doctrine arose out of the fact that Russia had obtained territory in the North-West of the American continent and laid claims to the Pacific Coast. Branch (3) was directed against any intervention on the part of the principal European Powers (the Triple Alliance) to restore the authority of Spain over the rebellious colonies in Latin America which had secured independence and recognition by the United States.
10. In 1923, Secretary of State Hughes referred to the Monroe Doctrine as being 'distinctively the policy of the United States', and of which the United States 'reserves to itself its definition, interpretation, and application'.

Powers.[11] Possibly, to this extent, the League of Nations Covenant in article 21 may now be regarded as correct in referring to the doctrine as a 'regional understanding'. But the Monroe Doctrine has not been completely multilateralised. To some extent, it still retains its unilateral significance for the United States Government, as indicated by the American 'quarantine' or 'selective' blockade of Cuba in October 1962, in order to forestall the further construction of, or reinforcement of Soviet missile bases on Cuban territory, and by the landing of United States units in the Dominican Republic in April 1965 to protect American lives and to ensure that no communist government was established in the Republic.

Sometimes by treaty, a state expressly excludes itself from intervention; cf article 4 of the Treaty of 1929 between Italy and the Holy See:

'The sovereignty and exclusive jurisdiction over the Vatican City which Italy recognises as appertaining to the Holy See precludes any intervention therein on the part of the Italian Government . . .'

Doctrine of the equality of states

The doctrine of the equality of states was espoused early in the modern history of international law by those writers who attached importance to a relationship between the law of nations and the law of nature. This is reflected in the following passage, for example, from Christian Wolff's major work:[12]

'By nature all nations are equal the one to the other. For nations are considered as individual free persons living in a state of nature. Therefore, since by nature all men are equal, all nations too are by nature equal the one to the other.'

That the doctrine of equality subsists today with added strength, but with some change of emphasis is shown by its reaffirmation and definition under the heading, 'The principle of sovereign equality of States', in the Declaration on Principles of International Law Concerning Friendly Relations and Co-operation Among States in Accordance with the United Nations Charter, adopted by the General Assembly in 1970. The Declaration proclaimed the following principle: 'All States enjoy sovereign equality. They have equal rights and duties and are equal members of the international community, notwithstanding differences of an economic, social, political or other nature.' In the Charter of the United Nations, drawn up at San Francisco in 1945, there is express recognition of the doctrine. Article 1 speaks of 'respect for the principle of equal rights', and article 2 says that the Organisation 'is based on the principle of the sovereign equality of all its Members'. The 'sovereign equality' of states was also reaffirmed in the General Assembly Declaration of 1974 on the Establishment of a New Economic Order (see paragraph 4(a) of the Declaration). From the doctrine of equality, stems the duty upon states, expressed in certain treaties,[13] and found in the law

11. This development can be traced through the Act of Chapultepec 1945, the Inter-American Treaty of Reciprocal Assistance of Rio de Janeiro 1947, and the Bogotá Charter of the Organisation of American States 1948, under which, inter alia, a threat to the independence and security of any one American state is regarded as a threat against all.

12. *Jus gentium methodo scientifica pertractatum* (1749) Prolegomena, para 16.

13. See, eg, art 7, para 2 (c) of the Geneva Convention on Fishing and Conservation of the Living Resources of the High Seas, of 29 April 1958, and the provision of a similar nature in art 119, para 3 of the United Nations Convention on the Law of the Sea of 10 December 1982.

concerning resident aliens, not to discriminate in favour of their own citizens as against the citizens of another state.

The doctrine imports not merely equality at law, but also the capacity for equal legal rights and equal duties. The results of the doctrine are seen particularly in the law and practice as to multilateral treaties where generally the rule used to prevail that unanimity was necessary for the adoption of these instruments by states in Conference. This necessity for unanimity rather hampered the progress of international legislation. Frequently small states were able to hold up important advances in international affairs by selfish obstruction under the shelter of the unanimity rule. To quote one authority:[14]

> 'The unanimity rule, conceived as the safeguard of the minority, has, through exaggerating the doctrine of equality, become an instrument of tyranny against the majority.'

But the recent trend is towards decisions and voting by a majority, instead of unanimously. This is particularly reflected in voting procedures in the United Nations, the International Labour Organisation, and other bodies.[15]

Another alleged consequence of the principle of equality is that, in the absence of a treaty, no state can claim jurisdiction over, or in respect of another sovereign state.[16] A more far-reaching proposition is that the courts of one state cannot question the validity or legality of the acts of state of another sovereign country or of its agents, and that such questioning must be done, if at all, through the diplomatic channel; this is the so-called 'Act of State' doctrine,[17] but it cannot as yet be said to be part of international law. There has so far been no conclusive decision by any international tribunal that a failure to apply the 'Act of State' doctrine constitutes a breach of an international obligation. The courts of particular countries may apply an 'Act of State' doctrine under their own municipal law system, or on grounds of domestic law or practice (eg, the consideration that the executive should not be embarrassed in the diplomatic sphere) refrain from ruling that an act of state of a recognised foreign sovereign country is invalid,[18] but this is not because of any mandatory principles of

14. Politis *Les Nouvelles Tendances du Droit International* (1927).
15. See below, pp 557 and 577–579.
16. Semble, this is rather an illustration of the sovereignty and autonomy of states than of the principle of equality; see Kelsen *General Theory of Law and State* (1961 edn) p 248. It involves the collateral rule that the servants or agents of one state cannot be tried in another state for acts done in their official capacity (sometimes characterised as the 'immunity of attribution' rule); semble, an exception to this collateral rule is that *in peacetime* the courts of a state are not prohibited from trying foreign agents of another state if the impugned act was committed in the territory of the state claiming jurisdiction. Thus it was lawful for a New Zealand court to try the French agents involved in the sinking in October 1986 in New Zealand internal waters of the Greenpeace vessel, the *Rainbow Warrior*.
17. The classic statement of the 'Act of State' doctrine is that by Chief Justice Fuller in the decision of the United States Supreme Court in *Underhill v Hernandez* 168 US 250 (1897) at 252. This statement was referred to, with approval, by the High Court of Australia in 1988 in the *'Spycatcher' Case, A-G for the United Kingdom v Heinemann Publishers Pty Ltd (No 2)* (1988) 165 CLR 30.
18. See, eg, decision of the US Supreme Court in *Banco Nacional de Cuba v Sabbatino* 376 US 398 (1964) (validity of Cuban sugar expropriation decrees, alleged to be in violation of international law, could not be questioned). The effect of the decision was restricted by the Hickenlooper Amendment (Foreign Assistance Act of 1965, re-enacting with amendments the Foreign

international law requiring them so to proceed. In any event, state courts remain free in accordance with the rules of their own municipal legal system to hold or abstain from holding that a foreign act of state is invalid because in conflict with international law. There may well be some overlap between the 'Act of State' doctrine and the more generic doctrine of non-justiciability whereby courts, as a matter of judicial restraint, decline to exercise jurisdiction over matters within the political or other domains of the 'public interest' of foreign states.[19]

There is indeed no general principle of international law obliging states to give effect to the administrative acts of other states. This is clearly illustrated by the prevailing 'nationalistic' system of patents, under which, subject to exceptions, patents are granted solely on a domestic national basis, without any general obligation to recognise a foreign grant. A fortiori, if civil liability is excluded under the laws of a country, no action will lie in the courts of another state to enforce such liability.[20]

Side by side with the principle of equality, there are, however, de facto inequalities which are perforce recognised. For example, the five great powers, the United States, the Soviet Union, the United Kingdom, France, and China are the sole permanent members of the United Nations Security Council, and may 'veto' decisions of the Council on non-procedural questions (see article 27 of the United Nations Charter).[1] Moreover, there is the distinction between developed and less-developed countries, expressly recognised in the new Part IV of the General Agreement on Tariffs and Trade of 30 October 1947 (GATT), added by the Protocol of 8 February 1965 (see the new articles 37–38). Then,

---

Assistance Act of 1964). Subsequently, the amendment was construed narrowly by a Circuit Court of Appeals as applying only to cases in which property was nationalised abroad, contrary to international law, and the property or its traceable proceeds came to the United States; see *Banco Nacional de Cuba v First National City Bank of New York* 431 F 2d 394 (1970), following and applying *Sabbatino's Case*. However, the judgment in this decision was set aside by the United States Supreme Court in the light of a letter from the Department of State intimating that American foreign policy would not be adversely affected by the court considering the merits; see 400 US 1019 (1971). Upon the Court of Appeals then adhering to its previous decision, the Supreme Court reversed it, holding that the Act of State doctrine was inapplicable; see 406 US 759 (1972), and ultimately the Court of Appeals applied international law. Cf *French v Banco Nacional de Cuba* 295 NYS 2d 433 (1968) (although a stringent Cuban currency control order constituted an act of state, its effect was outside the Amendment, which Amendment was said to be confined to claims of title in respect to specific property expropriated abroad). However, in *Alfred Dunhill of London Inc v Republic of Cuba* 425 US 682 (1976), a majority of the United States Supreme Court found that the mere refusal of a commercial agency of a foreign government to repay funds mistakenly paid to it did not constitute an act of state. See also now *Banco Nacional de Cuba v Chemical Bank New York Trust Co* 594 F Supp 1553 (1984) (exercise of jurisdiction held to be permissible).

19. Cf *Underhill v Hernandez* 168 US 250 at 252 (1897); *United States v Sisson* 294 F Supp 515 (1968); *Buttes Gas and Oil Co v Hammer* (No 2, 3) and *Occidental Petroleum Corpn v Buttes Gas and Oil Co* (No 1, 2) [1982] AC 888, [1981] 3 All ER 616, HL; and the decision of the High Court of Australia in the *'Spycatcher' Case, A-G for the United Kingdom v Heinemann Publishers Pty Ltd* (1988) 165 CLR 30. See also Henkin 'Is there a "Political Question" Doctrine?' (1976) 85 Yale LJ 597.

20. See *Chaplin v Boys* [1971] AC 356 at 389. For a division of views on this point see *Stevens v Head* (1993) 176 CLR 433 (High Court of Australia).

1. See below, pp 577–579. There are other somewhat similar cases in the membership of the 'executive' organs of other international organisations.

as mentioned in the early part of this chapter,[2] micro-states, with their limited resources and small population have had to be treated as incapable of coping with the full burdens of United Nations membership. An entity which cannot be received as a plenary member State of the United Nations is not in a practical sense one which has equal rights with a state actually admitted as a member.

The line between, on the one hand, equality of states, and, on the other hand, their independence, tends to become blurred. Thus it is maintained that the right of a state freely to choose and develop its political, social, economic, and cultural systems appertains to equality,[3] but stricto sensu this right is merely an expression of a state's independence.

Rules of neighbourly intercourse between states

There is one important qualification on the absolute independence and equality of states, which has found expression in the recent decisions of international courts and to some extent in the resolutions of international institutions. It is the principle, corresponding possibly to the municipal law prohibition of 'abuse of rights', that a state should not permit the use of its territory for purposes injurious to the interests of other states. Thus in the United Nations deliberations on the situation in Greece (1946–1949), it was implicitly recognised that, whatever the true facts might be, Greece's neighbours, Albania, Yugoslavia and Bulgaria, were under a duty to prevent their territory being used for hostile expeditions against the Greek Government.[4] Similarly, the *Trail Smelter Arbitration Case* of 1941[5] recognised the principle that a state is under a duty to prevent its territory from being a source of economic injury to neighbouring territory, eg, by the escape of noxious fumes. In the Declaration on the Human Environment adopted by the Stockholm Conference on the Human Environment in June 1972 (see Principles 21–22), it was proclaimed that states are responsible for ensuring that activities within their jurisdiction or control do not cause damage to the environment of other states, or of areas beyond the limits of national jurisdiction, thus affirming a more far-reaching principle than that of the *Trail Smelter Arbitration Case.* The Stockholm Principles were re-inforced and extended by the Rio Declaration on the Environment and Development, adopted in June 1992.[6] Another illustration is the *Corfu Channel Case (Merits)* (1949),[7] in which the International Court of Justice held that once the Albanian Government knew of the existence of a minefield in its territorial waters in the

2. See p 88 above.
3. See the Declaration on Principles of International Law Concerning Friendly Relations and Co-operation Among States in Accordance with the United Nations Charter, adopted by the General Assembly in 1970, where this right is stated to be one of the elements of the sovereign equality of states. The Declaration also affirms that the duty to respect the personality of other states is an element of equality, although such duty seems to be more concerned with preserving the independence of states.
4. Cf art 4 of the Draft Declaration on the Rights and Duties of States, prepared by the International Law Commission of the United Nations in 1949, imposing a duty upon every state 'to refrain from fomenting civil strife in the territory of another state, and to prevent the organisation within its territory of activities calculated to foment such civil strife'.
5. *United Nations Reports of International Arbitral Awards* Vol III, 1905.
6. See further below, ch 14.
7. ICJ 1949, 4 et seq.

Corfu Channel, it was its duty to notify shipping and to warn approaching British naval vessels of the imminent danger, and therefore it was liable to pay compensation to the British Government for damage to ships and loss of life caused through exploding mines. The Court stated that it was a 'general well-recognised principle' that every state is under an obligation 'not to allow knowingly its territory to be used for acts contrary to the rights of other States'.

In article 74 of the United Nations Charter, the general principle of 'good-neighbourliness' in social, economic, and commercial matters, is laid down as one which member states must follow in regard to both their metropolitan and their dependent territories.

The principle of neighbourly obligations between states also underlies the United Nations General Assembly Resolution of 3 November 1947, condemning propaganda designed or likely to provoke or encourage threats to the peace, breaches of the peace, or acts of aggression.

Opinions have differed, not over the existence of the principle, but as to the limits of its application; eg, it is questioned whether a state devaluing or 'freezing' its currency can be under any liability for the ensuing damage suffered by other states as a consequence. However, with respect to new technologies involving the risk of trans-border effects of an injurious nature, it is not now seriously questioned since the Chernobyl nuclear reactor accident of 1986 in the Soviet Union (see below, pp 378–379) that there should be close co-operation and/or consultation between states to ensure that countries that are likely to be injuriously affected by technological accidents or dangers, such as the release of spreading radio-activity, are duly warned immediately, so that joint measures may be taken to minimise the detrimental consequences.

2. THE DIFFERENT KINDS OF STATES AND NON-STATE ENTITIES

The position of states at international law often varies, and it is therefore necessary briefly to consider certain special cases which arise. There may also, equally briefly, be examined in this connection the cases of certain non-state entities, subjects of international law. Mention must also be made of the Holy See, which has international personality including the right of legation, but no territory. Its personality is distinct from that of the Vatican City State.[8] The Sovereign Military Hospitaller Order of St John of Jerusalem, Rhodes and Malta is regarded by many states as possessing international personality, although its 'territory', since its loss of the island of Malta in 1798, consists only of certain buildings in Rome having extra-territorial status under Italian law. The European Union has international personality to conclude treaties on subjects lying within Union competence and, like the Holy See and the Palestine Liberation Organisation, has Observer Mission status at the United Nations.

---

8. As to the Holy See, note that the relations between the Holy See and the Vatican City, on the one hand, and Italy, on the other hand, are now governed by an agreement concluded in February 1984. Cf as to the status of the Holy See and the Vatican City over which the Holy See exercises sovereignty, D. H. Ott *Public International Law in the Modern World* (1987) p 58.

Federal states and confederations

A confederation (*Staatenbund*) is constituted by a number of independent states bound together by an international treaty or compact into a union with organs of government extending over the member states and set up for the purpose of maintaining the external and internal independence of all. The historic example is the German Confederation, 1815-1866. The only modern example is the Commonwealth of Independent States (CIS), loosely linking all the former Soviet Republics except the Baltic States and Georgia.[9] The confederation is not a state at international law, the individual states maintaining their international position.

A federal state is, however, a real state at international law, the essential difference between it and the confederation being that federal organs have direct power not only over the member states, but over the citizens of these states. Examples include Australia, Canada, Germany, and the United States of America. In most federal states, external policy is conducted by the federal government, but historically there have been exceptions to this rule. For example, the member states of the pre-1919 Federal Germany were to some extent states at international law; they could conclude treaties, appoint and receive envoys, etc, and questions of law affecting their relations were decided according to international law.

Protected and vassal states and protectorates

A vassal state is one which is completely under the suzerainty of another state.[10] Internationally its independence is so restricted as scarcely to exist at all.

The case of a protectorate or a protected state arises in practice when a state puts itself by treaty under the protection of a strong and powerful state, so that the conduct of its most important international business and decisions on high policy are left to the protecting state.

Protectorates are not based on a uniform pattern. Each case depends on its special circumstances and more specifically on:

a.   the particular terms of the treaty of protection;[11]
b.   the conditions under which the protectorate is recognised by third Powers as against whom it is intended to rely on the treaty of protection.[12]

Although not completely independent, a protected state may enjoy a sufficient measure of sovereignty to claim jurisdictional immunities in the territory of another state (per Lord Finlay in *Duff Development Co v Kelantan Government*[13]). It may also still remain a state under international law.[14] Protectorates, in the strict sense, have for all practical purposes now disappeared from the international scene.

9.   Created by the Treaty signed at Minsk, 8 December 1991, and Protocol signed at Alma Ata, 21 December 1991: (1992) 31 ILM 138.
10. Vassalage is an institution that has now fallen into desuetude.
11. *The Ionian Ships* (1855) 2 Ecc & Ad 212, Spinks 193.
12. *Advisory Opinion of the Permanent Court of International Justice on the Nationality Decrees in Tunis and Morocco* (1923) PCIJ, Series B, No 4, p 27.
13. [1924] AC 797 at 814. This is one of the most important distinctions between a protected state and a vassal; cf *The Charkieh* (1873) LR 4 A & E 59.
14. See *Case Concerning Rights of Nationals of the United States of America in Morocco* ICJ 1952, 176.

Condominium

A condominium exists when over a particular territory joint dominion is exercised by two or more external Powers. A now historical example is that of the New Hebrides, in which the division of power was of some complexity, with some functions assigned to the joint administration, others residing in each of the national authorities (United Kingdom and France), subject to appropriate delegations of jurisdiction. This condominium, which had lasted for 74 years, ceased to exist when the New Hebrides attained independence on 30 July 1980, and assumed the name and style of the Republic of Vanuatu. It is not impossible that the current régime of collaboration in Antarctica[15] between the twelve parties to the 1959 Treaty on Antarctica could evolve into a condominium of a rather complex nature of division of powers and jurisdiction.[16]

Members of the Commonwealth

The position of members of the Commonwealth, the former British Commonwealth of Nations, has always been sui generis. It is only since the Second World War that they have finally completed a long process of emancipation, beginning as dependent colonies, next acquiring the status of self-governing colonies under the nineteenth century system of responsible government, and then as dominions moving towards the final goal of statehood. So it is that since 1948 even the name and style of 'dominions' had to be discarded.

The member states of the Commonwealth are now fully sovereign states in every sense. In the field of external affairs autonomy is unlimited; members enjoy and exercise extensively the rights of separate legation and of independent negotiation of treaties. They are capable of being subjects of international disputes and of conflicts as between themselves, and are at liberty to contract ties with non-Commonwealth states.[17] They may be separately and individually belligerents or neutrals. They have in fact concluded treaties with each other (cf the 'Anzac Pact' of 1944 between Australia and New Zealand). A marked development of the past thirty years has been the gradual supersession of inter se Commonwealth rules by the application of international law itself to practically all the relations between member states. Hence, also, the position of High Commissioners representing one member state in the territory of another has been assimilated to that of diplomatic envoys (cf the British Diplomatic Immunities (Commonwealth Countries and Republic of Ireland) Act 1952).

As for the Commonwealth itself, it is of course neither a super-state nor a federation, but simply a multi-racial association of free and equal states who value this association, who support the United Nations, who follow common

---

15. See pp 149–152 below.
16. *Division into Separate Zones:* Contrast with a condominium, a case of joint authority, the division of a territory or entity into two or more separate zones, each under the authority of a different state. Thus under the Memorandum of Understanding of 5 October 1954, signed in London by Great Britain, the United States, Italy, and Yugoslavia, the Free Territory of Trieste was divided into a Western and an Eastern Zone under the interim administration of Italy and Yugoslavia respectively.
17. Because of this freedom, among others, the Commonwealth has been described as the 'Open' Commonwealth; see, passim, M. Margaret Ball *The 'Open' Commonwealth* (1971).

principles of non-discrimination as to colour, race, and creed, who recognise for the purpose of their association, although most of them be republics, that the British Sovereign is head of the Commonwealth, and who, subject to exceptions, have somewhat similar institutions and traditions of government. There is no formal constitution, reliance being placed on accepted practices and consensus procedures. The Commonwealth possesses a Secretariat established in 1965 and located in London, yet the association is, to use an appropriate description given by one Commonwealth statesman,[18] 'functional and occasional'. Although it is sought through periodical Heads of Government Conferences, and latterly by Conferences of Chief Justices and Law Officers, to follow a common policy, differences of approach or of opinion are not excluded and may run a wide gamut (as in 1956, over the Anglo-French intervention in the Suez Canal zone, in 1962 and 1971 concerning the proposed terms of the United Kingdom's entry into the European Economic Community, in 1966 over the Rhodesian issue, and in 1971 over the question of the supply of arms by the United Kingdom to South Africa for joint defence of Indian Ocean sea routes). In ultimate analysis, the Commonwealth is held together by a web of mixed tangible and intangible advantages, that have evolved pragmatically, and are difficult to express in terms of legal relationships. Had the ties between member states of the Commonwealth been more formalised, it might have been appropriate to describe the Commonwealth as an international organisation, but it is at least correctly labelled as an 'association' of states.

The Declaration adopted on 22 January 1971, by the Commonwealth Heads of Government Conference at Singapore contained some pertinent statements as to the nature and purposes of the Commonwealth, which was defined as 'a voluntary association of independent sovereign States, each responsible for its own policies, consulting and co-operating in the common interests of their peoples and in the promotion of international understanding and world peace'. The Declaration also affirmed that 'membership of the Commonwealth is compatible with the freedom of member Governments to be non-aligned or to belong to any other grouping, association or alliance'. Emphasis was placed on the aspect of consultation; the Commonwealth was declared to be 'based on consultation, discussion and co-operation', and to provide 'many channels for continuing exchanges of knowledge and views on professional, cultural, economic, legal and political issues among member States'.

Recent developments in the areas of consensus and collaboration have included the establishment of working study groups in matters such as trade, energy and industry, and regional meetings, since 1978, of Commonwealth Heads of Government in the Asia/Pacific region (the so-called 'CHOGRM' meetings).

Trust territories

For all practical purposes, trust territories are now of historical interest only and will therefore be treated only briefly in the present edition of this book;[19] readers

18. The late Sir Robert Menzies, Prime Minister of Australia, 1939–1941, and 1949–1966.
19. For discussion of the system of trust territories and for a comparison with the League of Nations mandates system, see Duncan Hall *Mandates, Dependencies, and Trusteeship* (1948). The legal aspects of the system are analysed by Sayre in an article in (1948) 42 AJIL 263 et seq.

are referred to the 9th edition (1984) for a more detailed examination of the subject.[20]

Under Chapter XII of the United Nations Charter, there was established an International Trusteeship System for the supervision of trust territories placed under the United Nations by individual agreements with the states administering them, designated as 'Administering Authorities'. The System applied to: (i) territories then held under mandates established by the League of Nations after the First World War; (ii) territories detached from conquered enemy states as a result of the Second World War; and (iii) territories voluntarily placed under the System by states responsible for their government. The basic objectives of the System were to promote the political, economic and social advancement of the trust territories and their progressive development towards self-government or independence.

The Trusteeship Council was established under Chapter XIII of the Charter to supervise the administration of the trust territories and to ensure that governments responsible as Administering Authorities should take adequate steps to prepare them for the achievement of the above-mentioned objectives.

Eleven territories were placed under the System, but one only, the Trust Territory of the Pacific Islands, comprising former Japanese-mandated island territories, had the status of a 'strategic' trust territory, under the United States as Administering Authority according to an Agreement of 1947 approved by the United Nations Security Council. By 1981, all trust territories except the latter 'strategic' trust territory had either attained independence or were united with a neighbouring state to form an independent country. The Trust Territory of the Pacific Islands has been wound up, pending a referendum in Palau which is expected to exercise its right of self-determination in the form of a 'compact of free association' with the United States. The same option has already been exercised by two other parts of the Trust Territory—the Federated States of Micronesia, and the Marshall Islands—both of which were admitted to membership of the United Nations in 1991. Thus a 'compact of association' is not incompatible with full sovereignty. The fourth part of the former Trust Territory—the Northern Marianas—voted for 'commonwealth status' under the United States; thus, like Puerto Rico, it is not a sovereign state. It is unlikely that the institution of United Nations trusteeship will be revived in future, since it vests administration of a territory, for the time being unable to stand alone, in the hands of a particular administering power. However, as the instances of Cambodia and Somalia suggest, there are some similarities to trusteeship in certain recent examples of United Nations operations, mounted under collective authority, to restore or maintain order when that has broken down.

One matter of substantial significance concerning trust territories and the earlier mandates system needs to be mentioned. This concerns the South African mandate with respect to South West Africa, now known as Namibia. South Africa did not follow the example of other Mandatory Powers, and refused to bring South West Africa under the Trusteeship System. The questions of South Africa's obligations in that connection came before the International Court of Justice in 1950, which, although ruling by a majority that South Africa was not bound to place South West Africa under the Trusteeship System, nevertheless advised also

20. See pp 112–116 of the 9th edn of this book.

by a majority that the territory remained under the administration of South Africa subject to the terms of the original mandate, and subject to the supervision of the United Nations General Assembly, which by necessary implication stood in the place of the previous supervisory authority, the League of Nations.[1] In the *South West Africa Cases, 2nd Phase*[2] the International Court of Justice held that individual member States of the League had no legal standing or claim, by themselves, to enforce the terms of a mandate, this being a matter for organic or international action.[3] South Africa thus never became an Administering Authority in the strict sense under the United Nations Charter.[4] In 1989 South Africa acceded to demands by the United Nations that elections be held and independence granted. Namibia became independent on 21 March 1990. In 1993 South Africa ceded the enclave of Walvis Bay to Namibia, thus providing Namibia with a port.

Status of non-self-governing territories under United Nations Charter

The United Nations Charter accords a special status to colonial territories, possessions, and dependencies under the general designation of 'non-self-governing territories'. As in the case of trust territories, the concept of a trust reposing upon the administering states, is emphasised. By a Declaration regarding Non-Self-Governing Territories contained in Chapter XI of the Charter, members of the United Nations administering such territories recognised the principle that the interests of the inhabitants were paramount, accepted as a sacred trust the obligation to promote their well-being to the utmost, and undertook to develop self-government, and to assist in the evolution of free political institutions.

They also bound themselves to transmit regular information on conditions in these territories to the Secretary-General of the United Nations. The information thus transmitted came to be examined by a Committee of the General Assembly, known as the Committee on Information from Non-Self-Governing Territories. This Committee, formerly appointed on an ad hoc basis for renewable terms of three years, was converted into a semi-permanent organ as a result of a General Assembly Resolution in December 1961, appointing it until such time as the Assembly decided that the principles embodied in Chapter XI of the Charter, and in the Assembly's Declaration of 4 December 1960, on the Granting of Independence to Colonial Countries and Peoples[5] had been fully implemented. It was empowered to review, and make recommendations concerning social and economic conditions in non-self-governing territories, and it had in fact received

1. See ICJ 1950, 128. This view was upheld and reaffirmed by the international Court of Justice over twenty years later in its Advisory Opinion of 21 June 1971, on the *Legal Consequences for States of the Continued Presence of South Africa in Namibia (South West Africa)*. The Court ruled in addition that the failure of South Africa to comply with its obligation to submit to the supervision of United Nations organs made its continued presence in South Africa illegal; see ICJ 1971, 16 at 28, 35–43.
2. ICJ 1966, 6.
3. The Court was equally divided on the question, the President's casting vote being decisive under art 55 of the Court's Statute. For the history of the dispute see J. Dugard *The South West Africa/Namibia Dispute* (1973).
4. Semble, an Administering Authority cannot unilaterally modify the status of a trust territory without the authority of the United Nations.
5. See below, pp 111–113.

evidence other than information transmitted under Chapter XI of the Charter, including statements by governments of administering countries, and by international institutions. In December 1963, the General Assembly discontinued the Committee on Information, and transferred its functions to the Special Committee (the Committee of Twenty-four) on the Situation with regard to the Implementation of the Declaration on the Granting of Independence to Colonial Countries and Peoples.[6]

The provisions of Chapter XI of the Charter have been given, in practice, a rather wider operation than was probably contemplated when these were drafted. The General Assembly has apparently taken the view that Chapter XI has greater force than that of a merely unilateral undertaking. By various Resolutions, and by the appointment of ad hoc committees in respect to particular territories, the Assembly has sought to advance the attainment of independence by non-self-governing territories, to emphasise the obligations of states administering such territories, to promote the welfare of the inhabitants, and to procure a wider participation or association by the territories in, or with the work of the United Nations and its specialised agencies. A rather striking aspect is the extent to which thereby territories and dependencies have come under the cognisance of United Nations subsidiary organs. The decolonisation programme of the United Nations has progressed with such effectiveness that, at the date of writing, there are less than twenty territories, mainly small island territories, which can come within the cognisance of the United Nations organs administering Chapter XI of the Charter.[7]

Neutralised states

A *neutralised state* is one whose independence and political and territorial integrity are guaranteed *permanently* by a collective agreement of Great Powers subject to the condition that the particular state concerned will never take up arms against another state—except to defend itself—and will never enter into treaties of alliance, etc, which may compromise its impartiality or lead it into war.

The object of neutralisation is to safeguard peace by:

a. protecting small states against powerful adjacent states and thereby preserving the balance of power;
b. protecting and maintaining the independence of 'buffer' states lying between Great Powers.

The essence of neutralisation is that it is a *collective* act, ie the Great Powers concerned must expressly or impliedly assent to the status of neutrality

6. See below, p 112.
7. The cases of New Caledonia, Tahiti, Gibraltar, and the Falkland (Malvinas) Islands are complicated by arguments that their populations are largely imported from the metropolitan power, whose votes at referenda should on that account be ignored, and by rival claimants to sovereignty in the last two cases (Spain and Argentina, respectively). Notwithstanding the Advisory Opinion of the International Court of Justice in the *Western Sahara Case*, ICJ 1975, 12, that the people of Western Sahara have the right to self-determination, it has still not been possible to hold a definitive referendum, despite the establishment by the United Nations in 1991 of a supervisory mission (MINURSO) in the territory.

permanently conferred on the country, and that it is *contractual*, ie a state cannot be neutralised without its consent, nor can it unilaterally announce its neutralisation. Thus in 1938, when Switzerland took steps to obtain recognition of its full neutrality by the League of Nations, after a prior declaration of its independence and neutrality, the Soviet Foreign Minister—Monsieur Litvinoff—protested, perhaps correctly, that Switzerland could not so declare its neutrality in the absence of prior agreement with all other interested states. Nor is the case of the neutralisation of Austria in 1955 an exception to the principle. The Austrian legislature did, it is true, following upon the State Treaty of 15 May 1955, re-establishing an independent democratic Austria, enact a constitutional statute proclaiming Austria's permanent neutrality. But this self-declared neutrality was in pursuance of prior agreement[8] with the Soviet Union, and was recognised and supported by the other Great Powers, and by other states.

Neutralisation differs fundamentally from neutrality, which is a voluntary policy assumed temporarily in regard to a state of war affecting other Powers, and terminable at any time by the state declaring its neutrality. Neutralisation on the other hand is a permanent status conferred by agreement with the interested Powers, without whose consent it cannot be relinquished. It is thus also essentially different from 'neutralism', a newly coined word denoting the policy of a state not to involve itself in any conflicts or defensive alliances. (There can be some fine shades of distinction between 'neutralism' and another expression, 'non-alignment'.)

The obligations of a neutralised state are as follows:

a.　not to engage in hostilities except in self-defence;
b.　to abstain from agreements involving the risk of hostilities, or granting of military bases, or use of its territory for military purposes, for example, treaties of alliance, guarantee, or protectorate, but not from non-political conventions, for example, postal or tariff conventions;
c.　to defend itself against attack, even when calling on the guarantors for assistance, by all the means at its disposal;
d.　to obey the rules of neutrality during a war between other states;
e.　not to allow foreign interference in its internal affairs.[9]

The obligations of the states guaranteeing neutralisation are:

a.　to abstain from any attack or threat of attack on the neutralised territory;
b.　to intervene by force when the neutralised territory is violated by another Power, and the guarantors are called on to act.

It is believed that under current conditions, and having regard to the vast changes in the conditions of warfare and armed conflict, including subversion

---

8.　Indeed, under this agreement, Austria was to 'take all suitable steps to obtain international recognition' of such declared neutralisation. In the later case of the neutralisation of Laos, the unilateral Statement of Neutrality by Laos on 9 July 1962, was subsequently supported by a Thirteen-Power Declaration on 23 July 1962, that the sovereignty, independence, neutrality, unity, and territorial integrity of Laos would be respected (the thirteen Powers included Great Britain, the People's Republic of China, France, India, the United States and the Soviet Union).
9.　In its Statement of Neutrality of 9 July 1962, Laos also bound itself not to allow any country to use Laotian territory for the purposes of interference in the internal affairs of other countries.

and internal strife fomented from outside, together with the difficulty of circumscribing and localising any major conflict, the institution of neutralisation has only a limited, specific role to play in the context of international law.[10]

Outstanding cases of neutralised states have been Switzerland, Belgium and Austria. Belgium can no longer be regarded as a neutralised state because of its participation in certain pacts of security and mutual defence since the end of the Second World War (for example, the North Atlantic Security Pact of 4 April 1949), but Switzerland's status of permanent neutrality remains a fundamental principle of international law. Although more recent, Austria's neutralisation in 1955 is equally intended permanently to rest on the law of nations.

A neutralised state can become a member of the United Nations, for notwithstanding the provision in article 2 paragraph 5 of the United Nations Charter that member states must give the Organisation every assistance in any action taken in accordance with the Charter (which would include enforcement action), the Security Council may under article 48 exempt a neutralised state from any such duty. It is significant, in this connection, that Austria was admitted to the United Nations on 14 December 1955, that is to say, subsequent to the general recognition of its neutralisation. The Soviet Union objected to Austria's application to join the European Community in 1989, claiming this to be incompatible with neutrality, but these objections evaporated with the disintegration of the Soviet Union in 1990-91.

Right of self-determination of peoples and dependent entities

The right of self-determination of peoples and dependent entities has been expressly recognised by the United Nations General Assembly in its Resolution on Self-Determination of 12 December 1958, and in its Declaration of 14 December 1960, on the Granting of Independence to Colonial Countries and Peoples. The right was defined in some detail, under the heading 'The principle of equal rights and self-determination of peoples', in the Declaration on Principles of International Law Concerning Friendly Relations and Co-operation Among States in Accordance with the United Nations Charter, adopted by the General Assembly in 1970. On 10 November 1975, the General Assembly adopted a resolution reaffirming 'the importance of the universal realisation of the right of peoples to self-determination, to national sovereignty and territorial integrity, and of the speedy granting of independence to colonial countries and peoples as imperatives for the enjoyment of human rights'. The Covenant on Economic, Social and Cultural Rights, and the Covenant on Civil and Political Rights, unanimously approved by the General Assembly on 16 December 1966, and opened for signature on 19 December 1967, also recognise the right of peoples to self-determination.[11]

The right of self-determination has been treated as necessarily involving a number of correlative duties binding upon states, including the duty to promote

---

10. Cf C. E. Black, R. Falk, K. Knorr, and O. Young *Neutralisation and World Politics* (1968).
11. See also *Advisory Opinion on the Legal Consequences for States of the Continued Presence of South Africa in South West Africa (Namibia)* ICJ 1971, 16 at 54–56, where the International Court of Justice treated the people of the Mandated Territory of South West Africa as having an actual right of progress towards independence, which had been violated by South Africa's failure as Mandatory Power to comply with its obligation to submit to the supervision of United

by joint and separate action the realisation of the right of self-determination, and the transfer of sovereign powers to the peoples entitled to this right, and the duty to refrain from any forcible action calculated to deprive a people of this right. These duties have been expressed, or if not expressed are implied in the Declarations, above, adopted by the General Assembly, and in addition find some support in the practice of the past decade. First, there has been the rapid emancipation of many colonies and non-self-governing territories. Second, there has been the impact of the above-mentioned Declaration on the Granting of Independence to Colonial Countries and Peoples. In this Declaration, the General Assembly proclaimed the necessity of bringing to a speedy and unconditional end colonialism in all its forms and manifestations, and called for immediate steps to be taken to transfer all powers to the peoples of territories which had not yet attained independence. By a subsequent Resolution of 27 November 1961, the Assembly established a Special Committee of Seventeen to implement the Declaration, and this Committee, enlarged in 1962 to consist of 24 members, has since been active in all directions.[12] Third, the process of ratification and acceptance of the two Covenants mentioned above should consolidate acceptance of the duties correlative to the right of self-determination.

There still remains some difficulty as to what the expression 'self-determination' itself means, or includes. Some writers decline to treat it as a right of an absolute nature, stressing that it must be considered within the context of the people or group demanding to exercise it. Presumably it connotes freedom of choice to be exercised by a dependent people through a plebiscite or some other method of ascertainment of the people's wishes.[13] Another difficult problem is to determine which communities of human beings constitute 'peoples' (ie the 'self') for the purpose of enjoying the right of self-determination.[14] Aspects such as common territory, common language, and common political aims may have to be considered. Semble, there must normally be a territorial unit corresponding to the people to which the right may be regarded as attaching. Beyond this, there is the problem of whether, and, if so, to what extent the right of self-determination will permit secession of part of the territory of a state.[15] An unqualified right of secession, as a derivative of the right of self-determination, could lead to

---

Nations organs. See also the Advisory Opinion in the *Western Sahara Case*, ICJ 1975, 12. In s VIII of the Helsinki Declaration adopted on 1 August 1975, the states participating in the Declaration pledged themselves to respect the right of peoples to self-determination. See generally on the subject of self-determination, M. Pomerance *Self-Determination in Law and Practice* (1982).

12. The full title of the Committee is 'Special Committee on the Situation with regard to the Implementation of the Declaration on the Granting of Independence to Colonial Countries and Peoples'. It has taken cognisance, inter alia, of the emancipation of trust territories, and the termination of trusteeship agreements, as, eg, in August 1975, in connection with the termination of the trusteeship of Papua New Guinea and its achievement of independence on 16 September 1975.

13. Cf the provisions for freedom of choice to be exercised by the people of West New Guinea, according to article XVIII of the Netherlands-Indonesia Agreement of 15 August 1962.

14. See Eagleton 47 AJIL (1953) 88–93, D. B. Levin *Soviet Year Book of International Law* (1962) pp 24–48, and generally the article by Professor Østerud, an authority on self-determination, 'Varieties of Self-Determination: the Case of the Western Sahara' (1985) 10 *The Maghreb Review* 20–27.

15. Cf Bucheit *Secession: The Legitimacy of Self-Determination* (1978) and Østerud, op cit, n 10, ante.

disruption of state systems. In part for this reason, it is controversial according to the most recent practice and weight of opinion whether minority indigenous peoples or tribal groups in certain countries, eg, Canada and Australia, are 'peoples' entitled to self-determination.

Prior to 1958, it could be said that customary international law conferred no right upon dependent peoples or entities to statehood, although exceptionally some such right ad hoc might be given by treaty, or arise under the decision of an international organisation.[16] It is clear in the light of recent practice that such right is not conditioned upon the attainment of complete economic self-reliance, although economic viability may provide a ground, according to circumstances, to support entitlement to self-determination.

Self-determination may not necessarily involve solely and exclusively an absolute right to elect for autonomous statehood, but also an option to choose integration with the 'parent' state. Thus, eg, by the Act of Self-Determination of the people of the Cocos-Keeling Islands in December 1984, duly supervised by a United Nations mission, and later approved by the General Assembly (UN), the people voted for integration with Australia.

Sovereignty of peoples and nations over their natural wealth and resources
In a similar connection, is the so-called principle of 'economic self-determination', expressed in the United Nations General Assembly Resolution of 21 December 1952, affirming the right of peoples freely to use and exploit their natural wealth and resources. If the Resolution signified that, in the absence of treaty limitations or international law restrictions, a state was entitled to control the resources within its territory, it would merely enunciate a truism. The real object of the Resolution seems, however, to have been to encourage under-developed countries to make use of their own resources, as a proper foundation for their independent economic development, and to prevent their depletion by the action of other states.[17]

Later, fuller and more elaborate expression was given to the principle in Resolutions of the General Assembly dated respectively 14 December 1962, and 25 November 1966, and on 17 December 1973, by Resolution adopted at its 28th Session, the General Assembly extended the scope of the principle to 'permanent sovereignty' over natural resources in the seabed and subsoil of, and in the waters of the seas within national jurisdiction. The right of all peoples freely to dispose of their natural wealth and resources was affirmed in identical terms in article 1 of the Covenant on Economic, Social and Cultural Rights of 16 December 1966, and article 1 of the Covenant on Civil and Political Rights of the same date. Article 25 of the former Covenant also declared that nothing therein was to be interpreted as impairing the 'inherent right of all peoples to enjoy and utilise fully and freely their natural wealth and resources'. There have been other Resolutions of the General Assembly on the subject, more particularly

16. As, eg by the Resolution of the United Nations General Assembly in November 1949, that Libya and Italian Somaliland should become independent sovereign states, a Resolution adopted pursuant to the powers conferred by Annex XI, para 3, of the Treaty of Peace with Italy of 1947.
17. A somewhat related question concerns recent claims advanced for the general recognition of the 'right to development' of peoples (before self-determination), and of emancipated territories. See Dupuy (ed) *The Right to Development at the International Level* (1980).

its 1974 Resolution on Permanent Sovereignty over Natural Resources, its 1974 Declaration on the Establishment of a New Economic Order and the Charter of Economic Rights and Duties of States adopted by it in 1974, and these, together with the 1962 and 1966 Resolutions, reflect not only the idea of a state's sovereign control over its own resources, not to be surrendered but to be safeguarded even when foreign capital is imported to promote development, but also an insistence, implicitly, if not expressly, that it is the responsibility of the international community to assist in maximising the exploitation and use of the natural wealth of developing countries, and so contribute to strengthening their capability to promote their economic development by their own efforts. Since the ruling criterion is that of a state's permanent sovereignty over its own resources, it is this state's national law which according to the Resolutions must govern questions of compensation for nationalisation or expropriation of foreign enterprises, while remedies given in the national courts must be exhausted before seeking relief in the international forum.

One of the issues at the Stockholm Conference of June 1972 on the Human Environment was how to reconcile the sovereign rights of states to develop their own resources in their own way with the necessities of protection of the environment. In Principles 21 and 22 of the Declaration on the Human Environment adopted by the Conference, it was proclaimed, inter alia, that states have a sovereign right to exploit their own resources pursuant to their own environmental policies, while remaining responsible for ensuring that activities within their jurisdiction or control do not cause damage to the environment of other states.[18]

This affirmation and re-affirmation of the principle of a nation's sovereign control over its own resources has undoubtedly generated some new currents in international economic law. One important result has been the far-reaching United Nations programme for the evaluation and development of natural resources.

3. ASSOCIATIONS OR GROUPINGS OF STATES

States are free, consistently with their obligations under the United Nations Charter, to form associations or groupings for general or particular purposes. The Commonwealth, mentioned above,[19] remains an outstanding illustration, and so also the Organisation of American States (OAS), and the Organisation of African Unity. Some of these associations or groupings, for example the European Economic Community (EEC), and the North Atlantic Treaty Organisation (NATO), are, in effect, of the character of international organisations, and therefore come within the ambit of Chapter 20, below.

Since the end of the Second World War, the number of such associations or groupings of states has rapidly increased. The principal functions or purposes served by them are political, or economic, or related to the mutual defence and security of the members. The novel feature of these new associations or groupings

18. On the environment, see further below, ch 14.
19. See pp 105–106 above.

is not only their diversity, but the establishment in each instance of a permanent or semi-permanent machinery, to enable them to function as working unities. The majority of such bodies are regional in character or have regional implications, but sometimes include states not located in the region concerned, such as the Commonwealth.

The European Union is the most advanced example of regional economic and political integration.[20] The European Economic Community (EEC) was established by the Treaty of Rome of 25 March 1957, contemporaneously with the European Atomic Energy Community (Euratom). Together with the European Coal and Steel Community (ECSC), established earlier in 1951, the three legally distinct communities became known collectively as the European Communities. By virtue of the Merger Treaty of 1967, which established a single Council and Commission for the three Communities, the collective name became 'the European Community'. Somewhat confusingly, since 1993, the term 'European Community' (EC) is now taken to refer only to the former EEC, when it is necessary to refer to it separately; the three Communities collectively have been absorbed within the European Union, created by the Maastricht Treaty on European Union and Economic and Monetary Union, 7 February 1992, which entered into force on 1 October 1993. The Maastricht Treaty includes among its objectives the promotion of economic and social progress through, inter alia, the establishment of economic and monetary union, and ultimately of a single Union currency, the assertion of the Union's identity on the international scene by a common foreign and security policy, and the introduction of a common citizenship of the Union. There is a single institutional framework: the European Parliament, the European Council, the European Commission, and the European Court of Justice. These organs exercise their functions in accordance with the treaties establishing the three Communities and with the provisions of the Treaty on European Union.

Other economic groupings include the European Free Trade Association (EFTA), established by the Stockholm Convention of 20 November 1959,[1] the Latin American Free Trade Association, established by the Montevideo Treaty of February 1960, the ASEAN[2] Free Trade Area (AFTA), established by Brunei, Indonesia, Malaysia, the Philippines, Singapore and Thailand in 1992, the North American Free Trade Agreement (NAFTA), concluded by Canada, Mexico and the United States in December 1992, and the Asia-Pacific Economic Cooperation (APEC) process initiated by Australia in 1989, in which Australia, the ASEAN countries, Canada, China, Hong Kong, Japan, Korea, New Zealand, Taiwan and the United States participate.

20. The original members in 1957 were Belgium, France, the Federal Republic of Germany, Italy, the Netherlands, and Luxembourg. The EC was enlarged in 1972 by the accession of Denmark, Ireland, and the United Kingdom, in 1981 by the accession of Greece, and in 1986 by Portugal and Spain. Other European States are negotiating to join. The EC has also entered into conventions of 'association' with the ACP (African, Caribbean and Pacific) countries, which were formerly colonies of the EC member states.
1. EFTA members are Austria, Finland, Iceland, Liechtenstein, Norway, Sweden, and Switzerland. Most of these are negotiating to join the European Union. In the meantime the EU and EFTA have concluded an agreement for the creation of the European Economic Area (EEA), 2 May 1992.
2. ASEAN is the Association of South East Asian Nations, formed in 1967.

An example of a union or alliance for mutual security purposes, supported by permanent machinery, has been the North Atlantic Treaty Organisation (NATO) formed pursuant to the North Atlantic Security Pact of 4 April 1949.

CHAPTER 6

Recognition

1. RECOGNITION IN GENERAL[1]

The identity and number of states belonging to the international community are by no means fixed and invariable. The march of history produces many changes. Old states disappear or unite with other states to form a new state, or disintegrate and split into several new states, or former colonial or vassal territories may by a process of emancipation themselves attain statehood. Then, also, even in the case of existing states, revolutions occur or military conquests are effected, and the status of the new governments becomes a matter of concern to other states, which formerly had relations with the displaced governments, raising the question of whether or not to engage in formal or informal relations with the new régimes, either by recognition, or if a policy of not making formal statements of recognition of new governments is followed, solely by some kind of intercourse.

These transformations raise problems for the international community, of which one is the matter of *recognition* of the new state or new government or other change of status involved. At some time or other, this issue of recognition has to be faced by certain states, particularly if diplomatic intercourse must necessarily be maintained with the states or governments to be recognised.

It is important to distinguish between recognition of states and recognition of the governments of states. The former is the more important because it is fundamental to the international legal order; the state is the entity which is the bearer of international rights and obligations, not the government for the time being representing it. Thus these rights and obligations continue even though governments may come and go. To recognise a new state is therefore a serious step which other states take only after due deliberation and by formal statement. The matter will also nowadays usually be discussed in the United Nations in which a collective view may emerge. Changes in the governments of states, if ocurring by way of normal constitutional processes such as elections, do not

---

1. See Lauterpacht *Recognition in International Law* (1947); Chen *The International Law of Recognition* (1951); Jean Charpentier *La Reconnaissance Internationale et L'Evolution du Droit des Gens* (Paris, 1956); Hans-Herbert Teuscher *Die Vorzeitige Anerkennung im Völkerrecht* (1959); Dugard *Recognition and the United Nations* (1987).

require action by other states by way of recognition. Irregular changes of government, such as by coup d'état, military take-over, or revolution do require some response by other states, but most do not now issue formal statements; whether they are willing to deal with the new government or not will become evident from their behaviour, from which recognition or non-recognition can be inferred.

The subject is one of some difficulty, and at this stage of the development of international law, can be presented less as a collection of clearly defined rules or principles than as a body of fluid, inconsistent, and unsystematic state practice, involving as well the adoption by states of different policies.

The reasons for this are twofold:

a.　Recognition is, as the practice of most states shows, much more a question of policy than of law. The policy of the recognising state is conditioned principally by the necessity of protecting its own interests, which lie in maintaining proper relations with any new state or new government that is likely to be stable and permanent.[2] Besides this, other political considerations, for example, trade, strategy, etc, may influence a state in giving recognition. Consequently there is an irresistible tendency in recognising states to use legal principles as a convenient camouflage for political decisions.

b.　There are several distinct categories of recognition. At the outset there are the categories already mentioned—the recognition of new states, and the recognition of new heads or governments of existing states. Although very much the same principles are applicable to both, it is important that they should not be confused.[3] In addition to these two heads of recognition, there are the recognition of entities as entitled to the rights of belligerency, the recognition of entities entitled to be considered as insurgent governments, the recently proposed new category of recognition of national liberation or resistance movements, and the recognition of territorial and other changes, new treaties, etc (see below). Finally, there is the distinction to bear in mind between recognition de jure and de facto of states and governments.

It is important that in considering the international law and practice as to recognition, due allowance should be made for the exigencies of diplomacy. States have frequently delayed, refused, or eventually accorded recognition to newly-formed states or governments for reasons that lacked strict legal justification.[4] For example, in the First World War, Great Britain, France, the United States, and other Powers recognised Poland and Czechoslovakia before these latter actually existed as independent states or governments. Similarly, in the Second World War the grant of recognition was conditioned by the supreme necessity of strengthening the ranks in the struggle against the Axis Powers, as for example

2.　This conclusion is drawn by Professor H. A. Smith from a study of British practice; see Smith *Great Britain and the Law of Nations* (1932) Vol 1, pp 77–80.

3.　Hence, it is necessary when referring to a particular act of recognition to be most specific in stating what the state, government, or other entity is recognised as being. It is inadequate merely to state that some entity has been 'recognised'.

4.　Among such considerations have been the following: That the entity recognised could give valued help as a co-belligerent; that the entity recognised was willing to conclude a general settlement with the recognising state; that recognition or non-recognition might offend an ally.

in the case of the recognition of the governments-in-exile in London. Political and diplomatic considerations also explain the puzzling divergencies among states since 1948 so far as concerned the recognition of the newly emerged State of Israel, and after 1949 the government of the People's Republic of China.

Naturally, the question has been raised whether recognition in relation to governments of states is a necessary institution, and, if not, accordingly whether it ought to be discarded either generally or in most instances. This was the view indeed of Professor Richard Baxter, Judge of the International Court of Justice, 1979–1980, who felt that recognition caused more problems than it solved, and that its partial withdrawal would facilitate the maintenance of relations with states in which extra-constitutional changes of government were taking place.[5] In 1930, the then Minister for Foreign Affairs of Mexico, Mr Estrada, announced that his government would no longer issue declarations in the sense of grants of recognition of new governments inasmuch as 'such a course is an insulting practice and one which, in addition to the fact that it offends the sovereignty of other nations, implies that judgment of some sort may be passed upon the internal affairs of those nations by other governments . . .'.[6] This policy, as thus announced, has become generally known as the 'Estrada doctrine', and has been adopted by a certain number of other governments, but obviously, as subsequent experience has shown, it has not eliminated the responsibility falling on governments, from time to time, of deciding with which of two rival régimes relations or any form of intercourse should be conducted. The same difficulty would necessarily be faced by those states (eg, the United States, the United Kingdom and Australia) which have opted for a policy of not recognising or withholding recognition of new governments, but instead deciding according to the circumstances whether or not to maintain relations with them.[7]

In form and in substance, recognition has continued to remain primarily a unilateral diplomatic act on the part of one or more states. No collective, organic procedure for granting recognition based on established legal principles has yet been evolved by the international community, although the provisions in the United Nations Charter (articles 3–4) directed to the admission of states to membership of the Organisation may incidentally in most instances amount to a certificate of statehood.[8]

Accordingly, the recognition of a new state has been defined with some authority[9] as:

'. . . the free act by which one or more States acknowledge the existence on a definite territory of a human society politically organised, independent of any other existing State, and capable of observing the obligations of international law, and by which they manifest therefore their intention to consider it a member of the international community.'

5. See Galloway *Recognising Foreign Governments* (1978) Foreword, p xi.
6. See Whiteman *Digest of International Law* (1963) Vol 2, pp 85–86.
7. For the change in united Kingdom policy on recognition of irregular changes of government, announced by the Foreign Secretary in 1980, see (1980) 51 BYIL 367, and the analysis by Warbrick in (1981) 30 ICLQ 568.
8. J. Dugard *Recognition and the United Nations* (1987).
9. By the Institute of International Law; see Resolutions adopted at Brussels in 1936, art 1, 30 AJIL (1936) Supplement, p 185.

To express these two statements in another way, the state, to be recognised, must possess the four characteristics mentioned in the Montevideo Convention,[10] with particular regard to the capacity to conduct its international affairs, although the requirement of definiteness of territory is not generally insisted upon (cf the case of the recognition of Israel in 1949, while its boundaries were still not finally determined).

On the other hand, recognition as a government by those states which still follow the traditional course of recognising or withholding recognition of new governments and have not, like, eg, the United States, the United Kingdom and Australia, abandoned this practice, implies that the recognised government is, in the opinion of the recognising state, qualified to represent an existing state, but it does not necessarily signify approval of that government by the recognising state.

This act of recognition in both cases may be *express*, that is by formal declaration (which may be by diplomatic Note, *note verbale*, personal message from the head of state or Minister of Foreign Affairs, parliamentary declaration, or treaty),[11] or *implied* when it is a matter of inference from certain relations between the recognising state and the new state or new government. The manner of recognition is not material, provided that it unequivocally indicates the intention of the recognising state. There are no rules of international law restrictive of the form or manner in which recognition may be accorded.

Recognition under modern state practice involves more than *cognition*, that is to say more than an avowal of knowledge that a state or government possesses the requisite bare qualifications to be recognised. This is proved by the fact, inter alia, that substantial delays may occur before a state or government is recognised, notwithstanding that its status may be beyond doubt. The practical purpose of recognition, namely, the initiation of formal relations with the recognising state, must also always be borne in mind. Once granted, recognition in a sense estops or precludes the recognising state from contesting the qualifications for recognition of the state or government recognised.

Many writers have, however, sought to draw wider theoretical implications as to the object of recognition.

There are two principal theories as to the nature, function, and effect of recognition:

a.   According to the *constitutive* theory, it is the act of recognition alone which creates statehood or which clothes a new government with any authority or status in the international sphere.

b.   According to the *declaratory* or *evidentiary* theory, statehood or the authority of a new government exists as such prior to and independently of recognition. The act of recognition is merely a formal acknowledgment of an established situation of fact.

Probably the truth lies somewhere between these two theories. The one or the other theory may be applicable to different sets of facts. The bulk of

10. See p 85 above.
11. The minister concerned may also, by press statement, expressly declare that an otherwise ambiguous Note or *note verbale* constitutes formal recognition.

international practice supports the evidentiary theory, inasmuch as while recognition has often been given for political reasons and has tended therefore to be constitutive in character, countries generally seek to give or to refuse it in accordance with legal principles and precedents. Also recognition has frequently been withheld for political reasons[12] or until such time as it could be given in exchange for some material diplomatic advantage to be conceded by the newly recognised state or government—a clear indication that the latter already possessed the requisite attributes of statehood or governmental authority. Moreover, a mere refusal by a single state to recognise could not affect the situation if a great number of other states had already given their recognition. Nor have states in practice regarded non-recognition as conclusive evidence of the absence of qualifications to be a state or a government. Indeed by insisting that unrecognised states or governments must observe the rules of international law, they have implicitly acknowledged that they possess some status as such.

The evidentiary theory is further supported by the following rules:

a. The rule that if a question arises in the courts of a new state as to the date at which the state came into existence, it will be irrelevant to consider the date when treaties with other states recognising it came into operation. The date when the requirements of statehood were in fact first fulfilled is the only material date.[13]

b. The rule that recognition of a new state has retroactive effect, dating back to its actual inception as an independent state.[14]

These two rules which apply also to newly recognised governments are based principally on the necessary consideration that there should be no gap of time during which a state or government is out of existence. In other words, continuity is the essence of state sovereignty or of governmental authority. Otherwise, many transactions, contracts, changes of status, etc, of the utmost importance to private citizens, would be null and void because made in a period when the laws of the particular state or government under which they were effected were unrecognised.

The constitutive theory finds some support in the fact that upon recognition the recognised state or government acquires status, as such, in the municipal courts of the recognising state.[15]

---

12. As in the case of the early refusal to recognise the Soviet Union because of its failure to fulfil contractual obligations of the former Tsarist Government.
13. See *Rights of Citizenship in Succession States Cases*, Annual Digest of Public International Law Cases, 1919–1922, Nos 5, 6 and 7. See also art 9 of the Charter of the Organisation of American States, Bogotá, 1948: 'The political existence of the State is independent of recognition by other States'.
14. *A M Luther v James Sagor & Co* [1921] 3 KB 532; and as to the retroactive effect of recognition, see further below in this chapter, pp 137–138. Further authority against the constitutive theory is the *Tinoco Arbitration* (1923) where the Arbitrator held that the revolutionary Tinoco Government of Costa Rica which came into power in 1917 was a properly constituted government, although not recognised by Great Britain, and that Great Britain was not estopped (ie precluded in law) by such prior non-recognition from later alleging that the government was in fact a duly and properly constituted one; see *United Nations Reports of International Arbitral Awards* Vol I, pp 371 et seq.
15. See below, pp 134–135.

Is there a duty to grant recognition?
It has been urged that states are subject to a duty under international law to recognise a new state or a new government fulfilling the legal requirements of statehood or of governmental capacity.[16] However, the existence of such a duty is not borne out by the weight of precedents and practice, particularly the divergencies in 1949–1980 in the recognition of the People's Republic of China, although it could perhaps be said that in recognising certain newly emerged states (ie decolonised territories or emancipated trust territories) some states considered that they were bound to accord recognition.

If indeed there were such a legal duty to recognise, it is difficult to say by whom and in what manner it could be enforced. To each duty, there must correspond a correlative right, and how would one define this right? Is it a right of the state claiming to be recognised, or a right of the international community, and how would such claims of right be presented? The answer to these questions must be that there is no general acceptance of the existence of the duty or the right mentioned. No right to recognition is laid down in the Draft Declaration on the Rights and Duties of States, drawn up by the International Law Commission in 1949. The action of states in affording or withholding recognition is as yet uncontrolled by any rigid rules of international law; on the contrary recognition is treated, for the most part, as a matter of vital policy that each state is entitled to decide for itself.[17] Podesta Costa's view that recognition is a 'facultative' and not an obligatory act is more consistent with the practice. There is not even a duty on a state under international law not to recognise initially, or to withdraw recognition, if the qualifications of statehood or of governmental authority cease to exist. The apparent arbitrariness of state practice in this regard is tempered by the consideration that most states endeavour, as far as possible, to give recognition according to legal principles and precedents, to the extent at least that, although they may withhold recognition for political reasons, when they do grant it they generally make sure that the state or government to be recognised at least possesses the requisite legal qualifications. To this degree states do treat recognition as a legal act. Lastly, if there were such a duty under general customary international law, it would be one observed by all major states, yet no such duty is acknowledged by states following the Estrada doctrine of non-recognition (see above), nor so far as concerns the recognition of new governments is the existence of the duty recognised by states such as the United States, the United Kingdom and Australia, which have abandoned the policy of such recognition of new régimes.

16. In observations forwarded to the United Nations in 1948 on the Draft Declaration on the Rights and Duties of States (see above, pp 89–90), the British Government stated that it favoured a development of international law under which recognition would become a matter of legal duty for all states in respect of entities fulfilling the conditions of statehood. These observations of 1948 do not of course apply to the recognition of new governments, inasmuch as since 1980 the United Kingdom Government has abandoned the policy of such recognition (see below in this chapter).

17. Also municipal courts have adopted the view that the decision to recognise is a political one, to be performed by the executive, and not to be questioned in a court of law; cf *Oetjen v Central Leather Co* 246 US 297 (1918).

Implied recognition

Implied recognition is very much a matter of the intention of the state said to have given recognition. The implication is made solely when the circumstances unequivocally indicate the intention to establish formal relations with the new state or new government. Such clear-cut cases will naturally be limited. There are other cases in which a state may lay itself open to the inference of having recognised another state or government, for example, by entering into some form of relations with it. Such conduct can usually amount to no more than recognition de facto, or recognition of an entity as an insurgent authority, or indicate an intention to maintain, through agents, informal relations without recognition.

In practice, the only legitimate occasions for conclusively implying recognition de jure are:

1. The formal signature of a bilateral treaty by the recognised and recognising States (for example, the Treaty of Commerce between Nationalist China and the United States in 1928) as distinct from mere temporary arrangements or agreements. It is not necessary that the treaty be ratified.[18] The more recent practice, under which a state or government may, on occasions, conclude even a formal bilateral treaty with an unrecognised entity or régime, means that a close examination of the bilateral treaty concerned and its surrounding circumstances is necessary before an implication of recognition is valid.[19]
2. The formal initiation of diplomatic relations between the recognised and recognising state.
3. The issue of a consular exequatur by the admitting state for a consul of an unrecognised state.

In certain exceptional circumstances, but not otherwise,[20] recognition has been inferred from the following circumstances:

a. Common participation in a multilateral treaty. However, states such as Great Britain and the United States have, sometimes, when signing a convention, declared that their signature was not to be construed as the recognition of a signatory or adhering Power not recognised by them.
b. Participation in an international conference.
c. Initiation of negotiations between a recognising and a recognised state.

Recognition of the validity of the laws decreed or enacted by a particular entity, does not necessarily import recognition of the law-making entity.[1]

---

18. *Republic of China v Merchants' Fire Assurance Corpn of New York* 30 F 2d 278 (1929).
19. Cf B. R. Bot *Nonrecognition and Treaty Relations* (1968). Semble, the Treaty, initialled on 8 November 1972, between the Federal Republic of Germany (West Germany) and the German Democratic Republic (East Germany) by, inter alia, its preambular references to 'the two German States' and 'both German States' involved mutual recognition of each other's statehood.
20. Note, eg, the Protocol to the Declaration on the Neutrality of Laos, signed at Geneva on 23 July 1962. The United States, and the People's Republic of China, not then recognised by the United States, were both parties to the Protocol.
1. *Carl-Zeiss-Stiftung v Rayner and Keeler Ltd (No 2)* [1967] 1 AC 853 at 961, [1966] 2 All ER 536 at 581; *GUR Corpn v Trust Bank of Africa Ltd* [1987] QB 599, [1986] 3 All ER 449, CA.

Recognition subject to a condition

Sometimes states are recognised subject to a condition, generally an obligation which they undertake to fulfil. Thus, the Berlin Congress of 1878 recognised Bulgaria, Montenegro, Serbia, and Rumania, under the condition only that these states should not impose any religious disabilities on any of their subjects.

The effect of such conditional recognition is that failure to fulfil the obligation does not annul the recognition, as once given this is incapable of withdrawal. By breaking the condition, the recognised state may be guilty of a breach of international law, and it is open to the recognising states to sever diplomatic relations as a form of sanction, or otherwise to proceed. But the status which the recognised state has obtained from the act of recognition cannot then be retracted. By way of exception, however, the conditional recognition of states or governments which are just in process of emerging is probably revocable. Thus the recognition in 1919 by Great Britain of the Estonian National Council 'for the time being provisionally and with all necessary reservations as to the future'[2] was no doubt revocable in the sense that it did not constitute an undertaking to continue the recognition if conditions altered.

In this topic of conditional recognition, the term 'condition' is thus not used in its true legal connotation as a vital term going to the root of a legal act, so that if the term be not performed such act becomes void or inoperative.

In practice states have repeatedly, as consideration for the grant of recognition, exacted from states or governments to be recognised some guarantee or undertaking or stipulation (for example, respect for private property as in the case of the United States recognition in 1937 of the new Bolivian Government). This practice is consistent with the predominantly political character of the unilateral act of recognition. It is true, however, that if recognition should under international law become purely and simply the cognitive act of registering the existence of statehood or of governmental capacity, logically it could not be subject to any such extrinsic term or condition.

Collective recognition

The advantages of recognition taking place by some collective international act, or through the medium of an international institution cannot be denied. It would obviate the present embarrassments due to unilateral acts of recognition.[3]

In the light of the Advisory Opinion of the International Court of Justice, on *Conditions of Membership in the United Nations*,[4] which recognises statehood as a primary qualification for admission to the United Nations, it is clear that such admission is tantamount to recognition of the member admitted as a state.[5]

---

2.   *The Gagara* [1919] P 95.
3.   There are a number of historical precedents of collective recognition; eg, the recognition of Bulgaria, Montenegro, Serbia and Rumania by the Berlin Congress of 1878, and of Estonia and Albania by the Allied Powers in 1921. In principle, there is also no rule of international law which would preclude collective derecognition, ie collective withdrawal of recognition; more correctly, a number of states each withdrawing recognition pursuant to an agreement between them to that effect.
4.   ICJ 1948, 57 et seq.
5.   As distinct from the admission of a new member state to the United Nations, there is the question of the acceptance of the credentials of the government of an existing member state. Quaere whether accepting within the United Nations the credentials of a revolutionary government of

Although not as such an act of collective recognition, the European Community adopted principles and mechanisms to guide its Member States in recognition issues arising from the dissolution of the Soviet Union and of Yugoslavia, and from the division of Czechoslovakia into the separate Czech and Slovak Republics. The Council of the EC adopted on 16 December 1991 *Guidelines on the Recogntion of New States in Eastern Europe and in the Soviet Union*. These guidelines stated a common position of the Member States of the EC on the process of recognition of these states requiring:

a. respect for the provisions of the United Nations Charter and the commitments subscribed to in the Final Act of Helsinki[6] and in the Charter of Paris[7], especially with regard to the rule of law, democracy, and human rights;
b. guarantees for the rights of ethnic and national groups and minorities in accordance with the commitments subscribed to in the framework of the CSCE[8];
c. respect for the inviolability of all frontiers, which can only be changed by peaceful means and by common agreement;
d. acceptance of all relevant commitments with regard to disarmament and nuclear non-proliferation as well as to security and regional stability;
e. commitment to settle by agreement, including where appropriate by recourse to arbitration, all questions concerning state succession and regional disputes.

The Declaration concluded with a statement that the European Community and its Member States would not recognise entities formed as the result of aggression.

Although by their terms confined to Europe, and to a particular period of history, it is likely that these guidelines will be influential in shaping future state practice more widely, with necessary adaptations. At the very least they demonstrate that the Montevideo criteria of statehood (see above) are no longer considered in practice a sufficient basis for decision.

---

a member state involves the same considerations as the recognition of that government. In a memorandum circulated to the Security Council members on 8 March 1950, the Secretary-General adopted the view that the two matters rested on different considerations, and that United Nations representation must rest, inter alia, on plenitude of capacity to fulfil the obligations of membership of the United Nations. In this connection, see D. I. Feldman *Soviet Year Book of International Law* (1961) pp 50–64. A stage may be reached where, unless the credentials of the effective government are accepted in the same manner as it has been recognised, the member state concerned will for all practical purposes be denied its due right of participating in the Organisation. The matter had been raised repeatedly from 1950 onwards in connection with the claim by the Soviet Government and other governments of member states that the Nationalist Government of China could no longer represent China within the United Nations, but that the credentials of the Government of the Communist People's Republic of China, which had been recognised by a number of states, should for that and other reasons be accepted. While ultimately, in 1971, support was obtained for acceptance of the latter government's credentials, controversy centred on the point whether the former government should remain a member.

6. Final Act of the Conference on Security and Cooperation in Europe, Helsinki, 1975, (1975) 14 ILM 1292.
7. Charter of Paris for a New Europe, 1990, (1991) 30 ILM 190.
8. Conference on Security and Cooperation in Europe, a continuing process established under the Final Act of Helsinki, 1975.

Prior to the declaration of the above guidelines, the EC and its Member States established on 27 August 1991 the Conference on Yugoslavia with the purpose of helping the parties to the conflicts in the former Yugoslavia to achieve a peaceful solution. As part of its activities the Conference established an Arbitration Commission for the resolution of legal questions. This Commission consisted of five members, each a president of a constitutional court in an EC country. The presiding member of the Commission was Judge Badinter of France. In its first ten opinions, delivered between November 1991 and July 1992, the Commission had to decide on the qualifications for statehood and recognition, and aspects of state succession, in relation to the six former constituent parts of the Socialist Federal Republic of Yugoslavia.[9] These opinions held: (a) that the six republics - Bosnia-Herzegovina, Croatia, Macedonia, Montenegro, Serbia, and Slovenia were equally successor states to the Socialist Federal Republic of Yugoslavia (SFRY), which was 'in process of dissolution' (November 1991) and no longer in existence (July 1992); (b) that the Federal Republic of Yugoslavia (Serbia and Montenegro) (FRY) could not claim alone to be the successor of the SFRY; (c) that it was not possible in the present state of international law to specify with precision the rights to self-determination of the Serbian populations in Bosnia-Herzegovina and Croatia; but that it was clear that self-determination could not be carried out in such a way as to change the borders existing immediately prior to independence (the principle *uti possidetis juris*), unless with the consent of all interested states; moreover, ethnic, religious, and language groups within a state have a right to recognition of their identity under international law; (d) the pre-independence federal boundaries should be regarded now as the international boundaries, following the *uti possidetis juris* principle; (e) the application of Bosnia-Herzegovina, Croatia, Macedonia, and Slovenia for recognition as independent states should be granted, subject to the condition, in the first case, of full consultation among its people by referendum, and in the second case, to the passage of amendments to the Croatian Constitution incorporating more fully certain guarantees of human rights and the rights of minorities[10]; (f) the six successor states should settle all aspects of state succession by agreement, attempting to achieve an equitable solution by drawing on the principles contained in the Vienna Convention on State Succession in Relation to Treaties, 1978 and the Vienna Convention on State Succession in Respect of State Property, Archives and Debts, 1983, and, where appropriate, general international law.

Recognition of a head of state or of a new government

As already pointed out, this has nothing to do with the recognition of a state itself. It is well settled that if the government of one state should refuse the recognition of a change in the form of government of another well-established state, the latter does not thereby lose recognition of its statehood.

One must, however, be mindful of the fact, mentioned above, that since the late 1970s certain states follow a policy, varying in consistency from one state

9.   These opinions are published in (1993) 92 ILR 162-208.
10. Serbia and Montenegro (FRY) did not apply to the Commission for certification of statehood, since they regarded themselves as continuing the legal personality of the former SFRY. This has not been accepted by the EC countries, nor by the United Nations.

to another, of recognising states *only*, and of not granting or formally withholding recognition to new governments as such. This may be illustrated by a few examples. Thus in August 1977 the new development prior to that date in American recognition practice was summarised officially[11] as follows: 'In recent years, US practice has been to de-emphasise and avoid the use of recognition in cases of changes of governments and to concern ourselves with the question of whether we wish to have diplomatic relations with the new governments.' In April 1980, the then British Secretary of State for Foreign Affairs, Lord Carrington, announced in the House of Lords that from then on the United Kingdom Government would 'no longer accord recognition to governments', and that 'we shall . . . decide the nature of our dealings with régimes that come to power unconstitutionally in the light of our assessment of whether they are able of themselves to exercise effective control of the territory of the state concerned, and seem likely to continue to do so'. The announcement, however, made it clear that no change was intended in the practice of formally granting or withholding recognition of states. The most recent declaration of a policy of non-recognition of new governments was that made by Australia in January 1988 when it was announced that it would in the future not extend formal recognition whether de jure or de facto, to new governments taking power, but would replace recognition by the conduct of relations with new régimes 'to the extent and in the manner which may be required by the circumstances of each case'—thus in wider terms than the United Kingdom's declaration. It must therefore be stressed that the ensuing discussion of recognition of governments covers only the practice of states that do recognise governments as well as states and the practice previously followed by countries such as the United States, the United Kingdom and Australia (see above) which have ceased to follow a policy of recognising or withholding recognition of new governments.

In the case of *existing states*, no difficulty in recognising a government arises except when changes in the headship of the state or of its government take place in an abnormal or revolutionary manner.[12]

Where the change proceeds in a formal and constitutional way, recognition by other states is purely a matter of formality. But in the case of a revolution the recognition of the revolutionary government is a serious question and a decision thereon is only made with great care. It is practically impossible to lay down any definite legal principles on the matter, so materially do political

11. United States *Department of State Bulletin* 10 October 1977, p 463. For criticism of the new policy see Henkin, Pugh, Schachter and Smit *International Law: Cases and Materials* (2nd edn, 1987) pp 249 et seq. The non-recognition of the new government of the foreign state does not involve cessation of the recognition of that state; cf *Lehigh Valley Railroad Co v State of Russia* 21 F 2d 396 (1927).

12. Another category of recognition advocated in recent years is that of the recognition of national liberation or resistance movements, on the one hand, and also, on the other hand, of peoples having a right to self-determination. National liberation or resistance movements have been admitted as participants, or on the basis of observer status, to international conferences or meetings. Cf also the case of the recognition by the United Nations General Assembly (by its Resolution of 20 December 1976) of the South West Africa People's Organisation (SWAPO) as the 'sole and authentic' representative of the people of Namibia (South West Africa). Some states have declined to follow others in recognising some particular liberation movements as the sole representatives of peoples awaiting self-determination.

considerations usually impinge thereon, while the practice is, as may be expected, confused and conflicting. The recognising government should at least be satisfied as to the prospects of stability of the new government. Although the premature recognition of a revolutionary government may justifiably be treated by the legitimate government as an unfriendly act, it is questionable in the light of modern practice whether, in the absence of some display of force or threat of force by the recognising state towards the legitimate government, this can be illegal as amounting to a breach of international law (for example, as representing an unlawful intervention).[13]

In the case of *nascent* states, recognition raises many problems for the recognising states; first, because of the merging of the new state with its new government and the difficulty of recognising the one without recognising the other; secondly, most states prefer, in the matter of recognition of nascent states, to be as non-committal as possible and to preface the date of recognition de jure by a stage of recognition de facto.

There is no difficulty, of course, where the new state is a former dependency or trust territory, and the parent or tutelary state, itself already de jure recognised, has consented to emancipation. Recognition can be accorded automatically, and is essentially then a legal act of a cognitive nature. This is indeed what happened in the case of the recognition of the large number of African and Asian states, which have emerged since the end of the Second World War.

Withdrawal of recognition

As a rule, recognition de jure once given is irrevocable. This holds true even though recognition was given in the first instance from purely political motives to indicate to the world at large that relations with the recognised state or government were being initiated. It is a paradox that when a gesture is made in a contrary sense, indicating that no further relations will be maintained with the formerly recognised state or government, it is not in general attended by a withdrawal of recognition. A formal severance of diplomatic relations may be declared, but the once recognised state or government does not otherwise lose its status in the international community. Thus, Great Britain recognised the Soviet Government de jure in 1924, but later broke off relations in 1927, and although relations were subsequently resumed, participated in the vote of 1939 expelling the Soviet Union from the League of Nations. Neither the rupture of diplomatic relations nor the act of expulsion annulled recognition of the Soviet Government.

When the Khmer Rouge government came to power in Cambodia in 1975 it was generally recognised, and its delegates were seated at the United Nations. (From 1976 to 1990 the country was named Democratic Kampuchea). After the atrocities committed by that government against its own people came to light,

13. A historical instance of premature recognition which was in fact treated as an intervention was that of the recognition by France in 1778 of the United States Government. The weight of subsequent practice, leaning in favour of the claims of revolutionary governments commanding popular support, has tended to discount the view that any diplomatic assistance to such governments may represent an intervention. In 1968–1969, during the course of the Nigerian Civil War, it was claimed that the recognition of the Biafran Government might constitute an intervention.

a number of governments withdrew recognition, but did not recognise in its place the rival government which had driven the Khmer Rouge away from the main centres of the country, since that government had been installed and was maintained as a result of intervention by Vietnam. Thus, for those governments, a State of Cambodia existed but no government of that state was recognised— an unusual situation. Recognition was accorded universally to the government elected in 1993 following the interposition of the United Nations Transitional Authority in Cambodia (UNTAC), which prepared the way for, and supervised, the election process.

Refusal to recognise does not necessarily imply non-cognition. This is particularly well illustrated by the attitude of the United States of non-recognition of the Soviet Government before November 1933 when recognition was given. A communication of the United States Department of State to the New York Court of Appeals in 1933 characteristically defined this attitude:[14]

'The Department of State is cognisant of the fact that the Soviet regime is exercising control and power in territory of the former Russian Empire and the Department of State has no disposition to ignore that fact.

The refusal of the Government of the United States to accord recognition to the Soviet regime is not based on the ground that the regime does not exercise control and authority in territory of the former Russian Empire, *but on other facts*.'

Thus non-recognition of a new state or new government does not necessarily mean non-intercourse with non-recognising states, just as non-intercourse does not necessarily signify non-recognition.[15] For instance, even before its 1980 declaration of a policy of non-recognition of new governments (see above), the British Government had in practice never declined to have talks or to transact necessary business with the agents or ministers of unrecognised states or governments, as witness the discussions with the Rhodesian Government after its unilateral declaration of independence in November 1965, although it was made plain that such informal relations or non-committal exchanges did not in any sense amount to formal diplomatic intercourse. Thus frequently consular appointments had been made to such unrecognised entities, although care was taken to express the appointments in such a way as not to involve even de facto recognition.[16] The primary consideration is that of convenience, and there is not involved or implied any mark of approval of the régime concerned. In the opinion of the International Law Commission in 1967,[17] a state may send a special

14. *Salimoff & Co v Standard Oil Co of New York* 262 NY 220 (1933).
15. In *Compania de Transportes Mar Caribe SA v M/T Mar Caribe* (1961) 55 AJIL 749, a United States District Court appears to have treated the rupture of diplomatic relations with Cuba by the United States on 3 January 1961, as a withdrawal of recognition.
16. See Smith *Great Britain and the Law of Nations* (1932) Vol I, p 79. In 1949, Great Britain intimated to the newly formed Government of the Communist People's Republic of China that it was ready to conduct informal relations with authorities of that government through British consular officers, while stopping short of de facto recognition (see *Civil Air Transport Inc v Central Air Transport Corpn* [1953] AC 70 at 88–89).
17. See para 2 of draft art 7 of the Commission's Draft of Articles on Special Missions, and commentary thereon, in the *Report* of the Commission on the Work of its Nineteenth Session (1967). Art 7 of the Convention on Special Missions, opened for signature on 16 December 1969, merely provides that the existence of diplomatic or consular relations is not necessary for the sending or reception of a special mission, para 2 of draft art 7 having been omitted.

mission to, or receive a special mission from, a state not recognised by it. Perhaps, the most significant recent example is the fact that on a large number of occasions, during the period before it accorded recognition, the United States participated in discussions or negotiations with the People's Republic of China, including a series of exchanges and contacts in Warsaw, although refusing to grant formal recognition, and then later, some time after a meeting in Shanghai in 1972 between President Nixon and Chairman Mao-Zhedong, proceeded to maintain liaison offices in each other's capital, as a means, inter alia, of paving the way towards 'normalisation' of the relations between the two governments;[18] such 'normalisation' was fully achieved when recognition was accorded by the United States, taking effect as from 1 January 1979.[19] One may wonder whether this constitutes a tertium quid, in addition to recognition de jure and de facto (see below)—that is, a kind of non-formal tacit acceptance of the situation that a state or government is in control of the relevant territory.

2.   RECOGNITION DE JURE AND DE FACTO

The practice of most states draws a distinction between recognition de jure and de facto.

Recognition de jure means that according to the recognising state, the state or government recognised *formally* fulfils the requirements laid down by international law for effective participation in the international community.

Recognition de facto means that in the opinion of the recognising state, provisionally and temporarily and with all due reservations for the future, the state or government recognised fulfils the above requirements in fact (de facto).

It may be seen therefore that the epithets 'de jure' and 'de facto' are not, strictly speaking, descriptive of the process of recognition itself, but appertain to the status of the particular state or government, the recognition of which is in issue.

In modern times, the practice has generally been to preface the stage of de jure recognition by a period of de facto recognition, particularly in the case of a legally constituted government giving way to a revolutionary régime. In such a case, de facto recognition is purely a non-committal formula whereby the recognising state acknowledges that there is a legal de jure government which 'ought to possess the powers of sovereignty, though at the time it may be deprived of them', but that there is a de facto government 'which is really in possession of them, although the possession may be wrongful or precarious'.[20] Meanwhile de facto recognition secures considerable economic advantages to the recognising state, enabling it to protect the interests of its citizens in the territory of that state or government. At a later stage, when the need for reservations no longer exists because the future of the new state or new régime is completely assured, de jure recognition is formally given.

18. See United States *Department of State Bulletin* of 10 October 1977, p 463.
19. See (1979) 80 *Department of State Bulletin* 26.
20. See *AM Luther v James Sagor & Co* [1921] 3 KB 532 at 543.

If there be conclusive evidence of continuing de jure recognition, a court is not entitled to find that there has been de facto recognition, even of an entity subordinate to the de jure recognised government.[1]

Where a court sitting in a particular territory has to determine the status of a new government which has illegally assumed control of that territory, there can be no question of recognition de jure of the legitimate government and of recognition de facto, at the same time, of the new government. The court will have to decide, not merely whether the usurping régime is an established de facto government, but whether it is a lawful government at all.[2]

The point may be raised whether the jus of de jure recognition means: (a) state law, (b) international law, or (c) abstract justice, in the sense of 'right'. Ideally, it should mean international law, which in this regard should be guided by (c)—abstract justice—and should condition (a)—state law. Unfortunately, state practice falls far short of such standards, and the words de jure signify little more than the observation of legal or traditional forms in giving recognition, and a formal compliance by the recognised state or government with the requisite qualifications.

None the less, British practice in the matter of de jure recognition has been guided by a reasonably consistent policy based on precedent. To quote Professor H. A. Smith[3]:

'... The normal policy of this country for over a hundred years has been to insist upon certain conditions as a precedent to the grant of de jure recognition of a new State or a new Government. We have required, first, a reasonable assurance of stability and permanence. Secondly, we have demanded evidence to show that the Government commands the general support of the population. Thirdly, we have insisted that it shall prove itself both able and willing to fulfil its international obligations.'

As to de facto recognition, where given by such states as do not belong to the group of states following a policy of not making formal statements of recognition of new governments, it is misleading to regard this as always tentative or revocable; more generally it is simply a convenient prelude to the more formal and more permanent type of recognition—recognition de jure. Both types of recognition presuppose effective governmental control in fact.[4]

To take illustrations from British practice, the Soviet Government was recognised de facto on 16 March 1921, but only de jure on 1 February 1924. In 1936, Great Britain recognised de facto the Italian conquest of Abyssinia, and in 1938 recognised de jure Italy's sovereignty over that region. Also Great Britain recognised de facto the progressive occupation of different parts of Spain by the insurgent forces in the course of the Spanish Civil War 1936–1938, until finally

1. *Carl-Zeiss-Stiftung v Rayner and Keeler Ltd* (No 2) [1967] 1 AC 853 at 903, 925, [1966] 2 All ER 536 esp at 545, 559.
2. See *Madzimbamuto v Lardner-Burke* [1969] 1 AC 645 at 723–725.
3. See Smith *Great Britain and the Law of Nations* (1932) Vol I, p 239. US practice as to de jure recognition is to a similar effect; see M. M. Whiteman *Digest of International Law* (1963) Vol 2, pp 72–73. Cf the statement by Mr Herbert Morrison, Secretary of State for Foreign Affairs, on 21 March 1951, reported in 485 HC Official Report (5th series) cols 2410–2411.
4. *Carl-Zeiss-Stiftung v Rayner and Keeler Ltd* (No 2) [1967] 1 AC 853 at 956–957, [1966] 2 All ER 536 at 579.

de jure recognition was given to the Franco Government after all Spanish territory had been won over.

So far as concerns the legal incidents of recognition, there are few differences between de facto and de jure recognition.

The de facto recognition of a foreign government is as conclusively binding, while it lasts, as de jure recognition, for the reasons stated by Warrington LJ in *A M Luther v James Sagor and Co:*[5]

'In the latter case, as well as in the former, the Government in question acquires the right to be treated by the recognising State as an independent sovereign State, and none the less that our Government does not pretend to express any opinion on the legality or otherwise of the means by which its power has been obtained.'

It follows also that the act of recognition de facto has retroactive operation exactly as in the case of recognition de jure. Moreover, transactions with the government of a foreign state which has received de facto recognition are binding on that foreign state and cannot be repudiated by a subsequent government which has overthrown its predecessor by force.[6]

One material difference is that it is not the practice of most states to receive as properly accredited diplomatic envoys, representatives of states which have not been recognised de jure.

A conflict of authority between a displaced de jure government and a newly recognised de facto government may often arise. In such an event, an English court of law adopts the view that so far as concerns matters in the territory ruled by the de facto government, the rights and status of the de facto government prevail. This rule would seem to follow from two notable cases, *Bank of Ethiopia v National Bank of Egypt and Liguori*,[7] decided by Clauson J, and the *Arantzazu Mendi*,[8] decided by the House of Lords. The former decision arose out of the situation created by the Italian conquest of Abyssinia in 1936. After the Italian Government had been recognised de facto, it enacted certain laws which were in conflict with those issued by the exiled Emperor of Abyssinia—the de jure ruler who had been forced to flee from his conquered country. Clauson J held that as the authority of the de jure ruler was merely theoretical and incapable of being enforced, whereas actually the Italian Government was in control of Abyssinian territory and de facto recognised, effect must be given to the laws of this government over those of the de jure monarch.

The case of the *Arantzazu Mendi* involved a conflict of rights between the legitimate and the insurgent governments in Spain during the Spanish Civil War 1936–1938, at a period when the insurgents had won over the greater part of Spanish territory. At this stage Great Britain continued to recognise the Republican Government as the de jure government of Spain, but also recognised the insurgent administration as the de facto government of that portion of Spain occupied by it. Proceedings were initiated in the British Admiralty Court by the

5. [1921] 3 KB 532 at 551.
6. *Peru Republic v Dreyfus Bros & Co* (1888) 38 Ch D 348. Also, although a state is recognised only de facto as having authority over a particular area of territory, it is to be treated as having full jurisdiction over persons within that area; see *Schtraks v Government of Israel* [1964] AC 556, [1962] 3 All ER 529, HL.
7. [1937] Ch 513.
8. [1939] AC 256.

de jure government against the de facto government to recover possession of a certain ship, and the latter government claimed the usual immunity from suit accorded to a fully sovereign state. The ship was registered in a port under the control of the de facto government, and had been handed over to that government in England pursuant to a requisition decree issued by it. It was held that the writ must be set aside as the insurgent (or Nationalist) government was a sovereign state and was entitled to immunity. The argument put forward on behalf of the de jure government that the insurgent administration was not a sovereign state, since it did not occupy the whole of Spain, was rejected.

The decision in the *Arantzazu Mendi* has not escaped criticism, particularly on the ground that in such circumstances the concession of jurisdictional immunity to a de facto government without full sovereignty goes too far.[9] Properly considered, however, the case is merely a logical extension of the principles laid down in *A. M. Luther v James Sagor & Co* and in *Bank of Ethiopia v National Bank of Egypt.*[10] Taken together, the effect of the three decisions was virtually to erase a number of suggested distinctions between de jure and de facto recognition, so far as the municipal law effects of each are concerned.

None the less, recognition de facto may have a substantial function to perform in the field of international law for states which still follow a policy of expressly recognising or withholding recognition of new governments. In this regard, its difference from recognition de jure is not merely one of a political character. By recognising a state or government de facto, the recognising state is enabled to acknowledge the external facts of political power, and protect its interests, its trade, and citizens, without committing itself to condoning illegalities or irregularities in the emergence of the de facto state or government. To this extent recognition de facto is probably a necessary legal expedient.

Besides there are these important differences generally followed or applied between de jure and de facto recognition which render the distinction one of substance:

a.   only the de jure recognised state or government can claim to receive property locally situated in the territory of the recognising state;[11]
b.   only the de jure recognised state can represent the old state for purposes of state succession, or with regard to espousing any claim of a national of that state for injury done by the recognising state in breach of international law;
c.   the representatives of entities recognised only de facto are not as a rule entitled to full diplomatic immunities and privileges;[12]

9.   Counsel in *Civil Air Transport Inc v Central Air Transport Corpn* [1953] AC 70 at 75, described the decision as 'the high-water mark of recognition of jurisdictional immunity in the case of de facto sovereignty'. In this connection, there would now have to be considered the impact of s 21 of the State Immunity Act 1978 (UK), as to the giving of a certificate of statehood, etc, by the Secretary of State; see p 135 below.
10. See also for a decision on the same lines, *Banco de Bilbao v Rey* [1938] 2 KB 176, where it was held that the acts of the de jure government were a mere nullity in the area controlled by the de facto government.
11. *Haile Selassie v Cable and Wireless Co Ltd (No 2)* (1938) 54 TLR 1087, revsd by Court of Appeal [1939] Ch 182, after de jure recognition of Italy's conquest of Abyssinia. However, the recognition de jure of a new state or government cannot operate retroactively so as to invalidate acts of the previous de jure government (*Civil Air Transport Inc v Central Air Transport Corpn* [1953] AC 70).
12. *Fenton Textile Association v Krassin* (1921) 38 TLR 259. This point is, however, doubtful.

d. de facto recognition can, in principle, owing to its provisional character, be
    withdrawn on several grounds other than those normally justifying a
    withdrawal of de jure recognition; and
e. if a sovereign state, recognised de jure, grants independence to a dependency,
    the new state is to be recognised de jure and not otherwise.[13]

3. LEGAL EFFECTS OF RECOGNITION

Recognition produces legal consequences affecting the rights, powers, and
privileges of the recognised state or government both at international law and
under the municipal law of states which have given it recognition. Also, when
the subject of recognition arises for examination, however incidentally, by the
municipal courts of such states, various problems of evidence, legal interpretation
and procedure enter into consideration.

Here it is important to bear in mind the limits between international law and
state law. Recognition confers on the recognised state or government a status
under both international law and municipal law. In this section, we shall first
deal with the status under municipal law, and accordingly will examine for this
purpose the law and practice normally applied by Anglo-American courts.

The capacity of a recognised state or government may be considered from a
negative aspect, by ascertaining the particular disabilities[14] of one which is
unrecognised. The principal legal disabilities of an unrecognised state or
government may be enumerated as follows:

a. It cannot sue in the courts of a state which has not recognised it. The principle
    underlying this rule was well expressed in one American case:[15]

13. *Carl-Zeiss-Stiftung v Rayner and Keeler Ltd (No 2)* [1967] 1 AC 853 at 906, [1966] 2 All ER
    536 at 547.
14. There may, however, be other matters besides disabilities. One illustration is that of questions
    of nationality; eg, if a state is annexed by an unrecognised state, nationals of the annexed state
    will, in the municipal courts of a non-recognising country, be deemed to retain their citizenship.
    Acts or transactions, 'necessary to peace and good order among citizens', eg, marriages duly
    performed or transfers properly registered, and therefore not relevant to any question of power
    or disability of a state or government, may be valid notwithstanding the absence of recognition,
    the principle being that there should be no interruption of the administration of law and justice;
    see Grotius *De Jure Belli ac Pacis* Book I, Chapter IV, s xv 1; *Texas v White* 74 US 700 (1986)
    at 733; *Carl-Zeiss-Stiftung v Rayner and Keeler Ltd (No 2)* [1967] 1 AC 853, [1966] 2 All ER
    536; *Hesperides Hotels Ltd v Aegean Turkish Holidays Ltd* [1978] 1 All ER 277 at 285–286;
    GUR Corpn v Trust Bnk of Africa Ltd [1987] QB 599, [1986] 3 All ER 449, CA; and *Advisory
    Opinion of the International Court of Justice on the Legal Consequences for States of the
    Continued Presence of South Africa in Namibia (South West Africa)* 21 June 1971 ICJ 1971,
    16 at 56 (registrations of births, deaths, and marriages not invalidated). This 'necessity' doctrine
    does not apply to the administrative orders and judicial decrees of an illegal régime, the
    constitution and laws of which are illegal and void within the forum state's own legal order;
    see *Madzimbamuto v Lardner-Burke* [1969] 1 AC 645 at 727–729, and *Adams v Adams* [1971]
    P 188 at 208–211, [1970] 3 All ER 572 at 585–588.
15. See *Russian Socialist Federated Soviet Republic v Cibrario* (New York Court of Appeals) 235
    NY 255 (1923). Semble, however, an unrecognised government if truly exercising complete
    authority, cannot be sued in an American municipal court, inasmuch as it is to be regarded as
    a sovereign government (*Wulfsohn v RSFSR* 234 NY 372 (1923)). Cf *United States v New York
    Trust Co* 75 F Supp 583 (1946) at 587 and *Upright v Mercury Business Machines Inc* 213 NYS
    2d 417 (1961).

'. . . A foreign power brings an action in our Courts not as a matter of right. Its power to do so is the creature of comity. Until such Government is recognised by the United States, no such comity exists.'

b. By reason of the same principle, the acts of an unrecognised state or government will not generally be given in the courts of a non-recognising state the effect customary according to the rules of 'comity'.
c. Its representatives cannot claim immunity from legal process.
d. Property due to a state whose government is unrecognised may actually be recovered by the representatives of the de jure government which has been overthrown.

Recognition transmutes these disabilities into the full status of a sovereign state or government. Accordingly, the newly recognised state or government:

i. acquires the right of suing in the courts of law of the recognising state;
ii. may have effect given by these courts to its legislative and executive acts both past and future;
iii. may claim immunity from suit in regard to its property and its diplomatic representatives;
iv. becomes entitled to demand and receive possession of, or to dispose of property situate within the jurisdiction of a recognising state which formerly belonged to a preceding government.[16]

At international law, the status of a de jure recognised state or government carries with it the full privileges of membership of the international community. Thus it acquires the capacity to enter into diplomatic relations with other states and to conclude treaties with them. Also, such other states become subject to various obligations under international law in relation to the newly recognised state or government, which in its turn incurs similar reciprocal obligations. Upon it, therefore, as from the date of recognition, fall both the burden and bounty of international law.

Status of states and governments in the courts of law

The rule in British countries and in the United States is that though the existence of a new state or a new government is merely a question of fact, it is one involving important political considerations and is therefore primarily to be determined by the political and not by the judicial organs of the state. Accordingly, on this question the court is entitled to consult the executive on the principle that it must act in unison with the 'will of the national sovereignty', which is expressed in external affairs through the executive alone.

Considerations of evidentiary convenience have also conditioned this principle of consultation of the executive. According to Lord Sumner in *Duff Development Co v Kelantan Government*,[17] British courts act on the best evidence available, and the best evidence in this regard is a statement by the appropriate Secretary of State on behalf of the Crown.[18] This will be so even if the statement purports

16. See *The Jupiter* [1924] P 236, and *Bank of Ethiopia v National Bank of Egypt and Liguori* [1937] Ch 513.
17. [1924] AC 797 at 823.
18. See *Mighell v Sultan of Johore* [1894] 1 QB 149.

to set out facts which in principle ought to be attested by the British Government in conjunction with other governments concerned, or interested.[19] Now, under section 21 of the State Immunity Act 1978 (UK), a certificate by or on behalf of the Secretary of State as to whether, for the purposes of Part I of the Act (privileges and jurisdictional immunities) a country is a state, any territory is a constituent territory of a federal state, and what person or persons should be regarded as the head or the government of a state, has statutorily been given conclusive force; the certificate is to be treated as 'conclusive evidence'. However, a statement by the executive that a particular government is *not* treated as such does not preclude a British court from holding that such government is a sovereign government,[20] or is in control of the territory concerned,[1] especially in relation to questions not involving jurisdictional immunity.

The deference of American and British courts[2] to the attitude of the executive in this connection has not escaped criticism. It has been objected that this solicitude for the views of the executive is so exaggerated as almost to amount to an obsession. Moreover, it is asserted that often the courts have been more concerned not to embarrass the executive in its conduct of foreign affairs than to protect material interests of private citizens affected by changes in statehood or government. On the other hand, it is difficult to see how, on a contested issue of this nature, a court could take evidence or obtain the necessary materials for forming its judgment in any more satisfactory way. However, the executive now sometimes elects to give restrictively phrased certificates, in such form that the court may reach a decision uninfluenced by possible reactions on the executive's conduct of foreign policy. Such was the case in *GUR Corpn v Trust Bank of Africa Ltd*[3] where the executive certificate stated that 'Her Majesty's Government has not taken and does not have a formal position as regards the exercise of governing authority over the territory of Ciskei. Her Majesty's Government does not have any dealings with the "Government of the Republic of Ciskei".' The Court of Appeal was able to conclude nevertheless that the Government of Ciskei had locus standi in the English courts by virtue of its having been created by the Republic of South Africa, a recognised state, applying the same fiction of 'subordinate entity' as in the case of *Carl Zeiss Stiftung v Rayner and Keeler (No 2)*[4], where the German Democratic Republic was regarded as a subordinate body established by the de jure governing authority, the Soviet Union. These conclusions, impelled by practical considerations, are nevertheless strained, artificial, and fly in the face of international realities. Lord Wilberforce's alternative view that the courts might give effect to the laws and legal acts of unrecognised states or governments 'in the interests of justice and common sense,

19. Cf *Carl-Zeiss-Stiftung v Rayner and Keeler Ltd (No 2)* [1967] 1 AC 853, [1966] 2 All ER 536.
20. See *Luigi Monta of Genoa v Cechofracht Co Ltd* [1956] 2 QB 552.
1. See *Hesperides Hotels Ltd v Aegean Turkish Holidays Ltd* [1978] QB 205, [1978] 1 All ER 277. See also *GUR Corpn v Trust Bank of Africa Ltd* [1987] QB 599, [1986] 3 All ER 449, CA.
2. The American Department of State 'Suggestion' (or Certificate) has been able to go so far as to 'suggest' immunity from jurisdiction in the case of a foreign state or government, and this may be binding on an American court; see, eg, *Rich v Naviera Vacuba SA and Republic of Cuba* (1961) 56 AJIL (1962) 550–552. The Department might also appear as amicus curiae.
3. [1987] QB 599. See also critical comment by Crawford in (1986) 57 BYIL 405.
4. [1967] 1 AC 853.

where no consideration of public policy to the contrary has to prevail'[5] has yet to be accepted as the true rule.[6]

Generally speaking, a British court will take judicial notice of:

a. the sovereign status of a state or of its monarch;[7]
b. the existence as a matter of uncontested fact of a foreign state or government, and if in doubt will apply for information to the appropriate Secretary of State, whose answer is conclusive.

It is established by the authorities that a clear, complete and unambiguous answer by the Secretary of State dispenses with further inquiry by the court, and excludes other evidence, if offered.[8] Nor can the executive be cross-examined as to the terms of its statement or certificate,[9] although if these are not sufficiently plain the court is entitled in ultimate resort to make its own independent examination[10].

A formal statement by the appropriate Secretary of State tendered to the court is far from being the sole method of conveying the executive's views. The Law Officers may appear, either by invitation of the court or on an intervener,[11] to inform the court of the attitude of the Crown. Also, letters sent by the Foreign Office to the solicitors acting for one party to the proceedings, and submitted to the court, will be regarded as sufficient evidence of the Crown's views.[12]

Retroactive effect of recognition

As we have seen, the recognition of a new state or government has a retroactive operation, and relates back to the date of inception of the particular state or government concerned.

In British courts, such retroactive operation was extremely wide. Thus:

a. A cause of action based upon the existence of a particular state or government at the date of institution of proceedings, was nullified if before or at the time of the hearing, the British Government treated another state or government as having been in existence at the date the action was commenced.[13]
b. A judgment of a court of first instance based upon the existence of a particular state or government at the date of judgment might be set aside

5. Id, 954. See also the supporting dicta of Lord Denning MR in *Hesperides Hotels Ltd v Aegean Holidays Ltd* [1978] QB 205, [1978] 1 All ER 277, CA.
6. F.A. Mann in (1987) 36 ICLQ 348.
7. See *Mighell v Sultan of Johore* [1894] 1 QB 149.
8. *Carl-Zeiss-Stiftung v Rayner and Keeler Ltd* (No 2) [1967] 1 AC 853, at 956–958, [1966] 2 All ER 536, esp at 579, and *Van Heyningen v Netherlands East Indies* [1949] QSR 54. Nonetheless, the certificate or statement of the executive may always be interpreted by a British court; see *Gdynia Ameryka Linie (Zeglugowe Spolka Akcyjna) v Boguslawski* [1953] AC 11 at 43.
9. See *Sayce v Ameer Ruler Sadiq Mohammed Abbasi Bahawalpur State* [1952] 1 All ER 326; affd [1952] 2 QB 390.
10. See *Sultan of Johore v Abubakar Tunku Aris Bendahar* [1952] AC 318. In the *Feivel Pikelny Case* (1955) 22 ILR 97, Karminski J had recourse to *Hansard* (ie the record of the House of Commons debates) in order to determine the actual date of recognition, where the Foreign Office Certificate was ambiguous on the matter.
11. As to the Attorney-General's right of intervention, see *Adams v Adams* [1971] P 188 at 197–198, [1970] 3 All ER 572 at 576–577.
12. See, eg, *Banco de Bilbao v Rey* [1938] 2 KB 176 at 181.
13. *Bank of Ethiopia v National Bank of Egypt and Liguori* [1937] Ch 513.

on appeal if before or at the time the appeal was heard, the British Government treated another state or government as having been in existence at the time judgment was delivered.[14]

Two important decisions of the House of Lords, namely *Gdynia Ameryka Linie* (*Zeglugowe Spolka Akcyjna*) *v Boguslawski* [15] and *Civil Air Transport Inc v Central Air Transport Corpn*[16] further elucidated the retroactive effect, according to British courts, of recognition.

The former case showed that, in the matter of the retroactive operation of recognition, where applicable, the certificate of the executive was to be treated as of overriding importance; hence, if such certificate plainly showed that recognition was not intended to relate back, any retroactive effect was excluded. In other words, whether and to what extent the act of recognition was retroactive should be governed by the intention of the recognising state, and this was logically consistent with the nature of recognition.

The latter case showed that duly vested proprietorial or other rights, resting upon a duly effected disposition or other legal act by the formerly recognised de jure government could not be invalidated by the subsequent recognition de jure of the new government; prima facie, recognition, where applicable, operated retroactively not to invalidate the acts of a former government, but to validate the acts of a government which had become the new de jure government.

Both cases contain dicta in the judgments to the effect that, prima facie, recognition de jure could not operate retroactively to validate acts done otherwise than in the territory, and so within the sphere of de facto control of the government recognised; but this, it was emphasised, was only a prima facie rule.[17]

It should be pointed out that the case law, above, on the retroactive effect of recognition is, in the light of the abandonment by the United Kingdom since 1980 of the policy of formally recognising new governments, as distinct from states, applicable in British courts only to the recognition of states, although such case law may be of persuasive authority to provide relevant principles in circumstances where the government is ready to enter into relations with a new foreign government and to treat it as such, or is, for example, ready to provide certification of that government's sovereign status pursuant to s 21 of the State Immunity Act 1978 (UK) for the purposes of that Act.

4.   RECOGNITION OF INSURGENCY AND BELLIGERENCY

The problems which a civil war in a particular country may involve for outside Powers may be summed up as follows: These outside Powers will generally, except when they feel vital interests are at stake, maintain a policy of non-interference in the domestic affairs of another state. However, there may come a time when it becomes impossible as a matter of practical politics to continue such an attitude either because:

14. *AM Luther v James Sagor & Co* [1921] 3 KB 532.
15. [1953] AC 11.
16. [1953] AC 70.
17. See *Civil Air Transport Inc v Central Air Transport Corpn* [1953] AC 70 at 94.

a. The operations of insurgent forces may attain such a degree that they are in effective occupation of and constitute the de facto authority in a large part of the territory formerly governed by the parent government.[18] In this case the problem is at once raised for outside Powers of entering into some contact or intercourse with the insurgents as the de facto authorities in order to protect their nationals, their commercial interests and their sea-borne trade in regard to the territory occupied.
b. The actual war between the parent government and the insurgent forces may reach such dimensions that outside Powers will be compelled to treat the civil war as a real war between rival Powers, and not as a purely internecine struggle. In other words, these Powers will have to recognise belligerency. This is because difficult problems may arise which, unless outside Powers accept the risk of being drawn into the war, cannot be solved without treating the rival parties as belligerents. This usually occurs where the naval operations of the contending forces interfere with the sea-borne trade of a maritime Power. For instance, a maritime Power might find it difficult to resist an improper search of its ships for contraband by either party unless it were prepared to use force; on the other hand, the concession of belligerent rights would normalise the situation, by sanctioning the right of search, without compromising the maritime Power's authority and rights at international law.

On account of (a), external Powers may decide on the de facto recognition of the insurgents, limited to the particular territory of which they are in effective occupation. Thus in 1937, Great Britain conceded de facto recognition to the insurgents in the Spanish Civil War, in regard to the territory under their control, and also went so far as to exchange Agents. Alternatively, in the absence of any recognition, external states may enter into formal or informal relations with the body of insurgents in control of the relevant territory.

As to (b) certain conditions must exist before belligerency is recognised. First, the hostilities must be of a general character, as distinct from those of a purely local nature. Second, the insurgents must be in control of a sufficient portion of territory to justify the inference that they represent a rival Power of some magnitude. Third, both parties must act in accordance with the laws of war, and the insurgents in particular must have organised armed forces under a proper command. Even when all these conditions are present, the circumstances may preclude recognition of belligerency, as during the Spanish Civil War of 1936–1938 when the policy of 'Non-Intervention' of the European Powers and their desire to avoid complications leading to a general war, induced them to stop short of granting belligerent rights. It would appear, in other words, that the recognition of belligerency is facultative, and not a matter of duty.

The British practice in the matter of belligerent recognition was authoritatively stated by the Law Officers in 1867.[19] According to the terms of this statement, the mere declaration by insurgents that they have constituted a 'Provisional

18. There may, prior to this, be simply recognition of the rebel forces as *insurgents*, the purpose of which is to prevent the rebels being treated as mere criminals or pirates, and to preclude any suggestion that the legitimate government is to be held responsible for their acts. As to this distinction, see *The Ambrose Light* 25 Fed 408 (1885), and below, p 249.
19. Smith *Great Britain and the Law of Nations* (1932) Vol I, p 263.

Government' is insufficient to justify belligerent recognition. Before the grant is made, consideration should be given to the length of time that the insurrection has continued; the number, order, and discipline of the insurgent forces; and whether the newly constituted 'Government' is capable of maintaining international relations with foreign states.

The grant of recognition of belligerency entails the usual consequences, to the recognising state, of a declaration of neutrality in the case of a regular war. The recognising state becomes entitled to neutral rights, and these must be respected by rival parties. At the same time, the status of belligerency confers certain rights under the laws of war on the parent government and on the insurgents, which are of advantage as long as the struggle retains its pitch and intensity. In particular, the legitimate government is exonerated from responsibility for acts committed by the insurgents in territory occupied by them.

Belligerent recognition is quite distinct from the recognition of either the parent or insurgent governments as the legitimate government. As stated by the British Foreign Secretary, in 1937:[20]

'Recognition of belligerency is, of course, quite distinct from recognising any one to whom you give that right as being the legitimate Government of the country. It has nothing to do with it. *It is a conception simply concerned with granting rights of belligerency which are of convenience to the donor as much as they are to the recipients.*'

5. NEW TERRITORIAL TITLES, TERRITORIAL AND OTHER CHANGES, AND TREATIES; NON-RECOGNITION

Often states acquire new territorial or other rights by unilateral act on their part which may be:

a.   according to international law, or
b.   in violation of international law.

In case b, recognition may be sought in order to turn a doubtful title into a good one and because the recognition will amount to a waiver by the other states of claims or objections inconsistent with the title thus recognised. In this way, the possibility that non-recognition may defeat a claim based upon acquiescence or prescription is excluded. The continuance of formal relations with the state concerned, after such territorial acquisition, does not of itself imply the recognition of the new territorial title.

In January 1932, there was enunciated by Mr Stimson, United States Secretary of State, a doctrine of non-recognition, which has since become widely known as the *Stimson Doctrine of Non-Recognition*. This declaration of policy was due to events in the Far East. In 1931, Japan, then a member of the League of Nations, invaded Manchuria, which was legally under the sovereignty of China. Subsequently, the Japanese forces overran and conquered Southern Manchuria. The United States refused to recognise this new situation or any treaties with China legalising it, and to clarify this attitude, Mr Stimson, in a communication to the Chinese and Japanese Governments, announced that:

20. Then Mr Eden, later Sir Anthony Eden, and Lord Avon.

'The United States cannot admit the legality of any situation de facto nor does it intend to recognise any treaty or agreement between those Governments, or agents thereof, which may impair the treaty rights of the United States . . . and that it does not intend to recognise any situation, treaty or agreement which may be brought about by means contrary to the covenants and obligations of the Treaty of Paris of August 27, 1928.'

The Treaty of Paris referred to in Mr Stimson's communication was the General Treaty of 1928 for the Renunciation of War (known as the Briand-Kellogg Pact); this had been signed by the United States, as well as by China and Japan. Mr Stimson claimed that by the doctrine a caveat would 'be placed upon such actions which, we believe, will effectively bar the legality hereafter of any title or right sought to be obtained by pressure or treaty violation'.

The Stimson doctrine of non-recognition was explicitly a statement of United States national policy,[1] although at the same time it was, according to Professor Briggs,[2] 'in part, an attempt to establish the invalidity of treaties obtained through employment of duress in the wider sense of coercion against a State'. The Stimson declaration was followed some two months later by a Resolution adopted by the League of Nations Assembly on 11 March 1932, formulating a duty of non-recognition in these terms:

'It is incumbent upon the Members of the League of Nations not to recognise any situation, treaty, or agreement which may be brought about by means contrary to the Covenant of the League of Nations or to the Pact of Paris.'

In the events which happened during the period 1932–1940, both the Stimson doctrine and the Assembly Resolution proved ineffectual, although towards the end of, and after the Second World War, the principle which they sought to uphold was to some extent vindicated by the restoration to certain states of the territory which had previously been taken from them by force.

Since the adoption of the United Nations Charter in 1945, followed by the establishment of the United Nations as a working body, there has been a discernible trend towards a doctrine of the non-recognition of territorial changes and treaties that have resulted from the threat or use of force against the territorial integrity or political independence of any state, or in any other manner inconsistent with the Purposes of the United Nations.[3] This is reflected in the following:

a. The provision in the Bogotá Charter of the Organisation of American States, 30 April 1948 (see article 17) that 'no territorial acquisition or special advantages obtained either by force or by other means of coercion' should be recognised.[4]

b. Article 11 of the Draft Declaration on the Rights and Duties of States, prepared by the International Law Commission in 1949, to the effect that

1. Which could be made effective by executive action in countries such as the United Kingdom and the United States where, in respect to recognition matters, a certificate or expression of opinion of the executive in an appropriate case will bind domestic courts. See pp 135–137 above.
2. Herbert W. Briggs *The Law of Nations. Cases, Documents and Notes* (2nd edn, 1953) p 847. See also the statement by Mr Stimson, quoted in the preceding paragraph.
3. Such threat or use of force is prohibited by art 2, para 4, of the United Nations Charter.
4. Cf for prior covenants of non-recognition by American states, the undertaking to this effect in the Anti-War Pact of Non-Aggression and Conciliation of 1933, and the Lima Declaration of 1938 on Non-Recognition of the Acquisition of Territory by Force.

every state is under a duty to refrain from recognising any territorial acquisition by another state obtained through the threat or use of force against the territorial integrity or political independence of another state, or 'in any other manner inconsistent with international law and order'.

c. Article 52 of the Vienna Convention on the Law of Treaties of 22 May 1969, providing that a treaty is void if its conclusion has been procured by the threat or use of force 'in violation of the principles of international law embodied in the Charter of the United Nations'.

d. The Declaration on Principles of International Law Concerning Friendly Relations and Co-operation Among States in Accordance with the United Nations Charter, adopted by the General Assembly in 1970, proclaiming the following principle: 'No territorial acquisition resulting from the threat or use of force shall be recognised as legal'.

e. Paragraph 3 of article 5 of the Definition of Aggression Resolution adopted by the United Nations General Assembly on 14 December 1974, providing as follows: 'No territorial acquisition or special advantage resulting from aggression is or shall be recognised as lawful'.

The question of obligatory non-recognition arose in relation to the situation in South West Africa (Namibia), where in spite of United Nations Resolutions and rulings of the International Court of Justice to the contrary, South Africa continued to purport to exercise authority, as if it were not subject to the supervision of United Nations organs.[5] A Resolution adopted by the United Nations General Assembly on 27 October 1966, declared that South Africa had failed to fulfil its obligations as a Mandatory Power, with the result that the mandate was terminated and South West Africa came under the direct responsibility of the United Nations, thus carrying the implication that member states were bound to recognise this position, and not to recognise the continuance of South Africa's status as a Mandatory Power.

In its Advisory Opinion of 21 June 1971, on the *Legal Consequences for States of the Continued Presence of South Africa in South West Africa (Namibia)*,[6] the International Court of Justice ruled:

1. that inasmuch as the continued presence of South Africa in Namibia was illegal by reason of its refusal to submit to the supervision of United Nations organs, South Africa was under an obligation to withdraw its administration from the territory immediately, and to end its occupation there; and

2. that member states of the United Nations were under an obligation not to recognise the legality of South Africa's presence in Namibia, or the validity of South Africa's acts on behalf of or concerning Namibia, and were to refrain from any acts and any dealings with the South African Government implying recognition of the legality of, or lending support or assistance to, such presence and administration. Moreover, the validity or effects of any

5. The question of obligatory non-recognition also arose in regard to Rhodesia, following that territory's unilateral declaration of independence in November 1965. However, the matter is now of merely historical and academic significance, having regard to the establishment in 1980 of the new independent State of Zimbabwe.

6. ICJ 1971, 16 at 54, 56.

relations entered into by any state with South Africa concerning Namibia ought not to be recognised by the United Nations or its Member States.

Although the Advisory Opinion was confined to rulings upon the particular circumstances of South Africa's relationship to Namibia, these pronouncements may well be used in the future for wider purposes to support a generalised rule imposing a duty of non-recognition of all territorial and other situations brought about in breach of international law. In the meantime the Security Council has tended to include an express prohibition on recognition of new states, or territorial changes brought about by the use of force contrary to the United Nations Charter, in resolutions binding all Member States under article 25 of the Charter. These cases include the creation of the Turkish Republic of Northern Cyprus[7] and of the four states created by South Africa out of the 'independent homelands' (bantustans).[8] No explicit call for non-recognition was made in the case of the incorporation of the Portuguese colony of East Timor by Indonesia in 1975-76; that issue will be considered by the International Court of Justice in the forthcoming *Case Concerning East Timor* (Portugal v Australia).

7.   UNSC Res 541 (1983), 550 (1984).
8.   Transkei, Bophuthatswana, Venda, and Ciskei. UNSC Res 402 (1976), 407 (1977), UNGA Res 32/105N (1977), 34/93G (1979). See Dugard *Recognition and the United Nations* (1987) and *International Law —A South African Perspective* (1994), 77-81. See the same author (1987) 111-115, 155-156)—in respect of non-recognition of Israel's sovereignty over East Jerusalem and the Golan Heights.

CHAPTER 7

State territorial sovereignty and other lesser territorial rights of states

1. TERRITORIAL SOVEREIGNTY AND OTHER LESSER RIGHTS OF STATES

One of the essential elements of statehood is the occupation of a territorial area, within which state law operates. Over this area, supreme authority is vested in the state.

Hence there arises the concept of 'territorial sovereignty' which signifies that within this territorial domain jurisdiction is exercised by the state over persons and property to the exclusion of other states. This concept bears some resemblance to the patrimonial notions of ownership under private law, and in fact the early writers on international law adopted many of the civil law principles of property in their treatment of state territorial sovereignty. To this day, their influence has persisted so that in particular the rules as to acquisition and loss of territorial sovereignty plainly reflect the influences of the civil law, but it is manifest that there are certain dangers in having recourse to Roman law and civil law analogies. However, it may be that in certain areas of the subject there is room for a wider application of the uti possidetis principle ('as you possess, you shall continue to possess'), and indeed in 1986 in the *Burkina Faso-Republic of Mali Case*,[1] a special chamber of the International Court of Justice applied the principle of uti possidetis as having 'exceptional importance' for the African continent, by reason of the fact that the primary aim of the principle was to secure respect for territorial boundaries which existed at the time when an African territory acquired independence; the object was to accord pre-eminence to legal title, defined by frontiers, over effective possession as a basis of sovereignty. This principle was applied also in the *Land, Island and Maritime Frontier Dispute* (El Salvador/Honduras, Nicaragua intervening).[2]

1. ICJ 1986, 554, paras 20–26 of the Court's judgment. Cf observations of Judge Quintana in the *Frontier Lands Case* ICJ 1959, 209 at 255. In the award in the *Beagle Channel Arbitration* (Argentina–Chile) of 1977, 52 ILR 93, the Arbitral Tribunal took the view that the uti possidetis principle did not have such binding force with reference to the subject matter of the dispute before it as to govern overridingly a relevant boundary treaty between the parties (see paras 21–23 of the award).
2. ICJ 1992, 351. See below, p 236, n 2.

Territorial sovereignty was described by the learned Max Huber, Arbitrator in the *Island of Palmas Arbitration*, in these terms:[3]

'Sovereignty in the relation between States signifies independence. Independence in regard to a portion of the globe is the right to exercise therein, to the exclusion of any other State, the functions of a State.'

As the Advisory Opinion of the International Court of Justice on the *Western Sahara* (1975)[4] shows, legal ties of territorial sovereignty over people or land must be distinguished from ties of allegiance, in the case of persons, and mere customary rights in relation to land. On the other hand, state activity on an adequate scale, showing conclusively the exercise of authority, is one mark of the existence of territorial sovereignty. This corresponds to Max Huber's concept of the exercise of 'the functions of a state'.

It is sometimes said that territorial sovereignty is indivisible, but there have been numerous instances in international practice both of division of sovereignty, and of distribution of the components of sovereignty.

For instance, sovereignty may be shared jointly by two or more Powers as in the case of a condominium,[5] while states may by treaty restrict their right to transfer territory. Moreover, leases or pledges of a territory are sometimes made by one state to another, as for example the leases of Chinese territory to Russia, France, Germany, and Great Britain at the end of the last century during the so-called 'Battle of the Concessions' between these Great Powers, and the leases of British bases in the West Atlantic to the United States in 1940 in exchange for 50 American destroyers which were urgently needed in the war against Germany. In the case of a lease, temporary sovereignty is exercised by the lessee state, while the lessor state possesses a sovereignty in reversion. A recent example is the case of the lease by China to Great Britain in 1898 for a term of 99 years of what is known as 'British Hong Kong' (ie the Island of Hong Kong, the southern part of the Kowloon Peninsula and Stonecutters Island); the territory leased reverts to China in 1997, and an Anglo-Chinese Agreement was entered into on 19 December 1984 to arrange for the passing of sovereignty to China in that year. Again, sometimes sovereignty over a territory is held by one or more Powers in trust for the population of the territory concerned, as for example in the pre-war case of the League of Nations control over the Saar before its return to Germany in 1935. Thus, international law does not appear to restrict the manner in which the sovereignty as to particular territory can be bestowed on, or withdrawn from any state.

Acquisition of territorial sovereignty
The five traditional and generally recognised modes of acquiring territorial sovereignty are: occupation, annexation, accretion, prescription, and cession.

3. 22 AJIL (1928) 875.
4. ICJ 1975, 12. In 1982, before the United Nations, the United Kingdom Government also distinguished territorial sovereignty from the right of self-determination, maintaining that Argentinian claims of sovereignty and the factors involved could not be relied upon to override the right of self-determination of the population of the Falkland Islands, which population represented 'a people' for the purposes of self-determination; see UN document, A/37/582, dated 29 October 1982.
5. See p 105 above.

These modes are directly analogous to the civil law methods of acquiring private ownership.

As was pointed out in the *Island of Palmas Arbitration*,[6] these modes reduce essentially to the display of *effective* control and authority either by the state claiming sovereignty, or by a state from which the state claiming sovereignty can prove that title has been derived.[7] Thus occupation and annexation are based on an act of 'effective apprehension' of the territory, while accretion can only be conceived of as an addition to a portion of territory where there already exists an actual sovereignty. Prescription depends on the continuous and peaceful display of sovereignty over territory for a long period, while cession presupposes that the ceding state has the power of effectively disposing of the ceded territory. It is claimed by some writers, notably Kelsen, that cession per se does not operate to transfer territorial sovereignty until the receiving state has effectively established its authority over the ceded territory. Effectiveness is of course neither an absolute nor a self-evident concept, but is one to be judged and/or applied in relation to all the circumstances.

One additional mode of acquisition of territorial sovereignty, not included above, should be mentioned, namely adjudication or award by a Conference of states. This usually occurs where a Conference of the victorious Powers at the end of a war assigns territory to a particular state in view of a general peace settlement; for example, the territorial redistribution of Europe at the Versailles Peace Conference 1919. According to Soviet doctrine, territorial sovereignty may also be acquired by plebiscite, although this would appear to be less a mode of acquisition than a step preceding it.

Certain instances in the past of territorial sovereignty accruing to a state cannot readily be fitted into one or other of these traditional, generally accepted modes of acquisition. Such special cases have included, and may include the following:

a. territory accruing to a state by reason of a boundary delimitation effected by a mixed demarcation commission, or under an award ex aequo et bono by an arbitral tribunal settling a boundary dispute, or as the consequence of an adjudication by the International Court of Justice, determining the frontier between two states, as in its decision in 1986 in the *Burkina Faso-Republic of Mali Case*, above;

b. the grant of territorial rights to a state under a treaty between it and the rulers or representatives of some indigenous tribe or community, previously in sole and exclusive occupation of the area concerned;

c. long, continuous recognition by other states of a state's territorial sovereignty, notwithstanding obscurity or ambiguity surrounding the inception of that state's claim to title;

d. succession by a new state to the territory of its predecessor;

e. territory distributed as the result of a treaty of compromise or settlement in respect of disputed tracts of land, as eg, in the case of the Treaty of May 1985 between Chile and Argentina in settlement of their disputed territorial claims in the area at the eastern end of the Beagle Channel.

6. See 22 AJIL (1928) 875–876.
7. See Kelsen *General Theory of Law and State* (1961 edn) pp 213–216, for discussion of the extent to which effectiveness governs the operation of these modes of acquiring title.

As to e, the present writer would indeed favour a general head of acquisition under the provisions of a treaty, in the same way as the draftsmen of the *Code Napoléon* (1803) admitted the acquisition of property as the result of obligations (see Book III, General Provisions, article 711).

The modes-of-acquisition approach to the creation and transfer of territorial sovereignty is both sound in principle and of practical value, provided that care is taken, in using this approach, not to confuse the mode itself with its component elements or ingredients (eg, in the case of the mode known as 'occupation', the element of display of authority is an ingredient of, but not itself a mode of acquisition of territorial sovereignty).

Occupation

Occupation consists in establishing sovereignty over territory not under the authority of any other state whether newly discovered, or—an unlikely case—abandoned by the state formerly in control. Classically, the subject matter of an occupation is terra nullius, and territory inhabited by tribes or peoples having a social and political organisation cannot be of the nature of terra nullius.[8] Where land is inhabited by organised tribes or peoples, territorial sovereignty has been on occasions acquired by local agreements with the rulers or representatives of the tribes or peoples.

In determining whether or not an occupation has taken place in accordance with international law, the principle of effectiveness is applied for the most part. In the *Eastern Greenland Case*,[9] the Permanent Court of International Justice laid it down that occupation, to be effective, requires on the part of the appropriating state two elements:

i.   an intention or will to act as sovereign;
ii. the adequate exercise or display of sovereignty.

In the case mentioned, title to Eastern Greenland was disputed by Norway and Denmark, and Denmark was able to prove circumstances which established these two elements on its part.

The element of intention is a matter of inference from all the facts, although sometimes such intention may be formally expressed in official notifications to other interested Powers. There must be evidence of nothing less than a permanent intention to assume control; a mere transient passage by the alleged occupying Power is by itself insufficient to satisfy this test. Nor are the independent, unauthorised activities of private individuals, without subsequent ratification, valid for this purpose.[10] Hence, discovery alone, even if accompanied by a proclamation of sovereignty in situ, or the hoisting of a national flag, etc, has been regarded by writers as conferring an 'inchoate' title only, unless such

---

8. *Advisory Opinion of the International Court of Justice on the Western Sahara* ICJ 1975, 12. On the subject of 'colonisation' by occupation of African territory inhabited, at the time, by tribal peoples, see Malcolm Shaw *Title to Territory in Africa: International Legal Issues* (1984). The High Court of Australia held retrospectively, contrary to previous decisions, that the occupation of Australia by the British Crown was not of terra nullius: *Mabo v Queensland* (1992) 175 CLR 1.
9. (1933) PCIJ Series A/B, No 53.
10. See *Fisheries Case* ICJ 1951, 116 at 184.

discovery be consummated by some more significant acts or activity. As regards the second requirement of exercise or display of sovereignty, this may be satisfied by concrete evidence of possession or control, or according to the nature of the case, a physical assumption of sovereignty may be manifested by an overt or symbolic act[11] or by legislative or executive measures affecting the territory claimed, or by treaties with other states recognising the claimant state's sovereignty, by fixing of boundaries, and so on. The degree of authority necessary for this purpose will vary according to the circumstances; thus, a relatively backward territory does not require the same elaborate control and government as one more developed and civilised.

In the *Minquiers and Ecrehos Case*,[12] relating to disputed British and French claims to certain Channel islets, the International Court of Justice stressed the importance of actual exercise of 'State functions', eg, local administration, local jurisdiction, and acts of legislative authority, as proving the continuous display of sovereignty necessary to confirm title. For this reason, upon the evidence as to long continued exercise of state functions by British authorities, the Court preferred the claim of Great Britain. This same principle of the exercise of state activity on an adequate scale, as distinct from routine or inconclusive acts not necessarily evidencing a firm intention to establish territorial sovereignty, was applied also by the Court in 1975 in its Advisory Opinion on the *Western Sahara*.[13]

An act of occupation more frequently than not involves in the first instance an act of discovery. It now follows from the *Island of Palmas Arbitration*, above, decided by M. Huber as Arbitrator, that a mere act of discovery by one state without more is not sufficient to confer a title by occupation, and that such incomplete appropriation must give way to a continuous and peaceful display of authority by another state. In this arbitration, the contest of title lay between the United States, claiming as successor to Spain which had originally discovered the island disputed, and the Netherlands, which according to the historical evidence submitted to the Arbitrator, had for a very long period purported to act as sovereign over the island. The Arbitrator adjudged the island to the Netherlands, and in giving the reasons for his award laid supreme emphasis on the fact that long continuous exercise of effective authority can confer title at international law.

It may be important to determine what extent of territory is embraced by an act of occupation. Various theories on this point have been held from time to time,[14] and two such theories have assumed particular significance in connection with the claims of certain states in polar regions, namely:

11. See the *Clipperton Island Arbitration* (1931) 26 AJIL (1932) 390. As this Arbitration shows, an actual manifestation of sovereignty on the locus of the territory may serve to create a stronger title than a historic claim of right, unsupported by such a concrete act. In point of fact, the actual award indicated also that importance was attached to the circumstance, inter alia, that France, the claimant by virtue of the symbolic act, had given due notice to the world of what it had done by the publication of a declaration of sovereignty in English in a journal in Hawaii.
12. ICJ 1953, 47 at 68–70.
13. ICJ 1975, 12.
14. For discussion of the theories, see Westlake *International Law* (2nd edn, 1910) Vol I, pp 113 et seq.

1. The theory of *continuity*, whereby an act of occupation in a particular area extends the sovereignty of the occupying state so far as is necessary for the security or natural development of the area of lodgment.
2. The theory of *contiguity*, whereby the sovereignty of the occupying state reaches to those neighbouring territories which are geographically pertinent to the area of lodgment.[15]

Both theories are to some extent reflected in the claims made by states to polar areas according to the *sector principle*.[16] By claims based on this principle, certain states with territory bordering on the polar regions have asserted a sovereign title to land or frozen sea within a sector defined by the coastline of this territory and by meridians of longitude intersecting at the North or South Pole as the case may be. These claims have been advanced both in the Arctic[17] (by the Soviet Union and Canada, in particular) and in the Antarctic (by Argentina, Australia, Great Britain, Chile, France, New Zealand, and Norway).[18] The principal justification for sector claims is the inapplicability to polar regions, with their inaccessibility, climatic conditions, and lack of settlement,[19] of the normal principles of physical assumption of control implicit in the international law of occupation. Also the view has been advanced that the sectors themselves correspond to a just and equitable division. On the other hand, it is fairly arguable that the sector claims rest on no stronger basis than the mutual acquiescence of the claimant states. In effect, they amount to no more than notifications of future intention to assume full control, something akin to designations of spheres of influence or interest. Significantly, sector states have sought to fortify their title by the ordinary methods of administrative control, state activity, etc, traditionally

15. The theory of contiguity was rejected by Arbitrator Huber in the *Island of Palmas Arbitration*, p 145 above; he declared it to be 'wholly lacking in precision'. In the *North Sea Continental Shelf Cases* ICJ 1969, 3 at 30–31, the International Court of Justice preferred the theory of continuity to that of adjacency or proximity (ie contiguity) as an explanation of the coastal state's rights in regard to the continental shelf; see also pp 224, 244-245 below.
16. The sector claims of Chile and Argentina in the Antarctic, it would seem, rest on contiguity. For a map of the Antarctic sector claims, see *North Sea Continental Shelf Cases, Pleadings, Oral Arguments, Documents* (1968) Vol I, p 81; and ibid, p 82 for a map of the Arctic sectors.
17. The sector theory appears to have been first advanced in regard to the Arctic, and not in regard to the Antarctic. The Soviet sector claim rests mainly on a decree of 15 April 1926, but Canada's claim is founded, inter alia, on statements or declarations made at various times by Canadian political personages without explicit action by legislation or diplomatic exchanges to underpin such claim; see F. M. Auburn *Antarctic Law and Politics* (1982) pp 17–23. It is arguable that the Soviet and Canadian claims to exercise sovereign rights over certain Arctic areas were or could be founded on principles other than the sector theory. On the one hand, the Soviet claim could be considered as based on continuity (see above), while, on the other hand, the Canadian claim has been reinforced by reliance on the alleged necessity for anti-pollution measures in Arctic areas where the responsibility for enforcing these must be borne by Canada; cf the Canadian *Arctic Waters Pollution Prevention Act* 1970.
18. The British sector claim conflicts with the Argentinian and Chilean claims which themselves overlap.
19. These factors may be overcome by new technical developments in the field of aviation. Already, aviation has made it possible to supply winter bases in polar regions. In addition, 'great circle' air routes across the Arctic have been pioneered and are in regular use. Apart from aviation, there is the possibility that the inaccessibility of polar regions may be reduced through the use of nuclear submarines. On 31 July 1962, two United States nuclear submarines met at the North Pole.

employed by states desiring to acquire title by occupation. Other criticisms of sector claims are fairly and justly directed to the arbitrary character of the sector lines, and to the fact that these lines lie across large areas of the open sea.

One point is clear. The practice of a limited number of states in making sector claims has not created a customary rule that such a method of acquiring polar territory is admissible in international law. Here, it is only necessary to mention the reservations of non-sector states and doubts of jurists on the validity of sector claims, and the widely held view that polar areas should be subject to an international régime. Reference may be made in this connection to the Treaty on Antarctica signed at Washington on 1 December 1959, by the seven Antarctic sector states and Belgium, Japan, South Africa, the Soviet Union, and the United States. This treaty, which in effect created the whole area south of 60° south latitude a demilitarised and nuclear-free zone, provided, inter alia, that Antarctica should be used for peaceful purposes only, that there should be freedom of scientific investigation there, that the parties should exchange information regarding Antarctic scientific programmes, that nuclear explosions and the disposal of radioactive wastes in Antarctica should be prohibited, and that all areas in Antarctica should be freely available for inspection by observers of the contracting states. It was, however, expressly provided in article IV of the treaty that nothing therein was to be interpreted as a renunciation of claims or of any basis of claim in Antarctica, and that no acts or activities taking place while the treaty is in force were to serve as a basis for asserting, supporting, or denying a claim to territorial sovereignty in Antarctica, or create any rights of sovereignty there, while no new claim or enlargement of an existing claim was to be asserted. The result is that, during the currency of the Treaty, Antarctic sector claims are 'frozen', and the status quo of Antarctic non-sector bases of claim is preserved.[20]

In order to further the principles and objectives of the Antarctic Treaty, Consultative Meetings of the parties to the treaty have been held at different capital cities in turn. These Antarctic Treaty Consultative Meetings (ATCMs) have led to significant developments.[1] The Brussels Meeting of 1964 was especially notable for the adoption of the Agreed Measures for the Conservation of Antarctic Fauna and Flora, article VIII of which provided for the zoning of 'Specially Protected Areas'. A number of such areas have since been designated. At the Tokyo ATCM in 1970, two important Recommendations were adopted, one relating to human impact on the Antarctic environment, which provided for research in the matter and for interim measures to reduce harmful environmental interference, and the other for exchange of information concerning

20. Pursuant to art XIII, para 1 of the treaty, a number of states other than the twelve original signatories acceded to the treaty. Also under art IX, para 2 of the treaty certain states were granted consultative status, enabling them to participate in Consultative Meetings of the parties, on the basis that they had demonstrated interest in Antarctica by 'conducting scientific research there'; see F. M. Auburn *Antarctic Law and Politics* (1982) pp 147 et seq. At the date of writing there are twenty states having such consultative status in addition to the original signatories.
1. For text of the Recommendations and other measures adopted by the Consultative Meetings See W. M. Bush *Antarctica and International Law* 3 vols (1982-1988). See also G. Triggs (ed) *The Antarctic Treaty Regime* (1987). Cf also the Convention for the Conservation of Antarctic Seals negotiated by the signatories of the Antarctica Treaty in February 1972, which Convention has been regarded as a model of international law-making in the ecological domain of the preservation of living species.

launchings of scientific research rockets in the Treaty Area. The Eighth ATCM, held at Oslo in June 1975, was a milestone in this continuing process of consultation. Under the chairmanship of the late Dr Edvard Hambro of Norway[2] the Meeting made a start in examining the looming economic problems of the Treaty Area relating to future commercial exploitation of the area's resources. Special attention was paid to mineral resources, and inquiries were set in motion as to the ecological effects, and political and legal issues involved in Antarctic mineral exploitation, coupled with an understanding that, in the interim, there was to be abstention from exploitation. Other recommendations adopted at Oslo provided for the continuing protection of the Antarctic environment, with a prohibition of disposal of nuclear wastes there, and for scientific and technical co-operation between the treaty parties.

This interest in resource exploitation in Antarctica was continued at the important Tenth ATCM held at Washington in September–October 1979, which represented a further step in the process of establishing a mineral exploitation régime for the area, and also paved the way for the conclusion at Canberra on 20 May 1980 of a multilateral Convention on the Conservation of Antarctic Marine Living Resources.[3] This Convention embodied, inter alia, the concept that the relevant area in Antarctica, to which it applies, is a single ecosystem because of the interrelationships of the living species there. The discussions on a mineral exploitation régime in Antarctica continued after 1980, and culminated in the conclusion on 2 June 1988 at Wellington, New Zealand, of a Convention on the Regulation of Antarctic Mineral Resource Activities, the Final Act of which Convention was signed by the twelve original signatories, the twenty states with consultative status and some states not having such consultative status. The 1988 Convention, however, has effectively been superseded by a moratorium on all activities in Antarctica relating to mineral resources, other than scientific research, imposed by a protocol adopted by the parties at Madrid in 1991, which agreed to ban all such activities for a period of 50 years, owing to environmental concerns.[4]

The fact that the measures, arrangements and international conventions constituting the régime for the control of the Antarctic have been due primarily to the efforts of the twelve states which were parties to the Washington Treaty of 1959 has occasioned criticism and controversy, more especially by Third World countries at sessions of the United Nations General Assembly in recent years. First, it has been maintained that the present system should be replaced by direct involvement of the United Nations as the appropriate organisation for dealing with the affairs of the Antarctic. Second, it is claimed that like the high seas beyond national jurisdiction (see below, pp 230-232), the Antarctic is part of the common heritage of mankind, and any revenues obtained from the

2. See Dr Hambro's article 'Some Notes on the Future of the Antarctic Treaty Collaboration' 68 AJIL (1974) 217–226.
3. As to this Convention, see note in (1980) 54 ALJ 432–434. Under arts VII and XIII of the Convention, a Commission for the Conservation of Antarctic Marine Living Resources (CCAMLR) has since been established with headquarters at Hobart, Australia, the southernmost capital city of that country.
4. Protocol on Environmental Protection to the Antarctic Treaty, Madrid, 4 October 1991, (1991) 30 ILM 1455.

exploitation of the region should be shared with Third World countries. Third, it is proposed that the Antarctic area should become a kind of 'world heritage park', unspoiled by economic activity, environmentally intact, and protected in an appropriate manner.

In reply to these claims, the merits of the existing system have been vigorously defended by the Treaty states.

Annexation

Annexation[5] is a method of acquiring territorial sovereignty which is resorted to in two sets of circumstances:

a.   Where the territory annexed has been conquered or subjugated by the annexing state.
b.   Where the territory annexed is in a position of virtual subordination to the annexing state at the time the latter's intention of annexation is declared.

Case a. is the more usual, but there have been modern instances of case b., as, for example, the annexation of Korea by Japan in 1910, Korea having then been under Japanese domination for some years. Conquest of a territory as under a. is not sufficient to constitute acquisition of title; there must be, in addition, a formally declared intention to annex, which is usually expressed in a Note or Notes sent to all other interested Powers. It follows that sovereignty is not acquired by victorious states over the territory of a vanquished state, if they expressly disclaim an intention to annex it.[6] An annexation which results from aggression committed by one state against another, or which has been effected by force contrary to the provisions of the United Nations Charter, ought not, semble, to be recognised by other states.[7]

Accretion

Title by accretion[8] occurs where new territory is added, mainly through natural causes, which can be by fluvial action or otherwise (eg wind blown sand[9]), to territory already under the sovereignty of the acquiring state. No formal act or assertion of title is necessary. It is immaterial whether the process of accretion has been gradual or imperceptible, as in the normal case of alluvial deposits or alluvial formation of islands, or whether it has been produced by a sudden and abrupt transfer of soil, provided that this has become embedded, and was not

5.   Distinguish the so-called 'peaceful annexation', ie the taking over of territory in the name of a state, by proclamation followed by settlement, without the use of force to conquer the territory. Cf the use of the expression 'peaceful annexation' in *Cooper v Stuart* (1889) 14 App Cas 286 at 291, PC, with reference to the colonisation of Australia by Great Britain (but not followed by the High Court of Australia in *Mabo v Queensland* (1992) 175 CLR 1); and see also *Coe v Commonwealth of Australia and the United Kingdom Government* (1979) 53 ALJR 403.
6.   Cf the case of such a disclaimer by the allied Powers in 1945 in respect of Germany after the unconditional surrender by the German Government. According to Judge Jessup in *The South West Africa Cases*, 2nd Phase, ICJ 1966, 6 at 418–419: 'It is commonplace that international law does not recognise military conquest as a source of title'. Cf *Callas v United States* 253 F 2d 838 (1958).
7.   See above, pp 140-143.
8.   See Hyde *International Law* (2nd edn, 1947) Vol I, pp 355–356.
9.   See *Southern Centre of Theosophy v State of South Australia* [1982] AC 706, [1982] 2 All ER 283, PC.

in any event identifiable as originating from another location.[10] If gradual or imperceptible, this means gradual or imperceptible in its progress, rather than gradual or imperceptible after a long lapse of time.[11] The rules of Roman private law regarding the division of ownership over alluvial deposits in streams or rivers between the riparian owners are by analogy applicable to the problem of apportioning sovereignty between riparian states where similar deposits occur in boundary rivers.

Cession

Cession is an important method of acquiring territorial sovereignty. It rests on the principle that the right of transferring its territory is a fundamental attribute of the sovereignty of a state.

The cession of a territory may be voluntary, or it may be made under compulsion as a result of a war conducted successfully by the state to which the territory is to be ceded. As a matter of fact, a cession of territory following defeat in war is more usual than annexation. A cession by treaty is void where the conclusion of the treaty has been procured by the threat or use of force in violation of the principles of international law embodied in the United Nations Charter; see art 52 of the Vienna Convention of 1969 on the Law of Treaties. As examples of voluntary cession may be cited the sale of Alaska by Russia to the United States in 1867, and the exchange of Heligoland for Zanzibar by Germany and Great Britain in 1890. Compulsory cession is illustrated by the cession to Germany by France in 1871 of Alsace-Lorraine—subsequently returned to France at the end of the First World War.

Any transaction (such as a gift, sale, or exchange) will be valid as a cession if it sufficiently indicates an intention to transfer sovereignty from one state to another.

A ceding state cannot derogate from its own grant. Hence, there necessarily pass under a cession of territory all sovereign rights pertaining to the territory ceded. By parity of reasoning, a ceding state cannot transfer more than that over which it has been exercising sovereignty; therefore, the receiving state will take the ceded territory subject to any limitation of sovereignty or sovereign rights (eg, in respect to a particular area) that formerly bound the ceding state.

Prescription

Title by prescription (ie *acquisitive* prescription) is the result of the peaceable exercise of de facto sovereignty for a very long period over territory subject to the sovereignty of another, and this may be as the consequence of the immemorial exercise of such sovereignty (ie for such period of time as in effect to extinguish memories of the exercise of sovereignty by a predecessor) or as the result of lengthy adverse possession only.[12] A number of jurists (including Rivier and de Martens) have denied that acquisitive prescription is recognised by international

---

10. See Shalowitz *Shore and Sea Boundaries* (1964) Vol II, pp 537–539, as to the different meanings of accretion, alluvion, reliction, erosion, and avulsion.
11. See *Southern Centre of Theosophy v State of South Australia* above.
12. This distinguishes acquisitive prescription from occupation, which involves the acquisition of sovereignty over terra nullius.

law.[13] There is no decision of any international tribunal which conclusively supports any doctrine of acquisitive prescription, although it has been claimed that the *Island of Palmas Case*, represents such a precedent.[14] Nor is there any recognised principle of international law fixing in terms of years the period of time that will constitute a good root of title. As a practical matter it is also difficult to conceive of any case in which the lawful sovereignty of a state over territory would give way before possession and control by another. Indeed, it has never been accepted that the mere silence of a state with regard to territory claimed to belong to it could result in the divesting of its claim by anything less than the indicia of an effective occupation. In the *Frontier Lands Case* (Belgium-Netherlands),[15] it was held by the International Court of Justice that mere routine and administrative acts performed by local Netherlands officials in a certain area could not displace the legal title of Belgium to that area under a duly concluded convention.

On the other hand, it is true that if territory formerly belonging to State A is to be acquired by another entity or state, there is no requirement at international law that State A must evince an animus disponendi. If prescription is to be regarded as a good root of international legal title, the critical points are the length of the period of public and peaceful exercise of de facto sovereignty, whether this has remained uninterrupted, and the strength of the title displaced. The adequacy of length of the period would have to be decided by an international tribunal; and there should be caution in applying analogies from Roman law, or other systems of domestic law.

Acquisition of territorial sovereignty by newly emerged states
The acquisition of territorial sovereignty by newly emerged states, such as 'decolonised' dependencies or emancipated trust territories appears to be sui generis. The theoretical dilemma here is that territory is one of the components of statehood, yet until the new state comes into being, in principle, there is no entity capable of taking title. In the writer's view, this abstract difficulty can be resolved by treating the people of the territory, as such, provided they have a sufficient degree of political maturity, as having or acquiring sovereignty pending the attainment of statehood.[16] Upon the foundation of the new state, there is

13. Cf *Survey of International Law in Relation to the Work of Codification of the International Law Commission* (1949) published by the United Nations, p 39.
14. In that case, Arbitrator Huber did not expressly base his award on any doctrine of acquisitive prescription. See *United Nations Reports of International Arbitral Awards* Vol 2, 829.
15. ICJ 1959, 209. Also, subsequently, in the *Case Concerning the Temple of Preah Vihear (Merits)* (Cambodia-Thailand) ICJ 1962, 6, the Court declined to treat the acts of merely local administrative authorities in a certain disputed area, as negativing a consistent attitude of the central authorities of Thailand, accepting as valid a certain frontier line, which placed the area under the sovereignty of Cambodia.
16. Cf *Advisory Opinion of 21 June 1971, of the International Court of Justice on the Legal Consequences for States of the Continental Presence of South Africa in South West Africa (Namibia)*, treating the people of the Mandated Territory of South West Africa as having a right of progress towards independence, which had been violated by South Africa's failure as Mandatory Power to comply with its obligations to submit to the supervision of United Nations organs. The Court referred to the people as a 'jural entity'; see ICJ 1971, 16 at 56.

simply a crystallisation of the situation, the territorial sovereignty of the people then becoming that of the state itself.

This view as to the acquisition of territory by newly emerged states is consistent with the principle proclaimed in the Declaration on Principles of International Law Concerning Friendly Relations and Co-operation Among States in Accordance with the United Nations, adopted by the General Assembly in 1970, namely, that the territory of a colony or non-self-governing territory has under the Charter 'a status separate and distinct from the territory of the State administering it', which subsists until the people concerned has exercised its right of self-determination.

Loss of territorial sovereignty

To the modes of acquiring sovereignty over territory just considered, there correspond exactly similar methods of losing it. Thus territorial sovereignty can be lost by dereliction (corresponding to occupation on the acquisitive side, and which requires a converse intention on the part of the abandoning state to divest itself of effective control[17]) by conquest, by operations of nature (corresponding to accretion on the acquisitive side), and by prescription. There is, however, one method of losing territory which does not correspond to any mode of acquiring it, namely, revolt followed by secession of a part of the territory of the state concerned.

Sovereignty over the air space

The development of aviation as from the early years of the present century immediately raised problems as to the sovereignty of states over their superjacent air space.

Before the First World War (1914–1918) the only point on which there was universal agreement was that the air space over the open sea and over unappropriated territory was absolutely free and open. In regard to the air space over occupied territory and over waters subject to state sovereignty, there were a number of different theories,[18] but upon the outbreak of the First World War in 1914, it was found, as a matter of practical exigency, that the only one commanding acceptance by all states was the theory of sovereignty of the subjacent state over the air space to an unlimited height, ie usque ad coelum. This was adopted and enforced not merely by the belligerents, but also by neutral states. It was confirmed in article 1 of the Paris Convention of 1919 for the Regulation of Aerial Navigation, whereby the parties recognised that every state has 'complete and exclusive sovereignty' over the air space above its territory and territorial waters. As we shall see below,[19] this usque ad coelum principle

17. Cf *Clipperton Island Arbitration (1931) United Nations Reports of International Arbitral Awards* Vol II, p 1105, at pp 1110–1111.
18. These included, in addition to the usque ad coelum theory, the following: (a) complete freedom of the air space; (b) sovereignty of the subjacent state up to a specific height, the remaining air space being free; (c) sovereignty of the subjacent state up to a specific height, that state having a right to regulate the passage of aircraft through the remaining air space. In 1910 an inconclusive conference on the subject of air traffic under international law was held at Paris; for a first-hand account of the proceedings, see Sir Harold Butler's book *Confident Morning* (1950) pp 83–95.
19. See pp 161-171 below.

has been affected by recent developments in the upper strata of the atmosphere and in outer space.

The Paris Convention contained elaborate provisions for the international regulation of air navigation, partly with the object of establishing uniformity. It established the distinction, which is still currently maintained between (a) scheduled international airlines or air services (described in article 15 as 'regular international air navigation lines' and 'international airways'); and (b) aircraft not belonging to such scheduled airlines or air services. The latter aircraft, provided that they were of parties to the Convention, were to have 'freedom of innocent passage' through the air space of other parties, subject to their observance of the conditions laid down in the Convention (article 2). The former, however, were to have no right of operating, with or without landing, except with the prior authorisation of the states flown over (article 15). The Convention and its annexed Regulations provided also for the registration of aircraft, for certificates of airworthiness, for aircrew licences, for rules of traffic near aerodromes, etc. The Convention did not apply to certain American states, including the United States, but these[20] became party to the Havana Convention of 1928 on Commercial Aviation, containing substantially similar provisions, although differing from the former instrument in being primarily a commercial agreement and in containing no annexed technical regulations.

In general, prior to the Second World War, landing rights for foreign aircraft remained within the discretion of the state concerned.

The prodigious increase in trans-continental and inter-oceanic aviation, following on technical developments both before and during the Second World War, raised new problems as to freedom of air transit and landing rights for international airlines. States operating regular international airlines which did not possess convenient airports in other parts of the world naturally clamoured for such rights as against states which did have these landing grounds. Also, as between states which desired to maintain their own scheduled air services, even to distant countries, problems arose of the allocation of air traffic. These and allied questions formed the subject of an International Civil Aviation Conference which met at Chicago in November 1944. The object of this Conference at which over 40 states were represented was to conclude world-wide arrangements governing commercial air traffic rights as well as technical and navigational matters relating to international aviation. The main discussions were concerned with obtaining agreement by all states to the concession of the 'Five Freedoms of the Air', namely, the rights of the airlines of each state to:

1. fly across foreign territory without landing;
2. land for non-traffic purposes;
3. disembark in a foreign country traffic originating in the state of origin of the aircraft;
4. pick up in a foreign country traffic destined for the state of origin of the aircraft;
5. carry traffic between two foreign countries.

---

20. Chile, which was a party to the 1919 Convention, was also a party to the Havana Convention, but denounced the earlier Convention in 1936.

The proposal of the 'Five Freedoms' was fostered by the United States, at that time the most powerful operator state, but no unanimous enthusiasm was shown at the Conference for making these part of the law of nations. Only the first two 'Freedoms' appeared to obtain the support of a majority of the states represented. Accordingly, the Conference was constrained to draw up two Agreements:

a. The International Air Services Transit Agreement providing for the first two 'Freedoms', namely, flying without landing, and landing rights for non-traffic purposes in foreign territory. Subject to the provisions of this Agreement, a state party might designate the route to be followed within its territory, and the airports which could be used.
b. The International Air Transport Agreement embodying all 'Five Freedoms'. States parties to this Agreement might refuse to the aircraft of other states access to the internal air traffic within their territory. The majority of the states represented at the Conference signed the first Agreement, but less than half signed the second, and a few states abstained from signing either. It is clear from this that the third, fourth, and fifth 'Freedoms' do not command general acceptance as absolute principles of international law.

Besides these two Agreements, the Conference drew up a Convention on International Civil Aviation setting out general principles of international air law which were also to condition the privileges granted in the two Agreements, and establishing a permanent international civil aviation organisation. Further, the Convention provided codes of operation for aircraft and personnel and health and safety rules, and recommended customs and immigration methods and navigational facilities for member states of the Organisation. The permanent aviation organisation under the title of the International Civil Aviation Organisation (ICAO) has been actively functioning since 1947 with considerable achievements to its credit in the legal and technical fields, including the adoption of standards and recommended practices as annexes to the Convention, and the adoption or conclusion of the Geneva Convention of 1948 on the International Recognition of Rights in Aircraft, of the Rome Convention of 1952 on Damage Caused by Foreign Aircraft to Third Parties on the Surface, and of the Protocol of Amendment to the Warsaw Convention of 1929[1] concerning the Liability of the Air Carrier to Passenger and Cargo, concluded at The Hague in 1955.

1. The precise title of which is the Convention for the Unification of Certain Rules Relating to International Transportation by Air, concluded at Warsaw, 12 October 1929. The question of the revision of the Warsaw Convention, so far as concerns the upper limit of liability for passenger injury or death, the basis of responsibility, and related matters of insurance, became an acute issue in 1965–1966, arising out of the United States Government's dissatisfaction with the limit contained in the Convention, as amended at The Hague in 1955. This led to the negotiation in 1966 of the so-called 'Montreal Agreement', whereby a number of foreign and United States carriers operating in or into the United States undertook to accept a substantially higher limit and in effect acquiesced in the principle of absolute liability; cf R. H. Mankiewicz 'Air Transport Liability—Present and Future Trends' III J World Trade (1969) 32–48. The upper liability limit was raised in amendments to the Warsaw Convention effected by a Protocol adopted on 8 March 1971, by a conference convened at Guatemala under the auspices of the International Civil Aviation Organisation (ICAO). For all practical purposes, liability was to be strict and absolute, and provision was made for quinquennial conferences during the decade following the entry

The Chicago Conference did not result in material alterations to the international law of the air. This is apparent from a perusal of the more general chapters (Chapters I–III) of the Convention on International Civil Aviation which lay down principles very similar to those adopted in the Paris Convention of 1919; for example, the principle of a state's complete and exclusive sovereignty over the air space above its territory (articles 1–2), and the principles as to registration and nationality of aircraft (articles 17–21). The drafting was sharpened in many respects; for example, article 5, instead of granting 'freedom of innocent passage' according to the somewhat ambiguous terms of article 2 of the Paris Convention, granted to aircraft 'not engaged in scheduled international air services' the right to 'make flights into or in transit *non-stop*' across the territory of a state party, and to 'make stops for non-traffic purposes' without obtaining that state's prior permission, subject to the right of that state (for example, for security reasons) to require immediate landing.[2] 'Scheduled international air services' were not to be operated 'over or into the territory' of a contracting state, except with the special permission or other authorisation of that state, and in accordance with the terms of such permission or authorisation, although non-scheduled aircraft might discharge passengers, cargo, or mail, subject to the regulations, etc, of the state concerned. Thus the distinction between scheduled international air services, whose rights of overflight or landing depend on the consent of the subjacent state, and non-scheduled aircraft, with restricted rights of passage and landing, was continued. One point of interest was that internal air traffic, ie air *cabotage*, might be reserved entirely to the territorial state, and by the conjoint effect of articles 2 and 7, included traffic between the mother country and overseas territories or dependencies. Here again, the position under the Paris Convention remained unchanged.[3]

Other important points under the Convention are that state aircraft (including military aircraft) have no rights of flight over or landing in the territory of other states without special authorisation of the subjacent state, and that in time of war or duly notified emergency, declared to be such, states are free, whether as belligerents or neutrals, from obligations under the Convention, although they may opt to observe these. Reference should be made also to the duties laid down by the Convention in general terms that subjacent states should observe equality of treatment and non-discrimination in regard to other states using their air space, and that all states should take such measures as are necessary to make international air navigation safer and easier.

---

into force of the Protocol, to increase the upper liability limit. In 1975 at a conference convened by the ICAO at Montreal to deal with the problem of expressing limits in an appropriate currency, three Additional Protocols were approved, respectively amending the Warsaw Convention, that Convention as amended by the Protocol adopted at The Hague, and the Guatemala City Protocol of 1971.

2. Under the Convention, these rights of overflight and landing in territory are subject to a number of qualifications and restrictions; eg as regards routes, articles that may be carried, and areas that may be flown over.

3. The standard works on the law of international air transport are Bin Cheng *The Law of International Air Transport* (1962), and Shawcross and Beaumont *Air Law* (Loose Leaf Service to date, Butterworths, London). For a concise but very comprehensive treatment of the whole subject of international air law, see ch 19, 'Australia and International Air Law' by T. A. Pyman and L. C. Morris in K. W. Ryan (ed) *International Law in Australia* (1984) pp 456–523.

In times of armed conflict the belligerents have the right to prohibit overflight by the aircraft of all states, belligerent or neutral. Neutral states have the duty to prohibit overflight by military aircraft of all belligerents. The area of prohibition does not include the airspace over international straits or archipelagic sealanes, over which there exist non-suspendable transit rights under the conventional and customary international law of the sea. The position is different, however, when enforcement action is being taken against an aggressor state by or under the authority of the United Nations Security Council. By reason of the United Nations Charter, articles 43(1) and 49, which require all UN Member States to assist in an enforcement action — including the grant of rights of passage — the military aircraft of those members enforcing the UN resolutions may call upon the subjacent state to permit overflight.

The above-mentioned principles represent the main general rules of the international law of the air. They embrace an exceedingly narrow range, leaving unregulated a host of important matters affecting international air traffic. The need still remains for a multilateral convention to mitigate the effects of the current rivalry for air routes and air commerce, although such a convention seems a visionary ideal.

As was foreshadowed when the Chicago Conference terminated, the subject of allocation of traffic between competing scheduled international airlines, which the Conference was not able to regulate by multilateral general agrement, has come under regulation in particular cases by bilateral agreements between the states concerned.[4] One of the most important of these treaties was the Bermuda Agreement of February 1946 (replaced by another Bermuda Agreement of July 1977, known commonly as 'Bermuda 2'), between Great Britain and the United States, which has served as a model for later bilateral agreements. This mushrooming of bilateral treaties conferring, subject to ad hoc conditions, all or some of the 'Five Freedoms', has not been without its defects; it has, for instance seriously impaired the uniformity of law and practices which was one of the primary objects of the Chicago Conference. On the other hand, an examination of the treaties reveals a number of similar or common features, such as the dependence of transit and traffic rights upon reciprocity, the recognition of a principle that international air transport should be facilitated, and substantial uniformity in the drafting of administrative and technical clauses. In July 1946, the United States had withdrawn from the Air Transport or 'Five Freedoms' Agreement, thus recognising that the international regulation of air traffic by multilateral general agreement was impracticable. So, in respect at least of scheduled international airlines or air services, multilateralisation proved impossible, and as reflected in bilateral networks of intergovernmental agreements concerning transit, traffic, and landing rights, the doctrine of sovereignty in the 'closed air space' now prevails. Indeed, in other areas, states are extending rather than restricting this doctrine, for example by the

4. Non-scheduled air services also became the subject of bilateral agreements, and in one instance of a multilateral agreement, namely the Agreement on Commercial Rights of Non-Scheduled Air Services in Europe, concluded at Paris on 30 April 1956.

establishment for security purposes of 'air defence identification zones' (ADIZs) above the maritime approaches to their coasts,[5] and by other expedients.[6]

The recent emergence of wide-bodied airliners with greatly augmented passenger capacity and increased rate of frequency of journeys, by reason of higher speeds, has already pointed to some problems in the practical working of bilateralism, which is founded primarily upon the exchange of traffic rights. Such an exchange becomes difficult where, in respect of a particular country of embarkation and disembarkation, there is not enough volume of traffic for economic division among carriers, so that protectionist restrictions become necessary, unless it is clear that the volume will increase. For this reason, if the trend towards larger, speedier airliners continues upon a global scale, multilateral or regional solutions may perhaps be needed.

Apart from aviation traffic, problems of abuse of the air have come within the scope of international law. In respect of radiocommunications, two principles have emerged:

a.   That every state has a right to prevent its air space being traversed by injurious transmissions of radio waves.
b.   That every state is under a duty not to allow, and to prevent its territory being used for the transmission of radio waves injurious to other states.[7]

Then there is the Moscow Treaty of 5 August 1963, banning nuclear weapon tests in the atmosphere, in outer space, and under water; under this Treaty to which over 100 states currently are parties, the contracting states undertake to prohibit, to prevent, and not to carry out any nuclear weapon test explosion, at any place under their jurisdiction or control in the atmosphere, or beyond the limits of the atmosphere, including outer space, or under water including territorial waters or the high seas (see article I generally).[8] Other modern technological developments appear to require some principles for the protection of all states from injury through the air space; for example, states by the use of rain-making devices in their air space may deprive adjacent states of the benefit of rain-bearing clouds, thereby causing a drought, or again by the use of atomic energy for certain purposes, may cause dangerous radiations affecting the air or clouds above the territory of neighbouring states. In this connection, although no state is an insurer for neighbouring states against damage to the air space, there is probably a duty not to cause gross or serious damage which can be reasonably avoided, and a duty not to permit the escape of dangerous objects.

5.   Eg, by the United States and Canada. For bibliographical note on air defence identification zones, see Taubenfield *Review of International Commission of Jurists* December 1969, p 36, n 2. Aircraft of other states entering an ADIZ may be required to give notification beforehand of the course of flight, and even periodically to report their precise location.
6.   An interesting post-war development has been the practice of nominating 'air corridors', which may be used by approaching aircraft, leaving the remainder of the air space 'closed' and under the absolute control of the authorities of the subjacent state or territory.
7.   Cf Le Roy 32 AJIL (1938) 719 et seq. Quaere, whether the 'jamming' of international broadcasts is illegal. It is claimed that such local 'jamming' contravenes paragraph 2 of article 19 of the International Covenant of 1966 on Civil and Political Rights (freedom to impart information through any media 'regardless of frontiers') and article 35 (1) of the International Telecommunications Union (ITU) Convention of 1973 (prohibition of harmful interference with radio services).
8.   For the text of the Treaty, see *UK Treaty Series*, No 3 (1964) Cmd 2245.

The trend towards strict liability in this regard is reflected in the Treaty on Principles governing the Activities of States in the Exploration of Outer Space, including the Moon and Other Celestial Bodies, signed on 27 January 1967, and in the Convention on International Liability for Damage Caused by Space Objects, approved by the United Nations General Assembly in 1971, and signed in March 1972 (see below).

There are other problems concerning the air space and the atmosphere generally which have of necessity brought about developments in international law, or created problems requiring international legal solutions. Certain of these concern questions of pollution or the protection of the environment, which questions are considered in Chapter 14, below. The influence of modern technology on the evolution of new rules of international law could not be better illustrated. For example, thorough research demonstrated that the release of chlorofluorocarbons (CFCs) and other so-called 'greenhouse gases' (eg, those produced by the burning of fossil fuels) found their way into high levels of the atmosphere, and led to chemical reactions depleting to a dangerous extent the ozone layer that protected the earth from the sun's ultraviolet rays, and rendering possible a progressive warming of the atmosphere which could bring about melting of the polar ice caps, a consequent rise in the level of the oceans and radical climatic changes. A conference of 46 countries at Vienna in March 1985 adopted a Convention for the Protection of the Ozone Layer, and this was followed by another gathering (representing 27 of the 46 countries mentioned above) at Montreal in September 1987 which adopted a Protocol to that Convention for the reduction of the consumption of CFCs and other products likely to have similar consequences.[9] There has been support for the far-reaching suggestion that the international community should adopt a code of the International Law of the Atmosphere similar to the code of the International Law of the Sea contained in the United Nations Convention of 1982 on the Law of the Sea.[10]

Upper strata of the atmosphere, outer space and the cosmos

New problems of international law have been created by the greatly intensified activities of states in the upper strata of the atmosphere, in outer space, and in the cosmos,[11] and by the correspondingly spectacular advances in space technology, in aeronautical navigation, and in planetary exploration.[12]

9. See also Chapter 14, below, p 374.
10. See Chapter 9, below, pp 261ff.
11. The term 'cosmos' is used here to denote the remoter regions of outer space.
12. The following represents a short list of recommended books and articles on space law:W. Jenks *Space Law* (1965); J. E. S. Fawcett *International Law and the Uses of Outer Space* (1968); McWhinney and Bradley (eds) *New Frontiers in Space Law* (1969); D. Goedhuis 'Reflections on the Evolution of Space Law' XIII Netherlands ILR (1966) 109–149, and 'The Present State of Space Law' in *The Present State of International Law and Other Essays* (1973) pp 201–244; Professor Bin Cheng's articles 'The 1967 Space Treaty', Journal du Droit International, July–September 1968, pp 532–644, 'Analogies and Fiction in Air and Space Law' (1968) CLP 137–158, and 'The 1968 Astronauts Agreement or How not to Make a Treaty', Year Book of World Affairs (1969) pp 185–208; M Lachs *The Law of Outer Space* (1972); O. O. Ogunbanwo *International Law and Order Space Activities* (1975); G. C. M. Reijnen *Legal Aspects of Outer Space* (1976); N. Jasentuliyana and R. S. K. Lee *Manual on Space Law* (1981) Vols 1 and 2;

Into and through the upper strata of the atmosphere, that is beyond the present operating ceilings of conventional jet engine or piston engine aircraft,[13] states have been able to project balloons, rockets, and long-range missiles, and to transmit radio waves, while non-conventional machines, such as rocket-powered aircraft, have demonstrated a capability to reach unprecedented altitudes in the airspace.

As to outer space and the cosmos, the launching of the first artificial earth satellite in 1957 by the Soviet Union has been followed by space activities on a constantly increasing scale. First, there have been not only the number, weight, and orbital ranges of the satellites and sub-satellites projected, but also their functional diversity, for purposes, inter alia, of metereology, missile detection, espionage, navigation, earth survey, remote sensing of the resources of the earth,[14] monitoring of pollution, ionospheric measurement, solar radiation measurement, photography, and communications, including telecommunications. Second, the Soviet Union and the United States as the two principal space Powers have conducted far-reaching experiments in penetration of the cosmos, beginning with the Soviet Union's success in 1959 in hitting the moon and photographing its reverse side, and continuing with even more distant space probing, to planets such as Mars and Venus. Third, the man-in-space programmes of these two Powers resulted in sustained orbital flights by cosmonauts, and culminated in the lunar landings and explorations by United States cosmonauts in 1969–1971, while both manned and unmanned rover vehicles have traversed lunar territory and retrieved samples of lunar soil and rock. Apart from these concrete results, space shuttles, both reusable and otherwise, have been successfully launched and have completed missions, while the possibility of space stations, even of a permanent nature, appears to have been demonstrated.

In addition to the knowledge of the moon and planetary systems gained from the lunar landings and space probes, there have been the great discoveries contributing to extra-terrestrial science, namely those concerning the nature of space itself, the magnitude of the cosmic rays, the radiation zones surrounding the earth, the extent of the earth's magnetic field, the character of the ionosphere, and the measurement of micro-meteorite density.

It has been difficult indeed for the international law of space to keep up with the unflagging speed of this progress in space technology and exploration. Yet space law can only in a very limited way anticipate these advances, for the formulation of its rules is necessarily dependent upon reliable data obtained through activities in outer space and the cosmos. As Judge Manfred Lachs of

---

and M. Benkö, W. de Graaf and G. C. M. Reijnen *Space Law in the United Nations* (1985). For documents see K. Böckstiegel and M Benkö *Space Law: Basic Legal Documents*, 2 vols (1990).

13. Even high altitude flights of conventional aircraft have necessitated the establishment of special control centres.

14. *Remote sensing:* Unceasing international efforts have been in progress to ensure the continuity, compatibility and complementarity of systems employed by different states for the remote sensing of Earth. Some states may be concerned about being 'sensed' without their consent, and/or about the data thereby procured not being made available to them. In 1986, COPUOS was able to agree on a draft of principles to govern remote sensing from outer space. See generally N. M. Matte (ed) *Legal Implications of Remote Sensing from Outer Space* (1976).

the International Court of Justice, himself a distinguished space lawyer, has said in another connection:[15]

> 'Whenever law is confronted with facts of nature or technology, its solution must rely on criteria derived from them. For law is intended to resolve problems posed by such facts and it is herein that the link between law and the realities of life is manifest. It is not legal theory which provides answers to such problems; all it does is to select and adapt the one which best serves its purposes, and integrate it within the framework of law.'

It was recognised in fact at the Second United Nations Conference on the Exploration and Peaceful Uses of Outer Space held at Vienna in August 1982 ('UNISPACE 82', as the Conference was called) that legal controls over *all* activities in or related to outer space are out of the question. Apart from this, a large portion of future international outer space law will be institutional law, consisting of rules governing the relationships between the numerous international and national agencies concerned with space questions, such as the United Nations Committee on the Peaceful Uses of Outer Space (COPUOS), the International Telecommunications Satellite Organisation (INTELSAT), the International System and Organisation of Space Communications (INTERSPUTNIK), the European Space Agency (ESA), the United States National Aeronautics and Space Administration (NASA), and the Centre National d'Etudes Spatiales (CNES) in France.

It has been sought to formulate some of the rules applicable in this domain in the following instruments, namely:

a. The nuclear weapons test ban Treaty of 1963, referred to above, under which states parties undertake to prohibit, prevent, and not carry out nuclear weapon test explosions beyond the limits of the atmosphere, including outer space.

b. The Treaty on Principles governing the Activities of States in the Exploration and Uses of Outer Space, including the Moon and Other Celestial Bodies, signed on 27 January 1967 (referred to below as the 1967 Space Treaty).

c. The Agreement on the Rescue of Astronauts, the Return of Astronauts, and the Return of Objects Launched into Outer Space, signed on 22 April 1968 (referred to below as the 1968 Astronauts Agreement).

d. The Convention on International Liability for Damage Caused by Space Objects (referred to below as the Liability Convention of 1972), adopted in draft form on 29 June 1971, by the Legal Sub-Committee of the United Nations Committee on the Peaceful Uses of Outer Space (COPUOS),[16] and then by the General Assembly, being signed at Washington, London, and Moscow on 29 March 1972.

e. The Convention on Registration of Objects Launched into Outer Space, approved by the General Assembly on 12 November 1974, and opened for

15. In the *North Sea Continental Shelf Cases* ICJ 1969, 3 at 222.
16. The Committee was established by the General Assembly on 12 December 1959, and primarily through its Legal Sub-Committee and its Scientific and Technical Sub-Committee has proved to be the main forum for the initiation and adoption of law-making projects in the field of space law.

signature on 14 January 1975 (referred to below as the Registration Convention of 1975).

f.   The Agreement Governing the Activities of States on the Moon and Other Celestial Bodies, adopted by the General Assembly on 5 December 1979 (referred to below as the Moon Treaty of 1979).

There is also a large measure of agreement on broad principles as reflected in a number of hortatory General Assembly Resolutions.[17] The most important instrument to date is the 1967 Space Treaty which propounds in effect a first code of space law, although it must be borne in mind that all the instruments are interdependent, and were largely influenced and conditioned by the principles and guide-lines proclaimed by the General Assembly in its Resolutions.[18]

Upon the basis of these instruments and Resolutions, it is possible, allowing for the risks of generalisation, to formulate some of the fundamentals of the international law of space.

First, it is clear that the usque ad coelum rule, ie the doctrine of the sovereignty of the subjacent state to an unlimited height, cannot work in practice. States have not insisted on the rule, inasmuch as they have acquiesced, and still acquiesce in the repeated crossing, without their prior consent, of their superjacent space by orbiting satellites and capsules at heights of one hundred miles and more.[19] Apart therefrom, there is some difficulty in applying to space one of the considerations notionally underlying the usque ad coelum rule, namely, that of a vertical column which remains permanently and statically appurtenant to a particular subjacent state, because this does not strictly correspond to the scientific or astronomical facts.[20]

On the other hand, most states agree on the *principle* that, particularly for security purposes, there must be sovereignty up to some upper limit, ie some demarcation either in the upper atmosphere itself, or between the atmosphere and space, although there is no *consensus* as to a precise figure for this height.

---

17. As to the effect of the earlier Resolutions, see Bin Cheng 'United Nations Resolutions on Outer Space: "Instant" International Customary Law?' V Indian JIL (1965) 23.
18. The 1967 Space Treaty, the 1968 Astronauts Treaty, the Liability Convention of 1972, the Registration Convention of 1975, and the Moon Treaty of 1979 (see above) were in fact approved beforehand by General Assembly Resolutions.
19. On the other hand, the claim has been made on behalf of some states that the doctrine of the permanent sovereignty of every state over its natural resources (see pp 113-114) extends to information as to such natural resources, thereby constituting an objection to the acquisition of resource data, even for scientific purposes, by the employment of remote sensing satellites, and as well to the dissemination of such data, even for the benefit of science. This claim has been disputed, and it is said that such acquisition and dissemination of data, and the processing thereof, are not only compatible with the Space Treaty of 1967, but are unobjectionable as being for the benefit of the international community as a whole.
20. Cf Bin Cheng 'From Air Law to Space Law' (1960) CLP 228, at p 232 and McDougal 51 AJIL (1957) 74–77. There is, on the other hand, a division of opinion on the question whether the geostationary orbit (ie that orbit over the equator at such a height that the satellite there appears stationary) is within outer space, and therefore governed by the Space Treaty of 1967. It has been claimed that relevant segments of the geostationary orbit are part of the territory over which equatorial States exercise their national territorial sovereignty, but this is disputed. It is non-controversial that outer space has the status of a res extra commercium; see Bin Cheng 'The Legal Status of Outer Space and Relevant Issues: Delimitation of Outer Space and Definition of Peaceful Use' (1983) 11 Journal of Space Law 89 at p 91, and art II of the 1967 Space Treaty.

The suggested limits have ranged from 300 miles upwards, although latterly a well-founded course of opinion favours 110 kilometres or thereabouts above sea-level, out of regard for the lower limit of space in which artificial satellites have demonstrated ability to orbit.[1] There seems to be some apathy on the question of the necessity for fixing a demarcation height, and doubtless this reflects an underlying feeling that states may come to possess rights to a greater height than is now regarded as possible.[2] States appear ready to concede, albeit provisionally without any final waiver of their sovereignty, a right of innocent passage for objects launched for peaceful or scientific purposes, but not for military missiles. It seems undisputed that each state may claim sovereignty up to that height of the atmosphere where air density remains sufficient for the operation of conventional aircraft.

Second, outer space beyond this upper limit, whatever it may be, and celestial bodies, are subject to international law and the United Nations Charter, are free for exploration and use by all states on a basis of equality, in conformity with international law, such exploration and use to be carried on for the benefit and in the interests of all mankind, and are not subject to national appropriation. These principles were specifically commended to states by the United Nations General Assembly in its Resolutions of 20 December 1961, and of 13 December 1963, and were enunciated in articles 1–111 of the 1967 Space Treaty. Article IV indeed makes provision that the moon and other celestial bodies are to be used by all states parties exclusively for 'peaceful purposes', prohibiting thereon the establishment of military bases, installations, and fortifications, weapons testing, and military manoeuvres. It has been a matter of controversy whether the expression 'peaceful purposes' connotes 'non-military purposes' or, on the other hand, 'non-aggressive purposes'. Also under article II, outer space and celestial bodies are not subject to national appropriation by claim of sovereignty, by means of use or occupation, or by any other means (cf the provision of article XI of the Moon Treaty of 1979).

Third, it is the duty of every state launching a satellite or object into orbit or beyond, to give due notice of the launching thereof, and information concerning such matters as orbits, weights, and radio frequencies. In its above-mentioned Resolution of 20 December 1961, the General Assembly called on states to

1. Under a resolution adopted by the 1968 Conference of the International Law Association, the term 'outer space' as used in the 1967 Space Treaty should be interpreted so as to include all space at and above the lowest perigee achieved at the date of the Treaty (27 January 1967) by any satellite put into orbit, without prejudice to the question whether at some later date the term is held to include space below such perigee. At the eighteenth session of the United Nations Outer Space Committee in June 1975, the Italian delegation proposed a delimitation into two zones, atmospheric and outer space, with the 'vertical' frontier fixed at about 90 kilometres from the earth's surface. There is considerable support for the view that the upper limit of the atmosphere should be lowest altitude or perigee at which artificial earth satellites can remain in orbit without being destroyed by friction with the air; see Perek 'Scientific Criteria for the Delimitation of Outer Space' (1977) 5 Journal of Space Law 111 at p 118, and V. Kopal 'The Question of Defining Outer Space' (1980) 8 Journal of Space Law 154.
2. According to a working paper prepared by the United Nations Secretariat on the definition and/ or delimitation of outer space (see UN document A/AC.105/C.2/7, 1970) no proposal on the matter appears to command general support, while states are even divided about the necessity for such definition or delimitation, some countries being of the view that it might complicate and hinder progress in the peaceful exploration and use of outer space, or at least is irrelevant to the flight of space vehicles.

furnish such information promptly to the Committee on the Peaceful Uses of Outer Space, through the Secretary-General of the United Nations, and requested the Secretary-General to maintain a public registry of such information. Steps were subsequently taken to establish a public registry of information concerning outer space launchings. These principles received more detailed application and amplification in the Registration Convention of 1975 which, inter alia, makes provision for the national registration by launching states of space objects projected into outer space, and also for a central registry in respect to such objects to be maintained by the Secretary-General of the United Nations, while additional means and procedures were laid down for states to co-operate in the identification of space objects so as, inter alia, to mitigate hazards. Article XI of the 1967 Space Treaty casts a duty upon states parties to inform the United Nations Secretary-General, as well as the public and the international scientific community, of the nature, conduct, locations, and results of activities in space conducted by them, and such information is to be disseminated by the Secretary-General, immediately and effectively. This article stands in close relationship to article 5 of the 1968 Astronauts Agreement, obliging states, according to the circumstances, to give notice of the location of space objects returned to earth, or to recover them, or to restore them to, or hold them at the disposal of the launching authority.

Fourth, having regard to the discoveries concerning the nature of outer space, it is the duty of every state launching objects into orbit or beyond to take precautions to avoid injury to other states, or any permanent changes in the environment of the earth, or the contamination of the upper atmosphere and outer space, and of celestial bodies and the earth, or any impairment of the free use of scientific exploration of the upper atmosphere and outer space. This basic duty has received more ample expression in the provisions of articles VI, VII, and IX of the 1967 Space Treaty. Article VI sets out in the most general terms that states parties to the treaty are to bear international responsibility for national activities in outer space, while article VII, dealing specifically with the launching of space objects, lays down that each state party launching or procuring the launching of a space object, or from whose territory or facility an object is launched is internationally liable for damage to another state party or to its natural or juridical persons by such object on earth, in the airspace, or in outer space. Article IX imposes a duty of non-contamination, and of prevention of harm to the environment of earth resulting from the introduction of extra-terrestrial matter; there are also duties of consultation beforehand, if any activity or experiment is believed to be potentially harmful to the activities of other states parties in the exploration and use of space.

The liability of states for damage caused by space objects has been spelled out in more detail, as regards both substance and procedure, in the Liability Treaty of 1972. Under articles II–III, a launching state is to be 'absolutely liable' to pay compensation for damage caused by its space object on the earth's surface or to aircraft in flight, provided however that if damage be caused elsewhere than on the surface of the earth to a space object of another launching state or persons or property aboard this object, it is to be liable only if the damage is due to its fault[3] or the fault of persons for whom it is responsible; while there is

3.   Eg, liability would be excluded in case of vis major, such as lightning striking a space vehicle upon re-entry.

to be no liability for damage to nationals of the launching state or foreign nationals participating in the operation of the space object, or during the time when, by invitation, they are in the vicinity of the launching or recovery area (see article VII). There is provision for a Claims Commission to function where the question of compensation cannot be settled by negotiation. The law to be applied, and the measure of compensation are governed by the controversial article XII, according to which the matter is to be determined 'in accordance with international law and the principles of justice and equity', compensation being that which is required to restore the victim of damage to the condition which would have existed if the damage had not occurred.

Reference should also be made in this connection to article 5, paragraph 4 of the 1968 Astronauts Agreement, under which a launching state receiving notification of the locating of one of its space objects, believed to be of a hazardous or deleterious nature, is immediately to take steps to eliminate possible danger or harm.

It is nevertheless a moot question whether the provisions of the 1967 Space Treaty and of the Liability Treaty of 1972 are adequate to cover comprehensively all problems caused by nuclear-powered satellites, more particularly in the event of their disintegration with consequent earthbound scattering of debris, as occurred, for example, in the case of the Soviet nuclear-powered satellites 'Cosmos 954' in February 1978 and 'Cosmos 1402' in January 1983. There may be difficulties in locating all radioactive fragments, which unless deactivated can harm the environment. Although a new convention may not be necessary, there should perhaps be pre-agreed guidelines governing the precautions to be observed in the design, launching, and guidance, etc of such satellites, and providing for the co-ordination of emergency action and deactivation measures. Restrictions as to design may be of particular importance so far as concerns the prevention of fragmentation in outer space, and ensuring recoverability without damage to the earth and its environment. The matter was considered in a joint 15-Power working paper submitted in 1978 to the United Nations Committee on the Peaceful Uses of Outer Space.

One suggestion of some interest has been made, namely, that there be so-called 'crimes in space'; for example, the wilful disregard by a launching state of a patent risk of grave injury to the environment of the earth.

Fifth, communication by means of communication satellites should be freely available to all states upon a global and non-discriminatory basis.[4] This principle was laid down in the above-mentioned General Assembly Resolution of 20 December 1961, and was reaffirmed by the General Assembly in a Resolution of 16 December 1969. The arrangements for INTELSAT (ie International Telecommunications Satellite Consortium), constituting a global communi–

4. Copyright problems, inter alia, were raised by the advent of communication satellites. This is due to the ease with which signals can be received from the satellites, and be rebroadcast by the use of terrestrial transmission distribution systems. In order to prevent, so far as possible, unauthorised rebroadcasting of signals received from communication satellites a Convention Relating to the Distribution of Programme-Carrying Signals Transmitted by Satellite was signed at Brussels on 21 May 1974. In essence, the Convention binds the states parties to it by undertakings on their part (see article II) to prevent by adequate measures any ground station on its territory from picking up and redistributing, without authority, signals received from satellites, being signals not intended for such ground stations.

cations satellite system, which was first established in 1964,[5] are founded upon the principle that all states have the right of non-discriminatory access to the use of the system. The subject of direct satellite broadcasting, which has been under examination by a Working Group of the Committee on the Peaceful Uses of Outer Space,[6] involves a number of other legal implications. Although it is contemplated by the United Nations General Assembly that an international agreement should be concluded, formulating principles to govern direct satellite broadcasting,[7] it will be a long, hard haul towards the conclusion of such an international treaty or convention. The subject is bedevilled by technical problems and by thorny issues of state sovereignty. One difficulty is that of 'spillover'; current technology does not enable transmissions from satellites to be beamed with precision into most countries without spilling over into contiguous or adjacent countries. There seems to be a consensus that direct satellite broadcasting should be subject to the United Nations Charter, and the 1967 Space Treaty, that there should be an equitable sharing of radio frequencies, that transmission should be conducted within the limitations of the technical parameters and procedures established by the International Telecommunication Union (ITU) and its Radio Regulations, and that no country should have a monopoly in the launching or operation of broadcasting satellites, or preferential rights to the use of a geo-stationary orbit, or of frequency bands. Among the areas of controversy are the extent to which a receiving state is entitled to protect its sovereignty, its right to be consulted and to consent beforehand to transmissions, and its right to take counter-measures against allegedly illegal broadcasts.

Sixth, each state launching an object into outer space retains its sovereign rights over the object, no matter where it may be and where it may land. Correspondingly, the launching state remains responsible for damage done by its space objects to the extent set out above, while correlatively non-launching states are, under article 5 of the 1968 Astronauts Agreement, bound according to the circumstances to give notice of the location of space objects returned to earth, or to recover them, or to restore them to, or hold them at the disposal of the launching authority.

Seventh, states are under a duty to facilitate the passage of objects intended for the exploration for peaceful purposes of outer space,[8] and to give aid to space ships making forced landings on their territory.[9] It is questionable whether the duty of facilitation requires a state to make available its cosmodromes for use by another launching state. A further difficult point is whether a state which has granted tracking station facilities to one state should be bound to make these available to other states. In regard to rescuing astronauts, the principle of all

5.   For a summary-outline of the principal features of INTELSAT, see *Department of State Bulletin* 3 May 1971, pp 569–572.
6.   See Report of the Working Group on its Fifth Session (1974) for a survey of the legal and other problems involved.
7.   See, eg, para 4 of the General Assembly's Resolution of 18 November 1975.
8.   See Bin Cheng (1960) CLP 252–254, on the general duty of facilitation.
9.   This was referred to by Chairman Khrushchev of the Soviet Union in his letter of 20 March 1962, in reply to a letter by President Kennedy of the United States, dated 7 March 1962.

possible assistance in the event of accident, distress, or emergency landing is laid down in article V of the 1967 Space Treaty, coupled with provision for their safe and prompt return to the state of registry of the space vehicle. Astronauts are to be deemed 'envoys of mankind' in outer space, and as between themselves, astronauts of one state party are to render all possible assistance to astronauts of other states parties so far as concerns activities in outer space and on celestial bodies. Although the obligations of non-launching states in this connection have been set out more specifically in the 1968 Astronauts Agreement, it may still be necessary to rely upon the width of the provisions in article V of the 1967 Space Treaty, particularly for astronauts in distress in space itself, as distinct from their being in a plight upon their return to earth. The Astronauts Agreement imposes duties upon states parties of notification or public announcement regarding any plight or emergency landing of astronauts, of rescue and assistance where astronauts land in territory under the jurisdiction of the state concerned,[10] of contributing assistance to search and rescue operations in the event of their landing on the high seas or places not under the jurisdiction of any state, and of assuring the safe and prompt return of the astronauts to representatives of the launching authority.

Eighth, the issue of remote sensing from outer space has been controversial. Technologically advanced countries are able, through high resolution sensors, to obtain information about other countries having military or commercial value. Despite the views of some states, which argued for a requirement of prior consent for remote sensing above their territories, the United Nations General Assembly resolved in 1986 to allow open access for the use of remote sensing in outer space.[11]

As at the present date, no specific principles of international law concerning astronautical navigation, as such, have been formulated. It has been reasonably claimed that the freedom of the seas doctrine is applicable by analogy to outer space. To some extent, the analogy has already been applied, for under article VIII of the 1967 Space Treaty, the state of registry of a space object is to retain jurisdiction and control over the object, and over any personnel aboard while the object is in outer space or on a celestial body.[12] The Treaty does not however provide for the grant of nationality to spacecraft (contrast article 5 of the Geneva Convention of 1958 on the High Seas and article 91 of the United Nations Convention on the Law of the Sea of 10 December 1982). As more is known of the factors governing the paths and speeds of space vehicles, and the scientific forces operating in the cosmos, it may become necessary to impose restrictive rules for navigational safety and to prevent interference by space vehicles with each other, as well as to ensure that no damage be done to the earth itself or its environment. The successful development and possible uses of re-employable

---

10. In this case, the rescuing state is to have direction and control of the necessary operations, but acting in close and continuing consultation with the launching authority (article 2).
11. Resolution 41/65, 3 December 1986. Cf also the problem of direct satellite broadcasting: Fisher *Prior Consent to International Direct Satellite Broadcasting* (1990).
12. There would necessarily have to be subsidiary rules concerning the manner of identification of spacecraft. To some degree the subject of identification, primarily for purposes of registration, is covered in the Registration Convention of 1975.

space shuttles during the last five years have pointed to the necessity for such rules, especially rules for the definition or identification of orbit paths. Another need has also been demonstrated, namely the participation of states other than the United States and the Soviet Union in space shuttle programmes of greater magnitude so that the people of the world can more speedily reap the benefits of accelerated space exploration and exploitation.

It has been sought to denuclearise and demilitarise outer space. Absolute denuclearisation appears almost impossible to achieve. The Legal Sub-Committee of COPUOS has under consideration the elaboration of principles to regulate the use of nuclear power sources in outer space which would ensure safety assessment and due notification of such sources, and govern, as well the responsibility of user-states. As regards demilitarisation, under the first paragraph of article IV of the 1967 Space Treaty, states are under a duty not to place in orbit objects carrying nuclear or mass destruction weapons, or to install or station these on celestial bodies or in outer space. It is notorious that there has been no demilitarisation, strictly speaking, of outer space, as satellites have continued to be used for purposes of espionage and surveillance. Recently, also, the possibility of the use of laser weapons, based in space and with global capacity to attack a wide range of targets, has received attention. The demilitarisation of outer space was the subject of discussion at the Conference of 1982, UNISPACE 82 (see above). Administration of outer space by the United Nations has not been universally favoured by the states.[13] Nevertheless, the United Nations can, in line with the belief expressed by the General Assembly in its Resolution of 20 December 1961, reaffirmed in its Resolution of 18 November 1975, 'provide a focal point for international co-operation in the peaceful exploration and use of outer space'.

Apart from the matters of space law, referred to above, the United Nations has been concerned with the practical applications of space technology for the benefit of humanity, and the result of the United Nations Conference on the Exploration and Peaceful Uses of Outer Space, held in Vienna in 1968, was to promote certain steps for the transfer of space technology to the developing nations. In addition to the transfer of technology, these latter nations feel that they are entitled to reap the benefits of outer space developments, eg, those of an economic and medical nature, much to the same extent as in the case of the high seas beyond national jurisdiction (see chapter 9, below). Such space applications have a high priority in the view of the United Nations General

13. In 1959, the ad hoc United Nations Committee on the Peaceful Uses of Outer Space (COPUOS) reported to the General Assembly that it did not favour the establishment of an international agency to assume an overall responsibility for space matters. As Professor Taubenfeld has pointed out (see Review of International Commission of Jurists, December 1969, p 30), the current régime of space law is 'one of self-denial and is self-policed; the nations have firmly resisted creating any comprehensive, overall régime which would include the placing of authority and control for outer space activities in any international organisation'. The Conference of 1982, UNISPACE 82 (see above), likewise did not support specifically the creation at that stage of a new general international space agency, although the possibility of a Centre for Outer Space (which would not be such a major international agency) was noted.

Assembly (see, for example, its Resolution of 24 November 1975). The General Assembly has also attached high priority to the elaboration of an international agreement covering direct satellite broadcasting. As the discussions at the Conference of 1982, UNISPACE 82 (see above), showed, future problems are of infinite variety;[14] among these are the necessity or minimisation of 'space debris' (eg, dead satellites, spent rocket motors, etc) which, inter alia, may in outer space collide destructively with space vehicles or duly operating satellites, the use of space solar power systems, and international controls over aerospace scientific research. Space law cannot be static; through the very nature of its subject-matter, it is evolutionary.

Reference should be made finally to the impact of the Convention of 1986 on Early Notification of a Nuclear Accident and the Convention of 1986 on Assistance in the Case of a Nuclear Accident, both of which Conventions were concluded as a consequence of the Chernobyl nuclear reactor accident (see below, pp 378-379); these Conventions could be applicable to the consequences on Earth of accidents involving space objects carrying nuclear power sources.

Rights less than sovereignty—spheres of influence and spheres of interest

On many occasions, states have claimed in regard to certain regions or territories, rights less than territorial sovereignty, and falling short even of those exercised over a dependent territory or vassal state. Such inchoate rights were known in diplomatic terminology as 'spheres of influence' or 'spheres of interest', and were most commonly asserted in the late nineteenth century when international rivalry for the exploitation of weak or backward countries was historically at its peak. Although in view of such international engagements as those contained in the United Nations Charter to respect the territorial integrity of other countries it would not be politic today to use these terms, it is hardly open to question that the concrete conceptions underlying them are still applied by the Great Powers.

Perhaps the best definition of a 'sphere of influence' is that of Hall:[15]

'... an understanding which enables a State to reserve to itself a right of excluding other European powers from territories that are of importance to it politically as affording means of future expansion to its existing dominions or protectorates, or strategically as preventing civilised neighbours from occupying a dominant military position.'

A 'sphere of interest' differs only in direction of emphasis from a 'sphere of influence'. A state asserts a sphere of interest in a particular region when it claims to possess in that region exclusive economic or financial concessions or exclusive rights of exploitation, which it will not allow other Powers to exercise.

14. The particular problem of the geostationary orbit above the equator (due to the orbital speed being the same as that of the earth) calls for special mention. This is the only orbit capable of providing continuous contact with ground stations via a single satellite, but can accommodate only a limited number of satellites. This creates problems of radio frequencies, and COPUOS and its two Sub-Committees are endeavouring to frame principles for the rational and equitable use of the orbit without prejudice to the role of the International Telecommunication Union (ITU). See also n 20, above.
15. Hall *International Law* (8th edn, 1924) p 153.

2.   BOUNDARIES AND RIVERS

Boundaries

Boundaries are one of the most significant manifestations of state territorial sovereignty. To the extent that they are recognised expressly by treaty, or generally acknowledged without express declaration, they constitute part of a state's title to territory.

A boundary is often defined as the imaginary line on the surface of earth, separating the territory of one state from that of another. This is perhaps too artificial. As one writer says:[16]

> 'A boundary is not merely a line but a line in a borderland. The borderland may or may not be a barrier. The surveyor may be most interested in the line. To the strategist the barrier, or its absence, is important. For the administrator, the borderland may be the problem, with the line the limit of his authority.'

Where the borderland is of such a character that, notwithstanding the boundary line running through it, the territory itself and its inhabitants are fused for all practical purposes, the two or more states concerned may tolerate (either by treaty or by conduct) the existence in the borderland of administrative and other practices, for example the free movement of officials throughout the borderland, which would otherwise be in derogation of each other's sovereignty. The exceptional de facto relations between states and their citizens, arising out of such special conditions in a borderland area, are sometimes said to constitute relations of 'voisinage'.[17] Such relations could embrace arrangements between adjoining states for the joint exploitation of resources which straddle land boundaries (cf the use of the expression 'share-access zones' in boundary areas in the 1977 Joint Report by the Chief Negotiators on Canada–United States Maritime Boundaries and Related Resource Issues[18]).

Boundary disputes have occasioned many important international arbitrations; for example, the *Alaska Boundary Arbitration* (1903), between the United States and Great Britain. Such disputes were also the subject of two early instructive decisions of the International Court of Justice in 1959 and 1962 respectively, in the *Frontier Lands Case* (Belgium-Netherlands)[19] and in the *Case Concerning the Temple of Preah Vihear* (Merits) (Cambodia-Thailand).[20] In the former case, the Court gave effect to allocations of territory in a Boundary Convention of 1843,[1] thus deciding that Belgium was entitled to certain frontier lands; it refused to accept the contentions of the Netherlands that the Convention was vitiated by mistake, and that acts of sovereignty performed by local

16. Jones *Boundary-Making* (1945) p 7. As to the use of maps in boundary disputes, see Alastair Lamb *Australian Year Book of International Law* 1965, p 51. See also generally J. R. V. Prescott *The Geography of Frontiers and Boundaries* (London, 1965), and V. Adami *National Frontiers in Relation to International Law* (London, 1927).
17. See N. A. Maryan Green *International Law; Law of Peace* (1973) pp 190–191.
18. See United States *Department of State Bulletin*, 21 October 1977, pp 896–897.
19. ICJ 1959, 209.
20. ICJ 1962, 6. Note also the *Argentina-Chile Arbitration Award*, given 14 December 1966; see p 173 below.
1. Actually in a 'Descriptive Minute' annexed to the Convention, which had the same force as though inserted in the Convention.

Netherlands officials in the disputed areas could displace Belgium's title, holding that these acts were only of a routine and administrative character.[2] In the latter case, the disputed area was the region of a certain Temple sanctuary (Preah Vihear), and there was a conflict between the frontier according to a Treaty of 1904, whereby it was to follow a watershed line, and the frontier according to boundary maps completed in 1907, and communicated in 1908 to the Siamese (now Thai) Government. As the Siamese Government and later the Thai Government had by their conduct apparently accepted the map frontier line, and had not shown that any special importance was attached to the watershed line, the Court held that the map line should be preferred, and that the Temple area was under the sovereignty of Cambodia.[3] Following on these two early decisions of the International Court of Justice, there were, inter alia, three important arbitral awards in boundary disputes, that made in 1966 in regard to a boundary in the Andes area between Argentina and Chile,[4] that given in 1968 in the *Rann of Kutch Arbitration* between India and Pakistan,[5] and so far as concerns a maritime area and the islands located therein, that given in 1977 in the *Beagle Channel Arbitration*,[6] between Argentina and Chile.

In 1986, a special chamber of the International Court of Justice delivered another instructive judgment[7] in the frontier dispute between Burkina Faso (formerly Upper Volta) and the Republic of Mali—both African states. The importance of the decision lies in the principles relied upon by the chamber Judges and in the degree of weight attached to the materials before them. Due regard was paid to the principle of uti possidetis (see earlier in this chapter, p 144), to the role of equitable principles, to the prior history of the administrative organisation as to the relevant area, and to the extent to which the alleged acquiescence of one party might be taken into account. The materials treated as significant included legislative and regulatory texts, administrative orders and decrees, cartographic documentation and geographical contour features.

A Chamber of the International Court of Justice in the *Land, Island and Maritime Frontier Dispute*[8] decided a complex boundary dispute between El Salvador and Honduras as to its land and maritime borders, with Nicaragua intervening in the dispute so far as it related to the waters of the Gulf of Fonseca, an historic bay bounded by the three states. Regarding the territorial boundaries, the principal parties were in agreement on the primacy of application of the *uti possidetis juris* principle, which in this case transformed what were originally Spanish colonial administrative boundaries into international boundaries upon the advent of these former Spanish possessions to independence in 1821. They

2. The Court also attached importance to the fact that, in 1892, the Netherlands did not repudiate a Belgian assertion of sovereignty in an unratified convention.
3. It was incidentally held that Thailand should withdraw forces stationed in the Temple area and restore to Cambodia certain objects removed from the Temple.
4. For text of award, see HMSO publication 1966, bearing title, *Award of H.M. Queen Elizabeth II for the Arbitration of a Controversy between the Argentine Republic and the Republic of Chile, etc.* See also 38 ILR 10.
5. For an article on this Arbitration, see Wetter 65 AJIL (1971) 346–357.
6. For the material terms of the award in this Arbitration, see Wetter *The International Arbitral Process* (1979) Vol 1, pp 307 et seq. See also 52 ILR 93.
7. ICJ 1986, 554.
8. ICJ 1992, 351.

differed, however, as to the effect of 'colonial effectivités', ie 'the conduct of administrative authorities as proof of the effective exercise of territorial jurisdiction in the region during the colonial period' [9] on the determination of where these boundaries exactly lay. In respect of the Gulf of Fonseca, the Chamber refused to divide the waters but held, consistently with an earlier judgment of the Central American Court of Justice in 1917[10], that the Gulf was a pluristate historic bay in which the waters were held in condominium, with rights of passage thereover to the benefit of each party. Seaward of the closing line too, the territorial sea and EEZ would similarly project as a condominium (but not, of course, the waters seaward of the coasts proper); the parties were free to delimit these by agreement, if they wished

In the terminology of the subject of boundaries, there is a firmly established distinction between 'natural' and 'artificial' boundaries. Natural boundaries consist of mountains, rivers, the seashore, forests, lakes and deserts, where these divide the territory of two or more states. But used in a political sense, the term 'natural boundary' has a far wider significance; it denotes the line defined by nature, up to which a state considers its territory should be extended or delimited at the expense of, or as protection against, other states. Artificial boundaries consist either of signs purposely erected to indicate the course of the imaginary boundary line, or of parallels of longitude or latitude.

Most difficulty as regards boundary delimitation has arisen in the case of water boundaries. And of such water boundaries undoubtedly the most troublesome have been river boundaries, the problem being to decide what line in the river should be the boundary, and how it should be defined. In the case of a non-navigable river, the boundary line in the absence of contrary treaty provision runs down the middle of the river or down its principal arm if it has more than one, following all turnings of both banks. This line is known as the 'median line', and was adopted for non-navigable rivers by the Peace Treaties of 1919–1920. Where the river is navigable, the boundary line as a rule runs through the middle line of the deepest navigable channel, or as it is technically called—the *thalweg*. In the Peace Treaties of 1919–1920, the expression employed was 'the median line of the principal channel of navigation' (see, eg, Treaty of St Germain) which is more or less the same as the *thalweg*.[11] Where a bridge spans a boundary river, state practice favours the centre point of the bridge structure as the boundary line on the bridge rather than a point directly above the *thalweg* (which may, in any event, shift in the course of time) or the median line of the river, in order to preserve the equality of the riparian states with respect to their common interest in the integrity of the structure.[12]

9.   Cf *Frontier Dispute* (Burkina Faso/Mali) ICJ 1986, 554 at 586. See also the *Case Concerning the Territorial Dispute* (Libyan Arab Jamahiriya v Chad) ICJ 1994, 6.
10. *Gulf of Fonseca Case* 11 AJIL (1917) 674. That decision, however, was not treated by the ICJ as res judicata since Honduras had not been a party to those proceedings and Nicaragua was only an intervener in the present proceedings.
11. As to the *thalweg*, see the judgment of Mr Justice Cardozo in *New Jersey v Delaware* 291 US 361 (1934).
12. *Oppenheim's International Law* (9th ed by R. Jennings and A. Watts, 1992) 666; K. Bauer in (1976) 15 Zeitschrift für Wasserrecht 259-266.

Sometimes a boundary line lies along one bank of the river, while the whole bed is under the sovereignty of the other riparian state. This is an exceptional case arising under treaty or by long established peaceable occupation.

In the case of lakes and land-locked seas, the choice of the suitable boundary line depends on the depth, configuration, and use of the particular lake or sea concerned. In a shallow lake or sea, the navigable channel, if any, may be taken as a convenient boundary. More generally, the boundary line will be the 'median line', as in the case of a river. Many special apportionments have been made by treaty, but these have been of the most arbitrary character, and have followed no definite pattern or principle.

As to bays or straits, no general rules for boundary delimitation can be given, as considerations of history and geography come into play. On many occasions, however, the 'median line' has been accepted as the boundary.

Rivers

Where a river lies wholly within the territory of one state, it belongs entirely to that state, and generally speaking no other state is entitled to rights of navigation on it. Also where a river passes through several states, each state owns that part of the river which runs through its territory, but controversy has centred round the question of the rights of riparian and other states to navigate along the whole length of the river. Several writers on international law, commencing with Grotius, have been of opinion that there is a general right of passage for all states along such international rivers, but this view has never been generally accepted in practice, and is certainly not recognised as a customary principle of international law. Even writers who hold that there is freedom of navigation differ in their interpretation of the extent of this right:

a. some writers hold that such right of passage is confined to time of peace only;
b. others assert that only countries through which an international river passes have a right of passage;[13]
c. a third group maintains that the freedom of passage is without any limitation, subject only to the right of each state to make necessary and proper regulations in respect to the use of the river within its boundaries.

In principle, interpretation (b) is a reasonable one, as states located on the upper portion of a river should not be debarred from access to the sea.

However, such measure of freedom of navigation as became established on international waterways was almost entirely the creation of treaty. The process began with the Treaty of Paris 1814, and the Vienna Congress of 1815,[14] and continued with the Peace Treaties of 1919–1920, and the subsequent general conventions concluded under the auspices of the League of Nations. As a result, there was, before the Second World War, a limited freedom of navigation on

13. The Permanent Court of International Justice stressed the principle of 'community of interest' of riparian states in an international river; see the *River Oder Case* (1929) PCIJ Series A, No 23, at 27.
14. The Final Act of the Congress proclaimed the principle of freedom of navigation along the rivers of Europe, but in the events that happened, this principle did not receive full application.

most of the great river systems of Europe, while river systems in other continents[15] came under special regional agreements, or had been opened for navigation, subject to varying restrictions, by the states having sovereignty over them. Also, as the necessary framework for a free right of passage, international authorities had been set up to administer particular river systems. An outstanding example of a European river subject to such international control and regulation was the Danube. Under the Treaty of Paris 1856, a body called the European Commission of the Danube consisting of representatives both of riparian and non-riparian states was established to regulate navigation on the most important sector—the lower Danube, and on it were bestowed wide powers of administration. Under a 1921 convention which came into force in 1922, a Definitive Statute of the Danube was adopted confirming the powers of the Commission but setting up two Commissions in lieu thereof to manage the upper and lower portions of the river. These arrangements stabilised the situation on the river for many years, but were completely upset by the Second World War.

In 1946, the Paris Peace Conference caused to be inserted in the peace treaties with Bulgaria, Hungary and Romania a clause that navigation on the Danube, other than traffic between ports of the same state, should be free and open on a footing of equality. In 1948, a conference to work out a new convention to govern navigation on the Danube met at Belgrade. This conference by a majority and against the wishes of the delegations of France, Great Britain, and the United States adopted a new convention providing for a Commission composed entirely of representatives of riparian states. These three countries claimed that the new statute was invalid as displacing the acquired rights of non-riparian states under the earlier treaties. It should be added that by its article 1, this convention provided for freedom of navigation on the Danube.[16]

The Peace Treaties of 1919–1920 internationalised certain European rivers, and also laid the foundations of the work of the League of Nations through its Communications and Transit Organisation, whose avowed object was to achieve freedom of navigation on all rivers. The League sought to accomplish this by sponsoring the adoption of international conventions providing for freedom of passage, such as the Convention on the Régime of Navigable Waterways of International Concern, and the Convention on Freedom of Transit,[17] both adopted at Barcelona in 1921.

The League of Nations also endeavoured to unify river law by sponsoring the conclusion in 1930 of conventions dealing, for this purpose, with collisions between inland river vessels, the registration of inland shipping, and the flags of such vessels. More recent conventions on the same lines are the Bangkok Convention of 22 July 1956, for facilitating inland navigation between Asian countries, and the Geneva Convention of 15 March 1960, relating to the Unification of Certain Rules concerning Collisions in Inland Navigation.

15. For a brief account of the position in regard to river systems in other continents, see Fenwick *International Law* (4th edn, 1965) pp 459 et seq. As to rivers in the Middle East, see Hirsch 50 AJIL (1956) 81–100. As to the Moselle, see André Philippe *Le Port de Mertert et la Navigation de la Moselle* (1966).
16. But omitted the provision in art 1 of the 1921 Convention that there should be no differentiation of treatment as between riparian and non-riparian states.
17. The principle of international freedom of transit by the most convenient routes was again proclaimed in the General Agreement on Tariffs and Trade (GATT) of 30 October 1947 (see art V).

Yet, these treaties have neither singly nor cumulatively established a general right of passage along international rivers.

If general freedom of fluvial navigation appears too Utopian an ideal for international law to achieve, there is at least room for rules of more limited scope, tempering the restrictive practices followed by riparian states. Thus it might well be generally recognised that such states should not impose arbitrary or excessive dues and should not treat non-riparian states in a discriminatory or unequal manner, that access to fluvial ports should be free and equal, and that all navigable channels in internationally used waterways should be properly maintained, with due warning of dangers where necessary. Subject to this, the necessity for regional agreements dealing separately with the problems peculiar to each international river system cannot be gainsaid. As an example of regional co-operation, there may be cited the United States–Canada arrangements of 1954 for the St Lawrence Seaway, opened in 1959, as well as the International Joint Commission established by these two countries under their Boundary Waters Treaty of 1909.

So far as the injurious use of river waters or the diversion of and interference with the free flow of rivers are concerned, international law has not advanced to the stage of settled rules in either domain.[18] It is believed that there is a general readiness of states to admit that any such use or diversion or interference by one riparian state injuring the free navigability of a navigable international waterway to the detriment of a co-riparian state is a breach of international law. Short of this, it is perhaps only possible to say that there is a duty on a riparian state not, by any use of the river waters under its control to cause grievous or irreparable damage of an economic character to other riparian states, for example pollution,[19] which might reasonably have been prevented. In 1957, it was decided by the Arbitral Tribunal in the *Lake Lanoux Arbitration* (France–Spain)[20] that there was no duty on a riparian state under customary international law to consult, or obtain the prior agreement of a co-riparian, as a condition precedent of its right to begin new river works, although in carrying out the project it must take into account, in a reasonable manner, the interests of that co-riparian. Where the rivers concerned form part of a drainage basin, each riparian state is entitled to a reasonable and equitable share in the beneficial uses of the waters of the basin, a principle applied in numerous treaties. Essentially, such problems of the utilisation of rivers by one state to the injury of other states are a matter for treaty arrangement, or for settlement by arbitration or conciliation in the most equitable manner.[1]

18. Cf Hyde *International Law* (2nd edn, 1947) Vol I, pp 565 et seq.
19. A new problem of pollution has arisen in regard to navigation, through the recent more intensive use of tourist vessels plying in international rivers.
20. See 53 AJIL (1959) 156–171; [1957] ILR 101.
1. For the application of principles of equity in a case concerning a disputed use of river waters, see judgment of Judge Manley O. Hudson in the *Diversion of Water from the Meuse Case* (1937) PCIJ Series A/B, Fasc No 70, at pp 73 et seq. In past water disputes, the so-called principle of 'equitable apportionment' has been applied. Some such principle underlies the Agreement signed on 19 September 1960, by India, Pakistan, and the International Bank for Reconstruction and Development, in settlement of the dispute since 1948 relating to the Indus, Chenab, and Jhelum Rivers. Pakistan had claimed that Indian activities were interfering with its measures for flood control, irrigation, and developing hydro-electric power.

For some time now the idea has been mooted of a general convention on the law of international watercourses, analogous to the United Nations Convention on the Law of the Sea. It has been justly claimed that the customary law on the subject of international rivers is inadequate to deal with the newer technological uses of rivers, the problems of pollution, and the trend towards systematic development of river basins as one unit. On the other hand, it is an equally cogent objection to such a proposal that to attempt to draft a universal text, encompassing the various regional, local, and other aspects, peculiar to certain international rivers and certain international drainage basins, is not practicable, and that regional or local régimes are preferable to a universal régime, which in the nature of things can only consist of highly general, if not abstract rules.

At its 52nd Conference at Helsinki in 1966, the International Law Association approved a set of draft articles on the uses of waters of international rivers, and resolved that these should bear the title of the 'Helsinki Rules on the Uses of Waters of International Rivers'.[2] These Rules, which have commanded a large degree of approval, adopted the basic principle of the equitable utilisation of the waters of an international drainage basin, and broke new ground in certain respects, for example in the proposed rules to deal with water pollution and floating timber.[3] At least, the draft articles reflect an enlightened appreciation of the new problems connected with regulations for the waters of international rivers and drainage basins, and could well serve as a basic draft for a proposed general convention. Generally speaking, there is a movement to lay more stress on matters such as irrigation, hydro-electric power, flood control and pollution rather than on navigation simpliciter.

The law of the non-navigational uses of international watercourses has been one of the subjects under study or consideration by the International Law Commission. The use of the expression 'international watercourses' represents a shift of emphasis from concentration on rivers only to the wider subject of all trans-national waterways, whether these be rivers, on the one hand, or, on the other hand, lakes, canals, dams, reservoirs, and other surface waters, and as well underground waters. The International Law Commission gave consideration to waters flowing into mainstream rivers, and recognised that rules for the regulation of river systems could not serve, without more, to iron out inequalities in resources between states or to contribute to the solution of questions of the sovereign control of states over their natural territorial resources.[4] An international drainage basin is embraced in the expression 'international watercourses'; it involves the concept of an integrated area drained by a single river system passing through two or more states, and has been defined as 'a geographical area extending to or over the territory of two or more States ... bounded by the watershed extremities of the system of waters, including surface and underground waters, all of which flow into a common terminus'.[5] Each

2. See Report of the 52nd Conference of the Association 1966, pp 484–533 for text of the Rules, and commentary thereon.
3. See Chapters 3 and 5, respectively, of the Rules.
4. See pp 113-114 above.
5. See Garretson, Olmstead and Hayton *The Law of International Drainage Basins* (1968) p 4, and passim, B. R. Chauhan *Settlement of International Water Law Disputes in International Drainage Basins* (1981).

international drainage basin would in principle seem to require its own, peculiar, workable set of rules for co-basin states, rather than the application of global rules formulated in the abstract, or in an absolute manner for all international watercourses. Semble, there is at least a duty on a riparian state to consider the effect of its activities on co-riparian or co-basin states.[6] Finally, there is the problem of trans-border pollution of rivers and lakes, adding to the complexity of the whole subject.

3. SERVITUDES AND TERRITORIAL FACILITIES

Under present practice, an international servitude[7] may be defined as an *exceptional* restriction imposed by treaty on the territorial sovereignty of a particular state whereby the territory of that state is put under conditions or restrictions serving the interests of another state, or non-state entity. A well-known example is the condition that the frontier town of Hüningen in Alsace should in the interests of the Swiss Canton of Basle never be fortified.

Servitudes must be rights in rem, that is attached to the territory under restriction, and involving something to be done or something that the state bound by the servitude must refrain from doing on that territory,[8] for example, fishery rights in the maritime belt, the right to build a railway through a territory, the use of ports, rivers, and aerodromes, etc. Since the right is one in rem, it follows that the servitude remains in force whatever happens to the territory of the state bound by the servitude; for example, if it be annexed or merged in another state.

So far as government practice is concerned, the doctrine of international servitudes is relatively modern. In the *North Atlantic Coast Fisheries Arbitration* (1910),[9] the Permanent Court of Arbitration stated that there was no evidence that the doctrine was one with which either American or British statesmen were conversant in 1818.

Servitudes were, however, frequently referred to in books by writers on international law acquainted with the Roman and Civil law. In the late nineteenth and early twentieth century, there was some evidence that government advisers were becoming more familiar with the notion, and in 1910 in the *North Atlantic Coast Fisheries Arbitration* the argument was advanced that certain fishery rights granted to the United States by Great Britain constituted a servitude, but the Permanent Court of Arbitration refused to agree with this contention.

In a later case before the Permanent Court of International Justice, namely *The Wimbledon* (1923),[10] it was claimed that the right of passage through the Kiel Canal was a state servitude, but the majority of the Court did not accept this contention, although it found favour with Judge Schücking. In the *Right of*

6. Cf the Report of the International Law Commission on the Work of its 31st Session, 1979, para 130.
7. For a treatise on the subject, see Váli *Servitudes of International Law* (2nd edn, 1958).
8. An illustration is art 7 of the Lateran Treaty of 1929 (restriction upon construction in adjacent Italian territory of new buildings that may overlook the Vatican City).
9. *United Nations Reports of International Arbitration Awards* vol XI, 167.
10. (1923) PCIJ Series A, No 1.

Passage over Indian Territory Case (1960),[11] the International Court of Justice gave recognition to a customary right of passage for Portuguese private persons, civil officials, and goods over Indian territory between Daman and certain Portuguese enclaves, but inasmuch as it was held that such right was not general, being inapplicable to armed forces, armed police, and arms or ammunition, and was also subject to regulation and control by India, the right was hardly a servitude stricto sensu.

Initially, the doctrine of international servitudes was imported from the private law, and many authorities are of opinion that its translation to the international field has not been a success. There are cogent grounds for suggesting that the doctrine is not really a necessary one, and that international law can quite well dispense with its application. This view is at least supported by the rejection in the two cases mentioned of particular claims to servitudes.

If the term 'servitude' be inappropriate or legally inexact, there ought nevertheless to be some convenient expression to embrace the rights given to states under the numerous arrangements of recent years for the granting of air, naval, or military bases,[12] or for the establishment of satellite, space vehicle or missile tracking stations (for example the Exchange of Notes at Washington of 15 March 1961, between the British and United States Governments concerning the Establishment for Scientific Purposes of a Space Vehicle Tracking and Communications Station in Bermuda), or for permitting the installation of trans-border or trans-national pipelines.[13] Perhaps the expression 'territorial facilities' would be apt to cover these.[14] In regard to satellite and spacecraft tracking facilities, the point has been raised whether the grantor state is bound to extend the benefit of these to launching states other than the grantee state. This is certainly open to question.

11. ICJ 1960, 6.
12. A matter of controversy is the extent to which such bases may be contrary to international law. This turns, inter alia, on the point whether art 51 of the UN Charter ('inherent right of individual or collective self-defence' against armed attack) permits prior preparations and co-ordination for the contingency that an armed attack should occur against one state member of a collective defence grouping.
13. See article by J. B. Ballem QC 'International Pipelines: Canada–United States' in (1981) 18 Can YIL 146–160.
14. The word 'facility' is in fact used, apparently in this sense, in art 7 of the Treaty of 27 January 1967, on the Principles Governing the Activities of States in the Exploration and use of Outer Space, including the Moon and other Celestial Bodies (launching base of space objects).

PART 3

Rights and duties of states

CHAPTER 8
Jurisdiction

1. GENERAL OBSERVATIONS

The practice as to the exercise by states of jurisdiction[1] over persons, property, or acts or events varies for each state, and these variations are due to historical and geographical factors which are nonetheless coming to play a less important role in measure as, by reason of technological developments, countries have become geographically more knit together. Historically, states, such as Great Britain, in which sea frontiers predominated, paid primary allegiance to the *territorial* principle of jurisdiction, according to which each state might exercise jurisdiction over property and persons in, or acts or events occurring within its territory;[2] this was because the free or unrestricted movement of individuals or of property to or from other countries did not in the past occur so readily or frequently as between states bounded for the most part by land frontiers. On the other hand, most European states took a much broader view of the extent of their jurisdiction precisely because the continent is a network of land or river frontiers, and acts or transactions of an international character were more frequent owing to the facility and rapidity of movement across such frontiers.

However, with the increasing speed of communications, the more sophisticated structure of commercial organisations or enterprises with transnational ramifications, and the growing international character of criminal activities (eg, in the fields of narcotic drugs and currency transactions) there has been a noticeable trend towards the exercise of jurisdiction on the basis of criteria other than that of territorial location.

International law sets little or no limitation on the jurisdiction which a particular state may arrogate to itself. It would appear to follow from the much

1. See Judge Philip Jessup's study 'Jurisdiction', in U.S. Naval War College International Law Studies (1980) 303–318, and Mann 'The Doctrine of Jurisdiction in International Law' (1964) 111-I *Recueil des Cours* 9-162, (1984) 186-III *Recueil des Cours* 9-116. See also M. Akehurst in (1972-73) 46 BYIL 145-257, and L. Henkin in (1989) 216-IV *Recueil de Cours* 277-330. The three principal domains of jurisdiction are those of judicial process, administrative or other enforcement of laws and orders, and the so-called 'prescriptive' jurisdiction, ie amenability to legislation, regulations and judicial orders.
2. For affirmations of the territorial principle, see *Board of Trade v Owen* [1957] AC 602 at 625, 626, [1957] 1 All ER 411 at 416, and *Treacy v DPP* [1971] AC 537 at 561–564.

discussed *Lotus Case* (1927),[3] decided by the Permanent Court of International Justice, that there is no restriction on the exercise of jurisdiction by any state unless that restriction can be shown by the most conclusive evidence to exist as a principle of international law. In that case the Permanent Court did not accept the French thesis—France being one of the parties—that a claim to jurisdiction by a state must be shown to be justified by international law and practice. In the Court's opinion, the onus lay on the state claiming that such exercise of jurisdiction was unjustified, to show that it was prohibited by international law.

There is one practical limitation on the exercise of wide jurisdiction by a particular state. To quote a distinguished Judge,[4] 'no State attempts to exercise a jurisdiction over matters, persons or things with which it has absolutely no concern'. As, generally, persons or things actually in the territory of a state and under its sovereignty must affect that state, it will be found that the territorial basis of jurisdiction is the normal working rule.

2.   TERRITORIAL JURISDICTION

The exercise of jurisdiction by a state over property, persons, acts or events occurring within its territory is clearly conceded by international law to all members of the society of states. The principle has been well put by Lord Macmillan:[5]

> 'It is an essential attribute of the sovereignty of this realm, as of all sovereign independent States, that it should possess jurisdiction over all persons and things within its territorial limits and in all causes civil and criminal arising within these limits.'

According to the British practice, the mere physical presence of any person or thing within the territory is sufficient to attract jurisdiction without the necessity for either domicile or residence.[6] Indeed, under the so-called principle of 'transient jurisdiction', a British court may exercise jurisdiction in regard to a person, based on the service of proceedings on him during a mere fleeting visit to British territory.[7] Furthermore, the legislature is presumed to intend that its legislation shall be restricted in its application to persons, property and events in the territory over which it has territorial jurisdiction, unless a contrary intention appears, and statutes are construed with reference to this presumed intention.[8] A similar rule of construction is applied in the United States.[9]

3.   (1927) PCIJ Series A, No 10.
4.   Mr Justice H. V. Evatt in (1933) 49 CLR at 239.
5.   *Compania Naviera Vascongado v SS Cristina* [1938] AC 485 at 496–497.
6.   *Bank of Toronto v Lambe* (1887) 12 App Cas 575 at 584.
7.   Cf *Carrick v Hancock* (1895) 12 TLR 59. Under the Supplementary Protocol of 15 October 1966 to the Convention on the Recognition and Enforcement of Foreign Judgments in Civil and Commercial Matters of 26 April 1966 (Hague Conference on Private International Law), a judgment based on the exercise of such jurisdiction is not to be recognised or enforced by the courts of another state if the defendant so requests. Criminal jurisdiction may legitimately be exercised in criminal cases if the accused has been brought within British territory by irregular means but not if the British authorities were a knowing party to those means: *R v Horseferry Road Magistrates Court, ex p Bennett* [1994] AC 42. See further above, p 92.
8.   *Blackwood v R* (1882) 8 App Cas 82 at 98; *MacLeod v A-G for New South Wales* [1891] AC 455.
9.   *United States v Bowman* 260 US 94 (1922).

For the purposes of the exercise of territorial jurisdiction, it has been customary to assimilate to state territory: (a) the maritime coastal belt or territorial sea; (b) a ship bearing the flag of the state wishing to exercise jurisdiction; and (c) ports. The nature and extent of the jurisdiction permissible in the territorial sea, and by the flag state over ships of its nationality, are dealt with in Chapter 9, below, on the Law of the Sea, so that in the present chapter, discussion will be confined to jurisdiction with respect to ports.

Ports

A port is part of internal waters, and therefore is as fully portion of state territory as the land itself. Nevertheless, ships of other states are subject to a special régime in port which has grown from usage, and varies according to the practice of the state to which the port belongs.

The general rule is that a *merchant* vessel enters the port of a foreign state subject to the local jurisdiction. The derogations from this rule depend on the practice followed by each state. There is, however, an important exception which belongs to the field of customary international law, namely, that a vessel in distress has a right to seek shelter in a foreign port, and on account of the circumstances of its entry is considered immune from local jurisdiction, subject perhaps to the limitation that no deliberate breaches of local municipal law are committed while it is in port. On the other hand, some authorities concede only a qualified immunity to such vessels.

As we shall see below,[10] foreign *public* vessels are subject to special rules of jurisdiction and their status in port is considered in connection with these rules.

Where offences or misdemeanours are committed on board vessels berthed in foreign ports, jurisdiction depends on the practice followed by the territorial state of the port concerned. According to the British practice, foreign merchant vessels in British ports and British merchant vessels in foreign ports are subject to the complete jurisdiction and police regulations of the state of the port.[11] But in criminal matters, it is not usual for British authorities to intervene and enforce the local jurisdiction unless their assistance is invoked by or on behalf of the local representative—for example, a consul—of the flag state of the vessel, or those in control of the vessel, or unless the peace or good order of the port is likely to be affected. British practice maintains that in each case it is for the authorities of the territorial state to judge whether or not to intervene.

The practice of the United States and of France is somewhat different from that of Great Britain, a distinction being drawn between: (a) matters of internal discipline or internal economy of the vessel, over which the authorities of the flag state, including consuls, are considered to have primary jurisdiction; and (b) matters affecting the peace or good order of the port, which are reserved for the jurisdiction of local courts and local authorities. Thus, in *Wildenhus' Case*,[12] the United States Supreme Court held that the stabbing and killing of one Belgian seaman by another on board a Belgian ship in an American port was subject to local prosecution, and was excluded from the jurisdiction of the Belgian Consul.

10. See below, pp 203-205, 256.
11. See Smith *Great Britain and the Law of Nations* (1935) Vol II, pp 253–4.
12. 120 US 1 (1887).

The differences between the various state practices are far more a question of form than of substance, and it would appear possible by international agreement to bridge these artificial gaps (cf in this connection the Convention and Statute of 9 December 1923, on the International Régime of Maritime Ports).

Technical extensions of the territorial jurisdiction

Apart from the assimilation to territory of the territorial sea, of ships at sea, and of ports, certain technical extensions of the principle of territorial jurisdiction became necessary in order to justify action taken by states in cases where one or more constituent elements of an act or offence took place outside their territory. These extensions were occasioned by the increasing facilities for speedy international communication and transport, leading to the commission of crimes in one state which were engineered or prepared in another state. Some states in whose territory such ancillary acts took place, declined to prosecute or punish the offenders responsible on the ground that, as the acts were accessory to a principal offence committed elsewhere, the territorial jurisdiction did not apply.[13] But several states met the new conditions by technically extending the territorial jurisdiction:

a.   Applying the *subjective territorial principle*, these states arrogated to themselves a jurisdiction to prosecute and punish crimes commenced within their territory, but completed or consummated in the territory of another state. Although this principle was not so generally adopted by states as to amount to a general rule of the law of nations, particular applications of it did become a part of international law as a result of the provisions of two international conventions, the Geneva Convention for the Suppression of Counterfeiting Currency (1929), and the Geneva Convention for the Suppression of the Illicit Drug Traffic (1936).[14] Under these conventions, the states parties bound themselves to punish, if taking place within their territory, conspiracies to commit and intentional participation in the commission of counterfeiting and drug traffic offences wherever the final act of commission took place, as also attempts to commit and acts preparatory to the commission of such offences, and in addition agreed to treat certain specific acts as distinct offences and not to consider them

13. See in this connection, the House of Lords decision in *Board of Trade v Owen* [1957] AC 602, [1957] 1 All ER 411, to the effect that a conspiracy in England to commit a crime abroad is not indictable in England unless the contemplated crime is one for which an indictment would lie before an English court. More recently, it was held in the *A-G's Reference (No 1 of 1982)* [1983] QB 751, [1983] 2 All ER 721, that a conspiracy to defraud, to be carried out abroad, is not indictable in England, even if its performance would damage the property interests of a company within the English jurisdiction and even if its performance would injure a person resident in England or a company located in England by causing that person or company damage or loss abroad. See also *R v Cox* [1968] 1 All ER 410 (alleged conspiracy to commit fraud in France), *Treacy v DPP* [1971] AC 537, [1971] 1 All ER 110 (offence of blackmail may be committed through the posting in England of a letter with menaces, and which is received in a foreign state), and p 187, n 16, below.

14. This Convention has continued to remain in force as between its parties notwithstanding the penal repression provisions of the Single Narcotic Drugs Convention of 1961. A recent example of the application of the subjective territorial principle is the Australian case of *R v Nekuda* (1989) 39 A Crim R 5 (NSW, CCA); accused sentenced for sending poisoned chocolates from Australia to West Germany with intent to cause grievous bodily harm).

as accessory to principal offences committed elsewhere (in which case these specific acts would not have been punishable by the state in whose territory they took place).

b. Pursuant to the *objective territorial principle*, certain States applied their territorial jurisdiction to offences or acts commenced in another state, but: (i) consummated or completed within their territory; or (ii) producing gravely harmful consequences to the social or economic order inside their territory. The objective territorial theory was defined by Professor Hyde as follows:

'The setting in motion outside of a State of a force which produces as a direct consequence an injurious effect therein justifies the territorial sovereign in prosecuting the actor when he enters its domain.'

Illustrations of the theory were given in an official League of Nations report concerned with the criminal jurisdiction of states over offences committed outside their territory;[15] these were:

a. a man firing a gun across a frontier and killing another man in a neighbouring state;
b. a man obtaining money by false pretences by means of a letter posted in Great Britain to a recipient in Germany.[16]

The objective territorial principle was applied in the provisions of the two international conventions just referred to, and has also been recognised in decisions of English, German, and American courts.[17] But the most outstanding example of its application has been the decision of the Permanent Court of International Justice in 1927 in the *Lotus Case*.[18] The facts in that case were shortly, that a French mail steamer, the *Lotus*, collided on the high seas with a Turkish collier, due allegedly to the gross negligence of the officer of the watch on board the *Lotus*, with the result that the collier sank and eight Turkish

15. Report of Sub-Committee of League of Nations Committee of Experts for the Progressive Codification of International Law (1926), on Criminal Competence of States in respect of Offences committed outside their Territory.
16. Cf now *R v Baxter* [1972] QB 1, [1971] 2 All ER 359 (attempt to obtain property by deception by posting letters in Northern Ireland to England; offence committed in England, and subject to jurisdiction of English courts). As to a conspiracy entered into outside jurisdiction of English courts to commit an offence in England, see *DPP v Doot* [1973] AC 807, [1973] 1 All ER 940. The objective territorial principle applies a fortiori where the person committing the relevant offence *intends* to produce, and actually does produce detrimental consequences in the territory of the state seeking to exercise jurisdiction; see *United States v Fernandez* 496 F 2d 1294 (1974) (cashing in Mexico of stolen United States social security cheques drawn on the American Treasury).
17. See, for example, *R v Nillins* (1884) 53 LJMC 157; *R v Godfrey* [1923] 1 KB 24; *Ford v United States* 273 US 593 (1927); and *DPP v Stonehouse* [1978] AC 55; and for a discussion of the principle in the context of 'comity', the speech of Lord Diplock in *Treacy v DPP* [1971] AC 537 at 561–562. United States courts have exercised extra-territorial jurisdiction under anti-trust legislation in respect to such arrangements between foreign corporations as have or may have monopoly-producing effects or repercussions in the United States; and see also p 189 below. In the German Federal Republic, an alien may be rightfully convicted of an offence, committed abroad, of disclosing official secrets, if the result of such disclosure be to endanger the security of forces stationed in the Republic's territory; see 52 AJIL (1958) 799.
18. (1927) PCIJ Series A, No 10. The case no longer applies; see p 35, n 16 above.

nationals on board perished. The Turkish authorities instituted proceedings against the officer of the watch, basing the claim to jurisdiction on the ground that the act of negligence on board the *Lotus* had produced effects on the Turkish collier, and thus according to the rule mentioned above, in a place assimilable to Turkish territory. By a majority decision, the Permanent Court held that the action of the Turkish authorities was not inconsistent with international law.

The objective territorial principle plays a recognised role in respect of the exercise of jurisdiction as to multinational corporations, sometimes called 'transnational corporations'. The sociological and economic problems created by such corporations have for some time been under examination by certain international organisations, including the United Nations and the International Labour Organisation, which were responsible respectively for two pioneering studies published in 1973, namely, *Multinational Corporations in World Development* (UN), and *Multinational Enterprises and Social Policy* (ILO). In 1976, the Organisation for Economic Co-operation and Development (OECD) established a Committee on International Investment and Multinational Enterprises, which has continued since then to meet and examine the relevant problems of multinational corporations, and to secure wider recognition and acceptance of the Guidelines for Multinationals adopted by OECD governments in the same year, which Guidelines contained recommendations about such areas as the disclosure of information, competition, taxation, employment and industrial relations. However, consideration of the general international and trans-national problems related to multinational corporations and their extra-territorial ramifications lies beyond the scope of this book. The difficulties in applying to these enterprises traditional notions of jurisdiction have been well expressed[19] as follows:

> 'The multi-national corporation, by definition, is established and has activities in more than one State. If a strict territorial approach is adopted, each State may regulate only those activities within its borders. Such an approach could have serious effects. It might make it impossible for the corporation to do business by subjecting it to contradictory or confusing legal régimes, or on the other hand, it might allow the corporation to escape liability for conduct whose components are legal in each of the States in which they take place but which, taken as a whole, is illegal under the laws of some or all of the States concerned.'

One approach for which there is authority is that the country in the territory of which the effects or results are felt of action taken by the head office (in another country) of the multinational corporation is entitled to exercise jurisdiction, eg against the servants or assets of branches or subsidiaries locally situated.[20] It is

19. By John R. Stevenson in *Department of State Bulletin*, 12 October 1970, p 429. There have been endeavours (eg, by the United Nations) to circumvent such problems of jurisdiction by establishing codes of conduct for multinationals, such as the above-mentioned OECD Guidelines; see Horn (ed) *Legal Problems of Codes of Conduct for Multinational Enterprises* (1980); Feld *Multinational Corporations and U.N. Politics: The Quest for Codes of Conduct* (1980); Wells *Technology and Third World Multinationals* (Working Paper No 19, ILO, 1982); C. D. Wallace *Legal Control of the Multinational Enterprise: National Regulatory Techniques and the Prospects for International Controls* (1982); and F. E. Nattier 'Regulation of Transnational Corporations: Latin American Actions in International Fora' (1984) 19 Texas International Law Journal 265–283.

20. See, eg, *United States v Aluminium Co of America* 148 F 2d 416 (1945).

true that the head office's action may have concurrent effects in a large number of countries, the jurisdiction of all of which could then be attracted without being debarred by international law, so that ultimately it will be necessary to work out some appropriate code for the exercise of jurisdiction under international law over multinational corporations in order to avoid jurisdictional conflicts.

Apart from the application of the objective territorial principle, another possibility has been to treat the subsidiary as notionally an alter ego of the foreign parent corporation, so that jurisdiction may be exercised over the parent corporation by the state where the subsidiary is located, this being deemed the same as the exercise of jurisdiction over the subsidiary.[1] This, of course, is an extension of the nationality principle of jurisdiction considered below in this chapter, involving the attribution of what may be described as a 'notional' nationality to the subsidiary, thus allowing the exercise of extra-territorial jurisdiction over it; as applied by the Court of Justice of the European Communities, the approach is based on the doctrine of a 'single enterprise' theory of the nationality of related trans-national corporations, therefore discarding for this purpose the concept of separate identity of each member corporation of an integrated group of these.

Reference should be made to what apparently purports to be an extension by way of degree of the objective territorial principle, namely, the 'effects' doctrine adopted by American federal courts under which, especially in anti-trust proceedings, jurisdiction is exercised extra-territorially on the basis of the effects or consequences, however remote, within the United States and which are deemed to be of so reprehensible a nature (provided that they are *direct*), economic or otherwise, as to attract or necessitate such jurisdiction. Having regard to the possible serious results for their trading interests which the awards of American federal courts may involve (triple damages may be awarded), this 'effects' jurisdiction has been objected to by the United Kingdom,[2] Australia and other countries, and has led to the passage of local legislation to preclude the enforcement in the objecting countries of any element, evidentiary, procedural or otherwise of the American proceedings or judgments.[3] It is claimed that the 'effects' jurisdiction, as asserted by American courts, is contrary to international

1. Cf the decisions of the Court of Justice of the European Communities in Case 48/69: *Imperial Chemical Industries Ltd v EC Commission* [1972] CMLR 557 at 629, and Case 27/76: *United Brands Co v EC Commission* [1978] ECR 207, [1978] 1 CMLR 429.
2. But cf *DPP v Stonehouse* [1978] AC 55 at 59. For illustrations of the principles governing the application of the 'effects' doctrine, see *Grunenthal GmbH v Hotz* 511 F Supp 582 (1981), and *Schoenbaum v Firstbrook* 405 F 2d 200 (1968), revsd on other grounds, 405 F 2d 215. The 'effects' doctrine, as followed by American federal courts, is discussed in Buergenthal and Maier *Public International Law* (1985) pp 171 et seq, with references to leading United States decisions. The United States case law is not all one way on two points, namely: (i) whether or not the alleged 'effect' necessary to support extra-territorial jurisdiction must be substantial; and (ii) whether or not an intent to affect trade in the United States is alone sufficient for such jurisdiction.
3. Examples of such legislation are the United Kingdom Protection of Trading Interests Act 1980, and the Australian Foreign Proceedings (Excess of Jurisdiction) Act 1984. The disputed jurisdiction led to an Australia-United States Agreement of 29 June 1982, providing for consultation, inter alia, in respect to conflicts arising out of the extra-territorial application of anti-trust laws. The subject of the 'blocking' legislation is discussed by A. V. Lowe in 75 AJIL (1981) 257, and by D. L. Jones in (1982) 8 Commonwealth Law Bulletin 353. A useful collection of materials on this topic is A. V. Lowe *Extraterritorial Jurisdiction* (1985).

law, and that the local protective legislation is validly opposable to such American extra-territorial process.

Territorial jurisdiction over aliens

Territorial jurisdiction is conceded by international law as much over aliens as over citizens of the territorial state. As Judge J. B. Moore pointed out in the *Lotus Case*, no presumption of immunity arises from the fact that the person against whom proceedings are taken is an alien; aliens can claim no exemption from the exercise of such jurisdiction except so far as they may be able to show either: (i) that they are, by reason of some special immunity, not subject to the operation of the local law; or (ii) that the local law is not in conformity with international law.

Territorial jurisdiction over criminals

Great Britain (by long tradition), the United States, and several other countries, adhere for the most part to a territorial theory of criminal competence. Indeed, the British theory, which has been modified as a result of the two international conventions mentioned above,[4] goes so far as to deny to states the right to assume over non-nationals a criminal jurisdiction which is not properly territorial.[5] But the practice of most other states departs from an exclusive territorial theory.

The territorial criminal jurisdiction is founded on various principles. Its normal justification is that, as a matter of convenience, crimes should be dealt with by the states whose social order is most closely affected, and in general this will be the state on whose territory the crimes are committed.[6] Important considerations also are that the territorial state has the strongest interest, the greatest facilities, and the most powerful instruments for repressing crimes whether committed by subjects or citizens, or by aliens resident or domiciled within its territory.[7]

Although, as we have seen above, the territorial principle has been extended in several ways, it would appear from the *Cutting Case* (1887)[8] that such principle alone does not of itself justify a state prosecuting a non-national temporarily within its territory for an alleged offence against its laws, committed abroad on a prior occasion. The United States Government maintained this position in its exchanges with the Mexican Government over this case, which concerned the arrest in Mexico of an American citizen, Cutting, for having published in Texas an article alleged to constitute a libel on a Mexican citizen. On the other hand, the United States Supreme Court has recently upheld the right of United States courts to exercise jurisdiction over a Mexican citizen illegally abducted from Mexico in respect of crimes committed there against United States law.[9]

4. See above, p 186.
5. According to Lord Diplock in *Treacy v DPP* [1971] AC 537 at 561: 'It would be an unjustifiable interference with the sovereignty of other nations over the conduct of persons in their own territories if we were to punish persons for conduct which did not take place in the United Kingdom and had no harmful consequences there'.
6. See Report of Sub-Committee of League of Nations Committee of Experts for the Progressive Codification of International Law (1926), on Criminal Competence, etc, cited above, p 187, n 15.
7. Harvard *Research on International Law* (1935), Jurisdiction with respect to Crime, pp 483 et seq.
8. Moore's *Digest of International Law* (1906) Vol II, p 228.
9. *United States v Alvarez-Machain* 119 L Ed 2d 441 (1992). See further above, p 92.

Exemptions from and restrictions upon the territorial jurisdiction

A degree of immunity from the territorial jurisdiction may be enjoyed by:

a. Foreign states and heads of foreign states.
b. Diplomatic representatives, and consuls of foreign states.
c. Public ships of foreign states.
d. Armed forces of foreign states.
e. International institutions.

In the case of categories (a) and (c), whatever may have been the position historically before the developments in the weight of state practice in the 1970s, and also in the case of category (d), it would be now difficult completely and exhaustively to express the extent of their jurisdictional immunity in terms of recognised principles of international law,[10] except to say that international law permits or has been permitting to states a wide area of discretion in the degree to which jurisdictional immunity may be conceded to these categories, and in the manner in which limits may be set on the extent of such jurisdictional immunity. International law certainly does not now prohibit states from prescribing restrictions on the scope of such immunity from jurisdiction of these categories. So far as category (d), viz armed forces of foreign states, is concerned, it is difficult to extrapolate from the domestic legislation of states and from the welter of treaties and agreements concerning the status of foreign visiting forces located in the territory of host states any clear-cut general principles of international law binding states to concede a specific measure, if any, of jurisdictional immunity.

a. Foreign states and heads of foreign states

Historically, it was perhaps true to say that, save and except in the case of the involvement of states in transactions of a commercial or non-governmental nature, there was a general weight of practice supporting the existence of a principle of international law that foreign states and heads of foreign states might sue in territorial courts, but could not as a rule be sued there unless they voluntarily submitted to the jurisdiction of those courts either ad hoc or generally by a treaty or treaties. As pointed out in Chapter 6, above, such immunity was normally dependent on recognition by the state in the forum of which proceedings were brought against the foreign state or foreign head of state. In English courts, as distinct from the courts in a number of continental countries, the rule of absolute jurisdictional immunity prevailed, without exception, for the case of involvement of foreign states in transactions of a commercial or non-governmental nature.

The same principles were applicable to foreign states as to the sovereigns of such states, but it was a curious fact that the rule of jurisdictional immunity used to be stated—as for example by Chief Justice Marshall of the United States Supreme Court in 1812 in the classical case of *Schooner Exchange v*

---

10. The topic of jurisdictional immunities of states and of their property is one that the International Law Commission has been studying since 1978. The Commission adopted a set of draft articles on the subject in 1991; the text may be found in (1991) 30 ILM 1565

M'Faddon[11]—in terms which applied only to foreign sovereigns. The explanation perhaps was that the idea of the state as a juristic personality, distinct from its sovereign, was of recent origin only. Thus, as late as 1867, doubt existed in England whether a foreign state under a republican form of government could sue in English courts, although this right had always been conceded to foreign sovereigns.[12]

Several principles were suggested as the basis of this immunity:

i.   Par in parem non habet imperium. One sovereign power could not exercise jurisdiction over another sovereign power, but only over inferiors.
ii. Reciprocity or comity.[13] In return for a concession of immunity, other states or sovereigns of such states made mutual concessions of immunity within their territory.
iii. The fact that in general the judgment of a municipal court could not be enforced practically against a foreign state or sovereign thereof, or that the attempt to do so would be regarded as an unfriendly act.
iv. An implication from the circumstances; the very fact that a state allowed a foreign state to function within, or a foreign sovereign to visit, its territory, signified implicitly a concession of immunity, as no foreign state or foreign sovereign could be supposed to enter on any other terms. One judge well described this as 'an implied obligation not to derogate from a grant'.[14]
v.   The merits of a dispute involving the transactions or policy of a foreign government ought not to be canvassed in the domestic courts of another country.[15]

The rule of jurisdictional immunity of foreign states and foreign heads of states, as previously applicable in English courts and in the courts of certain other countries, had two aspects of significance:

1.   An immunity as to process of the court.
2.   An immunity with respect to property belonging to the foreign state or foreign sovereign.

Aspect (1) may best be considered in the light of the British practice. The English authorities laid it down that the courts would not by their process 'implead' a foreign state or foreign sovereign; in other words, they would not, against its will, make it a party to legal proceedings whether the proceedings involved process against its personality or aimed to recover from it specific property or damages. In the *Cristina*,[16] it was held that a writ in rem for the recovery of possession of a vessel, requisitioned by a government, impleaded that government since it commanded the defendants to appear or to let judgment

11. (1812) 7 Cranch 116.
12. *United States of America v Wagner* (1867) 2 Ch App 582.
13. But this was said by Lord Porter in *United States of America and Republic of France v Dollfus Mieg et Cie SA and Bank of England* [1952] AC 582 at 613 to be not a basis of, nor to limit, the immunity of a state.
14. Jordan CJ of the New South Wales Supreme Court, in *Wright v Cantrell* (1943) 44 SRNSW 45 at 52 et seq.
15. Per Lord Denning in *Rahimtoola v Nizam of Hyderabad* [1958] AC 379 at 422, [1957] 3 All ER 441 at 463, 464.
16. *Compania Naviera Vascongado v SS Cristina* [1938] AC 485.

go by default, thus imposing a clear alternative of submitting to jurisdiction or losing possession of the ship and ancillary rights. The writ and subsequent proceedings were accordingly set aside.

This aspect of the rule of immunity was so strictly applied that process even *indirectly* 'impleading' a foreign state or foreign sovereign was treated as to that extent bad. It was consistent with such strict application that British and American courts should hold state-owned commercial ships to be immune from all territorial process.[17]

As to aspect (2) of the rule of immunity, the courts applied the principle that they would not by their process, whether the foreign state or foreign sovereign was a party to the proceedings or not, allow the seizure or detention or judicial disposition of property which belonged to such state or sovereign, or of which it was in possession or control. If the foreign state or foreign sovereign had no title to the property alleged to be impleaded, it should at least show rights to possession or control in order to claim immunity. Aspect (2) was applied in the case mentioned above, the *Cristina*, in addition to aspect (1), the House of Lords ruling that a writ in rem issued in Admiralty against a vessel in the control of a foreign government for public purposes, imported process against the possessory rights of a foreign sovereign. As a condition of obtaining immunity, the foreign government needed only to produce evidence showing 'that its claim is not merely illusory, nor founded on a title, manifestly defective'.[18] It was not bound to give complete proof of its proprietary or possessory title.

The rule of immunity was not confined to proceedings in rem, for immunity could be claimed even if the proceedings were in personam but would if successful have the indirect effect of depriving the foreign state or foreign sovereign of proprietary or possessory rights, or of any rights of control.[19]

The immunity of a foreign state or foreign sovereign from jurisdiction was not in all cases an absolute one, as sometimes, depending on the nature of the remedy sought,[20] there was no exemption from process.[1] Thus the following proceedings appeared to be exceptions to the rule of immunity:

i.   Suits relating to the title to land within the territorial jurisdiction, not being land on which legation premises were established. The principle which was applied here was that the local state had too vital an interest in its land, to permit of any derogation from its jurisdiction over suits concerned with the title thereto.

17. See below, pp 205-207
18. See *Juan Ysmael & Co Inc v Government of Republic of Indonesia* [1955] AC 72, [1954] 3 All ER 236. Cf *Republic of Mexico v Hoffman* 324 US 30 (1945).
19. See *United States and Republic of France v Dollfus Mieg et Cie SA and Bank of England* [1952] AC 582, [1952] 1 All ER 572 where the doctrine of immunity of a foreign Sovereign state was applied to a claim to recover property in the hands of a bailee for a foreign Sovereign state. In *Rahimtoola v Nizam of Hyderabad* [1958] AC 379, [1957] 3 All ER 441, the House of Lords held that immunity might be claimed if an action brought against an agent of a foreign state, with legal title to a local debt, was calculated or intended to displace such title to the debt, nor could the action proceed against the debtor holding the moneys in question.
20. *Compania Naviera Vascongado v SS Cristina* [1938] AC 485 at 494.
1. It was expressly declared in the House of Lords decision, *Sultan of Johore v Abubakar Tunku Aris Bendahar* [1952] AC 318 at 343, that there was no 'absolute rule that a foreign independent Sovereign cannot be impleaded in our courts in any circumstances'.

ii. A fund in court (a trust fund) was being administered in which a foreign state or foreign sovereign was interested, but not if the alleged trustee happened also to be a foreign sovereign government.[2]

iii. Representative actions, such as debenture holders' actions, where a foreign state or foreign sovereign was a debenture holder.

iv. The winding-up of a company in whose assets the foreign state or foreign sovereign claimed an interest.

State practice also showed that not all states were ready to concede a full extent of immunity from jurisdiction. First, some states followed what was called a 'restrictive', as opposed to an 'absolute' theory, by applying the distinction mentioned above between state-like activities of foreign states or sovereigns (jure imperii) and their purely commercial activities (jure gestionis), allowing immunity only in the former instance.[3] Second, the municipal courts of certain states followed a practice of closely examining the nature and object of each particular transaction, in respect to which immunity was claimed, to determine whether or not the transaction really pertained to the functions of the foreign state. Third, there was no clear practice as regards the immunity of foreign governmental agencies or instrumentalities, and of foreign semi-public corporations. Some states were prepared here to follow the municipal law of the foreign state concerned, other states had regard to circumstances other than that municipal law, in order to ascertain whether the agency or corporation was part of the foreign state.

As to foreign semi-public corporations, in particular if they were not of the character of departments of state, but simply separate juridical 'entities', the privilege of jurisdictional immunity did not attach. It would seem from *Krajina v Tass Agency*[4] and *Baccus SRL v Servicio Nacional del Trigo*[5] that it was a question of degree whether separate juridical incorporation had proceeded so far as to deprive an agency or entity of its character as a department of state, or whether notwithstanding its incorporation, it still possessed that character. A separate, incorporated legal entity might, by reason of the degree of governmental control over it, nonetheless be an organ of the state.

2. See *Rahimtoola v Nizam of Hyderabad* [1958] AC 379 at 401, [1957] 3 All ER 441 at 450.
3. In *Rahimtoola v Nizam of Hyderabad* [1958] AC 379 at 422–424, [1957] 3 All ER 441 at 463, 464, such a distinction was also favoured by Lord Denning, but Viscount Simonds, Lord Reid, Lord Cohen, and Lord Somervell expressed their reservations as to Lord Denning's views. For illustrations of the 'restrictive' theory, see *The Philippine Admiral* [1977] AC 373, [1976] 1 All ER 78, a decision of the Privy Council (no immunity for an action in rem in respect to a state-owned vessel engaged in commerce), and for a contrary case *Heaney v Government of Spain* 445 F 2d 501 (1971) at 503–504 (contract by a government for propaganda against another government is a state transaction, in respect to which there is immunity). Article 5 of the European Convention on State Immunity of May 1972, provides that immunity does not attach to proceedings relating to a contract of employment between a state and an individual where the work is to be performed on the territory of the state of the forum. See also further, below, p 198.
4. [1949] 2 All ER 274.
5. [1957] 1 QB 438, [1956] 3 All ER 715. Where the major business of a bank is business of the state, the bank is to be considered as a department of state entitled to sovereign immunity; cf *Trendtex Trading Corpn v Central Bank of Nigeria* [1977] QB 529, [1977] 1 All ER 881.

A decisive criterion was whether the corporate entity was in effect the alter ego of a government.[6]

The immunity from process covered conduct by the foreign state or foreign sovereign which was a breach of local municipal law. In such case, if the territorial state felt aggrieved by the breach of its laws, the only course open to it was to seek diplomatic redress. The immunity extended also in respect of personal acts such as a promise of marriage, and even if the foreign sovereign was living incognito.[7]

As mentioned above, the immunity might be waived by express or implied consent. If express, the waiver had to be made with full knowledge of its consequences, and with the full authority of the sovereign government in question.[8] What amounted to an implied waiver depended on all the circumstances of the case, and the courts showed themselves extremely reluctant to infer a waiver of immunity. Thus it was held that the following acts did not amount to a submission to jurisdiction:

a. A submission to arbitration proceedings preceding action, or even a subsequent application to set aside these proceedings.[9]
b. Living in the jurisdiction and entering into contracts there.[10]
c. Seizure by the agents of a foreign state of a vessel within the jurisdiction.[11]
d. A clause in a contract,[12] to which the foreign sovereign was party, whereby it was agreed that the sovereign would submit to the jurisdiction of the territorial courts in matters arising out of the contract.

Nothing short of an undertaking given in face of the court at the time when the court was asked to exercise jurisdiction would suffice as a submission to jurisdiction.[12]

In this connection may be considered the matter of *set-offs* or *counter-claims* against a state which had begun suit in the courts of the territorial state. The principle was that a foreign state suing as aforesaid submitted itself to the ordinary incidents of the suit, so that, for instance, a defendant might set up a set-off or counter-claim arising out of the same matter in dispute, but not an independent and unrelated cross-claim, the test being whether the cross-claim was sufficiently connected with or allied to the subject-matter of the foreign state's claim as to make it necessary in the interests of justice that it should be disposed of along with that claim.[13] The justification of this principle was that if a foreign

6. *Mellenger v New Brunswick Development Corpn* [1971] 2 All ER 593 at 596.
7. *Mighell v Sultan of Johore* [1894] 1 QB 149.
8. See *Baccus SRL v Servicio Nacional del Trigo* [1957] 1 QB 438, [1956] 3 All ER 715.
9. *Duff Development Co v Kelantan Government* [1924] AC 797.
10. *Mighell v Sultan of Johore* [1984] 1 QB 149.
11. *Compania Naviera Vascongado v SS Cristina* [1938] AC 485. Yet a foreign sovereign who waived jurisdiction by instituting proceedings, was not immune from jurisdiction in respect of a continuation of such proceedings (see *Sultan of Johore v Abubakar Tunku Aris Bendahar* [1952] AC 318, [1952] 1 All ER 1261).
12. *Kahan v Pakistan Federation* [1951] 2 KB 1003, especially at 1016. Contrast art 2 (b) of the European Convention on State Immunity of May 1972.
13. See *High Comr for India v Ghosh* [1960] 1 QB 134, [1959] 3 All ER 659 (claim substantially for money lent; counterclaim for slander held inadmissible). Cf art 32, para 3 of the Vienna Convention on Diplomatic Relations of 18 April 1961, and art 1, para 2(a) of the European Convention on State Immunity of 24 May 1972.

state or foreign sovereign voluntarily chose to litigate, it has to abide by all the rules like any other litigant and ultimately take all the consequences of its decision to sue. The decisive test was, in effect, whether there had been on the part of the plaintiff state a definitive election to submit, for all purposes, to the court in which the suit was instituted. These principles applied mutatis mutandis to proceedings by diplomatic representatives and consuls (see below, and cf also article 32, paragraph 3 of the Vienna Convention on Diplomatic Relations of 18 April 1961).

Statutory and other developments in sovereign immunity

It is apparent from the analysis, above, of the English case law prior to the 1970s that for all practical purposes the United Kingdom was a country adhering to the 'absolute' doctrine of immunity, by contrast with a number of states which followed the 'restrictive' doctrine in this area (see above).

Consistently with developments in the 1970s, the position in the United Kingdom is now governed by the provisions of the State Immunity Act 1978, considered below in this chapter,[14] and which have served to alter radically in a number of respects the former 'absolute' doctrine applied by English courts. The passing of the Act had been preceded by a number of developments, even before the 1970s, that paved the way for the statutory erosion of the 'absolute' doctrine. Some, if not all, of these may be briefly mentioned. One early significant development was the notable 'Tate letter' sent in May 1952 by the Acting Legal Adviser to the United States Department of State (Mr Jack Tate) to the Acting United States Attorney-General (Mr Philip Perlman), containing, inter alia, a declaration that, having regard to the small support for the absolute doctrine of immunity, it would thereafter be the policy of the Department of State to follow the restrictive theory in the consideration of requests by foreign governments for the grant of sovereign immunity. The letter accordingly rejected the doctrine of absolute immunity.

Subsequently, in *Rahimtoola v Nizam of Hyderabad*,[15] Lord Denning indicated his opposition to the granting of immunity to foreign governments in respect of commercial transactions. In May 1972 the European Convention on State Immunity and Additional Protocol were adopted at Basle, and opened for signature; this was, of course, a purely regional convention. To a significant extent, it gave effect to a concept of 'relative' immunity as distinct from that of 'restrictive' immunity; thus, it enumerated a list of cases and situations in which jurisdictional immunity could not be claimed (see articles 1–14), while upholding as a basic precept that, otherwise, there should be absolute jurisdictional immunity for sovereign states and governments. In 1976, the Foreign Sovereign Immunities Act of 1976 was passed in the United States, following years of work on the subject of sovereign immunity by the Department of State and the Department of Justice.[16] This was a complex piece of legislation, one of the aims of which was to establish in statutory form principles of restrictive immunity, by way of exception to those of absolute immunity. Inter alia, foreign states were not to be immune from the jurisdiction of United States courts in any case in

14. See pp 197-199.
15. [1958] AC 379 at 422, [1957] 3 All ER 441 at 463.
16. As to this Act, see Buergenthal and Mair *Public International Law* (1985) pp 216 et seq.

which the relevant proceedings were based upon a commercial activity carried on in the United States by the foreign state in question, or based upon an act performed in the United States in connection with a commercial activity of that foreign state elsewhere, or based upon an act performed outside the United States territory in connection with a commercial activity of the foreign state elsewhere and that act caused a direct effect in the United States.

Following the enactment of the United States statute, there were two decisions of English courts in which the question of the applicability of the restrictive immunity doctrine was raised, namely *The Philippine Admiral (Owners) v Wallem Shipping (Hong Kong)Ltd*[17] and *Trendtex Trading Corpn v Central Bank of Nigeria.*[18] In the former case, the Judicial Committee of the Privy Council held in effect that a foreign state could not claim absolute immunity from jurisdiction when an action in rem was brought against a vessel, if that vessel was being put to commercial use by either the government of that state or a third party. In the latter case, the Court of Appeal held that the Central Bank established by Nigeria was not a government department, but a legal 'entity' of its own right, and therefore not entitled to jurisdictional immunity; but beyond this point, two members of the court, Lord Denning and Shaw LJ were prepared to hold that even if the Bank had been a government department, it would not have been entitled to immunity in proceedings in personam, because the letter of credit on which the plaintiff had sued the Bank was a commercial document. Lord Denning formulated obiter the principle that a foreign sovereign had no immunity when it entered into a commercial transaction with a trader in the United Kingdom and a dispute arose which *otherwise* was properly within the territorial jurisdiction of English courts.[19]

In 1978, as mentioned above, the State Immunity Act of the United Kingdom was passed. In a manner similar to that followed in the above-mentioned European Convention of 1972 on State Immunity, this Act reaffirmed essentially the general principle of absolute jurisdictional immunity of foreign states and governments, while listing in detail and with some elaborateness the statutory exceptions to the granting of immunity by British courts. The Act did not therefore necessarily supersede the principles laid down by previous British case law concerning the scope of operation of the doctrine of absolute immunity where it continued to apply by reason of the provisions of the Act, and where such operation was otherwise unaffected by the Act. It is beyond the scope of a book on international law to deal in detail with what is primarily a piece of domestic legislation, albeit the provisions thereof are largely in harmony with those of the European Convention of 1972 on State Immunity. Nevertheless, brief reference should be made to a number of significant points. First, British courts are required to give effect ex proprio motu to the absolute immunity of a foreign state, if such immunity is unaffected by provisions otherwise in the Act, even although the foreign state itself does not appear in the relevant proceedings (see section 1(2)). Second, there is no immunity if the state submits to the jurisdiction

---

17. [1977] AC 373, [1976] 1 All ER 78.
18. [1977] QB 529, [1977] 1 All ER 881.
19. On the point whether a matter, involving questions of sovereign immunity, is within the territorial jurisdiction, see the judgment of Lord Denning in *Thai-Europa Tapioca Service Ltd v Government of Pakistan* [1975] 3 All ER 961.

of British courts, ie if it waives immunity (see section 2(1)). Third, immunity is inapplicable in the case of, inter alia, proceedings in respect of the following:

a.   A commercial transaction as defined elaborately in subsection (3) of section 3.[20]

b.   An obligation of a foreign state falling to be performed wholly or partly in the United Kingdom.

c.   A contract of employment between the state and an individual where the contract was made in the United Kingdom or the work is wholly or partly performed there.

d.   Death or personal injury, or damage to or loss of property caused by an act or omission in the United Kingdom.

e.   Any interest of the state in, or its possession or use of, immovable property in the United Kingdom (section 6(1) (a)).

f.   Any obligation of the state arising out of its interest in, or its possession or use of property in the United Kingdom[1] (section 6 (1) (b)).

g.   Any patent, trade mark, design or plant breeders' rights belonging to the state and registered or protected in the United Kingdom, an alleged infringement by the foreign state in the United Kingdom of any patent, trade mark, design, plant breeders' rights or copyright, or the right to use a trade or business name in the United Kingdom.

h.   The foreign state's membership of a body corporate, an unincorporated body or a partnership which has members other than states, and is incorporated or constituted under the law of the United Kingdom or is controlled from or has its principal place of business in the United Kingdom.

i.   The foreign state's liability for value added tax, any customs or excise duty, any agricultural levy, or rates in respect of premises occupied by it for commercial purposes.

Apart from these points, special reference should be made to certain other provisions of the Act. Under section 9, where a state has agreed in writing to submit a dispute, which has arisen or may arise, to arbitration, the foreign state is not immune as respects proceedings in British courts that relate to the arbitration; this provision is to have effect subject to any contrary provision in the arbitration agreement, and does not apply to any arbitration agreement between states. Section 14 is of importance, particularly to the extent that it alters the prior law as to separate, non-governmental 'entities';[2] the section provides that the relevant immunities and privileges apply to any foreign or

20. In the light of this definition, it may still be necessary in some instances to determine whether the relevant transaction is one jure gestionis or jure imperii. Semble, there would appear to be a presumption that a transaction which is, in the first instance, 'commercial' within the meaning of s 3 of the State Immunity Act 1978, does not necessarily lose that character vis-à-vis the parties dealing initially with the foreign state by reason of subsequent political or governmental action by that state; cf *Playa Larga v I Congreso del Partido* [1983] 1 AC 244, [1981] 2 All ER 1064, HL. As to the garnishee orders on a foreign government's London bank account, see *Alcom Ltd v Republic of Colombia* [1984] AC 580, [1984] 2 All ER 6, HL.

1.   This would apply to the case of premises used as a private dwelling, and not part of the actual legation, where the proceedings are for damages for breaches of covenant in respect to the occupation of the premises; see *Intpro Properties (UK) Ltd v Sauvel* [1983] QB 1016, [1983] 2 All ER 495, CA.

2.   See p 194 above.

Commonwealth State, to the sovereign or other head of state in his public capacity, the government of that state, and any department of that government, but any entity which is distinct from the executive organs of the state and capable of suing or being sued (ie a separate entity) is jurisdictionally immune if, and only if, the relevant proceedings against it relate to anything done by it in the exercise of sovereign authority, and the circumstances are such that a state would have been so immune.

Section 10 of the Act, dealing, inter alia, with Admiralty proceedings and actions in rem against ships, will be considered below in connection with the jurisdictional immunity of state-owned commercial ships.[3]

It should be added finally that the examples of the United States and of the United Kingdom in enacting sovereign immunity legislation have been followed by other countries (eg, Canada, with the State Immunity Act 1981 and Australia with the Foreign States Immunities Act 1985).

b. Diplomatic representatives and consuls, of foreign states
The jurisdictional immunities of diplomatic agents are set out in articles 31–32 of the Vienna Convention on Diplomatic Relations of 18 April 1961.[4] They enjoy absolute immunity from the criminal jurisdiction of the receiving state, and immunity from its civil and administrative jurisdiction[5] except in three special cases specified in article 31, namely:

a. Actions for recovery of purely private immovable property.
b. Actions relating to succession in which they are involved in a purely private capacity.
c. Actions relating to any private, professional or commercial activity exercised by them.

In Great Britain, the immunity of diplomatic envoys rests partly on the common law, embodying the approved rules of customary international law, and partly on statutes, namely, the Diplomatic Privileges Act 1708, the International Organisations (Immunities and Privileges) Act 1950, the Diplomatic Immunities (Commonwealth Countries and Republic of Ireland) Act 1952, dealing with the privileges of High Commissioners from the Commonwealth and of the Ambassador of Ireland, and their staffs and families, the Diplomatic Immunities Restriction Act 1955[6] the Diplomatic Immunities (Conferences with Commonwealth Countries and Republic of Ireland) Act 1961, the Diplomatic Privileges Act 1964,[7] replacing the previous common law and statutory law, and

---

3. See pp 205-207 below.
4. Under art 29, the person of a diplomatic agent is inviolable, and he is not liable to any form of arrest or detention.
5. A person who acquires diplomatic status after proceedings have been instituted against him, becomes entitled to immunity, notwithstanding that he has previously taken steps in the action; see *Ghosh v D'Rozario* [1963] 1 QB 106, [1962] 2 All ER 640.
6. See p 202 below.
7. S 4 of the Act provides: 'If in any proceedings any question arises whether or not any person is entitled to any privilege or immunity under this Act a certificate issued by or under the authority of the Secretary of State stating *any fact* relating to that question shall be conclusive of that fact'; cf the reliance on such a certificate in *Empson v Smith* [1966] 1 QB 426, [1965] 2 All ER 881.

the Diplomatic and Other Privileges Act 1971. Under the 1708 Act, which has always been regarded as merely declaratory of the common law, all writs whereby the person of an ambassador might be arrested or his goods seized, were null and void. The 1950 Act, replacing prior statutory provisions, extended the privileges of immunity from diplomatic representatives proper to a wider class, including officers of approved international organisations, members of organisations or Committees thereof, and persons on special missions relating thereto. The 1964 Act was passed to give effect to the provisions of the Vienna Convention of 1961, above, and so to underpin ratification of the Convention.

This immunity of diplomatic envoys extends not merely to their own persons, but to their suite, and members of their family forming part of their household, provided that they are not nationals of the receiving state (see article 37 of the Vienna Convention).[8] Usually, the practice in most countries is to deposit periodically with the Foreign Office or similar government department a list of personnel for whom exemption from the territorial jurisdiction is claimed. In this list will be found the names of first, second, and third secretaries, counsellors, attachés, etc.[9]

In Great Britain, statements of the Foreign Office as to the diplomatic status of a particular person are accepted as conclusive by British courts in the same way as with foreign states and foreign sovereigns.[10] This was emphatically laid down by the House of Lords in the leading case of *Engelke v Musmann*.[11]

The immunity from jurisdiction is subject to waiver, which must be express (see article 32, paragraph 2 of the Vienna Convention). If the person claiming privilege is of lesser rank than the head of the legation, the waiver must be made by or on behalf of the superior envoy or his government, and must be made with full knowledge of the circumstances and of that person's rights; a waiver merely by a solicitor as such for that person is insufficient.[12] British courts usually insist on strict proof of waiver.

If the Ambassador or other head of mission waives the privilege of a subordinate diplomatic official, then that privilege ceases irrespective of the desire of that official to retain his or her immunity.[13]

A waiver of immunity from jurisdiction does not imply waiver of immunity in respect of the execution of the judgment, for which a separate waiver is necessary (see article 32, paragraph 4 of the Vienna Convention).

8. For the special conditions governing the immunity of administrative and technical staff, and members of their families, members of the service staff, and private servants of members of the mission, see paras 2–4 of art 37 of the Vienna Convention. See also *Re C (an infant)* [1959] Ch 363, [1958] 2 All ER 656 (a son of a diplomatic agent, ordinarily resident with him, cannot be made a ward of court without the latter's consent).
9. The mere possession of a diplomatic passport or visa, without actual membership of a diplomatic mission accredited to the territorial or any other state, is insufficient to confer immunity; see *United States v Coplon and Gubitchev* 88 F Supp 915 (1950), and *United States v Melekh* 190 F Supp 67 (1960) (United Nations employee with Soviet diplomatic passport). Cf *United States v Kostadinov* 734 F 2d 905 (1984). The publication of lists is provided for, in respect of persons covered by the International Organisations (Immunities and Privileges) Act 1950, by s 2 of that Act.
10. See Chapter 6 above, at pp 135-137. Cf *United States v Lumumba* 741 F 2d 12 (1984).
11. [1928] AC 433.
12. See *R v Madan* [1961] 2 QB 1, [1961] 1 All ER 588.
13. *R v AB* [1941] 1 KB 454, and see Diplomatic Privileges Act 1964, Sch 1, art 32.

When the mission terminates, immunity continues for a reasonable time to enable envoys to leave the receiving country, and in any event, as to acts performed by them in the exercise of their functions (see article 39, paragraph 2 of the Vienna Convention). This extension of the period of immunity does not apply to a diplomatic agent who has been dismissed, and whose immunity has been waived by the Ambassador or head of the mission.[14]

The principle on which the jurisdictional immunity of diplomatic envoys is based is that they should be free to perform official business on behalf of their country, without disturbance, interference, or interruption.[15] This principle applies so as to cast a shield of inviolability over the legation premises, all property owned by the legation, and means of transport (see article 22 of the Vienna Convention). Even if diplomatic premises are misused for such purposes as detaining persons, storing arms or narcotics, of even firing from the premises[16], the remedy of the receiving state lies only in isolating the premises, cutting off communications to them, and expulsion of the mission's staff, not in forcible entry.

Although not explicitly provided in the Vienna Convention, it is accepted that authorities of the receiving state may, in exceptional cases, temporarily arrest or restrain a diplomatic agent found in the act of committing a serious offence, especially an offence endangering public safety (such as drunken driving). Thereafter the diplomatic agent must be released as soon as possible. In serious cases the agent will then be declared persona non grata by the receiving state and required to leave. The latter is the standard procedure in the case of suspected espionage by a diplomatic agent.

If a diplomatic envoy passes through or is in the territory of a third state which has granted him a passport visa, if such visa was necessary, while proceeding to take up or to return to his post, or when returning to his own country, the third state must accord him inviolability and such other immunities as may be required to ensure his transit or return (article 40, paragraph 1 of the Vienna Convention).

Immunity from jurisdiction should not be confused with immunity from liability, for once the exemption from jurisdiction is effectively waived, liability may arise. The immunity, if any, is from suit, not from liability. The comments of Lord Hewart CJ in the case of *Dickinson v Del Solar*[17] are in point:

'. . . Diplomatic agents are not, in virtue of their privileges as such immune from legal liability for any wrongful act. The accurate statement is that they are not liable to be sued in the English Courts unless they submit to the jurisdiction. *Diplomatic privilege does not import immunity from legal liability, but only exemption from local jurisdiction.*'

---

14. *R v AB* [1941] 1 KB 454.
15. See *Engelke v Musmann* above, at 449–450. This is the so-called *functional* conception of immunity of diplomatic envoys. Cf the judgments of the International Court of Justice in the cases of *United States Diplomatic and Consular Staff in Tehran* ICJ 1979, 7 and ICJ 1980, 3.
16. Eg the Libyan Bureau incident in London in 1984 where shots were fired from the embassy premises at demonstrators outside, killing a policewoman: note in (1984) 55 BYIL 459, 471-472.
17. [1930] 1 KB 376 at 380. See to the same effect the judgment of Diplock LJ in *Empson v Smith* [1966] 1 QB 426, [1965] 2 All ER 881.

The new international organisations established during and immediately after the Second World War brought into being a class of international officials, such as the members of the Secretariat of the United Nations Organisation, and of delegates to meetings of international organs, whose duties and functions clearly required immunity from local jurisdiction of a similar kind to that enjoyed by diplomatic representatives of foreign states.

Accordingly, legislation was enacted both in the United States and in Great Britain to extend immunity to these persons, as well as to the international organisations of which they were members.[18] In Great Britain, this was effected by the above-mentioned International Organisations (Immunities and Privileges) Act 1950,[19] replacing earlier enactments, and the various Orders-in-Council pursuant to the Act, while in the United States there was passed the Federal International Organisations Immunities Act of 1945. The detailed provisions of the two Acts lie beyond the scope of this book, but in general it can be said that their effect is not as wide as is suggested by their titles. A limited but reasonably liberal immunity is conferred on international officials and delegates to international organs, which may, as in the case of diplomatic representatives, be waived by higher authority.[20] The extent of the immunity, where it exists, varies with the grade or category to which the particular official or delegate belongs. Also, as with diplomatic envoys, the immunity is one not from legal liability but from jurisdiction.

Finally, it should be emphasised that the immunity of diplomatic envoys is applicable in respect of acts in their private, as well as in their official capacity. Such immunity for private acts has not been conceded to all classes of international officials under the British and American legislation just referred to. In this connection, there was a novel enactment in Great Britain, the Diplomatic Immunities Restriction Act 1955, providing for the withdrawal by Order-in-Council of the immunity for private acts of foreign diplomatic envoys, their servants and staff, where British envoys are not accorded the same degree of immunity for private acts by the accrediting foreign states concerned.

Consuls

Consuls are not diplomatic agents, and in respect of private acts, are not immune from local jurisdiction, except where this has been specially granted by treaty. But apart from treaty provisions, as to official acts[1] within the limits of consular powers under international law, they are exempt from the jurisdiction of judicial or administrative authorities of the receiving state, unless the immunity is waived by the sending state. The rules applicable to the waiver of the immunity of diplomatic envoys apply mutatis mutandis. The justification of this limited consular immunity is that consuls are received by the country where they reside as officers of a foreign state charged with the performance of consular duties,

---

18. See also Ch 20 below, pp 558-561.
19. Other examples of enactments of this kind are the European Coal and Steel Community Act 1955, and the Geneva Conventions Act 1955.
20. Cf *The Ranollo Case* 67 NYS 2d 31 (1946), where the Secretary-General of the United Nations did not press the immunity of his chauffeur.
1. See *Waltier v Thomson* 189 F Supp 319 (1960) (consular immigration officer immune from suit for allegedly false representations concerning prospects for immigrants).

and to carry out these duties properly they obviously require immunity from local process.

Consuls who are at the same time diplomatic representatives of their states, are entitled to general immunity even in respect of private matters.[2]

The subject of consular immunities is now dealt with in detail in the Vienna Convention on Consular Relations, signed on 24 April 1963,[3] and is covered by legislation enacted subsequent to the Vienna Convention, such as the Consular Relations Act 1968 in the United Kingdom.

c. Public ships of foreign states

Warships and public vessels of foreign states, while in the ports or internal waters of another state, are in a great measure exempt from the territorial jurisdiction. For this purpose, a private vessel chartered by a state for public purposes, for example, the transport of troops, or transport of war materials, is a public vessel. Proof of character as warships or as public vessels is supplied by the ship's flag in conjunction with the ship's documents, for example, the commission issued and signed by the authorities of the state to which she belongs. Under article 29 of the United Nations Convention on the Law of the Sea of 10 December 1982, a 'warship' is defined as 'a ship belonging to the armed forces of a state bearing the external marks distinguishing ships of its nationality, under the command of an officer duly commissioned by the government of the state and whose name appears in the appropriate service list or its equivalent, and manned by a crew which is under regular armed force discipline'.

There are two theories as to jurisdiction in the case of public ships of a foreign state:

a. The 'floating island' theory according to which a public ship is to be treated by other states as part of the territory of the state to which she belongs. By this theory, the jurisdiction of the territorial court is excluded for all purposes where any act is done, or an offending party is found on board the ship.

b. The territorial court accords to the ship and its crew and contents certain immunities depending not on an objective theory that the public ship is foreign public territory, but on an implication of exemption granted by the local territorial law. These immunities conceded by local law are conditional and can in turn be waived by the state to which the public ship belongs.

In *Chung Chi Cheung v R*,[4] a case of a crime committed on board a Chinese public vessel in the territorial waters of Hong Kong (which was British territory), the Judicial Committee of the Privy Council rejected the former and approved the latter theory. On the particular facts of the case, it held that the Chinese Government had waived immunity, and that the Hong Kong Court had jurisdiction. It pointed out that theory (b) alone was consistent with the

---

2. See *Parkinson v Potter* (1885) 16 QBD 152; *Engelke v Musmann* [1928] AC 433, and *Afghan Minister (Consular Activities) Case* (1932) Annual Digest of Public International Law Cases 1931–1932, p 328. A consul who later acquires diplomatic status is immune from process as to acts outside the scope of his duties, committed while he was consul, so long as he retains his new status; see *Arcaya v Paez* 145 F Supp 464 (1956).
3. See pp 390-392 below.
4. [1939] AC 160.

paramount necessity for each nation to protect itself from internal disorder by trying and punishing offenders within its boundaries. In support of its views, it cited the classical judgment of Marshall CJ, of the United States Supreme Court, in *Schooner Exchange v M'Faddon*,[5] where the immunity of public vessels was based on an 'implied licence' to enter a port, the licence containing an exemption from the jurisdiction of the state which granted the rights of hospitality.

Where a public vessel is in port, no legal proceedings will lie against it, either in rem for recovery of possession, or for damages for collision or in respect of members of its crew. But the jurisdictional immunity extends only so far as necessary to enable such public vessel to function efficiently as an organ of the state and for state purposes.

> 'The foreign Sovereign could not be supposed to send his vessel abroad if its internal affairs were to be interfered with, and members of the crew withdrawn from its service, by local jurisdiction.'[6]

Therefore such vessel is bound to observe the ordinary laws of the port such as quarantine and sanitary regulations, and not to assist in breaches of local revenue laws. Any failure to respect these laws and regulations would be a ground for diplomatic representations, and possibly for expulsion, while the coastal state would be legitimately justified in requiring the vessel to leave the port.

Crimes committed on board the vessel while in port, except against a local subject, remain within the exclusive jurisdiction of the authorities of the vessel's flag state, including the commander of the vessel itself. Furthermore, some authorities maintain that individuals who do not belong to the crew, and who, after committing a crime on shore, board the vessel in order to take refuge, cannot be arrested by the local authorities and removed from the vessel if consent to this course is refused by the commander of the ship. Where such consent is refused, the local authorities have their remedy through the diplomatic channel against the government of the flag state. On the other hand, most authorities[7] have expressed the view that such fugitive criminals should be given up to the local police. Possibly, asylum may be granted on grounds of humanity, in cases of extreme danger to the individual seeking it. If members of the crew break the local laws while ashore, they are not protected, although normally the local police would hand them over to the ship's authorities for punishment or other action, if the offence is not serious or local interests are not greatly affected.

So far as concerns the innocent passage of a warship through the territorial sea (maritime belt), article 30 of the United Nations Convention on the Law of the Sea of 10 December 1982, provides that if any warship does not comply with the laws and regulations of the coastal state concerning such passage and disregards any request made to it for compliance therewith, the coastal state may require it to leave the territorial sea immediately. Moreover, under article 31 of the Convention, the flag state is to bear international responsibility for any loss or damage to the coastal state resulting from the non-compliance by a warship or other government vessel operated for non-commercial purposes with such

5. (1812) 7 Cranch 116.
6. *Chung Chi Cheung v R* [1939] AC 160 at 176.
7. Eg, Colombos *International Law of the Sea* (1967) 277-278; US Navy Regulations, 1973, art 0940.

laws and regulations, or with the provisions of the Convention, or other rules of international law.

State-owned commercial ships

For some time, foreign governments have embarked in trade with ordinary ships, and have been competing with shippers and ship-owners in the world's markets. The question has therefore arisen whether the ordinary principles as to immunity of public vessels should apply to such ships, and this has involved much the same considerations as touch the issue of the jurisdictional immunity of foreign states or foreign heads of state (see above in this chapter). The argument for the affirmative has been based on the government ownership of these vessels, and on the risk of 'impleading' a foreign state when exercising jurisdiction in respect of the ship. It has also been put that through trade conducted by way of shipping the 'maintenance and advancement of the economic welfare of a people in time of peace' is no less a public purpose than the maintenance and training of a naval force.[8]

On the other hand, severe criticism has been levelled at the immunity of public trading vessels. The objections to the concession of immunity were two principally:

1. The doctrine of the immunity of the property of foreign sovereigns is a concession to the dignity, equality, and independence of foreign sovereign powers and arises by virtue of the comity of nations. But it is not consistent with the dignity of sovereign states that they should enter the competitive markets of foreign commerce, and ratione cessante, the privilege of immunity should be withheld.
2. There is injustice to nationals of the territorial state when a foreign government may sue these nationals for matters arising out of its commerce by way of shipping, while at the same time enjoying absolute immunity should actions in rem or in personam be brought against it.

It has been said in answer to these objections that the remedy to a person injured is by diplomatic representations through his or her government. Lord Maugham's observations, made more than fifty years ago, on the uncertain value of diplomatic redress have continued to represent a trenchant but justifiable commentary on this argument:[9]

> 'In these days and in the present state of the world, diplomatic representations made to a good many States afford a very uncertain remedy to the unfortunate persons who may have been injured by the foreign government.'

As mentioned earlier in this chapter, with reference to the jurisdictional immunity of foreign states and foreign heads of state, there have been developments since 1972 paving the way for the restriction of the doctrine of absolute immunity in cases where states engage in commercial or non-governmental activities, and the proceedings are otherwise within the scope of the local territorial jurisdiction. What has been said in that connection is applicable mutatis mutandis to public ships of foreign states operated for

8. *The Pesaro* 271 US 562 (1926) at 574.
9. *Compania Naviera Vascongado v SS Cristina* [1938] AC 485 at 515.

commercial or non-governmental purposes. The developments referred to have included the European Convention of 1972 on State Immunity, the United States Foreign Sovereign Immunities Act of 1976, the decision of the Judicial Committee of the Privy Council in *The Philippine Admiral*,[10] and the dicta of two members of the English Court of Appeal in *Trendtex Trading Corpn v Central Bank of Nigeria*,[11] and the United Kingdom State Immunity Act 1978.

In this connection, it is also worthy of mention that under articles 27 and 28 of the United Nations Convention on the Law of the Sea of 10 December 1982, government ships operated for commercial purposes are not exempt from criminal and civil process by the coastal state if they are proceeding in passage through the territorial sea or are in course of such passage after leaving the internal waters of the coastal state. The extent to which the coastal state may exercise such criminal and civil process under these articles of the Convention is set out in Chapter 9, below.[12]

Apart from this, it is to be recalled that after the First World War, a number of international conferences discussed the subject of jurisdiction over commercial ships owned by foreign governments. There was an almost unanimous opinion that the same legal remedies and actions should apply as in the case of any other ship-owner. In April 1926, a large number of states, including Great Britain, signed at Brussels an International Convention for the Unification of Certain Rules concerning the Immunities of Government Vessels, as supplemented by a protocol of 1934. This Convention came into force in 1937, but was ratified or acceded to by only a small number of states. Its general effect was that ships and cargoes owned or operated by states were, in respect of claims relating to the operation of the ships or the carriage of cargoes, to be subject to the same rules of liability as privately-owned vessels. From these provisions, there were excepted ships of war, or government patrol vessels, hospital ships, and ships used exclusively on governmental and non-commercial service although even in regard to these, certain claims (for example, of salvage) were permissible. The International Law Commission has favoured the rules laid down in this Convention. Article 30 of the European Convention on State Immunity of May 1972, has provided that the Convention 'shall not apply to proceedings in respect of claims relating to the operation of seagoing vessels owned or operated by a Contracting State or to the carriage of cargoes and of passengers by such vessels or to the carriage of cargoes owned by a Contracting State and carried on board merchant vessels'. The United Kingdom ratified the Brussels Convention in 1979.

So far as concerns the position in the United Kingdom with respect to foreign government vessels operated commercially, that is now covered by section 10 of the State Immunity Act 1978, which section applies to Admiralty proceedings, and also proceedings on any claim which could be made the subject of Admiralty proceedings. It goes on to provide that a state is not immune as respects:

a.   an action in rem against a ship belonging to that state; or
b.   an action in personam for enforcing a claim in connection with such a ship, if at the time when the relevant cause of action arose, the ship was in use or intended for use for commercial purposes.

10. [1977] AC 373, [1976] 1 All ER 78.
11. [1977] QB 529, [1977] 1 All ER 881.
12. See pp 237-238 below.

Also, where an action in rem is brought against a ship belonging to a state for enforcing a claim in connection with another ship belonging to that state, the territorial courts will not have jurisdiction unless at the time when the cause of action relating to the other ship arose, both ships were in use or intended for use for commercial purposes. It is further provided that a state is not immune as respects:

a. an action in rem against a cargo belonging to that State, if both the cargo and the ship carrying it, were, at the time when the cause of action arose, in use or intended for use for commercial purposes; or

b. an action in personam for enforcing a claim in connection with cargo if the ship carrying it was then in use or intended for use as aforesaid.

The above-mentioned provisions are not to apply to proceedings where the foreign state concerned is a party to the Brussels Convention of 1926 and the claim relates to the operation of a ship owned or operated by that state, the carriage of cargo or passengers on any such ship or the carriage of cargo owned by that state on any other ship.

d. Foreign armed forces

Armed forces admitted to foreign territory enjoy a limited, but not an absolute, immunity from the territorial jurisdiction.

The extent of the immunity depends upon the circumstances in which the forces were admitted by the territorial sovereign, and in particular upon the absence or presence of any express agreement between the host and the sending state regulating the terms and conditions governing the entry of the forces in the territory.

In the absence of such an express agreement, the bare fact of *admission* of the forces produces certain generally recognised consequences of international law. The principle here applying was stated in classical terms by Marshall CJ of the United States Supreme Court in *Schooner Exchange v M'Faddon*[13] and were condensed by a very learned judge[14] into the following doctrine:

'A State which admits to its territory an armed force of a friendly foreign Power impliedly undertakes not to exercise any jurisdiction over the force collectively or its members individually which would be inconsistent with its continuing to exist as an efficient force available for the service of its sovereign.'

In other words, the principle is that the territorial or host state impliedly undertakes not to exercise any jurisdiction over members of the visiting force in such a way as to impair the integrity and efficiency of the force.[15]

Applying this principle, it follows that by implied grant or licence from the territorial state:

13. (1812) 7 Cranch 116. Note that in terms Marshall CJ's remarks were addressed to the *passage* of troops through foreign territory, and not to their sojourn.

14. Jordan CJ, of the New South Wales Supreme Court, in *Wright v Cantrell* (1943) 44 SRNSW 45 at 52–53.

15. Also, although normally entitled to exercise jurisdiction, the receiving State may, on the grounds of comity or courtesy, allow the authorities of the visiting force to deal with the alleged offenders; cf advice of Professor Yokota in connection with the arrest and prosecution of British naval ratings in Japan for robbery, London Times 9 October 1952.

1. The commander of the visiting force, and the courts of such force, have *exclusive* jurisdiction over offences committed by the members within the area in which the force is stationed, or in relation to matters of discipline, or over offences committed outside the stationing area, but while the members concerned were actually on duty.
2. The visiting force and its members are immune from the local jurisdiction, whether civil or criminal, in regard to matters of internal administration of the force, or necessarily involved in the performance by such force of its duties (for example, the bearing of arms, use of motor transport, etc). On the other hand, if the members of the force commit offences outside their area and while engaged on non-military duties, for example, recreation or pleasure, the territorial state may claim that they are subject to local law.

It follows further from the above principle that there is no complete waiver of jurisdiction by the territorial state when granting a licence or permission to an armed force to enter its territory; as one learned judge[16] has put it, 'the extent of the licence does not correspond with the extent of the waiver'.

Normally, the authorities or courts of the visiting force will, at least in matters of discipline or internal administration, be immune from the supervisory jurisdiction of the local courts by the exercise of the prerogative writs (for example, habeas corpus), unless perhaps there has been a clear case of exceeding their competence, such as a sentence passed upon a person who was not a member of the armed force.[17]

It is clear that opinions may differ as to how far immunity should be conceded to foreign visiting forces in order that military efficiency should be preserved. United States judicial pronouncements[18] and practice generally favour absolute immunity for this purpose; not so the British practice. Differences of opinion have indeed arisen with reference to the exercise of civil jurisdiction over members of a visiting force. In the case of *Wright v Cantrell*[19] an Australian court held as regards American forces on Australian territory for the purpose of the Pacific War, that the existence or efficiency of those forces would not be imperilled if an individual member were subject to a civil suit in the territorial courts for an injury caused to a local citizen even in the course of that member's duties.

The above principles apply if there is no express agreement between the state admitting and state sending the armed forces. If, however, there is such an agreement, then its terms will govern the jurisdiction of the courts; for example, if the admitting state agrees that the visiting forces shall be exempt from local jurisdiction in all civil and criminal matters, the courts are bound by the exemption so conceded.[20]

The exemption from jurisdiction is conceded only to visiting armed forces, and not a visiting band of persons without armed organisation and unconnected

---

16. *Chow Hung Ching v R* (1949) 77 CLR 449 at 463, per Latham CJ.
17. For an attempt to invoke this jurisdiction, see *Ex p Ortoli* (1942) 59 WNNSW 146. Cf also *Re Amand* [1941] 2 KB 239.
18. See, eg, *Tucker v Alexandroff* 183 US 424 (1901), and cf Canadian decision, *Reference Re Exemption of United States Forces from Canadian Criminal Law* [1943] 4 DLR 11.
19. (1943) 44 SRNSW 45.
20. See *Chow Hung Ching v R* (1949) 77 CLR 449, where it was so held by the High Court of Australia.

with military operations, although they may take orders from persons of military rank; nor is it to be conceded if the members of the visiting band mix freely with the local inhabitants and are not a body subject to proper military discipline and organisation.[1]

During the Second World War, Great Britain and other countries in the British Commonwealth enacted legislation conferring on certain (but not all) Allied forces within their territories, notably the United States forces, complete jurisdiction over the respective members of these forces and a correlative exemption from local criminal jurisdiction except where the visiting force waived its exclusive right of jurisdiction.[2]

In the post-war period, states have had to meet the impact of an important new development, the stationing of troops and of accessory civilian or depot personnel in foreign territory in pursuance of regional security arrangements such as the North Atlantic Security Pact of April 1949, or of international forces, including peacekeeping forces, under the United Nations Charter. A solution in this connection was adopted by the North Atlantic Powers in an Agreement signed in London on 19 June 1951, relative to the status of the forces of such Powers.[3] This provides that the sending and receiving states are to exercise concurrent jurisdiction over members of a visiting force of a North Atlantic Power and civilian component personnel, subject to:

a. exclusive jurisdiction being exercised by each State respectively in regard to offences which are punishable only by its laws;
b. the sending state having the primary right to exercise jurisdiction, in cases of concurrent jurisdiction, in relation to offences solely against the property or security of such sending state, or against the person or property of members of the force or civilian component personnel, or offences arising out of any act or omission in performance of official duty, with the receiving state entitled to the primary right to exercise jurisdiction as to other offences.

As to civil jurisdiction, no claim of immunity is to be pressed by the sending state except where members of the force act within the scope of their official duties. Other provisions in the Agreement enable review and modification of the subject of jurisdiction in the event of hostilities, and lay down certain minimum standards to be observed by the courts of the receiving state. This has been followed by a number of other status and stationing agreements, coupled with de facto practices and arrangements, sometimes not governed by any defined

1. See *Chow Hung Ching v R* above.
2. Jurisdiction was waived in 1944 by the American authorities in England in the celebrated case of *R v Hulten and Jones* (1945) Times, 20, 21 February.
3. This is discussed in an article by Rouse and Baldwin 51 AJIL (1957) 29–62. Somewhat similar principles have been followed in the stationing of forces agreements concluded by the Soviet Union; for texts, see 52 AJIL (1958) 210–227. Note also the Tokyo Agreement of 19 February 1954, regarding the Status of United Nations Forces in Japan. The subject of jurisdiction over armed forces stationed abroad is covered in three contributions in Vol 62 (1980) of the *U.S. Naval War College International Law Studies*, namely, Gordon B. Baldwin 'The International Law of the Armed Forces Abroad' (ibid, pp 667–675), Wilfred A. Hearn 'Status of Armed Forces Abroad' (ibid, pp 676–682), and Robert C. Grabb 'The Status of Armed Forces Abroad' (ibid, pp 683–689).

guidelines or sometimes not the subject of any uniform or consistent application. Most of these agreements or treaties are of a bilateral character.

The ultimate effect, however, may be to cut down the general principle that the sending state has exclusive jurisdiction over offences by servicemen within the limits of their quarters, or while on duty.[4]

e.   International institutions
International institutions such as the United Nations and the International Labour Organisation have been conceded immunity from the territorial jurisdiction both under international agreements (see the Conventions on the Privileges and Immunities of the United Nations and of the 'Specialised Agencies' adopted by the United Nations General Assembly in 1946 and 1947) and under municipal law (see, for example, the British International Organisations (Immunities and Privileges) Act 1950, and the United States Federal International Organisations Immunities Act of 1945).[5]

The subject of their general privileges and immunities is dealt with in Chapter 20 below.

3.   PERSONAL JURISDICTION

Personal, as distinct from territorial jurisdiction, depends on some quality attaching to the person involved in a particular legal situation which justifies a state or states in exercising jurisdiction in regard to that person. Practically, the jurisdiction is only employed when the persons concerned come within the power of the state, and process can be brought against them. This will occur generally when a person enters the territory of the state either voluntarily or as a result of successful extradition proceedings.

According to present international practice, personal jurisdiction may be exercised on the basis of one or other of the following principles:

(a)   Active nationality principle
Under this principle, jurisdiction is assumed by the state of which the person, against whom proceedings are taken, is a national. The active nationality principle is generally conceded by international law to all states desiring to apply it.[6] There is indeed a correlative principle of the law of extradition that no state is bound to extradite from its territory a national guilty of an offence committed abroad.

(b)   Passive nationality principle
Jurisdiction is assumed by the state of which the person suffering injury or civil damage is a national. International law recognises the passive nationality

---

4.   Nevertheless, the trend in the case of United Nations peacekeeping forces, of an international composition, is towards absolute immunity from the jurisdiction of the receiving state.

5.   Note also the various Headquarters Agreements concluded by the United Nations and the specialised agencies, referred to below, p 560.

6.   The active nationality principle has been extended 'notionally' in some instances to cover the foreign subsidiaries of a local principal corporation; see above in this chapter, at pp 188-189.

principle only subject to certain qualifications. Thus it would appear from the *Cutting Case*[7] that a state which does not admit the passive nationality principle is not bound to acquiesce in proceedings on this basis brought against one of its nationals by another state. The justification, if any, for exercising jurisdiction on this principle is that each state has a perfect right to protect its citizens abroad, and if the territorial state of the locus delicti neglects or is unable to punish the persons causing the injury, the state of which the victim is a national is entitled to do so if the persons responsible come within its power. But as against this, it may be urged that the general interests of a state are scarcely attacked 'merely because one of its nationals has been the victim of an offence in a foreign country'.[8] The passive nationality principle is embodied in several national criminal codes, in particular the codes of Mexico, Brazil, and Italy. Great Britian and the United States, however, have never explicitly admitted the propriety of the principle, but in the Diplomatic Security and Anti-Terrorism Act 1986, the United States claims jurisdiction over persons who kill US nationals abroad with the intention of coercing, intimidating, or retaliating against a government or people (whether that be the United States or not).

In the *Lotus Case*,[9] Judge J. B. Moore, an American judge on the Permanent Court of International Justice, declared that an article of the Turkish Penal Code whereby jurisdiction was asserted over aliens committing offences abroad 'to the prejudice' of a Turkish subject was contrary to international law, but it is not clear to what extent other members of the court shared or differed from this view.

4. JURISDICTION ACCORDING TO THE PROTECTIVE PRINCIPLE

International law recognises that each state may exercise jurisdiction over crimes against its security and integrity or its vital economic interests. Most criminal codes contain rules embodying in the national idiom the substance of this principle, which is generally known as the *protective* principle.

In *Joyce v DPP*,[10] the House of Lords seems to have held that the English common law recognises a principle of jurisdiction akin to the protective principle, namely that an alien owing some kind of allegiance to the Crown may be tried by British courts for the crime of treason committed abroad. Underlying the

7. See above, p 190.
8. See Report of Sub-Committee of League of Nations Committee of Experts for the Progressive Codification of International Law, *Criminal Competence of States etc* (1926) p 5.
9. See above, p 187.
10. [1946] AC 347. Cf American decision of *United States v Chandler* 72 F Supp 230 (1947). Also in *United States v Rodriquez* 182 F Supp 479 (1960), the protective principle was used to justify the prosecution of aliens for false statements in immigration applications, and in *Rocha v United States* 288 F 2d 545 (1961), the prosecution of defendants for being engaged in a 'war brides racket', ie conspiracy abroad to arrange sham marriages between aliens and American citizens, so as to gain preferential immigration status, thereby evading American immigration laws. See also *Stegeman v United States* 425 F 2d 984 (1970) (jurisdiction held to be exercisable in respect to debtors guilty of fraudulent concealment of assets abroad, in breach of the Federal Bankruptcy Act of the United States, upon the ground that the Act was designed to serve important interests of government, related to national commerce and credit).

House of Lords decision is the consideration that such a crime is one directly against the security and integrity of the realm, and its reasoning is applicable to other statutory offences of similar scope (for example, against the Official Secrets Acts).

The rational grounds for the exercise of this jurisdiction are two-fold:

i.   the offences subject to the application of the protective principle are such that their consequences may be of the utmost gravity and concern to the state against which they are directed;

ii. unless the jurisdiction were exercised, many such offences would escape punishment altogether because they did not contravene the law of the place where they were committed (lex loci delicti) or because extradition would be refused by reason of the political character of the offence.[11]

The serious objection to the protective principle is that each state presumes to be its own judge as to what endangers its security or its financial credit. Thus in many cases, the application of the protective principle tends to be quite arbitrary.

5. JURISDICTION ACCORDING TO THE UNIVERSAL PRINCIPLE: PIRACY

An offence subject to universal jurisdiction is one which comes under the jurisdiction of all states wherever it be committed. Inasmuch as by general admission, the offence is contrary to the interests of the international community, it is treated as a delict jure gentium and all states are entitled to apprehend and punish the offenders. Clearly the purpose of conceding universal jurisdiction is to ensure that no such offence goes unpunished.

There are probably today only two clear-cut cases of universal jurisdiction,[12] namely the crime of piracy jure gentium, and war crimes.[13] Other cases do not necessarily involve the exercise of universal jurisdiction by *all* states. All states are entitled to arrest pirates on the high seas, and to punish them irrespective of nationality, and of the place of commission of the crime. The subject of piracy is dealt with in Chapter 9, below. The principle of universality of punishment of war crimes was affirmed by the Geneva Conventions of 1949 relative to prisoners of war, protection of civilians, and sick and wounded personnel, as supplemented by the Protocols I and II adopted in 1977 by the Diplomatic Conference at Geneva on the Reaffirmation and Development of International Humanitarian Law Applicable in Armed Conflicts (see Chapter 18, below). In the *Eichmann Case* (1962),[14] the Supreme Court of Israel, sitting as a Court of

---

11. The principle of non-extradition for political crimes is now securely established; see pp 319-321 below.

12. The transport of slaves is not such a case; a state may prevent and punish the transport of slaves only in ships authorised to fly its flag, or prevent the unlawful use of its flag for that purpose (see article 13 of the Geneva Convention of 1958 on the High Seas, and article 99 of the United Nations Convention on the Law of the Sea, of 10 December 1982).

13. See pp 501-504

14. *Eichmann v A-G of Israel* (1962) 36 ILR 277 (judgment of court below reported in (1961) 36 ILR 5).

Appeal, relied in part upon the principle of universal jurisdiction in upholding the conviction by a court in Israel of Eichmann, a war criminal, for war crimes and crimes against humanity under an Israeli Law of 1951, thereby overruling objections that Eichmann's actions occurred in Europe during the Second World War before the state of Israel was actually founded, and that his offences were committed against people who were not citizens of that state.

Crimes or delicts jure gentium,[15] other than piracy and war crimes, raise somewhat different considerations. Thus the offences of drug trafficking, trafficking in women and children, and counterfeiting of currency have been brought within the scope of international conventions, but have been dealt with on the basis of *aut punire, aut dedere*, that is, the offenders are either to be punished by the state on whose territory they are found or to be surrendered (extradited) to the state which is competent and desirous of exercising jurisdiction over them.[16] This is so even with the international crime of genocide under the Genocide Convention of 1948 (see article VI, which provides for a trial by the courts of the state in the territory of which the crime was committed, or by an international tribunal, and hence not by the courts of all states). As for the provisions of the conventions considered below in section 6 of the present chapter, providing for international co-operation in the repression and punishment of certain crimes committed in or against aircraft, these may be said to have initiated a first phase in the process whereby such offences may ultimately be subject to universal jurisdiction, but the final point in such process is still far from being reached.

6. PROBLEMS OF JURISDICTION WITH REGARD TO AIRCRAFT[17]

One consequence of the increase in the volume, range, and frequency of the international air traffic, coupled with the growing number of countries in which the aircraft of regular airlines are registered, has been the emergence of difficult problems of jurisdiction in respect of offences committed on board aircraft in flight. If this were not enough, another development has been the grave menace to the safety and reliability of international civil aviation due to the multiplication of hijacking incidents, and of terrorist acts against aircraft about to take off or land, and against airline passengers.

The first major attempt to deal with these problems was made by the Tokyo Convention of 14 September 1963, on Offences and Certain Other Acts Committed on Board Aircraft. The main objects of the Convention were:

a.   to ensure that persons committing crimes aboard aircraft in flight, or on the surface of the high seas, or any area outside the territory of any country, or committing acts aboard such aircraft to the danger of air safety, would

---

15. As to which, see *Historical Survey of the Question of International Criminal Jurisdiction* (United Nations Secretariat, 1949) pp 1 et seq.
16. A recent example is that of article 8 of the International Convention against the Taking of Hostages, adopted by the United Nations General Assembly on 17 December 1979.
17. See generally on the subject Abramovsky (1974) 13 Columbia Journal of Transnational Law 381, and (1975) 14 Columbia Journal of Transnational Law 296.

not go unpunished simply because no country would assume jurisdiction to apprehend or try them;

b.   for protective and disciplinary purposes, to give special authority and powers to the aircraft commander, members of the crew, and even passengers.

Aircraft used in military, customs, or police services were excluded from the scope of the Convention. Normally, it is the subjacent state which exercises jurisdiction over offences committed in its airspace, but an over-flying aircraft may not have landed or been called upon to land, with the result that the subjacent authorities are deprived of the opportunity of taking police action, or the commission of the offence may not have been noticed until the aircraft reaches a destination outside the territory of the country in whose airspace the offence was committed. Object (a) was achieved principally by providing that the country of registration of the aircraft is competent to exercise jurisdiction over the offences and acts mentioned, and by obliging states parties to the Convention to take the necessary measures to establish their jurisdiction as the country of registration (see article 3). Coupled with this was the provision in article 16 that offences committed aboard an aircraft are for purposes of extradition to be treated as if they had occurred also in the territory of the country of registration; hence, if the offender takes refuge in a country which is party to the Convention and also party to an extradition treaty with the country of registration, making the alleged offence an extradition crime, the offender can be duly extradited. The convention did not exclude the criminal jurisdiction of countries which exercise this according to the active nationality principle or passive nationality principle.

The Convention contained detailed provisions giving effect to object (b), and enabling the aircraft commander to disembark an offender and deliver him, if necessary, to the competent authorities of a state party to the Convention. However, these provisions are not to apply in the airspace of the country of registration of the aircraft, and they apply to overflights across the high seas or territory outside the territory of any country only where:

i   the last point of take-off or next point of intended landing is situated in a country, not the country of registration; or

ii.   the aircraft subsequently flies into the airspace of a country not that of registration, with the offender still on board.

With regard to hijacking, it is fair to say that the Tokyo Convention made no frontal attack upon this offence, but dealt in only a limited manner with hijackers; for example, by enabling hijackers to be taken into custody or subjected to restraint in the same manner as other offenders, and by providing for restoration of control of the hijacked aircraft to the lawful commander, and for the continuance of the journey of passengers and crew.

A more ambitious, more elaborate effort to deal with hijacking was made in the Hague Convention for the Suppression of Unlawful Seizure of Aircraft, opened for signature on 16 December 1970. By this date, hijacking had assumed the proportions of a world-wide problem, which threatened to undermine international aviation. The Convention was confined to hijacking, leaving the matter of armed attacks, sabotage, and other forms of violent action directed against civil aviation and aviation facilities to be dealt with by a later diplomatic conference. The Convention did not fully apply the *aut punire, aut dedere* principle (ie the country where the offender might happen to be should prosecute him, or extradite him to a country having jurisdiction to try him for the offence), but provided a reasonably adequate framework for the exercise of jurisdiction, with obligations of extradition or rendition according to the existence of an extradition treaty or of a reciprocal practice of rendition.

The key provisions in the Convention are article 1, defining the offence of hijacking, although not calling it such, article 2, obliging each state party to make the offence punishable by severe penalties, and article 4, providing that states parties are to take measures to establish jurisdiction over the offence and related acts of violence against passengers or air crew. The offence is defined as unlawfully, by force or threat, or by any other form of intimidation, seizing or exercising control of an aircraft 'in flight', or attempting to commit such an act, or being the accomplice of any person performing or attempting to perform such an act. Under article 3, paragraph 1, an aircraft is considered to be 'in flight' at any time from the moment when all its external doors are closed following embarkation until the moment when any such door is opened for disembarkation. In the case of a forced landing—and experience has shown this may be an important point—the 'flight' is deemed to continue until the competent authorities take over responsibility for the aircraft and for persons and property on board. Under article 4 (see above), jurisdiction is to be established by contracting states in the following cases:

a. when the offence is committed on board an aircraft registered in the contracting state;
b. when the hijacked aircraft lands in a contracting state's territory with the alleged hijacker still on board;
c. when the offence is committed on board an aircraft leased without crew to a lessee who has his principal place of business in the contracting state, or—if no business—his permanent residence there.

The Convention applies only to civil aircraft, and not to aircraft used in military, customs, or police service, but it is immaterial whether the aircraft is engaged in an international or domestic flight. However, for general purposes, the Convention is only operative if the place of take-off, or the place of actual landing of the hijacked aircraft be situated outside the territory of the state in which the aircraft is registered. This restriction does not affect the far-reaching provisions in article 6 for taking custody of a hijacker or alleged hijacker present in a contracting state's territory, in article 7 for the obligatory prosecution of non-extradited alleged hijackers, in article 8 for the inclusion of hijacking as an extraditable offence in extradition treaties or the treatment of the offence as an extraditable one in the relations between states which surrender alleged offenders on a basis other than that of an extradition treaty, and in article 10 for mutual co-operation between states in relation to criminal proceedings against alleged hijackers, for these provisions in articles 6 to 10 are to apply whatever the place of take-off or the place of actual landing of the hijacked aircraft, if the hijacker or alleged hijacker is found in the territory of a state other than the state of registration of that aircraft.

The Hague Convention is not as stringent as it should be, and throughout reflects a compromise between different approaches to criminal law and to the rendition of offenders,[18] but its prompt conclusion, in the surrounding circumstances, did meet an urgent need.

The Hague Convention was supplemented nine months later by the Convention for the Suppression of Unlawful Acts against the Safety of Civil Aviation, concluded at Montreal on 23 September 1971. In the period 1968–1971 there had not only been hijackings, but the related aircraft crimes of armed attacks, sabotage, and other forms of violence and intimidation directed against civil aviation, including the appearance of bomb-hoax extortion as a new kind of menace undermining public confidence in the security of international air transport and prejudicing the administrative and financial conduct of air services. The objective of covering unlawful acts other than hijacking was reflected in article 1, the key article of the Montreal Convention, which was designed to cover those multiple forms of violence and intimidation which had occurred in the past as well as those which might emerge in the future. Because these aviation crimes might not necessarily be restricted to aircraft in flight, the draftsmen of the Montreal Convention were obliged to introduce the concept of an aircraft 'in service', in addition to that of an aircraft 'in flight', as in the Hague Convention. Instead of a single, comprehensive formula, article 1 enumerated as offences for the purposes of the Convention, five categories of unlawful acts:

a. acts of violence against a person on board an aircraft 'in flight', if that act is likely to endanger the safety of that aircraft;
b. destroying or causing damage to an aircraft 'in service' so as to render it incapable of flight, or which is likely to endanger its safety 'in flight';
c. placing or causing to be placed on an aircraft 'in service' any device or substance which is likely to have this effect;
d. the destruction or damage of air navigation facilities, or interference with their operation, if any such act is likely to endanger the safety of aircraft 'in flight';
e. the communication of information which is known to be false, thereby endangering the safety of an aircraft in flight, a category intended to cover bomb-hoax extortions.

As in the case of the Hague Convention, an aircraft is deemed to be 'in flight' at any time from the moment when all external doors are closed following embarkation until the moment when any such door is opened for disembarkation, or during the period of a forced landing pending the exercise of control by the authorities. 'In service' means the period from the beginning of the pre-flight preparation of the aircraft by ground personnel or by the crew for a specific flight until 24 hours after any landing.

So far as aircraft are concerned, the Montreal Convention applies only in the case of an 'international element', consisting of a place of take-off or landing, actual or intended, outside the territory of the state of registration, or if the offence committed against the aircraft is committed in a state other than the state

18. Cf Shubber 'Aircraft Hijacking under the Hague Convention 1970—A New Régime?' 22 ICLQ (1973) 714.

of registration. The Convention may apply if the alleged offender is found in the territory of a non-registration state.

Under other provisions of the Convention, countries parties to the Convention undertake to establish jurisdiction over certain categories of offences under the circumstances set out in article 5 (inter alia, if the offence is committed in the territory of that country, or against or on board an aircraft registered there); and they also bind themselves, in accordance with international law and national law, to take all practicable measures for the purpose of preventing the offences set out in article 1, and to co-operate with each other by communicating relevant information, and otherwise. Broadly speaking, the provisions of the Hague Convention regarding the taking into custody of alleged offenders, as to extradition and prosecution, and as to the reporting to the International Civil Aviation Organisation of offences and of action taken, are reproduced in the Montreal Convention; it was not found possible to adopt a more stringent, more far-reaching text.

It will be evident that the law of aviation crimes cannot under these Conventions of Tokyo, The Hague, and Montreal be efficacious in the absence of full co-operation between all states. Certain governments favour the provision of sanctions, or if not sanctions, means for bringing pressure to bear, where countries afford shelter to hijacked aircraft or are otherwise considered to be in breach of their obligations in that connection[19]. Moves and proposals to this effect have since 1971 been made or mooted at meetings within the framework of the International Civil Aviation Organisation and elsewhere. There are some almost insuperable obstacles to such moves and proposals bearing fruit in the shape of an international convention which will come into force with the necessary participation of a wide spread of countries. Alternatives to a multilateral convention or multilateral conventions are bilateral treaties, or domestic legislation enabling the suspension of flights to or from countries sheltering hijackers, or not co-operating in the prevention of aircraft crimes. Such treaties and such domestic legislation are not prohibited by international law.

19. Joint declarations of co-operation against hijacking and aircraft crimes were made in 1978 and 1988 at their summit meetings in West Germany, respectively, by the seven chief industrial powers, viz. the United States, the United Kingdom, Japan, Canada, the Federal Republic of Germany (West Germany), France and Italy. Thus, under the 1978 declaration, 'where a country refuses . . . the prosecution of those who have hijacked an aircraft' (emphasis added), immediate action was to be taken by those powers to cease all flights to that country, and to initiate action to halt all incoming flights therefrom. However, as was demonstrated, in particular in 1988, these measures apparently cannot be activated without the seven governments concerned being completely satisfied that the country to be subjected to these measures did in point of fact 'refuse' to prosecute the alleged hijacker or hijackers.

CHAPTER 9

The law of the sea and maritime highways

1. GENERAL AND HISTORICAL INTRODUCTION

No branch of international law has undergone more revolutionary changes during the past four decades, and especially during the immediate past decade and a half, than has the law of the sea and maritime highways. The final signature on 10 December 1982, at Montego Bay, Jamaica, by the great majority of the states represented at the Third United Nations Conference on the law of the Sea 1973–1982 (UNCLOS III) of a comprehensive code of rules of international law on the sea under the title, the United Nations Convention on the Law of the Sea, represented perhaps the most momentous development in the whole history of the rules of international law concerning the high seas. At this point, it need only be said that the greater part of the Convention, containing the more significant rules therein enunciated, however much the previous law was thereby changed, appear now to command the general consensus of the international community.[1]

This being said, it must be appreciated that one cannot just leap, without more discussion, into an analysis of this 1982 Convention as if it were self-explanatory of the present international law régime of the sea, the seabed, and maritime areas. To quote the eminent historian, Dr A. L. Rowse,[2] 'the bed out of which all the social sciences spring is history; there they find, in greater or lesser degree, subject-matter and material, verification or contradiction'. This observation applies with special force to the law of the sea. Leaving aside internal waters, such as, for example, ports, harbours, roadsteads and closed-in bays, it was historically the open sea or the high seas which primarily concerned statesmen and rulers of nations in the medieval and post-medieval periods, and writers on international law from the sixteenth century onwards. Initially, navigation on the high seas was open to everybody as were also fisheries, but in the fifteenth and sixteenth

---

1. The subject generally, including the impact of the 1982 Convention, is comprehensively covered in O'Connell *The International Law of the Sea* Vol I (ed I. A. Shearer, 1982) and Vol II (ed I. A. Shearer, 1984). For a shorter treatment see R. R. Churchill and A. V. Lowe *The Law of the Sea* (1983).
2. See his General Introduction to the Series, 'Teach Yourself History', in Christopher Hill *Lenin and the Russian Revolution* (1947) p v.

centuries—the periods of great maritime discovery by European navigators—claims were laid by the powerful maritime states to the exercise of sovereignty, indistinguishable from ownership, over specific portions of the open sea. For example, Portugal claimed maritime sovereignty over the whole of the Indian Ocean and a very great proportion of the Atlantic, Spain arrogated rights to herself over the Pacific and the Gulf of Mexico, and even Great Britain laid claim to the Narrow Seas and the North Sea.

Grotius was one of the first strenuously to attack these extensive claims to sovereignty. His objections were based predominantly upon two grounds:

1. No ocean can be the property of a nation because it is impossible for any nation effectively to take it into possession by occupation.
2. Nature does not give a right to anybody to appropriate things that may be used by everybody and are exhaustible — in other words, the open sea is a res gentium or res extra commercium.

In opposition to the principle of maritime sovereignty, the principle of the 'freedom of the high seas' (or 'freedom of the open sea') began to develop, in accordance with the mutual and obvious interests of the maritime nations. It was appreciated that too often, and to the great inconvenience of all states, conflicting claims were laid to the same parts of the open sea. Furthermore, it came to be realised that any claims to maritime sovereignty were of little practical value except in time of war when it was useless to assert them without the backing of a powerful navy. The freedom of the open sea was thus seen to correspond to the general interests of all states, particularly as regards freedom of intercourse between nations.

Perhaps, the more correct expression was 'freedoms', rather than 'freedom' of the high seas, because apart from the unrestricted liberties as to navigation and fisheries, the sea might be freely used for other purposes by all states, eg, scientific research. In more modern times, the freedoms came to include the 'freedom of immersion' (eg, the laying of submarine cables and of oil pipelines), and the free right of overflight for all aircraft. Nonetheless, these freedoms never warranted a state of unregulated maritime lawlessness, and certain rules for the exercise of jurisdiction over vessels at sea became essential in order to avoid conditions of anarchy.

Thus the concept of the freedom of the high seas was described as 'multiform and elusive', and as requiring the adaptation of old rules to new conditions, in the Memorandum presented by the United Nations Secretariat to the International Law Commission in 1950.[3] That the freedom of the high seas is a dynamic and not a static concept is of special contemporary importance when regard is had to the threat to the survival of whole species of marine life posed by unrestricted fishing on the high seas.

As a measure of necessary control, it was early established that all vessels, public or private, on the high seas were subject to the jurisdiction (in general, exclusive), and entitled to the protection, of the state under the maritime flag of

3. *Yearbook of the ILC*, 1950, ii. 67. The author of this Memorandum is known to have been the renowned French scholar Professor Gilbert Gidel, whose monumental work on the law of the sea, *Le Droit international de la mer*, was published in three volumes in 1932-1934.

which they might sail.[4] From this, there logically followed a number of corollary rules, namely, that in general no state might exercise jurisdiction over ships at sea not bearing its flag, that no ship might sail under a particular flag without proper authority from the flag state, nor under a flag other than the one which it was duly authorised to raise. Vessels sailing under an unauthorised flag were liable to capture and confiscation by the state whose flag had been wrongfully raised, and the warships of any state might call on suspicious vessels to show their flag.[5] If there was reasonable suspicion for suspecting that a vessel was engaged in piracy[6] or the slave trade,[7] it might be boarded, and, if necessary, searched.

It is necessary now to refer to the rights which came to be exercised by maritime states over a strip of waters immediately adjoining their coastlines, being such as was considered necessary to the safety of the state concerned, or which that state had power to dominate. This strip, named then more often as the 'maritime belt', and which has been universally known as the 'territorial sea' since its designation as such in the Geneva Convention of 1958 on the Territorial Sea and Contiguous Zone, was treated as being under the sovereignty of the coastal state, subject to a right of innocent passage by the vessels of other nations. By the beginning of the eighteenth century, this principle of the coastal state's sovereignty over the maritime belt had become completely established. It was indeed in 1702 that Bynkershoek[8] published his work, *De dominio maris dissertatio* (Essay on Sovereignty over the Sea), in which he adopted the rule that the littoral state could dominate only such width of coastal waters as lay within the range of cannon shot from shore batteries: *Terrae potestas ubi finitur armorum vis* (territorial sovereignty extends as far as the power of arms carries). Bynkershoek appears to have been the first notable jurist to enunciate the cannon shot rule in these terms, although there is historical evidence that the rule was already well-known and invoked in practice before the publication of his book. At a subsequent stage, an attempt was made to express the cannon shot range as a definite figure in nautical miles. It is controversial and far from clear when precisely, as a matter of history, this did occur. At all events the cannon shot rule became blended—some might say confused—with a three-mile limit, although it is possible that the three-mile limit had an independent historical origin. As will appear, the point is now purely academic.

In the nineteenth century, the three-mile limit received widespread recognition by the jurists, as well as by the courts,[9] and obtained adoption in the practice of important maritime states. This continued too in the twentieth century, with

4. For 'flag' purposes, the nationality of a vessel was determined by the state of registration. It was for each state to determine under its own law which ship had the right to fly its flag; see the *Muscat Dhows Case* (Permanent Court of Arbitration, 1905) UN Reports of International Arbitral Awards Vol IX, p 83.
5. A vessel, which was not sailing under the identifiable maritime flag of a state, was not entitled to protection, and might be seized in suspicious circumstances; see *Naim Molvan, Owner of Motor Vessel 'Asya' v A-G for Palestine* [1948] AC 351.
6. See pp 247-250 below.
7. See p 247 below.
8. See pp 11, 21 above.
9. Eg, by Lord Stowell in *The Anna* (1805) 5 Ch Rob 373.

two great maritime Powers, the United States and Great Britain, firm protagonists of the three-mile limit. Yet it failed to gain acceptance as a universal rule of international law. Numerous states adopted a wider breadth for the maritime belt, and as will be referred to later in the present chapter,[10] an increasing number of states became prompted to favour a limit as extensive as twelve miles, and even greater distances.

As a matter partly of customary international law and partly of certain conventions and treaties, maritime states acquired certain rights in regard to vessels not sailing under their flag. A major important right, initially of a customary nature, was the so-called right of 'hot pursuit', signifying that if the coastal state concerned had good reason to believe that a foreign ship had infringed its laws and regulations while passing through the maritime belt, that ship might be pursued and apprehended even on the high seas, provided:

a. such pursuit were commenced *immediately* while the alleged infringing vessel or its accessory boats were still within the coastal state's internal waters or maritime belt;
b. the pursuit was continuous and uninterrupted;[11]
c. a visual or auditory signal to stop had been given from such distance as to be seen or heard by the fugitive ship, ie a mere sighting would be insufficient; and
d. the pursuers were warships or other government ships specially authorised to that effect, although the craft making the arrest need not be actually the one which commenced the pursuit. Such right of hot pursuit ceased as soon as the vessel pursued entered the maritime belt of its own country, or of a third state.

Another more controversial right of the coastal state was that of the exercise of jurisdiction over foreign vessels outside the limits of the maritime belt where there was a grave suspicion that such vessels were a source of imminent danger to the sovereignty or security of the adjacent coastal state. This jurisdiction was permitted solely on the basis of, and as a measure of, self-protection.[12] The scope of this jurisdiction was at all times a debatable matter.[13]

The coastal state's sovereignty over the maritime belt itself was qualified to the extent that foreign vessels had a right of innocent passage through the waters of the belt.[14]

---

10. See pp 225 et seq below.
11. According to the standard work, Poulantzas *The Right of Hot Pursuit in International Law* (1969) p 43, the two most important elements of a valid hot pursuit are its conduct without interruption, and its immediate commencement.
12. See the case of the *Virginius*, Moore *Digest of International Law* Vol II, pp 895 et seq.
13. In more recent times enforcement action on the high seas has been taken against vessels suspected of carrying arms, narcotics, or illegal immigrants. In 1981 the United States concluded an agreement with Haiti whereby the latter permitted its flag vessels suspected of carrying illegal emigrants bound for the United States to be boarded and inspected by United States authorities. As to whether, in the case of refugees, this would constitute a refoulement see the decision of the Supreme Court of the United States in *Sale v Haitian Centers Council* 113 S Ct 2549 (1993).
14. Doubts had existed whether foreign vessels that were merely in transit through the maritime belt were subject for all purposes to the jurisdiction of the littoral state. In *R v Keyn* (*The Franconia*) (1876) 2 Ex D 63, it was held that, in the absence of an applicable statute, an English

States were also permitted to exercise jurisdiction on the high seas by reason of certain international conventions, whereby the states parties conceded to one another rights, in time of peace, of visiting and searching foreign vessels at sea. These rights were granted for limited purposes only, which are suggested by the title of the particular conventions concerned, for example, two such instruments concluded during the nineteenth century, namely the Convention for the Protection of Submarine Telegraph Cables of 1884, and the General Act of Brussels of 1890 for the Repression of the African Slave Trade.[15] Moreover, in time of war, the rights of jurisdiction of belligerent maritime states on the high seas were considerably extended, inasmuch as a belligerent state enjoyed a general right of visit and search of neutral shipping in order to prevent breaches of neutrality, such as the carriage of contraband. As has been pointed out in an earlier chapter,[16] rival parties in a civil war might obtain these powers of search as the result of the recognition of belligerency and the consequent grant of belligerent rights.

Beyond that, all states became bound to observe certain regulations relative to the safety of navigation at sea, and to ensure, by legislation or otherwise, that vessels flying their flags should act in conformity with these regulations. In the relevant historical period now under consideration, the practice of states as to the exercise of jurisdiction in the field of collision cases on the high seas could be described only as fluid. Some states claimed jurisdiction where the damaged vessel was under their flag; other states, where the vessels involved in the collision consented to the exercise of jurisdiction by such states; and certain other states where the ship primarily responsible for the collision was in one of their ports at the time that proceedings were instituted. In 1927 in the *Lotus Case*,[17] the Permanent Court of International Justice held, by a majority, that in collision cases on the high seas there was no rule of international law attributing exclusive penal jurisdiction to the flag state of a ship involved in the collision as regards an offence committed on that ship, and that jurisdiction could be exercised also by the flag state of the ship on which the offence had produced its effects in the course of the collision. The decision in the *Lotus Case* was not received with enthusiasm by international lawyers, and subsequently was in effect overruled,

---

Criminal Court had no jurisdiction over a crime committed by an alien on a foreign vessel in passage less than three miles from the coast. This decision surprised many English legal authorities, and was nullified by the enactment of the Territorial Waters Jurisdiction Act 1878, giving the courts jurisdiction over offences within a three-mile maritime belt; prosecutions could however be instituted only by leave of the Secretary of State. For discussion of the effect of *R v Keyn*, see the judgments of members of the High Court of Australia in *New South Wales v The Commonwealth of Australia* (1975) 135 CLR 337. As to the exercise of criminal jurisdiction over vessels in transit in the belt, according to the provisions now of the 1982 United Nations Convention on the Law of the Sea, see below, pp 237-238.

15. A much later example is that of the Interim Convention of 9 February 1957, for the Conservation of North Pacific Fur Seal Herds. For other instances of such conventions and treaties, see *Laws and Regulations on the Regime of the High Seas* (United Nations) (1951) Vol I, pp 179 et seq.
16. See pp 138-140 above.
17. (1927) PCIJ, Series A, No 10.

not by any decision of an international tribunal, but by the consensus generally of states acting officially and of international jurists.[18]

Considerations of space preclude detailed reference to other rules affecting the rights and duties of states with respect to the pre-1958 régime of the high seas and maritime belt. The relevant rules are now comprehensively covered in the United Nations Conventions on the Law of the Sea, 1958 and 1982 (see above), and the precise nature of the former rules is now of minimal historical significance.

It is nevertheless important to mention that at the Hague Codification Conference of 1930, the question of what should be the maximum breadth of the territorial sea was considered without agreement being reached, although there was such firm opposition to the general acceptance of the three-mile limit as a maximum that to quote Professor Gidel,[19] this limit emerged as the 'chief victim' of the Conference, as an 'idol dethroned and not restored'. At the same time the Conference did not generally support the concept of a 'contiguous zone',[20] that is to say, a belt of waters adjacent to the limits of the maritime belt, not subject to the sovereignty of the littoral state, but within which the littoral state could exercise certain rights of control for the purpose of its health or other regulations. As will be seen below, the concept of the contiguous zone was one which did find favour subsequently.

Two important developments following the end of the Second World War now need to be considered, first, the evolution and general acceptance of the doctrine of the continental shelf, and second, the decision of the International Court of Justice in the *Anglo-Norwegian Fisheries Case*[1] upholding the method in certain special cases of drawing baselines at some distance from the coastline of the littoral state concerned, from which baselines the breadth of the maritime belt was to be measured, instead of the low-water mark constituting the linear edge of the maritime belt.

Dealing with the first development, the general recognition of the continental shelf principle represented the culmination of a trend which began in 1945–1951 when, by unilateral declarations, a number of maritime states laid claim to exclusive jurisdiction, control or sovereign rights (as distinct from sovereignty) over the resources of the continental shelf and associated offshore areas.[2] What is commonly meant by the 'continental shelf' or the 'continental platform' is the submerged bed of the sea, contiguous to a continental land mass, and formed in

18. The rule in the *Lotus Case* was disapproved by the International Law Commission (the Commission's Report on the work of its *8th session* (1956)), and by the Conference at Brussels in 1952, which adopted the Convention for the Unification of Certain Rules relating to Penal Jurisdiction in Matters of Collision and other Incidents of Navigation. See now article 11 of the Geneva Convention of 1958 on the High Seas. See also p 247 below.
19. Gidel *Le droit international public de la mer* (1934) Vol 3, p 151.
20. The concept of the contiguous zone appears to have been first enunciated by the noted French jurist, M. Louis Renault; see Riesenfeld *The Protection of Coastal Fisheries under International Law* (1949) p 105.
1. ICJ 1951, 116-206.
2. In regard to the historical background of the continental shelf doctrine, see Anninos *The Continental Shelf and Public International Law* (1953) pp 11–34, and the *North Sea Continental Shelf Cases* ICJ 1969, 3 at 32–36. In 1916 and 1927 respectively, it was urged by De Buren and by Professor Suarez that the maritime belt should be extended to cover the continental shelf.

such a manner as to be really an extension of, or appurtenant to this land mass, but not situated in general at a greater depth beneath the sea level than 200 metres. At approximately this depth there occurs, as a rule, the first substantial 'fall-off' to the vastly greater ocean depths. Beyond such outer edge or declivity of the continental shelf, the deep seabed descends by further stages, known in accordance with accepted nomenclature[3] as the 'continental slope', and the 'continental rise', before sinking into the deeper ocean floor, or 'abyssal plain'. The expression 'continental margin' is in general use to encompass collectively the shelf, slope, and rise, the outer limit of such continental margin being the commencement, so far as it can be defined geomorphologically, of the abyssal plain. In the *North Sea Continental Shelf Cases*,[4] it was this geological context which persuaded the International Court of Justice, when seeking to rationalise the basis of shelf claims, to attach primary importance to the consideration that the shelf was a natural prolongation or continuation of the land domain, and therefore appurtenant to territory over which the coastal state already had dominion.

When initially claims over the continental shelf were laid by proclamation or other formal statement, the justification was usually by reference to, inter alia, considerations of geographical contiguity and of security. While the obvious purpose of the littoral states concerned was to reserve to themselves such oil and minerals as might lie in the seabed of the shelf, the exploitation of which had been rendered possible by advances in technology, the claims were expressed in terms sufficient to cover non-mineral resources. The actual extent of the claims varied; the Proclamation of the President of the United States in September 1945 reserved only rights of 'jurisdiction and control' over the natural resources of the subsoil and seabed of the shelf, expressly leaving intact the nature of the shelf waters as high seas and the right of free navigation, but in later declarations of other states claims were laid to sovereignty over and ownership of the seabed and subsoil as well as over the waters, of the shelf. Naturally, such claims involved an extension of jurisdiction or sovereignty beyond the maritime belt, even far beyond the width of the contiguous zones to which certain states had laid claim. For instance, the United States continental shelf was officially[5] described as:

'. . . almost as large as the area embraced in the Louisiana Purchase, which was 827,000 square miles, and almost twice as large as the original 13 colonies, which was 400,000 square miles. Along the Alaska coastline the shelf extends several hundred miles under the Bering sea. On the Eastern coast of the United States the width of the shelf varies 20 miles to 250 miles, and along the Pacific coast it is from 1 to 50 miles wide.'

Owing to the magnitude of the areas of the continental shelf, there was therefore little analogy between these claims and claims exclusively to control limited areas of the seabed outside the maritime belt for pearl, oyster and other sedentary fisheries. These more limited claims rested upon the occupation of a portion of the seabed as a res nullius, or upon some historical or quasi-historical

3. For the nomenclature adopted by the International Committee on Nomenclature of Ocean Bottom Features, Monaco, in 1952, see A.L. Shalowitz *Shore and Sea Boundaries* (1964) Vol II, pp 342–343.
4. ICJ 1969, 3 at 30–31.
5. *Annual Report* of the United States Secretary of the Interior for 1945, pp ix–x.

prescriptive title or upon some regional community of interest (eg, the pearl fisheries in the Persian Gulf). It was a controversial question whether the declaration of jurisdiction or sovereignty made by the littoral states concerned in 1945–1951 had contributed to the formation of a customary rule of international law giving coastal states such rights over their shelves.[6] As will be seen, however, the doctrine of the continental shelf was recognised by general consensus in the Geneva Convention of 1958 on the Continental Shelf.

The second major development, that of the delimitation of the maritime belt by reference to the 'baselines' method, was, as mentioned above, the consequence of the decision in 1951 of the International Court of Justice in the *Anglo-Norwegian Fisheries Case*.[7] There the Court held that a Norwegian Decree of July 1935 delimiting an exclusive fishery zone along almost 1,000 miles of coastline north of a certain latitude, being in effect a maritime belt of a breadth of four miles[8] extending from straight baselines drawn through 48 selected points on the mainland or islands or rocks at a considerable distance from the coast, was not contrary to international law. It emerged from the Court's judgment that this baselines method, rather than the low-water mark, was admissible where a coastline is deeply indented and cut into, or if there is a fringe of islands in the immediate vicinity, provided that the drawing of the baselines does not depart to any appreciable extent from the 'general direction'[9] of the coast, and that the areas lying within the baselines are sufficiently closely linked to the adjacent land domain as virtually to be akin to internal waters. If these conditions for permitting the drawing of the baselines are met, account may be taken in determining *particular* baselines of economic interests peculiar to the particular region concerned, where such interests are a matter of a long established usage. In other words, in the absence of the requisite geographical conditions referable to the nature of the coastline and adjacent islands, economic interests in the littoral State cannot alone justify recourse to the baselines method. The baselines would have to be duly notified and marked on charts subject to appropriate publicity. Underlying the reasoning of the International Court of Justice in the *Anglo-Norwegian Fisheries Case* was the consideration that the maritime belt was not so much a limited artificial extension of a state's territorial domain as an appurtenant contiguous area wherein for economic, security and geographical reasons the littoral state was entitled to exercise exclusive sovereign rights, subject only to qualifications such as the right of innocent passage of foreign vessels.

Meanwhile, beginning with its first session in 1949, the régime of the high seas and the régime of the maritime belt had engaged the attention of the United Nations International Law Commission as being among the topics in respect of which codification was considered by it as being necessary and feasible. The

6. In 1951, the existence of such a customary rule was denied by Lord Asquith, acting as Arbitrator in the *Arbitration between Petroleum Development and the Sheikh of Abu Dhabi* 47 AJIL (1953) 156–159.
7. ICJ 1951, 116.
8. Based on the Scandinavian marine league. This variation from the normal marine league of three nautical miles, used for measuring the territorial sea, seems to have secured international acquiescence and was not in issue in the case.
9. For critical comment on this concept of the 'general direction' of the coast, see Shalowitz *Shore and Sea Boundaries* (1962) Vol I, pp 74–75.

examination of the two subjects was spread over eight sessions, 1949–1956.[10] In the course of the fourth session in 1952, the Commission expressed a preference for the term 'territorial sea' to denote the maritime belt, and this has since come into universal currency of use, thereby displacing and rendering obsolete the expressions 'maritime belt' and 'territorial waters'[11] to denote the coastal strip subject to the sovereignty of the littoral state. At its eighth session in 1956 the Commission drew up a final set of draft articles on the territorial sea, incorporating changes based on communications from governments, and adopted a final report on the law of the high seas, containing a set of 73 draft articles, designed to constitute a single co-ordinated and systematic body of rules. These came before the United Nations General Assembly in 1956, and in accordance with the recommendation of the Commission, the Assembly by resolution of 21 February 1957, decided to convene an international conference of plenipotentiaries 'to examine the law of the sea, taking account not only of the legal but also of the technical, biological, economic and political aspects of the problem, and to embody the results of its work in one or more international Conventions or such other instruments as the conference may deem appropriate'.

The First United Nations Conference on the Law of the Sea met in Geneva from 24 February 1958 to 27 April 1958, and its labours resulted in the adoption of four conventions, namely the Convention on the Territorial Sea and the Contiguous Zone, the Convention on the High Seas, the Convention on Fishing and Conservation of the Living Resources of the High Seas and the Convention on the Continental Shelf.[12] Notwithstanding the large measure of agreement at the Conference on so many important points, two questions had been left unsettled by it, namely, the breadth of the territorial sea and fishery limits. After the conclusion of the 1958 Conference, the General Assembly by resolution adopted on 10 December 1958, asked the Secretary-General of the United Nations to convene a Second United Nations Conference on the Law of the Sea to consider further these two unsettled questions. Over 80 states were represented at this Second United Nations Conference, which was held in Geneva from 16 March 1960 to 26 April 1960 with inconclusive results as to the two questions, although the Conference did approve a resolution expressing the need for technical assistance to fishing.

One question which had not been covered in the report of the International Law Commission submitted to the General Assembly in 1956 (see above) was that of the free access to the sea of land-locked states. However, this question was dealt with in a memorandum submitted to the First United Nations Conference on the Law of the Sea by a preliminary conference of land-locked states which met in Geneva from 10 February 1958 to 14 February 1958, that is to say, little more than a week before the commencement of the United Nations Conference. This memorandum led to the latter Conference establishing as one

---

10. For a summary of the work of the Commission on these subjects see the United Nations publication, *The Work of the International Law Commission* (3rd edn, 1980) pp 36–38.
11. The Commission preferred the expression 'territorial sea', because 'territorial waters' may include internal waters; see *Report Concerning the Work of the Fourth Session of the Commission* (1952).
12. The texts of the four conventions are conveniently reproduced in the United Nations publication, *The Work of the International Law Commission* (3rd edn, 1980) Annex V, pp 140–165.

of its main Committees a Fifth Committee with the mandate of considering the question of access to the sea of land-locked states. In the result, no separate convention on the subject was adopted by the United Nations Conference, but in the wording of certain provisions of the Convention on the Territorial Sea and the Contiguous Zone and of the Convention on the High Seas due regard was had to the problem of access of land-locked countries, and article 3 of the latter convention dealt with the question explicitly and specifically.

Apart from this, pursuant to a resolution adopted by the First United Nations Conference on Trade and Development convened at Geneva in June 1964, the General Assembly decided, on 10 February 1965, to convene an international conference of plenipotentiaries to consider the subject of the transit trade of land-locked countries, and to embody the results of its work in a convention and such other instruments as the conference might deem appropriate. The United Nations Conference on the Transit Trade of Land-Locked Countries met in New York from 7 June 1965 to 8 July 1965, with a participation of the representatives of 58 states, and adopted the Convention on the Transit Trade of Land-Locked States.

The four Conventions of 1958 provided a régime for the use of, and rights to, the sea and the continental shelf. Most of their provisions have been incorporated with little or no change in the United Nations Convention on the Law of the Sea 1982. Thus there is no need to discuss these provisions separately from the 1982 Convention.

It is nevertheless necessary to consider the problem of the division of a common continental shelf which came before the International Court of Justice in 1969 in the *North Sea Continental Shelf Cases*.[13] In that connection, article 6 of the Geneva Convention of 1958 on the Continental Shelf had made provision for the manner of division of a shelf common to states with opposite coastlines (paragraph 1), or common to states adjacent to each other (paragraph 2). Paragraph 1 laid it down that, 'in the absence of agreement, and unless another boundary line is justified by special circumstances', the median line was to be the boundary in the former case, while, in the latter case, the matter, according to paragraph 2, was to be governed by the principle of equidistance from the nearest points of the baselines of the territorial sea. The Court held that in respect of the division of the common shelf of the German Federal Republic, the Netherlands and Denmark, paragraph 2 was not binding upon the German Federal Republic, a non-party to the Convention, inasmuch as:

a. that country had not accepted the rule in paragraph 2 in the manifest manner required for provisions in a multilateral Convention to bind a non-party to that instrument; and

b. the equidistance principle had not through its application by a certain number of countries become thereby a settled rule of customary international law, in the absence of evidence that in applying it those countries had considered that they were legally bound to follow it (opinio juris sive necessitatis[14]).

13. ICJ 1969, 3.
14. See pp 33-34 above.

The Court also ruled that, in the absence of the application to the instant cases of article 6 of the 1958 Convention, the governing principles of international law concerning delimitation of a common continental shelf were first, that such delimitation should be the object of agreement between the countries specially concerned, and second, that any arrangement for division should be arrived at in accordance with 'equitable principles'.

Developments since 1960 leading to the United Nations Convention of 1982 on the Law of the Sea

The First and Second United Nations Conferences on the Law of the Sea (see above) left unsettled numerous matters, including in particular:

1. the precise breadth of the territorial sea;
2. the question of innocent passage for warships at all times through straits constituting an international maritime highway, and consisting wholly of territorial waters;
3. the right of passage through, and overflight in relation to the waters of archipelagos; and
4. the problem of protection and conservation of marine resources beyond the territorial sea.

Beyond these specific points, it had since been claimed that the settlement achieved in the four Geneva Conventions of 1958 proved in the passage of time to be inadequate in the context of later conditions. These criticisms of the régime established by the 1958 Conference referred on the whole to matters of a more general nature than the technical legal questions left unsettled in 1958 and 1960. It was said, for example, that fishing grounds were faced with depletion, that the rules as to fisheries unfairly favoured the developed and disadvantaged the underdeveloped countries, that the enforcement of pollution control standards in the marine environment was proving to be unsatisfactory, that uncertainty surrounded the extent of the rights of littoral states over the resources of the continental shelf and areas beyond shelf limits, that land-locked states had inadequate access to the sea and that the 1958 Conventions would fail to halt a scramble by developed states to exploit resources in the seabed beyond national jurisdiction.

At all events, it was clear that taken together the four conventions were not acceptable as a whole to all states. As already indicated (see above) instead of ratifying or acceding to all four instruments en bloc, a number of states elected to become party to one or to some only, in a selective manner. Besides, the exploitability criterion adopted in the 1958 Convention on the Continental Shelf as marking the outer shelf limit was paradoxically viewed as unsatisfactory from two opposing standpoints. On the one hand, post-1958 advances in technology opened the way for mineral exploitation activities in ocean depths far beyond the limits envisaged in 1958. On the other hand, the newly emerged states became concerned that, on the basis of the exploitability criterion, they, without the technical know-how and being financially disadvantaged, would be powerless to prevent exploitation of the ocean floor resources by a monopoly of developed states possessing both finance and technological skills.

Another matter was the recurrence in the 1960s and 1970s of almost catastrophic oil spills from giant oil tankers running aground (eg, the *Torrey Canyon* off the southern coast of the United Kingdom in March 1967) or otherwise incurring damage. The result was to underscore boldly the deficiences of international maritime law with respect to the possibilities of such oil pollution. This had prompted legislation (eg, the Canadian Arctic Waters Pollution Prevention Act 1970) or administrative action by states for the purpose of establishing controls in pollution zones extending for one hundred miles or more offshore. Far more serious was the possibility that the seabed might be used for the emplacement of nuclear weapons, with incalculable consequences for navigation, fisheries and other uses of the superjacent waters, apart from other hazards of a wide-ranging nature. In the result, in the period 1969–1971, three instruments were adopted which represented a substantial addition to the corpus of the law of the sea.

On 29 November 1969, two conventions were adopted at Brussels to deal with oil pollution casualties of the *Torrey Canyon* genre (see above), namely the International Convention relating to Intervention on the High Seas in cases of Oil Pollution Casualties (which will be referred to as the Intervention Convention), and the International Convention on Civil Liability for Oil Pollution Damage (to be referred to as the Liability Convention). The Intervention Convention is of limited scope, inasmuch as states parties were given certain rights of taking defensive measures against pollution or threat of pollution only 'following' upon a maritime casualty or acts related to such a casualty; there were no specific provisions entitling coastal states to take preventive measures such as, for example, fixing sealanes or subjecting tankers to surveillance from shore-based stations, although states would not be debarred from making preparations beforehand to take such defensive measures as might conceivably become necessary in the event of a maritime casualty. In any event, the self-defensive measures were to be proportionate to the actual or threatened damage, while there were mandatory requirements for consultation with other states affected. The Intervention Convention was supplemented subsequently by a Protocol relating to Intervention on the High Seas in Cases of Marine Pollution by Substances other than Oil, adopted at London in November 1973; this applied to pollutants and also hazardous or injurious products other than oil, so that the expression 'Marine Pollution' is wider than its literal sense, as it covers injury and harm to humans and marine resources, damage to amenities, and interference with the use of the sea.

The Liability Convention applied exclusively to 'pollution damage caused on the territory including the territorial sea' of the coastal state. The tanker-owner was subjected to a principle of absolute liability, rather than liability based upon fault, but such absolute liability was one of a qualified character, for no liability for pollution damage attached to the owner if he proved (the onus of proof presumably being upon him) that the damage:

a. resulted from war, hostilities, civil war, insurrection or some unavoidable natural phenomenon; or
b. was caused by an act or omission with intent to cause damage by a third party; or

c. was wholly caused by the negligence or wrongful act of a government or authority responsible for maintaining lights or providing navigational aids.

A limit for liability was fixed, and fault came into account to the extent that if the casualty occurred as a result of the owner's actual 'fault or privity', the owner's liability was not restricted to the ceiling fixed by the Convention. Provision was made for the necessity of certificates of insurance or financial security where a tanker registered in a country party to the Convention carried more than 2,000 tons of oil in bulk as cargo. The Liability Convention of 1969 was followed in 1971 by a Convention for the Establishment of a Fund for Compensation for Oil Pollution Damage ('the Fund Convention') which provides for additional compensation to that provided under the Liability Convention, and for compensation even where no liability arises under that Convention. A Protocol of 1984 sought to raise the limits of liability but it is unlikely that a sufficient number of ratifications will be received in order for it to enter into force.[15]

An instrument of a different nature was the Treaty on the Prohibition of the Emplacement of Nuclear Weapons and Other Weapons of Mass Destruction on the Seabed and Ocean Floor and in the Subsoil Thereof, opened for signature on 10 February 1971. For the sake of brevity, this will be referred to as the Seabed Arms Control Treaty. It represented a first major step in preventing militarisation of the seabed and ocean floor. Under paragraph 1 of article 1 parties are prohibited from placing nuclear weapons or other weapons of mass destruction on the seabed and ocean floor beyond the limits of a twelve-mile coastal seabed zone, while paragraph 2 provided that this obligation was to apply also to the twelve-mile zone, except that within that zone the undertaking was not to apply either to the coastal state itself, or to the seabed beneath the coastal state's territorial sea. In other articles, provision was made for processes of verification, and for the continuance of negotiations for wider measures to prevent militarisation. The Seabed Arms Control Treaty was an arms control measure, and therefore did not prohibit or limit the use of peaceful nuclear explosive devices in the seabed or ocean floor in order to obtain minerals, or to drill for oil and gas. This consideration must be taken into account when assessing claims that the Treaty made a decisive contribution to the protection of the marine environment.

In 1967, before the adoption in 1969–1971 of the three last-mentioned instruments, the first step on the road to the conclusion of the 1982 Convention was taken when Mr Arvid Pardo of Malta pressed for United Nations action to be taken to have deep seabed resources beyond the continental shelf limits recognised as the common heritage of mankind, and to be developed in the interests of all states, with special regard to the needs of disadvantaged developing countries. This initiative influenced the recourse to far-reaching action within the framework of the United Nations. Mr Pardo had envisaged the adoption of

15. The International Maritime Organisation is working on new revisions of the Liability and Fund conventions. In the meantime the United States, which is a party to neither convention and is unhappy with the low limits of liability thereunder, enacted, following the *Exxon Valdez* disaster, the Oil Pollution Act 1990, which greatly increased the limits of liability under US law for oil pollution, and provides for unlimited liability in certain circumstances, including gross negligence.

a plan designed not only to avoid an unregulated scramble by developed countries to ravage the mineral wealth of the ocean floor beyond national jurisdiction, but also participation by rival states in an arms race which might ultimately conduce to the militarisation of the deep seabed. In December 1968, the United Nations General Assembly adopted four resolutions relating to the matter, the most important of which declared that the exploitation of the seabed and ocean floor 'beyond the limits of national jurisdiction' should be carried 'out for the benefit of mankind as a whole, with the United Nations system as the focal point of international co-operation in this domain, and which established a 42-member Committee on the Peaceful Uses of the Seabed and Ocean Floor beyond the Limits of National Jurisdiction (hereinafter referred to as the Seabed Committee) to make recommendations upon the related questions.

In 1969–1971, progress in the direction contemplated by the General Assembly resolutions was to a large extent activated by the labours of the Seabed Committee. Further resolutions were adopted by the General Assembly in 1969 after receiving a report from the Seabed Committee. Meanwhile, there had been other developments, including inter-state consultations for a general restructuring of the law of the sea and of oceanic resources, and the radical step taken by President Richard Nixon on 23 May 1970, when he issued a statement of a new United States Policy on the Oceans,[16] which was compatible with the approach favoured by the United Nations General Assembly, and the principles of which were embodied in a draft convention presented on 3 August 1970 by the United States Government to the Seabed Committee as a working paper for discussion purposes.[17]

The final result of these merging developments was the adoption by the General Assembly of two important resolutions on 17 December 1970, one consisting of a Declaration of Principles Governing the Seabed and Ocean Floor and the Subsoil Thereof beyond the Limits of National Jurisdiction, and the other representing a decision to convene a Third United Nations Conference on the Law of the Sea in 1973, later to be known under the acronym, 'UNCLOS III'. The Declaration proclaimed a number of principles and guidelines, including the following among others:

a. that the seabed and ocean floor and subsoil thereof, beyond the limits of national jurisdiction, as well as the resources of the area were the 'common heritage of mankind';
b. that the area was not subject to appropriation, or to be the object of claims of sovereignty or sovereign rights by states;
c. that all activities of exploration or exploitation in the area were to be governed by an international régime to be established;
d. that the area should be reserved exclusively for peaceful purposes; and
e. that measures should be taken in co-operation to prevent injury to the marine environment and its ecological balance, to protect and conserve natural resources of the area, and to prevent damage to the flora and fauna.

16. See the United States *Department of State Bulletin* 15 June 1970, p 737.
17. For a summary of the text of the Draft Convention, and for official statements thereon, see the *United States Department of State Bulletin* 24 August 1970, pp 209–218, and 19 April 1971, pp 529–533 (statements by Mr John R. Stevenson, Legal Adviser to the Department of State).

The terms of reference of the Third United Nations Conference of the Law of the Sea were extremely wide, embracing the establishment of the international régime for the area, a precise definition of the area (ie of its shoreward limit), and 'a broad range of related issues including those concerning the régimes of the high seas, the continental shelf, the territorial sea (including the question of its breadth and the question of international straits) and contiguous zone, fishing and conservation of the living resources of the high seas (including the question of the preferential rights of coastal states), the preservation of the marine environment (including, inter alia, the prevention of pollution) and scientific research'. This implied in fact a complete re-opening of the settlement reached at the First United Nations Conference on the Law of the Sea at Geneva in 1958, with no sanctity for any one of the four conventions then adopted by the Conference. The Seabed Committee was also enlarged to an 86-member body, to serve in effect as a preparatory committee for the Third United Nations Conference on the Law of the Sea.

It took no less than twelve sessions of the Conference, UNCLOS III, 1973–1982, for a result to be reached, beginning with an 'organisational' first session in 1973 and ending with the adoption of the final text of the Convention and its signature at Montego Bay on 10 December 1982, by 118 states. The formal story of the procedures adopted, and decisions reached at each stage, is recounted in the Final Act of UNCLOS III which was signed also on the same date; a detailed discussion of the matters narrated in the Final Act is beyond the confines of the present chapter. One virtually unprecedented feature of UNCLOS III considered as a lawmaking gathering may however be briefly referred to. The Conference at its second session at Caracas, Venezuela, in 1974 adopted a declaration that every effort should be made 'to reach agreement on substantive matters by way of consensus and there should be no voting on such matters until all efforts at consensus have been exhausted'.[18] Throughout the sessions preceding signature at Montego Bay, the consensus procedure was followed, and would not of course have been effective but for the work, inter alia, of Conference committees and of inter-sessional consultative gatherings. That the labours of UNCLOS III spanned a period of almost exactly nine years (the first session was held at New York from 3 December to 15 December 1973) is not surprising, having regard to the ambitious mandates to be fulfilled by the Conference, which were no less than the creation of complete and comprehensive international régimes for the high seas, the coastal waters and seabed, and the deep ocean floor, such régimes to embrace coverage of all relevant economic and environmental issues. Throughout the course of the Conference sessions, there was evidence of divisions on matters of principle between the developing countries and the developed countries, the latter wishing to retain as much freedom of enterprise as possible, as corresponding to the sophistication of the technology that they possessed, and reluctant to be bound by decisions of bodies in which they might lack representation. This was reflected in the decision, in particular, of the United States Government not to sign the 1982 Convention,[19] although apparently it

18. See Final Act of the Conference (Document A/CONF.62/121) pp 13–14.
19. According to the United Nations background Press Release of 3 December 1982 (Document SEA/498) p 6, the five principal objections of the United States to the Convention were as follows: (1) The seabed mining provisions would deter the exploitation of deep seabed mineral resources.

did not dissent from the provisions of the Convention which do not relate to the establishment of an International Seabed Authority and to controls over the exploitation of the resources of the seabed beyond the limits of national jurisdiction. Only three months later, the United States policy on the subject was apparently confirmed by the terms of the Presidential Proclamation of 10 March 1983 proclaiming an American Exclusive Economic Zone (see p 241 below), and in President Reagan's accompanying statement concerning the reach of his Proclamation. The group of non-signatory states also included the United Kingdom which declared that it would seek improvements in the seabed mining provisions.

Before dealing in the second section of this chapter with the substantive law of the sea it may be convenient to set out what the President of UNCLOS at its final session (Mr T.T.B. Koh) considered were the eight main achievements of the Convention. These, according to him, as set out in the United Nations Press Release on 10 December 1982 (Document SEA/514), were as follows:

1. The Convention would promote the maintenance of international peace and security because, instead of a plethora of conflicting claims by coastal states, there would be universally agreed limits on the territorial sea, on the contiguous zone, on the exclusive economic zone (EEZ) and on the continental shelf.
2. The international community's interest in the freedom of navigation in maritime waters would be facilitated by the important compromises in the Convention on the status of the EEZ, by the régime of innocent passage through the territorial sea, by the régime of transit passage through straits used for international navigation, and by the régime of archipelagic sea-lanes passage.
3. The international community's interest in the conservation and optimum utilisation of the living resources of the sea would be enhanced by the conscientious implementation of the provisions in the Convention relating to the EEZ.
4. Important new rules were laid down for the protection and preservation of the marine environment from pollution.
5. The Convention contained new rules on marine scientific research which struck an equitable balance between the interests of states conducting research and the interests of the coastal states in the EEZs or continental shelves of which the research was to be carried out.
6. The international community's interest in the peaceful settlement of disputes and the prevention of the use of force in the settlement of international disputes would be advanced by the mandatory system of dispute settlement provided for in the Convention.

(2) Access to these resources was not assured. (3) The countries most affected did not have a proportionate voice in decision-making on seabed policies, with the result that their interests would not be fairly reflected and effectively protected. (4) The procedure whereby future amendments to seabed provisions could come into force for a state without its consent was incompatible with United States processes for incurring treaty obligations. (5) The provisions as to the mandatory transfer of seabed technology, potential distribution of benefits to national liberation movements, and production limitations posed key problems for the United States Congress. For efforts in 1994 to meet these concerns, see below, p 259.

7. The principle that the resources of the deep seabed constituted the common heritage of mankind had been translated into fair and workable institutions and arrangements. (But for recent developments, see below, p 259.)
8. Elements of international equity were to be found in the Convention, such as revenue-sharing on the continental shelf beyond 200 miles, giving land-locked and geographically disadvantaged states access to the living resources of the EEZs of their neighbouring states, the relationship between coastal fishermen and distant-water fishermen, and the sharing of the benefits derived from the exploitation of the resources of the deep seabed.

2. THE LAW OF THE SEA UNDER THE REGIMES ESTABLISHED BY THE UNITED NATIONS CONVENTION OF 10 DECEMBER 1982[20]

At the outset, it must be stated that it would be beyond the scope of the present chapter to cover in full detail the elements and principles of the régimes established by the United Nations Convention on the Law of the Sea of 10 December 1982. Such a coverage can only be achieved, not in a single chapter, but in a major treatise of some length. The Convention consists of no less than 320 articles spread over 17 Parts, together with 9 Annexes. Apart from the Convention and its Annexes, there would also have to be considered the four important resolutions adopted by the Conference, and the Statement of Understanding Concerning a Specific Method to be Used in Establishing the Outer Edge of the Continental Margin (these are contained in pp 23–35 of the Final Act). Resolution I establishes the Preparatory Commission for the Seabed Authority and the Law of the Sea Tribunal. Resolution II, which is of some length, governs preparatory investment in pioneer activities by states and private consortia relating to polymetallic nodules in the deep sea area. Resolution III deals with the rights and interests of territories which have not attained independence or self-government. Resolution IV grants to recognised national liberation movements the right to sign the Final Act as observers.

The present treatment of the law of sea under the régimes created by the Convention will therefore necessarily be one of a condensed nature. Nonetheless, in its sequence this treatment will follow the arrangement in successive Parts, as employed in the Convention.

Definitions (Part I)
The principal definitions for the purposes of the Convention are contained in article 1, which constitutes Part I. The term 'Area' is defined to mean the seabed and ocean floor and subsoil thereof beyond the limits of national jurisdiction. The article also defines 'Authority' (the International Sea-Bed Authority), 'activities in the Area' (exploration and exploitation of resources), 'pollution of the marine environment' (emphasising deleterious effects, the creation of hazards

---

20. The Convention is being dealt with in a comprehensive manner, with annotations and commentary, in a multi-volume series, M. Nordquist (ed) *United Nations Convention on the Law of the Sea, 1982. A Commentary* (1985 and later years).

and the impairment of quality), 'dumping' (emphasising the deliberateness of the disposal of wastes, etc), and 'States parties'.

The Territorial Sea and Contiguous Zone (Part II)

Article 2 proclaims that the sovereignty of a coastal state extends beyond its land territory and internal waters, and in the case of an archipelagic state, its archipelagic waters, to the territorial sea, the superjacent air space and the bed and subsoil thereof (cf articles 1–2 of the Geneva Convention of 1958 on the Territorial Sea and Contiguous Zone). The breadths and limits of the territorial seas of states are covered in articles 3–7, under which the limit is not to exceed 12 nautical miles measured from baselines, the normal baseline being the low-water mark as shown on large-scale charts officially recognised by the coastal state. However, in the case of islands situated on atolls or of islands having fringing reefs, the baseline is the seaward low-water mark of the reef as shown by the appropriate symbol on charts officially recognised by the coastal state. Straight baselines are permissible according to the conditions laid down in article 7 (cf article 4 of the 1958 Convention), which to a large extent embodies the principles affirmed in the *Anglo–Norwegian Fisheries Case*.[1] Such lines joining 'appropriate points' may be drawn for 'localities' where the coastline is deeply indented and cut into, or if there is an offshore fringe of islands in the immediate vicinity. Where because of the presence of a delta and other natural conditions the coastline is highly unstable, the appropriate points may be selected along the furthest seaward extent of the low-water mark. Lines as drawn must not depart to any appreciable extent from the general direction of the coast, and the sea areas lying within the lines must be sufficiently closely linked to the land domain to be subject to the régime of internal waters. The lines are not to be drawn to and from low-tide elevations, unless lighthouses or similar permanent installations above sea level have been built thereon, except where the lines drawn in such circumstances have received 'general international recognition'. If the lines are, in principle, permissible, account may be taken in determining particular lines of economic interests peculiar to the region concerned, the reality and the importance of which are clearly evidenced by long usage. The system of such lines is not applicable if the effect is to cut off the territorial sea of another state from the high seas, or an EEZ.

Article 8 is similar to article 5 of the 1958 Convention, but, unlike the latter provision, reserves the position of archipelagic waters; subject to that position, waters on the landward side of the territorial sea baseline form part of the internal waters of the coastal state. Moreover, if a baseline has been drawn in compliance with article 7, thereby enclosing as internal waters areas not previously considered to be such, there shall exist a right of innocent passage in such waters. Article 9, dealing with the mouths of rivers, is similar to article 13 of the 1958 Convention; where a river flows directly into the sea, the baseline is to be a straight line across the river mouth between points on the low-water mark of the river banks.

Article 10 (cf article 7 of the 1958 Convention) deals with bays, the coasts of which belong to a single state. For the purposes of the Convention, a bay is in effect defined as 'a well-marked indentation whose penetration is in such

1.   ICJ 1951, 116; see p 225 above.

proportion to the width of its mouth as to contain land-locked waters and constitute more than a mere curvature of the coast', and the area of the indentation must be as large as, or larger than, that of the semi-circle whose diameter is a line drawn across the mouth of that indentation. Where, because of the presence of islands, an indentation has more than one mouth, the relevant semi-circle is to be drawn on a line as long as the sum total of the lengths of the lines across the different mouths, islands within the indentation being included as if they were part of the water area of the indentation. If the distance between the low-water marks of the natural entrance points of a bay does not exceed 24 nautical miles, a closing line may be drawn between the two marks so as to render the enclosed waters internal waters; but if the distance between the marks exceeds 24 nautical miles, a straight baseline of 24 nautical miles is to be drawn within the bay so as to enclose the maximum area of water possible with the line. The above-mentioned principles do not apply to 'historic bays',[2] or in any case where the baselines method under article 7 (see above) has been applied.

Articles 11–13 deal with harbour works, roadsteads and low-tide elevations (cf articles 8, 9 and 11 of the 1958 Convention). Under article 11, for the purpose of delimiting the territorial sea, the outermost permanent harbour works that form an integral part of the harbour system are to be regarded as forming part of the coast, but offshore installations and artificial islands are not to be considered as permanent harbour works. Article 12 provides that roadsteads normally used for the loading, unloading and anchoring of ships are to be included in the territorial sea. A low-tide elevation is defined by article 13 as a 'naturally formed area of land which is surrounded by and above water at low tide but submerged at high tide'. Where such an elevation is situated wholly or partly at a distance not exceeding the breadth of the territorial sea from the mainland or an island, the low-water mark on that elevation may be used as the baseline for measuring the territorial sea. On the other hand, where a low-tide elevation is wholly situated at a distance exceeding the breadth of the territorial sea from the mainland or an island, it has no territorial sea of its own.

Article 15 deals with the delimitation of the territorial sea between states with opposite or adjacent coasts (cf article 12 of the 1958 Convention); neither of the two states is entitled, failing agreement between them to the contrary, to extend its territorial sea beyond the median line every point of which is equidistant from the nearest points on the baselines from which the breadth of the territorial seas of each of the two states is measured. This rule is subject to the exception of cases of 'historic title' or other special circumstances of divergent limitation.

The rules concerning innocent passage in the territorial sea are contained in articles 17–32, and are more extensive in range than the corresponding articles 14–23 in the 1958 Convention, while also taking into account technological

2.　These are bays, the waters of which have come to be regarded as internal in the course of a long period of acquiescence by non-littoral states, irrespective of the distance between the headlands. See *Yearbook* of the International Law Commission, 1962, Vol II, pp 1–26 and generally G. Westerman *The Juridical Bay* (1986). In the unusual case of the historic Gulf of Fonseca, bordered by El Salvador, Honduras, and Nicaragua, the International Court of Justice held that the waters of the Gulf were owned in condominium by the three states: *Case Concerning the Land, Island and Maritime Frontier Dispute*, ICJ 1992, 351.

developments. The right of innocent passage attaches to ships of all states, whether coastal or land-locked, but there is no provision for innocent overflight by alien aircraft. The expressions 'passage' and 'innocent' are defined in article 18 and article 19 respectively. Normally, passage must be continuous and expeditious, but may include stopping and anchoring only in so far as these are incidental to ordinary navigation or are rendered necessary by force majeure (that is, Act of God), or distress, or for the purpose of rendering assistance to persons, ships or aircraft in danger or distress. To be 'innocent', passage must not be prejudicial to the peace, good order or security of the coastal state, nor in breach of the Convention or of other rules of international law. Twelve categories of activities are specified as rendering a passage by a foreign vessel 'prejudicial to the peace, good order or security' of the coastal state, including threats or use of force, weapon exercises, collecting information prejudicial to the defence of the coastal state, pollution, interference with systems of communication, and the launching or landing or taking on board any aircraft. Submarines and other underwater vehicles are required to navigate on the surface and to show their flag.

Article 21 deals with the subject matters of the laws and regulations which a coastal state may adopt with respect to innocent passage; as might be expected, they include the safety of navigation, protection of navigational aids, cables and pipelines, prevention of illegal fisheries, and prevention of customs, fiscal, immigration and health offences. Such laws and regulations are not to apply to the design or construction, etc, of foreign ships unless these were giving effect to accepted international norms. Foreign ships in innocent passage are to comply with duly made laws and regulations of the coastal state. Under article 22, the coastal state may designate sea lanes and prescribe traffic separation schemes, in particular for tankers, nuclear-powered vessels and ships carrying hazardous substances. These lanes and schemes must be clearly indicated. Foreign nuclear-powered ships and ships carrying nuclear or other hazardous substances must carry documents and observe the special precautionary measures established for such ships by international agreements (article 23). At the same time, duties have been imposed on coastal states by article 24, which prohibits requirements serving to hamper or impair innocent passage, or operate in a discriminatory manner. Nonetheless, article 25 empowers coastal states to take steps to prevent a passage which is not innocent, even to the extent of suspending a right of passage if the suspension is essential to protect the security of the coastal state concerned. No charge may be levied in respect of the exercise of a right of innocent passage, except non-discriminatory charges for services rendered (article 26).

The thorny subject of the exercise of criminal and civil jurisdiction on board foreign ships, whether merchant ships or government ships operated commercially, in passage through the territorial sea, is dealt with in article 27 and article 28, respectively (cf articles 19 and 20 of the 1958 Convention). Under paragraph 1 of article 27, the criminal jurisdiction of a coastal state is not to be exercised on board a foreign ship passing through the territorial sea to arrest any person or to conduct any investigation in connection with any crime committed on board the ship during its passage, save only in the following cases:

a. if the consequences of the crime extend to the coastal state concerned;

b. if the crime is of a kind to disturb the peace of the country or the good order of the territorial sea;
c. if the assistance of the local authorities has been requested by the master of the ship, or by a diplomatic agent or consular officer of the ship's flag state; or
d. if such measures are necessary for the suppression of the illicit traffic in narcotic drugs or psychotropic substances.

Except as provided in the Parts of the Convention dealing with the EEZ or the protection of the marine environment the coastal state may not exercise criminal process or undertake any criminal investigation on board a foreign ship in the territorial sea as to a crime committed before its entry therein. In determining whether or how an arrest is to be made, the authorities are to have regard to the interests of navigation.

Civil jurisdiction is provided for in a different manner. The coastal state is not to stop or divert a foreign ship in the territorial sea for the purpose of exercising civil jurisdiction in relation to a person on board the ship. Nor may the coastal state levy execution against or arrest the ship for the purpose of any civil proceedings, save only in respect of obligations or liabilities assumed or incurred by the vessel itself in the course of or for the purpose of its voyage through the coastal state's waters. These prohibitions are, however, without prejudice to the coastal state's right to take measures of civil process against a foreign ship in the territorial sea after leaving internal waters.

Warships are defined and treated in a separate category in articles 29–32 (cf article 23 of the 1958 Convention). A warship not complying with the coastal state's laws and regulations as to passage in the territorial sea and disregarding a request to conform thereto, may be required to leave the territorial sea immediately (article 30). The flag state is to bear 'international responsibility' for damage to the coastal state due to such non-compliance by a warship or other government ship operated for non-commercial purposes, or due to the breach by such vessels of the Convention or other rules of international law (article 31). Leaving aside articles 17–26 (see above) and articles 30–31, nothing in the convention is to affect the immunities of such ships.

The contiguous zone

As to the contiguous zone, article 33 (cf article 24 of the 1958 Convention) lays it down that the coastal state may in such zone exercise the control necessary to prevent infringement of its customs, fiscal, immigration or sanitary laws and regulations within its territory or territorial sea, and punish any such infringements. However, the contiguous zone is not to extend beyond 24 miles from the baselines from which the breadth of the territorial sea is measured.

Straits used for international navigation

Part III of the Convention (articles 34–45) provides a totally new international régime with regard to straits used for international navigation, representing one of the major achievements of UNCLOS III. It begins with general provisions to the effect, inter alia, that the régime of passage through such straits is not to affect the legal status of the waters thereof, or the exercise by countries bordering the straits of their sovereignty or jurisdiction over the waters, the bed, the subsoil and the superjacent air space concerned (article 34), that nothing in Part III is to affect any areas of internal waters within a strait except where the drawing of a baseline has served to enclose as internal waters areas not previously considered as such, the legal status of waters beyond the territorial seas of bordering countries that are of the nature of EEZs or high seas or the legal régime in straits in which passage has been governed by long-standing international conventions (article 35), and that Part III is not to apply to such straits if there exists through the strait concerned a route through the high seas or through an EEZ of similar convenience with respect to navigational and hydrographical characteristics, these routes to be governed by other relevant provisions of the Convention (article 36).

The concept of 'transit passage' is introduced in articles 37–44, and is applicable to straits used for international navigation between one part of the high seas or an EEZ and another part of the high seas or an EEZ (article 37), being defined as the exercise of the freedom of navigation and overflight 'solely for the purpose of continuous and expeditious transit' in the strait, the requirements of 'continuousness' and 'expedition' not precluding passage for the purpose of entering, leaving or returning from a bordering country (article 38). All ships and aircraft are to enjoy, *unimpeded*, this right of transit passage. The right is inapplicable if the strait concerned is formed by an island of a bordering country and its mainland, and there exists seaward of the island a route through the high seas or through an EEZ of similar convenience as to navigational and hydrographical characteristics (article 38). Articles 39–40 impose certain duties on, and set out certain prohibitions to be complied with by ships and aircraft in transit passage; there is nothing surprising about these, inasmuch as ships and aircraft, considered together, are required to proceed without delay, to refrain from the use or threat of force against bordering states and from non-transit activities unless rendered necessary by force majeure, or by distress, while, separately, and respectively, they are to comply with, broadly speaking, the relevant applicable international regulations governing safety at sea or in the air, and non-pollution from ships. There is a special prohibition on foreign vessels, including marine scientific research and hydrographic survey ships, conducting any research or survey activities without the prior authorisation of the bordering states.

Articles 41–42 do not call for detailed reference; in a manner to be expected, they contain provisions for the design by bordering states of sea lanes and traffic separation schemes, and for the adoption by such states of laws and regulations to govern transit passage. Under article 43, user states and bordering states are to co-operate by agreement with respect to safety aids and navigational aids and improvements in straits, and for the prevention, reduction and control of pollution from ships. Article 44 prohibits bordering states from hampering or suspending transit passage, and requires them to give due publicity to any danger to navigation or overflight of which they have knowledge.

The more limited right of innocent passage, as defined in articles 17 et seq (see above) is, however, to apply in straits used for international navigation, if the strait concerned is formed by an island of a bordering country and its mainland (see article 38 above), or is one between a part of the high seas or an

EEZ and the territorial sea of a foreign state. Such right may not be suspended (article 45).

The waters of archipelagic states

Another new régime, and one which is a major feature of the Convention, is created in Part IV of the Convention (articles 46–54) for archipelagic states and the waters of such states.

Definitions are of crucial importance in this connection. Both the expression 'archipelago' and the expression 'archipelagic state' had to be meticulously defined. The relevant definition article, article 46, sets out that the term 'archipelago' means 'a group of islands, including parts of islands, interconnecting waters and other natural features which are so closely interrelated that such islands, waters and other natural features form an *intrinsic* geographical, economic and political entity, or which *historically* have been regarded as such' (emphasis added for the words 'intrinsic' and 'historically'). 'Archipelagic state' is defined to mean 'a state constituted *wholly* [emphasis added] by one or more archipelagos and may include other islands'.

The method of straight baselines is adopted as a solution for the problem of archipelagic waters. The key provisions are contained in articles 47 and 49. An archipelagic state may draw straight archipelagic baselines joining the outermost points of the outermost islands and drying reefs of the archipelago, with the consequence that the archipelagic state's sovereignty extends to the waters thus enclosed, to the superjacent air space, the bed and subsoil thereof and the resources therein contained, but the following conditions and requirements must be met:

1. The baselines must include the main islands and an area in which the ratio of the water to the area of land is between 1:1 and 9:1.
2. The length of the baselines is not to exceed 100 nautical miles, except that up to 3% of the total number of baselines may exceed that length up to a maximum of 125 nautical miles.
3. The baselines must not depart to any appreciable extent from the general configuration of the archipelago.
4. The baselines must not be drawn to and from low-tide elevations (see above), unless lighthouses or similar installations permanently above sea level have been built thereon or where such an elevation is situated wholly or partly at a distance from the nearest island, not exceeding the breadth of the territorial sea.
5. The baselines must not be applied in such a way as to cut off from the high seas or the EEZ the territorial sea of another state.
6. If part of the archipelagic waters lies between two parts of an immediately adjacent neighbouring state, the traditionally exercised rights and legitimate interests of such latter state in the waters, and all rights stipulated by agreement between the two states shall continue and be respected. The breadth of the territorial sea, the contiguous zone, the EEZ and the continental shelf are to be measured from these baselines. Within these archipelagic waters, the archipelagic state may draw closing lines for the delimitation of internal waters, as under articles 9–11, above (mouths of rivers, bays and outermost harbour works).

In subsequent articles (articles 51–54), provision is made for respect to be given by the archipelagic state to existing agreements, traditional fishing rights and existing submarine cables lying entirely under water, for a right of innocent passage, as above, by foreign vessels, through archipelagic waters, for the designation in appropriate manner by the archipelagic states of sea lanes and air routes, and for the same duties to be observed by foreign ships and aircraft, and by archipelagic states, as mutatis mutandis in the case of transit passage through straits used for international navigation under the provisions of articles 39, 40, 42 and 44.

The Exclusive Economic Zone (EEZ)

UNCLOS III will perhaps always be remembered in the history of international law as having given birth to, or at least nurtured to full strength, the concept of the exclusive economic zone (EEZ). The Convention deals with the EEZ in Part V, consisting of no less than 21 articles (articles 55–75). The establishment of an acceptable régime for the EEZ occupied much of the time of UNCLOS III, although the concept itself found ready approval. It has revolutionised the law of the sea.[3] The United States, although opposed to the Convention, nevertheless by the Presidential Proclamation of 10 March 1983 (see above, p 233) explicitly recognised and adopted the concept.

First, there is its definition in articles 55 and 57 as an area beyond and adjacent to the territorial sea, not extending beyond 200 nautical miles from the baselines from which the breadth of the territorial sea is measured (that is, the 200 miles are not measured from the seaward outer limits of the territorial sea).

Second, within this zone, the adjacent coastal state does not have the equivalent of territorial sovereignty, but sovereign rights for the purpose of exploring, exploiting, conserving and managing the resources of the EEZ, and jurisdiction, with due regard to the rights of other states, with respect to the establishment and use of artificial islands and structures, marine scientific research, and the protection and preservation of the marine environment (article 56). Other rights are specified in the remainder of Part V. Broadly speaking, in the EEZ the traditional freedoms of the high seas, for example, navigation, overflight, and the laying of cables and pipelines are unaffected, but in the case of conflicts as to rights and jurisdiction, these are to be resolved 'on the basis of equity and in the light of all the relevant circumstances' (article 59).

Most of the thorny problems and difficulties relating to the working in practice of the coastal state's control over its EEZ are dealt with in articles 60–68, namely the construction of artificial islands, installations and structures by the coastal state (article 60), the conservation and utilisation of the living resources of the EEZ, with special provisions as to certain species, eg highly migratory species such as tuna, and marine mammals. It is beyond the scope and purpose of the present book to traverse in detail the provisions contained in these articles. Rights of participation by land-locked states and geographically disadvantaged states 'on an equitable basis' in the exploitation of an appropriate part of the surplus

3. See generally D. Attard *The Exclusive Economic Zone in International Law* (1986) and R. W. Smith *Exclusive Economic Zone Claims: An Analysis and Primary Documents* (1986). The International Court of Justice in the *Continental Shelf (Tunisia-Libya) Case* ICJ 1982, 18 treated the EEZ as now a settled part of modern international law.

of the living resources of the EEZ (to be worked out through agreements) are conferred by articles 69–70, which articles are, however, not to apply in the case of a coastal state 'whose economy is overwhelmingly dependent on the exploitation of the living resources' of its EEZ (article 71). It remains to be seen whether articles 69–70 will prove to be of concrete value to the states for the benefit of whom these articles were drafted. Being no more than agreements to agree, the articles are inherently weak.

As was to be expected, there is an article, article 73, setting out the limits subject to which a coastal state may enforce the laws and regulations governing the exercise of its sovereign rights and its jurisdiction in the EEZ. Article 73 instances such measures as boarding, inspection, arrest and judicial process, and the penalty of imprisonment for any breaches is excluded. It may be said that in this area a broad and general discretion in the exercise of their powers in the EEZ has been left to coastal states.

The continental shelf

Part VI (articles 76–85; cf articles 1–15 of the Geneva Convention of 1958 on the Continental Shelf) deals not only with the continental shelf, but with the continental margin. In fact, the continental shelf is defined by reference to the continental margin as follows (see paragraph 1 of article 76):

> 'The continental shelf of a coastal State comprises the seabed and subsoil of the submarine areas that extend beyond its territorial sea throughout the natural prolongation of its land territory to the outer edge of the continental margin, or to a distance of 200 nautical miles from the baselines from which the breadth of the territorial sea is measured where the outer edge of the continental margin does not extend up to that distance.'

This paragraph thus recognises both a fictitious and an actual continental shelf. The fictitious one is where the natural prolongation of a state's territory under the sea extends to a distance of less than 200 nautical miles; in that case the state is deemed to have a continental shelf extending beyond the geographical limit to the legal limit of 200 miles, which, in turn, is co-incident with national rights to the seabed granted to each coastal state as part of its EEZ (see above). This politically-inspired elision of two historically quite separate concepts has all but killed the relevance of geomorphological factors in the delimitation of overlapping continental shelves where the distance between the two opposite states is less than 400 nautical miles (see further below). It is only where the natural continental shelf extends beyond 200 nautical miles from the coastal state that the concept of natural prolongation again becomes pertinent.

The criterion of exploitability as determining the outer limit of the shelf, to be found in article 1 of the 1958 Convention, has been discarded. In paragraph 3 of article 76 the continental margin is described as comprising 'the submerged prolongation of the land mass of the coastal state', and as consisting of 'the seabed and subsoil of the shelf, the slope and the rise', but as not including 'the deep ocean floor with its oceanic ridges or the subsoil thereof'. Thus, geological criteria, both of a territorial and marine nature, have been adopted.

The outer limits of both shelf and margin are governed, albeit not very clearly, by paragraphs 4–7 of article 76. It is necessary first to refer to paragraph 7 which provides that, where a shelf extends beyond 200 nautical miles from the territorial sea baselines, the coastal state concerned shall delineate the shelf's outer limits by straight lines not exceeding 60 nautical miles in length, connecting fixed points defined by co-ordinates of latitude and longitude. Under paragraph 4 of the same article, wherever the continental margin extends beyond 200 nautical miles from the territorial sea baselines, the coastal state concerned is to establish the outer edge of the margin by either:

i.   a line delineated in conformity with paragraph 7 by reference to the outermost 'fixed points', at each of which the thickness of sedimentary rocks is at least 1% of the shortest distance from such point to the foot of the shelf; or

ii. a line delineated in conformity with paragraph 7 by reference to 'fixed points' not more than 60 nautical miles from the 'foot' of the continental slope, such foot to be normally the point of maximum change in the gradient at its base.

However, under paragraph 5, the 'fixed points' under (i) and (ii) either shall not exceed 350 nautical miles from the territorial sea baselines or shall not exceed 100 nautical miles from the 2,500 metre isobath. The convoluted if not turgid character of these provisions is further compounded by the declaration in paragraph 6 that, notwithstanding the provisions of paragraph 5, the position is that on 'submarine ridges', not being elevations that are natural components of the continental margin such as the plateaux, rises, caps, banks and spurs of the margin, the outer limit of the continental shelf is not to exceed 350 nautical miles from the territorial sea baselines.

There is somewhat more precision in the remaining paragraphs, 8–10 of article 76. Information on shelf limits outside the 200-mile belt is to be submitted by the coastal state to the Commission on the Limits of the Continental Shelf set up under Annex II of the Convention. Shelf limits established by the coastal state on the basis of the Commission's recommendations are to be 'final and binding' (paragraph 8). The coastal state is also to deposit with the United Nations Secretary-General charts and relevant information permanently describing the shelf's outer limits, to which the Secretary-General shall give due publicity (paragraph 9). Nothing in article 76 is to prejudice the question of delimiting the shelf between states with opposite or adjacent coasts (paragraph 10).

Article 77 defines the rights of the coastal state over the shelf in a manner which differs but little from article 2 of the 1958 Convention. That state has sovereign rights over the shelf for the purpose of exploring and exploiting its 'natural resources', these rights being exclusive in the sense that if it does not explore or exploit these, nobody can undertake activities without its express consent; nor do the rights depend on occupation, effective or notional, or on any express proclamation. The expression 'natural resources' embraces not only the mineral and other non-living resources of the seabed and subsoil, but also living organisms belonging to sedentary species, ie organisms which, at the harvestable stage, either are immobile on or under the seabed, or are unable to move except in constant physical contact with the seabed or subsoil. Thus free-swimming fish or free-moving crustaceans are not, in this context, within the meaning of the expression 'natural resources'. Articles 78–81 clarify some of the limits of these rights; they are not to affect the legal status of the superjacent waters or the air space above these, nor is their exercise to impair navigation or other rights and freedoms of other states under the Convention, such as, specifically, the laying of submarine cables and pipelines, although the delineation of the course of the pipelines is subject to the coastal state's consent. As in the case of the EEZ, under article 60 (see above), the coastal state is to have the exclusive right to construct, etc, artificial islands, installations and structures on the shelf, and the provisions otherwise of article 60 are to apply mutatis mutandis in respect of these. Moreover the coastal state is to have the exclusive right to authorise and regulate drilling on the continental shelf for all purposes.

Article 82 provides, in effect, for a penalty to be paid by states blessed by nature with a continental shelf extending beyond 200 miles. Where exploitation of the natural non-living resources occurs on a shelf area seaward of 200 nautical miles to the edge of the continental margin, the coastal state must make payments, or contributions in kind, to the International Sea-Bed Authority, established under Part XI of the Convention (see below). The first five years of production are free of the duty to make payment, but 1% of the volume or value of production becomes payable in the sixth year, rising annually by 1% until pegged at 7% after the twelfth year of production. The Authority will distribute the payments or contributions to other states parties to the Convention 'on the basis of equitable sharing criteria, taking into account the interests and needs of developing states, particularly the least developed and land-locked among them' (article 82(4)). Obviously, these provisions cannot be regarded as customary law; their practical effect will depend upon the participation of the 'margin states' and the major sea-bed mining states in the Convention regime.

Delimitation of the continental shelf and of the EEZ

It was thought at an early stage of UNCLOS III that the notion and the regime of the continental shelf would become subsumed within those of the exclusive economic zone (EEZ). That proved not to be the case. However, for the purposes of delimitation of seabed areas between adjacent and opposite states the presence of a co-extensive EEZ regime depending on distance as its sole criterion put great pressure on the criterion of natural prolongation, declared by the International Court of Justice in 1969 to be the root of claim to the continental shelf.[4] It is possible for states with overlapping EEZ claims to adopt separate boundaries for the EEZ and the continental shelf[5], but in nearly all recent instances of delimitation states have preferred to negotiate or arbitrate a single boundary for both the EEZ and the continental shelf. Arbitral tribunals[6], and the International Court of Justice itself[7], have since 1978 moved steadily away from

4. *North Sea Continental Shelf Cases*, ICJ 1969, 3.
5. Eg the Treaty on the Zone of Co-operation in the Area between the Indonesian Province of East Timor and Northern Australia, 1989, (1990) 29 ILM 469 applies only to the seabed in respect of oil and gas resources, and not to the living or other resources.
6. *Anglo-French Continental Shelf Arbitration* (1978) 18 RIIA 3, 18 ILM 397; *Guinea-Guinea Bissau Maritime Boundary Delimitation* (1986) 25 ILM 2511 *Canada-France Maritime Boundary between Newfoundland and St Pierre and Miquelon* (1992) 31 ILM 1145.
7. *Tunisia-Libya Continental Shelf Case* ICJ 1982, 18; *Gulf of Maine Case* (Canada/USA) ICJ 1984 246; *Libya-Malta Continental Shelf Case* ICJ 1985; 13, esp at 35; *Maritime Delimitation in the Area between Greenland and Jan Mayen Case* (Denmark v Norway) ICJ 1993, 38.

natural prolongation — and with it, away from geomorphological factors — towards tempering a prima facie equidistance or median line[8] with equitable considerations so as to produce the 'equitable solution' referred to as the sole criterion in articles 74(1) and 83(1) of the 1982 Convention and which now appears to be regarded as customary international law.[9] Emphasis is now placed not on natural prolongation but on the geography of the immediate area in which delimitation is to take place[10], on disparity in coastal lengths[11], and — to a limited extent — economic factors affecting the immediate area.[12] Political factors may also be taken into account: for example, that islands on the 'wrong side' of the median line are dependent territories of the more distant state[13]; but not such factors as the relative wealth or power of the states delimiting their areas. Where it has not been possible for states to agree on a delimitation line, or where for other reasons (such as unity of oil or gas deposits) it is seen as desirable, a joint development zone may be the agreed solution.[14]

The high seas

The régime of the high seas is covered in Part VII, divided into two sections, section 1, 'General Provisions' (articles 86–115; cf articles 1–37 of the Geneva Convention of 1958 on the High Seas), and section 2, 'Conservation and Management of the Living Resources of the High Seas' (cf articles 1–22 of the Geneva Convention of 1958 on Fishing and Conservation of the Living Resources of the High Seas).

Dealing first with the provisions in section 1, one may see from article 86 how the Convention has revolutionised the traditional concept of the high seas. The area of waters corresponding to the concept has shrunk drastically, so that Part VII, bearing the title 'High Seas' applies only to all those parts of the sea not included in the EEZs, in the territorial seas or internal waters of states or in the archipelagic waters of archipelagic states. It is thus in regard to this negatively defined maritime area alone that the freedoms of the high seas specified in article 87 are solely applicable; under this article, such 'high seas' are entirely and fully open to all states, coastal or land-locked, with freedoms of navigation, overflight, laying of submarine cables and pipelines, construction of artificial islands and other installations, fishing and scientific research (subject to Part VI on the continental shelf and Part XIII as to marine scientific research), all such freedoms

---

8. *Jan Mayen Case* (supra), at 60: '[J]udicial decisions on the basis of customary law governing continental shelf delimitation between opposite coasts have . . . regarded the median line as a provisional line that may then be adjusted or shifted in order to ensure an equitable result.'
9. See generally M. D. Evans *Relevant Circumstances and Maritime Delimitation* (1989); LDM Nelson in (1990) 84 AJIL 837.
10. *Gulf of Maine Case*, supra.
11. *Libya-Malta Case; Greenland/Jan Mayen Case*, both supra.
12. *Greenland/Jan Mayen Case*, supra, where a median line would have affected adversely access by East Greenlanders to the capelin fishery on which they were dependent.
13. *Anglo-French Continental Shelf Arbitration*, supra. In the *Newfoundland/St. Pierre and Miquelon Case* (supra), by contrast, no diminished effect was given on that account to those remote French islands since Newfoundland itself was regarded merely as an island of Canada: 31 ILM 1148 at 1165-66; Marston in (1993) 17 Marine Policy 155.
14. Eg the Timor Gap Treaty between Australia and Indonesia, note 5 above; Japan-Korea Agreement of 5 February 1974. See generally H. Fox et al *Joint Development of Offshore Oil and Gas* (1989).

to be exercised with due regard to the interest of other states exercising the same freedoms.

A number of fundamental propositions are enunciated in the subsequent articles. The high seas (within the meaning of Part VII) are to be reserved for peaceful purposes (article 88), no part thereof may be the subject of a claim of sovereignty (article 89), every state has the right to sail thereon ships flying its flag (article 90), and every state is to fix the conditions for the grant of its nationality to ships, for the registration of ships in its territory, and the right to fly its flag, while ships have the nationality of the state whose flag they are entitled to fly, provided that there exists a 'genuine link' between the state and the ship (article 91). Article 92 (similar to article 6 of the 1958 Convention) is concerned with the status of ships as such; they may sail under the flag of one state only, and save in exceptional cases provided for in international treaties or in the Convention, are to be subject to the *exclusive jurisdiction* of that state on the high seas (emphasis added; by thus subjecting ships to the exclusive jurisdiction of the flag State, the doctrine laid down by the decision of the Permanent Court of International Justice in the *Lotus Case*[15] was negated).

The principle laid down in article 92 of the Convention does not necessarily endorse the doctrine that a ship bearing the national flag of a state is for purposes of jurisdiction treated as if it were territory of that state, on the principle that it is in effect a 'floating island'.[16] The latter expression is purely a metaphor, and is one which was criticised in *R v Gordon-Finlayson, ex p An Officer*;[17] in that case, it was pointed out that a ship is not part of the territory of the flag state, but jurisdiction is exercisable over the ship by that state in the same way as over its own territory.[18] Nonetheless, this concept of the notional territoriality of vessels on the high seas had continued, prior to the United Nations Convention on the Law of the Sea of 1982, to receive recognition and application.[19]

A ship may not change its flag during a voyage, or while in a port of call, save in the case of a real transfer of ownership or change of registry. A ship that sails under the flags of two or more states, using them according to convenience, may not claim any of the nationalities with respect to any other state, and may be assimilated to a ship without nationality (article 92). Article 92 does not address what is more popularly called a 'flag of convenience', namely the case where a ship has only one flag but is registered in a state offering favourable 'open registry' conditions for foreign shipowners. These states are nevertheless subject to the stipulations of articles 91 (genuine link between ship and flag state)

---

15. (1927) PCIJ Series A, No 10. See pp 35, 187-188 above.
16. See *R v Anderson* (1868) LR 1 CCR 161, 11 Cox CC 198; the *Lotus Case* (1927) PCIJ Series A No 10; and the *Costa Rica Packet* (1897) 5 Moore's International Arbitrations 4948.
17. [1941] 1 KB 171. For comment on this decision see *Oteri v R* [1976] 1 WLR 1272, PC and cf the American decision of *Cunard SS Co v Mellon* 262 US 100 (1923) at 123. For criticism of the 'floating island' doctrine, see also Hall *International Law* (8th edn, 1924) pp 301–304.
18. Yet a crime committed on board a ship is, for the purposes of an extradition treaty, deemed to have been committed in the territory of the flag state, which is a party to the treaty; see *R v Governor of Brixton Prison, ex p Minervini* [1959] 1 QB 155, [1958] 3 All ER 318.
19. See article 23 of the Rome Convention of 7 October 1952, on Damage Caused by Foreign Aircraft to Third Parties on the Surface, providing that for the purposes of the Convention, a ship or aircraft on the high seas is to be regarded as part of the territory of the state in which it is registered.

and 94 (effective exercise of control). These provisions do not affect the case of ships in the official service of the United Nations and its related agencies which fly the flag of the organisation in question (article 93).

Article 94 proceeds to detail the duties lying upon a flag state with respect to its ships on the high seas. The general principle is proclaimed in paragraph 1 that 'every state shall effectively exercise its jurisdiction and control in administrative, technical and social matters' over its ships. The rest of the article sets out the measures which are to be taken, including, in particular, the maintenance of a proper register, and an elaborate enumeration of steps to be taken for the maintenance of safety at sea.

The question of jurisdictional immunity is dealt with in articles 95–96. Warships on the high seas are completely immune from the jurisdiction of any state other than the flag state, and so also are ships owned or operated by a state and used only on government non-commercial service.

Article 97 deals with the important matter of penal jurisdiction in cases of collisions or other incidents of navigation. Like article 92, which was in more general terms (see above), it negates the doctrine laid down by the Permanent Court of International Justice in the *Lotus Case*,[20] above, by providing that where, in such cases, the penal or disciplinary responsibility of the master or of any other person in the service of the ship is involved, no penal or disciplinary proceedings may be instituted against such latter persons except before the judicial or administrative authorities of the flag state or of the state of which such person is a national. No arrest or detention of the ship, even as a measure of investigation, shall be ordered by any authorities other than those of the flag state.

Under article 98 states are under a duty to require masters of ships flying their flags to render assistance in cases of danger, distress and collisions.

Slavery

Every state is under article 99 to take effective measures to prevent and punish the transport of slaves in ships of its flag, and to prevent the unlawful use of its flag for that purpose. Any slave taking refuge on board *any ship, whatever its flag* [emphasis added] shall ipso facto be free (cf article 13 of the 1958 Convention).

Piracy jure gentium

The subject of piracy jure gentium, dealt with in articles 100–107 of the Convention, can be adequately treated only in the context of the traditional international law on the subject, considered in conjunction with these articles of the Convention.

Traditionally, in its jurisdictional aspects, the offence of piracy jure gentium was unique. Pirates were subject to arrest, trial, and punishment by all states on the ground that they represented an enemy of the human race (hostis humani generis).[1] The vessel (or aircraft) involved was similarly subject to seizure by all

20. (1927) PCIJ Series A, No 10. See pp 35, 187-188 above.
1. So far was this the case that the taking of property by a pirate jure gentium did not divest the title of the true owner (pirata non mutat dominium); see Oppenheim *International Law* (9th edn, 1992), 754, n 2.

states. By their conduct, persons committing the offence were deemed automatically to lose the protection of the vessel's flag state and any privileges that might be due to them by virtue of their nationality.

Formerly, it sufficed to define piracy as meaning simply murder or robbery on the high seas by persons who were in effect outlaws, but this definition was gradually widened to bring it into line with conditions not prevalent when the customary rules on the subject were first evolved. This is reflected in the definition of piracy in article 101 (cf the definition in similar terms in article 15 of the 1958 Convention) as consisting of the following acts:

'(a) any illegal acts of violence or detention, or any act of depredation, committed for private ends by the crew or the passengers of a private ship or a private aircraft, and directed:
  (i)   on the high seas, against another ship or aircraft, or against persons or property on board such ship or aircraft;
  (ii) against a ship, aircraft, persons or property in a place outside the jurisdiction of any State;
(b) any act of voluntary participation in the operation of a ship or of an aircraft with knowledge of facts making it a pirate ship or aircraft;
(c) any acts of inciting or intentionally facilitating an act described in subparagraph (a) or (b).'

Thus accessory conduct is included within the scope of the definition.[2] It follows from this now extended meaning of piracy that the offence may be prompted by motives other than gain, eg revenge. Moreover, the instrument of the offence may be an aircraft as well as a ship while the victim may be another aircraft, provided that it is on the high seas or in terra nullius (ie an area outside the jurisdiction of any state).

The expression 'pirate ship or aircraft' in article 101 is defined in article 103 as connoting a ship or aircraft intended by the persons in dominant control to be used for the purpose of committing the piratical acts specified in article 101.

Because of the operative words 'committed for private ends' in the definition in article 101, acts inspired by political motives and which would otherwise be treated as piratical, do not constitute piracy jure gentium. With respect to the other operative words '*against* another ship or aircraft or *against* persons or property' on board, it has been claimed that the hijacking of an aircraft can never be piracy jure gentium, because the offence is committed 'within' and not against the aircraft, nor against the persons or property on board.[3]

At the outset, it is necessary to distinguish piracy at international law and piracy at municipal law. Under the laws of certain states, acts may be treated as piratical which are not strictly speaking acts of piracy jure gentium. For example, under English criminal law the transport of slaves on the high seas is piracy, but is not so according to international law. In the same way, one must distinguish

2. In 1934, it had been held by the Judicial Committee of the Privy Council in *Re Piracy Jure Gentium* [1934] AC 586, that actual robbery was not an essential element of the crime of piracy, and that a frustrated attempt to commit a robbery on the high seas could be considered as piracy.
3. Hence the adoption of the Hague Convention for the Suppression of Unlawful Seizure of Aircraft 1970. Following the internal seizure of the cruise ship *Achille Lauro* for political purposes in 1985, the International Maritime Organisation sponsored in 1988 the Convention on the Suppression of Unlawful Acts against the Safety of Maritime Navigation.

piracy jure gentium from acts (such as, arms running) which may be deemed to be piracy under bilateral treaties or under joint declarations of policy by states, for the strict meaning of piracy jure gentium cannot be extended by such treaties,[4] or by joint declarations, designed to govern only the relations between the states subscribing to them.

Private vessels or aircraft only can commit piracy, except that a public vessel or aircraft under the control of a crew which has mutinied may be treated as private, if the crew commit piratical acts (see article 102 of the Convention). A warship or other public ship under the orders of a recognised government or recognised belligerent Power cannot be a pirate ship because any unlawful acts committed by it are imputable to the flag state and engage the latter in responsibility. Difficulties in this connection have arisen when hostilities at sea have been conducted by insurgents in the course of a civil war. Obviously it is in the interests of the legitimate parent government to declare that those in control of insurgent vessels are pirates and to put them at the mercy of the navies of the great maritime Powers. The British practice however, has been not to treat these insurgent vessels as pirate vessels as long as they abstain from repeated or wilful acts of violence against the lives and property of British subjects. It would seem, however, that insurgent units, which commit acts of violence or depredation, in no way connected with the insurrection, such as entirely arbitrary attacks upon foreign shipping, may legitimately be treated as guilty of piracy jure gentium.

A test is sometimes suggested for distinguishing the unlicensed violence of piracy from the recognised action permitted to insurgents, namely that there is an insurgent government or administration with which foreign states may conduct relations, and which is capable of assuming responsibility for the acts of those serving in its armed forces. The test therefore is whether the insurgent vessels are acting under the orders of a responsible government[5] against which a state, affected by any injury to its citizens, may obtain redress according to the recognised principles of international law. Inasmuch as the essence of piracy is the absence of any government which can be held responsible for the piratical acts, it follows that generally speaking, apart from the circumstances in which the acts were committed (eg, if such acts consist of entirely arbitrary attacks upon foreign shipping), the offence of piracy is negatived if there be such a government.

All states are under a duty to co-operate to the fullest possible extent in the suppression of piracy on the high seas, or in any other place outside the jurisdiction of any state (article 100). Other relevant provisions in the Convention concerned with piracy are to the following effect:

4. Examples of such treaties are: (a) the abortive treaty concluded at the Washington Naval Conference of 1922 providing that persons violating the humane rules of maritime warfare should be tried and punished 'as if for an act of piracy'; and (b) the Nyon Arrangement of 1937 for joint action by the European Powers to prevent sinkings of merchant vessels in the Mediterranean by unidentified submarines during the course of the Spanish Civil War, which attacks were referred to as 'piratical acts'. As to the inapt use of the word 'pirate' as applied to offshore radio stations in the North Sea area, see p 250 below. More recently the term 'pirate' has been applied to the maker of unlawful copies of musical records or cassettes.

5. In the case of *The Ambrose Light* 25 Fed 408 (1885), an American federal court held that an armed vessel commissioned by Colombian insurgents was properly seized as a pirate ship because there had been no express recognition of the insurgents as belligerents.

a. A ship or aircraft may retain its nationality although it has become a pirate
    ship or aircraft. The retention or loss of nationality is determined by the
    law of the state from which such nationality was derived (article 104).
b. Every state may seize a pirate ship or aircraft, or one taken by piracy and
    under the control of pirates, and arrest the persons concerned for trial by
    the courts of the seizing state (article 105). This signifies that the jurisdiction
    exercisable in regard to pirates is of a 'universal' nature (see Chapter 8 above
    at pp 212-213).
c. Such seizure may be carried out only by warships or military aircraft, or
    other ships or aircraft clearly marked and identifiable as being on government
    service and authorised to that effect (article 107).

Traffic in narcotic drugs or psychotropic substances
All states are to co-operate in the suppression of the illicit traffic in narcotic drugs
and psychotropic substances engaged in by ships on the high seas contrary to
international conventions (article 108).

Unauthorised broadcasting from the high seas
Article 109 deals with problems of jurisdiction occasioned by unauthorised or
unregulated broadcasting from vessels stationed in, or installations in the high
seas—problems which had become acute in the 1960s, and which had then not
previously engaged the attention of authorities of coastal states. For the purposes
of the Convention, 'unauthorised broadcasting' is defined as 'the transmission
of sound radio or television broadcasts from a ship or installation on the high
seas intended for reception by the general public contrary to international
regulations, but excluding the transmission of distress calls'. All states are to
co-operate in the suppression of such broadcasting, and any person engaged
therein may be prosecuted before the courts of:

a. the ship's flag state;
b. the state of registry of the installation;
c. the state of the person's nationality;
d. any state where the transmissions are receivable; or
e. any state where authorised radio communication is suffering interference.

Such states may arrest the person concerned on the high seas, and seize the
broadcasting unit concerned.

Right of visit
An important article, article 110, confers on warships a right of boarding foreign
vessels, in addition to treaty rights permitting such interference, provided that
the vessel visited is not immune under articles 95–96 (see above), and that there
is reasonable ground for suspecting that the vessel is engaged in piracy, the slave
trade, unauthorised offshore broadcasting with the flag state having jurisdiction
under article 109 (see above), or is without nationality, or though flying a foreign
flag or refusing to show its flag, is of the same nationality as the warship. These
provisions apply mutatis mutandis to military aircraft.

Hot pursuit
The right of hot pursuit[6] is covered in a long and comprehensive article, article 111 (cf article 23 of the 1958 Convention). Hot pursuit of a foreign vessel may be undertaken if there is good reason to believe that the vessel has violated the laws and regulations of the coastal state, but it must be commenced when the vessel or one of its boats is within internal waters, archipelagic waters, the territorial sea or the contiguous zone, and may only be continued outside the territorial sea or contiguous zone if the pursuit has not been interrupted. It is not necessary that at the time when the vessel within the territorial sea or contiguous zone receives the order to stop that the signalling ship should likewise be within these waters. If the foreign vessel is within the contiguous zone, pursuit is permissible only if there has been a violation of the rights for the protection of which the contiguous zone was established. Such right of pursuit applies mutatis mutandis to the EEZ and continental shelf. Pursuit may be commenced only after a visual or auditory signal to stop has been given at a distance which enables it to be seen or heard by the vessel signalled. Pursuit is permissible only by warships or military aircraft or other ships or aircraft clearly marked and identifiable as being on government service and authorised to that effect. The right ceases as soon as the pursued vessel enters the territorial sea of its own state or of a third state.

Cables and pipelines
Articles 112–115 deal with the free right of all states to lay submarine cables and pipelines on the bed of the high seas beyond the continental shelf, and with the duties of states to adopt laws and regulations in regard to the breaking of, or injury to such cables and pipelines.

Conservation and management of living resources
The subject of conservation and management of the living resources of the high seas is dealt with in section 2 of Part VII in a manner reconcilable with the economic considerations governing articles 61–62 on the same matter in Part V on the EEZ (see above), which articles contain the key concepts. Paragraph 1 of article 61 (the article in respect to conservation of living resources) requires that the coastal state 'shall determine the allowable catch of the living resources' in the EEZ; while the use of the word 'shall' suggests a mandatory determination, article 297 (3)(a) on the settlement of fisheries disputes refers to the coastal state's 'discretionary' powers for determining the allowable catch. These provisions can be reconciled by treating paragraph 1 of 61 as involving a mandatory exercise of a discretion, the discretion being in regard to the end result. The remaining paragraphs of article 61 are drafted with due regard to the perils of over-exploitation and the necessity of proper management. Paragraph 1 of article 62 (on utilisation of the living resources) requires the coastal state to 'promote the objective of optimum utilisation of the living resources' of the EEZ. Although not specifically defined, the expression 'optimum utilisation' receives some elaboration in the succeeding paragraphs of the article. Thus, paragraph 2

6.   See generally P. Poulantzas *The Right of Hot Pursuit in International Law* (1969).

provides that the coastal state is to allow other states access to[7] any surplus beyond its own national requirements as determined by it. Moreover, under paragraph 3, in granting access to the surplus, the coastal state is to take into account all relevant factors, including inter alia 'the significance of the living resources of the area to the economy of the coastal state concerned and its other national interests', so that possibly political considerations may be relevant. The terms of both articles leave the coastal state with considerable latitude in the choice of the particular measures that may be adopted to achieve the declared objectives of management and utilisation of the living resources.

In section 2 of Part VII, article 116 proclaims that all states have the free right for their nationals to fish on the high seas subject to their treaty obligations, while the rights and duties, as well as the interests of coastal states are provided for, inter alia, in those articles on the protection or preservation of certain species in the EEZ. Articles 117–119 impose duties on the states parties to co-operate with other states in the conservation and management of the living resources of the high seas, to the extent that in determining the allowable catch and adopting other conservation measures, the best scientific evidence available is to be taken into account, as qualified by relevant environmental and economic factors, while also regard is to be had to the effect on species associated with the 'harvested' species. Provision is made also for exchanging scientific information, catch statistics and other relevant data. Measures taken are not to be discriminatory against the fishermen of any state.

Section 2 of Part VII is weaker than the corresponding provisions of the 1958 Convention on the Conservation of the Living Resources of the High Seas, which allowed for unilateral measures of conservation to be taken by coastal states in circumstances of urgency. But then it must be remembered that in 1958 the high seas began at 12 nautical miles from shore; now they begin at 200 miles. Even so, pressure on particular species, resulting from unrestrained fishing practices, especially the use of drift gill-nets, has become intense in recent years, prompting studies by the Food and Agriculture Organisation of the United Nations, and other concerned bodies, the declaration of a moratorium on the use of drift gill-nets in the Pacific Ocean approved by the United Nations General Assembly in 1989[8], and even the threat by certain states (eg Canada) of unilateral action. In this respect the 1982 Convention is already outdated.

Islands

A short Part VIII, comprising one article only, article 121, deals with the régime of islands. An island is defined as a naturally formed area of land, surrounded by water, and which is above water at high tide. The territorial sea, the contiguous zone, the EEZ and the continental shelf are determined for islands in the same way as the provisions of the Convention otherwise make such determination in respect to land territory, but mere rocks which cannot sustain human habitation or economic life of their own are not to have an EEZ or a continental shelf.[9]

7.   With regard to the acquired or traditional fishing rights of non-littoral states, cf the *Fisheries Jurisdiction Case* (Iceland-United Kingdom) ICJ 1974, 3.
8.   (1990) 29 ILM 1555. See also the Wellington Convention on Drift Gill-net Fishing in the South Pacific: ibid, 1449.
9.   The *Greenland/Jan Mayen Case* confirms that an island populated only by research scientists and their staffs can generate an EEZ: ICJ 1993, 38, at 73-74.

Enclosed or semi-enclosed seas

Part IX introduces the concept of an 'enclosed or semi-enclosed sea' defined in article 122 as:

a. a gulf, basin or sea surrounded by two or more States and connected to another sea or the ocean by a narrow outlet; or

b. consisting entirely or primarily of the territorial seas and EEZs of two or more coastal states.

Under article 123, states bordering on such a sea are to co-operate with each other with respect to their rights and duties under the Convention, and are required to 'endeavour', directly or through an appropriate regional organisation, to co-ordinate their rights, duties and scientific research policies (enumerated in paragraphs (a)–(c) in that connection), and to invite, as appropriate, other interested States or international organisations to co-operate with them in furtherance of the provisions of the article.

Right of access of land-locked states to and from the sea and freedom of transit

The detailed provisions in Part X (articles 124–132) for the right of access of land-locked states to and from the sea and for the related privilege of passage through states lying between them and the coast (defined in article 124 as 'transit states') represent distinctly another major feature of the Convention. Such right of access and freedom of transit are conferred or purported to be conferred by article 125, for the purpose of land-locked states exercising their rights otherwise under the Convention. The terms and modalities of such freedom of transit are to be settled by agreement, but transit states are entitled to ensure that this freedom of passage shall in no way infringe their legitimate interests. It may reasonably be objected that the Convention in effect bestows on land-locked states no definitive right of transit. Much depends on the transit states concerned acting in good faith in the implementation of article 125.

The remaining articles of Part X contain provisions, more or less to be expected, or of a self-evident nature. Transit traffic is not to be subject to customs or other charges, except for specific services rendered, or to taxes or charges that are discriminatory vis-à-vis local transport; free zones may be provided by agreement; transit states and land-locked states may co-operate in the provision of adequate means of transport; and transit states are to take steps to avoid delays or technical difficulties for transit traffic, while ships flying the flag of land-locked states are to enjoy in maritime ports treatment equal to that accorded to foreign ships.

The 'Area' and related provisions

Part XI deals with the 'Area', ie, the seabed and ocean floor and subsoil thereof, and related provisions, and may be regarded as directed to the future establishment of a deep seabed mining régime (DSBM). As to this Part, it cannot yet be said that it commands universal consensus, and in these circumstances, it is believed that it would be inappropriate at this juncture to examine Part XI in any detail in this book, save broadly to describe its content. It is divided into five sections, namely, section 1 consisting of general provisions defining the scope of the Part, section 2 enunciating the fundamental principles concerning the legal status, responsibilities of States, etc, so far as concerns the Area, section 3 dealing with the development of the resources of the Area, and the relevant policies to be applied as to such development, section 4 providing for the establishment of an 'International Sea-Bed Authority' for the purposes, inter alia, of organising and controlling activities in the Area, and administering its resources, and defining also the function and composition of the proposed organs of the Authority, together with the related matters of financial arrangements for the Authority and the legal status, privileges and immunities of the Authority and its organs, and section 5 containing provisions for the settlement of disputes by, and for advisory opinions to be given by the Sea-Bed Disputes Chamber of the International Tribunal of the Law of the Sea, the Statute of which Tribunal is set out in Annex VI to the Convention. Reference perhaps should be made to article 136 proclaiming the doctrine which influenced the taking of the steps leading to the convening of UNCLOS III, viz that 'the Area and its resources are the common heritage of mankind', and to article 137 defining generally and consistently with the doctrine of article 136 the legal status of the Area and its resources (no state to claim or exercise sovereignty or sovereign rights over any part of the Area or its resources).

It is well known that the objections of the developed states to the 1982 Convention were substantially confined to certain provisions of Part XI. As a result they failed altogether to sign (eg Germany, the United Kingdom, the United States), or have withheld ratification (eg France, Japan, Russia) of, the 1982 Convention.[10] Most of these states before and after 1982 passed national legislation authorising interim arrangements for licensing exploration and exploitation of the deep sea bed, with provision for eventual contributions to such international authority as might later come into existence.[11] Some have entered into a 'reciprocating states agreement' in order to avoid overlapping grants of national licences[12]. The prospects for the entry into force of the 1982 Convention with a modified form of Part XI are discussed below, p 259.

Protection and preservation of the marine environment
Part XII deals with the protection and preservation of the marine environment, and is one of the longest Parts in the Convention containing 11 sections comprised of no less than 46 articles (articles 192–237). It could not really be claimed, however, that Part XII is one of the best drafted Parts of the Convention. In a number of the articles, there appears to be unnecessary verbosity, with the consequence here and there of a degree of ambiguity. Some provisions are self-evident and throughout the Part there is a certain degree of repetitiousness. It would not be consistent with the purpose of this book to attempt an analysis of Part XII other than one of the broadest nature.

10. For the objections of the United States see (1982) 82 AJIL 364.
11. Eg Deep Sea Bed Hard Mineral Resources Act 1980 (USA); Deep Sea Mining (Temporary Provisions) Act 1981 (UK).
12. Agreement Concerning Interim Arrangements relating to Polymetallic Nodules of the Deep Sea Bed, 1982, 21 ILM 950, and Provisional Understanding, 1984, 23 ILM 1354 (Belgium, France, Germany, Italy, Japan, Netherlands, UK, USA).

Section 1 (articles 192–196) bears the title, 'General Provisions', and the general obligation is proclaimed in article 192 that states have the obligation to protect and preserve the marine environment, while in recognition nonetheless of the resource policies of developing and other states. It is provided that states have the sovereign right to exploit their natural resources pursuant to their environmental policies, and in accordance with their duty to protect and preserve the marine environment. The two articles thus reflect the same kind of relationship between development and environmental considerations that manifested itself in the course of the Stockholm Conference of 1972 on the Human Environment (see Chapter 14, below, on Development and the Environment, at pp. 358, 367-369).

These general articles are followed by articles 194–196 on measures to prevent, minimise and control pollution of the marine environment, or the creation of additional damage or hazards, and on measures to prevent, etc, pollution of that environment by new technologies or the introduction of alien or new species.

Section 2 (articles 197–201) deals in a manner to be expected with global and regional co-operation, section 3 (articles 202–203) with scientific and technical assistance in this area to developing states and provides for preferential treatment to be afforded to such states, section 4 (articles 204–206) with the monitoring of the risks or effects of pollution, the publication of results of such monitoring, and the assessment of the potential effects of activities as to which there may be reasonable grounds for believing that these could cause substantial or significant and harmful changes to the marine environment, and section 5 (articles 207–212), bearing the title, 'International Rules and National Legislation to Prevent, Reduce and Control Pollution of the Marine Environment', contains provisions as to pollution from land-based sources, pollution from seabed activities subject to national jurisdiction, pollution from activities in the 'Area', the adoption by states of laws and regulations to prevent, minimise and control the pollution of such an environment by dumping, pollution from vessels, and pollution from or through the atmosphere.

Section 6 on Enforcement (articles 213–222) is of some significance by reason of the duties, inter alia, imposed on states, according to the source of pollution, to enforce anti-pollution or anti-dumping regulations. The enforcing state may be that state having territorial jurisdiction (land-based sources of pollution; article 213), or the exploiting state (pollution from seabed activities; article 214), or in the case of dumping, the coastal state where dumping occurs within its territorial sea, EEZ or continental shelf, the flag state of the vessel or aircraft responsible for dumping, or the state having territorial jurisdiction as to acts of loading of wastes, etc occurring within its territory (article 216). Special articles deal with enforcement by flag, port and coastal states, and with measures to be taken by a port state as to the seaworthiness of vessels within one of its ports or at one of its offshore terminals. There is a special article also with respect to enforcement of measures as to pollution from or through the atmosphere (article 222), while under article 221 nothing in Part XII is to prejudice the right of states under international law to take and enforce measures beyond the territorial sea proportionate to the actual or threatened damage to protect their coastline or related interests, including fishing, from pollution or threat thereof, following upon a maritime casualty or acts relating thereto, which may reasonably be expected to have major harmful results (cf the Brussels Conventions of 1969 as to Oil Pollution Casualties and Oil Pollution Damage, referred to above, pp 229-230).

Section 7 (articles 223–233) is entitled 'Safeguards', which does not appear to be a very appropriate heading, in the light of the content of the section, which deals with measures to facilitate proceedings (tendering of evidence, etc), by what agencies the powers of enforcement are to be exercised, the manner of investigation of foreign vessels, the limitation of penalties to those of a monetary nature, notifications of action taken by the flag state or other state concerned, the liability of states for unlawful or excessive measures and safeguards in respect of passage through straits used for international navigation (see above, pp 238-240).

Section 8 on ice-covered areas, containing the one article, article 234, confers important rights on coastal states that have jurisdiction over such areas; they are entitled to 'adopt and enforce' non-discriminatory laws and regulations for the prevention, reduction and control of marine pollution from vessels in ice-covered areas within the limits of the EEZ, where particularly severe climatic conditions and the presence of ice over such areas for most of the year create obstructions or exceptional hazards to navigation, and pollution of the marine environment would cause major harm to, or irreversible disturbance of, the 'ecological balance'. Due regard is to be had to navigation and the preservation of the marine environment based on the best available scientific evidence.

Section 9 on responsibility, also containing the one article, article 235, renders states responsible for the fulfilment of their international obligations as to the marine environment. This again seems to be either a self-evident provision or redundant. It also provides, inter alia, that states are to ensure that their legal systems afford prompt and adequate remedies for damage caused by pollution of the marine environment by persons under their jurisdiction.

Under section 10 on sovereign immunity (containing only article 236), the above-mentioned provisions are not to apply to any warships, naval auxiliary, other vessels or aircraft owned or operated by a state and used, for the time being, only on government non-commercial service. However, states are to ensure that such vessels or aircraft act in a manner consistent, so far as is reasonable and practicable, with the Convention.

Finally, section 11, the concluding section of Part XII (containing only article 237) endeavours to reconcile the provisions of that Part with the obligations of states under other conventions on protecting and preserving the marine environment; if previously concluded, Part XII is not to prejudice the special obligations of states thereunder. This applies also to agreements concluded in furtherance of the general principles laid down in the Convention.

Marine scientific research, development and transfer of marine technology, settlement of disputes, general provisions and final provisions

The remaining Parts of the Convention, Parts XIII, XIV, XV, XVI and XVII, deal respectively with the subjects of marine scientific research, the development and transfer of marine technology, the settlement of disputes, the general provisions and the final provisions of the Convention. It is proposed to examine these Parts only in a broad manner, and without going into detail.

Part XIII enunciates general principles concerning what is declared to be the right of all states to conduct marine research; eg this must be exclusively for peaceful purposes, and without interfering with the legitimate uses of the sea compatible with the provisions of the Convention. International co-operation in this area is to be promoted through such means as the publication and dissemination of information and knowledge, and in particular the furnishing of information to affected coastal states. All such research in the EEZ and in the waters of the continental shelf is to be subject to the consent of the coastal state, but when the proposed research is solely for peaceful purposes and is in conformity with a number of other criteria laid down in Part XIII, consent is normally to be given. The development of scientific research installations and equipment in the marine environment must be effected in such a way as to conduce to safety, and so as not to interfere with shipping routes; also, identification markings must be borne, and warning signals are required to be given. States and international organisations are to be held responsible for damage caused by their own research activities, or for action taken against research conducted by others, when such action is in breach of the Convention. Inter alia, in the event of certain disputes, the researching state may require the coastal state to submit to international conciliation upon the ground that the coastal state had not acted in a manner compatible with the Convention.

Part XIV contains somewhat ambitious provisions concerned with promoting the development, transfer and dissemination of marine technology, international co-operation to implement these objectives (including in that regard co-operation with the projected International Sea-Bed Authority), the establishment of national and regional marine scientific and technological centres and co-operation among and with international organisations. Some of the provisions of Part XIV, although expressed in the language of obligations, appear nevertheless to be of a hortatory character. Part XIV imposes upon States the duty to promote marine technology on fair and reasonable terms and conditions, with due regard for all legitimate interests, including the rights and duties of holders, suppliers and recipients of technology. Broadly speaking, international co-operation will be promoted through the establishment of guidelines, criteria and standards for technology transfer, and the co-ordination of international programmes.

Part XV on the settlement of disputes likewise contains a number of ambitious provisions. States are obliged to settle by peaceful means any disputes over the interpretation or application of the Convention. When they cannot reach agreement on a negotiatory basis, they will have to submit most types of disputes to a compulsory procedure involving a binding decision; provision in that regard is made in section 2 bearing the title 'Compulsory Procedures Entailing Binding Decisions'. States have four options in such compulsory procedure. Under paragraph 1 of article 287 (the second article in section 2) a state, when signing, ratifying or acceding to the Convention or at any time thereafter, shall be free to choose by means of a written declaration, one or more of the following means for the settlement of disputes concerning the interpretation or application of the Convention:

a. The International Tribunal for the Law of the Sea, to be established in accordance with Annex VI to the Convention (see ante).
b   The International Court of Justice.
c. An arbitral tribunal constituted in accordance with Annex VII.
d. A special arbitral tribunal constituted in accordance with Annex VIII for particular categories of disputes (fisheries, the marine environment, marine scientific research or navigation, etc).

Paragraph 2 of article 287 provides that such a declaration under paragraph 1 is not to affect or be affected by the obligation of a state party to accept the jurisdiction of the Sea-Bed Disputes Chamber of the International Tribunal as provided for in section 5 of Part XI (settlement of disputes relating to the 'Area'). Then, under paragraph 3, a state party which is party to a dispute not covered by a declaration in force, is to be deemed to have accepted arbitration in accordance with Annex VII. Section 3 sets out the limitations on the applicability of section 2. Certain categories of disputes will have to be submitted to conciliation (Annex V), which procedure is in its results not binding on the parties. The most notable exception to the binding procedures of section 2 is the interpretation or application of the Convention's provisions on fisheries; coastal states are not obliged to accept binding forms of settlement in the case of disputes concerning their sovereign rights in the EEZ, including the exercise of their discretionary power of determining the allowable catch, their harvesting capacity, and the allocation of surpluses to other states. States have the option of declining to accept compulsory settlement processes in the case of certain categories of disputes as to specially sensitive matters, eg, boundaries and military activities.

Part XVI, entitled 'General Provisions', proclaims a number of general principles which are to govern the conduct of states parties. Two at least of these seem redundant, inasmuch as they are expressive of already established principles; eg, article 300 declaring that states parties are to fulfil in good faith their obligations under the Convention, and are to exercise their jurisdictions, etc, without abuse of any right, and article 301 which reiterates the prohibition in paragraph 4 of article 2 of the United Nations Charter (no threat or use of force against the territorial integrity or political independence of any state, or conduct in any manner inconsistent with the principles of international law contained in the United Nations Charter). States are not bound to disclose information contrary to their essential security interests. Coastal states have jurisdiction over archaeological objects and objects of historical origin found at sea up to the outer edge of their contiguous zone. States parties are under a duty to protect such objects found at sea, and to co-operate in the performance of this duty (article 303).

Part XVII contains the final provisions. Reservations to the Convention are prohibited by article 309. This is understandable, having regard to the arduously negotiated 'package' nature of the Convention and the stated goal of achieving a uniform text with universal participation. Article 310 permits the making of declarations designed to harmonise the Convention with domestic laws (eg to state that such national institutions as a 'patrimonial sea' will be applied in accordance with the Convention's regime of the EEZ), but not such as to seek to qualify the application of the Convention (eg the declarations made by the Philippines to which objections have been lodged by several states). The non-seabed provisions of the Convention can be amended by two-thirds of the states parties, but the amendments will apply only to those states which ratify or accede thereto. The seabed provisions can be amended with the approval of the Assembly and the Council of the Authority, but only if they do not prejudice the system of exploration and exploitation pending a review conference to be held fifteen years after commercial exploitation begins. The Convention remained open for signature until 9 December 1984, at the Jamaica Ministry of Foreign Affairs, and, also from 1 July 1983 until 9 December 1984, at the United Nations Headquarters in New York. As a consequence, there were 159 signatory states ie 41 more than the original signatories on 10 December, the major non-signatories being the United States, the United Kingdom and Federal Republic of Germany. With the deposit of the 60th instrument of ratification (by Guyana) on 16 November 1993, in accordance with article 308 the Convention entered into force one year later on 16 November 1994.

General

At the time of writing (April 1994) there were signs of an important breakthrough in efforts to achieve universal participation in the Convention, Part XI of which had represented the sole stumbling block. Informal consultations under the auspices of the Secretary-General of the United Nations began in 1990 with a view to exploring the possibilities of modifying the implementation of Part XI upon entry into force of the Convention without resorting to the formal amendment procedure provided for in article 304 which would, in any event, have had to await the outcome of the Review Conference provided for in article 155 and which, in turn, could not have been held until 15 years after the earliest commercial production had begun under a plan of work approved by the Authority. A Resolution and Implementing Agreement were drafted for presentation to a special session of the United Nations General Assembly in mid-1994. The Resolution calls on states to accept both the Implementing Agreement and the 1982 Convention and to apply them together as one instrument. The effect of the Implementing Agreement is to modify substantially the provisions of Part XI of the Convention, most notably by reducing the costs to state parties, and the size, of institutional arrangements, removing the obligation of authorised contractors to fund a parallel mining site of the Enterprise, giving greater weight to the role of the developed states in decision-making through chambered voting procedures, applying market principles to the transfer of technology, and bringing the production policy of the Authority into line with GATT and other market principles and rules. The general effect of the Implementing Agreement is to go a long way towards meeting the objections of the technologically advanced states to the provisions of Part XI in their original form and to make possible the wide and representative participation in the Convention necessary to ensure an international regime for the exploration and exploitation of the deep sea bed.

That, for all practical purposes, the four Geneva Conventions of 1958 (see above) have ceased to be operative, except as between a minority of states inter se seems clear; article 311 paragraph 1 of the Convention provides that the

Convention shall prevail, as between states parties, over the Geneva Conventions of 1958, and this would imply that the latter conventions can, at the free discretion of non-parties, remain operative between them inter se, although as a practical matter they are more likely to accept the main provisions of the Convention (ie other than those concerning the 'Area' and the Sea-Bed Authority) as governing their activities at sea. Article 311 paragraph 2 lays it down that the Convention is not to alter the rights and obligations of states parties under agreements compatible with the Convention, and which do not affect the enjoyment by other states parties of their rights or the performance of their obligations under the Convention. This reflects the fact that certain maritime matters remain outside the scope of the Convention. An illustration is that of the general regulations to be observed for preventing collisions at sea. These regulations were originally set out in an Annex to the Final Act of the London Conference of 1960 on the Safety of Life at Sea, but they were superseded by the revision thereof effected by the Convention of 1972 on the International Regulations for Preventing Collisions at Sea, which came into force on 15 July 1977, and to which, at the date of writing, 113 states are parties. Amendments to this Convention were adopted on 19 November 1981 by the resolution of the Assembly of the Intergovernmental Maritime Consultative Organisation (IMCO)—the name of which Organisation was changed as from 22 May 1982, to that of the 'International Maritime Organisation' (IMO).

The United Nations Convention on the Law of the Sea is an instrument without precedent in the history of international legislation, and its impact on the domain of international law generally can or will be measured only with any certainty in the course of time.

3. MARITIME CANALS

Canals which are inland waterways are part of the territory of the territorial states through which they pass, and by analogy are subject to the rules as to rivers.

As to maritime canals, special treaty rules are or have been applicable to the Suez, Panama and Kiel Canals. The Suez Canal was to some extent neutralised and demilitarised by the Convention of Constantinople of 1888, under which it was to be freely open in time of peace[13] as well as of war to merchant vessels and warships of all nations. It was not to be blockaded, and in time of war no act of hostility was to be allowed either in the canal itself or within three sea miles from its ports. These provisions could not, and did not in practice preclude a strong naval power, such as Great Britain, in time of war, from blockading access for enemy vessels to the Canal beyond the limit of three sea miles. Men-of-war were to pass through the Canal without delay, not staying longer than

13. In September 1951, the United Nations Security Council affirmed the principle of freedom of transit through the Suez Canal under this Convention by adopting a Resolution calling upon Egypt to terminate certain restrictive practices in respect to shipping passing through the Canal, which were designed by Egypt to operate as a 'blockade' of the ports of Israel. From the comments of certain delegates, it appeared that the Constantinople Convention was regarded as dedicating an international maritime highway.

24 hours in Port Said and Suez. Troops, munitions, and other war material were not to be shipped or unshipped inside the Canal or in its harbours, and no permanent fortifications were allowed in it, or the stationing of men-of-war. Subject to the provisions of the 1888 Convention, the Canal was territorially part of Egypt.

In 1956, Egypt purported to nationalise the Suez Canal Company which enjoyed a concession to operate the Canal. It thereupon became a vital question, as to what extent the free rights of states to use the Canal might be subject to impairment in the future. In ultimate analysis, the issue lay at the root of the Anglo-French intervention against Egypt in the Canal zone, in October–November 1956.

There is an opinion of some weight to the effect that the rights to use the Canal are not dependent on the former concession, nor exercisable only on sufferance by Egypt, but are vested rights of an international character, guaranteed by international law. Reference may be made, apart from the 1888 Convention, to the Anglo-Egyptian Agreement of 19 October 1954, under which the parties recognised that the Canal was 'a waterway economically, commercially and strategically of international importance', and to the principles approved by the United Nations Security Council on 13 October 1956—among them, that freedom of passage should be maintained 'without discrimination, overt or covert', that the Canal should be 'insulated' from the politics of any country, and that tolls and charges should be fixed by agreement. Egypt's Declaration of 24 April 1957,[14] in which it affirmed that it would respect the terms and spirit of the 1888 Convention, has, however, prevented the issue from becoming clarified.

The Panama Canal stands in an entirely different position from the Suez Canal. The status of, and the respective rights of the United States and Panama with respect to that Canal are now governed by a set of treaties and arrangements concluded by the two governments at Washington on 7 September 1977 and consisting, inter alia, of the Panama Canal Treaty and Annex thereto, a Treaty concerning the Permanent Neutrality and Operation of the Panama Canal (hereinafter referred to as 'the Neutrality and Operation Treaty'), and a Protocol to the latter treaty.

By these arrangements a new régime has been created for the Panama Canal, superseding the four treaties which had previously regulated the status of the Canal as an international waterway and the respective rights in respect thereto of the United States, Panama and third countries, namely the Hay-Pauncefote Treaty of 1901 between the United States and Great Britain, the Hay-Varilla Treaty of 1903 between the United States and Panama, the Treaty of Friendship and Co-operation between the United States and Panama signed in March 1936, and the Treaty of Mutual Understanding and Co-operation between the United States and Panama concluded in January 1955. The 1901 Treaty had provided that the Canal should be free and open to the vessels of commerce and war of

---

14. For the text of the Declaration, see 51 AJIL (1957) 673–675. The Canal was opened to Israel-bound cargoes in pursuance of article 5 of the Egypt-Israel Peace Treaty, thus ending restrictions imposed since 1948 on the basis of self-defence on Egypt's part.

all nations on terms of entire equality,[15] and that the Canal was not to be blockaded, nor any act of hostility committed within it. Under the 1903 Treaty the United States was to enjoy rights of operation and control over the Canal Zone in perpetuity, and for all practical purposes continued de facto to exercise sovereign rights in regard to the area.

Under the Panama Canal Treaty of 1977, however, Panama's territorial sovereignty over the Canal and the Canal Zone is explicitly recognised, while the United States Government is to relinquish control at the end of 1999; Panama, as 'territorial sovereign', grants to the United States 'for the duration of the Treaty' rights of operation of, maintenance of and protection of the Canal, and rights to regulate the orderly transit of vessels. Implicit in these provisions is the continuance of the Canal as an international maritime and access route—a status spelled out in more detail in the Neutrality and Operation Treaty, and in the Protocol thereto. In article I of the Neutrality and Operation Treaty, Panama declared that the Canal *as an international transit waterway*, shall be permanently neutral in accordance with the régime established in the Treaty', and in article II it has made a declaration of the neutrality of the Canal 'in order that both in time of peace and in time of war it shall remain secure and open to *peaceful transit* by the vessels of all nations on terms of entire equality', without discrimination as to conditions or charges of transit.[16] Under article V, at the end of 1999, when the United States Goverment is to relinquish control, only Panama is to operate the Canal and to maintain military forces, defence sites and military installations in the Canal Zone. The Protocol is significant as enabling participation in the new régime of countries other than Panama and the United States; under Article III, the Protocol is open to accession 'by all States of the world'. Thus the Protocol serves to multilateralise the provisions for non-discriminatory access and neutrality, in effect as part of general international law, by its impact on the position bilaterally created between the United States and Panama under the Neutrality and Operation Treaty.

Some commentators have entered reservations with respect to the question whether this will necessarily represent the purported effect of the 1977 arrangements between the United States and Panama. They have raised the point that the word 'transit', introduced into the provisions of the treaties, is ambiguous, and might not be wide enough to cover all such movements and operations by commercial vessels and warships as might conceivably become necessary; for example, for the defence of the Canal. On the other hand, the provisions are open to the interpretation that they constitute a 'dedication'[17] of the Canal as an international non-discriminatory maritime highway.

The Kiel Canal was made freely open to the merchant vessels and warships of all nations under the Treaty of Versailles of 1919, but in 1936 Germany denounced the relevant provisions contained in article 380 of the Treaty. In the

15. Although it did not contain an express provision that the Panama Canal was to be open to all vessels in time of peace as well as of war. Ideally, the principle of non-discrimination should apply to all canals which are international highways; and cf Baxter *The Law of International Waterways* (1964) p 183.
16. Cf as to the principle of non-discrimination and international maritime highways, Baxter, op cit, p 183.
17. Cf Baxter, op cit, pp 182-183.

Wimbledon Case,[18] the Permanent Court of International Justice held in respect of the Kiel Canal, and applying the precedents of the Suez and Panama Canals, that the passage of a belligerent warship through an interoceanic canal would not compromise the neutrality of the riparian state. However, following apparent acquiescence by other states in the assertion of full sovereignty over the Canal in 1936, it would appear that the Kiel Canal is no longer subject to the international regime.[19]

18. (1923) PCIJ , Series A, No 1, at 25, 28.
19 *Ari Case* (1957) 7 Jahrbuch für internationales Recht 405. An earlier German case left the point open: (1950) 17 ILR 133.

CHAPTER 10

State responsibility

1. NATURE AND KINDS OF STATE RESPONSIBILITY

Frequently action taken by one state results in injury to, or outrage on, the dignity or prestige of another state. The rules of international law as to state responsibility concern the circumstances in which, and the principles whereby, the injured state becomes entitled to redress for the damage suffered.[1] State responsibility has been authoritatively stated to be confined to 'the responsibility of states for internationally wrongful acts'.[2] This is state responsibility in the strict sense, the source of such responsibility being an act or acts in breach of international law. But can liability be cast upon states in respect of acts not constituting a violation of any rule of international law, eg, private conduct, regardless of whether such conduct is or is not in contravention of domestic law? This subject has for some time now been under consideration by the International Law Commission under the heading 'International Liability for Injurious Consequences Arising out of Acts not Prohibited by International Law'. It is almost entirely of the nature de lege ferenda, ie an area in which the law has yet to be formulated, and is regarded as being mainly concerned with the duties of governments to oversee activities which may lead to trans-border environmental damage.

Obviously the redress to be obtained for internationally wrongful acts will depend on the circumstances of the case. Most usually the injured state will attempt to get *satisfaction* (as it is called) through diplomatic negotiations, and if only its dignity has been affected, a formal apology from the responsible state or an assurance against the repetition of the matters complained of, will generally be regarded as sufficient. Pecuniary reparation, as distinct from satisfaction, is, however, sometimes necessary, particularly where there has been material loss or damage, and in many instances the question of liability and the amount of compensation have to be brought for adjudication before an international arbitral tribunal.

1. With regard to the work of the International Law Commission 1973–1980 on state responsibility, a subject that it had commenced considering in 1955, see S. Rosenne *The International Law Commission's Draft Articles on State Responsibility* (1991). See also generally I. Brownlie *System of the Law of Nations: State Responsibility* (pt 1), (1983).
2. *Report* of the International Law Commission on the Work of its *27th Session* (1975) para 33, p 6.

The wrongs or injuries which give rise to state responsibility may be of various kinds. Thus a state may become responsible for breach of a treaty, in respect of the non-performance of contractual obligations, for injuries to citizens of another state, and so on. The breach of duty may be: (a) an act, or (b) an omission.

In ultimate analysis, state responsibility is governed by international standards (although in particular branches an international standard may incorporate a national standard), and it depends on international law whether and to what extent the act or omission of a particular state is deemed legitimate or wrongful. Where the acts or omissions of a state measured by such standards are held to be legitimate, state responsibility does not arise. For example, as all states are generally conceded to have complete power to refuse to admit aliens into their territory, the states of which the aliens are nationals have no claim against any state which has refused ingress. Similarly, where international law concedes jurisdiction to a state which proceeds to exercise it, there is no breach of duty for which that state is responsible.

The law of state responsibility is still in evolution, and may possibly advance to the stage where states and individuals are fixed also with responsibility for breaches of international law which are 'international crimes'[3] as distinct from normal responsibility for breaches giving rise ordinarily to an obligation only to make reparation or pay compensation. Indeed the United Nations General Assembly since 1978 and the International Law Commission since 1982 have continuously been concerned with the subject of international criminal responsibility, to be formulated in a Code of Offences against the Peace and Security of Mankind (to include, inter alia, the crime of apartheid, and that of racial discrimination). Some Western countries are unenthusiastic about the project of such a Code, because, among other considerations, it might lead to the review of treaties which are working reasonably well, or because of problems concerning what sort of tribunal or tribunals would be needed to exercise jurisdiction over offending states or individuals.

Another important matter which will have incidence on the developing law of state responsibility is the extent to which states are or may become involved in the control of ultra-hazardous activities, eg, nuclear experiments, the

---

3. At the 1962 session of the International Law Commission, some members were of the opinion that 'under modern international law, State responsibility arose less in connection with the treatment of aliens than as a result of acts which endangered or might endanger international peace, such as aggression, denial of national independence, or of exchange of friendly relations with States, and violation of provisions of the United Nations Charter' (see *Report* of Commission on the Work of its *14th Session* (1962) p 31). One of the principles proclaimed in the Declaration on Principles of International Law Concerning Friendly Relations and Co-operation among States in accordance with the United Nations Charter, adopted by the General Assembly in 1970, is: 'A war of aggression constitutes a crime against the peace, for which there is responsibility under international law'. Draft article 19 on state responsibility, as adopted by the International Law Commission, deals with 'international crimes', defined (in para 2) as resulting from the breach by a state of an international obligation so essential for the protection of the fundamental interests of the international community that such breach is recognised by that community as a whole as an international crime—a somewhat circular definition. Para 3 of the same article goes on to illustrate this definition by examples, such as a breach of the prohibition against aggression, maintaining colonial domination by force (contrary to self-determination), and breaches of a serious nature of the prohibitions against slavery, genocide, apartheid and massive pollution of the atmosphere or seas.

development of nuclear energy, space exploration[4] and the 'sonic boom' or 'sonic bang' of new types of aircraft. This is not a domain in which traditional diplomatic procedures of protest, demands for satisfaction, and claims can be of avail. Dangers must be anticipated, and if possible completely excluded; eg, if there be such a risk as an alteration of the environment of the earth. It may be necessary to impose strict duties of consultation, notification, registration and providing information, while even a process of injunction, mandatory or restraining, may need to be developed. There may be room for other international safeguards.

Federal states, protected states, and component territorial government entities
The question frequently arises as to the *incidence of liability* when injury is done by or through a state member of a federation, or by or through a protected state. The accepted rule appears to be that the federal state and the protecting state are responsible for the conduct respectively of the member state and the protected state, inasmuch as in the realm of foreign affairs they alone are recognised as having capacity to enter into relations with other states. This is true even although the facts and events which give rise to liability are actually matters constitutionally within the exclusive competence of the member state or the protected state. According to the International Law Commission[5] 'a consistent series of legal decisions', cited by it in the report, 'has affirmed the principle of the international responsibility of the Federal State for the conduct of organs of component States amounting to a breach of an international obligation of the Federal State, even in situations in which internal law does not provide the Federal State with means of compelling the organs of component States to abide by the Federal State's obligations'. In the same report[6] reference was made to two other suggested justifications for this principle of the international responsibility of the federal state, namely:

a. The conduct of the component state is imputed or attributed to the federal state, in the same way as the conduct of its federal organs.
b. The rationale that the federal state is in a sense vicariously responsible for the conduct of a component state.

It follows that it will be no defence to an international claim as to conduct by a component state to plead the provisions of the federal constitution or—in the case of a claim relating to the conduct of the protected state—the terms of the treaty of protection. British practice has long adhered to these principles, and as long ago as in the course of the preparatory work for the Hague Codification Conference of 1930, it was officially stated on behalf of Great Britain that 'the distribution of powers between [a federal state] and the other or subordinate units on whose behalf it is entitled to speak is a domestic matter with which foreign states are not concerned', thus corresponding to the first rationale stated above.

4. See pp 161-171 above.
5. *Report* of the Commission on the Work of its *26th Session* (1974) para 123, in its commentary on draft art 7 on State Responsibility.
6. Ibid.

A like doctrine applies in respect to other component units of states in general, whether federal or unitary. In its above-mentioned report of 1974, the International Law Commission stated:[7]

'The principle that the State is responsible for acts and omissions of organs of territorial governmental entities, such as municipalities, provinces and regions, has long been unequivocally recognised in international judicial decisions and the practice of States.'

With respect to the normal overall responsibility of the federal state for a component state's breach of international obligations, there is one qualification which was specifically referred to by the International Law Commission in its above-mentioned report of 1974.[8] In certain federations, the position is that the component state may for some purposes or in some degree be treated as a subject of international law, and, as such, may have international obligations which are incumbent on it, but not on the federal state of which it is a member. The conduct of the component state, if in breach of its international obligations, is then imputable or attributable solely to it, and not to the federal state.

Limits between international law and municipal law

It is important when considering practical cases of state responsibility to keep clearly in mind the limits between international law and municipal law. This distinction has a particular bearing on two matters:

a.   the breach of duty or non-performance by a state of some international rule of conduct which is alleged to give rise to responsibility;[9]
b.   the authority or competence of the state agency through which the wrong has been committed.

As to a., the breach or omission must in ultimate analysis be a breach of, or omission to conform to, some rule of international law. It is immaterial that the facts bring into question rights and duties under municipal law as between the state alleged to be responsible and the citizens of the claimant state. Further, it is no answer to an international claim to plead that there has been no infraction of municipal law if at the same time a rule of international law has been broken, or, as it has been put by the International Law Commission, the fact that an act may be characterised as internationally wrongful 'cannot be affected by the characterisation of the same act as lawful by internal law'.[10]

As to b., it is in general not open to any state to defend a claim by asserting that the particular state agency which actually committed the wrongful act exceeded the scope of its authority under municipal law. A preliminary inquiry as to the agency's authority under municipal law is necessary as a matter of

---

7.   Ibid; cf *Heirs of Duc de Guise Award* (1951), United Nations Report of International Arbitral Awards, Vol XIII, 161 (responsibility of Italy for the region of Sicily).
8.   Ibid.
9.   The International Law Commission currently prefers that the breach be referred to as a 'breach of an international obligation', rather than as a breach of a rule or norm of international law; see Professor Ago's Fifth Report (1976) on State Responsibility to the Commission, paras 5–6, pp 3–4.
10. See draft art 4 on State Responsibility, in *Report* of the Commission on the Work of its *27th Session* (1975) para 52, p 11.

course, but if, notwithstanding that the agency acted beyond the scope of its authority, international law declares that the state is responsible, international law prevails over municipal law.

It follows from these two principles, a. and b., that, as already mentioned in Chapter 4 above[11] a state may not invoke its municipal law as a reason for evading performance of an international obligation.

Defences and justifications

The subject of defences and justifications with respect to a claim of state responsibility—a subject not generally elaborated upon in some international law treatises—did, however, occupy the attention of the International Law Commission at its sessions, in particular, in 1979 and 1980. In 1979, it adopted draft articles as regards the following defences:

a.   The alleged wrongful act has been committed by a state in circumstances where it is subject to the power of direction or control of another state, as the result of coercion exerted by that other state.
b.   Consent by the state affected by the alleged wrongful act to its commission.
c.   Countermeasures (eg, by way of legitimate reprisals) permissible in international law and not involving armed force.
d.   Situations of irresistible force majeure or of extreme distress, contributing to the commission of the unlawful act, where there was an absence of wilfulness on the part of the officials concerned.

In 1980, the International Law Commission adopted two important articles on the justifications, respectively, of necessity and self-defence. The provision as to a state of necessity (draft article 33) imposed somewhat severe restrictions on this defence; it was as follows:

'1.   A state of necessity may not be invoked by a State as a ground for precluding the wrongfulness of an act of that State not in conformity with an international obligation of the State unless:

a.   the act was the only means of safeguarding an essential interest of the State against a grave and imminent peril; and
b.   the act did not seriously impair an essential interest of the State towards which the obligation existed.

2.   In any case, a state of necessity may not be invoked by a State as a ground for precluding wrongfulness:

a.   if the international obligation with which the act of the State is not in conformity arises out of a peremptory norm of general international law[12]; or
b.   if the international obligation with which the act of the State is not in conformity is laid down by a treaty which, explicitly or implicitly, excludes the possibility of invoking the state of necessity with respect to that obligation; or
c.   if the State in question has contributed to the occurrence of the state of necessity.'

11. See above, pp 78-79.
12. Ie a rule of jus cogens; see pp 48-50 above.

The draft article (article 34) adopted as to self-defence was phrased in general terms so far as concerns lawful acts of self-defence in response to an armed attack within the meaning of article 51 of the United Nations Charter, or in other words, it did not enumerate or specify what particular acts should be deemed to possess the character of self-defensive measures; it was in these terms:

'The wrongfulness of an act of a State not in conformity with an international obligation of that State is precluded if the act constitutes a lawful measure of self-defence taken in conformity with the Charter of the United Nations.'

2. RESPONSIBILITY FOR BREACH OF TREATY, OR IN RESPECT OF CONTRACTUAL OBLIGATIONS; EXPROPRIATION OF PROPERTY[13]

State responsibility for breach of a treaty obligation depends upon the precise terms of the treaty provision alleged to have been infringed. More often than not this raises purely a question of construction of the words used. If the treaty provision is broken, responsibility follows. According to the Permanent Court of International Justice in the *Chorzów Factory (Indemnity) Case*[14] it is a principle of international law that 'any breach of an engagement involves an obligation to make reparation'. Reparation must, so far as possible, wipe out the consequences of the illegal act and re-establish the situation that would have existed had the illegality not occurred. Depending on the nature of the illegality and the seriousness of the consequences reparation may range in form from apology, punishment of individuals responsible for the unlawful act[15], and repeal of offensive legislation[16], to restitution in kind or the payment of monetary compensation.

Somewhat different considerations apply to the case of contracts entered into between a state and alien citizens or corporations. Such contracts are typically governed by the municipal law of the state party. A breach by a state of such a contract will not necessarily engage its responsibility at international law, nor will such responsibility, when it exists, be identical in kind with the liability under the contract. Here, the responsibility at international law arises only if the state breaks some duty extraneous to the contract, for example, if it be guilty of a denial of justice to the other contracting party. A state may, however, impliedly contract with another state that it will observe the terms of arrangement with a citizen of the latter state, although it would seem from the decision of the

---

13. See generally on the rules of international law as to expropriation, Wortley *Expropriation in Public International Law* (1959); G. White *Nationalisation of Foreign Property* (1961); I. Foighel *Nationalization: A Study in the Protection of Alien Property in International Law* (1982). In regard to recent developments and changed approaches, see M. Sornarajah *The Pursuit of Nationalised Property* (1986); R. Lillich (ed) *The Valuation of Nationalized Property in International Law 1972-75* (1976); W. Mapp *The Iran-United States Claims Tribunal* (1993).
14. (1928) PCIJ Ser A, No 17, p 29.
15. Eg the Rainbow Warrior affair, above pp 91-92.
16. Among the many measures ordered against Iraq by the Security Council in Resolution 687 of 3 April 1991, as conditions under which the enforcement action would cease, was the demand that the legislature of Iraq pass a formal act rescinding its purported annexation of Kuwait.

International Court of Justice in the *Anglo-Iranian Oil Co Case* (*Jurisdiction*) that weighty proof is required of such an implied treaty.[17]

A private contractor may also seek to 'internationalise' the contract by the insertion of clauses in it that make international law the governing law of the contract expressly, or impliedly by clauses referring disputes under the contract to binding international arbitration.[18] This type of contractual provision is often allied with a 'stabilisation clause' which declares that the state party will not alter its laws to the disadvantage of the private party during the currency of the contract.[19] The internationalisation of a contract may not always be effective in practice to prevent a state from altering the contract contrary to a stabilisation clause or to enable the private party to secure an order of specific performance of it, but it will afford a basis in international law for compensation for breach of it.[20]

The responsibility of a state for expropriating[1] foreign private property is an entirely different matter. Concessionary contracts, if regarded as such by the municipal law of the state party, are also treated much as though they were property rights; typical examples are concessions relating to mining, manufacturing, transportation, utilities and communications.[2] In the nineteenth century any expropriation of the property of an alien would have been regarded as a clear basis for an international claim. At the present time, however, the widened control by states over their national economies and of almost every aspect of private enterprise, together with the advent of colonial territories to independence desirous of economic self-determination, make it impossible to treat, as necessarily contrary to international law, an expropriation of foreign private property[3]. This movement has been reflected in a series of United Nations General Assembly resolutions confirming the rights of states to manage their

---

17. ICJ 1952, at 109 et seq; there the British Government claimed that when, in 1933, it sponsored the conclusion of a new oil concession contract between Persia and the Anglo-Iranian Oil Company, Persia engaged itself towards Great Britain not to annul or alter the concession. The Court rejected the contention, holding that there was no privity of contract between Persia and Great Britain (ibid, at 112).
18. See eg *BP Exploration Co v Libya* (1974) 53 ILR 297; *Texaco v Libya*, ibid 389; *Aminoil v Kuwait* (1982) 66 ILR 518.
19. See eg *LIAMCO v Libya* (1981) 62 ILR 140; El Chiati in (1987-IV) 204 Recueil des Cours 9-170.
20. *Texaco v Libya*, above.
1. The terms 'nationalisation' and 'confiscation' have also been used. The term 'expropriation' appears, however, to be the generic term, and to include 'nationalisation', ie the taking of property by a state with a view to its continued exploitation by that state in lieu of the exploitation by private enterprise; see *Anglo-Iranian Oil Co v Idemitzu Kosan Kabushiki Kaisha* [1953] ILR 305, for the view that nationalisation is merely a species of expropriation. The term 'confiscation' is used to denote a temporary acquisition of property, as in time of war or an arbitrary or penal taking of property, without compensation (cf Garcia Amador's Fifth Report on International Responsibility, presented in 1960 to the International Law Commission). For what measures may constitute an expropriation when the state has not formally so acted but has intervened heavily in the affairs of the concern see *Starrett Housing Corpn v Iran* (1983) 4 Iran-US CTR 122.
2. O'Connell *International Law* (2nd edn, 1970) p 992.
3. See generally Jiminéz de Aréchaga in (1978-79) 11 NYU J1 Int L & Pol 179; Dolzer in (1981) 75 AJIL 553; Higgins in (1982-III) 176 Recueil des Cours 259; Bowett in (1988) 59 BYIL 49; Norton in (1991) 85 AJIL 474.

own economies. In the Resolution on Permanent Sovereignty over Natural Resources, 1962, the General Assembly declared that:

> 'Nationalisation, expropriation or requisitioning shall be based on grounds or reasons of public utility, security or the national interest which are recognised as overriding purely individual or private interests, both domestic and foreign. In such cases the owner shall be paid appropriate compensation in accordance with the rules in force in the state taking such measures in the exercise of its sovereignty and in accordance with international law....'[4]

An attempt was made in later resolutions of 1973 and 1974 leading to the Charter of Economic Rights and Duties of States, 1974, (associated with the concept of 'the New International Economic Order') to state these principles in terms more agreeable to developing states, in particular by removing the public purpose requirement and the reference to international law, and by purporting to confine compensation questions to the domestic law and tribunals of the expropriating state.[5] This formulation has not been accepted by arbitral tribunals as having changed customary law, the relevant paragraph of the 1974 Resolution having failed to gain the support of the developed and capital exporting states and thus lacking in the widespread and representative support in practice and opinio juris necessary to demonstrate an emerged norm.[6]

Practice, doctrine and case law unite in showing that, to be valid under international law, an expropriation of foreign private property must:

1. be for a public purpose in accordance with a declared national policy;
2. not discriminate between aliens and citizens, or as between different foreign nationalities;
3. not involve the comission of an unjustified irregularity;
4. be accompanied by the payment of appropriate compensation.

A distinction is drawn, for the purpose of adjudging appropriate reparation, between lawful and unlawful expropriations, as defined above. Nothing less than *restitutio in integrum*, or its monetary equivalent, is held to be the appropriate level of reparation in the case of unlawful takings.[7] Where monetary compensation in lieu of restitution is deemed appropriate, the amount will include not only the market value of the assets (*damnum emergens*) but also damages representing the loss of expected profits (*lucrum cessans*). For lawful takings the standard of compensation is less easy to state authoritatively, as it has varied in state practice and arbitral opinion, and has also been affected, in some cases, by the desire to achieve a lump-sum settlement in respect of a number of claims

---

4. Resolution 1803(XVII), para 4.
5. General Assembly Resolution 3281(XXIX), para 2(c): '[Each state has the right to] nationalise, expropriate, or transfer ownership of foreign property, in which case appropriate compensation should be paid by the state adopting such measures, taking into account its relevant laws and regulations and all circumstances that the state considers pertinent. In any case where the question of compensation gives rise to a controversy, it shall be settled under the domestic law of the nationalising state and by its tribunals, unless it is freely and mutually agreed by all states concerned that other peaceful means be sought on the basis of sovereign equality of states and in accordance with the principle of free choice of means.'
6. See, eg, *Texaco Overseas Petroleum v Libya* (1977) 53 ILR 389, per Arbitrator Dupuy; the *Sedco Case* (1986) 10 Iran-US CTR 180; Weston in (1981) 75 AJIL 437.
7. *Chorzów Factory Case*, above.

by dispossessed property owners of the same nationality.[8] The prescription of a 'prompt, adequate, and effective' level of compensation (usually referred to as 'the Hull formula' after United States Secretary of State Cordell Hull's representations to the Mexican Government in 1938) has been qualified in more recent times by recognition that developing economies are not always able to afford the payment of immediate compensation in full, and that 'adequacy' is to be assessed against such factors as whether the nationalisation programme was wide-ranging, and whether the foreign investment concerned was recent or had delivered substantial profits for many years. It seems that adequacy tends now to be influenced by the negative measure of what would be unjust enrichment to the expropriating state if the taking were uncompensated, and to be assessed against other equitable criteria.[9] The measure of compensation due in the case of an expropriated business is normally to be assessed on a 'going concern' valuation, which includes as well as the physical assets of the enterprise such components as contracts, patents and goodwill, and 'future prospects'; but the last is not to be equated with loss of future earnings, a component added only in the case of unlawful expropriations.[10]

In the case of an unlawful expropriation, the expropriating state must, in addition to paying the compensation due in respect of a lawful expropriation, pay also damages for any loss sustained by the injured party.[11]

In recent times, problems as yet unsolved by international law have been created by the emergence of various forms of so-called 'creeping expropriation' (eg, restriction of profits by discriminatory price control, taxes on the repatriation of capital, high discriminatory taxation, etc).[12] One method of mitigation of the difficulties involved is by the negotiation of bilateral treaties of friendship and commerce, with provisions, among others, for consultation between the parties.

So far as the status of foreign expropriation decrees in municipal courts is concerned, it seems that in general the rules of private international law will apply. The normal rule as to property is that the *lex situs* of a recognised state applies. Thus the English courts will give effect to the foreign expropriatory decree, even if the expropriation is contrary to international law[13], if the property concerned was situated within, or was under the control of, the expropriating state at the time of the expropriation.[14] Where the property was in England at the time of the expropriation then it will be unaffected, whether the expropriation

8. As in the cases of nationalisations in Eastern Europe after World War II.
9. See the Iran-US Claims Tribunal in the *INA Case* (1985) 8 Iran-US CTR 371, per Judge Lagergren at 389-390.
10. *Amoco International Finance Corpn v Iran (the Khemco Case)* (1987) 15 Iran-US CTR 189.
11. See *Chorzów Factory (Indemnity) Case* (1928) PCIJ Series A, No 17 pp 46–48.
12. Cf D. H. Ott *Public International Law in The Modern World* (1987) pp 188–189. One suggested solution is the payment of partial compensation of an appropriate nature, having due regard fairly to the internal needs of the compensating state; see C. P. Bauman in (1987) 19 *Case Western Reserve Journal of International Law* pp 103–119.
13. A case to the contrary is the decision of the Supreme Court of Aden in *Anglo-Iranian Oil Co v Jaffrate (The Rose Mary)* [1953] 1 WLR 246, but this is now not regarded as good law in England.
14. *Williams & Humbert Ltd v W & H Trade Marks (Jersey) Ltd* [1986] AC 368, [1986] 1 All ER 129.

was contrary to international law[15], or not, or even for a purpose approved of according to the public policy of the forum state.[16]

The 'Calvo Clause'

It is convenient at this point to discuss the clauses of the type known as the 'Calvo Clause'. These clauses (named after the Argentinian jurist, Calvo) were at one time very frequently inserted in contracts between Central and South American governments and foreign companies or persons to whom concessions or other rights are granted under the contracts. Under such a clause foreign concessionaires renounced the protection or assistance of their government in any matters arising out of the contract. The following clause, which was adjudicated upon in the *North American Dredging Co Case*[17] before the United States–Mexico General Claims Commission, is an example:

'The contractor and all persons, who, as employees or in any other capacity, may be engaged in the execution of the work under this contract either directly or indirectly, shall be considered as Mexicans in all matters, within the Republic of Mexico, concerning the execution of such work and the fulfilment of this contract. They shall not claim, nor shall they have, with regard to the interests and the business connected with this contract, any other rights or means to enforce the same than those granted by the laws of the Republic to Mexicans, nor shall they enjoy any other rights than those established in favour of Mexicans. They are consequently deprived of any rights as aliens, and under no conditions shall the intervention of foreign diplomatic agents be permitted, in any matter related to this contract.'

The object of such a clause is to ensure that legal disputes arising out of the contract shall be referred to the municipal courts of the state granting the concession or other rights, and to oust the jurisdiction of international arbitral tribunals or to prevent any appeal for diplomatic action to the national state of the company or individual enjoying the concession, etc. Its insertion in so many contracts with Latin American states was due to the number of occasions when on rather weak pretexts concessionaire companies or persons in these states sought the intervention of their own governments to protect their interests without any recourse to the remedies available in local municipal courts.

There have been several conflicting decisions by international arbitral tribunals on the legality of the Calvo Clause. In a number of cases it has been held null and void on the ground that individuals cannot contract away the right of their governments to protect them. In other cases the arbitrators have treated it as valid and as barring the claim before them. Thus, in the *North American Dredging Co Case*,[18] the United States–Mexico General Claims Commission dismissed the claim on the ground that under the clause it was the duty of the claimant company to use the remedies existing under the laws of Mexico, and

---

15. Eg confiscatory decrees against Jews in Germany and Austria: *Frankfurther v WL Exner Ltd* [1947] Ch 629.
16. As, eg, in the case of foreign legislation designed to protect national art treasures or cultural property by declaring forfeit to the state any such items exported without authority, provided that such forfeiture was operative before the item left the prescriptive state: *A-G for New Zealand v Ortiz* [1984] AC 1.
17. Annual Digest of Public International Law Cases, 1925–1926, No 218.
18. See n 17 above.

on the facts the company had not done this. This decision has been accepted by the British Government as good law. On the other hand, in the case of the *El Oro Mining and Rly Co Ltd*[19] where the Calvo Clause was pleaded as a defence, the British–Mexican General Claims Commission declined to dismiss the claim inasmuch as the claimant company had actually filed suit in a Mexican court, and nine years had elapsed without a hearing. Therefore, it could not be said that the claimant company had sought to oust the local jurisdiction.

Perhaps the better opinion as to the Calvo Clause may be summed up as follows:

1. Insofar as such clause attempts to waive *in general* the sovereign right of a state to protect its citizens, it is to that extent void.
2. But, to quote a statement of the British Government, 'There is no rule to prevent the inclusion of a stipulation in a contract that in all matters pertaining to the contract, the jurisdiction of the local tribunals shall be complete and exclusive'. In other words, it would be obviously improper for individuals to treat the state against which they seek redress as an inferior and untrustworthy country, and to apply for their government's intervention without making any claim in the local courts.
3. Where such a stipulation purports to bind the claimant's government not to intervene in respect of a clear violation of international law, it is void.

To sum up, it may be said that the Calvo Clause is ineffective to bar the right of states to protect their nationals abroad, or to release states from their duty to protect foreigners on their territory.

Debts

Claims asserting the responsibility of a state for debts more frequently arise in cases of state succession where an annexing or successor state seeks to evade the financial obligations of its predecessor. Such claims also occur, however, in many other cases where governments fail in the service of loans or default in contributions to international institutions of which they are members.

Three theories have been advanced as to the right of a state to protect subjects, creditors of another state:

1. Lord Palmerston's theory, enunciated in 1848, that the former state is entitled to intervene diplomatically, and even to resort to military intervention as against a defaulting debtor state.
2. The 'Drago Doctrine' (so called after the Argentinian Minister of Foreign Affairs who first affirmed it in 1902) that states are duty bound not to use against a defaulting debtor state compulsory measures such as armed military action. This doctrine was intended to apply in favour of Central and South American states as a virtual corollary to the Monroe Doctrine;[20] accordingly, in its later form, it laid down that the public debts of such American states could not 'occasion armed intervention nor even the actual occupation of the territory of American nations by a European Power'. Drago's objections were principally confined to the use of armed force in the collection of public

19. Annual Digest of Public International Law Cases, 1931–1932, No 100.
20. See above, pp 98-99.

debts; he was not directly opposed to diplomatic intervention or to claims before international tribunals. Subsequently, the Hague Convention of 1907 for limiting the Employment of Force for the Recovery of Contract Debts provided that the states parties to the Convention would not resort to armed force in order to recover contract debts due to their nationals by another state, except where the state refused to accept arbitration or to submit to an arbitral award.[1]

3. According to the most generally accepted theory, the obligation of a debtor state is similar in all respects to obligations under international agreements in general. Therefore no special rules nor special methods of redress are applicable where a debtor state defaults.

3. RESPONSIBILITY FOR INTERNATIONAL DELINQUENCIES (WRONGS UNCONNECTED WITH CONTRACTUAL OBLIGATIONS)

In practice, most cases of state responsibility, at least before international tribunals, arise out of wrongs alleged to have been committed by the state concerned. By wrong in this connection is meant the breach of some duty which rests on a state at international law and which is not the breach of a purely contractual obligation. To such wrongs, more frequently the term 'international delinquency' is applied. It is too early yet to measure the effects of the impact on the present topic of the increasing tendency under international law to cast responsibility on individuals for delinquencies (see Chapter 3, above).

Most of the cases which come under this head concern injuries suffered by citizens abroad. Indeed, the topic of protection of citizens abroad makes up much of the law on this subject. These injuries may be of different kinds, for example, injuries to property in the course of riots, personal injuries, improper arrests by the local authorities, the refusal of local judicial tribunals to accord justice or due redress, and so on. Generally speaking, a person who goes to live in the territory of a foreign state must submit to its laws; but that is not to say that certain duties under international law in respect to the treatment of that person do not bind the state. Examples are the duty on the state to provide proper judicial remedies for damage suffered, and the duty to protect alien citizens from gratuitous personal injury by its officials or subjects.

It may be said that according to international law, aliens resident in a country have a certain minimum of rights necessary to the enjoyment of life, liberty and property, but these are most difficult to define.

In the subject of international delinquencies, it is important to apply the notion of *imputability*. This notion assists in clarifying the subject and in providing a proper framework for its theory. To take a practical example, if an agency of state X has caused injury to a citizen of state Y in breach of international law, technically we say that state X will be responsible to state Y for the injury done.

---

1. Having regard to the obligations of states members of the United Nations to settle their disputes peacefully, and to refrain from the threat or use of force against other states (see art 2 of Charter), the 'Drago Doctrine' has lost much of its importance and application.

What this means is that the organ or official of state X has committed a wrongful act, and the conduct in breach of international law is *imputed* from the organ or official to the state. The *imputation* is thus the result of the intellectual operation necessary to bridge the gap between the delinquency of the organ or official, and the attribution of breach and liability to the state.[2]

The practical necessity of the notion is founded on the importance of keeping clear the limits between international law and municipal or state law. Breaches of duty by state agencies may be imputed to the respondent state according to rules of international law, even though under municipal law such acts would not have been imputed to that state, because, for example, the agency concerned had acted outside the scope of its authority.

Imputability therefore depends on the satisfaction of two conditions:

a.   conduct of a state organ or official in breach of an obligation defined in a rule of international law;
b.   that according to international law, the breach will be attributed to the state.

It is only if the breach is imputable that the state becomes internationally responsible for the delinquency. Responsibility begins where imputability ends. As has been emphasised by the International Law Commission:[3]

'. . . The attribution of an act or omission to the State as an international legal person is an operation which of necessity falls within the scope of international law. As such it is distinct from the parallel operation which may, but need not necessarily, take place under internal law.'

In establishing the incidence of state responsibility, the inquiry proceeds as follows:

1.   It is first of all necessary to determine whether the state organ or official guilty of the relevant act or omission had or had not authority under municipal law in that connection, apart from the case where a specific instruction from a superior instrumentality was acted on.

2.   If it be found that the state organ or official has such authority, the next matter to be investigated is whether the breach of duty is or is not imputable, so as to make the state responsible at international law. Here international law acts entirely autonomously.[4] For instance, it may be that although the state organ or official exceeded the authority conferred by municipal law, international law

2.   The *Harvard* Draft Convention on the International Responsibility of States for Injuries to Aliens uses the expression 'attributable' rather than 'imputable' (see arts 1 and 15). In connection with state responsibility, the International Law Commission also preferred 'attribution' to 'imputation', upon the ground that this would obviate the ambiguities inherent in the notions of 'imputation' and 'imputability', which are used in an entirely different sense in certain systems of internal criminal law; see *Report* of the Commission on the Work of its *22nd Session* (1970) para 77. In the draft articles adopted by it at its 25th–27th Sessions, 1973–1975 (see arts 7–10), the International Law Commission adhered to the term 'attribution'.
3.   *Report* of the Commission on the Work of its *22nd Session* (1970) para 77.
4.   See *Report* of the International Law Commission on the Work of its *27th Session* (1975) commentary on draft art 10, pp 12 et seq.

will none the less impute liability to the state. Thus, in the *Youmans Case*[5] a lieutenant of state forces in a town in Mexico was ordered by the mayor of the town to proceed with troops to quell riots against and stop attacks being made on certain American citizens. The troops, on arriving at the scene of the riot, instead of dispersing the mob, opened fire on the house in which the Americans were taking refuge and killed one of them. The other two American citizens were then forced to leave the house, and as they did so were killed by the troops and the mob. The troops had disobeyed superior orders by their action in opening fire. It was held that the Mexican Government was responsible for the wrongful acts of the soldiers even though they had acted beyond the scope of their authority.

3.   But if it be ascertained that the state organ or official had no such authority under municipal law, so that the acts were completely ultra vires, no imputation of liability arises. Where an incompetent state agency commits an ultra vires act, it cannot be said to have acted on behalf of the state. To quote the Report of a League of Nations Sub-Committee:[6]

'If the act of the official is accomplished outside the scope of his competence, that is to say, if he has exceeded his powers, we are then confronted with *an act which, judicially speaking, is not an act of the State*. It may be illegal, but from the point of view of international law, the offence cannot be imputed to the State.'

However, even in these circumstances a state may become responsible if through the omissions or default of other officials or organs it has facilitated the commission of the ultra vires act, or has broken an independent duty of international law, such as a duty to take steps to restrain the commission of the wrongful act, or to take measures to prevent the recurrence of the offence.[7] Thus the state may incur an indirect responsibility arising out the ultra vires acts. It may possibly also be liable in such circumstances if it has 'held out' the incompetent agency as having authority (unless there be some constitutional or legal prohibition of the acts of 'holding out' relied upon by the claimant state), but even then the 'holding out' would still necessitate an imputation to the respondent state of conduct by some instrumentality other than the incompetent agency which tortiously acted or omitted to act.

4.   Where the illegal acts are committed by private citizens and not by an organ or official of the state the grounds for not imputing liability to the state are much stronger, for the doctrine of imputability rests on the assumption that the delinquency has been committed by an agency *at least* of the state concerned, or by persons actually acting on behalf of the state.[8] But here again, by their

5.   Annual Digest of Public International Law Cases, 1925–1926, p 223. See also *Royal Holland Lloyd v United States* (1932) 26 AJIL (1932) 410, and cf the *La Masica Case* (1916) *United Nations Reports of International Arbitral Awards* Vol XI, 560.
6.   Report of Sub-Committee of Committee of Experts for the Progressive Codification of International Law (1927) in League of Nations Doc C.196, M.70, 1927, V, p 97.
7.   See report of Sub-Committee of Committee of Experts for the Progressive Codification of International Law, op cit, p 97.
8.   Cf *British Property in Spanish Morocco Case* (1925) *United Nations Reports of International Arbitral Awards* Vol X, 689.

omissions, or default, the agencies of the state may have broken some independent duty of international law, and liability may then be imputed to the state; for example, if it fails in its duty of repression and punishment of the guilty persons[9] or if it has actually inspired the illegal act or acts committed, or if it has become an accessory after the fact by wilfully benefiting from the wrongful act or acts of the private citizen or citizens concerned, or if, by conduct or declaration (oral or written) it has authorised or ratified the unlawful act or acts.[10] It is sometimes said that before a state is liable in this connection, there must be some implied complicity in the wrongful act either by negligent failure to prevent the injury, or to investigate the case, or to punish the guilty offender. In this connection, the inordinate upsurge during recent years of terrorist acts committed by individuals or groups has raised problems concerning the extent to which the states, in the territory of which these acts have been perpetrated, may be liable in respect of the injuries or losses caused by these acts. Inter alia, it has been suggested that the local state may incur liability by reason of the negligent creation of opportunities for the commission of terrorist acts, or by the failure to punish terrorists adequately for their crimes or at all, or because of the failure to permit their extradition to a state competent to try and punish them.

One particular example of damage done by private individuals has several times come before arbitral tribunals[11] namely, that inflicted on the property or persons of aliens in the course of mob riots. It has been ruled on these occasions that the state is responsible for the acts of the rioters only if it is guilty of a breach of good faith or has been negligent in preventing the riots. If the state reasonably affords adequate protection for the life and property of aliens, it has fulfilled its duty at international law towards these persons. To quote the Report of the League of Nations Sub-Committee mentioned above:

'Damage suffered by foreigners in case of riot, revolution or civil war does not involve international responsibility for the State. In case of riot, however, the State would be responsible if the riot was directed against foreigners, as such, and the State failed to perform its duties of surveillance and repression.'

Thus a state is liable if it promotes or finances groups to engage in injurious mob rioting, or encourages or instigates this activity on their part.[12]

In two of the draft articles adopted by it in 1973–1975 on state responsibility and remaining unaltered by it at its 32nd Session in 1980, the International Law Commission considered it appropriate that the doctrine of imputability or attributability should extend, but only in exceptional circumstances, to certain

9.   Art 13 of the above-mentioned *Harvard* Draft Convention (p 276, n 2 above), limits the scope of this duty by relation to criminal acts, and stipulates that the injured alien or some other alien (eg a relative) must have thereby been deprived of the opportunity to recover damages from the delinquent; otherwise such inadequacy of efforts of apprehension or prosecution are not of themselves grounds of an imputable liability.
10. *Case of United States Diplomatic and Consular Staff in Tehran* ICJ 1980, 3; and cf *Nicaragua v United States* ICJ 1986, 14 (alleged laying of mines by agents of the United States in Nicaraguan waters). It follows from the latter case that the individuals need not be nationals of the state to which imputability is attached (see paras 75 et seq of the judgment).
11. See, eg, the *Home Missionary Society Case*, Annual Digest of Public International Law Cases, 1919–1922, pp 173–174. This case is referred to by the International Law Commission in the *Report* on the Work of its *27th Session* (1975) pp 26–27.
12. *Report* of the International Law Commission on the Work of its *27th Session* (1975) p 31.

entities and persons other than state organs or state officials, stricto sensu, provided that there was some genuine connection of the entities and persons with state activities.[13]

First, in paragraph 2 of draft article 7, it was provided:

'The conduct of an organ of an entity which is not part of the formal structure of the State or of a territorial government entity, but which is *empowered by the internal law of that State to exercise elements of the governmental authority*, shall also be considered as an act of the State under international law, provided that organ was acting in that capacity in the case in question.'

The purpose was to cover entities such as public or public utility corporations, empowered to exercise governmental authority, the International Law Commission's view being that it was 'important that the State should not be able to evade its international responsibility in certain circumstances solely because it has entrusted the exercise of some elements of the governmental authority to entities separate from the state machinery proper'. The Commission used the descriptive words 'empowered by the internal law of that State to exercise elements of the governmental authority' because the real common feature of these entities was that they were 'empowered, if only exceptionally and to a limited extent, to exercise specified functions which are akin to those normally exercised by organs of the State'.

Second, draft article 8 made provision for attribution to the state of the conduct of persons acting in fact on behalf of the State in these terms:

'The conduct of a person or group of persons shall also be considered as an act of the State under international law if

a. it is established that such person or group of persons was in fact acting on behalf of that State; or

b. such person or group of persons was in fact exercising elements of the governmental authority in the absence of the official authorities and in circumstances which justified the exercise of those elements of authority.'

Paragraph a. was intended by the International Law Commission to cover cases in which the action of state organs is supplemented by the action of private persons or groups who act as 'auxiliaries' on the state's behalf, while ostensibly remaining outside the official structure of the state. Paragraph b., on the other hand, was intended to embrace the cases of persons who had assumed public functions in order to carry on services which could not be interrupted or which had to be provided because of exceptional circumstances; for example, the discharge of such public functions during a military invasion in the absence of officials or official bodies, or during natural disasters, such as earthquakes or floods, again in the absence of state officials. The qualification is that the circumstances must justify the exercise by private persons of the necessary elements of authority.

Paragraph a. is illustrated to a striking extent by the prosecution in New Zealand of the agents of the French Government involved in the sinking of the Greenpeace vessel the *Rainbow Warrior* in New Zealand internal waters in July

13. See *Report* of the International Law Commission on the Work of its *26th Session* (1974) para 123.

1985.[14] France admitted liability for the acts of the agents, and those prosecuted and convicted could not rely on the so-called doctrine of 'immunity of attribution' in order to avoid trial and punishment for contravening New Zealand criminal law. It was also immaterial so far as the responsibility of France was concerned that the agents concerned were of subordinate status.

General principles as to protection of citizens abroad[15]

The rules of state responsibility under this head depend on keeping a proper balance between two fundamental rights of states:

i.   the right of a state to exercise jurisdiction within its own territory, free from control by other states;

ii. the right of a state to protect its citizens abroad.

Most frequently claims are laid on the basis of what is termed 'denial of justice'.[16] Although used in quite a range of different meanings, in a broad sense, the expression covers all injuries inflicted on citizens abroad in violation of international justice, whether by judicial, legislative or administrative organs, for example, maltreatment in gaol, or arbitrary confiscation of property; but in its narrow and more technical sense it connotes misconduct or inaction on the part of the judicial agencies of the respondent state, denying to the citizens of the claimant state the benefits of due process of law. To constitute a 'denial of justice' in this narrow sense there must be some abuse of the judicial process or an improper administration of justice, for example, wrongful arrest and detention, obstructing access to the courts, unwarranted delays in procedure, a manifestly unjust judgment of the court, a refusal to hear the defendant, or a grossly unfair trial.[17] However, a mere error in a domestic court's decision is, semble, not sufficient; the decision must be so obviously wrong that it cannot have been made in good faith, and/or with reasonable care.

In the *Chattin Claim* (1927)[18] the United States–Mexico General Claims Commission found that a denial of justice had occurred on Mexico's part, and it cited certain facts in support:

'Irregularity of Court proceedings is proven with reference to absence of proper investigations, an insufficiency of confrontations, withholding from the accused the opportunity to know all of the charges brought against him, undue delay of the

---

14. 74 ILR 241, 259; (1987) 26 ILM 1346.
15. A state may also, under this heading of 'protection of citizens abroad', become liable towards an international institution for injuries done to officials of the institution, while acting within the scope of their duties; see Advisory Opinion of the International Court of Justice, *Reparation for Injuries Suffered in the Service of the United Nations* ICJ 1949, 174 et seq.
16. See, on the whole subject, Freeman *The International Responsibility of States for Denial of Justice* (1938).
17. The provisions of arts 9–11 and 14 of the International Covenant of 1966 on Civil and Political Rights, that, inter alia, prohibit arbitrary arrest or detention, or delay in trial proceedings, and that lay down (in art 14) minimum guarantees for the due determination of a criminal charge necessarily have an impact upon the scope of liability for denial of justice. This point is recognised in §711 of the American Restatement of the Foreign Relations Law of the United States (Revised, 1985). Bilateral treaties may also contain standards for the treatment of aliens, to be respected by the contracting states.
18. See (1928) 22 AJIL 667.

proceedings, making the hearings in open Court a mere formality, and a continued absence of seriousness on the part of the Court.'

The Commission also pointed out that the relevant procedure followed (in 1910–1911) was insufficient by international standards. Similarly, in the *Cutting Case*[19] the United States intervened with Mexico in regard to the trial of an American citizen who had been arrested on a charge of criminal libel.[20]

Important in this connection is the matter of *exhaustion of local remedies*, particularly where claims for denial of justice are brought before international tribunals. It appears to be the rule that no state should intervene or claim in respect of an alleged denial of justice to a national or other wrong until all local remedies open to that national have been exhausted without result. The obvious principle underlying the rule is that until there has been recourse to the proper final courts or authorities of the respondent state it cannot be said that there has been a denial of justice. Another consideration is that every opportunity for redress in the municipal sphere should be sought before the matter assumes the more serious aspect of a dispute between states.

It is not easy to reconcile draft article 22, as adopted by the International Law Commission, with this conception of exhaustion of local remedies. This article provides that when a state's conduct has created a situation not complying with an obligation as to the treatment of aliens, but such obligation may allow compliance or an equivalent result to be achieved by subsequent conduct of that state, 'there is a breach of the obligation *only* if the aliens concerned have exhausted the *effective* local remedies available to them without obtaining the treatment called for by the obligation or, where that is not possible, an equivalent treatment'. Semble, however, a breach always remains a breach, irrespective of whether or not local remedies have been exhausted.

A detailed consideration of the local remedies rule lies outside the scope of this book, but certain principles may be briefly formulated:

a.   a local remedy is not to be regarded as adequate and need not be resorted
     to if the municipal courts are not in a position to award compensation or
     damages;
b.   a claimant is not required to exhaust justice if there is no justice to exhaust;
     for example, where the supreme judicial tribunal is under the control of the
     executive organ responsible for the illegal act, or where an act of the
     legislative organ has caused the injury suffered;
c.   where the injury is due to an executive act of the government as such, which
     is clearly not subject to the jurisdiction of the municipal courts[1], semble,
     the injured foreign citizens are not required to exhaust local remedies;
d.   states may waive the condition that local remedies should be exhausted,
     although it is not clear whether an agreement between the disputant states
     to arbitrate the relevant issues will of itself operate as an implied waiver.

---

19. See above, p 190.
20. A mere error in judgment of an international tribunal does not amount to a denial of justice; see *The Salem Case* (1932) *United Nations Reports of International Arbitral Awards* Vol II, p 1202.
1. However, if this is not clearly shown, only the municipal courts themselves can determine the issue of jurisdiction, so that the local remedies rule applies; see *Panevezys-Saldutiskis Rly Case* (1939) PCIJ Series A/B No 76.

On the other hand, as the *Ambatielos Arbitration* (1956), between Greece and Great Britain, shows[2] local remedies are not exhausted if an appeal to a higher Court is not definitely pressed or proceeded with, or if essential evidence has not been adduced, or if there has been a significant failure to take some step necessary to succeed in the action.

According to the decision of the International Court of Justice in the *Interhandel (Preliminary Objections) Case*[3] the local remedies rule applies a fortiori where the national of the claimant state concerned is actually in the course of litigating the matter before the municipal courts of the respondent state, and the municipal suit is designed to obtain the same result as in the international proceedings. Moreover, the rule applies even though the municipal courts may be called upon to apply international law in reaching a decision on the matter. The decision of the International Court of Justice to some extent demonstrates that international tribunals will not be easily persuaded that local remedies are unavailable or have been exhausted, but will closely consider all the circumstances in that connection.

State responsibility and the fault theory[4]

It is often said that a state is not responsible to another state for unlawful acts committed by its agents unless such acts are committed wilfully and maliciously or with culpable negligence.[5]

It is difficult to accept so wide a conclusion and so invariable a requirement. A general floating condition of malice or culpable negligence rather contradicts the scientific and practical considerations underlying the law as to state responsibility. Few rules in treaties imposing duties on states contain anything expressly in terms relating to malice or culpable negligence, and breaches of those treaties may without more involve the responsibility of a state party. It is only in specific cases when particular circumstances demand it that wilfulness or malice, or negligence may be necessary to render a state responsible; for example, if the state knowingly connives in the wrongful acts of insurgents or rioters, it would become liable, although not generally otherwise, or if it were negligent in failing to provide adequate police protection for diplomatic premises against the injurious acts of demonstrators or rioters, and damage occurred.[6] Moreover, fault can seldom enter into account in the case of alleged breaches of international law by legislative or judicial organs, or where the relevant state agency is acting in the exercise of a statutory discretion, and there is no evidence of arbitrariness or capriciousness.

2.   23 ILR 306.
3.   ICJ 1959, 6.
4.   The subject is discussed in Garcia Amador's Fifth Report to the International Law Commission on International Responsibility; see *Yearbook* of the Commission 1960, Vol II, 41, pp 61–64. Cf the *Report* of the International Law Commission on the Work of its *25th Session* (1973) para 58, in its notes on draft art 3 on State Responsibility, as to what constitutes objectively 'an internationally wrongful act'.
5.   Cf Judge Krylov's dissenting opinion in the *Corfu Channel (Merits) Case* ICJ 1949, 4, and his insistence that state responsibility presupposes culpa.
6.   Cf *Report* of the International Law Commission on the Work of its *25th Session* (1973) para 58, in notes on draft art 3 on State Responsibility, referring to this case of negligence.

Further, the actual decisions of international arbitral tribunals fail to justify a general or absolute condition of malice or culpable negligence. An instructive precedent is supplied by the case of the *Jessie* which came before the British–American Claims Arbitral Tribunal in 1921. There the United States was held responsible to Great Britain for the action of its officers, although such action was bona fide and in the belief that it was justified by a joint regulation adopted by the two countries. The tribunal laid down the wide principle that:

'Any government is responsible to other governments for errors in judgment of its officials purporting to act within the scope of their duties and vested with power to enforce their demands.'[7]

Thus the tribunal did not hold that the presence of malice or culpable negligence was a condition precedent of state responsibility.

In the field of state responsibility for nuclear activities, there has to be, subject to the nature of the situations arising and subject to reasonable general qualifications, some form of strict or absolute liability. The difficulties here are not to be minimised.[8] The safety of the international community cannot be ensured under a system whereby a state would be responsible only if it were proved to be negligent in the management of nuclear fuels and nuclear installations. This involves the additional difficulty which in some instances, may require the problem of insurance to be dealt with, of the availability of sufficient financial resources to meet large-scale liabilities for major damage.

The unavoidable dangers involved in nuclear activities, particularly those related to the use of, and experiments with, nuclear weapons, together with the increase in the number of non-nuclear-weapon states engaged in the development of nuclear energy, partly explain the signature on 1 July 1968, of the Treaty on the Non-Proliferation of Nuclear Weapons (currently referred to as 'the NPT'), which is the principal international instrument aimed at preventing the spread of nuclear weaponry. The dangers inherent in the nuclear arms race also materially influenced the conclusion of the treaty. The two key provisions are contained in articles I and II. Article I provides that each nuclear-weapon state party to the treaty is not to transfer to any recipient whatsoever nuclear weapons or other nuclear explosive devices or control over such weapons or explosive devices directly, or indirectly, and also is not to assist, encourage, or induce any non-nuclear-weapon state to manufacture or acquire or control such weapons or devices. Article II obliges each non-nuclear-weapon state party to the treaty not to receive the transfer from any transferor whatsoever of nuclear weapons or devices, directly or indirectly; and not to manufacture or acquire these, or to seek or receive assistance in their manufacture. Under article IV, the right of all parties, subject to articles I and II, to use nuclear energy for peaceful purposes is preserved, while non-nuclear-weapon states parties are through agreements

---

7.   6 RIAA 57.
8   Cf R. Fornasier 'Le Droit International Face au Risque Nucléaire' *Annuaire Français de Droit International* Vol X (1964) pp 303–311. Note also the following instruments: (1) Convention on Third Party Liability in the Field of Nuclear Energy, Paris, 29 July 1960, with Supplementary Convention. (2) Convention on the Liability of Operators of Nuclear Ships, Brussels, 25 May 1962. (3) Convention on Civil Liability for Nuclear Damage, Vienna, 21 May 1963. (4) The Convention on the Physical Protection of Nuclear Material, Vienna, 26 October 1979. On the validity at international law of the use of nuclear weapons, see p 498, n 2 below.

negotiated with the International Atomic Energy Agency (IAEA), pursuant to article III, to accept the safeguards system evolved by that organisation.[9]

The treaty is a compromise, and possibly does not represent an ideal solution, but without it nuclear proliferation would have been removed from the major controls established under its provisions.

In relation to this subject of nuclear activities, reference should be made lastly to the two conventions adopted in the wake of the Chernobyl nuclear reactor accident in April 1986, namely the Convention of 1986 on Early Notification of a Nuclear Accident, and the Convention of 1986 on Assistance in the Case of a Nuclear Accident or Radiological Emergency. Under the terms of the former Convention, a state is, *inter alia*, under a duty to notify and to provide information both to states which might be adversely affected, on the one hand, and to the International Atomic Energy Agency (IAEA) at Vienna, on the other hand, of the occurrence of a nuclear accident involving its civil and military facilities and activities, except nuclear weapons. This seems to be a duty of a strict nature, for the breach of which the non-notifying state incurs absolute liability.

Possible state responsibility in relation to other forms of environmental harm are dealt with in Chapter 14, below.

4.   CLAIMS

Inasmuch as a state has a right to protect its citizens abroad, it is entitled to intervene diplomatically or to lodge a claim for satisfaction before a competent international tribunal if one of its subjects has sustained unlawful injury for which another state is responsible. The claimant state is deemed to be injured through its subjects, or to be asserting its right to ensure respect for the rules of international law vis-à-vis its own nationals[10], and once the intervention is made or the claim is laid, the matter becomes one that concerns the two states alone. The injured subject's only right is to claim through his or her state as against the state responsible. Some writers indeed hold the view that if injured subjects waive their rights of compensation, their state can nonetheless prosecute a claim for the injury done to them.

Sometimes it is expressed that this right corresponds to an administrative duty of the state towards such of its nationals as have suffered injury.[11] But state practice (for example, of the Department of State of the United States) shows that most states regard the sponsoring of claims by nationals as entirely within

9.   This is a truly international system, involving both reporting and inspection. Prior to the treaty, a large number of countries were subject to the system; see the address, 21 September 1966, by the Director-General of IAEA to the 10th General Conference, and M. Willrich 60 AJIL (1966) 34–54. Also, since the NPT (see above), and more particularly since 1977, a large number of bilateral safeguards agreements have been concluded between uranium-exporting countries, on the one hand, and uranium-importing countries, on the other hand. On the treaty generally, see M. I. Shaker *The Nuclear Non-Proliferation Treaty: Origin and Implementation, 1959–1979* (3 vols, 1980).
10. See *Panevezys-Saldutiskis Rly Case* (1939) PCIJ Series A/B No 76.
11. See *Gschwind v Swiss Confederation* Annual Digest of Public International Law Cases, 1931–1932 at 242–243.

their discretion. Whether or not protection be a right or a duty of the state, it is now well established that in the international forum, as a rule, the only recognised claimants are states. To quote the Permanent Court of International Justice:[12]

'Once a State has taken up a case on behalf of one of its subjects before an international tribunal, in the eyes of the latter the State is the sole claimant.'

It follows from the general principle that once compensation has been assessed and paid by the defendant state to the claimant state, the defendant state, apart from express contract, is not interested in nor entitled to concern itself with the manner in which the complainant state disposes of the sum of money awarded. The complainant state need not in fact remit to its injured citizen the whole of the compensation received by it.[13]

The persons on behalf of whom a state is entitled to propound an international claim are primarily its nationals, but may include also 'protected' subjects such as those placed under that state's diplomatic protection, and even aliens who have complied with almost all the conditions of naturalisation. In the majority of cases, international arbitral tribunals have applied the rule that the injured person must have the nationality of the claimant state or other recognised status at the time the injury was suffered and must retain it until the claim is decided (or at least until the claim is presented), but other requirements and refinements in connection with the nationality of the injured party have also been adopted by different arbitrators. The necessity for the rule was expressed by the United States–Germany Mixed Claims Commission as follows:[14]

'The reason of the rule is that the nation is injured through injury to its national and it alone may demand reparation as no other national is injured. As between nations the one inflicting the injury will ordinarily listen to the complaint only of the nation injured. . . . *Any other rule would open wide the door for abuses and might result in converting a strong nation into a claim agency on* behalf of those who after suffering injuries should assign their claims to its nationals or avail themselves of its naturalisation laws for the purpose of procuring its espousal of their claims.'

Where the party injured is a company or corporation, the matter is likewise governed by the 'nationality of claims' canon. Only the national state is entitled to espouse the claim of the company or corporation, the nationality of which is determined by tests referred to in Chapter 12 below.[15] Difficulties may arise, however, in the case of the so-called 'triangular' situation, namely:

a. Injury in breach of international law is done to a company incorporated and with its registered office in state A.
b. The act occasioning the injury has been committed by state B, where the company has carried on its operations.
c. The principal shareholders of the company are nationals of, and resident in state C.

---

12. *Mavrommatis Palestine Concessions Case (Jurisdiction)* (1924) PCIJ Series A, No 2, p 12.
13. Cf *Civilian War Claimants Association Ltd v R* [1932] AC 14.
14. See Report of Decisions of the Commission (1924), pp 175 et seq. Cf also the difficult case of *The Bathori* [1934] AC 91.
15. See p 313.

Is state C entitled to espouse the claims of the shareholders who have incurred loss through the act of state B?

The principles governing such a situation were clarified in 1970 by the International Court of Justice in the *Barcelona Traction Case* (Belgium–Spain)[16] where the Court ruled in favour of the respondent state, Spain, upon the antecedent ground that Belgium had no locus standi to espouse before the Court claims of Belgian nationals who were shareholders in the subject company, Barcelona Traction, Light and Power Company, Limited, inasmuch as the latter was incorporated in Canada and was, in an international legal sense, of Canadian nationality. The reasoning relied upon by the Court may be expressed as follows:

a.   International law was bound to have regard to the general tenor of rules of national legal systems, which was to the effect that an infringement of a company's rights by outsiders did not involve liability towards the shareholders, even if their interests were detrimentally affected by the infringement. Consistently, therefore, the *general* rule of international law was that only the national state of the company concerned was entitled to exercise diplomatic protection for the purpose of seeking redress for an international wrong done to the company.

b.   A different principle might apply if the wrong were aimed at the direct rights of the shareholders as such (eg, the right to attend and vote at general meetings), but in the instant case, Belgium had conceded that its claim was not based upon upon any infringement of the direct rights of shareholders, but only upon the alleged illegal measures taken in Spain against the company.

c.   The general rule of the exclusive entitlement of the national state of the company might conceivably, in certain cases, give way to the right of the national state of the shareholders, for example where the company itself had ceased to exist, or the protecting national state of the company lacked capacity to exercise diplomatic protection;[17] however, in the instant case the Barcelona Traction, Light and Power Company, Limited, had not ceased to exist as a corporate entity in Canada, nor was the Canadian Government incapable of exercising diplomatic protection, although for reasons of its own, its interposition on behalf of the company had ceased as from 1955.

The Court did not accept certain propositions, namely:

i.   If investments formed part of a country's national economic resources, and these were prejudicially affected contrary to that country's right to have its nationals enjoy a certain standard of treatment, it could claim for breach of international law done to it. A claim of this nature would have to be based on treaty or special agreement, which did not exist between Belgium and Spain.

ii.   For reasons of equity, a country should be entitled in certain cases to take up the protection of its nationals who were shareholders in a company, the

16.   *Case Concerning the Barcelona Traction, Light and Power Co Ltd* (*Second Phase*) ICJ 1970, 3. For the background to this case, see J. Brooks *The Games Players* (1980).
17.   Where, eg, the company is a national of the respondent state: *Elettronica Sicula (ELSI) Case* (USA v Italy) ICJ 1989, 15.

victim of a breach of international law. Any such alleged equitable justification would open the door to competing claims on the part of different states, thereby creating insecurity in international economic relations.[18]

The net effect of the Court's decision is then that an international court ought to be reluctant to 'pierce the corporate veil' in order to allow a country other than the national state of the company to seek redress for an international wrong done to the company.

According to the decision of the International Court of Justice in the *Nottebohm Case (Second Phase)*[19] where the person, whose claim was being propounded by the claimant state, was a national of it by naturalisation, the claimant state will not be entitled to proceed, if such person has no close and genuine connection with that state, at least against a respondent state in which he was habitually resident. A somewhat similar principle applies if the person is of dual nationality; the 'real and effective nationality' must be that of the claimant state.[20]

In the *I'm Alone Case*[1] between Canada and the United States, the Canadian Government was held entitled to claim although only the nominal or de jure owner of the vessel—the *I'm Alone*—was of Canadian nationality, the real or de facto owners being Americans. Counsel for the United States urged that the damages awarded would ultimately go into the pockets of American citizens, but this was treated as an irrelevant consideration.

This doctrine of 'nationality of claims' has with some justification been condemned as artificial, and the theory that a claimant state is injured through its subjects has been described as a pure fiction, but they are both supported by the weight of state practice and arbitral decision.

It remains to point out that states may by treaty lay down special principles or provide for a special procedure inter partes for claims in respect of disputes, or for tortious injuries received by their citizens.[2] In that connection, reference may be made to article 25 of the Convention of 18 March 1965, on the Settlement of Investment Disputes between States and Nationals of Other States, enabling private investors who are nationals of a state party to settle investment disputes with the government of another state party. In the case of private investors, who are natural persons, they are to have the nationality of the state concerned on

18. In its judgment (see para 99) the Court referred to the case of a company established in a foreign country in order to obtain tax or other advantages, and said that it did not seem 'to be in any way inequitable' that these advantages should be balanced by the risk that a state other than the national state of shareholders would be solely entitled to exercise diplomatic protection.
19. See ICJ 1955, 4.
20. Cf *Florence Strunsky Mergé Case* (1955) 50 AJIL (1956) 154.
1. See *United Nations Reports of International Arbitral Awards* Vol III, p 1609. This case arose out of the sinking in 1929 of the *I'm Alone*, a British schooner of Canadian registry, by a United States coastguard vessel at a point on the high seas more than 200 miles from the United States coast. The *I'm Alone* was engaged in the smuggling of alcoholic liquor into the United States, but the Canadian Government claimed that the sinking was illegal and not justified by any convention with the United States.
2. See, eg, art VIII of the Agreement of the North Atlantic Powers of 19 June 1951, regarding the Status of their Forces (claims in respect to acts or omissions of members of the forces or civilian components), and cf the claims provisions in the stationing of forces agreements concluded by the Soviet Union.

the date of the consent of the parties to submit the dispute to settlement and on the date of the *registration* of the relevant request for settlement by arbitration or conciliation; but a person who on either date possessed the nationality of the investment-receiving state is ineligible to use the machinery of the Convention, even if the investment-receiving state consented to access being given. However, in the case of a private investor who is a body corporate or other entity, the position is not so rigid; not only is access allowed to corporations, etc, which had the nationality of a state party other than the investment-receiving state on the date of the consent to submit, but also to those who on that date held the nationality of the investment-receiving state, provided that the latter state agrees to treat the claimant as the national of another state, because of foreign control. This is a radical advance, enabling regard to be had to the realities of control of corporations and companies.

Damages
Under international law, in matters of state responsibility, a claimant state is always entitled to some damages where its claim has been sustained, irrespective of whether the wrongful act subject of the claim has caused material damage, or injury, or pecuniary loss. Further, if the wrongful act be an infringement, contrary to international law, of the rights of a private citizen whose claim has been espoused by that state, the damage deemed to have been suffered by the claimant state is an independent damage not identical with that suffered by the individual. To quote the Permanent Court of International Justice in the *Chorzów Factory (Indemnity) Case*[3]

> 'The damage suffered by an individual is never . . . identical in kind with that which will be suffered by a State; *it can only afford a convenient scale for the calculation of the reparation due to the State.*'

This principle is consistent with the award in the *Lusitania Death Claims*, arising out of the sinking of the British vessel, the *Lusitania*, by a German submarine in 1915. The United States–Germany Mixed Claims Commission, in claims by the United States on behalf of American citizens drowned when the vessel sank, refused to grant vindictive or exemplary damages[4] against the German Government.[5] On the other hand, such damages appear to have been awarded by the United States–Mexico General Claims Commission in the *Janes Case* (1926), where the claim was lodged by the United States in regard to the failure of the Mexican authorities to take prompt and effective action to apprehend the murderer of an American citizen. The Commission awarded damages for the 'indignity' done to the relatives of the victim by the murderer's non-punishment.[6]

The normal rule, having regard to the fact that usually exact restitution may be impossible, is that an award by way of reparation should be for the payment

3. (1928) PCIJ Series A, No 17, p 28.
4. Vindictive or exemplary damages are damages given on an increased scale in respect of acts committed maliciously or with gross negligence or in other circumstances of aggravation.
5. Annual Digest of Public International Law Cases, 1923–1924, No 113.
6. Annual Digest of Public International Law Cases, 1925–1926. No 158. Apart from arbitral awards, states have in practice repeatedly paid indemnities in the form of vindictive damages to other states for breaches of duty of more than ordinary concern.

of monetary compensation.[7] In some instances, however, restitution may necessarily be the more appropriate remedy.[8]

In several instances, international arbitral tribunals have awarded two separate heads of damage, one in respect of the damage suffered by individuals, and the other in respect of injury to the claimant state. Such an award was made in the *I'm Alone Case*, above, and is consistent with the views expressed by the International Court of Justice that the United Nations can claim compensation both in respect of itself and of the damage to individuals arising out of injuries suffered by its officials in the course of their duties.[9]

In practice, however, most states limit their claims to the loss actually suffered by the individual[10] and such loss is also usually the measure of the arbitral tribunal's award, irrespective of the degree of blame attachable to the delinquent or respondent state.[11]

Finally, reference may be made to the significant course taken by the International Court of Justice in 1986 in its judgment in the case of *Nicaragua v United States*.[12] The Court had found in favour of Nicaragua that the United States had been in breach of certain obligations under customary international law (including the wrongful use of force) and also in breach of a Treaty of 1956 of Friendship, Commerce and Navigation entered into by the two parties. Nicaragua, as the successful complainant, requested the Court to adjudge and declare that compensation was due to Nicaragua, the quantum thereof to be fixed subsequently, and to make an interim award. In response to this request, the Court made the following rulings: (a) it had jurisdiction to order reparation; (b) the request by Nicaragua for the nature and amount of the reparation to be determined in a subsequent stage was appropriate; and (c) there was no provision in the Court's Statute either specifically empowering it or debarring it from making an interim award, as requested. Notwithstanding these rulings, this was a case in which one party, the United States, had not appeared, and the Court should refrain from any unnecessary act which might prove an obstacle to a negotiated settlement. It therefore did not consider that it could accede *at that stage* to Nicaragua's request. The order made by the Court was accordingly 'that the form and amount of [the] reparation, failing agreement between the Parties, will be settled by the Court, and reserves for this purpose the subsequent procedure in [the] case'.

---

7. But cf *Chorzów Factory (Indemnity) Case* (1928) Pub PCIJ Series A, No 17, pp 47–48.
8. See the award in *Texaco v Libya* (1978) 17 ILM 1.
9. See Advisory Opinion on *Reparation for Injuries Suffered in the Service of the United Nations* ICJ 1949, 174 et seq.
10. In the *Chorzów Factory (Indemnity) Case* (1928) PCIJ Series A, No 17, pp 46–48, the Permanent Court of International Justice laid it down that the measure of damages for an international wrong is determined by what is necessary to make restitution, together with special damages for loss not covered by such restitution. The International Court of Justice awarded to Great Britain the replacement of one destroyer that had been lost through explosions for which Albania was held liable; see the *Corfu Channel (Assessment) Case* ICJ 1949, 244.
11. This is not, however, an absolute or invariable rule. In the *I'm Alone Case* (1935), referred to at p 287 above, no damages were awarded corresponding to the loss of the vessel sunk, the award being primarily for the lack of respect for the flag of the vessel subject of the alleged unlawful act of sinking.
12. ICJ 1986, 14, paras 283–285.

CHAPTER 11

Succession to rights and obligations

1. SUCCESSION IN GENERAL

The subject discussed in the present chapter is more frequently treated in the textbooks under the titles of 'State Succession'[1] and 'Succession of Governments', although this terminology is somewhat inappropriate.[2]

In the former case of so-called 'State Succession' we are principally concerned with the transmission of rights or obligations from states which have altered or lost their identity to other states or entities, such alteration or loss of identity occurring primarily when complete or partial changes of sovereignty take place over portions of territory. In article 2 of the Vienna Convention of 23 August 1978, on Succession of States in respect of Treaties, and in article 2 of the Vienna Convention of 7 April 1983, on Succession of States in respect of State Property, Archives and Debts (as to both conventions, see below in this chapter), 'succession of states' was defined to mean 'the replacement of one state by another in the responsibility for the international relations of territory'. This is somewhat confusing, and would be unacceptable regarded as an absolute proposition to cover all cases where, by operation of law, international rights and obligations may pass to a successor state, eg, the case where the sovereignty of a lessee state over particular territory reverts to the lessor state, as will be the position in 1997 when China resumes sovereignty over Hong Kong territories, now exercised by

---

1. The standard work on succession in international law is O'Connell *State Succession in Municipal Law and International Law* (2 vols, 1967). The subject has also been covered in a number of valuable studies and documents prepared or circulated by the United Nations Secretariat, and submitted to the International Law Commission for the purpose of its work on succession; the earlier documentation is listed in the *Report* of the Commission on the Work of its *22nd Session* (1970) para 36, and the lengthy footnote 53 to this para, and see generally the *Report* of the Commission on the Work of its *24th Session*.
2. It bears the title 'Succession of States and Governments' in the *Report* of the International Law Commission on the Work of its *21st Session* (1969) (see title of Chapter III), and the title 'Succession of States' in the *Report* of the Commission on the Work of its *22nd Session* (1970) (see title of chapter III), and in *Reports* subsequent to the 1970 Report.

Great Britain as the lessee from China. The questions of international law involved may be summarised as:

1. To what extent are the existing rights and obligations of the predecessor state extinguished, or—where there is a change of sovereignty over portion only of the territory of that state—to what extent do they remain vested in that state?
2. To what extent does the successor state, ie the state to which sovereignty has passed wholly or partially, become entitled to such rights or subject to such obligations?

In this connection the term 'state succession' is a misnomer, as it presupposes that the analogies of private law, where on death or bankruptcy, etc, rights and obligations pass from extinct or incapable persons to other individuals, are applicable as between states. The truth, however, is that there is no general principle in international law of succession as between states, no complete juridical substitution of one state for the old state which has lost or altered its identity. What is involved is primarily a change of sovereignty over territory, through concurrent acquisition and loss of sovereignty, loss to the states formerly enjoying sovereignty, and acquisition by the states to which it has passed wholly or partially. It is not feasible to carry over to international law analogies concerned with the transmission of a universitas juris under domestic law. So far as rights and duties under international law are concerned, no question whatever of succession to these is involved. The state which has taken over is directly subject to international law, simply by virtue of being a state, not by reason of any doctrine of succession.

In the second case of the so-called 'Succession of Governments', a different problem is involved. The change of sovereignty is purely *internal*, whether it takes place through constitutional or revolutionary processes. A new government takes up the reins of office, and the question is to what extent are the rights and obligations of the former government extinguished, and to what extent does the new government become entitled to such rights or bound by such obligations.

In more correct terminology, the two cases therefore resolve themselves into:

a. The passing of rights and obligations upon *external* changes of sovereignty over territory.[3]
b. The passing of rights and obligations upon *internal* changes of sovereignty, irrespective of territorial changes.

Each of these cases will be discussed in turn.

---

3. The case must involve a real external change of sovereignty; thus when Austria was liberated from German control in April 1945, that liberation did not create a new state for the purposes of succession to Germany; see *Jordan v Austrian Republic and Taubner* (1947) Annual Digest of Public International Law Cases 1947, No 15. Similarly, the emergence of Estonia, Latvia and Lithuania from the Soviet Union in 1991, into which they had been forcibly incorporated in 1940, is regarded as instances of restoration of suspended sovereignty rather than of the creation of new states.

2.   PASSING OF RIGHTS AND OBLIGATIONS UPON EXTERNAL CHANGES OF SOVEREIGNTY OVER TERRITORY

The most common situations in which external changes of sovereignty over territory take place are these:

i.   Part of the territory of state A becomes incorporated in that of state B, or is divided between several states, B, C, D, and others.

ii.   Part of the territory of state A is formed as the basis of a new state. (This has been illustrated most frequently since the end of the Second World War, and especially since 1960, by the emergence of new states from the colonies, trust territories or protectorates of a distant power by way of independence. Secession is also a form of external change of sovereignty, eg the emergence of the new state of Bangladesh in the territory previously constituting the eastern part of Pakistan).

iii.   The whole of the territory of state A becomes incorporated in that of state B, state A in effect becoming extinguished.

iv.   The whole of the territory of state A becomes divided between several states, B, C, D, and others, again involving the extinction of state A.

v.   The whole of the territory of state A forms the basis of several new states, state A again becoming extinguished.[4]

vi.   The whole of the territory of state A becomes part of the territory of a single new state, again involving the extinction of state A.

These cases of external changes of sovereignty by no means exhaust the multifarious situations which may arise. Changes of sovereignty over territory may take place not only from states to states, but also from states to non-state entities, for example, international institutions,[5] or from lessee state to lessor state, as will occur in 1997 when sovereignty over Hong Kong territories reverts from Great Britain to China; and non-state entities, for example, trust territories and protectorates, may themselves acquire sovereignty on attaining statehood. Besides, the diversity of situations and factors involved must not be overlooked. There may be variations in the *mode* of the change of sovereignty, which may be by annexation, adjudication by international Conference, voluntary cession, secession or revolution. Much may depend also on the size of the territory concerned, the number of inhabitants affected, and the social and economic

---

4.   The break-up of the former Socialist Federal Republic of Yugoslavia in 1991 and the emergence on its territory of the new states of Bosnia-Herzegovina, Croatia, [the former Yugoslav Republic of] Macedonia, and Slovenia has left in doubt whether the remaining portions — Serbia and Montenegro, united as the Federal Republic of Yugoslavia — constitute the same entity in international law as the former Socialist Federal Republic of Yugoslavia. At the time of writing, the Federal Republic of Yugoslavia (Serbia and Montenegro) was not permitted to be seated as a continuing member of the United Nations. The other four nations were admitted to the United Nations as new members. See also Opinion No 9 (1992) of the Badinter Commission that state succession by the new states emerging from the former Socialist Federal Republic of Yugoslavia was to be governed by agreement between the parties, attempting to achieve an equitable solution by drawing on the principles embodied in the Vienna conventions of 1978 and 1983 (see below) and, where appropriate, general international law: 92 ILR 203; and see above, p 126.

5.   Eg, the temporary legal sovereignty of the League of Nations, 1920–1935, over the German territory of the Saar.

interests involved, which inevitably play a role in these days of modern states with their complex structure. Finally, the nature of the particular rights and obligations, which are alleged to pass, must be considered.

For all these reasons, it is difficult to present the subject as a body of coherent principles. No facile criteria can be offered as a guide.[6] As Professor H. A. Smith said:[7]

'. . . The complexity and variety of the problems which arise in practice are such as to preclude accurate and complete analysis within narrow limits.'

Nonetheless, a consideration of the practice, and of judicial authority and doctrine,[8] as well as of the above-mentioned Vienna Convention of 23 August 1978, on Succession in respect of Treaties and of the above-mentioned Vienna Convention of 7 April 1983, on Succession of States in respect of State Property, Archives and Debts, suggests a tendency to pay regard to the question whether it is just, reasonable, equitable, or in the interests of the international community that rights or obligations should pass upon external changes of sovereignty over territory. It is significant that criteria of justice and reasonableness seem to have been applied in modern succession practice, for example, in the understandings of 1947–1948 between Pakistan and India on the occasion of the division of the Indian Empire and their emergence as two new states.[9] Moreover, treaties providing expressis verbis for the transfer of certain obligations upon changes of sovereignty have generally been interpreted by international tribunals in the light of considerations of reason and justice.[10]

Yet state practice on the subject is unsettled and full of inconsistencies, nor, in that connection, have all the difficulties been removed by the provisions of the two above-mentioned conventions, viz. the Convention of 23 August 1978 on Succession of States in respect of Treaties, and the Convention of 7 April 1983 on Succession of States in respect of State Property, Archives and Debts. Possibly, owing to the uncertainty of the international law of succession, the

---

6. Suggested tests or distinctions in the literature have included: (a) the distinction between *universal* and *partial* succession; (b) whether the international personality of the predecessor state has substantially continued through the change of sovereignty; (c) the distinction between *personal* and *territorial* rights and obligations.
7. *Great Britain and the Law of Nations* (1932) Vol I, p 334.
8. See, eg, Opinion on *Claims against Hawaii* (1899) of US Attorney-General Griggs *Opinions of Attorneys-General* Vol 22, pp 583 et seq, *Advisory Opinion on the Settlers of German Origin in Territory ceded by Germany to Poland* (1923) PCIJ Series B, No 6, pp 36 et seq, and Hurst *International Law* (Collected Papers, 1950) p 80. Cf upon the aspect of whether it is reasonable that obligations should pass, *Szcupak v Agent Judiciaire du Trésor Public* (1966) 41 ILR 20.
9. Eg, in the solution adopted of India remaining a member of the United Nations and Pakistan applying separately for membership. See memorandum prepared by the United Nations Secretariat in 1962 on succession of states in relation to United Nations membership; *Yearbook of the ILC*, 1962, Vol II, pp 101–103. See, eg, cl 3 of the Anglo-Chinese Agreement of 19 December 1984 dealing with the recovery by China from Great Britain as lessee of Hong Kong territories to occur in 1997, designed to permit Hong Kong to continue for a certain period its current activities as an economic and financial centre, a transitional provision which is pragmatically just and reasonable. The Agreement was in the form of a Joint Declaration with three Annexes.
10. See, eg, the *Case of Certain German Interests in Polish Upper Silesia* (1926) PCIJ Series A, No 7.

modern tendency is to deal expressly with all possible cases under a treaty between the parties affected (the so-called 'voluntary succession').[11]

It is, however, a sound general working rule, and one applied in the case law, to look at the texts of any relevant laws, treaties, declarations, and other arrangements accompanying the change of sovereignty, and ascertain what was the intention of the state or states concerned as to the continuance or passing of any rights or obligations.

The nature of the subject requires that each of the categories of rights and obligations be dealt with in turn.

(1) Succession to treaty rights and obligations[12]

There is no general rule that all treaty rights and obligations pass, nor any generally accepted principle favouring the greatest possible continuity of treaty relations.

The absence of any general or generally accepted principle in respect of succession to treaty rights and obligations may be discerned from consideration of the practice of states and of the views expressed by writers on international law, while it also finds support in the provisions of the above-mentioned Vienna Convention of 23 August 1978 on Succession of States in respect of Treaties, which instrument was based upon draft articles adopted prior to 1977 by the International Law Commission. The Convention was intended to codify the rules of customary international law on the subject, but closer examination shows that a number of its provisions are not in point of fact declaratory of such law. Nonetheless, it is necessary in the present chapter to set out in juxtaposition what appear, on the one hand, to be accepted principles as to certain situations involving treaties, and, on the other hand, the provisions of the Convention formulated for like situations. It should be pointed out, too, that the Convention is expressly confined to international agreements in written form and governed by international law (see article 2) and that rules of customary international law will continue to govern questions not regulated by the Convention (see the preamble).

One must also add, not unfairly, that a number of the provisions of the Convention seem to have little to do with succession stricto sensu, that is to say, succession by operation of law, and that in these no distinctly clear line appears to be drawn between the passing of rights or obligations by such operation of law, on the one hand, and, on the other hand, the passing of rights or obligations by assignment, or novation (ie a fresh agreement between the predecessor state,

11. The particular treaty concerned may, or may not, provide for succession to rights or obligations; see, eg, art 37, para 1 of the Rome Convention on Damage Caused by Foreign Aircraft to Third Parties on the Surface, signed at Rome on 7 October 1952, according to which, when the whole or part of the territory of a contracting state is transferred to a non-contracting state the Convention is to cease to apply to the territory so transferred as from the date of transfer. A good example of voluntary succession is the Agreement of 7 August 1965, relating to the Separation of Singapore from Malaysia as an Independent and Sovereign State; cf S. Jayakamur 'Singapore and State Succession. International Relations and Internal Law' (1970) 19 ICLQ 398–423.

12. Under art 4 of the Convention of 1978 on Succession in respect of Treaties, treaties to which the Convention applies are to include treaties which are the constituent instruments of international organisations and treaties adopted within an international organisation. On the 1978 Convention see the critique of O'Connell in (1979) 39 ZaöRuVR 725-739.

the successor state and the other party or other parties to the treaty concerned), or fresh treaty arrangement. An illustration is paragraph 1 of article 9 which reads as follows:

'1. Obligations or rights under treaties in force in respect of a territory at the date of a succession of States do not become the obligations or rights of the successor State or of other States parties to those treaties by reason only of the fact that the successor State has made a unilateral declaration providing for the continuance in force of the treaties in respect of its territory.'

Does this paragraph mean any more than that it takes two or more parties to make a treaty, and that there must be a novation before the successor state is bound?

Where a state becomes extinguished by the loss of all its territory, prima facie no rights and obligations of an executory[13] character under treaties pass to the successor state, with the exception of:

a.   Such treaties as pertain directly to the territory that has changed masters, for example, treaties creating a boundary régime, a servitude[14] or quasi-servitude such as a right of passage, or treaties neutralising or demilitarising the territory concerned. In this connection, articles 11 and 12 of the Vienna Convention of 1978 provide, in effect, that a 'succession of states' is not, as such, to affect a boundary established by treaty, a régime of rights and obligations established by treaty relating to a boundary, and rights, obligations or restrictions (as defined) involved in a territorial régime for the benefit of the territory concerned and attaching thereto. These provisions are not to apply to agreements for the establishment of foreign military bases, so that the state owning such bases cannot claim that the agreements are binding on a successor state.

b.   Multilateral conventions relative to health, narcotics, human rights, and similar matters, which are intended to apply, notwithstanding such changes, in respect of the territory. It is to be noted that under Annexe 1 of the Anglo-Chinese Agreement of 19 December 1984 as to the return of sovereignty to China over Hong Kong territories (Annexe 1 of the Joint Declaration; see n 8 above), the two International Covenants of 1966 on Civil and Political Rights and on Economic, Social and Cultural Rights are to continue to be applicable to Hong Kong when China resumes sovereignty in 1997.

This prima facie rule may have to give way to controlling facts or circumstances rendering it reasonable or equitable that certain treaty rights and obligations should pass; for example, if the particular treaty were one under which the consideration had been executed in favour of the extinct state, and the successor state had taken the benefit of that consideration, the latter would become liable to perform the corresponding obligations.[15] Semble, also, if the successor state

---

13. In the case of *executed* obligations under certain treaties, eg, treaties of cession or boundary demarcation, where there is a subsequent change of sovereignty, no question of succession of treaty rights is involved, but the territory, boundary, etc, simply passes to the successor state.

14. See above, pp 179-180.

15. Cf Opinion of US Attorney-General Griggs, p 293, n 8 above, that the successor state 'takes the burdens with the benefits'.

represents merely an enlargement of the predecessor state (as in the case of the incorporation of Prussia into the German Empire), prior treaty rights and obligations would pass in principle.

Where the predecessor state does not become extinguished, for instance, where part only of its territory is lost to it, prima facie the passing of treaty rights and obligations depends on the nature of the treaty. As regards succession in respect of a part of a territory, article 15 of the Vienna Convention of 1978 provides that where such part is incorporated in another state:

a.   treaties of the predecessor state are to cease to be in force in relation to the territory thus passing; and

b.   treaties of the successor state are to be in force in respect of the territory thus passing, unless it 'appears from the treaty or is otherwise established that the application of the treaty to that territory would be incompatible with the object and purpose of the treaty or would radically change the conditions for its operation'.

The rule thus formulated in article 15 of the Convention is often referred to as the 'moving treaty-frontiers rule'. Rights or obligations under political treaties, for example, of alliance, or as to landing and pick-up rights for foreign scheduled air services,[16] are as a rule deemed not to pass, and this on the whole seems reasonable, particularly where the treaty presupposes that the predecessor state shall be the only entity with which the other states parties were prepared to enter into a political arrangement or air services agreement. There is, however, an absence of agreement as to what constitutes a political treaty. Rights or obligations under multilateral conventions intended to be of universal application on health, technical, and similar matters may pass,[17] except those conventions which are the constituent instruments of international organisations, and which require the admission of the successor state by decision of an international organ before it can become a party,[18] or conventions which by their express or implied terms preclude the successor state from becoming a party to the convention, or from becoming a party except with the consent of all existing parties. In the same way as provided in articles 11–12 of the Vienna Convention of 1978, obligations under treaties creating a boundary régime or creating servitudes or quasi-servitudes, or obligations pertaining to, or for the benefit of the territory subject of the change of sovereignty or adjoining territory, may also pass.[19] Treaties

---

16.   Article IX of Annex 1 of Anglo-Chinese Agreement of 19 December 1984 as to the recovery by China of sovereignty over Hong Kong territories (Annex 1 of the Joint Declaration; see n 8 above) specifically makes reference to air services agreements.

17.   Thus, after becoming separated from India in 1947, Pakistan was recognised as becoming party automatically to certain multilateral conventions of universal application binding India. See memorandum prepared by the United Nations Secretariat in 1962, *Yearbook of the ILC*, 1962, Vol II, pp 101–103.

18.   See below, pp 554-555.

19.   For a detailed treatment of doctrine and practice on the point, see the commentary on draft arts 11 and 12 on succession in respect of treaties, adopted by the International Law Commission at its 26th Session, 1974; these articles deal respectively with boundary régimes, and other 'territorial' régimes (see *Report* of the Commission on the Work of its *26th Session* (1974)). Cf also the *Case of the Free Zones of Upper Savoy and Gex* (1932) PCIJ Series A/B, No 46, p 145,

outside these categories, such as of commerce, and extradition, do not pass unless some strong consideration requires this. In the case of a treaty of extradition, it would generally be unreasonable to bind the successor state under it, because normally such a treaty relates to special offences and procedure under the municipal criminal law of the predecessor state, and a different penal code may be in force in the case of the successor state.[20]

Part IV of the Vienna Convention of 1978 (articles 31–38) contains special provisions relating to the cases where two or more states unite to form one successor state, or where a part or parts of the territory of a state should separate to form one or more states. The general principle adopted here is that the relevant existing treaties continue in force, in regard to both the successor state and predecessor state, unless the parties concerned otherwise agree, or it appears from the treaty in question or is otherwise established that the application of the treaty to the successor state or to the predecessor state, as the case may be, would be incompatible with the object and purpose of the treaty or would radically change the conditions of its application. In certain cases, eg, where a treaty has a restricted operation in regard to certain territory only, provision is made for a written notification by the successor state that the treaty may apply in regard to the whole of the territory.

Most of what is provided otherwise in articles 31–38 of the Convention appears to be descriptive of what would be ordinary practice upon changes of sovereignty. It is difficult to conceive instances in which states would be constrained expressly to invoke or rely upon the provisions as to such practice in complicated situations of unions of states or separations of territory to form new states.

The extensive decolonisation or emancipation of dependent and trust territories in the period since 1953, produced a welter of practice concerning the extent to which:

a. treaties formerly applying to them, eg, under 'territories clauses' of conventions, continued to apply to them in their new international capacity;
b. treaty rights and obligations generally of the parent or tutelary state passed to them.[1]

It is a bewilderingly hopeless exercise to seek to spell out from this practice any new *general* customary principles of international law; one circumstance alone would be sufficient to negate the value and significance of any such effort, namely the number and nature of the different expedients adopted by newly emerged states to deal with the question of what treaties they would either recognise or refuse to acknowledge as applicable to them; among such expedients were 'devolution agreements' and 'inheritance agreements' with the parent or tutelary

---

under which France was regarded as having succeeded to Sardinia in the matter of an obligation to respect a territorial arrangement between Sardinia and Switzerland.
20. For three exceptional decisions (unreported) upholding the continued application of an extradition treaty, see *Report of the 53rd Conference of the International Law Association* 1968, p 628.
1. On post-decolonisation succession practice in the Pacific region, see Peter Sack (ed) *Pacific Constitutions* (1982) p 65 (article by Professor I. A. Shearer) and 189 (article by G. E. Fry).

state,[2] or unilateral declarations,[3] including the 'declaration of succession' (eg, that made by Tuvalu in March 1986 of succession as party to the Convention of 1951 relating to the status of Refugees) and the so-called 'temporising declaration' whereby the newly emerged state agreed to accept, wholly or partially, upon a basis of reciprocity, the former treaty régime pending a treaty-by-treaty review, and a final decision based upon such investigation.[4] In principle, devolution agreements between the parent tutelary state and the emancipated territory becoming a state could not automatically operate to bind third states, parties to the treaties concerned. Some newly emerged states preferred indeed to give general notice that they were beginning with a 'clean slate', so far as their future treaty relations were concerned, or to give so-called 'pick-and-choose' notifications as to treaties that were formerly applicable to it through its dependence on the parent tutelary state. Indeed the work of the International Law Commission on succession from 1972 onwards and debates in the United Nations General Assembly revealed considerable support for a 'clean slate' or 'free choice' doctrine applicable to newly emancipated states—a doctrine closely linked to the principles of self-determination, and of sovereignty of the new state over its own resources, and as will be seen, the 'clean slate' doctrine was ultimately adopted in the relevant provisions of the Vienna Convention of 1978.

This very diversity of action, apart from other considerations, appears inconsistent with the proposition that the practice has given rise to rules of general customary law as to succession stricto sensu. Moreover, when it is claimed, for example, that a devolution agreement may, with regard to a particular treaty, operate by way of novation between the parent state, the new state, and the other state party, or that a unilateral declaration or notification of accession may have effect upon the basis of estoppel or preclusion so as to bind the new state, these are not illustrations of the application of principles of succession, but rather of the incidence of the law of treaties or of the rules as to estoppel. Some devolution agreements are, on their true interpretation, no more than purported assignments of treaty rights and obligations, without relevance to the passing of such rights and obligations by way of state succession. Not to be overlooked also is the practical problem in many cases of determining, in the light of the law of treaties and of general principles of international law, whether a former treaty is inherently or by its terms invokable against the new state; in this connection, the provisions of the devolution agreement or unilateral declaration may be legally irrelevant.[5]

2. For the practice concerning these agreements, see the *Report of the 53rd Conference of the International Law Association* 1968, pp 610–627.
3. See Report, op cit, p 624, describing the practice in regard to Conventions of the International Labour Organisation (ILO) previously in force in a dependent territory; upon attaining independence, the new state should make a declaration that such conventions will continue to be respected.
4. An example of such a 'temporising' declaration is the note sent by Nauru on 28 May 1968, to the United Nations Secretary-General, some four months after attaining independence. The similar Lesotho declaration of 1967 was considered by the Privy Council in *Molefi v Principal Legal Adviser* [1971] AC 182, [1970] 3 All ER 724, to be more than a mere declaration of policy, and as an acceptance of temporary obligations rather than a mere offer to other state parties to continue such obligations on a basis of reciprocity.
5. On this matter of the practical difficulties, see Lawford 'The Practice Concerning Treaty Succession in the Commonwealth', Can YIL (1967) 3–13.

In regard to this subject, Part III of the Vienna Convention of 1978 (articles 16–30) contains special provisions dealing with 'newly independent States', defined in article 2 as those which immediately before the date of the succession of states were dependent territories for the international relations of which the predecessor states were responsible. The general rule for newly independent states laid down in the Convention is that of the 'clean slate', or as it is expressed in article 16 (representing section 1 of Part III) such a newly independent state 'is not bound to maintain in force, or to become a party to, any treaty by reason only of the fact that at the date of the succession of States the treaty was in force in respect of the territory to which the succession of States relates'. Strictly speaking, this is a rule not of succession, but of non-succession. Sections 2, 3, 4 and 5 of Part III deal respectively with multilateral treaties, bilateral treaties, provisional application and newly independent states formed from two or more treaties. Largely, the provisions thereof are framed in facultative terms, not in the phraseology of obligations under international law, and for the most part set out what may be done by a newly independent state and/or by other parties to the relevant treaty to enable the burden or bounty of the treaty to pass to the newly independent state; an illustration is that of the provisions in articles 17, 18 and 22 as to written notifications to be given by such states of accession to a multilateral treaty. The device of a notification of succession represents, of course, a useful addition to treaty practice, but as may be appreciated, to the extent that it represents a *consensual* measure on the part of the state assuming obligations or acquiring rights, it is inconsistent with any doctrine of succession by operation of law.

(2) Succession to non-fiscal contractual rights and obligations

The extent to which these pass is highly debatable. The following principles may perhaps be formulated:

a. A contractual right which is solely of the nature of a claim to unliquidated damages, and which cannot be alternatively enforced as a quasi-contractual right against the predecessor or successor state (for example, by reason of some benefit taken over by such state) does not survive the change of sovereignty. But if some element of quasi-contract is involved, for example, unjustified enrichment to the predecessor or successor state, the right and corresponding obligation may survive.[6]

b. A contractual right which is of the nature of a *vested* or *acquired* right ought to be respected by the successor state. To be such a vested or acquired right, it must be liquidated in nature and correspond to some undertaking, or enterprise, or investment of a more or less established character;[7] or—in more general terms—the right must be such that it would be unjust for the

---

6. There was some difference of opinion in the International Law Commission at its Session in 1969 concerning the current applicability of the principle of unjust enrichment, particularly its applicability in the context of decolonisation, having regard to the possible necessity for new states to nationalise and exploit their natural resources in the manner best suited to their economic development; see *Report* of the Commission on the Work of its *21st Session* (1969) paras 47–55.
7. Cf *Jablonsky v German Reich* Annual Digest of Public International Law Cases, 1935–7, Case No 42.

successor state not to give effect to it. Hence a merely executory contractual right, without more, is not a vested or acquired right. This concept of vested or acquired rights has been accepted by municipal and international tribunals,[8] although in view of the element of appreciation involved, there still remains some uncertainty regarding its scope, while latterly it has not escaped criticism. On the one hand, it is claimed that the concept of vested or acquired rights cannot be applied except subject to certain qualifications, one such qualification being that rights not in conformity with the public and social order of the successor state, even if vested or acquired, ought not to be binding upon that state. On the other hand, some would reject the concept altogether, or at least in relation to newly emerged states having problems of development, except in very special cases (eg debts of public utility).[9]

The doctrine of vested or acquired rights did operate to temper the stringency of earlier rules relating to succession to contractual rights and obligations, including the rule of non-succession laid down by the English Court of Appeal in *West Rand Central Gold Mining Co v R*[10] in 1905 to the effect that in the case of extinction of a predecessor state by conquest and annexation, the successor state as conqueror remains entirely free to decide whether or not to become subrogated to the contractual rights and duties of its predecessor. The latter view was indeed to some extent inconsistent with prior opinion and practice, and semble would not be followed today as an absolute principle.

(3) Succession and concessionary contracts

The general weight of practice and opinion[11] lies in the direction of holding that obligations under concessionary contracts are terminated upon changes of sovereignty resulting in the extinction of the predecessor state,[12] unless indeed the successor state renews the concession.[13] It is not clear why this is necessarily so in every case,[14] because even the executory rights and obligations under the

8. See, eg, *Advisory Opinion on the Settlers of German Origin in Territory ceded by Germany to Poland* (1923) PCIJ Series B, No 6, and *United States v Percheman* (1833) 7 Peters 51.
9. See *Report* of the International Law Commission on the Work of its *21st Session* (1969) paras 43–46 and 52–55.
10. [1905] 2 KB 391.
11. See First Report of 1968 by the Special Rapporteur of the International Law Commission on succession in respect of non-treaty rights and duties, para 139, YILC (1968) Vol II, p 115. See also paras 144–145, where the views are propounded that the economic conditions in which the concession was granted and the requirements of the new economic policy of the successor state should be taken into consideration, and that the right of new states to carry out nationalisations cannot be impeded by concessionary contracts. In respect of the rights of a successor state to succeed to the title of a predecessor state as to public property covered by a concession in the territory which has undergone a change of sovereignty, see Sixth Report by Mr Bedjaoui to the International Law Commission on Succession of States in Respect of Matters other than Treaties, 1973, commentary on draft art 10.
12. If only part of the territory of the predecessor state is transferred, and the concession relates to the resources of the remaining territory, presumably concessionaires retain their rights against the predecessor state.
13. In practice successor states have frequently renewed concessions, although it could not be inferred from this that they acknowledged a legal obligation to do so.
14. The intentions of the predecessor and successor states may in fact be that the concession should continue; see Hyde *International Law* (2nd edn, 1947) Vol I, pp 425–428.

concession may correspond to some substantial benefit which has accrued to the successor state, making it only just and reasonable that concessionaires should continue to enjoy their rights. As against that consideration, concessionaires are in theory always entitled to obtain compensation on just terms for the loss of their rights, including the loss of executory rights, so that these rights would terminate subject only to an obligation upon the successor state to make due compensation. The concessionaire is often said to retain an interest in the money invested and the labour expended, and this, whether classified as an acquired right or otherwise, should be respected by a successor state.[15]

(4) Succession and public debts

Both practice and doctrine reveal great divergencies on the question whether the successor state is obliged to take over public debts, and also on the question whether the creditor rights of a predecessor state pass to the successor.[16]

On the face of it, the successor state, having obtained the benefit of the loan by the very fact of taking over the territory, should be responsible for the public debts of the predecessor state relating to the territory that has passed. This principle of responsibility, resting on the basis of 'taking the burden with the benefits' has been repeatedly upheld by the United States.[17] The same principle applies with particular force where the visible benefits of the loan are directly associated with the territory that has passed, for instance, if the proceeds of the loan have been devoted to the erection of permanent improvements on the territory.[18]

At the same time, regard must be paid to the terms of the actual contract of loan, and if the debt be secured on the revenues of the predecessor state, and in respect of the territory which passed, it would be unreasonable to make the successor state liable beyond the taxable capacity of the territory which has changed sovereigns.[19]

No obligation accrues for a successor state in respect of a public debt incurred for a purpose hostile to the successor state, or for the benefit of some state other than the predecessor state.[20]

A difficult problem is that of the incidence of a public debt of the predecessor state, the territory of which becomes separated into several parts, each under the sovereignty of new or existing states. The rule that the debt becomes divided

15. Cf also with regard to a concessionary contract, although the case rests on its own peculiar facts, the *Mavrommatis Palestine Concessions Case* (1924) PCIJ Series A, No 2, p 28, and (1925), Series A, No 5.
16. See generally on the subject, Feilchenfeld *Public Debts and State Succession* (1931). Under draft art 11 on Succession to State Property, adopted by the International Law Commission (see *Report of the Commission on the Work of its 27th Session* (1975) para 76), 'debts owed to the predecessor State by virtue of its sovereignty over, or its activity in, the territory to which the succession of States relates shall pass to the successor State'.
17. Eg, in 1938 when it claimed that Nazi Germany, having absorbed Austria by bloodless conquest, was liable to service former Austrian loans; see Hyde, op cit, Vol I, pp 418–419. Cf O'Connell *State Succession in Municipal Law and International Law* (1967) Vol 1, pp 373, 375.
18. See Hyde, op cit, Vol I, pp 409–410.
19. See Hyde, op cit, Vol I, pp 413–414 and 416–417.
20. Thus in 1898 at the peace negotiations between Spain and the United States, which gained control over Cuba during its successful war with Spain, the American Peace Commissioners refused to recognise a so-called Cuban public debt, which had been raised by Spain for its own national purposes, and for interests in some respects adverse to those of Cuba.

among the successors is favoured by doctrine, although not supported by the award in the *Ottoman Debt Arbitration* (1925).[1] In practice, the debts of a predecessor state have been apportioned by treaty[2] among the successor states according to some equitable method of distribution, for example, proportionately to the revenues of each parcel of transferred territory or rateably in some other reasonable manner.

Part IV of the recently concluded Vienna Convention of 7 April 1983, on Succession of States in respect of State Property, Archives and Debts contains provisions as to the obligations of the successor state in respect of state debts. It is there laid down as a general rule (in article 36) that a succession of states does not as such affect the rights and obligations of creditors; thus an agreement between the predecessor state and the successor state governing the parts of state debts that are to pass cannot be relied on against a creditor third state or a creditor international organisation. On the transfer of part of the territory of a state, in the absence of agreement, an 'equitable' proportion is to pass, having regard to the property, rights and interests passing to the successor state in relation to the relevant debt (article 37). If the successor state is a newly independent state, no debt passes, unless an agreement provides otherwise in view of the link between the debt, on the one hand, and, on the other hand, the property, rights and interests passing to the newly independent state, which agreement is not to infringe the principle of the permanent sovereignty of a people over its wealth and natural resources, nor should its implementation endanger the fundamental economic equilibrium of that state (article 38). When part of the territory of a state separates to form a new state, or a state ceases to exist and parts of its territory form two or more states, an 'equitable' proportion of the predecessor's state debt, having regard to the property, rights and interests accruing to the successor state in relation to the debt concerned, is to pass to the successor state or to each of the successor states, as the case may be (articles 40–41).

(5) Succession and private[3] or municipal law rights

Such of these rights as have crystallised into vested or acquired rights must be respected by the successor state, more especially where the former municipal law of the predecessor state has continued to operate, as though to guarantee the sanctity of the rights.[4]

However, the continuance of any such rights is subject to any alterations affecting them made to the former municipal law by the successor state, for there is no rule of international law obliging the latter to maintain the former municipal legal system. The successor state can always displace existing rights and titles by altering the former municipal law, unless in doing so, it breaks some other independent duty under international law, for instance, by expropriating the property of aliens arbitrarily, and not for a public purpose.

1. See *United Nations Reports of International Arbital Awards* Vol I, pp 571–572.
2. See, eg, art 254 of the Treaty of Versailles, 1919.
3. The traditional view regarding *public* law rights is that the public law of the predecessor state is not automatically taken over by the successor state. However, some writers are of the view that there is a rebuttable presumption that the predecessor state's public law is incorporated into the legal system of the successor state.
4. See *Advisory Opinion on Settlers of German Origin, etc* (1923) PCIJ Series B No 6.

(6) Succession and claims in tort (or delict)

There is no general principle of succession to delictual liabilities.

According to the principles enunciated in two well-known cases, the *Robert E. Brown Claim*[5] and the *Hawaiian Claims*,[6] the successor state is not bound to respect an unliquidated claim for damages in tort.[7] If, however, the amount of the claim has become liquidated by agreement of the parties or through a judgment or award of a tribunal, then in the absence of any suggestion of injustice or unreasonableness, the successor state may be bound to settle the amount of this liquidated claim. This rule is irrespective of whether the change of sovereignty is forcible or voluntary. It is not clear even from the justifications given for the rule, why it should apply as an invariable proposition; for instance, where a tort relates to territory, as where there has been a wrongful diversion of water, or where some permanent benefit has accrued to the successor state, it may in some circumstances be reasonable to bind the successor state to respect the unliquidated claim against its predecessor.[8]

(7) Succession and public funds and public property

It is generally recognised that the successor state takes over the public funds and public property, whether movable or immovable, of the predecessor state, if such property is linked with or located in the territory to which the question of succession relates.[9] This principle of succession extends to public franchises and privileges, as well as to rights of a proprietorial or pecuniary character.

Part II of the above-mentioned Vienna Convention of 7 April 1983 on State Succession in respect of State Property, Archives and Debts contains provisions as to the passing of state property. In general, the successor state is to take over the predecessor's state property without compensation (article 11). When part of the territory of a state is transferred to another state, in the absence of agreement, immovable property situated in the territory taken over by the successor state is to pass to it, as does also movable property connected with the activity of the predecessor state in relation to the territory taken over. When the successor state is a newly independent state, the following rules apply (article 15):

i.   Immovable state property of the predecessor state situated in the territory passing, is to pass to the successor state.

ii. Immovable property, having belonged to the territory passing, being situated outside such territory, and being the state property of the predecessor state, is to pass to the successor state.

5. See 19 AJIL (1925) 193 et seq.
6. See 20 AJIL (1926) 381 et seq, and O'Connell *State of Succession in Municipal and International Law* (1967) Vol 1, pp 482–486.
7. See also *Kishangarh Electric Supply Co Ltd v United States of Rajasthan* (1959) 54 AJIL (1960) 900–901.
8. See Hyde, op cit, Vol 1, pp 437–440.
9. See the *Peter Pázmány University Case* (1933) PCIJ Series A/B, No 61 237, and see draft art 9 on Succession to States adopted by the International Law Commission (*Report* of the Commission on the Work of its *27th Session* (1975), para 76). As to the relevance of a distinction between movables and immovables in that connection, see Mr Bedjaoui's Eighth Report to the Commission on Succession of States in Respect of Matter other than Treaties, April 1976, para 30 et seq.

iii.   Immovable state property of the predecessor state not within (ii) and situated outside the territory passing, and movable property, to the creation of both of which the dependent territory has contributed, are to pass to the successor state in proportion to its contribution.
iv.   Movable state property connected with the activity of the predecessor state in regard to the territory passing, is to pass to the successor state.

There are also special rules in Part II covering the cases of separation of part or parts of a state's territory, or of a dissolution of a state. In the former case, the rules, in the absence of agreement, are as follows (article 17):

a.   Immovable state property of the predecessor state is to pass to the successor state in the territory in which it is situated.
b.   Movable state property of the predecessor state connected with the activity of the predecessor state in respect of the territory passing, is to pass to the successor state.
c.   Movable state property of the predecessor state other than property within (b) is to pass to the successor state in an equitable proportion.

In the latter case, when the parts of the territory of the dissolved state form two or more states, and unless the successor states otherwise agree, the rules are as follows (article 18):

a.   Immovable state property of the predecessor state is to pass to the successor state in the territory of which it is situated.
b.   Immovable state property of the predecessor state situated outside its territory is to pass to the successor states in equitable proportions.
c.   Movable state property of the predecessor state connected with the activity of the predecessor state in respect of the territories passing, is to pass to the successor state concerned.
d.   Movable state property of the predecessor state other than that within (c) is to pass to the successor states in equitable proportions.

(8) Succession and state archives

Elaborate provisions concerning succession in respect of state archives are contained in Part III of the above-mentioned Vienna Convention of 7 April 1983, on Succession of States in respect of State Property, Archives and Debts. Detailed consideration of these lies beyond the scope of the present chapter. More often, the matter will be one for negotiation. The provisions reflect the general principle that archives pertinent to the territory that passes or to the normal administration of that territory, or (in cases of transfers or separations of part or parts of territory) that part of the archives relating exclusively or principally to the territory passing, is to pass to the successor state.

(9) Succession and nationality

The problem here is whether and to what extent the successor state can claim as its nationals citizens of the predecessor state.[10] Prima facie, persons living or

10.   See Weis *Nationality and Statelessness in International Law* (2nd edn, 1979) pp 144–145.

domiciled in the territory subject of change, acquire the nationality of the successor. Difficulty arises in formulating rules concerning the position of citizens of the predecessor, normally living or domiciled in such territory, but outside it at the time of change.

There is no duty at international law upon the successor state to grant any right of option as to citizenship, nor, correspondingly, is there any duty upon the predecessor state to withdraw its nationality from persons normally living or domiciled in the transferred territory. Most cases, it will be found, have been regulated in detail by treaty or agreement.

(10) Succession and customary rights relating to territory

In principle, a customary right relating to territory, which has become established in favour of one state against the predecessor state, must be respected by the successor state in whom the particular territory subject to the right becomes vested. The decision of the International Court of Justice in the *Right of Passage over Indian Territory Case* (1960)[11] to the effect that Portugal was entitled to a certain right of passage over Indian territory, which had first become established by custom during British rule over India, is not a clear authority for this proposition, because the practice constituting the custom had continued as such for some time after India succeeded to Great Britain so as in effect to amount to a custom as between India and Portugal.[12]

3. PASSING OF RIGHTS AND OBLIGATIONS UPON INTERNAL CHANGES OF SOVEREIGNTY

The principle which applies here is known as the principle of *continuity*, namely, that notwithstanding internal alterations in the organisation of government, or in the constitutional structure of a particular state, the state itself continues to be bound by its rights and obligations under international law, including treaty rights and obligations.[13] Hence each successive government is, as a rule, liable for the acts of its predecessors.

This principle received an extended application in 1947 in the view which commanded general support that, despite the considerable alterations to its constitution when India emerged as an independent state, it continued as an original member of the United Nations with all former rights and obligations. That opinion prevailed in practice, the new India being automatically recognised as a member of the United Nations.[14]

11. [1960] ICJ 6.
12. It was held that the right was subject to regulation and control by India, and that under the circumstances in question, passage might be refused.
13. See the *Tinoco Arbitration* (1923) *United Nations Reports of International Arbitral Awards* Vol I, 369 at p 377.
14. See memorandum prepared by the United Nations Secretariat in 1962 on succession of states in respect to United Nations membership; YILC (1962) Vol II, pp 101–103. Quaere whether if a predecessor government withdraws from membership of an international organisation, the successor government is necessarily bound by such withdrawal and even after a period of inactive non-participation in the organisation is entitled to enjoy rights of continued membership. The

Even if the internal change in sovereignty has been brought about by revolution and has been accompanied by profound constitutional or social change, the principle of continuity applies. Thus, in the case of Iran, which underwent radical internal change after the deposition of the Shah in 1979, the basis of the jurisdiction of the International Court of Justice in the *Case Concerning United States Diplomatic and Consular Staff in Tehran* (the Hostages Case)[15] rested on the optional protocols to the Vienna Conventions on Diplomatic Relations (1961) and Consular Relations (1963) investing the Court with compulsory jurisdiction, to which the previous governments of Iran and the United States had both adhered, and on the Treaty of Amity, Economic Relations and Consular Rights, 1955, between Iran and the United States. It may, however, not always be easy in practice to enforce this rule against an unwilling state; the Soviet Union after 1917, and the People's Republic of China after 1949, in general rejected succession to the pre-revolutionary treaties of Russia and China.[16]

A problem of a special nature may arise in regard to a government which usurped office by illegal or unconstitutional means, and established de facto control for a period during which various obligations were incurred towards other states. If such other states had notice from the displaced government that no new treaty engagements entered into by the usurping government would be recognised if the displaced government re-established control, then prima facie such treaties would be entered into at the peril of the parties concerned, and the government displaced could claim not to be bound thereby when it resumed office.

Another special case arises where an insurgent government is established temporarily as the de facto government in control of a portion of the territory of the whole state and is subsequently suppressed by the parent government, as occurred in the American Civil War when the Confederate Government of the Southern States was overthrown. In such a case, the parent government is not responsible for the debts or delinquencies of the insurgent government[17] unless, perhaps, the debt be one incurred for the benefit of the state as a whole, and in regard to alleged delinquencies, unless the parent government has itself broken some independent duty of international law, for example, by facilitating the commission of the delinquency.

---

point recently arose in regard to the present government of mainland China and the membership of GATT (the General Agreement on Tariffs and Trade of 30 October 1947), from which the Nationalist Chinese Government withdrew in 1950. Semble, all the circumstances should be considered, including the views of the members and of competent organs of the organisation concerned.

15. ICJ 1979, 7; ICJ 1980, 3.
16. For discussion of the refusal of the Soviet Government to be bound by Tsarist treaties, see Taracouzio *The Soviet Union and International Law* (1935) pp 235–290.
17. For opinion of Sir Robert Phillimore to this effect, see Smith *Great Britain and the Law of Nations* (1932) Vol I, pp 412 et seq. Cf also draft arts 14–15 on state responsibility adopted by the International Law Commission, and commentary thereon, in the Commission's *Report* on the Work of its *27th Session*, (1975) pp 12, 44–47 and 51–53. These articles deal respectively with the question of responsibility for the conduct of organs of an insurrectional movement, and the attribution to the state of the act of an insurrectional movement which becomes the new government of a state, or which results in the formation of a new state.

CHAPTER 12

The state and the individual

1. NATIONALITY

Nationality is the most frequent and sometimes the only link between an individual and a state, ensuring that effect be given to that individual's rights and obligations at international law. It may be defined as the legal status of membership of the collectivity of individuals whose acts, decisions, and policy are vouchsafed through the legal concept of the state representing those individuals. One of the best passages descriptive of the status is that contained in the judgment of the British-Mexican Claims Commission in *Re Lynch*:[1]

'A man's nationality forms a continuing state of things and not a physical fact which occurs at a particular moment. A man's nationality *is a continuing legal relationship between the sovereign State on the one hand and the citizen on the other. The fundamental basis of a man's nationality is his membership of an independent political community*. This legal relationship involves rights and corresponding duties upon both—on the part of the citizen no less than on the part of the State.'

Most of the rules as to nationality are the sole concern of municipal law. It has long been conceded that it is the prerogative of each state to 'determine for itself, and according to its own constitution and laws what classes of persons shall be entitled to its citizenship'.[2]

Under changes in 1948 to the legislation of each of the member states of the British Commonwealth, the law as to British nationality was revised.[3] Each

1. Annual Digest of Public International Law Cases, 1929–1930, p 221 at 223. See also definition by the International Court of Justice in the *Nottebohm Case (Second Phase)* ICJ 1955, 23.
2. Per Gray J in *United States v Wong Kim Ark* 169 US 649 (1898) at 668. See also *Nationality Decrees in Tunis and Morocco Case* (1923) PCIJ, Ser B, No 4, at 24, and *Oppenheimer v Cattermole* [1973] Ch 264 at 270, 273, per Buckley LJ. Nonetheless no state may arbitrarily impress its nationality on persons outside its territory, having no genuine connection with it, or on persons residing in its territory without any intention of permanently living there; see Moore *Digest of International Law* (1906) Vol III, pp 302–310, and *Nottebohm Case (Second Phase)* ICJ 1955, 4. Nor are states under a duty to recognise a nationality acquired by fraudulent misrepresentation or non-disclosure of essential facts.
3. For a general treatise on the law of nationality in the Commonwealth, see Parry *Nationality and Citizenship Laws of the Commonwealth and of the Republic of Ireland* Vol 1 (1957) and

member state had its own 'citizens' (ie nationals), but in addition there was the status of British 'subject' which denoted membership of this Commonwealth and comprised certain privileges. The terminology in the 1948 Commonwealth-wide legislation was perhaps open to the objection that it might serve to cause confusion. If the objection were valid, the position appears to have been compounded by the provisions of the British Nationality Act 1981 which, inter alia, in addition to providing for a class of British citizens belonging to the United Kingdom, introduced other categories, namely, citizens of British dependent territories, and British 'overseas' citizens, that is to say, persons belonging to a territory previously subject to British sovereignty and who had retained their British nationality upon the dependent territory in question attaining independence.

Varied indeed are the different rules on nationality found in state laws, this lack of uniformity being most manifest in the divergencies relating to original acquisition of nationality. Thus the laws of one group of states provide that a person's nationality is determined by that of his or her parents at birth (jus sanguinis), those of a second group equally by parentage (jus sanguinis) and by the state of the territory of birth (jus soli), those of a third group principally by parentage (jus sanguinis) and partly by the state of territory of birth (jus soli), and those of a fourth group principally by the state of territory of birth (jus soli) and partly by parentage (jus sanguinis).

The lack of uniformity in state nationality laws has resulted in troublesome problems of multiple nationality, statelessness, and disputed nationality of married women. An attempt to cope with such problems was made in 1930, when the Hague Codification Conference adopted a Convention on the Conflict of Nationality Laws, two ancillary Protocols on, respectively, Military Obligations and Double Nationality, and a Certain Case of Statelessness, and a Special Protocol with regard to Statelessness. More recent instruments include the Convention on the Nationality of Married Women opened for signature on 20 February 1957, the Convention relating to the Status of Stateless Persons of 28 September 1954, and the Convention on the Reduction of Statelessness of 30 August 1961.

Nationality should be distinguished from the following:

a.   Race.[4]
b.   Membership or citizenship of the states or provinces of a federation. This local citizenship falls short of the international status of nationality, although it may entitle the holder eventually to claim these fuller and wider rights.
c.   The right to diplomatic protection. For example, under United States law and practice many persons enjoy a right to protection without being

---

Vol 2 (1960). On the law of nationality generally, see V. Bevan *The Development of British Immigration Law* (1986) ch 3, 'Citizenship', pp 104–163, and at pp 112 et seq for the legislation as to British nationality.

4.   Note in this connection para 2 of art 1 of the Convention of 1965 on the Elimination of all Forms of Racial Discrimination: 'This Convention shall not apply to distinctions, exclusions, restrictions or preferences made by a State Party to this Convention *between citizens and non-citizens*'.

American subjects.[5] Similarly, it has been held that French protected subjects do not necessarily become French nationals.[6]

d. Rights of citizenship, which may be denied to persons who are nationals. Disabilities in citizenship, even of a serious nature, do not involve loss of nationality. This is shown by the case of *Kahane v Parisi and the Austrian State*[7] where it was held that Jews in Rumania who were denied many privileges and subjected to many severe restrictions were none the less Rumanian nationals.

International importance of nationality

It is always material to know of which state a particular person is a national. The reason is that nationality has various important incidents at international law:

i. Entitlement to diplomatic protection abroad is an essential attribute of nationality. We have already seen that in questions of state responsibility, it is regarded as a vital right of each state that it should be entitled to protect its subjects abroad. The English common law conception of nationality coincides with this principle; as early as *Calvin's Case*,[8] it was ruled that allegiance and protection were the correlative aspects of nationality— '*Protectio trahit subjectionem et subjectio protectionem*'.

ii. The state of which a particular person is a national may become responsible to another state if it has failed in its duty of preventing certain wrongful acts committed by this person or of punishing the person after these wrongful acts are committed.[9]

iii. Generally, a state does not refuse to receive back on its territory its own nationals. Paragraph 4 of article 12 of the International Covenant on Civil and Political Rights of 1966 provides: 'No one shall be arbitrarily deprived of the right to enter his own country'.

iv. Nationality imports allegiance, and one of the principal incidents of allegiance is the duty to perform military service for the state to which such allegiance is owed.

v. A state has a general right, in the absence of a specific treaty binding it to do so, to refuse to extradite its own nationals to another state requesting surrender.

vi. Enemy status in time of war may be determined by the nationality of the person concerned.

vii. States may frequently exercise criminal or other jurisdiction on the basis of nationality.[10]

---

5. See *The Costello Case* Annual Digest of Public International Law Cases, 1929–1930, pp 188–9.
6. Decision of the Franco-German Mixed Arbitral Tribunal in *Djevahirdjhian v Germany* Annual Digest of Public International Law Cases, 1927–1928, pp 310 et seq.
7. Decision of the Austro-German Mixed Arbitral Tribunal, Annual Digest of Public International Law Cases, 1929–1930, pp 213 et seq.
8. (1608) 7 Co Rep 1a. Yet, semble, there is no legally enforceable right to be granted diplomatic protection; cf *China Navigation Co Ltd v A-G* [1932] 2 KB 197.
9. See, however, above, pp 275-280.
10. See above, pp 210-211.

Clearly difficulties may arise in many cases where the nationality of a particular individual is in doubt. The authorities have long established that the question is to be decided by the municipal law of the state whose nationality such person is alleged to possess; according to Russell J in *Stoeck v Public Trustee*:[11]

> 'The question of what State a person belongs to must ultimately be decided by the municipal law of the State to which he claims to belong or to which it is alleged that he belongs.'

This principle is supported by articles 1 and 2 of the Hague Convention of 1930 on the Conflict of Nationality Laws. These provisions are as follows:

> '*Article 1*.   It is for each State to determine under its own law who are its nationals. This law shall be recognised by other States in so far as it is consistent with international Conventions, international custom, and the principles of law generally recognised with regard to nationality.
> *Article 2*.   Any question as to whether a person possesses the nationality of a particular State shall be determined in accordance with the law of that State.'

It should be added that there are authorities to the effect that a duly authorised passport is prima facie evidence of nationality,[12] but there have also been decisions, both reported and unreported, that a passport is not to be relied on except in conjunction with other evidence of nationality, and is not conclusive on the question in the absence of such other evidence.

Acquisition of nationality

The practice of states shows that nationality may be acquired in the following principal ways:

1.   By birth either according to jus soli—the territory of birth—or jus sanguinis—the nationality of the parents at birth—or according to both.
2.   By naturalisation, either by marriage, as when a wife assumes her husband's nationality, or by legitimation, or by official grant of nationality on application to the state authorities. According to the decision of the International Court of Justice in the *Nottebohm Case* (*Second Phase*),[13] states are not under a duty to recognise a nationality acquired by a person who has no genuine link or connection with the naturalising state.
3.   The inhabitants of a subjugated or conquered or ceded territory may assume the nationality of the conquering state, or of the state to which the territory is ceded.[14] Quaere, also, whether a state may purport to naturalise persons who do not have their habitual residence in that state's territory.

11.   [1921] 2 Ch 67 at 78; applied by Buckley LJ in *Oppenheimer v Cattermole* [1973] Ch 264 at 270, 273.
12.   See Sandifer *Evidence Before International Tribunals* (1939) pp 154–5; Luke T. Lee *Consular Law and Practice* (1961) p 175; *R v Brailsford* [1905] 2 KB 730 at 745; and cf *Joyce v DPP* [1946] AC 347. The subject of passports is not as yet governed by international law or by any definitive international practice; see Bevan, op cit, n 3 above at pp 141 et seq. Moreover, at common law the limits marking the prerogative to issue passports are uncertain; cf *Council of Civil Service Unions v Minister for the Civil Service* [1985] AC 374, [1984] 3 All ER 935.
13.   ICJ 1955, 4.
14.   Other methods of acquiring nationality are by option, entry into the public service of the state concerned, and by registration.

Loss of nationality
According to the practice of states, nationality may be lost by:

1. Release, or renunciation, for example, by deed signed and registered at a consulate, or by declaration of alienage upon coming of age.
2. Deprivation, for example, under special denationalisation laws passed by the state of which the person concerned is a national.[15]
3. Long residence abroad.

So far as both international law and municipal law are concerned, there is a presumption against the loss of one nationality that has been held for some time, and a heavy onus of proof must be discharged before the loss is recognised. For instance, by article 7 of the Hague Convention of 1930 on the Conflict of Nationality Laws, the mere grant of an expatriation permit is not to entail the loss of nationality of the state issuing the permit. Under English law, an individual seeking to establish loss of nationality of a particular state must not merely satisfy the court by positive evidence as to the facts of the municipal law under which such loss is alleged,[16] but must also prove that nationality has been lost for all purposes and with all its incidents, and any possibility that a right of protection or a chance of resumption of nationality still exists will prevent the onus being discharged.[17]

Dual nationality, statelessness, and nationality of married women
Owing to the conflict of nationality laws and their lack of uniformity, it often arises that certain individuals possess dual nationality.[18] A frequent instance is the case of a woman who, marrying somebody not of her own nationality, may retain her nationality according to the law of the state of which she is a national and acquire the nationality of her husband according to the law of the state of which her husband is a national. Dual nationality may also result from birth in the territory of a state, not the state of which the parents are nationals, although usually a minor is given a chance to opt for one or the other nationality on the attainment of the age of majority. A right of option, otherwise, may be conferred by treaty.

Articles 3 to 6 of the Hague Convention of 1930 on the Conflict of Nationality Laws deal with some difficulties arising out of dual nationality. Of particular importance is article 5, which provides that within a third state persons of more

15. According to *R v Home Secretary, ex p L* [1945] KB 7, the municipal courts of a belligerent state are not bound in time of war to give effect to the denationalisation laws of an enemy belligerent state. Contra, *United States (ex rel Schwarzkopf) v Uhl* 137 F 2d 898 (1943). English courts will only refuse to recognise a change in the status of an enemy alien effected under the law of the enemy country during wartime so long as the war subsists; *Oppenheimer v Cattermole* [1973] Ch 264, [1975] 1 All ER 538. Semble, a denationalisation decree, which is a grave infringement of human rights, ought not to be recognised by English courts; ibid.
16. *Hahn v Public Trustee* [1925] Ch 715.
17. *Stoeck v Public Trustee* [1921] 2 Ch 67; *Ex p Weber* [1916] 1 AC 421 at 425.
18. For general treatise on this subject, see Bar-Yaacov *Dual Nationality* (1961). International law recognises the possibility of dual nationality (see below), although where a question of nationality of claims is involved, an international tribunal will not admit the locus standi of a claimant state if that state relies on one of the nationalities which is not the 'real and effective' nationality of the individual concerned; see p 287, n 20. Nor does international law prevent states passing legislation to prohibit dual nationality; eg, dual nationality is prohibited by Zimbabwe's Citizenship Act 1984.

than one nationality shall be treated as if they only had one nationality, and such third state shall recognise exclusively either:

a.   the nationality of the country in which they are habitually and principally resident, or

b.   the nationality of the country with which in the circumstances they appear to be in fact most closely connected.

Articles 8–11 of the Convention deal with the nationality of married women, containing provisions mitigating the artificial and technical principle that their nationality follows that of their husbands, and enabling them under certain conditions to retain premarital nationality. An advance on these provisions was made in the Convention on the Nationality of Married Women opened for signature on 20 February 1957, under which each contracting state agrees that neither the celebration nor the dissolution of marriage between one of its nationals and an alien, nor a change of nationality by the husband during marriage, shall have any automatic effect on the wife's nationality, and provision is made for facilitating, through naturalisation, the voluntary acquisition by an alien wife of her husband's nationality. Article 5 of the Declaration on the Elimination of Discrimination against Women, adopted by the United Nations General Assembly in November 1967 provided more broadly: 'Women shall have the same rights as men to acquire, change or retain their nationality. Marriage to an alien shall not automatically affect the nationality of the wife either by rendering her stateless or by forcing upon her the nationality of the husband'. This proposed principle was spelled out in more elaborate terms in article 9 of the Convention of 1979 on the Elimination of All Forms of Discrimination Against Women. Paragraph 1 of the article provided: '1. States Parties shall grant women equal rights with men to acquire, change or retain their nationality. They shall ensure in particular that neither marriage to an alien nor change of nationality by the husband during marriage shall automatically change the nationality of the wife, render her stateless or force upon her the nationality of husband'. Paragraph 2 was in these terms: '2. States Parties shall grant women equal rights with men with respect to the nationality of the children'.

Statelessness is a condition recognised both by municipal law[19] and by international law. It has indeed become in recent years a major problem of international law, the very urgency and acuteness of which prompted the insertion of article 15 in the Universal Declaration of Human Rights of December, 1948, that 'everyone has the right to a nationality', and that 'no one shall be arbitrarily deprived of his nationality'. Statelessness may arise through conflicts of municipal nationality laws, through changes of sovereignty over territory, and through denationalisation by the state of nationality.[20] It is a condition which not only means great hardship and lack of security for individuals; but involves the existence of a serious gap in the application of international law.[1]

---

19. See *Stoeck v Public Trustee* [1921] 2 Ch 67.
20. See 'A Study of Statelessness' (United Nations Department of Social Affairs, 1949), Weis *Nationality and Statelessness at International Law* (2nd edn, 1979), and A. P. Mutharika *The Regulation of Statelessness under International and National Law* (2 vols, 1980).
1.   See *Report* of the International Law Commission on the work of its *5th Session* (1953) para 22.

Remedial action for the condition lies in:

a. Imposing duties upon states to regard a certain nationality as acquired, or not to regard a certain nationality as lost, or to grant a nationality upon special grounds or subject to special conditions. Limited progress in this field was achieved by certain treaty provisions adopted in 1930 at the Hague Codification Conference,[2] and later by the Convention on the Reduction of Statelessness, adopted at New York on 30 August 1961.[3]
b. Obliging states to refrain from denationalisation measures unless there be just cause.
c. The conferment by liberal-minded states of their nationality upon stateless persons. Many states have begrudged this solution.
d. Relief from the disadvantages of this unprotected status through international conventions allowing the use of identity or travel documents, and privileges of admission by foreign states with rights of residence, of practising an occupation, etc. In this regard, the Convention on the Status of Refugees signed at Geneva on 25 July 1951,[4] and the Convention relating to the Status of Stateless Persons signed at New York on 28 September 1954, conferred important benefits on stateless persons.

The subject of statelessness, and of remedial action in regard to it, was under study for some time by the International Law Commission,[5] and by the General Assembly of the United Nations.

Nationality of corporations and unincorporated associations

The nationality of corporations and unincorporated associations is entirely a modern conception, and becomes relevant when it is necessary to determine the nationality of such corporations or associations for the purpose of applying the 'nationality of claims' principle[6] in a case before an international tribunal, or for giving effect to a treaty applying to 'nationals' of a state.

There is no unanimity of opinion regarding the tests to be applied for ascertaining the nationality of these bodies. Prima facie, the nationality of a corporation or limited company is that of the state of incorporation, and this test is also adopted by some treaties. However, for different purposes, other tests of the nationality of a corporation have been adopted; eg, the principal place of business test for exchange control purposes, and the location of central control test for the purpose of determining the right to take advantage of double taxation treaties.[7] The national status of the individual corporators or shareholders is not

2. See arts 13 and 15 of the Convention on the Conflict of Nationality Laws, the Protocol on a Certain Case of Statelessness, and the Special Protocol with regard to Statelessness.
3. This Convention contains, inter alia, provisions enabling persons who would otherwise be stateless to acquire the nationality of the country of birth, or of one of the parents at the date of birth, and also provides that a loss of nationality, which would otherwise take place under certain circumstances, is to be conditional upon the acquisition of another nationality.
4. Note also the Protocol of 31 January 1967, in extension of this Convention.
5. See *The Work of the International Law Commission* (3rd edn, 1980) pp 33–36.
6. See pp 284-288 above.
7. See M. Tedeschi 'The Determination of Corporate Nationality' (1976) 50 ALJ 521. The location of central control test, coupled with the test of location of primary profit-making functions, was applied for double taxation treaty purposes in *Compagnie Financière de Suez, etc v United States* 492 F 2d 798 (1974).

generally a material consideration in this connection.[8] Prima facie, also, the nationality of an unincorporated association is that of the state in which the association has been constituted, or of the state in which the governing body of the association is normally located for administrative purposes.

2.   RIGHTS AND DUTIES OF STATES WITH REGARD TO ALIENS

Admission of aliens

Four principal opinions have been held regarding the admission of aliens into countries not of their nationality:

a.   A state is under a duty to admit all aliens.
b.   A state is under a duty to admit all aliens, subject to the qualification that it is entitled to exclude certain classes, for example drug addicts, persons with diseases, and other undesirables.
c.   A state is bound to admit aliens but may impose conditions with regard to their admission.
d.   A state is fully entitled to exclude all aliens at will.

So far as state practice is concerned, it may be said that the first view has never been accepted as a general rule of international law.

Most states claim in legal theory to exclude all aliens at will, affirming that such unqualified right is an essential attribute of sovereign government.[9] The courts of Great Britain and the United States have laid it down that the right to exclude aliens at will is an incident of territorial sovereignty.[10] Unless bound by an international treaty to the contrary, states are not subject to a duty under international law to admit aliens or any duty thereunder not to expel them. Nor does international law impose any duty as to the period of stay of an admitted alien.

The absence of any duty at international law to admit aliens is supported by an examination of state immigration laws, showing that scarcely any states freely admit aliens. The practice of most states is to reserve the right to exclude entry to foreign nationals deemed undesirable for any reason. Moreover, most states require all entrants, or certain categories of entrant, to have obtained in advance of arrival at the border a stamp in their passport called a visa, certifying that the passport has been sighted by the receiving state's representatives abroad and that the holder is qualified to seek entry. Even then the holder of a visa may be excluded; the visa does not necessarily operate as a guarantee that entry will be allowed. States often enter into agreements with other states waiving the visa requirement for citizens of those states, or have laws permitting visa-free entry

8.   As to the question of the legal capacity of the national state of the shareholders to espouse a claim by them for injury done to the company itself, see *Case Concerning the Barcelona Traction, Light and Power Co Ltd (Second Phase)* ICJ 1970, 3 discussed pp 286-287 above.
9.   See Nafziger 'General Admission of Aliens under International Law' (1983) 77 AJIL 804.
10.   As to Great Britain, see *Musgrove v Chung Teeong Toy* [1891] AC 272, and as to the United States, see *Nishimura Ekiu v United States* 142 US 651 (1892) and *Fong Yue Ting v United States* 149 US 698 (1893). See also Henkin, Pugh, Schachter and Smit *International Law: Cases and Materials* (2nd edn, 1987) p 1040.

for certain categories of traveller, eg tourists with onward pre-paid travel tickets. Visa and entry permits will normally be subject to restrictions, such as on the permitted length of stay and on engaging in paid local employment.

Among the member states of the European Union there is freedom of movement and the 'right of establishment', ie the right to reside and work in any part of the Union, for citizens of the Union.[11]

Legal position of aliens when admitted

An alien entering the territory of a state becomes subject to its laws in the same way exactly as citizens of that state. Most states, however, place aliens under some kind of disability or some measure of restrictions of varying severity. Frequently they are denied voting rights or the right to practise certain professions or the power of holding real estate.

In 1924, the Economic Committee of the League of Nations classified the treatment of aliens abroad under the following headings:

a. Fiscal treatment, for example, in respect of taxation.
b. Rights as to the exercise of professions, industries, or occupations.
c. Treatment in such matters as residence, the holding of property, and civil privileges and immunities.
d. Conditions of admission and immigration.

As to (a) unless possessing diplomatic immunity, resident aliens are not exempt from ordinary civil taxes or customs dues. Leading English and American decisions have also affirmed the right of all states at international law to tax property physically within their jurisdiction belonging to non-resident aliens.[12]

As to (c), aliens are exempt from any compulsory obligation to serve in the armed forces of the country in which they reside, unless the state to which they belong consents to waive this exemption.[13] This rule, however, does not prevent compulsory service in a local police force, or, apparently, compulsory service for the purpose of maintaining public order or repelling a sudden invasion.[14] During the Second World War most belligerent states compelled resident aliens to perform some kind of service connected with the war effort, even to the extent of making voluntary service in the armed forces an alternative to the performance of compulsory civilian duties. In certain instances, this was sanctioned by agreement or treaty between the states concerned.

As noted above in Chapter 10 on State Responsibility, aliens carry with them a right of protection by their national state, although the latter is not duty bound to exercise that right. Grossly unfair discrimination or outright arbitrary

11. EC Treaty, 1957 (as amended by the Maastricht Treaty, 1993), arts 8a, 48, 49, and EC Council Regulation 1612/68 of 15 October 1968 (as amended by Regulation 2434/92).
12. *Winans v A-G* [1910] AC 27; *Burnet v Brooks* 288 US 378 (1933).
13. In the US, aliens can be called up for service, but have the right to opt out, in which event: (a) if they subsequently leave the US, they cannot return; and (b) if they stay, they will not be granted US citizenship. The position as to alien migrants, as distinct from temporarily resident aliens, is at least open to doubt. In 1966, the Australian Government purported to make alien migrants subject to compulsory service, formal protests being received from the USSR, Italy, Spain, and other countries.
14. See judgment of Latham CJ in decision of Australian High Court, *Polites v The Commonwealth* (1945) 70 CLR 60 at 70–71.

confiscation of the alien's property would, for example, be legitimate ground for intervention by that state. Aliens' *vested rights* in their country of residence are also entitled to protection. But as the decision of the Permanent Court of International Justice in the *Oscar Chinn Case*[15] shows, protection of vested rights does not mean that the state of residence is duty bound to abstain from providing advantages for local enterprises, which may cause loss to aliens in their businesses. A number of states, including the Afro-Asian group, hold that the national standard of treatment should apply, inasmuch as aliens entering impliedly submit to that standard, otherwise they could elect not to enter.

Resident aliens owe temporary allegiance or obedience to their state of residence, sufficient at any rate to support a charge of treason.[16]

Expulsion and reconduction[17] of aliens

States are generally recognised as possessing the power to expel, deport, and reconduct aliens. Like the power to refuse admission, this is regarded as an incident of a state's territorial sovereignty.

The *power* to expel and the *manner* of expulsion are, however, two distinct matters. Expulsion (or reconduction) must be effected in a reasonable manner and without unnecessary injury to the alien affected. Article 13 of the International Covenant of 1966 on Civil and Political Rights provides that aliens lawfully in the territory of a state party to the Covenant may be expelled only pursuant to a decision reached by law, and, except where compelling reasons of national security otherwise require, are to be allowed to submit the reasons against their expulsion and to have their case reviewed by, and to be represented for the purpose before, the competent authority or a person or persons especially designated by the competent authority. Detention prior to expulsion should be avoided, unless the alien concerned refuses to leave the state or is likely to evade the authorities. Also aliens may not be deported to a country or territory where their person or freedom would be threatened on account of their race, religion, nationality, or political views.[18] Nor should they be exposed to unnecessary indignity.

Mass expulsion of aliens would almost inevitably be unlawful as breaching norms of human rights, including article 13 of the International Covenant on Civil and Political Rights, referred to above. Uganda's expulsion of its Indian population group in 1972 was doubly objectionable, since many of those expelled possessed Ugandan citizenship and had no right to reside in any other country.[19]

---

15. (1934) Pub PCIJ, Series A/B, No 63. For certain prohibitions against discrimination in regard to resident refugee aliens, see arts 3, 4, 14 and 16 of the Geneva Convention on the Status of Refugees, of 25 July 1951.
16. *De Jager v A-G of Natal* [1907] AC 326.
17. As distinct from expulsion, reconduction amounts to a police measure whereby the alien is returned to the frontier under escort.
18. See below, p 325.
19. See *R v Secretary of State for the Home Office, ex p Thakrar* [1974] QB 684, CA; and the *East African Asians Cases*, (1981) 3 EHRR 76. After nearly 20 years the expelled citizens have been allowed to return to Uganda.

3. EXTRADITION, RENDITION AND ASYLUM

The liberty of a state to accord asylum to a person overlaps to a certain extent with its liberty to refuse extradition or rendition of that person at the request of some other state, an overlapping best seen in the grant, commonly, of asylum to political offenders, who correspondingly are not as a rule extraditable. Asylum stops, as it were, where extradition or rendition begins, and this interdependence[20] makes it convenient to consider the two subjects together.

Extradition

The term 'extradition' denotes the process whereby under treaty or upon a basis of reciprocity one state surrenders to another state at its request a person accused or convicted of a criminal offence committed against the laws of the requesting state, such requesting state being competent to try the alleged offender. Normally, the alleged offence has been committed within the territory or aboard a ship[1] flying the flag of the requesting state, and normally it is within the territory of the surrendering state that the alleged offender has taken refuge. Requests for extradition are usually made and answered through the diplomatic channel.

The following rational considerations have conditioned the law and practice as to extradition:

a. The general desire of all states to ensure that serious crimes do not go unpunished. Frequently a state in whose territory criminals have taken refuge cannot prosecute or punish them purely because of some technical rule of criminal law or for lack of jurisdiction. Therefore to close the net round such fugitive offenders, international law applies the maxim, *'aut punire aut dedere'*, ie offenders must be punished by the state of refuge or surrendered to the state which can and will punish them.

b. The state on whose territory[2] the crime has been committed is best able to try the offender because the evidence is more freely available there, and that state has the greatest interest in the punishment of the offender, and the greatest facilities for ascertaining the truth. It follows that it is only right and proper that to the territorial state should be surrendered such criminals as have taken refuge abroad.

With the increasing rapidity and facility of international transport and communications, extradition began to assume prominence in the nineteenth

---

20. No question of asylum, and therefore of interdependence between it and extradition, arises, however, where a state is requested to extradite its own resident nationals. Also, art 1 of the Declaration on Territorial Asylum adopted by the United Nations General Assembly on 14 December 1967, recommends that all states should 'respect' (this would include refraining from an application for extradition) asylum granted to persons who have sought refuge from persecution, including persons struggling against colonialism. On extradition under international law, see generally Bassiouni *International Extradition* (1983) and Henkin, Pugh, Schachter and Smit *International Law: Cases and Materials* (2nd edn, 1987) pp 885–890.
1. *R v Governor of Brixton Prison, ex p Minervini* [1959] 1 QB 155, [1958] 3 All ER 318.
2. 'Territory' can cover, for this purpose, also ships and aircraft registered with the requesting state; see, eg, art 16 of the Tokyo Convention of 14 September 1963 on Offences and Certain Other Acts Committed on Board Aircraft (offences committed on board aircraft in flight to be treated for purposes of extradition as if committed also in country of registration).

century, although actually extradition arrangements date from the eighteenth century. Because of the negative or neutral attitude[3] of customary international law on the subject, extradition was at first dealt with by bilateral treaties. These treaties, inasmuch as they affected the rights of private citizens, required in their turn alterations to the laws and statutes of the states which had concluded them. Hence the general principle became established that without some formal authority either by treaty or by statute, fugitive criminals would not be surrendered nor would their surrender be requested. There was at international law neither a duty to surrender, nor a duty not to surrender. For this reason, extradition was called by some writers a matter 'of imperfect obligation'. In the absence of treaty or statute, the grant of extradition depended purely on reciprocity or courtesy.[4]

As regards English municipal law, the special traditions of the common law conditioned the necessity for treaty and statute. At common law the Crown had no power to arrest a fugitive criminal who was a foreign subject and to surrender him or her to another state; furthermore, so far as the surrender of subjects of the Crown was concerned, treaties as to extradition were deemed to derogate from the private law rights of British citizens, and required legislation before they could come into force in England.[5] Thus from both points of view legislation was essential, and the solution adopted was to pass a general extradition statute—the Extradition Act 1870—which applied only in respect of countries with which an arrangement for the surrender of fugitive offenders had been concluded, and to which the Act itself had been applied by Order-in-Council.[6] This structure has been retained by the Extradition Act 1989. Extradition between the United Kingdom and Commonwealth countries is also governed by the same act, replacing the Fugitive Offenders Act 1967, but is not dependent on treaty arrangements.

International law concedes that the grant of and procedure as to extradition are most properly left to municipal law, and does not, for instance, preclude states from legislating so as to refuse the surrender by them of fugitives, if it appears that the request for extradition had been made in order to prosecute the fugitive on account of race, religion, or political opinions, or if the fugitive may be prejudiced thereby upon eventual trial by the courts of the requesting

3. On the one hand, customary international law imposed no duty upon states to surrender alleged or convicted offenders to another state, while on the other hand, it did not forbid the state of refuge to deliver over the alleged delinquent to the state requesting his surrender.
4. Reference should be made to the European Convention on Extradition, 13 December 1957 (Council of Europe) as an illustration of a multilateral extradition treaty. On the necessity of a treaty to confer a right on a state to request the surrender of a fugitive from justice and to impose a correlative duty on the requested state to hand the fugitive over see *Factor v Laubenheimer* 290 US 276 (1933) at 287. A bilateral extradition treaty should be liberally and pragmatically interpreted, eg, as to the time-limit for adducing evidence to the local court; see *Belgian Government v Postlethwaite* [1988] AC 924; [1987] 2 All ER 985, HL.
5. See above, pp 71-72. See also Shearer 'Extradition without Treaty' (1975) 49 ALJ 116 at 118.
6. For an analysis of the effect of, and the procedure related to the British Extradition Act 1870 and subsequent Extradition Acts, see the speech of Lord Diplock in *Re Nielsen* [1984] AC 606 at 614–616, and see also *Government of Federal Republic of Germany v Sotiriadis* [1975] AC 1.

state. There are some divergences on the subject of extradition between the different state laws, particularly as to the following matters: extraditability of nationals of the state of refuge; evidence of guilt required by the state of refuge; and the relative powers of the executive and judicial organs in the procedure of surrendering the fugitive criminal.

Before an application for extradition is made through the diplomatic channel, two conditions are as a rule required to be satisfied:

a. There must be an extraditable person.
b. There must be an extradition crime.

We shall discuss each of these conditions.

(a) Extraditable persons
There is uniformity of state practice to the effect that the requesting state may obtain the surrender of its own nationals or nationals of a third state. But many states usually refuse the extradition of their own nationals who have taken refuge in their territory, although as between states who observe absolute reciprocity of treatment in this regard, requests for surrender are sometimes acceded to. This does not necessarily mean that a fugitive from justice escapes prosecution by the country of his or her nationality, for that country (and especially Civil Law countries) may assert jurisdiction on the basis of nationality[7], over all crimes committed by their citizens abroad.

(b) Extradition crimes
The ordinary practice as to extradition crimes is to list these in each bilateral extradition treaty. However, it is becoming increasingly common to define extradition crimes in terms of a given minimum level of punishment provided under the laws of each state, however the offence may be denominated.

Generally, states extradite only for serious crimes,[8] and there is an obvious advantage in thus limiting the list of extradition crimes since the procedure is so cumbrous and expensive. Certain states, for example, France, extradite only for offences which are subject to a definite *minimum* penalty, both in the state requesting and in the state requested to grant extradition. This is also the case in the United Kingdom under the Extradition Act 1989.

As a general rule, the following offences are not subject to extradition proceedings:

i.   political crimes;
ii. military offences, for example, desertion;
iii. religious offences.

7. On nationality as a basis of State jurisdiction see above, p 210.
8. Recent practice shows a general disposition of states to treat alleged 'war crimes' as extradition crimes. However, there are a number of decisions of municipal courts treating war crimes as political offences for the purpose of extradition (cf *Karadzole v Artukovic* 247 F 2d 198 (1957)), so that extradition is refused. In one decision, *Re Wilson, ex p the witness T* (1976) 135 CLR 179, the High Court of Australia declined to treat war crimes as being offences of a political character; and see also *Re Gross, ex p Treasury Solicitor* [1968] 3 All ER 804.

The principle of non-extradition of political offenders crystallised in the nineteenth century, a period of internal convulsions, when tolerant, liberal states such as Holland, Switzerland, and Great Britain, insisted on their right to shelter political refugees. At the same time, it is not easy to define a 'political crime', although a clear case would be that where it is evident that the fugitive is to be punished for political activities or beliefs rather than for the offence itself.[9] Different criteria have been adopted:

a. the motive of the crime;
b. the circumstances of its commission;
c. that it embraces specific offences only, eg, treason or attempted treason;[10]
d. that the act is directed against the political organisation, as such, of the requesting state;
e. the test followed in the English cases, *Re Meunier*,[11] and *Re Castioni*,[12] that there must be two parties striving for political control in the state where the offence is committed, the offence being committed in pursuance of that goal, thereby excluding anarchist and terrorist acts from the category of 'political crimes'.

In *R v Governor of Brixton Prison, ex p Kolczynski*,[13] the court favoured an even more extended meaning, holding in effect that offences committed in association with a political object (eg anti-Communism), or with a view to avoiding political persecution or prosecution for political defaults, are 'political crimes', notwithstanding the absence of any intention to overthrow an established government. Whether an alleged crime is 'political' is a question to be determined by reference to the circumstances attending its alleged commission at the material time, and not in the light of the motives of those who have instituted the prosecution proceedings and the corresponding application for extradition.[14]

A number of decisions by municipal courts show that extradition will not be denied for actual offences, including crimes of violence, having no direct and close relation to political aims, although committed in the course of political controversy, or by persons politically opposed to the requesting government.[15] In this connection, the question of war crimes gives rise to difficulties; to some

9. Cf *R v Governor of Winson Green Prison, ex p Littlejohn* [1975] 3 All ER 208.
10. A number of bilateral and other treaties after the Second World War, including the Paris Peace Treaties of 1946 with Italy, Rumania, Bulgaria, Hungary, and Finland, provided for the surrender of 'quislings', persons guilty of treason, and so-called 'collaborationists' with the enemy occupying authorities.
11. [1894] 2 QB 415.
12. [1891] 1 QB 149.
13. [1955] 1 QB 540.
14. See *Re Extradition of Locatelli* 468 F Supp 568 (1979).
15. Cf *Schtraks v Government of Israel* [1964] AC 556 esp at 591–592, per Viscount Radcliffe, upholding the view that to be a political offence, the relevant act must be committed in the course of political opposition to a government, or in the course of political disturbances. See also *Cheng v Governor of Pentonville Prison* [1973] AC 931, [1973] 1 All ER 935. There is a recent trend to exclude from the 'political crime' exception crimes of violence typically committed by terrorists, international or otherwise; note, eg, in that connection the Supplementary Extradition Treaty of June 1985 between the United States and the United Kingdom and, earlier, the European Convention of 1977 on the Suppression of Terrorism (Council of Europe).

extent the issues involved are matters of degree, insofar as a war crime may or may not transcend its political implications.[16]

International law leaves to the state of refuge the sovereign right of deciding, according to its municipal law and practice, the question whether or not the offence which is the subject of a request for extradition is a political crime.[17]

As regards the character of the crime, most states follow the rule of *double criminality*, ie that it is a condition of extradition that the crime is punishable according to the law both of the state of asylum and of the requesting state. The application of the rule to peculiar circumstances came before the United States Supreme Court in 1933 in the case of *Factor v Laubenheimer*.[18] There, proceedings were taken by the British authorities for the extradition of Jacob Factor on a charge of receiving in London money which he knew to have been fraudulently obtained. At the time extradition was applied for, Factor was residing in the State of Illinois, by the laws of which the offence charged was not an offence in Illinois. It was held by the Supreme Court that this did not prevent extradition if, according to the criminal law generally of the United States, the offence was punishable; otherwise extradition might fail merely because the fugitive offender would succeed in finding in the country of refuge some province in which the offence charged was not punishable. Substantial similarity of the alleged extradition crime to the crime punishable according to the legal system of the state of refuge is sufficient to bring into effect the double criminality rule so as to justify a grant of extradition.[19]

A further principle sometimes applied is known as the *principle of specialty*, ie the requesting state is under a duty not, without the consent of the state of refuge, to try or punish the offender for any other offence than that for which he was extradited. This principle is frequently embodied in treaties of extradition and is approved by the Supreme Court of the United States. In Great Britain its application is a little uncertain; in *R v Corrigan*[20] the Extradition Act was held to prevail over a Treaty of Extradition with France embodying the specialty principle, and it was ruled that the accused there could be tried for an offence

16. Cf *Re Wilson, ex p the witness T* (1976) 135 CLR 179 (decision of High Court of Australia), and *Re Gross, ex p Treasury Solicitor* [1968] 3 All ER 804.
17. Quaere, whether an English court should accept an unconditional undertaking by the requesting state not to apply a particular law to the extraditee; see *Armah v Government of Ghana* [1968] AC 192, [1966] 3 All ER 177. An English court will assume that the requesting government will honour its obligations under law or any arrangement; see *Royal Government of Greece v Brixton Prison Governor* [1971] AC 250 at 278–279.
18. 290 US 276.
19. *R v Governor of Pentonville Prison, ex p Budlong* [1980] 1 All ER 701; there the alleged extradition offence was burglary, and it was held to be immaterial that entry as a trespasser was not an essential element of the crime in the District of Columbia (USA), whereas it was an essential element under s 9(a) of the English Theft Act 1968. Cf also *Re Locatelli* 468 F Supp 568 (1979). The House of Lords held in *Re Nielson* [1984] AC 606, followed in *United States Government v McCaffery* [1984] 2 All ER 570; [1984] 1 WLR 867, that on the true construction of the Extradition Act 1870 an English committing magistrate is, in the absence of special provision in the relevant extradition treaty, concerned with English law alone in determining whether the conduct of the accused amounted to an extradition crime, and has no jurisdiction to inquire into or receive evidence of the substantive criminal law of the requesting state so as to determine, for the purposes of the double criminality rule, whether the offence for which extradition is sought is substantially similar in both countries. To that extent, *ex p Budlong* (above) is overruled in part.
20. [1931] 1 KB 527.

for which he was not extradited, but one which was referable to the same facts as alleged in the extradition proceedings.[1]

Human rights as embodied in national legislation or in international instruments may constitute further restrictions on extradition. In the *Soering Case* the United Kingdom intended to extradite a person to the United States for a crime carrying a possible penalty of death. The European Court of Human Rights held that such circumstances, where a fugitive might spend years on 'Death Row' awaiting the result of appeals, would constitute inhuman and degrading treatment contrary to the European Convention on Human Rights, and that extradition was thus inadmissible.[2]

Rendition

This more generic term 'rendition' covers instances where an offender may be returned to a state to be tried there, under ad hoc special arrangement, or on the basis of reciprocity[3] in the absence of an extradition treaty, or even if there be such a treaty between the states concerned, irrespective of whether or not the alleged offence is an extraditable crime.

A deportation or refusal of asylum may have the *effect* of a rendition, although from the point of view of the deporting state or state of purported entry, it is not of this nature stricto sensu.[4] As pointed out by Barwick CJ in a decision of the High Court of Australia,[5] 'there are obvious objections to the use of immigration or expulsive powers as a substitute for extradition'.[6] The House of Lords in *R v Horseferry Road Magistrates, ex p Bennett*[7] declared that to invoke the criminal jurisdiction of the English courts over an accused deported from South Africa by prior arrangement with English police constituted an abuse of process, and that jurisdiction should be declined for that reason.[8]

1. Cf *R v Aubrey-Fletcher, ex p Ross-Munro* [1968] 1 QB 620, [1968] 1 All ER 99. Moreover, in *R v Davidson* (1976) 64 Cr App Rep 209, the court did not pay regard to the treaty in question as compelling the application of the specialty principle.
2. (1989) 11 EHRR 439. The death penalty as such is not contrary to either the European Convention on Human Rights or the International Covenant on Civil and Political Rights, but optional protocols to both instruments allow parties to declare that they will not apply it.
3. See *Barton v Commonwealth of Australia* (1974) 48 ALJR 161 (High Court of Australia) where the question or reciprocity was discussed, in relation to an Australian request to Brazil for extradition, the Brazilian extradition law being based on either bilateral treaty or assured reciprocity of treatment; and cf Shearer 'Extradition Without Treaty' (1975) 49 ALJ 116.
4. Cf *R v Governor of Brixton Prison, ex p Soblen* [1963] 2 QB 243 (deportation allowable under aliens legislation, even though alleged offence is non-extraditable, and even if there be a request for rendition).
5. *Barton v The Commonwealth of Australia* (1974) 48 ALJR 161 at 162.
6. Cf O'Higgins 'Disguised Extradition' (1964) 27 MLR 521, 539; *Shearer Extradition in International Law* (1971) pp 19, 87–90. It would seem to follow from the decision of the European Court of Human Rights in *Bozano v France* (1987) 9 EHRR 297 that deportation, preceded by detention, when obviously employed as a 'disguised' form of non-treaty extradition, may be illegal, either on the ground of breach of human rights to lawful procedures or because it would constitute an improper exercise of the administrative discretion to exclude aliens.
7. [1994] AC 42. Cf the converse Australian case of *Schlieske v Minister for Immigration* (1988) 84 ALR 719 (Full Federal Court) where the court allowed deportation to the state of the person's nationality, after failed extradition proceedings instigated by that state, but only on condition that no collaboration occurred between the two national authorities. It may be questioned how effective such a condition might prove to be in reality.
8. See further above, p 92.

Asylum
The conception of asylum[9] in international law involves two elements:

a.   shelter, which is more than merely temporary refuge; and
b.   a degree of active protection on the part of the authorities in control of the territory of asylum.

Asylum may be *territorial* (or internal), ie granted by a state on its territory; or it may be *extra-territorial*, ie granted for and in respect of legations, consular premises, international headquarters and warships to refugees from the authorities of the territorial state. The differences between the principles applying to the two kinds of asylum flow from the fact that the power to grant *territorial* asylum is an incident of territorial sovereignty itself, whereas the granting of *extra-territorial* asylum is rather a derogation from the sovereignty of the territorial state insofar as that state is required to acquiesce in fugitives from its authorities enjoying protection from apprehension.[10]

Consistently with this distinction, the general principle is that every state has a plenary right to grant territorial asylum unless it has accepted some particular restriction in this regard, while the right to grant extra-territorial asylum is exceptional and must be established in each case.

Both types of asylum have this in common, that they involve an adjustment between the legal claims of state sovereignty, and the demands of humanity.

(1) Territorial asylum
A state's liberty to grant asylum in its territory is of ancient origins, and extends not only to political, social, or religious refugees, but to all persons from abroad, including criminal offenders; it is merely one aspect of a state's general power of admission or exclusion from its territory. Normally, however, persons not being nationals of the territorial state, and who are held in custody on foreign vessels within that state's waters, will not be granted asylum. It is a matter of controversy whether a state may grant asylum to prisoners of war detained by it, but unwilling to be repatriated.[11] In the light of recent events it has been claimed that territorial asylum should be sub-classified into: (a) 'political asylum', eg, for so-called 'defectors'; (b) 'refugee asylum', for refugees with a well-founded fear of persecution in their own country; and (c) 'general asylum', ie for persons who have fled from their country to seek economic betterment, but do not have the status of immigrants.

(a) 'Political' asylum. It is sometimes said that the fugitive has a 'right of asylum'.[12] This is inaccurate, as fugitives have no enforceable right in international law to

---

9.   See for treatment of various aspects of asylum, Report of the 51st Conference of the International Law Association, Tokyo (1964), pp 215–293, and for an excellent, more recent examination of the subject in the light of new developments, V. Bevan *The Development of British Immigration Law* (1986) pp 213–223, and R. C. Hingorani (ed) *Humanitarian Law* (1987) pp 121–131 (mass trans-border flow of refugees in Asia).
10.   See *Asylum Case* ICJ 1950, 274–275.
11.   See also below, pp 505–506.
12.   It has been claimed that there is such an individual right of asylum because the fugitive is not usually surrendered, in the absence of an extradition treaty, and because if the offence is political, the fugitive is not generally subject to extradition, but the flaw in this proposition is that it takes account only of persons to whom asylum has been granted, not of those to whom asylum has been refused.

enjoy asylum. The only *international* legal right involved is that of the state of refuge itself to grant asylum. Municipal legal systems (see, for example, the constitutions of France, Germany, and Italy) do indeed sometimes provide for a right of asylum to individuals fleeing from persecution, and an example of the provision of a modern international instrument (not being a binding convention) providing for an individual right of asylum from persecution is article 14 of the Universal Declaration of Human Rights 1948 which rather weakly refers to a right to 'seek' asylum. But, so far, no such individual right is guaranteed by international law, although a Declaration on Territorial Asylum adopted by the United Nations General Assembly on 14 December 1967, recommended that, in their practices, states should follow a number of standards and desiderata, among which are the following:

a. Persons seeking asylum from persecution (see article 14, above, of the Universal Declaration of Human Rights) should not be subject to rejection at the frontier, or if they have already entered the territory in which they seek asylum, to expulsion or compulsory return. If there are overriding reasons of national security, or if it be necessary to safeguard the population, as in the case of a mass influx, asylum may be refused, but the state concerned should consider granting the person seeking refuge an opportunity, by way of provisional asylum or otherwise, of going to another state (art 3).
b. Where a state finds difficulty in granting or continuing to grant asylum, states individually or jointly or through the United Nations should consider, 'in a spirit of international solidarity', appropriate measures to lighten the burden on that state (article 2).
c. Asylum granted to persons seeking refuge from persecution should be respected by all other states (article 1).

The liberty of states to grant asylum may, of course, be cut down by treaties of the states concerned of which, as we have seen, extradition treaties are the commonest illustration. In principle, asylum ought not to be granted to persons, with respect to whom there are well-founded reasons for considering that they have committed a crime against peace, a war crime, or a crime against humanity (see article 1, paragraph 2 of the Declaration on Territorial Asylum, referred to above).

A draft Convention on Territorial Asylum emerged in 1974–1975 from discussions in the United Nations General Assembly, and the work of a group of experts and of the United Nations Secretariat. This draft instrument spelled out with more precision the principles enunciated in the Declaration on Territorial Asylum, and likewise stopped short of conferring an *absolute* right to asylum. Article 1 of the draft convention recognised that the grant of asylum pertained to the sovereign rights of a state, but that states parties should use their 'best endeavours' in a 'humanitarian spirit' to grant asylum in their territory to persons eligible under the draft convention, by reason of fear of persecution or punishment for reasons set out in article 2.

The text of the draft convention constituted the basis of discussions at the United Nations Conference on Territorial Asylum, in which 85 countries participated, held at Geneva from 10 January to 4 February 1977, and which was convened in order to adopt a convention on the subject. However, the

Conference came to a close without reaching consensus; a 'Committee of the Whole' of the Conference succeeded in adopting the text of five articles on the grant of asylum, the non-rejection of persons seeking it, and the standards of conduct to be observed by asylees in countries of refuge, but no final or definitive vote was taken on these articles. The consequence may be said to be one of confirmation of the untrammelled nature of the discretionary right of a State of proposed refuge to grant or withhold the grant of asylum, as the case may be, according to its own domestic laws, policies, and practices.

(b) Refugees.[13] The principles outlined above with respect to 'political' asylum apply also to refugees. Indeed, most applicants for territorial asylum will also claim status as refugees. A refugee is defined in article 1 of the Convention on the Status of Refugees, 1951, as a person who, owing to a well-founded fear of being persecuted for reasons of race, religion, nationality, membership of a particular social group, or political opinion, is outside the country of which that person is a national and is unable or, owing to such a fear, is unwilling to return to it. The convention was limited at first to a fear based on events occuring in Europe prior to 1 January 1951, but these geographical and temporal restrictions were removed as between the parties to the supplementary Protocol of 1967. Nonetheless the Convention clearly betrays its dated origins as an instrument designed to deal with the problems posed by millions of people displaced by World War II in Europe and unwilling to return to countries which they had left because those countries now had Marxist-Leninist governments or, in the case of some, because they had been rendered stateless by reason of territorial changes. The issue of reception and admission of refugees did not arise; they were already present in the territories of contracting parties. The primary focus of the Convention therefore was the conditions of treatment of refugees. Hence the Convention does not address the more important issue of refugee law at the present time, namely under what circumstances should a person seeking admission to a state as a refugee be recognised as such and be granted permanent or temporary asylum by way of being accorded refugee status. This vital issue continues to be regulated solely by national laws and practice; states are apparently for the most part unwilling to subordinate their sovereignty to acceptance of any international standard of obligation to receive refugees, no doubt out of fear that they might be swamped by an intolerable influx.

The Convention did succeed in achieving a principle of special importance. Article 33 of the Convention provides that, even if for any reason a state no longer desires that a refugee remain in its territory, it 'may not expel or return ("refouler") a refugee in any manner whatsoever to the frontiers of territories where his life or freedom would be threatened on account of his race, religion, nationality, membership of a particular social group, or political opinion.' This article, establishing the principle of non-refoulment, is now regarded as having

13. The literature on refugee law is voluminous, and the case law of states parties to the Convention on the Status of Refugees, 1951, applying the principles of that Convention as part of municipal law, ever growing. See inter alia A. Grahl-Madsen *The Status of Refugees in International Law*, vol 1 (1966), vol 2 (1972); G. Goodwin-Gill *The Refugee in International Law* (1983); D. Martin (ed) *The New Asylum-Seekers: Refugee Law in the 1980s* (1988); J.C. Hathaway *The Law of Refugee Status* (1991).

the status of a binding rule of general international law.[14] However, the same vice remains that article 33 does not apply except in the case of refugees determined to be such by the host state, according to the definition in article 1, but as to which no procedure for determination is laid down.[15] The test for refugee status under both articles has been held to be the same.[16] An extension of the principle of non-refoulment to a wider category of persons who might qualify as refugees, because they are fleeing from 'persecution', as set out in article 14 of the Universal Declaration of Human Rights, 1948, but have not yet been determined to be such by the host state, can be argued to arise on the basis of the Declaration on Territorial Asylum of the United Nations General Assembly, 1967, which provides that no person entitled to invoke article 14 of the General Declaration shall be subjected to rejection at the frontier or expulsion or return to any state where that person may be subjected to persecution. However, the 1967 Declaration has only recommendatory status; moreover, it is subject to exception 'for over-riding reasons of national security or in order to safeguard the population, as in the case of a mass influx of persons.'

Despite the legal and moral strength of the principle of non-refoulment it has been difficult in practice to secure an even observance of it. Some states have come under great pressure from large numbers of claimants to refugee status and have found the task of assessing each case individually to be arduous and lengthy. Faced with a mass influx, some states have resorted to forcible measures of repulsion or exclusion, or of detention of claimants to refugee status in rigorous camps, by way of discouraging further inflows. The United Nations High Commissioner for Refugees (UNHCR), and other concerned humanitarian organisations, have promoted a concept of 'temporary refuge' that would fall short of asylum or refugee status in the technical sense but would allow for the determination of the status of the claimant and for the finding of 'durable solutions', such as resettlement in a third state or even eventual repatriation. The object of the concept is to relieve the fear of the state of first resort that it will carry the burden of looking after refugees for an indefinite period; UNHCR actively seeks places in other countries for persons granted temporary refuge, and calls upon all states to assist materially in the alleviation of what has become a major world problem, under the principle of international solidarity.

(c) 'General' asylum. At the base of the concerns of many states faced with an actual or threatened influx of asylum-seekers is the reality that some of these may not qualify as refugees in the sense of the Convention, or as victims of persecution in the sense of the Universal Declaration, but are seeking a better life elsewhere for economic or social reasons. This can only be determined on a case by case basis. Such persons are not asylum-seekers but would-be immigrants. Other persons may be genuine asylum-seekers, not for political or similar reasons but as a result of civil war in their own countries, or natural disasters such as famine or flood. Normally the need for such asylum will not be lengthy before

14. Goodwin-Gill, supra, 97-100. The word refouler means to drive back.
15. See the High Court of Australia in Simsek v Macphee (1982) 148 CLR 636.
16. R v Secretary of State for the Home Department, ex p Sivakumaran [1988] AC 958. See also the decision of the United States Supreme Court in Immigration and Naturalization Service v Cardoza-Fonseca 94 L Ed 2d 434 (1987).

repatriation can take place, but the states offering temporary asylum may need international assistance in order to bear the burdens.

(2) Extra-territorial asylum

(a) Asylum in legations. Modern international law recognises no general right of a head of mission to grant asylum in the premises of the legation.[17] Such grant seems rather prohibited by international law where its effect would be to exempt the fugitive from the regular application of laws and administration of justice by the territorial state. The lack of any such general right of diplomatic asylum was affirmed by the International Court of Justice in the *Asylum Case*,[18] which dealt with the application of alleged regional Latin-American rules of international law concerning such asylum. It has been claimed that the Latin-American practice and doctrine of diplomatic asylum 'operated in large measure not through treaties alone [such as the Montevideo Convention of 1933 on Political Asylum] but by common unarticulated understandings'[19] and should not be regarded as capable of generalisation. In any event such asylum was usually granted for only a limited time.

Exceptionally, but without acknowledgement of any absolute right in a fugitive to require this, asylum may be granted in legation premises:

i.   As a temporary measure, to individuals physically in danger from mob disorder or mob rule, or where the fugitive is in peril because of extreme political corruption in the local state, the justification being presumably that by the grant of asylum, an urgent threat is temporarily tided over.[20] In certain instances, the legation would not provide asylum without the authority of the accrediting government

ii. Where there is a binding local custom, long recognised, that such diplomatic asylum is permissible.

iii. Under a special treaty (usually allowing such right in respect of political offenders only) between the territorial state and the state which is represented by the legation concerned.

There is, in the light of recent events, a need for clarification of the rules and practice as to diplomatic asylum. At its 29th Session in 1974, the United Nations General Assembly adopted a Resolution inviting member states to communicate their views on diplomatic asylum to the United Nations Secretary-General, and

---

17. See Satow *Guide to Diplomatic Practice* (1957) (ed Bland) p 219. It is significant that the Vienna Convention on Diplomatic Relations of 18 April 1961 provides for no such right, and see article 41(3) of the Convention providing that the premises of a mission shall not be used in a manner 'incompatible' with the functions of the mission.

18. See ICJ 1950, 266 et seq. In the *Haya de la Torre Case* ICJ 1951, 71 et seq, arising out of the same facts, the court held that where asylum in legation premises has been granted without justification, the head of the mission concerned is not obliged to deliver the fugitive to the local authorities, in the absence of a treaty binding him to do so.

19. Mr Surena, United States delegate to the Sixth Committee of the United Nations General Assembly, speaking on the subject on 29 November 1974; see 69 AJIL (1975) 389.

20. Lengthy periods of refuge afforded to certain persons in foreign embassies, eg Cardinal Mindszenty in the American legation in Budapest 1956-1971, extending beyond the period of the possibility of extra-legal punishment, are not regarded as creating a general rule or tolerance.

requesting the latter to circulate a report containing an analysis of the subject. The Secretary-General's report on diplomatic asylum is a valuable study which, in conjunction with General Assembly discussions, has paved the way for further clarification and development. Some countries have continued to favour and to press for such clarification and development of the principles and practice as to diplomatic asylum, and it may be hoped that such a desirable result on the scale and at the level sought will ultimately be achieved.

(b) Asylum in consulates or consular premises. Similar principles, subject to the same exceptions, apply as in the case of legation premises.

(c) Asylum in the premises of international institutions. The Headquarters Agreements of the United Nations and of the specialised agencies reveal no general right of international institutions to grant asylum or even refuge in their premises to offenders as against the territorial state, and semble not even a right of protection on humanitarian grounds. It is difficult to conceive, however, that a right to grant temporary refuge in an extreme case of danger from mob rule would not be asserted and conceded.

(d) Asylum in warships. This has been discussed in a previous chapter.[1]

(e) Asylum in merchant vessels. Merchant vessels are not exempt from the local jurisdiction, and therefore cannot grant asylum to local offenders.

4.   HUMAN RIGHTS AND FUNDAMENTAL FREEDOMS[2]

For a long time, the formulation and due implementation of binding general rules of international law for the protection of human rights and fundamental freedoms by adequate machinery for their enforcement have remained more a promise than an achievement. It is true that in Europe there have been established an international administrative body and an international court for the purpose of protecting human rights, namely the European Commission of Human Rights and the European Court of Human Rights, but these two organs operate under jurisdictional and procedural restrictions, and in respect to that limited number of states only which have accepted their competence. There is also a large number

---

1.   See above, p 204.
2.   See on the whole subject A. L. del Russo *International Protection of Human Rights* (1971); L. B. Sohn and T. Buergenthal *International Protection of Human Rights* (1973); E. Kamenka and A. Erh-Soon Tay (eds) *Human Rights* (1978); and Nagendra Singh *Human Rights and International Co-operation* (1969). For general bibliography, see Rhyne *International Law* (1971) p 391 n 1, and p 395 n 3, and for critical analysis, see Richard Falk *Human Rights and State Sovereignty* (Oxford, 1981). A comprehensive work is Sieghart *The International Law of Human Rights* (Oxford, 1983). See also now Meron *Human Rights Law-Making in the United Nations: A Critique of Instruments and Processes* (1986); Nagendra Singh *Enforcement of Human Rights in Peace and War and the Future of Humanity* (1986); and P. Alston (ed) *The United Nations and Human Rights* (1992).

of international conventions, mentioned below, including the Covenant on Economic, Social and Cultural Rights, and the Covenant on Civil and Political Rights adopted 16 December 1966, both of which came into force in 1976, when each had been ratified by the required number of 35 ratifications (the absence of ratification by a larger number of states after ten years was in itself significant). Apart therefrom, however, there has been limited concrete progress in the direction of establishing effective international machinery to protect individual rights beyond the point of proclaiming conceptions, attempting definitions, making programmatic statements or hortatory declarations, establishing organs with limited powers of promotion, investigation, bringing pressure to bear on governments, or recommendation,[3] and encouraging the mass communication of the aims and ideals to be realised.[4] A number of human rights and fundamental freedoms are not the subject of protection by any binding general international convention or conventions, while it would of course be wrong to maintain that there is in existence a complete body of general or universal norms of international law binding all states to protect human rights.

One material achievement, however, is the general recognition today that a state, qua the protection of the human rights of its subjects, does not possess in this regard an absolute sphere of reserved jurisdiction into which international law or outside diplomacy may not penetrate. Moreover, to the extent that states do observe human rights standards, individuals receive protection regardless of whether or not they are nationals of the conforming state.

The following are the principal instruments in which attempts have been made to enunciate or guarantee human rights standards:

(1) The United Nations Charter[5] and the constitutions of the specialised agencies. These neither impose binding obligations on member states to observe human rights, nor concretely define such rights. Pledges are expressed in the most general language, and the powers of the United Nations and its organs laid down in terms only of recommendation, promotion, and encouragement. It could not really be said that there was any binding obligation on member states *immediately* to protect and respect human rights.

(2) The Paris Peace Treaties of 1946 with Italy, Rumania, Bulgaria, Hungary, and Finland. These contained general pledges only to respect human rights, unsupported by any court or machinery to enforce them. They proved of little value in 1948–1950 when the matter of alleged breaches of human rights by

3. Eg, the Human Rights Commission, a Functional Commission of the United Nations Economic and Social Council, and its Sub-Commission on the Prevention of Discrimination and Protection of Minorities. Another example is the Inter-American Commission on Human Rights established in August 1959, by the Organisation of American States (OAS).
4. For pertinent criticism of the position, see the *United States Department of State Bulletin* 27 December 1976, pp 745–749. A special matter calling for improvements is the more general application by national courts of international human rights standards and principles; this was the subject of an international Colloquium, 'The Domestic Application of International Human Rights Norms', at Bangalore, India in February 1988.
5. See as to the effect of these provisions in United States municipal law, above, p 75, n 17.

Rumania, Bulgaria, and Hungary was raised in the United Nations General Assembly.[6]

(3) The Universal Declaration of Human Rights, adopted by the United Nations General Assembly in December 1948. This Declaration represented the first of three stages of a programme designed to achieve an International Bill of Rights, based upon universally binding obligations of states, and reinforced by effective curial and administrative machinery. Chronologically, the three stages were to be: (i) a Declaration defining the various human rights which ought to be respected; (ii) a series of binding covenants on the part of states to respect such rights as defined; and (iii) measures and machinery for implementation.

Consequently, the Declaration could not and did not purport to be more than a manifesto, a statement of ideals, a 'pathfinding' instrument.[7] To that extent, it has achieved as much as could be expected. Its most important contribution lies in the pioneering formulation of the principal human rights and fundamental freedoms that ought to be recognised. To reproach the Declaration for the absence of provision of enforcement machinery or for the fact that it is not a binding legal instrument, is to misconstrue its original limited purpose—to provide a generally acceptable catalogue of inalienable human rights. Yet it has had a remarkable influence on further developments, at both the international and domestic levels, as is reflected in the number of instances of conventions and other instruments referring to, or invoking its provisions.

(4) The European Convention for the Protection of Human Rights and Fundamental Freedoms signed by the member states of the Council of Europe at Rome, 4 November 1950.[8] Sponsored by the Council of Europe, this important regional Charter of human rights went beyond the Universal Declaration of Human Rights in: (a) imposing binding commitments to provide effective domestic remedies with regard to a number of the rights specified in the Universal Declaration; (b) the close and elaborate definition of such rights as it embraced, and of the exceptions and restrictions to each of such rights; (c) the establishment of a European Commission of Human Rights to investigate and report on violations of human rights at the instance of states parties, or—if the state against which complaint is laid, has so accepted—upon the petition of any person, non-

6. As to which see Renouf 'Human Rights in the Soviet Balkans' *World Affairs* (1950) pp 168–80; and Advisory Opinion of the International Court of Justice on the *Interpretation of the Peace Treaties* ICJ 1950, 65, 221.
7. Although the Teheran United Nations Conference of 1968 on Human Rights was able to declare that the Declaration constituted 'an obligation' for the members of the international community.
8. The Convention has since been amended by a number of Protocols, adding to the list of rights protected by the Convention, enabling the European Court of Human Rights, inter alia, to give advisory opinions on the interpretation of the Convention, for improving the internal procedure of the European Commission of Human Rights, eg, allowing the use of special chambers, abolishing the death penalty and providing procedural safeguards as to the expulsion of aliens. On the operation and application of the Convention, see F. G. Jacobs *The European Convention of Human Rights* (1975); P. Van Dijk and G.J.H. van Hoof *Theory and Practice of the European Convention on Human Rights* (2nd edn, 1990); and D. Kinley *The European Convention on Human Rights: Compliance Without Incorporation* (1993).

governmental organisation, or group of individuals within that state's jurisdiction. In time of war or other public emergency threatening the life of a nation, a state party may take measures derogating from the Convention. The Commission became competent to receive applications of the latter type in July 1955, after (as required by the Convention) six states had accepted the right of individual recourse; the number of accepting states has since increased. The Convention also provided for a European Court of Human Rights with compulsory jurisdiction, to come into being upon at least eight states accepting such jurisdiction.[9] This was achieved in September 1958, and the Court was set up in January 1959; it delivered its first judgment on 14 November 1960, in the *Lawless Case*. On 21 December 1965, the British Government accepted the relevant optional provisions, so recognising the right of recourse to the Commission, and the jurisdiction of the Court.

Although the Commission has been very active and has dealt with hundreds of applications, the great majority of these have been declared inadmissible under the Convention because of failure to exhaust local remedies, lapse of a period of six months or more after final decision by a domestic court (article 26), activities of applicants aimed at the destruction of the rights and freedoms guaranteed by the Convention (article 17),[10] and other grounds, such as the anonymity of the applicant. Since 1981–1982, however, the Commission has followed a policy of referring some cases to the Court even where the Commission itself has reached the conclusion that there had been no breach of the Convention. If the application is admissible, or is deemed referable, the Commission's primary action, if it has been unable to dispose of the matter by conciliation, is to transmit its report on the question of a breach of a right under the Convention to the Committee of Ministers of the Council of Europe, which may decide on the measures[11] to be taken if there has been a breach, unless the matter is referred to the Court within a period of three months. As to the Court, only the states accepting its jurisdiction and the Commission, and not individuals, have the right to bring a case before it.[12] The technicalities and limitations which surround the exercise of jurisdiction by the Court in a matter referred to it by the Commission are well illustrated in its two rulings in the *Lawless Case*,[13] one dealing with

9. An abortive move was made in 1946 at the Paris Peace Conference to create a European Court of Human Rights.
10. In 1957, the Commission held that, for this reason, the German Communist party was not entitled to make an application against the German Federal Republic complaining of a violation of the right to freedom of association, in that an order for its dissolution had been made in 1956 by the Federal Constitutional Court. On the other hand, in the *Lawless Case* in 1961, the Court held that even if the applicant were a member of the Irish Republican Army and this organisation were engaged in such destructive activities as mentioned, this did not absolve the respondent state, Ireland, from observing those provisions of the Convention conferring freedom from arbitrary arrest and from detention without trial.
11. These measures may include requiring action to correct the breach; if satisfactory action has not been taken in the prescribed period, the Committee of Ministers is to decide what effect should be given to its decision.
12. Cf *Guilfoyle v Home Office* [1981] QB 309 at 316, 319, 322.
13. See reports in (1958) 25 ILR 216; (1960) 31 ILR 31, 276, 290. Considerations of space preclude discussion of this case.

questions of procedure concerning inter alia the complainant's right to receive a copy of the Commission's report, the other with the merits of the application, that is to say the allegation of breach of human rights.[14] Yet the influence of the Court is not to be minimised; the possibility of proceedings has contributed towards a settlement in advance of a Court hearing, as in the *Knechtl Case* of 1969–1971 (access of prisoner to legal advice); while both directly and indirectly, it has led to changes in legislation,[15] and this has occurred, in particular, where a government sought to avoid an anticipated adverse decision. In other cases which have come before it, raising questions as to the scope and effect of rights in the Convention and the Protocols thereto, the Court has given important rulings, to which due respect will be and has already been paid by the domestic courts and legislators of states parties.[16]

Some of the more important decisions of the European Court of Human Rights—important because of the wide general reach of the implications of the Court's pronouncements—have included the following:

a.   *Golder v United Kingdom* (1975). In that case the Court ruled, inter alia, that the right to a fair and public hearing before an independent and impartial tribunal under article 6 of the 1950 Convention involved necessarily a right of a prisoner to have free communication with, and access to legal advisers for the purpose of instituting legal proceedings.[17] The *Golder* ruling was followed in *Silver v United Kingdom*, in which the Court held that the Convention was violated by censorship of prisoners' letters to solicitors and relatives, with respect to prison conditions, etc.

b.   *Tyrer v United Kingdom* (1978). There, among other points, the Court held that the infliction of corporal punishment by birching (on the Isle of Man) amounted to 'degrading punishment', thereby violating article 3 of the 1950

14. On the questions of procedure, the Court ruled that the complainant was entitled to receive a copy of the report, but not to publish it, and that the complainant's point of view could be put before the Court, not directly by himself, but through delegates of the Commission, or in the Commission's report, or in his evidence, if called as a witness. On the merits, the Court held that the complainant's arrest and detention without trial were justified by a public emergency threatening the life of the respondent country, Ireland, within the meaning of article 15 of the Convention, and that this emergency had been duly notified under this article to the Secretary-General of the Council of Europe. Under a revision of the Court's procedural rules in 1981–1982, it is possible now for individual complainants to be separately represented in proceedings before the Court.
15. The *De Becker Case*, as to which see *Yearbook of European Convention on Human Rights* 1962 (1963) pp 320–337, resulted in a change of legislation, namely amendments to the Belgian Penal Code. So also as a consequence of the Belgian *Vagrancy Cases* (1966–1972), Belgian law was amended, revising the former rules under which vagrants might be imprisoned without right of appeal.
16. As, eg, in 1968 in the *Wemhoff* and *Neumeister Cases* (right to trial within a reasonable time, and questions of length of detention pending trial), and in the *Belgian 'Linguistic' Case* (the right to education does not oblige governments to educate in a particular language, and what constitutes discriminatory treatment). Cf the later *Stögmüller* and *Matznetter Cases* of 1972 and the *Ringeisen Case* of 1973 (whether the preventive detention of the complainants extended beyond a reasonable time).
17. For discussion of the *Golder Case*, see G. Triggs' article in (1975) 50 ALJ 229–245. See also generally N. S. Rodley *The Treatment of Prisoners under International Law* (1986).

Convention, which article prohibited 'inhuman or degrading treatment or punishment'.[18]

c. *The Sunday Times (Thalidomide) Case* (1979). The Court in this case ruled that an injunction, upheld by the House of Lords in *A-G v Times Newspapers Ltd* [1974] AC 273, [1973] 3 All ER 54, restraining the newspaper, *The Sunday Times*, from publishing critical material on the detrimental effects of the drug thalidomide, upon the ground of alleged contempt of court in view of pending civil litigation, contravened the provisions of article 10 of the 1950 Convention, conferring, inter alia, a right to freedom of expression.

d. *The Dudgeon Case* (1981). There the Court took the view that legislation in Northern Ireland rendering homosexual relations between consenting adults a crime contravened article 8 of the 1950 Convention which required respect for a 'person's private and family life', and that the legislation was 'not necessary in a democratic society . . . for the protection of . . . morals' within the meaning of the article.

e. *The Case of Young, James and Webster* (1981). In this decision the Court held that the dismissal by British Rail of three railwaymen because of their refusal to join a union when a new 'closed shop' arrangement came into force represented a breach of article 11(1) of the 1950 Convention, providing for a right of freedom of association. The Court, however, stressed that it was not called upon to review the legality of the 'closed shop' system generally. It was significant that the breach had occurred through action by a governmental entity.

Since 1983 there have been a great variety of decisions of the Court covering a wide range of alleged breaches of the Convention and Protocols thereto, including *Malone* (1984) on the privacy of mail and telephone calls, *Barthold* (1985) on the right of freedom and expression, *Gillow* (1986) on the right to respect for one's home, *H v Belgium* (1987) on the right to a fair and public hearing, *Bozano* (1987) on the right not to be illegally detained and deported and *Berrehab* (1988) on the right of respect for the family life of resident aliens. Due, however, to considerations of space, it is not possible in the present book to deal with all the significant decisions in detail, and readers are referred to textbooks containing analyses of cases considered by the Court.[19]

(5) The Covenant on Economic, Social and Cultural Rights, and the Covenant on Civil and Political Rights adopted by the United Nations General Assembly on 16 December 1966 and opened for signature on 19 December 1966. These two Covenants which came into force in 1976 have represented an attempt to

18. However, a threat of corporal punishment for juveniles in Scottish schools did not, in the circumstances of the case, represent 'degrading treatment' within the meaning of article 3; see the *Campbell and Cosans Case* (1982) 4 EHRR 293 decided by the Court in 1982. The subject of alleged inhuman and degrading treatment was also considered by the Court in its decision of 1978 in *Ireland v United Kingdom* (alleged ill-treatment for purposes of interrogation).
19. See, eg, J.E.S. Fawcett *The Application of the European Convention on Human Rights* (2nd edn, 1987); P. Van Dijk and G.J.H. van Hoof *Theory and Practice of the European Convention on Human Rights* (2nd edn, 1990).

complete the second stage, referred to above, of binding covenants to observe human rights. A single Covenant was first contemplated, but the United Nations General Assembly reversed its directive to the Human Rights Commission, requesting it to prepare two separate covenants dealing respectively with economic, social, and cultural rights, and with civil and political rights. These instruments were the subject of continuous consideration and revision by the General Assembly.

Although the two Covenants recognise different sets of rights, they contain some common provisions, for instance as to the recognition of the right of self-determination, and as to the prohibition of discrimination. On the other hand, they differ with respect to the machinery set up under each. The Covenant on Civil and Political Rights provides for a committee with the responsibility of considering reports from states parties, and of addressing comments, if necessary, to these states and to the Economic and Social Council of the United Nations. Inasmuch as it was felt that economic, social and cultural rights could be achieved less quickly than civil and political rights, because the latter could be safeguarded by immediate legislation, whereas the former depended upon resources becoming progressively available to each state, the Covenant on Economic, Social, and Cultural Rights provided merely for the submission of periodical reports to the Economic and Social Council upon the progress made and measures taken to advance the rights concerned. Thus, the rights and obligations under the Covenant on Civil and Political Rights are more immediate. In 1987 there was established a Committee on Economic Social and Cultural Rights to monitor compliance with the terms of the other Covenant, particularly so far as concerns duties of states vis-à-vis developing states.

Under Optional Protocol I to the International Covenant of Civil and Political Rights parties may declare that they recognise the competence of the Human Rights Committee to receive communications from individuals subject to its jurisdiction who claim to be victims of a violation by that party of any of the rights set out in the Covenant. The Committee, which consists of 18 members chosen from states parties to the Covenant, but acting in their personal capacities, will consider such a complaint provided that it is not being examined under any other international procedure and that the complainant has exhausted local remedies. The Committee then communicates its views to the individual complainant and to the state party. Although the Committee has no power to make a binding decision, its powers being essentially recommedatory in nature, it nevertheless exercises considerable influence through the publication of its views and through its reasoned conclusions.[20] In 1994 71 states had become parties to this Optional Protocol.[1]

(6) Obligations to respect or enforce certain human rights are contained in the Convention for the Suppression of Traffic in Persons and of the Exploitation or

---

20. For the work of the Committee see D. McGoldrick *The Human Rights Committee: Its role in the development of the International Covenant on Civil and Political Rights* (1991).
1.   When account is taken that little or no purpose would be served by the states of the European Union in becoming parties to the Optional Protocol, by reason of the alternative (and binding) procedures of the European Commission and Court of Human Rights, the number of parties to the Optional Protocol can be viewed as impressive.

the Prostitution of Others opened for signature on 31 March 1950, the Convention on the Status of Refugees of 25 July 1951, the Supplementary Geneva Convention of 7 September 1956, for Abolishing Slavery, the Slave Trade, and Institutions and Practices Similar to Slavery (eg serfdom, debt bondage), and the International Convention on the Suppression and Punishment of the Crime of Apartheid adopted on 30 November 1973; in five conventions adopted by Conferences of the International Labour Organisation, namely, the Freedom of Association and Protection of the Right to Organise Convention 1948,[2] the Right to Organise and Collective Bargaining Convention 1949, the Equal Remuneration Convention 1951, the Abolition of Forced Labour Convention 1957, and the Discrimination (Employment and Occupation) Convention 1958; and in the important International Convention on the Elimination of All Forms of Racial Discrimination, of 21 December 1965. Under the last-mentioned convention, provision was made for the establishment of a Committee on the Elimination of Racial Discrimination, consisting of eighteen experts serving in their personal capacity, to deal with allegations of violations of human rights, and to consider reports from states parties on measures adopted to give effect to the Convention. The committee commenced work in 1970, after the entry into force of the Convention in 1969. In December 1979, the United Nations General Assembly also adopted the Convention on the Elimination of All Forms of Discrimination against Women, and in November 1981 the United Nations Declaration on the Elimination of All Forms of Intolerance and Discrimination Based on Religion or Belief.[3] Following the adoption by the United Nations General Assembly in 1975 of a Declaration of Torture, in 1984 the General Assembly opened for signature a Convention against Torture and other Cruel, Inhuman or Degrading Treatment or Punishment; the Convention serves to amplify the provisions of article 7 of the International Covenant of 1966 on Civil and Political Rights. Similarly, the Declaration on the Rights of the Child, 1975, was followed by the opening for signature of the International Convention on the Rights of the Child, 1989.

Reference should also be made to:

a.   The influence upon municipal law of these Charters and instruments relating to human rights; for example, as revealed in the decisions of certain municipal courts, that contracts which conflict with human rights should be held illegal and invalid on the ground of public policy,[4] and as shown in the guarantees for human rights contained in the constitutions of certain new states which attained independence after 1945.[5]

2.   In implementation of this Convention, the International Labour Organisation established special investigatory and supervisory machinery, consisting, inter alia, of the Freedom of Association Committee of the Governing Body of the Organisation, to examine alleged infringements of the freedom of association. It is claimed that during the period 1951–1971 more than 700 complaints were examined by the Committee, in many cases with 'positive results'; see *ILO Information*, October 1973, p 6. Since 1971, a large number of complaints have also been investigated under the above-mentioned procedure.
3.   On discrimination, see generally McKean *Equality and Discrimination under International Law* (1983).
4.   See, eg, *Re Drummond Wren* [1945] 4 OR 778.
5.   See, eg, ss 17–32 of the Constitution of Nigeria, which became independent in 1960.

b.   The undertakings by Italy and Yugoslavia under the Memorandum of Understanding of 5 October 1954, as to Trieste, to apply the Universal Declaration of Human Rights in their respective administrative zones in Trieste.

c.   The formulations or definitions of human rights in such programmatic statements as the American Declaration of the Rights and Duties of Man of 1948, the Declaration of the Rights of the Child adopted by the General Assembly on 20 November 1959, and the Fifteen General Principles on Freedom and Non-Discrimination in the Matter of Political Rights adopted by the United Nations Sub-Commission on Prevention of Discrimination and Protection of Minorities in January 1962.[6]

d.   The Inter-American Convention on Human Rights, opened for signature on 22 November 1969, coming into force in 1978. In addition to detailed definitions of over twenty human rights, provision is made for establishing an Inter-American Court of Human Rights; states parties wishing to accept the Court's jurisdiction may make declarations to this effect when ratifying or adhering to the Convention (see article 62). In this connection, reference may be made also to the revision by the 1967 Protocol of Buenos Aires to the Charter of the Organisation of American States (OAS), establishing the Inter-American Commission on Human Rights (originally set up by the OAS in 1960) as a principal organ of OAS, with the function of promoting respect for the human rights declared in the American Declaration of the Rights and Duties of Man of 1948.[7] With the coming into operation of the above-mentioned Inter-American Convention, the Inter-American Commission became one of two organs having competence in regard to the investigation of matters relating to the fulfilment of the obligations of states parties to the Convention (see articles 33 and 48 of the Convention). The Inter-American Court of Human Rights exercises both an advisory and a contentious jurisdiction, and in the latter jurisdiction has power to award damages and, as well, to make declaratory decrees or orders.

e.   Under the Helsinki Declaration adopted on 1 August 1975, by over 30 European states, together with Canada, the Holy See, and the United States, at the Conference on Security and Co-operation in Europe, the participating states reaffirmed in Part VII pledges to respect human rights and fundamental freedoms, to respect the rights of minorities to equality before the law, and to endeavour jointly and separately, including in co-operation with the

6.   Reference should also be made to the various Resolutions, from time to time, of the Human Rights Commission for promoting and developing human rights throughout the world. These are transmitted for approval or other action to the Economic and Social Council. The Commission has evolved a procedure (known as the '1503' procedure because of its latest authorisation by Council Resolution No 1503), whereby a Working Group of its Sub-Commission on Prevention of Discrimination and Protection of Minorities meets in separate session to consider human rights complaints reaching the United Nations, for the purpose of referring to the Sub-Commission those complaints revealing a consistent pattern of gross violations of human rights. This procedure was authorised by Council Resolutions of 1967 and 1970; prior to these Resolutions the Commission was not entitled to take action upon individual human rights complaints. The Commission also has recourse to other expedients; eg fact-finding, negotiation, conciliation, and inducing governments to initiate legislation.

7.   See T. Buergenthal 'The Revised OAS Charter and the Protection of Human Rights' 69 AJIL (1975) 828–836 and Buergenthal and Maier *Public International Law* (1985) pp 131–138.

United Nations, to promote universal and effective respect for such rights and freedoms. One significant affirmation was that in the penultimate paragraph of Part VII: 'They [the participating States] confirm the right of the individual to know and act upon his rights and duties in this field'. Even if the Helsinki Declaration is not to be deemed a binding international treaty, these statements represent an acknowledgement that the subject of human rights is not one within the sphere of a state's reserved jurisdiction, but is of international concern. Human rights problems were further discussed at the Madrid meeting of 1980–1983, held by way of a follow-up to the Helsinki Conference.[8]

f. Fundamental human rights have been recognised both in the Treaties of the European Communities (eg, freedom of movement and freedom of establishment in, respectively, articles 48 et seq, and articles 52 et seq of the Treaty of Rome of 25 March 1957, establishing the European Economic Community) and by the Court of Justice of the Communities.[9]

g. Since 1967–1968, as will be seen below in Chapter 18, a process has been set in motion of importing human rights rules and standards into that branch of international law traditionally known as the 'law of war' or the 'law of armed conflict', so that the expression 'international humanitarian law applicable in armed conflicts' has come now to replace these phrases 'law of war' and 'law of armed conflict'. A bridge has in effect been created between the doctrine of human rights and the rules of international law applicable in armed conflicts;[10] this indeed represents one of the most significant contributions of the human rights movement to the development of international law.

h. The protection of the right of privacy to a certain extent by the Guidelines Governing the Protection of Privacy and the Trans-Border Flows of Personal Data, adopted in 1980 in the form of a Recommendation by the Council of the Organisation for Economic Co-operation and Development (OECD) in Paris.

i. The adoption in 1981 of the African Charter of Human Rights by the Organisation of African Unity (OAU), providing, inter alia, for an African Commission on Human and Peoples' Rights, which is a body of a quasi-judicial character, empowered to deal with inter-state and individual petitions.

j. The United Nations World Conference on Human Rights, and the adoption, on 25 June 1993, of the Vienna Declaration and Programme of Action.[11] On the recommendation of the Conference, the United Nations General Assembly, at its 48th session in 1993, established the office of the United Nations High Commissioner of Human Rights.[12]

8. See generally A. Bloed and P. Van Dijk (eds) *Essays on Human Rights in the Helsinki Process* (1985).
9. See above, p 330.
10. See G.I.A.D. Draper 'Human Rights and the Law of War' (1972) 12 Virginia JIL 326 at 337.
11. Text in (1993) 32 ILM 1661.
12. Resolution 48/141, 20 December 1993. Ambassador Jose Ayala Lasso of Ecuador was appointed to the post. The High Commissioner operates with the support of the United Nations Centre for Human Rights in Geneva.

One point is that a number of important human rights are not rights of individuals, but collective rights, ie the rights of groups or of peoples.[13] This is clear so far as concerns the right of self-determination, which has been considered in Chapter 5, above. Apart from this right, there is the right of an ethnic group or of a people to physical existence as such, a right which is implicit in the provisions of the Genocide Convention of December 1948. Then also there is the right of certain groups or minorities to maintain their own identity; thus article 27 of the Covenant on Civil and Political Rights provides: 'In those States in which ethnic, religious or linguistic minorities exist, persons belonging to such minorities shall not be denied the right, in community with other members of their group, to enjoy their own culture, to profess and practise their own religion, or to use their own language'. A further illustration is that of the emerging principle that states should co-operate in the relief of peoples affected by disasters or disaster situations,[14] such as those due to volcanic eruptions, drought and the shortage of food supplies.

Finally, reference should be made briefly to the moves to bring about general recognition, as human rights, of the right to peace and the right to development, in particular by the adoption of Declarations to that effect by the United Nations General Assembly as, for example, in 1984, 1985 and 1986. These moves have not been universally favoured by states. It is questioned whether these two suggested rights can be regarded as 'human rights' in the accepted sense of that expression, more particularly as the concepts of peace and development are in themselves of some complexity and of a scope difficult to define.

13. See Y. Dinstein 'Collective Human Rights of Peoples and Minorities' (1976) 25 ICLQ 102–120. As to the rights of ethnic groups to the protection of their cultural identity, heritages and relics, see articles 2 and 14 of the Algiers Declaration of the Rights of Peoples, 4 July 1976; O'Keefe and Prott, *Law and the Cultural Heritage* Vol I (1984) pp 28–29; and *Onus v Alcoa of Australia Ltd* (1981) 149 CLR 27.
14. See generally P. Macalister-Smith *International Humanitarian Assistance: Disaster Relief Actions in International Law and Organisation* (1985).

CHAPTER 13

The state and economic interests— international economic and monetary law[1]

Modern states exercise wide control over the economy, including such aspects of private economic enterprise as the export and import trade, internal and external investment, shipping, agricultural production, and private banking. It is only natural that they should enter into agreements with each other to regulate those economic and monetary matters which affect two or more of them jointly. Most of these agreements are bilateral, eg, trade treaties, or treaties of commerce and navigation, or treaties of establishment, but there have been also treaties and multilateral agreements of a more general character, including the Articles of Agreement, respectively, of the International Monetary Fund, of the International Bank for Reconstruction and Development, and of the International Finance Corporation,[2] the Convention of 18 March 1965 on the Settlement of Investment Disputes between States and Nationals of Other States, the Treaty of Rome of 25 March 1957, establishing the European Economic Community, the General Agreement on Tariffs and Trade (GATT) of 30 October 1947, the Constitution of the Food and Agriculture Organisation (FAO), the Convention of 1985 establishing the Multilateral Investment Guarantee Agency (MIGA), and the international commodity agreements that are continually under revision and re-evaluation, such as those with regard to tin, sugar, dairy products, cocoa, meat, coffee, rubber, wheat, jute and jute products and tropical timber.[3]

---

1. Jackson and Davey, *Legal Problems of International Economic Relations* (2nd edn, 1986); D. Carreau, P. Juillard and T. Flory *Droit International Economique* (1978); Sir Joseph Gold *Legal and International Aspects of the International Monetary System: Selected Essays* Vol I (1979) and Vol II (1984); P. T. B. Kohona *The Regulation of Economic Relations Through Law* (1985); and E. McGovern *International Trade Regulation* (2nd edn, 1986).
2. The Articles of Agreement of the Fund and of the Bank were adopted at the Bretton Woods Conference, 1–22 July 1944, while the Articles of Agreement of the International Finance Corporation were adopted at Washington on 25 May 1955. The First and Second Amendments to the Articles of Agreement of the Fund became effective, respectively, in 1969 and 1978.
3. As to the principles involved in these commodity agreements, see Kabir-ur-Rahman Khan *The Law and Organisation of International Commodity Agreements* (1982) and E. McGovern *International Trade Regulation* (2nd edn, 1986) ch 15, 'Commodity Arrangements', pp 461 et seq.

There has thus developed a new field of the regulation by treaty of international economic matters.[4] Apart from these economic and monetary treaties, the period since 1972 has seen the adoption also of a number of declaratory or hortatory instruments, representing not binding engagements, but rather a series of blueprints for the evolution in due course of a new economic order. These texts have included the United Nations General Assembly's Consensus Declaration of 1974 on the Establishment of a New International Economic Order, the Charter of Economic Rights and Duties of States adopted by the Assembly by Resolution of 12 December 1974, the Final Statement Resolution adopted by it at its Seventh Special Session on economic co-operation and development in September 1975, the Rambouillet Declaration adopted on 17 November 1975 by an economic 'summit' Conference of the major industrial powers (Canada, France, West Germany, Italy, Japan, the United Kingdom, and the United States), and reaffirmed by them at subsequent annual conferences, the most recent being those at London in 1991, at Munich in 1992, at Tokyo in 1993, and at Naples in 1994, and the *Revised Program of Action Towards Reform of the International Monetary and Financial System*, adopted in 1984 by the Ministers of the Group of Twenty-Four. The difficulty, however, is to extract from these numerous treaty provisions and manifesto-type instruments principles of general application, which can truly be postulated as binding rules of international law. It is really only possible to indicate the main directions in which progress is being made towards an international economic legal order.

First, a principle appears to be taking shape, imposing upon every state a duty not to institute discriminatory trade restrictions, or discriminatory taxes or levies upon trade against another state, unless genuinely justified by balance-of-payments difficulties. There does not appear to be any distinction in this connection between wilful and unintentional discrimination, as it is sufficient if there be discrimination de facto. In either event, as the practice of the contracting parties to the General Agreement on Tarriffs and Trade (GATT) of 30 October

---

4. The importance of this field of regulation of international economic matters was recognised by the United Nations General Assembly in its Resolution of 17 December 1966, establishing the United Nations Commission on International Trade Law (UNCITRAL) with the functions, inter alia, of harmonising and unifying the law of international trade, promoting wider participation in international conventions and preparing new conventions, and promoting the codification of international trade customs and practices. The Commission held its first session in January–February, 1968. The substantive work of UNCITRAL has since been carried out through Working Groups preparing draft uniform laws and conventions in various specialised fields. Among the conventions that have emerged from the labours of UNCITRAL have been the Convention of 1974 on the Limitation Period in the International Sale of Goods, the Convention adopted at Hamburg in 1978 on the Carriage of Goods by Sea, the Convention adopted at Vienna in 1980 on Contracts for the International Sale of Goods, the Convention adopted at Geneva in 1980 on the International Multimodal Transport of Goods, and the Model Law on International Arbitration adopted in 1985. On the work of UNCITRAL in formulating rules and procedures to govern arbitration and conciliation in the field of international trade, see I. I. Dore *Arbitration and Conciliation under the UNCITRAL Rules: A Textual Analysis* (1986). Also active in this field of harmonisation and unification of international commercial law have been the Rome Institute for the Unification of Private Law (UNIDROIT), the Hague Conference on Private International Law, and the International Chamber of Commerce (ICC), which latter body promulgated in 1978 a set of Uniform Rules for Contract Guarantees (ICC Publication No 325).

1947 shows, it is the duty of states to correct or remove the element of discrimination. Reference should be made also to article 4 of the above-mentioned Charter of the Economic Rights and Duties of States of 12 December 1974, which provides:

'Every State has the right to engage in international trade and other forms of economic co-operation irrespective of any differences in political, economic and social systems. No State shall be subject to discrimination of any kind based solely on such differences.'

Unfortunately, there is bound to be controversy as to what constitutes discrimination. If under a trade treaty between State A and State B, the parties agree to grant to each other special reciprocal state privileges, eg, by way of reduced customs duties, is State X entitled to complain of discrimination if goods exported from its territory to these states continue to be subject to the former amount of duty? If State X were a party to a treaty with these states, providing for most-favoured-nation treatment, the inequality of customs privileges would clearly amount to discrimination.[5] In the absence of any such treaty with a most-favoured-nation clause or obligation, it is difficult to accept the view that the grant of reciprocal trade privileges between two states inter partes can represent a discrimination as against a third state, and the decision of the Permanent Court of International Justice in the *Oscar Chinn Case*[6] provides persuasive authority against such a view. It was the object of the General Agreement on Tariffs and Trade, above, to extend the most-favoured-nation obligation,[7] so as to ensure non-discrimination generally in customs and taxation matters (see article I). In the Final Act of the Conference on Security and Co-operation in Europe adopted at Helsinki on 1 August 1975, the participating states recognised 'the beneficial effects which can result for the development of trade from the application of the most-favoured-nation treatment'. At the same time, there has been developing an emergent, intermediate principle that states or associations of states, taking measures in their own interests by way of extending most-favoured-nation treatment or applying discrimination even legitimately, should have regard to the possible harmful effects of such steps upon the economies of other countries.

Second, insofar as private foreign investment is concerned, there is emerging a principle that the state in which such investment is made should not by its

---

5. See *Case Concerning Rights of Nationals of the United States of America in Morocco* ICJ 1952, 176 at 192 et seq. Two respects in which the standard of non-discrimination is not identical with that of most-favoured-nation treatment (MFN) may be noted: (1) MFN can hardly be applied to quantitative restrictions except by allocating equal quotas to all countries, which could result in unfairness. (2) Non-discrimination could allow favours to be given to some states in a special relationship, whereas this would not be admissible under MFN. See E. McGovern *International Trade Regulation* (2nd edn, 1986) p 254.
6. (1934) PCIJ Series A/B, No 63.
7. *Most-favoured-nation clause:* The most-favoured-nation clause which, notwithstanding erosions under recent developments, still governs a large part of the world trade, was the subject of consideration and study by the International Law Commission from 1967 onwards. The reports to the Commission and the discussions by it in 1967–1980 reflected the fact that the clause could not be studied in isolation from other economic developments (eg, the needs of developing countries, customs unions, and free trade areas); see *The Work of the International Law Commission* (3rd edn, 1980) pp 73–77. The possibility of the conclusion of a convention on the subject of the clause has been under consideration within the United Nations General Assembly.

exchange control laws and regulations hamper or prevent the payment of profits or income to the foreign investors, or the repatriation of the capital invested (although there is no absolute or unconditional right to repatriate capital), unless: (a) such restrictions are essential for the maintenance of monetary reserves; or (b) semble, the restrictions are temporarily necessary for reasons of the health and welfare of the people of the country of investment. Any such restrictions should also be non-discriminatory.[8] With regard to the *entry* of capital, although the general trend of international law is towards the promotion of investment, investment-receiving states are not debarred from prescribing requirements for the screening, approval, and registration of any capital inflow.[9] It is to be observed that article 2, paragraph 2 (a) of the above-mentioned Charter of Economic Rights and Duties of States of 12 December 1974, provides: 'Each State has the right: (a) to regulate and exercise authority over foreign investment within its national jurisdiction in accordance with its laws and regulations and in conformity with its national objectives and priorities. No State shall be compelled to grant preferential treatment to foreign investment'.

A number of proposals have been made for the protection and encouragement of private foreign investment, including a suggested international convention defining the fundamental mutual rights of private foreign investors and capital-importing countries,[10] a project for an international investments tribunal, and a code of multilateral investment insurance. These proposals provided the background for the first major step taken in investment protection under international law, namely the above-mentioned Convention of 18 March 1965 for the Settlement of Investment Disputes between States and Nationals of Other States, setting up international conciliation and arbitration machinery on a consensual basis so that private foreign investors might have direct access thereto to settle legal disputes with investment-receiving states.[11] On the aspect of investment-promotion, there should not be overlooked the expansion of the activities in this area since 1977 of the International Finance Corporation (IFC), established originally in 1956 for the purpose, among others, of stimulating productive investment.[12] A major step in the direction of the protection of foreign

8. Although discriminations in favour of the foreign investor, eg, by granting specially attractive terms, are not prohibited.
9. See *The Protection and Encouragement of Private Foreign Investment* (Butterworths, 1966, ed J. G. Starke) on the subject of foreign investments legislation and practice, and cf Schwarzenberger *Foreign Investments and International Law* (1969), *International Investment and Multinational Enterprises* (OECD, Paris, 1979); S. Sekiguchi *Japanese Direct Foreign Investment* (1979) and B. Zagaris *Foreign Investment in the United States* (1980).
10. See as to the Abs-Shawcross Draft Convention on Investments Abroad, of April 1959, *The Encouragement and Protection of Investment in Developing Countries* (1961) (British Institute of International and Comparative Law) pp 10–11.
11. Conciliation and arbitration proceedings are administered by the International Centre for Settlement of Investment Disputes (ICSID) set up under the Convention. See, for authoritative treatment of the Convention, lectures by Aron Broches on the Convention, published in (1972) II Hague Recueil 337–410, and more recently the article by Ibrahim F. I. Shihata, 'Towards a Greater Depoliticization of Investment Disputes: The Roles of ICSID and MIGA [Multilateral Investment Guarantee Agency]' (1986) 1 Foreign Investment Law Journal 1, especially at pp 3–12.
12. See article by Carl Bell 'Promoting private investment: the role of the International Finance Corporation' (1981) 18 Finance and Development 16–19.

investment was the adoption in 1985 of the Convention establishing the Multilateral Investment Guarantee Agency (MIGA), representing the culmination of efforts spanning a period of over thirty years to implement the concept of a multilateral investment guarantee scheme in respect of non-commercial risks, which scheme would be both protective and promotional of foreign investment.

As pointed out by the International Court of Justice in the *Barcelona Traction Case*,[13] one overriding general principle is that an investment-receiving state, while bound to extend some protection in law to the investments concerned, does not thereby become an insurer of that part of the investing state's wealth corresponding to such investments. Certain risks must remain.

A trend of the past decade, reflecting the above-mentioned developments concerning private foreign investment, is towards the negotiation of bilateral treaties for the mutual encouragement and protection of investments; one example of this is the United States—Morocco Treaty of July 1985 Governing the Encouragement and Reciprocal Protection of Investments, with ancillary Protocol, signed at Washington.

Third, the international commodity agreements, mentioned at the commencement of this chapter, indicate a movement towards rules of international law, obliging producing and purchasing states to co-operate in ensuring the stability of commodity prices, and in equating supply with demand by, inter alia, controlling and regulating the maintenance of desirable levels of production in each producing country or territory. Negatively, they show that there is no rule of international law, which prevents a state from restricting production, having regard to economic exigencies. However, as a different regulatory system is followed by the contracting states in each of the commodity agreements, lack of uniformity precludes the drawing of any more general conclusions.[14]

A broad principle governing the obligations of states in regard to international commodity supplies was proclaimed in article 6 of the above-mentioned 1974 Charter of Economic Rights and Duties of States, as follows:

> 'It is the duty of States to contribute to the development of international trade of goods particularly by means of arrangements and by the conclusion of long-term multilateral commodity arrangements, where appropriate, and taking into account the interests of producers and consumers. All States share the responsibility to promote the regular flow and access of all commercial goods traded at stable, remunerative and equitable prices, thus contributing to the equitable development of the world economy, taking into account in particular the interests of developing countries.'

As was reflected in the terms of this article, current emphasis in this connection was placed upon the needs and interests of developing countries. Such emphasis was also apparent in the proposals of UNCTAD (United Nations Conference on Trade and Development) at the Nairobi Conference of May, 1976, involving, inter alia, the establishment of buffer stocks, financed by a common fund for all products, and a system of export controls and production controls. These

13. *Case Concerning the Barcelona Traction, Light and Power Co Ltd (Second Phase)* ICJ 1970, 3 (see para 87 of the judgment of the Court).
14. Cf article by Kenneth Klein 'International Commodity Agreements' (1976) 6 Georgia JIL 275–307.

proposals received Conference endorsement, but not all developed countries were prepared to accept them unreservedly. On 13 June 1976, a United Nations Conference adopted an Agreement creating the International Fund for Agricultural Development, one of the purposes of which was the improvement and mobilisation of additional resources to be furnished on a concessional basis for agricultural development in developing states, members of the Fund. Then, on 29 June 1980 the parties concerned adopted an Agreement for a Common Fund for Commodities to be established, in effect implementing the Nairobi proposals, in order to provide finance for buffer stocking and other commodity stabilisation measures, in the context of producer-consumer agreements.

Fourth, there appears to be an emerging principle[15] that states should avoid practices such as dumping and the unrestricted disposal of accumulated stocks that may interfere with the industrial development of developing countries. This principle is no doubt merely a particular illustration of the rule of economic good neighbourliness which should be followed by all states; it underlies the basic purposes of the International Monetary Fund and of the Meeting of the Contracting Parties to the General Agreement on Tariffs and Trade of 30 October 1947, that the growth of international trade should be facilitated in order to contribute to the promotion of full employment and the development of national productivity. In general, states taking measures for their own economic protection should have regard to the possible harmful effects upon the economies of other states,[16] a principle reflected in article 24 of the above-mentioned Charter on Economic Rights and Duties of States of 12 December 1974, which provides:

'All States have the duty to conduct their mutual economic relations in a manner which takes into account the interests of other countries. In particular, all States should avoid prejudicing the interests of developing countries.'

Fifth, international law is moving towards the abolition of quantitative restrictions on imports and exports, except where these are temporarily and urgently required to solve problems of maintenance of currency reserves (see articles XI to XIV of the General Agreement on Tariffs and Trade, above) or for other legitimate special reasons.

Sixth, states appear ready to recognise a principle that in matters not materially involving the revenue, or balance-of-payments issues, customs formalities should be simplified, and administrative restrictions on, or barriers to trade, whether in goods or in services, should be minimised. This is illustrated not only by the General Agreement on Tariffs and Trade of 30 October 1947, but by conventions such as the International Convention to Facilitate Importation of Commercial Samples and Advertising Material signed at Geneva on 7 November 1952, by the Resolution of 20 December 1965 of the United Nations General Assembly favouring the 'progressive unification and harmonisation of the law of

15. See the Resolution of the United Nations General Assembly of 19 December 1961, on International Trade as the Primary Instrument for Economic Development.
16. This principle to some extent underlies the work of the Organisation for Economic Co-operation and Development (OECD), established in 1961, as a permanent institution for the harmonisation of national economic policies, with the express purpose of making available to its members all knowledge relevant to the formulation of rational policy in every economic field, and of sharing experiences through meetings at ministerial and official levels.

international trade', and the betterment of conditions to facilitate trade, and much more recently the communiqué of the ministerial meeting of the Organisation for Economic Co-operation and Development (OECD), of 10 May 1983, expressing a joint resolve 'to relax and dismantle progressively trade restrictions and trade-distorting measures' (paragraph 14 of the communiqué). Indeed the OECD is continually updating, for this purpose, its Code of Liberalisation of Invisible Transactions and its Code of Liberalisation of Capital Movements. At their 'economic summit' held in Venice in June 1987, the seven major industrial powers (Canada, France, West Germany, Italy, Japan, the United Kingdom and the United States) made a call for the preservation of 'an open world trading system by reducing trade barriers'.

Seventh, there are indications that an important branch of international economic law in the future will consist of rules to regulate and oversee the sharing of natural resources such as energy, raw materials, and food.[17] The necessity for establishing such a sharing régime in the case of oil and oil products was brought home to the nations of the world in the energy crisis of 1973–1974 with the restrictions on oil exports by producing countries and the unprecedented increase in oil prices. These circumstances led to the World Energy Conference in September, 1974, and the establishment by the OECD of the International Energy Agency in 1974, with the function, inter alia, of ensuring a rationalised sharing and distribution of energy base products. Further, in August 1981, a United Nations Conference on New and Renewable Energy Sources was held at Nairobi, resulting, inter alia, in the acceptance of an Agreed Programme of Action which could serve as a possible platform for the eventual formation of new rules of international law concerning energy-sharing. The keynote of such future rules would appear to be, above all, international co-operation in the identification of new energy sources (such as geothermal and wind power, tidal power, wave power and the thermal gradient of the sea, etc), and in the development of mature technologies, involving as far as possible the utilisation of renewable sources. The necessity for co-operation between nations in respect to these and other crucial matters has clearly been one of the main preoccupations of the Governing Board of the International Energy Agency at the Board's periodical meetings.

Studies have been initiated of areas in which sharing will involve critical problems, as, eg, in the case of uranium.[18] At the United Nations Conference held at Geneva in March–April 1987 (attended by 106 states) there was emphasis by states on the assurance of supply of nuclear materials and equipment by states able to provide these, and more specifically attention was drawn to article IV of the Nuclear Non-Proliferation Treaty of 1968 requiring that parties to the Treaty facilitate to the fullest possible extent the exchange of materials for the peaceful uses of nuclear energy, with due consideration for the needs of the world's developing areas. The question of sharing is closely linked to international monetary law and practice, as was reflected in the proposal by the United States, put to the UNCTAD Conference at Nairobi in May 1976, and not approved by

17. Cf address by Joseph A. Greenwald 'Sharing the World's Natural Resources; Prospects for International Co-operation' *Department of State Bulletin* 30 August 1976, pp 294–299.
18. See OECD study, *Uranium Resources, Production and Demand* (1976).

that Conference, of an International Resources Bank. Producing and consuming States would doubtless accept the existence of a rule of international law that there is at least a duty to consult about sharing problems, and consuming countries might acknowledge an obligation inter se to share equitably resources in short supply, and if necessary for the purposes of conservation to reduce consumption jointly on an equitable basis, but otherwise no firm rules can be postulated.

Eighth, the principle that the developing (or under-developed) countries are entitled to special economic assistance and special trade preferences is firmly established, and is reflected in the provisions of the new Part IV, added by the Protocol of 8 February 1965 to the General Agreement on Tariffs and Trade, referred to above, in the current and continuing work of the United Nations Conference on Trade and Development (UNCTAD), and as well of the International Bank for Reconstruction and Development and its affiliates, and the Development Assistance Committee (DAC) of the Organisation for Economic Co-operation and Development (OECD), in numerous subsequent instruments and reports including the Report of the Independent Commission on International Development Issues (the Brandt Report) presented on 12 February 1980, and in the continuing discussions between the world of developed countries and the 'Third World' of developing countries, that has become known as the 'North-South dialogue'. Indeed, it may be said that by way of exception to the concept of development of free and open trading relationships, the extension of new preferences, subject to consultation with the countries significantly affected, as an expedient for encouraging the export of selected products from less-developed countries, is not excluded by any general rules of international law; this seems to be shown by the 'waivers' granted by the GATT Contracting Parties in 1966 and 1971 to enable Australia and other developed countries to grant tariff preferences to under-developed states, and in the steps taken by the Organisation for Economic Co-operation and Development (OECD) in 1970–1971 and since to procure the introduction of, and extend as far as possible, a generalised system of trade preferences in favour of developing countries, so as to increase their export earnings and make possible further economic development, preferences being in this case an instrument for promoting rather than for restricting trade.

In 1974–1976, in particular, the subject of assistance to developed countries obtained emphatic expression in various resolutions adopted. In the above-mentioned Charter of Economic Rights and Duties of 12 December 1974, article 18 provided that 'developed countries should extend, improve and enlarge the system of generalised non-reciprocal and non-discriminatory tariff preferences to the developing countries consistent with the relevant agreed conclusions and relevant decisions as adopted on this subject in the framework of the competent international organisations', and that 'developed countries should also give serious consideration to the adoption of other differential measures, in areas where this is feasible and appropriate and in ways which will provide special and more favourable treatment, in order to meet trade and development needs of the developing countries'. Article 19 of the same Charter provided, in more general terms, that 'with a view to accelerating the economic growth of developing countries and bridging the economic gap between developed and developing countries, developed countries should grant generalised preferential, non-reciprocal and non-discriminatory treatment to developing countries in those fields of international economic co-operation where it may be feasible'. The Resolution adopted by the Seventh Special Session of the United Nations General Assembly on 16 September 1975, reaffirmed an earlier commitment of the developed countries to provide 0.7% of their gross national product (GNP) by way of development assistance to developing countries. At the UNCTAD Conference at Nairobi in May 1976, Resolutions were adopted, inter alia, to the effect that there should be duty-free entry into developed countries for the manufactured exports of developing countries, that the continuing multilateral trade negotiations should provide special and more favourable treatment for developing countries, and that an expert group should meet to draft a code of conduct for the transfer of technology to developing countries.

The subject of assistance to developing countries ought not to be viewed in isolation, inasmuch as since 1974 it has represented one element of a wider movement, continually growing in reach and strength, for the establishment of what is designated as the 'New International Economic Order' (NIEO), to involve a radical restructuring of the rules and institutions of international economic law.[19] The initial formal starting points of the NIEO were the two Resolutions adopted in 1974 by consensus at the Sixth Special Session of the United Nations General Assembly, namely, the Declaration on the Establishment of a New International Economic Order, and the Programme of Action on the Establishment of a New International Economic Order. These two Resolutions have set the pattern for the intensified efforts since 1974, continuing at the date of writing, both within and outside the framework of the United Nations, to provide firmer foundations for, and to extend the scope of the NIEO. For instance, in June 1978, the United Nations Commission on International Trade Law (UNCITRAL) establishing a Working Group on the NIEO, which Group met for the first time in January 1980 and has held further meetings since. The precise scope of the régime of the NIEO remains to be finalised, but it consists at least of the principles, considered above in this chapter, to the extent that they serve to further the advancement of developing countries (eg, preferential treatment, stabilisation of export earnings, and access to technology), and embraces also the participatory equality of developing countries in international economic relations and the right to nationalise. Even if the proclaimed rules and precepts of the NIEO have not yet attained the force of law, binding non-developing countries, the latter must nonetheless be influenced by the content of the NIEO in their negotiations and arrangements with developing countries. At their above-mentioned 'economic summit' in Venice in June 1987 the seven major industrial powers declared that they attached 'particular importance to fostering stable economic progress in developing countries', while the United

19. There is already an immense bibliography on the NIEO; however reference may be made to four valuable studies relative thereto, namely, Robert F. Meagher *An International Redistribution of Wealth and Power: a Study of the Charter of Economic Rights and Duties of States* (1979); M. Bedjaoui *Towards a New International Economic Order* (1979); K. Hossain (ed) *Legal Aspects of the New International Economic Order* (1980); and A. Akinsanya and A. Davies 'Third World Quest for a New International Economic Order: An Overview' (1984) 33 ICLQ 208.

Nations General Assembly at its sessions in 1986 and subsequently has had under consideration the progressive development of principles and norms, to be part of international law, relating to the NIEO.

The matter of access of developing countries to the technology of developed countries has been one to which the developing countries attach cardinal importance. It forms in fact one of the key doctrines of the NIEO. On one level, it is regarded as primarily referable to the obligation, legal or moral, of states to promote international co-operation in scientific and technological questions, although ultimately bearing upon the economic developments of developing countries. Thus in paragraphs 1 and 2 of article 13 of the above-mentioned Charter of Economic Rights and Duties of States of 12 December 1974, it was provided that 'every State has the right to benefit from the advances and developments in science and technology for the acceleration of its economic and social development' and that 'all States should facilitate the access of developing countries to the achievements of modern science and technology, the transfer of technology and the creation of indigenous technology for the benefit of the developing countries in forms and in accordance with procedures which are suited to their economies and their needs'. A more recent illustration is that of the provisions for the transfer of technology contained in article 144 of the United Nations Convention on the Law of the Sea of 10 December 1982, which Convention was considered in detail in Chapter 9, above. There has continued to be pressure for a code of binding rules or principles for the transfer of technology to developing countries; however, this is not favoured by some states not classified as 'developing', partly because it is considered that the complexities of trade and industry are such as to warrant guidelines rather than binding rules, partly because they are themselves to some extent importers of technology, and binding rules could discriminate against them in favour of developing countries.

In the matter of consultation, it may be added that economic good-neighbourliness makes it incumbent upon states to consult with each other, and to be accessible for the receipt of representations, in connection with the application of the above-mentioned principles. All this is, however, expressed or implied in the provisions of the Articles of Agreement of the International Monetary Fund, of the General Agreement on Tariffs and Trade, and of other multilateral and bilateral instruments. As will be seen (p 351, below), regular consultations between the International Monetary Fund (IMF) and member states constitute an important part of the process of surveillance by the IMF of the policies of members, and by a decision of the Fund's Executive Board in 1986, the influence of IMF-member consultations was strengthened by a requirement of direct contact, at the conclusion of a consultation, between the Managing Director of the IMF and the member state's Finance Minister in those cases where such high-level contact was deemed particularly necessary.

These are among the evolving principles of international economic law of general significance, and they embrace only a limited field, leaving a whole range of international economic questions not even subject to emergent doctrines.

Apart from these areas of tentative acceptance, there are a number of growing international economic doctrines, eg, the promotion by international action of policies conducive to balanced economic growth, and the obligation on a state, in technical economic terms, to keep demand at an appropriate level and to graduate national expenditure in line with the growth of production, that may be yet translated into ruling principles of international law.[20] It would, however, be bold to predict that this will take place in the very near future.

This overview of international economic law would be incomplete without some particularisation of the role of the General Agreement on Tariffs and Trade (GATT) which, to illustrate its durability, celebrated its 45th anniversary in 1992. GATT is not in the strict sense an international organisation, but an association of the contracting parties to the Agreement providing a régime with many of the features of an international institution; it serves pragmatically as a forum for international trade regulation and international trade law initiatives. It was originally conceived as no more than a temporary measure pending the formation of an international trade organisation, the ITO, and was based on the same rationale as would have provided the core justification for the ITO, namely, that, as proclaimed in the Atlantic Charter of 1941, all countries, great or small, should enjoy access on equal terms to the trade and to the raw materials of the world. GATT has been metaphorically described as furnishing the 'highway rules' for the free flow of the 'traffic' of world trade. Thus, the GATT rules, broadly speaking, provide for non-discrimination, fair competition, the rational settlement of international trade disputes, the liberalisation of trade and the use of tariffs rather than quotas or other non-tariff barriers to trade. Most countries operate under the GATT rules: upwards of 100 countries are full contracting parties, and about 30 more apply the GATT rules de facto or provisionally. Even the countries not participating in the GATT at all benefit to some extent from the GATT rules under the umbrella of the most-favoured-nation rule (MFN treatment).

GATT has also been involved in multilateral trade negotiations for the purposes, inter alia, of the progressive lowering of tariffs and of the elimination or mitigation of non-tariff barriers, as for instance with the sponsorship of the so-called 'Tokyo Round' of negotiations, 1973–1979, and the 'Uruguay Round' 1986-1994. In its efforts to increase the momentum of trade liberalisation and trade growth, GATT has been hampered by an unprecedented conjunction of disastrous features of the global economy, including unstable exchange rates, massive debts incurred by developing countries, trade and budgetary imbalances, rising fuel prices and curtailments in economic growth. Not unnaturally, there have been claims that, although GATT provides the principal machinery for the international surveillance of trade liberalisation, there is room for improvement in its policies if existing problems are to be solved and difficulties surmounted. GATT can, however, hardly be blamed for not coping with situations such as those created by the rapid movements of capital around the world and the large-scale subsidisation of commodity producers.

---

20. These doctrines are to some extent reflected in s 1 of art IV of the Articles of Agreement of the International Monetary Fund, as amended in 1976 (see below in this chapter) stipulating in sub-ss (i) and (ii) that member states of the Fund should endeavour to direct their economic and financial policies towards fostering orderly economic growth, with reasonable price stability, and that they should seek to promote stability by encouraging orderly economic and financial conditions.

The Uruguay Round of negotiations within the GATT concluded in April 1994 with the adoption of the Marrakesh Declaration, which officially endorsed the results of these protracted and complex negotiations.[1] The Declaration also approved the creation of a new World Trade Organisation (WTO) to forward many of the objectives intended by the unrealised ITO (above).

International monetary law

International monetary law consists of the complex of international rules and guidelines which have been created, largely upon the basis of traditional banking and trading practices, in an effort to ensure fair and efficient methods of conducting international financial transactions, to promote international monetary co-operation, and to maintain an orderly exchange system. It includes, for example, the following:

a.   the rules and principles embodied in the Articles of Agreement of the International Monetary Fund (IMF), referred to above, the principal object of which is to establish a system for stabilising and regulating in an orderly manner international currency relationships;
b.   the provisions of the Articles of Agreement of the Fund and of the General Agreement on Tariffs and Trade (GATT), under which restrictions on trade and on current payments are generally allowable only in situations of balance-of-payments difficulties and are subjected to international control;
c.   the provisions of the Articles of Agreement of the Fund, and related arrangements and practices, designed to mitigate the effect of exchange controls and restrictions, and so far as possible, without making this an absolute goal, to foster the interconvertibility of currencies;
d.   the de facto arrangements implementing the above-mentioned rules, and serving to preserve monetary stability.

One keystone of the system is the International Monetary Fund established under the above-mentioned Articles of Agreement, and of which the purposes are, inter alia, to serve as a permanent institution for providing the machinery for consultation and collaboration on international monetary problems, to promote exchange stability, to maintain orderly exchange arrangements among members, to avoid competitive exchange depreciation (see article 1, s (iii) of the Articles of Agreement), to make its resources available to members for correcting maladjustments in their balance of payments without detriment to their economies and social structures, and to shorten the duration and lessen the degree of disequilibrium in the international balances of payments of members. The Fund, which is independent of other international organisations and cannot delegate its functions to other international agencies, is prohibited from intervening in the domestic or social policies of its members, and must, particularly having regard to the diversity of its membership, treat all members

1.   The Final Act of 15 December 1993 embodying the results of the Uruguay Round, the Agreement Establishing the World Trade Organisation, the Agreement on Trade in Goods, the General Agreement on Trade in Services, the Agreement on Trade-related Aspects of Intellectual Property Rights Including Trade in Counterfeit Goods, the Understanding on Rules and Procedures Governing the Settlement of Disputes, and Ministerial Decisions and Declarations are reprinted in (1994) 33 ILM 1-152.

of the Fund uniformly.[2] Throughout the history of the Fund to date, notwithstanding new year-by-year developments, there has been a measure of consistency in the discharge of its functions and in its practices, almost equivalent to a set of established international norms, namely regular consultations by the Fund with its members, the financing of balance of payments shortfalls, the exercise of surveillance or regulatory authority over international monetary affairs and constant attention to exchange rates.

It will be apparent that there is a large measure of interdependence between international economic law and international monetary law. As was implicit in the above-mentioned Rambouillet Declaration of 17 November 1975, and Joint Declaration of Puerto Rico of 28 June 1976, and as reflected in s 1 of article IV, as amended, of the Articles of Agreement of the International Monetary Fund, a stable system of exchange rates is a prerequisite for the development of stable underlying economic and financial conditions, and in their turn stable national economic and financial policies provide a good basis for stable monetary conditions. The principles of stability of monetary exchange and of co-operation with the International Monetary Fund in, inter alia, the Fund's surveillance activities, were also affirmed at the 'summit' conferences of the major industrial powers (Canada, France, West Germany, Italy, Japan, the United Kingdom and the United States) at Versailles in 1982, Williamsburg in 1983, Tokyo in 1986, Venice in 1987 and Toronto in 1988, supporting also the theme that orderly economic and financial conditions and policies of international co-ordination could contribute to better stability of exchange rates.

The interdependence between international economic law and international monetary law may be illustrated also by the de facto development in more recent years of a closer working relationship between the International Monetary Fund and the World Bank (the International Bank for Reconstruction and Development), the principal respective fields of which are, for the Fund, acting as guardian of the international monetary system, eliminating competitive exchange depreciations practices and promoting orderly exchange arrangements, on the one hand, and, for the Bank, development programmes and the promotion of private foreign investment and international trade, on the other hand; eg, the Fund has recently given increasing attention to savings, investment, and production in programmes supported by its lending activities so as to foster economic growth, which is a World Bank function.[3]

However, it is not to be doubted that international monetary law has during the past twenty years continued to be to some extent at the cross-roads. The fragility of the system was demonstrated in a series of international crises from 1968 to 1974, which included the gold crisis of March 1968, the dollar-mark crisis in Western Europe in April–May 1971, the crisis in August 1971, arising

---

2. See discussion of these points by Sir Joseph Gold in the *IMF Survey*, 23 May 1983, pp 146–148. Also for valuable discussions of the role of the Fund, see Margaret G. de Vries *The IMF in a Changing World* 1945-1985.

3. See article on this relationship by Sir Joseph Gold in (1982) 15 Creighton Law Review 499–521. The importance of co-operation between the Fund and the Bank, and, as well, between these two bodies and GATT, was stressed by the seven major industrial powers at the Venice 'economic summit' in 1987.

out of the United States Government's decision to cease conversion into gold of foreign-held dollars, the British Government's decision in June 1972, to 'float' the pound sterling from 23 June and to suspend currency trading in London for four days, the disruption of exchanges in February–March 1973, leading to joint and separate 'floating' exchange rates, and the crisis produced by the curtailing of oil exports and the rise in oil prices, coupled with a surging world-wide inflation, in 1973–1974. It was generally accepted that the recurrence of these crises attested the breakdown of the original International Monetary Fund par value system under which each member was to maintain a fixed value of its currency relative to gold and other currencies, with alterations of the value being confined to circumstances of fundamental disequilibrium, and generally requiring the consent of the Fund. There were those who maintained that as soon as national economies came out of alignment by reason of different degrees of inflation and economic productivity, exchange rates were thrown out of gear and financial crises occurred, giving rise to urgent demands for additional liquidity, and encouraging movements of capital, partly speculative and partly conditioned by a natural desire to obtain security or a higher return. A par value régime depends essentially on a reasonable measure of certainty and confidence, but these conditions tend to disappear when exchange rates become unstable for more than a reasonable period or when inflation continues unchecked. It was claimed indeed that the par value régime would have broken down earlier if it had not been for practices such as stringent national action to reduce excess of internal spending, and the increasing recourse to transactions by way of 'Euro-dollars' ('Euro-dollars' are in effect no more than the dollar liabilities of banks in certain Western European countries, including the United Kingdom).

In July 1972, mainly as a consequence of the above-mentioned events of 1971–1972, a resolution of the Board of Governors of the International Monetary Fund created a Committee of Twenty with the mandate of producing a plan for a new international monetary order, and of reporting on all aspects of international monetary reform. This Committee, the formal title of which was the Committee on Reform of the International Monetary System and Related Issues, began work at the end of September 1972. It was hopefully envisaged that two years would suffice for the formulation of a new comprehensive code of rules of international monetary behaviour. A First Outline of Reform, presented at a Fund meeting in Nairobi in September 1973, reflected some measure of agreement upon certain basic principles of a reconstructed monetary order, namely, allowance for greater flexibility of exchange rates, acceptance of a certain role within limits for 'floating' exchange rates, acknowledgment of the status of the Fund's new liquidity facility created in 1969 following a decision reached in 1967—special drawing rights— as the principal reserve asset, and of the declining position of gold and reserve currencies, and recognition of the principle that import and export controls ought not to be used for balance-of-payments purposes.

The energy crisis which arose in October 1973, with the curtailment of oil exports and the increase in oil prices, involving a possibility of unpredictable movements of capital and consequent uncertainty, rendered imperative the deferment of the process of general revision of the international monetary system. It was also clear that, under the new conditions, states would not be prepared to accept any long-term binding monetary commitment of a changed nature. At the end of March 1974, it was officially announced[4] that the process of putting a reformed international monetary system into practice would be 'evolutionary', and was not to be achieved within the two-year period first envisaged, and would be conducted with 'some aspects of reform . . . pushed forward and implemented early, while other aspects could be developed over time'.

In the result, the Committee of Twenty concluded its work at Washington in meetings of 12 and 13 June 1974. It recommended a programme of immediate action, which included the establishment of an Interim Committee of the Board of Governors and the formulation of guidelines for the management of floating exchange rates, and it transmitted to the Governors a final Report on its work, together with an *Outline of Reform* and Annexes,[5] recording the outcome of the Committee's discussions, indicating the general direction in which the Committee believed the international monetary system could evolve in the future, and treating in the Annexes a number of technical and other points. Thus goals only of future 'evolutionary' reform were fixed.

Subsequently, discussions within the framework of the Fund centred on what immediate reforms could be made by amendment of the Fund's Articles of Agreement, leaving other general and particular aspects to be dealt with in the future. At Jamaica in January 1976, the Interim Committee, which had been established as recommended, reached agreement on a set of reforms as a basis of a proposed amendment of the articles, and this amendment, known as the Second Amendment,[6] was approved by the Board of Governors at the end of April 1976, and the machinery for bringing the amendment into force was set in motion.

This Second Amendment, which entered into force on 1 April 1978, represented the immediate steps required to be taken to initiate the 'evolutionary' process of reform of the international monetary system recommended by the Committee of Twenty. In some degree, the Second Amendment constituted a root and branch adjustment of some of the main elements of the original International Monetary Fund structure; nevertheless, certain basic principles were to remain intact, and the Fund was to continue as one cornerstone of the revised system.

First, significant changes were made to the par value régime. Under the amended provisions, members of the Fund are to have the right to maintain exchange arrangements of their own choice, whereas previously they undertook to maintain exchange rates on the basis of fixed par values, adjustable within certain margins, with alterations in value being confined to circumstances of fundamental disequilibrium, subject generally to the consent of the Fund. As pointed out on 2 April 1976, by the then Managing Director of the Fund, Mr Witteveen, this change would 'legalise the present situation in which some countries are having independently floating currencies; others are floating jointly; others are pegged to a currency or to some combination of currencies or to the special drawing right'. It would also, according to him, terminate for the purposes

4. By the Chairman of the Deputies of the Committee of Twenty on 29 March 1974, at Washington; see *IMF Survey*, 8 April 1974, p 97.
5. For text, see *Supplement* to *IMF Survey*, 17 June 1974.
6. The First Amendment was that constituted by the alterations of 1969 to the Articles of Agreement for the creation of special drawing rights.

of the articles the par values established under the articles in their present form. The change was nevertheless to remain subject to the general obligation of member states to collaborate with the Fund in order to ensure orderly exchange arrangements and to promote a stable system of exchange rates. According to Mr Witteveen's statement on the same above mentioned date, there was to be 'a freedom of choice of exchange arrangements, but not a freedom of behaviour'.

Under the new system, the Fund was given power by a decision taken by an 85% majority of total voting power to 'recommend' exchange arrangements that accord with the development of the international monetary system, and by a similar majority—in all probability unlikely to be achieved except at economic crisis point—the Fund might determine that international economic conditions permit the introduction of a system based on stable but adjustable par values, whereupon each member would establish a par value unless it intends to apply other arrangements. The Fund was also given an overseeing role in order to ensure the effective operation of the international monetary system, and the performance by member states of their obligations. The effectiveness of these safety valves against the hazards involved in the dropping of the par value régime depended essentially upon the willingness of the members of the Fund to co-operate.

Second, the Amendment involved the reduction of the role of gold in the international monetary system. The following were the main points:

a. the function of gold was no longer to be that of the 'common denominator' of the par value régime;
b. gold would also not be the 'common denominator' of any future par value régime decided upon by the Fund;
c. there would no longer be obligatory payments of gold by members to the Fund, or by the Fund to members, and the Fund might be able to accept gold only in payments from members under decisions taken by a very substantial majority of the total voting power of the Fund; and
d. the Fund would be required, in its dealings (if any) with gold, to avoid the management of the price or the establishment of a fixed price of gold in the gold market.

Correlative to these changes for diminishing the role of gold were the alterations for the enhancement of the functions of special drawing rights, designed to assist such special drawing rights to become the principal reserve asset of the international monetary system, and better to ensure the international supervision of global liquidity. Possible uses of special drawing rights in operations and transactions of the Fund were to be expanded, and the Fund was empowered to determine the mode of valuation of such rights. These alterations were largely confirmatory of the developments of the previous years.

When the consequences of the changes wrought by the Second Amendment to the Articles of Agreement of the Fund fully took effect, it was hoped that a pattern would be set for further progress in the 'evolutionary' method of international monetary reform contemplated by the Committee of Twenty, and accepted by the members of the Fund. Since 1976 some of the major steps and decisions taken within the framework of the Fund have included the following:

a. The establishment in August 1977 of a supplementary financing facility.

b. The decision in April 1980 that assistance for the adjustment and financing of imbalances in payments should be provided for over larger periods and in larger amounts.
c. The decision in September 1980 to unify and simplify the currency 'baskets' that determine and govern the value of, and the interest on special drawing rights.
d. More attention being given in recent years to the importance of the promotion of balance of payments adjustments and to the Fund's surveillance functions. There was general consensus at the Fund Annual Meeting in September 1983 (a consensus confirmed in the review, concluded by the Executive Board of the Fund in February 1986) on the need to strengthen surveillance.
e. The establishment by the Fund in March 1986 of a Structural Adjustment Facility (SAF) and in December 1987 of an Enhanced Structural Adjustment Facility (ESAF), each funded from a different source, to provide balance of payments assistance upon concessional terms to low-income developing countries according to separate criteria.
f. The call in April 1986 by the Interim Committee of the Fund's Board of Governors on the International Monetary System for improved policy co-ordination among member countries to improve the functioning of the floating exchange rate system.

Nevertheless, there has continued to prevail a feeling that more should be done to strengthen the international monetary system, so as to cope with future contingencies. This has been reflected in a number of reports since 1983, including the above mentioned Report in September 1984 of the Ministers of the Group of Twenty-Four, bearing the title the *Revised Program of Action towards Reform of the International Monetary and Financial System*, and in a notable IMF paper on the reform of the system.[7] Proposals have also been put forward for restricting the area within which there is latitude for currencies to float[8], as distinct from the 'pegging' of exchange rates. The debate is not about whether the Fund should cease to operate, but about its future role and responsibilities in the context of more orderly economic and financial conditions due to better co-ordination between member states.

By way of completion of this brief account of international monetary law, reference should be made to the key role, different from that of the International Monetary Fund, played by the Bank for International Settlements (BIS) at Basle, founded in 1930, and the current principal function of which are, inter alia, to promote the co-operation of Central Banks, to provide a clearing-house for facilitating inter-Bank settlements, and to act as a trustee in respect to certain international financial operations.[9] In the last two decades, the BIS has grown

7. Andrew Crockett and Morris Goldstein *Strengthening the International Monetary System: Exchange Rates, Surveillance and Objective Indicators* (1987: Occasional Paper No. 50).
8. One proposal is to adopt so-called 'target zones'; major states would agree to criteria to govern their rates of exchange relationships, and then set bands of up to 20% on the basis of these criteria. Corrective action would be taken whenever rates edged towards the outer limits of the 'zones'.
9. See passim *BIS Handbook* (1980), published by the Bank for International Settlements. As to the regulation of international banking, see R. Dale *Regulation of International Banking* (1986).

from strength to strength, and will and must continue to be a permanent element in the infrastructure of international monetary law. Its influential annual reports have done much to clarify the needs and defects of the international monetary system in measure as these emerge.

CHAPTER 14

Development and the environment

1. GENERAL

Two of the most pressing problems confronting the international community at the present time are those of development, and of the protection and improvement of the human environment, and, as will appear, both problems have been given priority within the framework of the United Nations and other international bodies.

The link between these two areas in which international law is currently feeling its way may not be immediately obvious. It could be said, for instance, that the former topic of development is concerned with the situation of developing countries, whereas the degradation of the environment is a state of affairs with which, primarily, the developed, and not the developing countries, are afflicted. In such a statement, a number of relevant matters are overlooked. First, any multilateral agency responsible for the promotion of development projects, involving large scale financial aid, must concern itself with the ecological effects of the projects in developing countries, otherwise ecological detriments would have to be set off against the benefits to accrue to the developing country concerned.[1] Second, so far as development has been treated as a branch of the general science of economics, and so far as criteria and indicators of the quality, as distinct from the quantity of development have been evolved, one of the accepted indicators of development quality is the standard of environment of the country subject of development.[2] Third, it may be remembered, as referred to in Chapter 5, that the General Assembly has in a number of Resolutions proclaimed the inalienable right of all countries (particularly developing

---

1. In 1970, the President of the International Bank for Reconstruction and Development instructed the Bank's staff to evaluate the ecological consequences of Bank-financed development projects; see *Finance and Development*, Part No 3, 1970, p 3. Seventeen years later, in May 1987, the current President of the Bank announced the creation of a new Environmental Department in the Bank to help set the direction of Bank policy, planning and research on the environment so as to integrate environmental considerations into Bank activities. Moreover, Bank resources would be devoted, inter alia, to programmes to help governments assess environmental threats, to arresting desertification and to the encouragement of forest conservation.
2. See *Department of State Bulletin* 24 August 1970, pp 230–231.

countries) to exercise permanent sovereignty over their natural resources in the interest of their national development; in the 1966 Resolution, such proclamation was made in the context of a recital in the preamble that 'natural resources are limited and in many cases exhaustible and that their proper exploitation determines the conditions of the economic development of the developing countries both at present and in the future'. But the depletion of exhaustible natural resources represents one of the identifiable problems involved in the protection of the human environment. Thus Principles 2 and 3 of the Declaration on the Human Environment adopted by the Stockholm Conference of June 1972 and Principles 3 and 4 of the Declaration on Environment and Development adopted by the Rio Conference of June 1992 (see below in this chapter) provided that the natural resources of the earth must be safeguarded for the benefit of present and future generations through careful planning or management, and that the capacity of the earth to produce vital renewable resources must be maintained and, wherever practicable, restored or improved. Fourth, as was said by writers of a notable article published in 1986[3]: 'Sound management of the environment and natural resource base has come to be seen as a prerequisite, not an obstacle, to sustainable economic development, and a vital element in any program designed to raise the living standards of the poor'. In particular, the writers said: 'Proper management of the natural resource base is especially important in developing countries, because, inter alia, such countries can least afford efforts to remedy environmental damage'.

In the International Development Strategy for the Third United Nations Development Decade (1981–1990) adopted by the United Nations General Assembly at its Eleventh Special Session in August–September 1980, the following was said:

'Accelerated development in the developing countries could enhance their capacity to improve their environment. The environmental implications of poverty and under-development and the interrelationships between development, environment, population and resources must be taken into account in the process of development. ... There is need to ensure an economic development process which is environmentally sustainable over the long run and which protects the ecological balance. Determined efforts must be made to prevent deforestation, erosion, soil degradation and desertification.'

It is for these reasons that the two subjects of development and of the human environment are treated together in the present chapter.

2. DEVELOPMENT

The international law of development has not yet reached the stage where it can be set down as a substantial body of binding rules, conferring specific rights upon developing states and imposing duties on developed countries.[4] For the most part,

---

3. See James Lee and Robert Goodland 'Economic Development and the Environment' *Finance and Development* December 1986, p 36.
4. The right to development, as proclaimed by UN General Assembly Resolution 41/128 (1986), is conditioned by respect for the principles of international law concerning friendly relations

it is best described as institutional law, that is to say the law of the various bodies and agencies through which development is promoted and development aid is channelled.[5] At the same time, a large number of standards and guidelines have been defined or proclaimed, and these enter into the province of international law no less than do the Recommendations adopted by the International Labour Conference, or the Recommendations adopted by the Antarctic Treaty Powers. The special needs of development of developing countries have nevertheless had an impact upon certain general principles of international economic law, and have served to reduce the stringency of the duty of non-discrimination between states, and to exclude in favour of the doctrine of 'national treatment' the international standard of treatment of resident aliens in developing countries from the point of view of local mercantile operations, and international trading. Development represents in point of fact a key objective of the New International Economic Order (NIEO), referred to in Chapter 13, above.

The definition of 'development' presents insuperable difficulties by reason of the range of operations encompassed. This largely explains the lack of acceptance of the view that there is a 'right to development' which can be characterised as a human right in the strict sense. According to the Report in 1970 of the United Nations Committee for Development, containing proposals for the Second United Nations Development Decade: 'It cannot be over-emphasised that what development implies for the developing countries is not simply an increase in productive capacity but major transformations in their social and economic structures'. The Report went on to point out that 'the ultimate purpose of development is to provide opportunities for a better life to all sections of the population', and to achieve this, it would be necessary in developing countries to eliminate inequalities in the distribution of income and wealth, and mass poverty and social injustice, including the disparities between regions and groups, while there would have to be arrangements for new employment opportunities, greater supplies of food and more nourishing food, and better education and health facilities. On a different level, there should be international co-operative measures to establish, strengthen, and promote scientific research and technological activities which have a bearing upon the expansion and modernisation of the economies of developing countries. The Committee recognised that 'at the present state of knowledge, the intricate links permeating the process of development are not all amenable to quantification on the basis of a common framework'. Ten years later, in 1980, the Report of the Independent Commission on International Developments Issues (the Brandt Commission) dealt with the matter under the heading 'What Does Development Mean?', stating that 'the focus has to be not on machines or institutions but on people', and

---

and co-operations. For an analysis of the emerging rules in this area, see M. Bulajic *Principles of International Development Law* (1986).

5. An illustration is that of the United Nations Industrial Development Organisation (UNIDO), established in 1966, and restructured as a specialised agency with a constitution that came into force in mid-1985, in which year its first General Conference of over 100 members was held. Its principal functions are to promote and accelerate the industrialisation of developing countries, and to raise the world share of developing countries in manufacturing production. See Henkin, Pugh, Schachter and Smit *International Law; Cases and Materials* (2nd edn, 1987) pp 1229–1230.

added: 'One must avoid the persistent confusion of growth with development, and we strongly emphasise that the prime objective of development is to lead to self-fulfilment and creative partnership in the use of a nation's productive forces and its full human potential'.

As these general objectives have to be tailored to the requirements of each individual developing country, the difficulty in framing general rules of law as to development can be appreciated.

Ten objectives, which may be regarded as standards of development, were proposed in the Report in 1969 of the Commission on International Development[6] established by the President of the World Bank Group, namely:

1. The creation of a framework for free and equitable trade, involving the abolition by developed countries of import duties and excessive taxes on those primary commodities which they themselves do not produce.
2. The promotion of private foreign investment, with offsetting of special risks for investors.
3. Increases in aid should be directed at helping the developing countries to reach a path of self-sustained growth.
4. The volume of aid should be increased to a target of 1% of the gross national product of the donor countries.
5. Debt relief should be a legitimate form of aid.
6. Procedural obstacles should be identified and removed.
7. The institutional basis of technical assistance should be strengthened.
8. Control of the growth of population.
9. Greater resources should be devoted to education and research.
10. Development aid should be increasingly multilateralised. Such multi-lateralisation would contribute to a uniform development of the principles governing the grant and receipt of aid.

On 24 October 1970, the United Nations General Assembly adopted a policy statement under the title of the 'International Development Strategy', to be applied during the Second Development Decade (1971–1980). This laid down desiderata consistent with the above-mentioned ten objectives, including the requirement that economically advanced countries should endeavour to provide by 1972, if possible, 1% of their gross national product in aid to the developing countries. In the light of experience during the Second Development Decade, the United Nations General Assembly, at its Eleventh Special Session in August–September 1980, in proclaiming a Third United Nations Development Decade to commence on 1 January 1981, adopted a similar policy statement, namely, an International Development Strategy for that Decade, in which far-reaching policy measures and methods for achieving optimum development were outlined. The facts that a Third Decade was proclaimed and a new Strategy for that Decade was adopted serve to emphasise that development is and will be a continuing problem for the international community for many years to come.

The cornerstone of the present evolving law of development is the institutional structure, heterogeneous as it is, which contributes to making possible development on an international scale. The various principal organisations,

6. The Report has become known as the 'Pearson Report', by reason of Mr Lester Pearson's chairmanship of the Commission.

bodies, and agencies involved in the process include the United Nations, working through such organs and channels as the United Nations Conference on Trade and Development (UNCTAD) and the United Nations Development Programme (UNDP), the related agencies of the United Nations including the International Bank for Reconstruction and Development and its affiliates, the United Nations Industrial Development Organisation (UNIDO) the Development Assistance Committee of the Organisation for Economic Co-operation and Development (OECD), the European Economic Community, and the Committee of the Colombo Plan for Co-operative and Economic and Social Development in Asia and the Pacific (which Plan was inaugurated in July 1951). In addition, an important role is played by the regional development banks, such as the Asian Development Bank, the Inter-American Development Bank and the African Development Bank. One area of the international law of development is represented by the rules and practice that are evolving for the co-ordination of the efforts of these different agencies. Not to be overlooked also, in this connection, are the regulations governing the various funds and financial facilities involved in the process, either of development assistance or of trade stabilisation in respect to developing countries.

The problem of development concerns not only developing countries, but also under-developed regions in developed countries. This is well illustrated by the efforts made within the framework of the European Communities, by such measures as the establishment of a European Regional Development Fund and a European Investment Bank, to provide finance, resources and other assistance for under-developed areas in Community member countries.[7]

Development, while it has primarily concerned the operations of the International Bank for Reconstruction and Development ('the World Bank'), has also required support from the other Bretton Woods institution, the International Monetary Fund (IMF). While the Bank and the IMF do not exactly work in tandem, their roles in the domain of development are characterised by what is said to be 'complementarity'. In the course of the last two decades, during which the world economy has suffered afflictions with an inevitable impact upon developing countries, three important concepts have emerged in the development work of both the Bank and the Fund, namely: (i) adjustment; (ii) structural adjustment; and (iii) conditionality.

The term 'adjustment' denotes a process or programme in the particular developing country receiving support, whereby that country is encouraged to follow policies aimed at achieving a better balance of payments equilibrium and more lasting economic growth; this would involve normally greater domestic price stability, control over budget deficits, and rational allocation of resources.[8] The aim is more orderly economic management warranting assistance from the IMF and, if necessary, from the Fund.

'Structural adjustment' refers to a programme of reforms designed to enable the developing country to achieve a more permanent ability to cope with the external economic environment, including sustained growth, rationalisation of

7.   See *Regional Development and the Economic Community* (European Community Doc 8/81, European File series, April 1981).
8.   See passim *Theoretical Aspects of the Design of Fund-Supported Adjustment Programs* IMF Occasional Paper No. 55, September 1987.

the scope of the public sector, providing incentives for the private sector, and increasing the efficiency of use of resources.[9] The reforms can extend to institutions and to technology.

'Conditionality' signifies a requirement by the IMF that a country making use of the Fund's resources should carry out an economic policy programme aimed at producing a 'viable' balance of payments position over an appropriate period of time.[10] The requirement is not rigid and absolute, but tailored to the specific set of circumstances.

3. PROTECTION AND IMPROVEMENT OF THE HUMAN ENVIRONMENT

It is a commonplace now that a crisis of global proportions is, and has been affecting the human environment, through pollution of the atmosphere and of maritime, coastal, and inland waters, through degradation of rural lands, through destruction of the ecological balance of natural areas, through the effect of biocides upon animal and plant life, and through the uncontrolled depletion and ravaging of the world's natural resources, partly by reason of the explosive growth of human populations and partly as a result of the demands of industrial technology. The problems involved in this environmental crisis, and the various causes and factors which brought it about were analysed in detail by the Secretary-General of the United Nations in a Report on the Problems of the Human Environment, dated 26 May 1969 (Document E/4667), prepared in relation to the summoning of the Stockholm Conference of June 1972 on the Human Environment (see below), pursuant to a Resolution of the United Nations General Assembly of 3 December 1968. In a subsequent Resolution of 15 December 1969, the United Nations General Assembly endorsed the Report, assigned to the Secretary-General overall responsiblity for organising and preparing the Conference, and established a 27-member Preparatory Committee to assist him.

The Report identified three basic causes as responsible for the deterioration of the environment, namely, accelerated population growth, increased urbanisation, and an expanded and efficient new technology, with their associated increase in demands for space, food, and natural resources (see paragraph 8 of the Report).

As was stressed by the Secretary-General, the subject had to date been dealt with by international law-making conventions in only a fragmentary manner, with room for much progress. Illustrations of such piecemeal measures were at that time provided by article IX of the Treaty of 1967 on the Principles Governing the Activities of States in the Exploration and Use of Outer Space including the Moon and Celestial Bodies, obliging states parties to conduct space studies and exploration in such manner as to avoid adverse changes in the environment of the earth from the introduction of extra-terrestrial matter, by the African Convention on the Conservation of Natural Resources adopted by the

9. *Finance and Development* June 1987, p 12 (article by Marcelo Selowsky).
10. *IMF Survey, Supplement on the fund* September 1985, p 1.

Organisation for African Unity (OAU) in 1968, by the International Convention of 1954, as amended, for the Prevention of the Pollution of the Sea by Oil, by the International Plant Protection Convention of 1951, by the two Brussels Conventions of 29 November 1969, relating to Intervention on the High Seas in cases of Oil Pollution Casualties and on Civil Liability for Oil Pollution Damage,[11] and by a number of arrangements designed to control pollution in particular river systems. The Nuclear Weapons Tests Ban Treaty of 1963,[12] the Treaty of 1967 for the Prohibition of Nuclear Weapons in Latin America, the Treaty of 1968 on the Non-Proliferation of Nuclear Weapons,[13] and the Treaty of 1971 on the Prohibition of the Emplacement of Nuclear Weapons on the Seabed and Ocean Floor and Subsoil Thereof,[14] could at that time also be regarded as measures of environmental protection, insofar as their object was to prevent radioactive contamination of the environmental areas to which they related. Also paragraph 11 of the General Assembly's Declaration of 17 December 1970, of Principles Governing the Seabed and the Ocean Floor, and the Subsoil Thereof beyond the Limits of National Jurisdiction,[15] affirmed that states were to take appropriate measures for, and co-operate in establishing a régime to govern the prevention of pollution and contamination to the marine evironment, and of interference with the ecological balance of this environment, and to govern also the protection and conservation of the natural resources of the seas, and the prevention of damage to the flora and fauna of the marine environment. As pointed out in Chapter 9, above, this Declaration contributed towards the developments which led ultimately to the adoption on 10 December 1982 of the United Nations Convention on the Law of the Sea, which contained Part XII on the Protection and Preservation of the Marine Environment (articles 192–237).

The Secretary-General's Report also detailed the various activities of the related or specialised agencies of the United Nations, bearing upon the human environment (see Annex to the Report). These included, for example, various standard-setting instruments (Recommendations and Codes) of the International Labour Organisation (ILO) for protection of workers against pollution of the working atmospheric environment, or against radioactive contamination (eg the Convention on Protection of Workers against Ionising Radiations); the work of the Food and Agriculture Organisation of the United Nations (FAO) in the domain of water development, management, and conservation, of conservation and development of plant resources, and of the scientific aspects of marine pollution; the studies on the scientific problems of the environment under the auspices of the United Nations Scientific, Educational and Cultural Organisation (UNESCO), including the Conference of 1968 convened by it on the Scientific Basis for Rational Use and Conservation of the Resources of the Biosphere; the work of the World Health Organisation (WHO) in the definition of environmental standards, the identification of environmental hazards, and the study of induced changes in the environment; and investigations by the

11. See pp 229-230 above.
12. See p 160 above.
13. See pp 283-284 above.
14. See p 230 above.
15. See p 231 above.

International Civil Aviation Organisation (ICAO) of the problems of aircraft noise in the vicinity of airports, and of sonic boom due to supersonic aircraft.

It emerged from the Secretary-General's Report that international regulatory action was in principle appropriate for the following:

a. Problems of pollution and contamination of the oceans and atmosphere, partly because these might be the object of general use, partly because of the impossibility in certain cases of localising the effects of polluting or contaminating agents.

b. Wild species and nature reserves, upon the basis that these are a common heritage of mankind. International agreement might be necessary to control the export, import, and sale of endangered species.

c. The depletion of marine resources, having regard to the dependence of mankind upon the sea as a source of protein.

d. The monitoring of changes in the earth's atmosphere, climate, and weather conditions.

e. The definition of international standards of environmental quality.

f. Reciprocal controls of, and restraints upon certain industrial operations in all countries, where such operations could endanger the environment, so as to remove inducements to obtain competitive advantages by ignoring the consequences of the processes which were a hazard to the environment.[16] Precedents for international action in this case were represented by International Labour Conventions, one of the aims of which is to ensure that economic competition between states does not thwart the realisation of proper standards of working conditions.

4. STOCKHOLM CONFERENCE OF 1972 ON THE HUMAN ENVIRONMENT

The historic United Nations Conference on the Human Environment which met at Stockholm from 5–16 June 1972, pursuant to the United Nations General Assembly's above-mentioned Resolution of 3 December 1968, represented the first major effort to solve the global problem of protection and improvement of the human environment by international agreement on as universal a level as possible.

The principal decisions, resolutions, and recommendations of the Conference were as follows:

1. A resolution in plenary session condemning nuclear weapons tests, especially those carried out in the atmosphere, and calling on states intending to carry out such tests to refrain from doing so, as these might lead to further contamination of the environment.[17]

---

16. See Report, para 75.
17. See also the first sentence of Principle 26 of the Declaration on the Human Environment adopted by the Conference: 'Man and his environment must be spared the effects of nuclear weapons and all other means of mass destruction'.

2. A unanimous recommendation that a World Environment Day be observed on 5 June each year.

3. A so-called 'Action Plan' for the protection and enhancement of the environment. This Plan was in effect a grouping in a more or less logical fashion of all recommendations for international action adopted by the Conference. The rearrangement involved three parts, an 'Earthwatch' programme to identify problems of international significance so as to warn against impending environmental crises; recommendations concerning 'environmental manage-ment', or in other words the application in practice of what was shown to be desirable or necessary in regard to the environment; and 'supporting measures' such as education, training, public information, and finance. 'Earthwatch' was to encompass not only a projected network of atmospheric monitoring stations, but also existing programmes of international bodies for the detection of climatic changes and of marine pollution. An interesting recommendation was that for an International Referral Service to provide liaison between those persons or institutions seeking environmental information, on the one hand, and persons or institutions, on the other hand, able to furnish the information desired.

Other important recommendations were directed to the identification and control of pollutants. In that connection, reference should be made to Recommendation 79 which was to the following effect:

a. That approximately ten baseline stations be set up, with the consent of the states involved, in areas remote from all sources of pollution, in order to monitor long-term global trends in atmospheric constituents and properties which may cause changes in meteorological properties, including climatic changes.
b. That a much larger network of not less than 100 stations be set up, with the consent of the states involved, for monitoring properties and constituents of the atmosphere on a regional basis and especially changes in the distribution and concentration of contaminants.
c. That these programmes be guided and co-ordinated by the World Meteorological Organisation.

It may be said that the main contribution of the 'Action Plan' lay in its emphasis upon national and international action and co-operation for the identification and appraisal of environment dangers and problems of global significance.

4. The adoption of the Declaration on the Human Environment. This Declaration may be regarded as doing for the protection of the environment of the earth what the Universal Declaration of Human Rights of 1948 accomplished for the protection of human rights and fundamental freedoms, that is to say it was essentially a manifesto, expressed in the form of an ethical code, intended to govern and influence future action and programmes, both at the national and international levels. Although the Declaration was adopted by acclamation by the Conference, its fate lay in the balance until the last day of the session, when adoption took place. The text was the subject of intensive and protracted discussion, involving fifteen meetings of the Working Group on the Declaration.

Partly this was due to dissatisfaction with the draft prepared by the Working Group, partly to a torrent of amendments which endangered the balance of consensus underlying the text, and partly to the injection of highly political issues.[18]

It must be acknowledged that the Declaration on the Human Environment is an uneven document—certainly more uneven and less precisely drafted than the Universal Declaration of Human Rights of 1948—so that there is some ground for the dissatisfaction expressed at the Conference. The text represents an odd mixture of political declarations, scientific generalities, banalities, propositions of international law, and well-phrased environmental guidelines. It was divided into two Parts, a Preamble proclaiming certain truths about the human environment and an operative part, enunciating 26 principles to govern international and national action in the environmental field. A large number of these merely enunciate non-controversial environmental guidelines or truisms, such as Principle 2, that the natural resources of the earth must be safeguarded for the benefit of present and future generations through careful planning or management, as appropriate, Principle 3, that the capacity of the earth to produce vital renewable resources must be maintained and wherever practicable, restored or improved, and Principle 18, that science and technology, as part of their contribution to economic and social development, must be applied to the identification, avoidance and control of environmental risks and the solution of environmental problems and for the common good of mankind. There was perhaps some value in codifying these by general consensus. States are not committed in a legally binding manner to observe any of these principles, however much they corresponded to the consensus of the Conference. The non-mandatory nature of the Declaration was reflected in the different descriptions of it by delegates and writers as:

a.   an 'aspirational' document;
b.   a platform for future action;
c.   a moral code;
d.   a first step towards the development of international environmental law; and
e.   the recognition and acceptance of an 'environmental ethic'. Some think that the main value of the Declaration lay in its future educational effects.

5.   Recommendations were made to the United Nations General Assembly for the creation of new international machinery. The Conference did not approve the establishment of a new major international organisation, but favoured instead the setting up of a United Nations Environment Programme (UNEP), with a Governing Council for Environmental Programmes, elected triennially by the General Assembly on the basis of equitable geographical distribution, to act as a central organ, with its operations annually reviewed by the Economic and Social Council and the General Assembly. The Council promotes environmental co-operation among governments, and guides and co-ordinates the existing environmental work being done by various international organisations, which

18. See also Louis B. Sohn 'The Stockholm Declaration on the Human Environment' (1973) 14 Harvard ILJ 423 at pp 430–431.

continue to carry on as before within the ambit of their responsibilities. The Council is supported by a small Environment Secretariat, which co-ordinates United Nations programmes, advises international organisations, secures the co-operation of world scientists, and submits plans, both medium-range and long-term, for United Nations action.

6. The Conference recommended that the draft articles of a Convention on Ocean Dumping be referred for adoption to a Conference to be convened by the United Kingdom towards the end of 1972 (see below). The United Kingdom delegation had stressed the necessity for a convention to prevent marine pollution by the ocean dumping of wastes, and for a world programme to make rivers cleaner. It was felt that such a convention would represent a major step towards reducing marine pollution, notwithstanding the views of certain marine biologists that the bulk of the pollution of the seas was not due to dumping, or the emptying of wastes from rivers, but to the deposit of wind-blown materials from the land. Another significant recommendation was that a Conference be summoned to prepare and adopt a convention on the exports and imports of certain species of wild animals and plants, primarily with a view to conservation (see below).

7. It was recommended that the General Assembly should decide to convene a second United Nations Conference on the Human Environment, preparations in respect to which should be carried out by the environmental machinery referred to above. This was realised by the Rio Conference, held in 1992 (see below).

Before the Conference, the link between development, on the one hand, and environmental considerations, on the other hand, mentioned at the commencement of this chapter, had been foreseen,[19] and indeed had occasioned some controversy about the drafting of the Declaration on the Human Environment by the Inter-Governmental Working Group, during the preparatory work for the Conference, when the Preparatory Committee for the Conference had felt that the first draft unduly dissociated environmental issues from the general framework of development and development planning.[20] Few persons would, however, have predicted that the link between development and the environment would have become so dominant an issue at the Stockholm Conference in 1972. Delegate after delegate from the developing and other countries urged that the preservation of the environment should not be at the expense of development in the developing countries, or be used as a pretext for discriminatory practices in trade or otherwise affecting these countries, that new industries in developing countries should not be compelled to bear the costs of anti-pollution campaigns, and that the protection of the environment should be integrated with development planning. This fear of environmental 'neo-protectionism' and this stress upon the overriding importance of development were ultimately reflected in the texts of the 'Action Plan' and of the Declaration on the Human Environment. At least eight important 'Action Plan' recommendations for international action were coloured by this emphasis upon the development-environment relationship, including recommendations that

19. See, eg, 22nd Report of the Commission to Study the Organisation of Peace (Louis B. Sohn, Chairman) on the United Nations and the Human Environment, April 1972, pp 21–27.
20. See Louis B. Sohn, article, loc cit, p 428.

'environmental concerns' should not be invoked by governments as a pretext for trade discrimination or for reduced access to markets, that the emergence of tariff and non-tariff barriers to trade as a result of environmental policies ought to be monitored and reported upon by the competent international bodies, and—more controversially—that if environmental concerns or standards should lead to trade restrictions upon or adversely affect exports from developing countries, appropriate measures for compensation should be worked out.

The link between development and the environment found expression in two recitals in the Preamble to the Declaration on the Human Environment (see recital 4 which affirms that environmental problems are caused by under-development, and recital 7 which advocates international co-operation to raise resources to help developing countries meet their environmental responsibilities), and in no less than nine principles in the second part of the Declaration, namely Principles 8–14,[1] 20 and 23, declaring, inter alia, that environmental policies should enhance the development of developing countries, and be integrated with development planning, and that environmental standards might not always be appropriate for developing countries.

It is clear then that the necessities and problems of development must for some time continue as an obstacle to the growth of generalised rules of international law for the environment. Moreover, according to their special approach, developing countries attach importance to the social environment as well as to the physical environment (see, eg, the condemnation of apartheid and of racial discrimination in Principle 1 of the Declaration on the Human Environment).

In Principles 21 and 22 of the Declaration on the Human Environment, three principles of international law were proclaimed:

1. States have a sovereign right to exploit their own resources pursuant to their own environmental policies.
2. States are responsible for ensuring that activities within their jurisdiction or control do not cause damage to the environment of other states, or of areas beyond the limits of national jurisdiction.[2]
3. States are under a duty to co-operate to develop further the international law as to liability and compensation for the victims of pollution and other environmental damage caused by such activities to areas beyond national jurisdiction.

It is clear that, apart from all its worthwhile results, the Stockholm Conference served to identify those areas in which rules of international environmental law, acceptable to the international community as a whole, can be laid down, and as well as those areas in which the formation of environmental rules must encounter

1. For commentary on these Principles, see Louis B. Sohn, article, loc cit, pp 464–474.
2. For commentary on this principle of international law, see Louis B. Sohn, article, loc cit, pp 485–593. Cf the principle in the *Trail Smelter Case (US v Canada)* (1938) *United Nations Reports of International Arbitral Awards* Vol III, p 1905, which is confined to damage to the environment of neighbouring States, whereas the principle enunciated in the Declaration on the Human Environment extends to damage in areas beyond the limits of national jurisdiction (eg high seas). As to the developing principles in the subject, see C. Flinterman, B. Kwiatkowska and J. G. Lammers (eds) *Transboundary Air Pollution* (1986). There is a trend towards dealing with trans-border pollution by bilateral treaties or bilateral agreement; eg, the Bulgaria-Romania agreement of 20 February 1988 to take joint measures to prevent cross-border atmospheric pollution.

serious obstacles. To that extent, it provided foundations for the development of international environmental law.

Some of the principal decisions and recommendations of the Conference were implemented subsequently by resolutions of the United Nations General Assembly at its 27th session later in 1972. By the main resolution 2997 (XXVII) adopted on 15 December 1972, and bearing the title 'Institutional and Financial Arrangements for International Environmental Co-operation', the General Assembly broadly gave effect to the organisational recommendations made at Stockholm. The executive body of the United Nations Environment Programme (UNEP) was, as proposed at Stockholm, to be a representative Governing Council, with a mandate 'to keep under review the world environmental situation'. The Council was, as previously recommended, to be supported by an Environment Secretariat—to be headed by an Executive Director—and backed financially by a voluntary Environment Fund. In order to provide for the most efficient co-ordination of United Nations Environmental programmes, the resolution provided for the establishment of an Environmental Co-ordination Board under the chairmanship of the Executive Director, and under the auspices and within the framework of the Administrative Committee on Co-ordination of the United Nations. By other resolutions, the General Assembly designated 5 June as World Environment Day, referred the main recommendations of the Stockholm Conference to the newly established Governing Council, emphasised that in the exploration, exploitation, and development of their natural resources states must not produce significant harmful effects in zones situated outside their national jurisdiction, decided to hold a Conference on Human Settlements in 1975, later scheduled to meet at Vancouver in 1976 (see below as to this Conference), and determined that the Environment Secretariat should be located in Nairobi, Kenya, by way of preference for a site in a developing country.

With regard to the draft Convention on Ocean Dumping which was before the Conference, and which was to be referred for adoption to a later diplomatic conference to be convened at the end of 1972, such conference actually met at London from 30 October to 13 November 1972. The text of a Convention on the Prevention of Marine Pollution by Dumping of Wastes and Other Matter was adopted and opened for signature; it entered into force on 30 August 1975. The Convention binds the states parties individually and collectively to promote the effective control of all sources of pollution of the marine environment, and to take all practicable steps to prevent the pollution of the sea by the dumping of harmful wastes which may affect health, injure living resources and marine life, or damage amenities (article I), while also the states parties are to take effective measures individually, according to their scientific, technical and economic capabilities, and collectively, to prevent marine pollution caused by dumping, and are to harmonise their policies in this regard (article II). In an important Annex I the Convention listed matter and items, the dumping of which should be absolutely prohibited. Thus the Convention has covered one of the most important environmental areas for which the Stockholm Conference was summoned in the first place.

Apart from the last-mentioned convention, the following instruments, conventions, or declaratory documents have been concluded or adopted since the Stockholm Conference, to deal with matters of a direct or indirect bearing upon the protection or improvement of the human environment and upon the quality of human life:

a. The Convention for the Protection of the World Cultural and Natural Heritage, adopted at Paris on 16 November 1972, under the auspices of the United Nations Educational Scientific and Cultural Organisation (UNESCO).

b. The Convention on International Trade in Endangered Species of Wild Fauna and Flora, concluded at Washington on 3 March 1973.

c. The International Convention for the Prevention of Pollution from Ships, and its six Annexes and two Protocols, concluded on 2 November 1973, together with the related Convention of 1974 on the Prevention of Marine Pollution from Landbased Sources.

d. The Action Plan adopted by the United Nations World Population Conference at Bucharest, Romania, 19–30 August 1974, containing statements and recommendations directed to the control of population growth, and related demographic goals, and calling, inter alia, for the continuous monitoring of population trends by the United Nations, but involving no binding commitments for States in this area.

e. The Convention on Long-Range Trans-Boundary Air Pollution, done at Geneva on 13 November 1979, and the Protocol of 1992.

f. The United Nations Convention Law on the Sea of 10 December 1982, containing its Part XII on the Protection and Preservation of the Marine Environment, which Part consists of articles 192–237.[3]

g. The World Charter for Nature, adopted in 1982 by United Nations General Assembly Resolution 37/7, a non-binding instrument directing efforts to ensure genetic viability through the maintenance of the population levels of all life forms, wild and domesticated, sufficient for their survival.

h. The Convention for the Protection of the Ozone Layer, concluded at Vienna in 1985, and the Protocol on Substances that Deplete the Ozone Layer, done at Montreal in 1987 (further amended in 1990 and 1992) limiting the use of chlorofluorocarbons (CFCs) which deplete the ozone layer and contribute to 'the greenhouse effect' warming the earth's atmosphere. An important step in assisting the developing countries in implementing the Convention and Protocol was taken by the World Bank in 1991 in establishing the Global Environment Facility.[4]

i. The Vienna Conventions on Early Notification of a Nuclear Accident, and on Assistance in the Case of a Nuclear Accident or Radiological Emergency, both concluded in 1986.

j. The Basel Convention on the Control of Transboundary Movements of Hazardous Wastes and Their Disposal, 1989.

k. The Wellington Convention for the Prohibition of Fishing with Long Driftnets in the South Pacific, 1989.

l. The International Convention on Oil Pollution Preparedness, response and Co-operation, signed at London in 1990.

3. As to these provisions, see Chapter 9, above, pp 254-256.
4. For documentation see (1991) 30 ILM 1735.

m. The United Nations Convention on Environmental Impact Assessment in a Transboundary Context, 1991.

n. The United Nations Convention on Transboundary Watercourses and International Lakes, 1992.

o. The Rio Declaration on the Environment and Development, 1992, and the three associated instruments: the Framework Convention on Climate Change, the Convention on Biological Diversity, and the Statement of Principles for a Global Consensus on the Management, Conservation, and Sustainable Development of All Types of Forests. (See further below).

In addition to the above there have also been numerous conventions concerned with the environment concluded on the bilateral and regional levels.

Following its initial session in 1973, the Governing Council of the United Nations Environment Programme (UNEP) was in the first instance concerned with the establishment of necessary machinery, the determination of priority areas for action, and the approval or implementation of projects calling for special attention. Machinery matters included initially the creation of an International Habitat and Human Settlements Foundation within the UNEP framework for the improvement of housing and community conditions for the world's disadvantaged peoples, and the activation of two important components of the 'Earthwatch' system, namely, on the one hand, a Global Environment Monitoring System (GEMS) for monitoring the more dangerous and injurious pollutants, and focussing otherwise on the long-range transport of pollutants, renewable natural resources, climate, health and water quality, and, on the other hand, as mentioned above, an International Referral System for Sources of Environmental Information (INFOTERRA), to constitute a global directory and network of information sources and information seekers, thereby facilitating access to knowledge and experience as to environmental matters. INFOTERRA has grown in the period since its establishment to a network of over 100 partner countries with established National Focal Points (NFPs) that co-ordinate national INFOTERRA activities. In connection with INFOTERRA, there is published annually an *International Directory of Sources* by the INFOTERRA Programme Activity Centre (PAC). INFOTERRA has contributed towards satisfying the world demand for precise information on environmental planning, development and technology. Another network established within the framework of UNEP has been the International Register of Potentially Toxic Chemicals (IRPTC), an important component of Earthwatch, which disseminates, through national correspondents and others, information on hazardous chemicals, and since 1980 has been concerned with the trans-boundary transport and disposal of hazardous wastes. Mention should also be made of the International Programme on Chemical Safety and of the Background Atmospheric Pollution Monitoring System.

One of the main achievements of UNEP[5] has been the United Nations Conference on Human Settlements held at Vancouver, 31 May–11 June 1976,

5. See article by T. C. Bacon 'The Role of UNEP in the Development of International Environmental Law' (1974) 12 Can YIL 255 at pp 260–261; and cf L. A. Teclaff and A. E. Utton (eds) *International Environmental Law* (1974) ch 4. Detailed information as to the work of UNEP in its initial years may be found in its *Annual Reviews* (see particularly the UNEP *Annual Review*

known familiarly as the 'Habitat Conference', which represented another significant step in giving effect to the principles proclaimed at the Stockholm Conference. The Conference will be remembered, in addition to its numerous wide-ranging recommendations, for the Declaration on Human Settlements adopted by it; this was a kind of manifesto, a programmatic charter in 55 paragraphs analogous to the Universal Declaration of Human Rights of 1948, serving to mark a first phase in the progress towards the establishment in due course of effective machinery and the acceptance of more specific rules and standards in the domain of human settlements. The Declaration sets out principles that are designed to prevent aggravation of the deteriorating circumstances of vast numbers of people in human settlements, to achieve action at both the national and international levels to deal with such factors as uncontrolled urbanisation, rural backwardness and dispersion, and to attend to the basic needs of disadvantaged peoples for food, shelter, clean water, and leisure. It can thus be seen that underlying the Declaration on Human Settlements is the general principle of respect for human rights, a principle intimately connected with the evolution of rules of international law as to the interrelated subjects of development and the environment.[6]

Dealing generally with the work of UNEP since 1977, it may be said that UNEP has served primarily as a catalyst agency[7] to encourage and co-ordinate national and regional environment protection activities, rather than itself engaging in implementation of environmental projects. True, it has been instrumental in the setting up of working groups of experts in specialised fields, in the publication of documentation and its dissemination, and in the systematic collation of information. The functions of UNEP were in this initial period 1977–1982 much more of a promotional than of an operational nature. Within these limitations, it nonetheless achieved much. Some examples may be referred to. In 1978, it sought to achieve formulations of principles to guide states with respect to co-operation as to shared resources, and with respect to problems of liability and compensation for pollution and environmental damage. In 1978–1979, UNEP took the initiative of proposing a World Conservation Strategy in regard to living resources; this was formally endorsed by the United Nations General Assembly in 1979 and was successfully launched in 34 countries in March 1980, with general endorsement from governments and scientists. Another domain of activity in this period was the regional seas programme; for instance, in 1978 it convened a regional Conference, as a result of which the eight coastal states in the Kuwait region adopted an Action Plan for the protection and development of the marine environment and coastal areas, and also adopted and signed a Kuwait Regional Convention on the subject, together with a Protocol for Co-operation in Combating Oil Pollution and Pollution by other Harmful Substances. In 1981 a similar regional Conference was convened for

---

1980, passim) and in its valuable publication UNEP Report No 2 (1981) under the title *Environmental Law; An In-Depth Review*.
6. See also W. Paul Gormley *Human Rights and Environment; The Need for International Co-operation* (1976) passim.
7. In para 10 of the Nairobi Declaration of 18 May 1982 (see below), UNEP was described as 'the major catalytic instrument for global environmental co-operation' (see the *Report* of the Governing Council of UNEP on its *Tenth Session* (1982) p 51).

the West and Central African region, with the result that ten coastal states adopted an Action Plan, and a Convention and Protocol similar to the instruments adopted for Kuwait in 1978.

Commencing in 1979, UNEP was given the responsibility of administering three environmental trust funds, one for the protection of the Mediterranean against pollution, a second fund for the protection and development of the marine environment and coastal areas of Bahrain, Iran, Iraq, Kuwait, Oman, Qatar, Saudi Arabia and the United Arab Emirates, and a third fund for the Convention of 1973 on International Trade in Endangered Species of Wild Fauna and Flora.

In 1981 UNEP adopted a Programme for the Development and Periodic Review of Environmental Law, known as 'the Montevideo Programme'. The Programme was to be implemented by UNEP, the UNEP Environmental Law Unit, other UN agencies, and relevant intergovernmental and non-governmental organisations. The Programme has been broadly successful under the three categories of action envisaged: (1) the promotion of international conventions on various aspects of environmental protection; (2) the development of standard-setting by encouraging declarations of principles and guidelines by competent bodies; and (3) the provision of assistance to states in developing their legislative and executive powers in relation to the environment. The Montevideo Programme constituted a significant dynamic element in the lead-up to the United Nations Conference on the Environment and Development (UNCED) in 1992 (see below).

In order to commemorate the tenth anniversary of the Stockholm Conference of 1972, 105 states assembled at Nairobi from 10–18 May 1982, and adopted a special Declaration, known as the 'Nairobi Declaration' on 18 May 1982.[8] Apart from this Declaration, other significant resolutions were adopted, including one for the creation of a special commission to propose long-term environmental strategies for achieving 'sustainable development to the year 2000 and beyond'.[9]

The Governing Council of UNEP has continued to formulate programmes and priorities in the following areas among others: (a) the better development of human settlements, taking advantage of improved technology; (b) human and environmental health, free of hazards to humans; (c) integration of the management of ecosystems, encouraging these where sustainable; (d) the continued protection and enhancement of the marine environment; (e) ensuring that governments and other bodies have regard to environmental considerations in development planning (see the early part of this chapter); (f) the prevention of, or the mitigation of the consequences of, natural disasters; (g) the use of environmentally sound forms of energy; (h) plans to combat desertification; (i) the development of guidelines and principles for the harmonious utilisation by States of shared natural resources and of offshore mining and drilling. The sharing of natural resources with developing countries is now considered as one of the possible solutions to overcome the tendency of such countries to prefer

8. For the text of the Declaration, see the *Report* of the Governing Council of UNEP on its *Tenth Session* (1982) pp 49–51. The Nairobi Declaration was supplemented by the elaborate World Charter for Nature (on conservation of nature) adopted by the UN General Assembly in a Resolution of 20 October 1982.
9. Ibid, p 41.

exploitation of their own resources for their much needed gain as against the application of principles of environmental protection.

By way of complementing, in effect, the work of the above-mentioned Intergovernmental Committee on New and Renewable Sources of Energy, UNEP has supported various pilot projects for producing energy from the sun, wind and household and agricultural wastes, and, as well, a comprehensive study on the environmental impact of the production, use and transport of various types of energy. In 1987 the Governing Council endorsed a long-term programme of international environmental strategies under the title of a 'World Environmental Perspective to the Year 2000 and Beyond'.

Perhaps the most notable achievement of UNEP in the period 1984–1988 was its sponsorship of the historic Vienna International Convention for the Protection of the Ozone Layer concluded in March 1985, and of the Protocol to that Convention signed at Montreal in September 1987. The Convention was designed to combat the threat to the ozone layer—a layer in the upper atmosphere serving to protect life on earth from the risks occasioned by ultra-violet radiation—by the control of the spread of chlorofluorocarbons (CFCs). Research also revealed that certain CFCs and certain halons used in chemical fire extinguishers might also result in a concentration in the upper atmosphere possibly culminating in a progressive warming of the earth's atmosphere, with the consequences of melting of polar icecaps causing rises in sea levels and, as well, far-reaching climatic changes. Broadly speaking, the Montreal Protocol provides for the halving by the year 2000 of the consumption of five kinds of CFCs and for a freeze on the consumption of three categories of halons. It is critical for the success of both instruments that all countries should co-operate meticulously in their implementation.

Another recent problem is that of so-called 'acid rain', capable of environmental damage damage to, inter alia, forests and crops. On the one hand, it may involve solely a matter of trans-border damage in one country caused allegedly by activities in an adjoining country; this could be solved possibly by bilateral treaty. On the other hand, there may be a group of countries affected by the scourge of acid rain, in which event a multilateral or regional treaty or convention becomes necessary.[10]

5. THE UNITED NATIONS CONFERENCE ON ENVIRONMENT AND DEVELOPMENT, 1992.

The United Nations Conference on Environment and Development (UNCED) took place at Rio de Janeiro on 3-14 June 1992. It was deliberately scheduled to occur in the year of the 20th anniversary of the Stockholm Conference on the Human Environment, 1972, and designed to build on that foundation with a particular focus on development. The preparatory document for UNCED, running to some 800 pages and negotiated by representatives of governments at frequent meetings between 1990 and 1992, was called 'Agenda 21', which

10. On the subject, see P. Ballantyne 'International Liability for Acid Rain' (1983) 41 Univ of Toronto L Rev pp 63–70.

was regarded as referring to the need to create a better environment for the 21st century but which, in some minds at least, perhaps also recalled Principle 21 of the Stockholm Declaration (see above).

Aside from the activities of UNEP, and of the Agenda 21 negotiations, the most important other influence on the Rio Conference was the Report of the World Commission on Environment and Development, commissioned by the United Nations General Assembly by Resolution 38/161 in December 1983. The Commission was chaired by Mrs Gro Harlem Brundtland, Prime Minister of Norway, and published its report — 'Our Common Future' — in 1987. Annexed to the report was a set of 'Proposed Legal Principles for Environmental Protection and Sustainable Development' prepared by a group of experts on environmental law.

Since so much preparatory work was done before the Conference, UNCED was comparatively brief in duration. The Conference achieved the following results[11]:

1. The opening for signature of the Framework Convention on Climate Change, the text of which had been adopted previously in New York on 9 May 1992. This Convention deals with the control of 'greenhouse gases' which affect the world's climate; these gases include not only carbon dioxide (such as in car exhaust fumes and industrial smoke) but also any gases that absorb and re-emit infra-red radiation. The chief feature of the Convention is the establishment of a procedure by which the parties will monitor and control the emission from their territories of greenhouse gases. The monitoring process includes the establishment of national inventories of, and reports on, the sources and sinks of gases (ie processes, activities or mechanisms which release or remove, respectively, into or from the atmosphere gases, aerosols, and their precursors), which will be subject to regular review by the parties.

2. The opening for signature of the Convention on Biological Diversity, the text of which had been adopted previously at Nairobi in 22 May 1992. This Convention aims to conserve biological diversity by obliging state parties to adopt national programmes, and to co-operate with each other, to protect against decline or extinction animal, plant, and microbial organisms, and to preserve them for sustainable human use. The United States declined to sign this Convention at Rio, stating its concerns regarding the Convention's provisions on the transfer of technology, intellectual property rights, biotechnology and biosafety, and other matters.

3. The adoption of the Statement of Principles for a Global Consensus on the Management, Conservation, and Sustainable Development of All Types of Forests. This Statement, which expressly states that it is 'non-binding', but also that it is 'authoritative', has a bearing not only on forests as a national and international resource but also on their functions as habitats of biological diversity and as sinks for greenhouse gases. Its careful wording reflects the difficulty of achieving a balance between conservation and sustainable

---

11. The texts of the Rio Declaration and of the associated Conventions and Declaration described below are printed in (1992) 31 ILM 814-887.

development on the one hand, and national economic, trade, and social policies on the other, and indicates the need for further work on the subject.

4.   The Rio Declaration on the Environment and Development, drafted at the preparatory meeting in March 1992 and not changed when adopted on 14 June 1992. The Declaration contains 27 Principles which aim to establish 'a new and equitable global partnership through the creation of new levels of co-operation among states, key sectors of societies, and people.' Of particular note are:

a.   '*Principle 2*. States have, in accordance with the Charter of the United Nations and the principles of international law, the sovereign right to exploit their own resources pursuant to their own environmental and developmental policies, and the responsibility to ensure that activities within their jurisdiction or control do not cause damage to the environment of other states or of areas beyond the limits of national jurisdiction.' This Principle repeats exactly the wording of Principle 21 of the Stockholm Declaration, 1972 (see above), but with the addition of the words 'and developmental [policies]'.

b.   '*Principle 3*. The right to development must be fulfilled so as to equitably meet developmental and environmental needs of present and future generations.' This statement reflects the principle of intergenerational equity, ie the notion that the environment must be managed and protected so as to continue to serve the needs of future generations of human beings.

c.   *Principles 5 and 6* link the problems of sustainable development, the eradication of poverty, and the granting of assistance to developing countries.

d.   *Principle 11* calls on all states to enact effective national laws for the protection of the environment. However, the Principle notes that 'standards applied by some countries may be inappropriate and of unwarranted economic and social cost to other countries, in particular developing countries.'

e.   '*Principle 13*. States shall develop national law regarding liability and compensation for the victims of pollution and other environmental damage. States shall also co-operate in an expeditious and more determined manner to develop further international law regarding liability and compensation for adverse effects of environmental damage caused by activities within their jurisdiction or control to areas beyond their jurisdiction.' This principle may be said to recognise the 'polluter pays' principle. It also recognises that much work remains to be done in order to develop the international law principles and rules on state responsibility (see Chapter 10 above).

f.   '*Principle 15*. In order to protect the environment, the *precautionary approach* shall be widely applied by states according to their capabilities. Where there are threats of serious or irreversible damage, lack of full scientific certainty shall not be used as a reason for postponing cost-effective measures to prevent environmental degradation.'

g.   *Principle 17* encourages the use of the instrument of environmental impact assessment in decision-making by national authorities on

   proposed activities likely to have a significant adverse effect on the
   environment.

h. *Principles 18 and 19* direct states to notify other states of natural
    disasters, emergencies, or activities having potential transboundary
    consequences and to consult with them at an early stage with a view to
    preventing those consequences.

The Agenda 21 negotiating process, which preceded the Rio Conference,
resulted also in the establishment of a new Commission on Sustainable
Development which will monitor and review progress and report to the United
nations Economic and Social Council.

   Considerations of space prevent discussion of an exhaustive nature regarding
the contribution of bodies other than UNEP to the protection of the environment.
However, reference may be made briefly to the participation of the International
Labour Organisation (ILO) and of the European Community in the processes
of international environmental protection. The ILO has been responsible,
following a decision by its Governing Body in 1982, for the establishment of an
International Occupational Safety and Health Alert System, which has operated
as a clearing-house for the transmission of warnings, or requests for information
to a world-wide network in regard to newly-discovered or suspected occupational
hazards. Moreover, the ILO has sought to promote and influence the widespread
application of what is known as an 'Environmentally Sound Technology' (EST),
ie a technology the object of which is to minimise the generation of pollution or
waste and, at the same time, to conserve resources liable to depletion. In another
area, the ILO has endeavoured to foster the environmental training of managers
and employers to ensure that they pay due regard to the human environment,
to environmental planning and to the planning of systems for the prevention of
pollution in and outside the workplace.[12] The European Community, on its side,
has by means of far-reaching directives followed since 1983 a more intensified
environmental policy.[13] This has included the observance of defined priorities,
namely, inter alia, the carrying out beforehand of environmental impact studies
before taking decisions that might affect the environment, the prevention of
pollution in the atmosphere, water or soil, action against noise nuisances, the
management of waste and dangerous chemical substances or processes, the
promotion of 'clean' technologies, the protection of the marine environment (the
North Sea and Mediterranean), control of energy supply and the conservation
of fauna and flora. The quality of the living environment is assured by the
designation of protected areas.

   The work of the International Maritime Organisation (IMO) in the
sponsorship of conventions on the pollution of the marine environment by ships
has been noted already above, and in Chapter 9. Other United Nations
Specialised Agencies, such as the Food and Agriculture Organisation (FAO), the
United Nations Educational, Scientific and Cultural Organisation (UNESCO),
and the International Atomic Energy Agency (IAEA), also play important roles
in promoting environmental objectives through their activities.

---

12. See passim H. Z. Evan *Employers and the Environmental Challenge* (1987).
13. See Johnson and Corelle *The Pollution Control Policy of the European Communities* (1979);
    Haigh *European Community Environmental Law in Practice*, 4 vols (1986).

There are numerous non-governmental organisations actively engaged in promoting concern for the environment, including Friends of the Earth, Greenpeace, and the World-Wide Fund for Nature. Of particular importance is the International Union for the Conservation of Nature (IUCN), founded in 1948; it is an unusual example of an organisation which includes governments, governmental agencies, and non-governmental groups in its membership. The IUCN operates the Environmental Law Centre in Bonn, and has collaborated with UNEP on a number of projects involved with the UNCED process.

6. NUCLEAR SAFETY AND THE ENVIRONMENT

The accident at the Chernobyl nuclear power plant in the Soviet Union on 25–26 April 1986 revealed a number of serious gaps and flaws in the rules of international law concerning nuclear safety and the environment, although the subject of the possible international environmental implications of such an accident had already been the subject of discussion by concerned experts as a consequence of the earlier 'Three Mile Island' accident in the United States. Chernobyl demonstrated definitively that the environmental damage to humans medically and to natural resources could be widespread across neighbouring countries, and led to a special session of the General Conference of the International Atomic Energy Agency (IAEA) in Vienna, where two previously unheralded historic Conventions were adopted on 26 September 1986, namely: (1) the convention on Early Notification of a Nuclear Accident or Radiological Emergency (entered into force on 27 October 1986); (2) the Convention on Assistance in the Event of a Nuclear Accident or Radiological Emergency (entered into force on 26 February 1987). Under the Notification Convention, a state party is bound to notify and inform states likely to be adversely affected and also the IAEA of a nuclear accident involving its civil and military facilities and activities, except nuclear weapons.[14] Five nuclear weapon states have indicated that they would, within the framework of the Convention, give notice of any nuclear accident which might have significant radiological effects in another state. The European Community was galvanised into taking appropriate action, in addition to already existing measures, to supplement the two Conventions in the Community region, and to ensure the safety of nuclear installations in use, as well as closer co-operation between members. Earlier, there had been concluded a Convention in 1979 on the Physical Protection of Nuclear Material, adopted as a result of one of the recommendations at the first Review Conference on the Nuclear Non-Proliferation Treaty of 1968 (NPT); this Convention entered into force on 26 February 1987. It binds parties to take measures to deter or defeat deliberate acts such as theft, sabotage or removal and use of nuclear materials, whether in transit, storage or otherwise.

Finally, there should be mention of: (a) the Treaty of 6 August 1985, signed by 14 Pacific states, establishing a South Pacific Nuclear Free Zone; (b) the

---

14. Cf the OECD publication, *Chernobyl and the Supply of Nuclear Reactors in OECD Countries* Report by a Nuclear Energy Agency Group of Experts (June 1987).

problem of removal of nuclear wastes; this is almost insoluble, if the aim is the complete elimination of hazards, insmuch as any disposal must to some extent affect the environment, marine or otherwise, selected as the final site for such wastes.[15]

15. Cf G. Handl 'Managing Nuclear Wastes: The International Connections' (1981) 21 Natural Resources Journal pp 621–690.

PART 4

International transactions

CHAPTER 15

The agents of international business: diplomatic envoys, consuls, and other representatives

1. DIPLOMATIC ENVOYS

Nearly all states today are represented in the territory of foreign states by diplomatic envoys and their staffs. Such diplomatic missions are of a permanent character, although the actual occupants of the office may change from time to time. Consequent on a development over some hundreds of years, the institution of diplomatic representatives has come to be the principal machinery by which intercourse between states is conducted.

The general rise of permanent as distinct from temporary diplomatic missions dates from the seventeenth century. The rights, duties, and privileges of diplomatic envoys continued to develop according to custom in the eighteenth century, and by the early nineteenth century the time was ripe for some common understanding on the subject, which as we shall see, took place at the Congress of Vienna in 1815. Developments in diplomatic practice since 1815 rendered necessary a new and more extensive codification[1] and formulation of the laws and usages as to diplomatic envoys, which was achieved in the Vienna Convention on Diplomatic Relations concluded on 18 April 1961.[2] Customary international law will, however, continue to govern questions not expressly regulated by the Convention (see Preamble). In the case of the *United States Diplomatic and Consular Staff in Tehran*,[3] the International Court of Justice described the rules of diplomatic law as 'a self-contained régime which, on the one hand, lays down the receiving state's obligations regarding the facilities, privileges and immunities to be accorded to diplomatic missions and, on the

1. In the case of the *United States Diplomatic and Consular Staff in Tehran* ICJ 1980, 3, para 45, the International Court of Justice referred to the Vienna Convention of 1961 on Diplomatic Relations as codifying the law of diplomatic relations. This seems to be only partially correct, as some provisions of the Convention cannot definitely be attributed to customary international law.
2. Based on Draft Articles prepared by the International Law Commission; for commentary thereon, which is applicable to the corresponding Articles of the Vienna Convention, see *Report* of the Commission on the Work of its *Tenth Session* (1958). Effect was given to the Vienna Convention in the United Kingdom by the Diplomatic Privileges Act 1964 and in the United States by the provisions of legislation of 1982, namely, USC §254a–e.
3. ICJ 1980, 3 at para 86.

other, foresees their possible abuse by members of the mission and specifies the means at the disposal of the receiving state to counter any such abuse'.

Classification of diplomatic envoys

Originally, some controversy centred around the classification of diplomatic representatives, particularly as regards matters of precedence and relative status. Ambassadors sent on a temporary mission were called 'Extraordinary' as contrasted with resident envoys. Later the title 'Extraordinary' was given to all Ambassadors whether resident or temporary, and the title of 'Plenipotentiary' was added to their designation. In its literal sense the term 'Plenipotentiary' signified that the envoy was fully empowered to transact business on behalf of the Head of State who had sent him on the mission.

The designation 'Envoy Extraordinary and Minister Plenipotentiary' came to be applied to almost all diplomatic representatives of the first rank, such as Ambassadors and ministers, with the exception of ministers resident. This titular nomenclature survives today, although the reasons for its use are not commonly appreciated.

The Congress of Vienna in 1815 attempted to codify the classifications and order of precedence of diplomatic envoys. This codification, better known as the 'Regulation of Vienna', was, subject to certain adjustments, incorporated in the provisions of articles 14 to 18 of the Vienna Convention on Diplomatic Relations of 18 April 1961. According to these provisions, heads of diplomatic mission are divided into three classes:

1. Ambassadors or nuncios accredited to Heads of State, and other heads of mission of equivalent rank.[4]
2. Envoys, ministers, and internuncios accredited to Heads of State.[5]
3. *Chargés d'affaires* accredited to Ministers for Foreign Affairs.

Except in matters of precedence and etiquette,[6] there is to be no differentiation between heads of mission by reason of their class. The class to which heads of their missions are to be assigned is to be agreed between states. Heads of mission are to take precedence in their respective classes in the order of the date and time of taking up their functions; for this purpose, they are considered as taking up their functions either when they have presented their credentials, or when they have notified their arrival and a true copy of their credentials has been presented to the Minister for Foreign Affairs of the receiving state, or other ministry according to the practice of this state. Alterations in the credentials of a head of mission not involving any change of class, are not to affect precedence.

4. This class does not include Legates, as previously under the Regulation of Vienna, because the new codification purports to deal only with heads of mission. Also, the provisions of article 2 of the Regulation of Vienna that only Ambassadors, Legates, or nuncios should possess the representative character in relation to the accrediting Head of State, were not adopted. The words 'other heads of mission of equivalent rank' would, semble, include Ambassadors accredited to international organisations (eg the United Nations and UNESCO) or to certain long-term conferences, eg an Ambassador for Disarmament.
5. No provision was made for the class of 'Ministers resident', which was established by the Conference at Aix-la-Chapelle in 1818, in modification of the Regulation of Vienna. As to this former class, see Twiss *The Law of Nations* (2nd edn, 1884) Vol I, p 344.
6. 'Etiquette' includes ceremonial matters, and matters of conduct or protocol.

These provisions as to precedence are to be without prejudice to any practice of the receiving state regarding the precedence of the representative of the Holy See. The procedure to be observed in each state for the reception of heads of mission is to be uniform in respect of each class.

The attribution of the title of Ambassador, as distinct from minister, to the head of a diplomatic mission depends on various factors, including the rank of the states concerned. Sometimes an embassy is a matter of tradition, as for example between France and Switzerland. Usually, however, now, the population and importance of the country of mission are the determining factors.[7] There are none the less many cases of anomalies in the allocation of embassies, which reflect a lack of uniformity of practice. This is illustrated, eg, by the appointment in recent years of Ambassadors-at-large and of Ambassadors as to disarmament questions. A distinctive mark of membership of the Commonwealth of Nations[8] is that an embassy of one member accredited to another is called a High Commission and the term High Commissioner substituted for ambassador.

Envoys on an ad hoc mission are usually furnished with a document of Full Powers[9] setting out their authority which in due course they present to the authorities of the state with whom negotiations are to be conducted, or to the Committee on Full Powers of the Conference at which they are to represent their country.

Appointment and reception of diplomatic envoys

The machinery of diplomacy used to be attended by a good deal of ceremony and ritual, and to a certain extent this still applies. Ceremonial procedure, for instance, is generally observed with regard to the arrival and departure of diplomatic envoys.

The appointment of an individual as Ambassador or minister is usually announced to the state to which he or she is accredited in certain official papers, with which the envoy is furnished, known as Letters of Credence or *Lettres de Créance*; these are for remission to the receiving state. Apart from the Letters of Credence envoys may take with them documents of Full Powers relating to particular negotiations or other specific written instructions.

States may refuse to receive diplomatic envoys either: (a) generally, or in respect to a particular mission of negotiation; or (b) because a particular envoy is not personally acceptable. In the latter case, the state declining to accept the envoy is not compelled to specify its objections to the accreditation or to justify them (see article 4, paragraph 2 of the Vienna Convention). Consequently, to avoid any such conflict arising, a state wishing to appoint a particular person as envoy must ascertain beforehand whether that person will be persona grata. Once such assent or *agrément* is obtained, the accrediting state is safe in proceeding with the formal appointment of its envoy. Nonetheless, at any later time, the receiving state may, without having to explain its decision, notify the sending

---

7. In its *Report*, op cit, the International Law Commission made significant mention of the growing tendency of most states today to appoint Ambassadors, rather than ministers, as heads of missions. The titular rank of minister is now, in fact, being used more and more for a responsible or senior member of the legation.
8. See above, p 105.
9. See also below, pp 407-408.

state that the envoy is persona non grata, in which case the envoy is recalled, or the envoy's functions are terminated (article 9 of the Vienna Convention).

Rights, privileges, and immunities of diplomatic envoys[10]

These are primarily based on the need to ensure the efficient performance of the functions of diplomatic missions (see Preamble to Vienna Convention), and to a secondary degree on the theory that a diplomatic mission personifies the sending state (the 'representative character' theory). The theory of 'exterritoriality', whereby the legation premises represent an extension of the sending state's territory, is no longer accepted. In the Australian case of *R v Turnbull, ex p Petroff*[11] where two persons had been charged with throwing explosive substances at the Chancery of the Soviet Union's Embassy in Canberra, in the Australian Capital Territory, it was sought to argue in prerogative writ proceedings that the magistrate concerned had no jurisdiction to deal with the alleged offences as these were committed on foreign territory. The court rejected this contention and expressly held, after a full review of the authorities, that an embassy is not a part of the territory of the sending state, and that the accused could be prosecuted for such alleged offences against the local law.

As we have seen,[12] diplomatic envoys enjoy exemption from local civil and criminal jurisdiction.

They also have a right to inviolability of the person. This protects them from molestation of any kind, and of course from arrest or detention by the local authorities (see article 29 of the Vienna Convention). Inviolability attaches likewise to the legation premises and the archives and documents of the legation (see articles 22 and 24 of the Vienna Convention).

In the case of the *United States Diplomatic and Consular Staff in Tehran*[13] the International Court of Justice upheld the principle of the inviolability of the premises of a diplomatic mission and the correlative duty of the receiving state to protect the premises, and the documents and archives of the mission, as well as the receiving state's obligation to protect the personnel of the mission. The circumstances were that in November 1979 a strong group of militant Iranians overran the compound of the Embassy of the United States at Tehran, seized buildings there, entered the Chancery and gained control of the main vault, and also detained diplomatic and consular staff and other persons as hostages.

10. Arts 20 to 41 of the Vienna Convention deal with these rights, privileges, and immunities in detail. Considerations of space have precluded a full treatment in the text, or an examination of the position of the subordinate personnel of diplomatic missions, as provided for in the convention. As to the determination of the status of a diplomatic envoy for the enjoyment of immunities, etc, see ante p 200, and cf *United States v Kostadinov* 734 F 2d 905 (1984); *United States v Lumumba* 741 F 2d 12 (1984); and *R v Lambeth Justices, ex p Yusufu* [1985] Crim LR 510 (unilateral action of sending government, eg, providing applicant with a diplomatic passport, insufficient for diplomatic status without notification to, or acceptance by, host state of accreditation).
11. (1971) 17 FLR 438.
12. See above pp 199-202. In this connection, note that certain governments (eg the United States Government) may require diplomatic missions to insure against liability for the benefit of persons who may be injured by members of the mission, the procurement of such insurance not being treated as a waiver of immunity; cf Buergenthal and Maier *Public International Law* (1985) p 211.
13. ICJ 1980, 3.

Embassy documents and archives were destroyed and ransacked or taken away. On the facts, the Court held that it was satisfied that the Iranian Government had failed to take appropriate steps within the meaning of article 22 of the Vienna Convention on Diplomatic Relations to protect the premises, staff and archives of the mission against attack by the militants, or to take appropriate steps to protect American consulates at Tabriz and Shiraz. Other provisions of the Vienna Convention were relied upon, namely article 25 imposing a duty on a receiving state to accord full facilities for a mission to perform its functions, article 26 providing for freedom of movement and travel of mission personnel, and article 27 imposing a duty to permit and protect free communication on the part of the mission for all official purposes. The analogous or corresponding provisions of the Vienna Convention of 1963 on Consular Relations (see below in this chapter) were relied upon so far as concerned the consular staff held as hostages, and the American consulates at Tabriz and Shiraz.[14] The Iranian Government, so it was ruled, had also failed in its duty to restore the status quo and to bring the infringements by the militants to an end.

The question of inviolability of a legation's premises arose in England in 1984 when shots were fired from the Libyan People's Bureau in London at demonstrators outside the Bureau, killing a woman police officer.[15] The British Government abstained from authorising any entry of the premises, but insisted on the recall of the Bureau's staff, thus complying strictly with the principles laid down by the International Court of Justice.

Articles 34 and 36 of the Vienna Convention provide that diplomatic agents are exempt from all dues and taxes,[16] other than certain taxes and charges set out in article 34 (eg charges for services rendered), and also from customs duties. The latter exemption was formerly a matter of comity or reciprocity.

A new right is conferred by article 26 of the Convention, namely a right of members of a diplomatic mission to move and travel freely in the territory of the receiving state, except in prohibited security zones. Other privileges and immunities dealt with in detail in the Convention include the freedom of communication for official purposes (article 27), exemption from social security provisions (article 33), and exemption from services and military obligations (article 35).[17]

Prevention and punishment of crimes against diplomatic envoys
The increase in the number of serious crimes committed against diplomatic envoys and diplomatic missions, such as the murder and kidnapping of envoys, and attacks directed against the premises of legations, led to the adoption by the United Nations General Assembly on 14 December 1973, of a Convention

14. Ibid, at paras 62–63.
15. See note in (1984) 55 BYIL 459, 471-472. Despite its singular name the Bureau was regarded as in law and in fact an embassy.
16. As to the exemption in respect of the legation premises, see art 23 of the Vienna Convention.
17. As to the studies made by the International Law Commission of the questions of the status of diplomatic couriers, and of the diplomatic bag, not accompanied by a diplomatic courier, see *The Work of the International Law Commission* (3rd edn, 1980) pp 94–96. In 1989 the Commission adopted draft articles and referred them to the United Nations General Assembly: *Report of the International Law Commission to the 41st Session*, 1989, paras 17-72. This text has not yet been formalised in a convention.

on the Prevention and Punishment of Crimes against Internationally Protected Persons, including Diplomatic Agents.[18] The text of this Convention was based on draft articles on the subject prepared by the International Law Commission at its 24th Session in May–July 1972. The matter had been treated by the Commission as being of such special urgency that the draft text was prepared through a Working Group, without the appointment of a Special Rapporteur. The Convention follows closely, in most major respects, the relevant provisions appropriate to the subject of the Convention for the Suppression of Unlawful Seizure of Aircraft concluded at The Hague on 16 December 1970, and the Convention for the Suppression of Unlawful Acts Against the Safety of Civil Aviation, concluded at Montreal on 23 September 1971.[19]

Diplomatic envoys are, under article 1 of the Convention, included in the class of 'internationally protected persons' who are possible victims of crimes under the Convention, but that class encompasses also heads of state and of government, and ministers for Foreign Affairs, whenever such persons are in a foreign state, as well as members of their family accompanying them, and 'any representative or official of a state or any official or other agent of an international organisation of an intergovernmental character who, at the time when and in the place where a crime against him, his official premises, his private accommodation or his means of transport is committed, is entitled pursuant to international law to special protection from any attack on his person, freedom or dignity, as well as members of his family forming part of his household'. The key provision is article 2, which sets out the acts against which the Convention is directed, and which each state party is to make punishable as a crime under its internal law by appropriate penalties, taking into account their grave nature; these are the intentional commission of:

1.   a murder, kidnapping or other attack upon the person or liberty of an internationally protected person;
2.   a violent attack upon the official premises, the private accommodation or the means of transport of an internationally protected person likely to endanger his person or liberty; and
3.   threats or attempts to commit, or participation as accomplices in the commission of such attacks.

Article 2 is not to derogate from the obligations of states parties otherwise under international law to prevent attacks on the person, freedom or dignity of internationally protected persons, as, eg, under the Vienna Convention of 1961 on Diplomatic Relations. Under article 3, paragraph 1, states parties are to take such measures as may be necessary to establish jurisdiction over the crimes specified in article 2 when the crime is committed in the territory of the state concerned or on board a ship or aircraft registered in that state, when the alleged

18.   See article on this Convention by Michael C. Wood, (1974) 23 ICLQ 791–817. The disputes article (art 13) of the Convention was invoked by the United States in the case of *United States Diplomatic and Consular Staff in Tehran* before the International Court of Justice which, however, did not find it necessary to enter into the question of jurisdiction under the provisions relied upon; see ICJ 1980, 3 at para 55.
19.   As to these two conventions, see Chapter 8, above, pp 214–217.

offender is a national of that state, and when the crime is committed against an 'internationally protected person' who enjoys status as such by virtue of functions exercised on behalf of that state. States parties are also under paragraph 2 of the same article to take such measures as may be necessary to establish jurisdiction over these crimes in cases where the alleged offender is present in its territory and is not extradited under article 8 of the Convention, which deals with the extradition of alleged offenders (see below).

Articles 4–6 and 10 provide for co-operation and various measures of collaboration in the prevention and apprehension of alleged offenders. Article 7 provides that the state party in whose territory the alleged offender is present shall, if it does not extradite him, submit, 'without exception whatsoever and without undue delay', the case to its competent authorities for the purpose of prosecution, through proceedings in accordance with the laws of that state.

Article 8 deals comprehensively with the subject of extradition. To the extent that the crimes under the Convention are not listed as extraditable offences in any extradition treaty between states parties, they shall be deemed to be included as such therein, and states parties undertake to include those crimes as extraditable offences in every future extradition treaty to be concluded between them. If a state party which makes extradition conditional upon the existence of an extradition treaty receives a request for extradition from another state party with which it has no extradition treaty, it may, if it decides to extradite, consider the Convention as the legal basis for extradition in respect of those crimes, but extradition is to be subject to the procedural provisions and the other conditions of the law of the requested state. States parties which do not make extradition conditional upon the existence of a treaty are to recognise those crimes as extraditable offences between themselves subject to the procedural provisions and the other conditions of the law of the requested state. Each of the crimes is to be treated, for the purpose of extradition as between states parties, as if it had been committed not only in the place in which it occurred, but also in the territories of the states required to establish their jurisdiction in accordance with paragraph 1 of article 3 (see above).

Termination of diplomatic mission
A diplomatic mission may come to an end in various ways:

1. Recall of the envoy by the accrediting state. The letter of recall is usually handed to the Head of State or to the Minister of Foreign Affairs in solemn audience, and the envoy receives in return a *Lettre de Récréance* acknowledging the recall. In certain circumstances, the recall of an envoy, eg a head of mission, will have the gravest significance; for example, where it is intended to warn the receiving state of the sending state's dissatisfaction with their mutual relations. Such a step is only taken where the tension between the two states cannot otherwise be resolved.
2. Notification by the sending state to the receiving state that the envoy's function has come to an end (article 43 of the Vienna Convention).
3. A request by the receiving state that the envoy be recalled. The host country need not give any explanation for such a request (see article 9 of the Vienna Convention).

4. Delivery of passports to the envoy and the envoy's staff and suite by the receiving state, as when war breaks out between the accrediting and receiving states.
5. Notification by the receiving state to the sending state, where the envoy has been declared persona non grata and where the envoy has not been recalled or his or her functions terminated, that it refuses to recognise the envoy as a member of the mission (articles 9 and 43 of the Vienna Convention).
6. Fulfilment of the object of the mission.
7. Expiration of Letters of Credence given for a limited period only.

From time to time declarations as personae non gratae[20] occur in relation to diplomatic personnel, usually following allegations of espionage or of 'activities incompatible with their diplomatic status'. There is a tendency in these cases for the sending state to take retaliatory action against diplomatic personnel of the expelling state; but such 'reciprocity' is not warranted by any provision of the Vienna Convention and is against the spirit, if not the letter, of that Convention.

2. CONSULS

Consuls are agents of a state in a foreign country, but are not diplomatic agents. Their primary duty in such capacity is to protect the commercial interests of their appointing state, but commonly a great variety of other duties are performed by them for the subjects of their state; for example, the execution of notarial acts, the granting of passports, the solemnisation of marriages, and the exercise of a disciplinary jurisdiction over the crews of vessels belonging to the state appointing them.[1]

The laws and usages as to the functions and immunities of consuls were codified, subject to certain adaptations, alterations, and extensions, in the Vienna Convention of 24 April 1963, on Consular Relations (based on draft articles adopted in 1961 by the International Law Commission). The Convention covers a wide field, but does not preclude states from concluding treaties to confirm, supplement, extend, or amplify its provisions (article 73), and matters not expressly regulated by the Convention are to continue to be governed by customary international law (see Preamble).

The institution of consuls is much older than that of diplomatic representatives, but the modern system dates from the sixteenth century. Originally consuls were elected by the merchants resident in a foreign country from among their own number, but later the Great Powers established salaried consular services and consuls were despatched to different countries according to the requirements of the service. Consuls are frequently stationed in more than one city or district in the state to which they are sent, thus differing from

20. *Persona non grata* (plural *personae non gratae*) means 'person(s) not pleasing' [to the receiving state].
1. Formerly, in certain countries, consuls exercised extra-territorial jurisdiction over their fellow-nationals to the exclusion of local municipal courts. As to this, see the decision of the International Court of Justice in the *Case Concerning Rights of Nationals of the United States of America in Morocco* ICJ 1952, 176 and 198 et seq.

diplomatic envoys. There are, of course, other differences. Consuls are not equipped with Letters of Credence, but are appointed under a commission issued by their government; the appointment is then notified to the state where the consul is to be stationed, the government of which is requested to issue an exequatur or authorisation to carry out the consular duties. If there is no objection to the appointment of the person concerned as consul, the exequatur is issued. Normally consuls do not enter on their duties until the grant of an exequatur. If, subsequently, their conduct gives serious grounds for complaint, the receiving state may notify the sending state that they are no longer acceptable; the sending state must then recall them or terminate their functions, and if the sending state does not do so, the receiving state may withdraw the exequatur, or cease to consider them as members of the consulate. Article 23 of the Vienna Convention of 1963 goes much further than this accepted practice, permitting a receiving state at any time to notify the sending state that a consular officer is persona non grata, or that any other member of the consular staff is not acceptable.

Heads of consular posts are divided into four classes: (a) Consuls-general; (b) Consuls; (c) Vice-consuls; (d) Consular agents (see article 9 of the Vienna Convention of 1963, above). Generally speaking, they take precedence according to the date of grant of the exequatur.

Rights and privileges of consuls

Consuls seldom have direct communication with the government of the state in which they are stationed except where their authority extends over the whole area of that state, or where there is no diplomatic mission of their country in the state. More usually, such communication will be made through an intermediate channel, for example, the diplomatic envoy of the state by which they are appointed. The procedure is governed by any applicable treaty, or by the municipal law and usage of the receiving state (see article 38 of the Vienna Convention of 1963).

As pointed out above,[2] consuls do not, like diplomatic envoys, enjoy complete immunity from local jurisdiction. Commonly, special privileges and exemptions are granted to them under bilateral treaty, and these may include immunity from process in the territorial courts. Apart from this it is acknowledged that as to acts performed in their official capacity and falling within the functions of consular officers under international law, they are not subject to local proceedings unless their government assents to the proceedings being taken.

In practice a great number of privileges have attached themselves to the consular office. In the absence of such privileges, consuls would not be able to fulfil their duties and functions, and accordingly as a matter of convenience they have become generally recognised by all states. Examples of such privileges are the consul's exemption from service on juries, the right of safe conduct, the right of free communication with nationals of the sending state, the inviolability of official papers and archives,[3] and the right if accused of a crime to be released

---

2. See above, p 202.
3. There is, semble, no such corresponding general inviolability of the consular premises, nor are such premises *extra-territorial* in the sense that consuls may there exercise police powers, exclusive of the local authorities, over the citizens of their state. Thus, in 1948, in the *Kasenkina Case* in the United States, where a Russian woman, presumably detained by Soviet consular

on bail or kept under surveillance until his exequatur is withdrawn or another consul appointed in his or her place. Certain states also grant consuls a limited exemption from taxation and customs dues.

In general, however, the privileges of consuls under customary international law are less settled and concrete than those of diplomatic envoys, although in the Vienna Convention of 24 April 1963, referred to above, it was sought to extend to consuls mutatis mutandis, the majority of the rights, privileges, and immunities applying under the Vienna Convention on Diplomatic Relations of 18 April 1961, subject to adjustments in the case of honorary consuls. In that connection, it is significant that in recent years, both Great Britain[4] and the United States have negotiated standard consular conventions or treaties with a number of states in order that the rights and privileges of consuls may be defined with more certainty, and placed on as wide and secure a basis as possible.

The modern tendency of states is to amalgamate their diplomatic and consular services, and it is a matter of frequent occurrence to find representatives of states occupying, interchangeably or concurrently,[5] diplomatic and consular posts. Under the impact of this tendency, the present differences between diplomatic and consular privileges may gradually be narrowed.

3. SPECIAL MISSIONS OF A NON-PERMANENT NATURE

In addition to their permanent diplomatic and consular representation, states are often obliged to send temporary missions to particular states to deal with a specific question or to perform a specific task, and such missions may be accredited, irrespective of whether in point of fact permanent diplomatic or consular relations are being maintained with the receiving state. Of course, it is fundamental that a special mission of this nature may be sent only with the consent of the state which is to receive it.

The rules governing the conduct and treatment of these special missions of a non-permanent character were the subject of a Convention on Special Missions

---

officers, jumped to the street from the window of a room in the Soviet Consulate, the United States Government insisted on the position that consular premises were subject to local police control in a proper case; cf Preuss 43 AJIL (1949) 37–56. But see now the rule of inviolability of consular premises laid down in article 31 of the Vienna Convention of 1963; this prohibits authorities of the receiving state from entering, without consent, only that part of the consular premises used exclusively for the work of the consular post, and provides that consent to enter may be assumed in case of fire or other disaster requiring prompt protective action.

4.   Cf the series of such consular treaties concluded by Great Britain with Norway, the United States, France, Switzerland, Greece, Mexico, Italy, the Federal Republic of Germany, and other states.

5.   See, eg, *Engelke v Musmann* [1928] AC 433. Consular functions may be performed by a diplomatic mission; see art 3, para 2 of the Vienna Convention on Diplomatic Relations, above. Similarly, diplomatic functions may be carried out by a Consular Officer (not necessarily a head of the post) in a state, where the sending state has no diplomatic mission, and with the consent of the receiving state; see art 17 of the Vienna Convention of 1963. In a United States Department of State Circular of 16 January 1958, it was stated that the United States Government would continue to recognise in a dual capacity members of diplomatic missions in Washington who also performed consular functions.

adopted by the United Nations General Assembly on 8 December 1969, and opened for signature on 16 December 1969. The Convention was based on the final set of draft articles prepared in 1967 by the International Law Commission, which had had the subject under consideration since 1958.[6]

The Convention is largely modelled on provisions of the Vienna Convention on Diplomatic Relations of 1961, while there has also been some borrowing from the text of the Vienna Convention on Consular Relations of 1963. No distinction was made by the Convention between special missions of a technical nature and those of a political character, and its provisions apply also to the so-called 'high level' special missions, that is, missions led by heads of state or cabinet ministers, subject however to the special recognition of the privileged status of the leader of the mission in such a case. Privileges and immunities are conferred upon the members of special missions to an extent similar to that accorded to permanent diplomatic missions, the justification being that the like privileges and immunities are essential for the regular and efficient performance of the tasks and responsibilities of special missions (see seventh recital of the preamble to the Convention).

The Convention on Special Missions of 1969 contains, inter alia, the following provisions which differentiate it from the Vienna Convention on Diplomatic Relations of 1961, while at the same time reflecting differences between the nature of special missions, on the one hand, and that of permanent diplomatic missions, on the other hand:

a.   Two or more states may each send a special mission at the same time to another state in order to deal together with a question of common interest to all of them (article 6).

b.   Before appointing members of a special mission, the sending state must inform the receiving state of the size of the mission, and of the names and designations of its members (article 8).

c.   The seat of the mission is to be in a locality agreed by the states concerned, or, in the absence of agreement, in the locality where the Ministry of Foreign Affairs of the host state is situated, and there may be more than one seat (article 17).

d.   Only such freedom of movement and travel is allowed as is necessary for the performance of the functions of the special mission (article 27; contrast article 26 of the Vienna Convention).

e.   An action for damages arising out of an accident caused by a vehicle used outside the official functions of the person sought to be sued is not within the scope of immunity from the civil and administrative jurisdiction of the host state (article 31 paragraph 2 (d)).

f.   Immunities are allowable to a mission representative in transit through a third state only if that state has been informed beforehand of the proposed transit, and has raised no objection (article 42 paragraph 4).

6.   For text of draft articles and commentary thereon, see *Report* of the Commission on the Work of its *19th Session* (1967).

4. OTHER CATEGORIES OF REPRESENTATIVES AND AGENTS

Representatives and observers accredited in relation to international organisations

The increasing establishment of permanent missions and delegations accredited in relation to international organisations prompted the United Nations General Assembly in 1958 to invite the International Law Commission to consider the subject of the relations between states and inter-governmental international organisations. As a result of the Commission's labours at its sessions in 1968, 1969, 1970, and 1971[7] a composite set of draft articles was prepared dealing with the conduct and treatment of:

a. permanent missions to international organisations;
b. permanent observer missions of non-member governments to international organisations; and
c. delegations to organs of international organisations, and to conferences of states convened by or under the auspices of international organisations.

After these draft articles had been submitted to governments for comment and observations, and after further consideration of the subject by the United Nations General Assembly, a Conference was convened to be held in Vienna in 1975 to examine the subject, and to adopt a convention or other instruments upon the basis of the draft text. In the result a Convention on the Representation of States in their Relations with International Organisations of a Universal Character was adopted at Vienna on 14 March 1975, governing the status, functions, and immunities of the above-mentioned classes of representatives. On the face of it, this instrument seemed to be a worthwhile, comprehensive attempt to stabilise the practice as to these new classes of representatives and delegates. The contrary position of representatives of international organisations accredited to states was not dealt with, mainly because these representatives would of necessity be officials of the organisation concerned, and therefore their status would normally be covered by the appropriate rules and regulations of the organisation. Moreover, the Convention did not purport to regulate the position of representatives or observers accredited to regional organisations or organs of, or conferences convened by these regional bodies; only general or universal international organisations were within the scope of its provisions. However, for a number of reasons this Convention of 1975 is most unlikely to result in a substantial contribution to the body of universal diplomatic international law, although it may become operative as between those states which accept, ratify, or adopt it; even if it is in force as between them, such operative effect would be largely abstract or academic, as the majority of host states of international organisations have indicated their reluctance to become parties. The very necessity for the Convention has been questioned, on the ground that much of its content is covered to a substantial extent by Headquarters Agreements, and by the conventions on privileges and immunities of the relevant international organisations, while the host states entertain serious reservations regarding the

---

7. For text of the principal draft articles and commentary thereon, see the *Reports* of the Commission on the Work of its *20th* (1968), *21st* (1969), and *22nd* (1970) Sessions.

extent of the privileges and immunities granted to representatives, delegates, and observer missions, etc, which generally speaking are on a par with those accorded under the Vienna Convention of Diplomatic Relations of 1961. Some of the exemptions accorded by the Convention are regarded as excessive or unnecessarily generous.[8] Nevertheless, if the Convention fails to mature into an instrument of general international law, this does not mean that, in practice, a special status is not to be accorded to such representatives commensurate with what may be duly required for the performance of their functions.

It may also be recalled that under article 1 of the Convention on the Prevention and Punishment of Crimes against Internationally Protected Persons, Including Diplomatic Agents, adopted on 14 December 1973, and considered above in this chapter, 'representatives' or 'officials' of a state may in appropriate circumstances come under the ambit of protection of the provisions of this Convention.

Three advisory opinions of the International Court of Justice have related to the status of persons employed by or accredited to the United Nations. In the *Reparations for Injuries Suffered in the Service of the United Nations* case[9] the Court held that the United Nations had the independent right to exercise diplomatic protection of one of its officials and to pursue a claim against a state causing injury to such officials. In the *Applicability of the Obligation to Arbitrate under Section 21 of the United Nations Headquarters Agreement of 26 June 1947* case[10] the Court held that the United States was under an obligation to submit to arbitration the dispute between itself and the United Nations respecting the establishment of an Observer Mission by the Palestine Liberation Organisation at the United Nations. The Mission had been authorised by the United Nations and thus came under the protection of the Headquarters Agreement between the United States and the United Nations, but appeared to conflict with the terms of the Anti-Terrorism Act of the United States which required the closure of offices of the PLO in the United States. The dispute was resolved when a United States court held that the Anti-Terrorism Act did not apply to the Observer Mission at the United Nations, since express words would be required in order to ascribe an intention to Congress to override the provisions of the Headquarters Agreement.[11] In the *Applicability of Article VI, Section 22, of the Convention on the Privileges and Immunities of the United Nations* case[12] the Court held that the national state of an official of the United Nations was not permitted to deny access to that official while he or she was still accredited to the United Nations as an official.

Non-diplomatic agents and representatives

States may employ for various purposes agents, other than regularly accredited diplomatic envoys or consuls. These may be of a permanent character, such as

8. Cf article on this Convention by J. G. Fennessy 70 AJIL (1976) 62–72.
9. ICJ 1949, 167.
10. ICJ 1988, 12.
11. *United States v Palestine Liberation Organisation* (1988) 27 ILM 1055 (SDNY).
12. ICJ 1989, 177. The case concerned Mr Mazilu, a special rapporteur of the UN Subcommission on Prevention of Discrimination and Protection of Minorities, access to whom was denied by his national state, Romania.

Trade Commissioners[13] and officers of independent information or tourist services. No special rules of international law have developed with respect to such agents. Their rights and privileges may be the subject of specific bilateral arrangement, or simply a matter of courtesy. Normally, they may expect to be treated with consideration by receiving states.

---

13. Independent representatives unlike the commercial counsellors or commercial attachés of permanent diplomatic missions.

CHAPTER 16

The law and practice as to treaties

1. NATURE AND FUNCTIONS OF TREATIES

Prior to 1969 the law of treaties consisted for the most part of customary rules of international law. These rules were to a large extent codified and reformulated in the Vienna Convention on the Law of Treaties, concluded on 23 May 1969 (referred to below in the present chapter as 'the Vienna Convention'[1]). Apart from such codification, the Convention contained much that was new and that represented development of international law, while also a number of provisions resulted from the reconciliation of divergent views and practices. The Vienna Convention was not, however, intended as a complete code of treaty law, and in the preamble it is in fact affirmed that rules of customary international law will continue to govern questions not regulated by the provisions of the Convention. In 1971, it was declared by the United States Department of State that the Vienna Convention was 'recognised as the authoritative guide to current treaty law and practice'.[2]

A treaty may be defined, in accordance with the definition adopted in article 2 of the Convention, as an agreement whereby two or more states establish or seek to establish a relationship between themselves governed by international law. So long as an agreement between states is attested, provided that it is not one governed by domestic national law, and provided that it is intended to create a legal relationship,[3] any kind of instrument or document, or any oral exchange

---

1. In the footnotes to this chapter, the Convention will also be referred to as 'the Vienna Convention', while the abbreviation 'Draft Arts ILC' will denote the draft articles on the law of treaties drawn up by the International Law Commission, and contained in Chapter II of its *Report* on the Work of its *18th Session* in 1966 (these Draft Articles were used as a basic text by the Vienna Conference of 1968–1969 which drew up the Convention). For an analysis of the Vienna Convention and of its drafting history at the Conference, see R. D. Kearney, and R. E. Dalton 'The Treaty on Treaties' 64 AJIL (1970) 495–561. See also Sir Ian Sinclair *The Vienna Convention and the Law of Treaties* (2nd edn, 1984) and T. O. Elias *The Modern Law of Treaties* (1974).
2. Quoted in Henkin, Pugh, Schachter and Smit *International Law; Cases and Materials* (2nd edn, 1987) p 387.
3. This would exclude 'gentlemen's agreements' such as those relating to the distribution of seats on the United Nations Security Council, or as to the regions from which Judges of the

between states involving undertakings may constitute a treaty, irrespective of the form or circumstances of its conclusion. Indeed, the term 'treaty' may be regarded as nomen generalissimum in international law,[4] and can include an agreement between international organisations inter se, or between an international organisation on the one hand, and a state or states on the other,[5] although it should be borne in mind that the provisions of the Vienna Convention do not apply to such other instruments, but are confined to treaties between states, concluded in a written form.[6]

At the same time, merely considering the treaty as an agreement without more is to over-simplify its functions and significance in the international domain. In point of fact, the treaty is the main instrument which the international community possesses for the purpose of initiating or developing international co-operation.[7] In national domestic law, the private citizen has a large variety of instruments from which to choose for executing some legal act or for attesting a transaction, for example, contracts, conveyances, leases, licences, settlements, acknowledgments, and so on, each specially adapted to the purpose in hand. In the international sphere, the treaty has to do duty for almost every kind of legal act,[8] or transaction, ranging from a mere bilateral bargain between states to such

International Court of Justice are elected; see p 5, above. See also E. Lauterpacht in *Festschrift für F.A. Mann* (1977), 381-398, and Schachter in (1977) 71 AJIL 296-304. Also excluded are political declarations, or the accords spelled out in communiqués of 'summit' Conferences.

4.   A League of Nations mandate was a 'treaty'; *South West Africa Cases (preliminary objections)*, ICJ 1962, 319 at 330.

5.   That subject is now covered by the Vienna Convention of 1986 on the Law of Treaties between States and International Organisations or between International Organisations. This Convention is based on a set of draft articles adopted by the International Law Commission, and although there is a close resemblance between its provisions and the provisions of the Vienna Convention on the Law of Treaties of 1969, a number of the situations covered are more varied than those applicable to states alone. Cf *The Work of the International Law Commission* (1980) pp 88–91.

6.   Art 3 of the Vienna Convention provides nevertheless that the fact that the Convention does not apply to agreements between states and non-state entities, or between non-state entities themselves, or to unwritten agreements is not to affect: (a) the legal force of such agreements; (b) the application to them of any rules in the Convention to which they would be subject under international law apart from the Convention; and (c) the application of the Convention to the relations of states as between themselves under agreements to which non-state entities may also be parties.

7.   For treatments of the subject of treaties, see Rosenne *The Law of Treaties* (1970); Kaye Holloway *Modern Trends in Treaty Law* (1967); Ingrid Detter *Essays on the Law of Treaties* (1967); T. O. Elias *The Modern Law of Treaties* (1974); Henkin, Pugh, Schachter and Smit *International Law; Cases and Materials* (2nd edn, 1987) ch 6 'The Law of Treaties' pp 386 et seq. The United Nations publication, *Laws and Practices concerning the Conclusion of Treaties* (1953) is a valuable compilation of state practice, with a bibliography. For a selected bibliography on the law of treaties, see the Vienna Conference document, A/CONF.39/4.

8.   *Unilateral acts:* The difference between treaties proper and certain unilateral acts, commonly recognised in international practice, should be noted. As to unilateral acts, see Schwarzenberger *International Law* (3rd edn, 1957) Vol 1, pp 548–561, and Dr E. Suy *Les Actes juridiques unilatéraux en droit international public* (1962). These include acts of protest, notification, renunciation, acceptance, and recognition, and serve the following purposes, inter alia: (a) assent to obligations; (b) cognition of situations; (c) declaration of policy; (d) notice to preserve rights; (e) reservation, in respect to a possible liability. According to the decision of the International Court of Justice in the *Nuclear Tests Case (Australia v France)* ICJ 1974, 253 at 267–70, a declaration may be made by way of unilateral act by a state concerning a legal or factual situation

a fundamental measure as the multilateral constituent instrument of a major international organisation (eg the United Nations Charter of 1945).

In nearly all cases, the object of a treaty is to impose binding obligations on the states who are parties to it. Many writers on the theory of international law have put the question—why do treaties have such binding force? Perhaps the only answer to this query is that international law declares that duly made treaties create binding obligations for the states parties. Certain theorists, for example, Anzilotti, have rested the binding force of treaties on the Latin maxim pacta sunt servanda, or in other words that states are bound to carry out in good faith the obligations they have assumed by treaty.[9] Once a state has bound itself by agreement in a treaty, it is not entitled to withdraw from its obligations without the consent of the other states parties. In 1871, Great Britain, France, Italy, Prussia, Russia, Austria, and Turkey subscribed to the following Declaration made at a Conference in London:

> 'That the Powers recognise it an essential principle of the Law of Nations that no Power can liberate itself from the engagements of a treaty nor modify the stipulations thereof, unless with the consent of the contracting parties by means of an amicable understanding.'

Treaties proper must be distinguished from a contract between a state and an alien citizen or corporation; although in ultimate analysis such a contract may raise questions of international concern between the contracting state and the state to which the citizen or corporation belongs, it is not a treaty, and is not subject to the rules of international law affecting treaties.[10]

Two further points should be mentioned. The law and practice of treaties naturally include rules relating to agreements on international matters made by international institutions, whether inter se, or with states, or perhaps even with individuals. With the establishment of the United Nations and the 'specialised agencies' (see Chapter 20, below), the number of such transactions is rapidly increasing. The matter has now been dealt with to some extent in the Vienna Convention of 1986 on the Law of Treaties between States and International Organisations or between International Organisations.

The second point is that care must be exercised in assessing whether a particular document is intended to create legal relations between the parties or not. This is especially so in the case of the increased use made in international practice of the 'memoradum of understanding' as a method of regulating bilateral relations in relation to particular matters on the political, but not the legal, level. 'Memorandum of Understanding' (MOU) is not a term of art, and may indeed be a treaty; but it will more often than not be found that the wording itself expressly or impliedly excludes an intention to create binding legal relations.

---

under such circumstances (eg publicly and erga omnes) as to have the effect of creating a legal obligation on that state (in that case an obligation on France's part to hold no further nuclear atmospheric tests in the South Pacific).

9. Cf Vienna Convention, 3rd recital of preamble (affirming that the principles of free consent, good faith, and pacta sunt servanda are 'universally recognised'), and art 26 (all treaties are binding on the parties thereto, and must be performed by them in good faith).

10. See *Anglo-Iranian Oil Company Case (Jurisdiction)* ICJ 1952, 93 at 112. As to what instruments are not treaties, see Myers, 51 AJIL (1957) 596–605. A League of Nations mandate is a treaty; *South West Africa Cases (preliminary objections)* ICJ 1962, 319, 330.

The MOU has been found useful in circumstances where confidential matters of a political or military nature are concerned, or in such cases as the provision of development assistance or humanitarian aid, where flexibility and lack of insistence on reciprocal legal rights and obligations are deemed more appropriate. MOUs are often not published in national treaty collections; nor, if they are regarded as non-binding in law, are they registered with the United Nations.[11]

2. FORMS AND TERMINOLOGY

In regard to the forms and terminology of modern treaties the present-day practice is far from systematic, and suffers from a lack of uniformity. This is due to several factors, principally the survival of old diplomatic traditions and forms not easily adaptable to modern international life and to a reluctance on the part of states to standardise treaty usage.

The principal forms in which treaties are concluded are as follows:

i. Heads of states form. In this case the treaty is drafted as an agreement between Sovereigns or heads of state (for example, the British Crown, the President of the United States) and the obligations are expressed to bind them as 'High Contracting Parties'.[12] This form is not now frequently used, and is reserved for the more solemn kinds of treaties.

ii. Inter-governmental form. The treaty is drafted as an agreement between governments. The difference between this and the previous form is not a matter of substance; usually, however, the inter-governmental form is employed for technical or non-political agreements. One notable exception to this rule was the Anglo-Japanese Treaty of Alliance 1902, which was expressed to be made between the Government of Great Britain and the Government of Japan as contracting parties.

iii. Inter-state form. The treaty is drafted expressly or impliedly as an agreement between states. The signatories are then most often referred to as 'the Parties' (see, eg, the North Atlantic Security Treaty of 4 April 1949).

iv. A treaty may be negotiated and signed as between ministers of the countries concerned, generally the Ministers of Foreign Affairs.[13]

v. A treaty may be an inter-departmental agreement, concluded between representatives of particular government departments, for example, between representatives of the Customs Administrations of the countries concerned.

vi. A treaty may be made between the actual political heads of the countries concerned, for example, the Munich Agreement of September 1938, which was signed by the British and French Premiers, Chamberlain and Daladier, and by the German and Italian Leaders, Hitler and Mussolini, and the United States–Soviet Union Treaty on Anti-Ballistic Missile Systems signed at Moscow on 26 May 1972 by President Nixon and General Secretary Leonid

---

11. As to registration pursuant to art 102 of the United Nations Charter see below, p 418.
12. As to this phrase, see *Philippson v Imperial Airways Ltd* [1939] AC 332, and Henkin, Pugh, Schachter and Smit *International Law; Cases and Materials* (2nd edn, 1987) p 443, para 4.
13. The United States–Soviet Union Maritime Agreement concluded at Washington on 14 October 1972, was signed by the American Secretary of Commerce (Mr Peterson) and the USSR Minister of Merchant Marine (Mr Guzhenko).

Brezhnev.[14] A more recent example is the Joint Declaration of 19 December 1984 on the reversion of Hong Kong to Chinese sovereignty; this was signed by the British Prime Minister (Mrs Thatcher) and the Premier of the People's Republic of China (Mr Zhao Ziyang).

The form in which treaties are concluded does not in any way affect their binding character. To take an extreme illustration of this principle it is not even necessary that a treaty be in writing. An oral declaration in the nature of a promise made by the Minister of Foreign Affairs of one country to the Minister of Foreign Affairs of another and in a matter within his or her competence and authority may be as binding as a formal written treaty.[15] International law does not as yet require established forms for treaties, and here content and substance are of more importance.[16]

Treaties go under a variety of names, some of which indicate a difference in procedure or a greater or a lesser degree of formality.[17] Thus besides the term 'treaty' itself, the following titles have been given: (1) *Convention*. (2) *Protocol*. (3) *Agreement*. (4) *Arrangement*. (5) *Procès-Verbal*. (6) *Statute*. (7) *Covenant* (8) *Declaration*. (9) *Modus Vivendi*. (10) *Exchange of Notes* (*or of Letters*). (11) *Final Act*. (12) *General Act*. Each of these titles will be commented on in turn. As to the term 'treaty' itself, this tends to be given to formal agreements relative to peace, alliance, or the cession of territory, or some other fundamental matter.

(1) Convention

This is the term now ordinarily reserved for a proper formal instrument of a multilateral character. The term also includes the instruments adopted by the organs of international institutions, for example, by the International Labour Conference and the Assembly of the International Civil Aviation Organisation.[18] Until World War II the term was sometimes used for a bilateral treaty, but this is now unusual.

(2) Protocol

This signifies an agreement less formal than a treaty or convention proper and which is generally never in the heads of state form. The term covers the following instruments:

a.   An instrument subsidiary to a convention, and drawn up by the same negotiators. Sometimes also called a Protocol of Signature, such a Protocol deals with ancillary matters such as the interpretation of particular clauses

14. To this list may be added military treaties made between opposing commanders-in-chief, eg, the Korean Armistice Agreement of 27 July 1953. Another special case is that of a *Concordat*, ie an agreement between the Pope and a head of state; see Oppenheim *International Law* (8th edn, 1955) Vol I, p 252, and Satow's *Guide to Diplomatic Practice* (4th edn, 1957) pp 343–344.
15. See the decision of the Permanent Court of International Justice in the *Eastern Greenland Case* (1933) PCIJ Series A/B, No 53. See also the decision of the International Court of Justice in the *Nuclear Tests Case* (*Australia v France*) ICJ 1974, 253 at 267–270, noted at pp 398-399, n 8 above.
16. Cf Oppenheim *International Law* (8th edn, 1955) Vol 1, pp 898–900.
17. See Myers 51 AJIL (1957) 574–605.
18. It is still sometimes used for a bilateral treaty; note, eg, the Franco-Dutch General Convention on Social Security of January 1950.

of the convention, any supplementary provisions of a minor character, formal clauses not inserted in the convention, or reservations by particular signatory states. Ratification of the convention will normally ipso facto involve ratification of the Protocol.

b.   An ancillary instrument to a convention, but of an independent character and operation and subject to independent ratification, for example, the Hague Protocols of 1930 on Statelessness, signed at the same time as the Hague Convention of 1930 on the Conflict of Nationality Laws.

c.   A supplementary treaty, concluded at a later date, eg the Protocol of 1967 to the Refugees Convention, 1951.

d.   A record of certain understandings arrived at, more often called a *Procès-Verbal*.

(3)   Agreement

This is an instrument less formal than a treaty or convention proper, and generally not in heads of state form. It is usually applied to agreements of more limited scope and with fewer parties than the ordinary convention.[19] It is also employed for agreements of a technical or administrative character only, signed by the representatives of government departments, but not subject to ratification.

(4)   Arrangement

The observations above as to Agreements apply here. It is more usually employed for a transaction of a provisional or temporary nature.

(5)   Procès-Verbal[20]

This term originally denoted the summary of the proceedings and conclusions of a diplomatic conference, but is now used as well to mean the record of the terms of some agreement reached between the parties; for example, the Procès-Verbal signed at Zurich in 1892 by the representatives of Italy and Switzerland to record their understanding of the provisions of the Treaty of Commerce between them. It is also used to record an exchange or deposit of ratifications, or for an administrative agreement of a purely minor character, or to effect a minor alteration to a convention. It is generally not subject to ratification.

(6)   Statute

a.   A collection of constituent rules relating to the functioning of an international institution, for example, the Statute of the International Court of Justice 1945.

b.   A collection of rules laid down by international agreement as to the functioning under international supervision of a particular entity, for example, the Statute of the Sanjak of Alexandretta 1937.[1]

19. *Partial Agreements*: The term 'Partial Agreement' is used for an Agreement prepared and concluded within the framework of the Council of Europe, but between only a limited number of interested states.

20. For a note on the generic practice of drawing up a Procès-Verbal as a legal record, or as a minute of proceedings, see note by Pierre Crabites in the 1927 Volume of the American Bar Association Journal p 439.

1.   See the decision of the Permanent Court of International Justice on the *Interpretation of the Statute of Memel Territory* (1932) Pub PCIJ Series A/B, No 49, p 300, which shows that this type of statute must be interpreted in the same way as a treaty.

c.   An accessory instrument to a convention setting out certain regulations to be applied; for example, the Statute on Freedom of Transit annexed to the Convention on Freedom of Transit, Barcelona, 1921.

(7)   Covenant

This term was first used as a synonym for 'treaty' or 'convention' in the Covenant of the League of Nations, adopted at Versailles in 1919. The term 'pact' also came into vogue with the League of Nations to designate the Covenant itself, and other particularly important documents, such as the Kellogg-Briand Pact, more formally known as the General Treaty for the Renunciation of War, 1928. The term has more recently been revived in order to designate as engagements of fundamental importance the United Nations Covenant on Civil and Political Rights and the Covenant on Economic, Social and Cultural Rights, 1966.

(8)   Declaration

The term denotes:

a.   A treaty proper, for example, the Declaration of Paris, 1856. A recent significant example is that of the Joint Declaration, 19 December 1984, of the United Kingdom and the People's Republic of China on the reversion of Hong Kong to Chinese Sovereignty in 1997; cl 7 of the Declaration declared that the two Governments 'agree to implement the preceding declarations and the Annexes to this Joint Declaration', thereby converting the documentation into a binding treaty arrangement.
b.   An informal instrument appended to a treaty or convention interpreting or explaining the provisions of the latter.
c.   An informal agreement with respect to a matter of minor importance.
d.   A resolution by a diplomatic conference, enunciating some principle or desideratum for observance by all states; for example, the Declaration on the Prohibition of Military, Political or Economic Coercion in the Conclusion of Treaties, adopted by the Vienna Conference of 1968–1969 on the Law of Treaties.[2]

Declarations may or may not be subject to ratification.

(9)   Modus vivendi

A modus vivendi is an instrument recording an international agreement of a temporary or provisional nature intended to be replaced by an arrangement of a more permanent and detailed character. It is usually made in a most informal way,[3] and never requires ratification.

2.   In addition the term 'Declaration' can denote: (i) a unilateral declaration of intent by a state; eg, a declaration accepting the compulsory jurisdiction of the International Court of Justice under art 36, para 2 of its Statute; (ii) resolutions of the United Nations General Assembly, intended to affirm a significant principle; eg, Declaration on the Rights of the Child, adopted in 1959.
3.   Eg, being made in the names of the negotiating plenipotentiaries only, or initialled without being signed.

(10)   Exchange of notes (or of letters)

An exchange of notes is an informal method, very frequently adopted in recent years,[4] whereby states subscribe to certain understandings or recognise certain obligations as binding them. Sometimes the exchange of notes is effected through the diplomatic or military representatives of the states concerned. Ratification is not usually required, but will be necessary if this corresponds to the intention of the parties.

There have been also instances of multilateral exchanges of notes.

(11)   Final Act

The Final Act is the title of the instrument which records the winding up of the proceedings of the Conference summoned to conclude a convention (see, for example, the Final Act of the Vienna Conference of 1968–1969 on the Law of Treaties and the Final Act of the Third United Nations Conference on the Law of the Sea, signed on 10 December 1982, at Montego Bay, Jamaica). It summarises the terms of reference of the Conference, and enumerates the states or heads of states represented, the delegates who took part in the discussions, and the instruments adopted by the Conference. It also sets out resolutions, declarations, and recommendations adopted by the Conference which were not incorporated as provisions of the convention. Sometimes it also contains interpretations of provisions in the formal instruments adopted by the Conference. The Final Act is signed but normally does not require ratification.

There have been several instances of a Final Act which was a real international treaty, for example, the Final Act of the Conference of Countries Exporting and Importing Wheat, signed in London in August 1933.

(12)   General Act

A General Act is really a treaty but may be of a formal or informal character. The title was used by the League of Nations in the case of the General Act for the Pacific Settlement of International Disputes adopted by the Assembly in 1928, of which a revised text was adopted by the United Nations General Assembly on 28 April 1949.[5]

3.   PARTIES TO TREATIES

Generally only states which fulfil the requirements of statehood at international law, or international law, or international organisations can be parties to treaties.

---

4.   See Oppenheim *International Law* (9th edn, 1992) Vol I, p 1210, and cf art 13 of the Vienna Convention (exchange of instruments constituting a treaty—consent to be bound is expressed by such exchange), and Satow's *Guide to Diplomatic Practice* (4th edn, 1957) pp 340–342.

5.   Other titles for treaty instruments, sometimes used, are: *Accord; Act* (French equivalent—*Acte*) for a treaty laying down general rules of international law or setting up an international organ; *Aide-Mémoire; Articles*, or *Articles of Agreement* (eg, Articles of Agreement of the International Monetary Fund, 1944); *Charter* and *Constitution* for the constituent instruments of international organisations; *Compact, Instrument, Memorandum, Memorandum of Agreement*; and *Minute* or *Agreed Minutes* to record in a less formal manner some understanding or to deal with a minor procedural matter; *Note verbale; Pact*, to record some solemn obligation; and *Public Act* (similar to *Act*, above).

Modern developments have made it almost impossible to apply this rule in all its strictness. Sometimes agreements of a technical character are made between the government departments of different states, being signed by representatives of these departments. Sometimes also conventions will extend to the dependent territories of states.

As a general rule a treaty may not impose obligations or confer rights on third parties without their consent (Vienna Convention, art 34), and, indeed, many treaties expressly declare that they are to be binding only on the parties. This general principle, which is expressed in the Latin maxim *pacta tertiis nec nocent nec prosunt*, finds support in the practice of states, in the decisions of international tribunals,[6] and now in the provisions of the Vienna Convention (see arts 34–38). The exceptions to it are as follows:

a.   Treaties under which the intention of the parties is to accord rights to third states, with their express or presumed assent, such as treaties effecting an international settlement or conferring an international status on ports, waterways, etc, or creating what is called an 'objective régime', may reach out to states non-parties. The best illustration of this is the Convention of 1856 between France, Great Britain, and Russia, concerning the non-fortification of the Aaland Islands. In 1920, after Sweden, a non-party, had insisted that the provisions of the Convention should be complied with, a League of Nations Committee of Jurists expressed the opinion that, though Sweden was a non-party and had no contractual rights, the Convention in fact created objective law, with benefits extending beyond the circle of the contracting parties. As the Permanent Court of International Justice has pointed out,[7] the operation of such a third party right is not lightly to be presumed and much depends on the circumstances of each case. But if the parties intended to confer rights on a state which was not a party, this intention may be decisive. The test is 'whether the states which have stipulated in favour of a third state meant to create an actual right which the latter has accepted as such'.

Article 36 of the Vienna Convention purports to declare a general principle covering the case of such treaties intended to confer third party rights. On the matter of third party assent, it lays down that such assent 'shall be presumed so long as the contrary is not indicated, unless the treaty otherwise provides'. Article 37, paragraph 2, provides that such a third party right may not be revoked or modified by the parties 'if it is established that the right was intended not to be revocable or subject to modification without the consent of the third state'.

b.   Multilateral treaties declaratory of established customary international law will obviously apply to non-parties, but the true position is that non-parties are bound not by the treaty but by the customary rules, although the precise formulation of the rules in the treaty may be of significance. Also treaties, bilateral or otherwise, may, by constituting elements in the formation of customary

6. For discussion, see C. Chinkin *Third Parties in International Law* (1993), chs 2–6; and commentary on arts 30–32, Draft Arts ILC (this includes some useful references to the case law).
7. *Case of the Free Zones of Upper Savoy and Gex* (1932) Pub PCIJ Series A/B, No 46 p 147. These observations were, however, of the nature of obiter dicta.

international law, come to bind third parties by virtue of the same principle (cf Vienna Convention, article 38).

c.   Multilateral treaties creating new rules of international law may bind non-parties in the same way as do all rules of international law,[8] or be de facto applied by them as standard-setting instruments.

d.   Certain multilateral conventions which are intended to have universal operation, may provide in terms for their application to non-parties. Thus, the Geneva Drugs Convention of 1931 now replaced by the Single Convention on Narcotic Drugs concluded at New York on 30 March 1961, as amended in 1975, enabled an international organ finally to determine the estimates for legitimate narcotic drug requirements of states, not parties to the Convention. Moreover, if a state non-party exceeded these estimates by obtaining or producing larger supplies of drugs, it became liable to an embargo on imports in the same way as states parties.[9]

e.   Article 35 of the Vienna Convention declares that an obligation arises for a third state from a treaty provision, if the parties to the treaty intend the provision to be the means of establishing the obligation, and the third state expressly accepts the obligation in writing. It is questionable whether this is a real exception; an arguable point is that the treaty itself in conjunction with the written acceptance of the obligation may constitute a composite tripartite arrangement, and such an interpretation seems to be supported by article 37, paragraph 1, providing that the obliga-tion may be revoked or modified only with the consent of the treaty parties and the third state 'unless it is established that they had otherwise agreed'.

In the light of the impact of the above-mentioned articles 34–38 of the Vienna Convention upon the admissibility of third party rights and obligations, the practical course for states not wishing, in any treaty concluded by them, to confer such rights or impose such obligations is to stipulate expressly against this result, while a non-party state, unwilling to be saddled with an external treaty obligation, should ensure that neither by its conduct nor by its declarations has it assented to the imposition of the obligation.

Assignment of treaty rights and obligations

It has been sometimes stated as a general proposition that treaty rights and obligations are not assignable. Thus in the *Report* of its *28th Session* in 1972, the International Law Commission declared that assignability was not an institution recognised in international law, and that 'in international law the rule seems clear that an agreement by a party to a treaty to assign either its obligations

8.   See above, p 37. Cf the Briand-Kellogg Pact of 1928 for the Outlawry of War which under the Nuremberg Judgment of 1946 was regarded as creating general law for signatories and non-signatories alike.
9.   For the practice and procedure, see *Study of the Convention* published by the League of Nations (1937), Doc. C. 191, M.136, 1937, XI, pp 183–187. Cf also para 6 of art 2 of the United Nations Charter (enforcement of principles of Charter upon non-members), and art 32 (non-members attending Security Council discussions). Cf the position under certain provisions of the Articles of Agreement of the International Monetary Fund; Gold, op cit, pp 40–42.

or its rights under the treaty cannot bind any other party to the treaty without the latter's consent'. Such a generalisation although largely correct cannot be accepted without certain reservations and qualifications.

First, treaty rights and obligations may be assignable by way of novation, ie by a fresh agreement between the states parties to the treaty and the assignee state non-party. Just as in the case of a novation of a contract in private law, all parties to the old treaty must be parties to the new treaty with the assignee, and it must clearly appear that the treaty rights and obligations of the assigning state are to be extinguished, these being replaced by rights and obligations acknowledged to be those of the assignee state. Moreover, there must similarly be clear evidence of an animus novandi, that is to say an intention to enter into a new arrangement for the replacement of the assigning state's rights and obligations by rights and obligations of the assignee state.

Second, a treaty may expressly or by necessary implication permit a state party to assign to a non-party state; rights and obligations under the treaty are then assignable, provided that any restrictions laid down in the treaty as to notice to be given to other states parties, and as to the categories of states to which such an assignment is permissible, are duly observed by the assigning state.

Third, there seems to be no reason why a liquidated debt or claim arising under a treaty may not be assigned by the beneficiary state, unless such assignment be clearly prejudicial to the debtor state.

Of course many treaty rights and obligations are clearly unassignable; eg, if the treaty itself expressly prohibits any such assignment, or in the case of rights or obligations under treaties of a purely political nature, or under extradition treaties.

4. PRACTICE AS TO CONCLUSION AND ENTRY INTO FORCE OF TREATIES

The various steps in the creation of obligations by treaty are:

1. The accrediting of persons who conduct negotiations on behalf of the contracting states.
2. Negotiation and adoption.
3. Authentication, signature and exchange of instruments.
4. Ratification.
5. Accessions and adhesions.
6. Entry into force.
7. Registration and publication.
8. Application and enforcement.

(1) Accrediting of negotiators; full powers and credentials

Once a state has decided to commence negotiations with another state or other states for a particular treaty, the first step is to appoint representatives to conduct the negotiations. It is clearly important that representatives should be properly accredited and be equipped with the necessary authority proving not merely their status as official envoys, but also their power to attend at and to participate in the negotiations, as well as to conclude and sign the final treaty, although, strictly speaking, a power to sign is unnecessary for the stage of negotiations. In practice representatives of a state are provided with a very formal instrument given either by the head of state or by the Minister of Foreign Affairs showing their authority in these various regards. This instrument is called the Full Powers or *Pleins Pouvoirs*.[10] According to British practice, two kinds of Full Powers are issued to plenipotentiaries:

a.   If the treaty to be negotiated is in the heads of state form, special Full Powers are prepared signed by the Sovereign and sealed with the Great Seal.

b.   If the treaty to be negotiated is in the inter-governmental or inter-state form, government Full Powers are issued, signed by the Secretary of State for Foreign Affairs and bearing the official seal.

Full Powers are not necessary if it appears from the practice of the negotiating states that their intention was to consider the person concerned as representing the sending state, and to dispense with Full Powers (Vienna Convention, article 7, paragraph 1 (b)). Nor are Full Powers normally issued for the signature of an agreement to be concluded between the departments of two governments. This is rather a manifestation of the principle that the negotiating states concerned may evince an intention to dispense with Full Powers. Such relaxation in the practice has been rendered necessary by the growing practice of concluding agreements between governments in a more simplified form.

When bilateral treaties are concluded, the representatives exhibit their Full Powers. Sometimes an actual exchange of these documents is effected, in other cases only an exchange of certified copies takes place. Practice in this matter is far from settled.

In the case of diplomatic conferences summoned to conclude a multilateral instrument, a different procedure is followed. At the beginning of the proceedings a Committee of Full Powers is appointed to report generally to the Conference on the nature of the Full Powers which each representative at the Conference possesses.[11] The delegates hand in their Full Powers to the Secretary of the Committee of Full Powers. It may be, for instance, that Full Powers possessed by a particular delegate authorise negotiation but give no power to sign. In that case the Committee reports the fact to the Conference and the delegate is specifically requested to obtain from his or her government the necessary authority to sign. In practice, Committees of Full Powers do not, as a rule, insist on the presentation of formal instruments of Full Powers, but sometimes temporarily accept as credentials far less formal documents such as telegrams

10.   See, as to the whole subject, Jones *Full Powers and Ratification* (1946), and Sir Ian Sinclair, op cit, p 397, n 1 above, pp 29–33 et seq. Full powers can authorise the representative to negotiate, adopt, or authenticate a treaty text, or to express a state's consent to be bound by a treaty, or to accomplish any other act with respect to a treaty (Vienna Convention, art 2); possibly, for example, to terminate or denounce a treaty.

11.   Under art 7, para 2 (c) of the Vienna Convention, representatives accredited to an international conference, or to an international organisation or one of its organs, for the purpose of adopting a treaty text in that conference, organisation, or organ, are considered as representing their sending state, without the necessity of producing Full Powers.

or letters emanating from Prime Ministers, Ministers for Foreign Affairs, or Permanent Delegates to the United Nations.[12]

In the case of the International Labour Conference, Full Powers are generally not given to the various government, employers' and workers' delegates of each state represented. As a rule credentials are issued by the government authorising delegates to the Conference merely to attend it, but of course giving them no power to agree to or to conclude or to sign conventions adopted by the Conference, since these conventions are not signed by delegates but merely authenticated by the signatures of the President of the Conference and the Director-General of the International Labour Office, and since the Conference adopts a text in a different manner from diplomatic Conferences.

Acts relating to the conclusion of a treaty performed by a person who has either not produced appropriate Full Powers or who, in the absence of Full Powers, has not been considered as representing the sending state, are without legal effect unless subsequently confirmed by that state (Vienna Convention, article 8).

(2) Negotiation and adoption

Negotiations concerning a treaty are conducted either through discussions in the case of bilateral treaties or by a diplomatic Conference, the more usual procedure when a multilateral treaty is to be adopted. In both cases the delegates remain in touch with their governments, they have with them preliminary instructions which are not communicated to the other parties, and at any stage they may consult their governments and, if necessary, obtain fresh instructions. As a matter of general practice, before appending their signature to the final text of the treaty, delegates do obtain fresh instructions to sign the instrument whether with or without reservations.

The procedure at diplomatic Conferences runs to a standard pattern. Apart from Steering Committees, Legal and Drafting Committees are appointed at an early stage to receive and review the draft provisions proposed by the various delegations. Usually, too, the Conference appoints a prominent delegate to act as rapporteur in order to assist the Conference in its deliberations. Besides the formal public sessions of the Conference, many parleys are conducted in the 'corridors', in hotel rooms, and at special dinners and functions. The results of these appear in due course in the decisions reached by the Conference.

Article 9, paragraph 2 of the Vienna Convention provides that the adoption of a treaty text at an international conference is to take place by the vote of two-thirds of the states present and voting, unless by the same majority these states decide to apply a different rule.

It should be mentioned that in respect of certain subjects at least, the procedure of adoption of multilateral instruments by diplomatic Conferences has been replaced by the method of their adoption by the organs of international institutions; for example, by—among others—the United Nations General

12. Heads of state, heads of government, and Ministers for Foreign Affairs, negotiating in person, do not need Full Powers, but are treated as representing their state for the purpose of performing all acts relating to the conclusion of a treaty, and the same applies to the head of a diplomatic mission for the purpose of adopting a treaty between the sending and the receiving state (Vienna Convention, art 7, para 2 (a) and (b)).

Assembly, the World Health Assembly, and the Assembly of the International Civil Aviation Organisation. The Conventions adopted by any such Assembly are opened for signature or acceptance by member or non-member states.

Provisions of a treaty may be adopted by consensus, as in the case of the United Nations Convention of 10 December 1982 on the Law of the Sea.

(3)   Authentication, signature and exchange of instruments

When the final draft of the treaty has been agreed upon, the instrument is ready for signature. The text may be made public for a certain period before signature, as in the case of the North Atlantic Security Treaty, made public on 18 March 1949, and signed at Washington on 4 April 1949. The act of signature is usually a most formal matter, even in the case of bilateral treaties. As to multilateral conventions, signature is generally effected at a formal closing session (*séance de clôture*) in the course of which each delegate steps up to a table and signs on behalf of the head of state or government by whom they were appointed.

Unless there is an agreement to dispense with signature, this is essential for a treaty, principally because it serves to authenticate the text. The rule, as stated in article 10 of the Vienna Convention, is that the text may be authenticated by such procedure as is laid down in the treaty itself, or as is agreed to by the negotiating states, or in the absence of such agreed procedure, by signature, signature ad referendum,[13] initialling,[14] or by incorporation in the Final Act[15] of the conference. In practice, also, the text of an instrument may be authenticated by the resolution of an international organisation. If a treaty is signed, it is important that the signature should be made by each of the delegates at the same time and place, and in the presence of each other. Furthermore, the date of the treaty is usually taken to be the date on which it was signed.

Sometimes not merely a delegate but a head of state will sign a treaty. Thus, in 1919, Woodrow Wilson, as President of the United States, signed the Treaty of Versailles, the preamble reciting that he acted 'in his own name and by his own proper authority', and President Nixon signed the United States–Soviet Union Treaty on the Limitation of Anti-Ballistic Missile Systems concluded at Moscow on 26 May 1972.

As mentioned above, the conventions adopted by the International Labour Conference are not signed by the delegates but are simply authenticated by the signatures of the President of the Conference and the Director-General of the International Labour Office. There have also been cases of instruments adopted by international organs, which are accepted or acceded to by states, without signature.

13. As to which see p 412, n 18, below.
14. In which case, formal signature of an instrument in proper form, takes place later; eg, the Security Treaty between Australia, New Zealand, and the United States (ANZUS), initialled at Washington on 12 July 1951, and signed at San Francisco on 1 September 1951. Other cases of initialling occur where a representative, without authority to sign or acting generally without instructions, prefers not to sign a text. The initialling may indeed be intended to convey only that the negotiating plenipotentiaries have reached agreement on a text, to be referred to their governments for consideration. In special circumstances, an initialling may be intended to operate as a signature; and cf Vienna Convention, art 12.
15. See p 404 above.

It is a common practice to open a convention for signature by certain states until a certain date after the date of the formal session of signature. Generally, this period does not exceed nine months. The object is to obtain as many parties to the convention as possible, but inasmuch as new signatories can only be allowed with the consent of the original signatories, a special clause to this effect must be inserted in the convention. A current practice is to open a convention for signature to all members of the United Nations and the specialised agencies, to all parties to the Statute of the International Court of Justice, and to any other state invited by the General Assembly. During the period mentioned, each state may sign at any time, but after the expiration of the period no further signatures are allowed and a non-signatory state desiring to become a party must accede or adhere to the convention but cannot ratify, inasmuch as it has not signed the instrument. In the case of the nuclear weapons test ban treaty of 1963 referred to above,[16] the instrument was opened for the signature of all states (see article III).

A further expedient has been, by the so-called *acceptance formula clause*, to open an instrument for an indefinite time for: (a) signature, without reservation as to acceptance; (b) signature subject to, and followed by later acceptance; and (c) acceptance simpliciter, leaving states free to become bound by any one of these three methods. The term 'acceptance', used in this clause, has crept into recent treaty terminology to denote the act of becoming a party to a treaty by adherence of any kind, in accordance with a state's municipal constitutional law.[17] The principal object of the clause was indeed to meet difficulties which might confront a potential state party under its municipal constitutional rules relative to treaty approval. Some states did not wish to use the term 'ratification', as this might imply an obligation to submit a treaty to the legislature for approval, or to go through some undesired constitutional procedure. In general, it may be said, the formula of 'signature subject to acceptance' is employed more particularly in the case of treaties of such a kind that normally ratification would be inappropriate or legally inconvenient for certain of the states that are signatories.

Effect of signature
The effect of signature of a treaty depends on whether or not the treaty is subject to ratification, acceptance, or approval.

If the treaty is subject to ratification, acceptance, or approval, signature means no more than that the delegates have agreed upon a text and are willing to accept it and refer it to their governments for such action as those governments may choose to take in regard to the acceptance or rejection of the treaty. It may also indicate an intention on the part of a government to make a fresh examination of the question dealt with by the treaty with a view to putting the treaty into

16. See p 160 above.
17. On the meaning of 'acceptance', see Yuen-Li Liang 44 AJIL (1950) 342 et seq. It means in effect a decision to become definitively bound, in accordance with a state's municipal constitutional rules. As to the term 'approval', see commentary on art 11, Draft Arts ILC. Art 11 of the Vienna Convention provides that the consent of a state to be bound by treaty may be expressed by signature, exchange of instruments constituting a treaty, ratification, acceptance, approval or accession, or any other means, if so agreed.

force.[18] In the absence of an express term to that effect, there is no binding obligation on a signatory state to submit the treaty to the national legislature for action or otherwise. On the other hand, it is laid down in the Vienna Convention that, where a treaty is subject to ratification, acceptance, or approval, signatory states are under an obligation of good faith to refrain from acts calculated to defeat the object of the treaty until they have made their intention clear of not becoming parties (see article 18[19]).

Where a treaty is subject to ratification, acceptance or approval, it is sometimes expressly stipulated in the treaty or in some related exchange of notes that, pending ratification, acceptance, or approval, the instrument is to operate on a provisional basis as from the date of signature, as with the Japan-Australia Trade Treaty of 6 July 1957.

If the treaty is not subject to ratification, acceptance, or approval, or is silent on this point, the better opinion is that, in the absence of contrary provision, the instrument is binding as from signature. The ground for this opinion is that it has become an almost invariable practice where a treaty is to be ratified, accepted, or approved, to insert a clause making provision to this effect, and where such provision is absent, the treaty may be presumed to operate on signature. Some treaties may by their express provisions operate from the date of signature, for example, the Anglo-Japanese Treaty of Alliance of 1902, and Agreements concluded within the framework of the Council of Europe, which are expressed to be signed without reservation in respect to ratification.[20] Also many treaties relating to minor or technical matters, generally bearing the titles 'Agreement', 'Arrangement' or 'Procès-Verbal', are simply signed but not ratified, and operate as from the date signature is appended.[1] Indeed, if there is direct evidence of intention to be bound by signature alone, as, for example, in the terms of the Full Powers, this is sufficient to bind the states concerned without more. Article 12 of the Vienna Convention upholds the autonomous right of the negotiating states so to agree, expressly or impliedly, that they shall be bound by signature alone,[2] or by initialling treated as equivalent to signature, or by signature ad referendum[3] confirmed by the sending state.

18. The common practice of signature ad referendum generally denotes that the signatory state is unable at the time to accept definitively the negotiated terms expressed in the treaty. It has also been interpreted as indicating that the plenipotentiary concerned had no definite instructions to sign, and no time to consult his government. If signature ad referendum be confirmed by the state concerned, the result is a full signature of the treaty; cf Vienna Convention, art 12.
19. Under this article, also, a state which has expressed a consent to be bound by a treaty, is similarly obliged to refrain from such acts, pending the entry into force of the treaty, and provided that such entry into force is not unduly delayed.
20. Sometimes, a treaty signed, without being subject to ratification, may provide for entry into force as from a date later than the date of signature; eg, the United States–Soviet Union Maritime Agreement signed at Washington on 4 October 1972, was expressed to enter into force on 1 January 1973.
1. As to treaties in simple form, see generally Smets *La Conclusion des Accords en Forme Simplifiée* (Brussels, 1969).
2. Para 1 of art 12 provides that the consent of a state to be bound by a treaty is expressed by the signature of its representative when: (a) the treaty provides that signature shall have that effect; (b) it is otherwise established that the negotiating states were agreed that signature should have that effect; or (c) the intention of the state to give that effect to the signature appears from the full powers of its representative or was expressed during the negotiation.
3. See n 18 above.

Exchange of instruments

Where a treaty is constituted by instruments exchanged by representatives of the parties, such exchange may result in the parties becoming bound by the treaty if: (a) the instruments provide that the exchange is to have this effect; or (b) it can otherwise be shown that the parties were agreed that this would be the effect of such exchange (Vienna Convention, article 13).

Sealing

Treaties and conventions are nearly always sealed, although this is not the case with the less formal types of international agreements. Sealing appears now to have lost its prior importance, and is not necessary either for the authentication or the validity of the treaty. Formerly, with the exception of notarial attestation for special instruments, it was, however, the only recognised mode of authenticating the text of a treaty.

(4) Ratification

The next stage is that the delegates who signed the treaty or convention refer it back to their governments for approval, if such further act of confirmation be expressly or impliedly necessary.

In theory, ratification is the approval by the head of state or the government of the signature appended to the treaty by the duly appointed plenipotentiaries. In modern practice, however, it has come to possess more significance than a simple act of confirmation, being deemed to represent the formal declaration by a state of its consent to be bound by a treaty. So in article 2 of the Vienna Convention, ratification was defined to mean 'the international act . . . whereby a state establishes on the international plane its consent to be bound by a treaty'. Consistently with this, ratification is not held to have retroactive effect, so as to make the treaty obligatory from the date of signature.

At one time, ratification was regarded as so necessary that without it a treaty should be deemed ineffective. This point was referred to by Lord Stowell:[4]

'According to the practice now prevailing, a subsequent ratification is essentially necessary; and a strong confirmation of the truth of this position is that there is hardly a modern treaty in which it is not expressly so stipulated; and therefore it is now to be presumed that the powers of plenipotentiaries are limited by the condition of a subsequent ratification. The ratification may be a form, but it is an essential form; *for the instrument, in point of legal efficacy, is imperfect without it.*'

According to Judge J. B. Moore in the *Mavrommatis Palestine Concessions Case*[5] the doctrine that treaties may be regarded as operative before they have been ratified is 'obsolete, and lingers only as an echo from the past'.[6]

These judicial observations apply with less force and cogency at the present time, when more than two-thirds of currently registered treaties make no provision whatever for ratification, and when most treaties make it quite clear

4. See *The Eliza Ann* (1813) 1 Dods 244 at 248.
5. (1924) PCIJ, Series A, No 2, p 57.
6. In modern practice, the express or implied waiver of ratification is so common that, today, the more tenable view is that ratification is not required unless expressly stipulated. Ratification is, of course, unnecessary if the treaty provides that parties may be bound by signature only, or if the treaty be signed by heads of state in person; and see also art 12 of the Vienna Convention.

whether or not signature, or signature subject to ratification, acceptance, etc is the method chosen by the states concerned. The more acceptable view today is that it is purely a matter of the intention of the parties whether a treaty does or does not require ratification as a condition of its binding operation. Consistently, article 14 of the Vienna Convention provides that the consent of a state to be bound by a treaty is expressed by ratification if: (a) the treaty expressly so provides; or (b) the negotiating states otherwise agree that ratification is necessary; or (c) the treaty has been signed subject to ratification; or (d) an intention to sign subject to ratification appears from the Full Powers or was expressed during negotiations.

The practice of ratification rests on the following grounds:

a.   States are entitled to have an opportunity of examining and reviewing instruments signed by their delegates before undertaking the obligations therein specified.

b.   By reason of its sovereignty, a state is entitled not to become a party to any treaty should it so choose.

c.   Often a treaty requires amendments or adjustments in municipal law. The period between signature and ratification enables states to pass the necessary legislation or obtain the necessary parliamentary approvals, so that they may thereupon proceed to ratification. This consideration is important in the case of federal states, where, if legislation to carry into effect treaty provisions falls within the powers of the member units of the federation, these may have to be consulted by the central government before it can ratify.

d.   There is also the democratic principle that the government should consult public opinion either in Parliament or elsewhere as to whether a particular treaty should be confirmed.

Ratification and municipal constitutional law

The development of constitutional systems of government under which various organs other than the head of state are given a share in the treaty-making power has increased the importance of ratification.[7] At the same time in each country the procedure followed in this regard differs. For instance, often states will insist on parliamentary approval or confirmation of a treaty although the treaty expressly provides that it operates as from signature, whereas other states follow the provisions of the treaty and regard it as binding them without further steps being taken.

In British practice there is no rule of law requiring all treaties to be approved by Parliament prior to ratification. It is customary to submit certain treaties to Parliament for approval,[8] for example, treaties of alliance, and ratification is only effected after this approval is given. Theoretically, however, the Crown is constitutionally free to ratify any treaty without the consent of Parliament. By reason of their subject matter some treaties necessitate the intervention of Parliament, for example, treaties derogating from the private rights of citizens,

7.   See as to the subject of ratification, Jones *Full Powers and Ratification* (1946), Oppenheim *International Law* (9th edn, 1992) Vol I, pp 1226-1235, and the commentary by the International Law Commission in (1966) 2 *Yearbook of the International Law Commission* p 197.

8.   See eg p 72 above.

treaties imposing a charge on public funds, etc. In practice the text of every treaty subject to ratification is, as soon as possible after signature, laid before Parliament for a period of at least 21 days before ratification.[9]

Usually the ratification is an act executed only by the head of state, but in the case of treaties of lesser importance the government itself or the Minister for Foreign Affairs may effect the ratification. The document of ratification is generally a highly formal instrument, notwithstanding that international law neither prescribes nor insists on any degree of formality for such instruments.

Some treaties make signature subject to 'acceptance'[10] or 'approval'; these terms may then denote a simplified form of ratification. In fact, in article 2 of the Vienna Convention, 'acceptance' and 'approval' have received the same definition as ratification, while the provisions of article 14 as to when ratification imports consent to be bound by a treaty apply mutatis mutandis to acceptance and approval.

Absence of duty to ratify

The power of refusing ratification is deemed to be inherent in state sovereignty, and accordingly at international law there is neither a legal nor a moral duty to ratify a treaty. Furthermore, there is no obligation other than one of ordinary courtesy to convey to other states concerned a statement of the reasons for refusing to ratify.

In the case of multilateral 'law-making' treaties, including the conventions of the International Labour Organisation, the delays of states in ratifying or their unexpected withholding of ratifications have caused much concern and raised serious problems. The practical value of unratified conventions scarcely calls for comment. The principal causes of delay were acutely investigated and reported on by a Committee appointed by the League of Nations to consider the matter, and the conclusions reached by the Committee appear to be more or less valid in the context of present-day conditions, more than half a century later.[11] To borrow from the study made by this Committee the causes may be briefly summarised as:

a. the complicated machinery of modern government involving protracted administrative work before the decision to ratify or accede;
b. the absence of thorough preparatory work for treaties leading to defects which entitle states to withhold or delay ratification;
c. the shortage of parliamentary time in countries where constitutional practice requires submission of the instrument to the legislature;
d. serious difficulties disclosed by the instrument only after signature and calling for prolonged examination;
e. the necessity for new national legislation or the need for increased expenditure as a result;
f. lack of interest by states.

The International Labour Office has over a period of years developed a specialised technique for supervising the ratification of conventions and their

9. See p 72, n 18 above.
10. See p 411 above.
11. See *Report* of the Committee, League of Nations Doc. A.10, 1930, V.

application by municipal law, partly through a special Committee which regularly deals with the matter, partly through the work of special sections of the Office.

The delays in ratification may explain the recent tendency in treaty practice to dispense with any such requirement, and the growth in the practice of concluding arrangements between governments in more simplified forms.

Obligation not to defeat the object and purpose of a treaty prior to its entry into force

The rule stated by article 18 of the Vienna Convention is regarded as one of customary international law[12]:

> 'A State is obliged to refrain from acts which would defeat the object and purpose of a treaty when: (a) it has signed the treaty or has exchanged instruments constituting the treaty subject to ratification, acceptance or approval, until it shall have made its intention clear not to become a party to the treaty; or (b) it has expressed its consent to be bound by the treaty, pending the entry into force of the treaty and provided that such entry into force is not unduly delayed.'

The effect of this rule is not to make an unratified treaty, or one not yet in force, in all respects binding, for that would be to deprive those steps of meaning. Rather, a state is bound by good faith not to take up or persist in an action or posture fundamentally at variance with the treaty until it has definitively disavowed its intention to proceed to the ratification of the treaty that it has signed.

Exchange or deposit of ratifications

Unless the treaty itself otherwise provides, an instrument of ratification has no effect in finally establishing consent to be bound by the treaty until the exchange or deposit, as the case may be, of ratifications, or at least until some notice of ratification is given to the other state or states concerned, or to the depositary of the treaty (see Vienna Convention, article 16). The same rule applies to an instrument of acceptance or approval.

In the case of bilateral treaties, ratifications are exchanged by the states parties concerned and each instrument is filed in the archives of the Treaty Department of each state's Foreign Office. Usually a Procès-Verbal is drawn up to record and certify the exchange.

The method of exchange is not appropriate for the ratification of multilateral treaties. Such a treaty usually provides for the deposit of all ratifications in a central headquarters such as the Foreign Office of the state where the treaty was signed. Before the Second World War, ratifications of conventions adopted under the auspices of the League of Nations were deposited in the League Secretariat, and the Secretary-General used to notify all states concerned of the receipt of ratifications. The Secretariat of the United Nations now carries out these chancery functions.[13] In the case of the nuclear weapons test ban treaty of 1963 referred

---

12. *Certain German Interests in Polish Upper Silesia* case (1926) PCIJ, Ser A, No 7.
13. The Secretary-General has exercised depositary functions in respect to a large number of conventions, treaties, etc. For his practice as depositary, see *Summary of the Practice of the Secretary-General as Depositary of Multilateral Agreements*, published in 1959. The Vienna Convention contains provisions setting out the functions of a depositary of a treaty (see arts

to above,[14] the treaty was to be deposited in the archives of each of the three original signatories, the USSR, the USA, and the UK.

(5) Accessions and adhesions

In practice, when a state has not signed a treaty it can only accede or adhere to it. According to present practice, a non-signatory state may accede or adhere even before the treaty enters into force.[15] Some writers profess to make a distinction between accession and adhesion. Thus it is sometimes said that accession involves being party to the whole treaty by full and entire acceptance of all its provisions precluding reservations to any clause, whereas adhesion may be an acceptance of part only of the treaty. Again, it is maintained by some that accession involves participation in the treaty with the same status as the original signatories, whereas adhesion connotes merely approval of the principles of the treaty. These suggested distinctions are not generally supported by the practice of states.

The term 'accession' has also been applied to acceptance by a state of a treaty or convention after the prescribed number of ratifications for its entry into force have been deposited. Thus, assuming ten ratifications are necessary for entry into force, and ten have been deposited, subsequent ratifications or acceptances would be termed 'accessions'. The use of the term 'accession' in this sense is not generally approved. In fact, in article 2 of the Vienna Convention, 'accession' has received the same definition as 'ratification', while under article 15 accession imports consent to be bound much in the same way mutatis mutandis as under article 14 dealing with ratification (see p 413 above). Similarly, unless the treaty otherwise provides, an instrument of accession does not finally establish such consent, until exchange or deposit, or notice thereof to the contracting states, or to the depositary (Vienna Convention, article 16).

No precise form is prescribed by international law for an instrument of accession, although generally it is in the same form as an instrument of ratification. A simple notification of intention to participate in a treaty may be sufficient.

Strictly speaking, states which have not signed a treaty can in theory accede only with the consent of all the states which are already parties to the instrument. The reason for this rule is that the states parties are entitled to know and approve of all other parties to a treaty binding them, so that the equilibrium of rights and obligations created by the treaty is not disturbed. Usually, therefore, states accede to a treaty in virtue of a special accession clause, enabling them to accede after the final date for signature of the treaty, and prescribing the procedure for deposit of accessions.

(6) Entry into force

The entry into force of a treaty depends upon its provisions, or upon what the contracting states have otherwise agreed (Vienna Convention, article 24, paragraph

---

76–80), and cf in that connection the depositary functions cast upon the Secretary-General of the United Nations by art 319 of the United Nations Convention on the Law of the Sea of 10 December 1982.

14. See p 160 above.
15. See commentary on art 12, Draft Arts ILC.

1). As already mentioned, many treaties become operative on the date of their signature, but where ratification, acceptance, or approval is necessary, the general rule of international law is that the treaty concerned comes into force only after the exchange or deposit of ratifications, acceptances, or approvals by all the states signatories. Multilateral treaties now usually make entry into force dependent on the deposit of a prescribed number of ratifications and like consents to be bound—usually from six to about thirty-five.[16] Sometimes, however, a precise date for entry into force is fixed without regard to the number of ratifications received. Sometimes, also, the treaty is to come into operation only on the happening of a certain event; for example, even after its ratification by all states signatories, the Locarno Treaty of Mutual Guarantee of 1925 was to enter into force only after Germany's admission to the League of Nations (see article 10).

As to states parties desiring to ratify, accept, approve, or accede, it is usually provided that the treaty or convention will enter into force for each such state on the date of deposit of the appropriate instrument of consent to be bound, or within a fixed time—usually 90 days—after such deposit.[17] Sometimes also it is specified that the treaty will not be operative for a particular state until after the necessary legislation has been passed by it.

Another frequently adopted expedient is that of the provisional or de facto application of a treaty, or a part thereof, pending its de jure entry into force, as for example in the case of the Protocol of 8 February 1965, adding a new Part IV to the General Agreement on Tariffs and Trade (GATT) of 30 October 1947. This method of provisional application is recognised by the Vienna Convention (see article 25).[18] The provisional application of a bilateral treaty is terminated if one party to the treaty informs the other of its intention not to become a party thereto.[19] In the case of the provisional application of a treaty, the obligation not to defeat the object and purpose of the treaty prior to its entry into force (see article 18 of the Vienna Convention discussed above) imports a duty to refrain from taking steps that would render impossible the future application of the treaty if and when it is ratified.[20]

(7)   Registration and publication

The United Nations Charter 1945, provides by article 102 that all treaties and international agreements entered into by members of the United Nations Organisation shall 'as soon as possible' be registered with the Secretariat of the Organisation and be published by it. No party to a treaty or agreement not registered in this way 'may invoke that treaty or agreement before any organ of the United Nations'. This means that a state party to such an unregistered treaty

16. In the unusual case of the United Nations Convention on the Law of the Sea, 1982 (Chapter 9, above), where universal participation was especially desired, the prescribed number was 60. In the absence of such a prescribed number of consents to be bound, a treaty enters into force only when all negotiating states are shown to have consented to be bound (Vienna Convention, art 24, para 2).
17. In principle, the act of deposit is sufficient without notification to other states concerned; cf commentary on art 13, Draft Arts ILC.
18. Other precedents for the provisional application of treaties, including maritime boundary treaties and international commodity arrangements, are referred to in 74 AJIL (1980) 931–932.
19. Para 2 of art 25 of the Vienna Convention.
20. 74 AJIL (1980) 933.

or agreement cannot rely upon it in proceedings before the International Court of Justice or in meetings of the General Assembly or Security Council. Apparently the provision does not invalidate an unregistered treaty, or prevent such a treaty from being invoked before bodies or courts other than United Nations organs.

The object of article 102 was to prevent the practice of secret agreements between states, and to make it possible for the people of democratic states to repudiate such treaties when publicly disclosed.

It has been suggested that article 102 gives member states a discretion in deciding whether or not to register treaties, and, by electing not to register, voluntarily to incur the penalty of unenforceability of the instrument, but the better view, adopted by the Sixth Committee (Legal) of the United Nations General Assembly in 1947, is that it imposes a binding obligation to effect registration.

The following points may be briefly referred to:

a. In the interim period pending registration 'as soon as possible', the unregistered treaty can be relied upon before the Court or any United Nations organ, subject presumably to an undertaking to register.
b. Notwithstanding a failure to register 'as soon as possible', the lapse can be cured by subsequent registration.
c. Although, in principle, the functions of the Secretariat are purely ministerial, and it cannot reject an illegal treaty for registration, it would seem that an instrument, obviously on the face of it neither a treaty nor an international agreement, ought to be refused registration.
d. Under a direction from the General Assembly, the Secretariat receives for filing and recording (as distinct from registration and publication), instruments entered into before the date of coming into force of the Charter, and instruments transmitted by non-member states,[1] but in substance this process amounts to voluntary registration.
e. Certified statements as to changes in the parties, or the terms, scope, and application of registered treaties, are also received for registration.[1]

The duty of publication[2] by the Secretariat is performed by publishing the instruments concerned in the *United Nations Treaty Series* (cf the former *League of Nations Treaty Series*), together with lists from time to time of ratifications, acceptances, etc. A failure to publish does not render the instrument unenforceable (see terms of article 102).

Instruments that have been lodged with the Secretariat, include treaties or agreements made by or with the specialised agencies of the United Nations, trusteeship agreements, declarations accepting compulsory jurisdiction of the International Court of Justice, and even unilateral engagements of an

---

1. See the Regulations adopted by the General Assembly on 14 December 1946, as amended on 12 December 1950; these Regulations enable a certificate of registration of a treaty to be issued, and also permit the filing and recording (as distinct from registration) of agreements entered into by the United Nations and its specialised agencies (for text, see *Report* of the International Law Commission for 1962, Annex, pp 37–38). Art 80 of the Vienna Convention provides that treaties shall, after their entry into force, be transmitted to the Secretariat of the United Nations for registration or filing and recording, as the case may be, and for publication.
2. Under municipal law, treaties are often required to be promulgated or published officially.

international character, such as the Egyptian Declaration of 24 April 1957, regarding the future use of the Suez Canal.

Certain international organisations other than the United Nations have their own system of registration, etc, for treaties related to such organisations.

(8)   Application and enforcement

The final stage of the treaty-making process is the actual incorporation, where necessary, of the treaty provisions in the municipal law of the states parties, and the application by such states of these provisions, and, also, any required administration and supervision by international organs. As already mentioned above, there may be, if the treaty so provides or the parties so agree, a provisional application of the treaty pending its entry into force. In practice, vigilant 'follow-up' work is needed to ensure that states parties do actually apply instruments binding them. Some international organs (for example, the International Labour Organisation with its Committee of Experts on the Application of Conventions and Recommendations, and its tripartite Conference Committee on the application of these instruments) have special Committees to discharge this function, work which may be supplemented by the sending of official visiting missions. One innovation has been the drawing up of special model codes for the legislative application of conventions.

Structure of conventions and treaties

The principal parts of conventions or treaties in their usual order are:

1.   The preamble or preliminary recitals, setting out the names of the parties (heads of state, states, or governments), the purpose for which the instrument was concluded, the 'resolve' of the parties to enter into it, and the names and designations of the plenipotentiaries.
2.   The substantive clauses, sometimes known as the 'dispositive provisions'.
3.   The formal (or final) clauses or 'clauses protocolaires'[3] dealing with technical or formal points or matters relative to the application or entry into force of the instrument. The usual such clauses relate separately to the following: (i) the date of the instrument; (ii) the mode of acceptance (signature, accession, etc); (iii) opening of the instrument for signature; (iv) entry into force; (v) duration; (vi) denunciation by the parties; (vii) application by municipal legislation; (viii) application to territories, etc;[4] (ix) the authoritative status of different languages in which the instrument is drafted; (x) settlement of disputes; (xi) amendment or revision; (xii) registration; (xiii) custody of, and the functions of the depositary of the original instrument.
4.   Formal attestation or acknowledgment of signature, and of the date and place of signature.
5.   Signature by the plenipotentiaries.

3.   See *Handbook of Final Clauses*, prepared by Legal Department of United Nations Secretariat, August 1951, and the document on standard final clauses, A/CONF.39/L. 1, prepared for the Vienna Conference of 1968–1969 on the Law of Treaties. In 1962, the Committee of Ministers of the Council of Europe adopted texts of model final clauses of Agreements and conventions.
4.   For the British practice regarding this so-called 'Territories' Clause, see the United Nations publication, *Laws and Practices Concerning the Conclusion of Treaties* (1953) pp 122–124. In the light of decolonisation, territorial application clauses became less frequent after 1960.

5.   RESERVATIONS[5]

A state may often wish to sign or ratify or otherwise consent to be bound by a treaty in such manner that certain provisions of the treaty do not bind it, or apply to it subject to modifications. This can be effected principally by: (1) express provision in the treaty itself; or (2) by agreement between the contracting states; or (3) by a reservation duly made.

Where a state wishes to become bound by a specific part only of a treaty, its consent to be so bound can be effective only if this is permitted by the treaty or is otherwise agreed to by the contracting states; and where a treaty allows a contracting state to become partially bound by exercising a choice between differing provisions, the consent must make clear to which provisions it relates (Vienna Convention, article 17).

A reservation is defined in article 2 of the Vienna Convention as a unilateral statement, however phrased or named, made by a state, when signing, ratifying, accepting, approving, or acceding to a treaty, whereby it purports to exclude or modify the legal effect of certain provisions of the treaty in their application to that state. For example, a reservation may stipulate for exemption from one or more provisions of the treaty, or the modification of these provisions or of their effect, or the interpretation of the provisions in a particular way. A declaration by a signatory as to how the treaty will be applied, which does not vary the obligations of that signatory vis-à-vis other signatories, is not however a true reservation.[6] An example of the latter is the United Nations Convention on the Law of the Sea, 1982, article 309 of which forbids the making of reservations or exceptions, but article 310 of which allows the making of declarations intended to harmonise the provisions of the Convention with those of municipal law in particular cases.[7]

---

5.   See commentary on arts 16–20, Draft Arts ILC for the 1966 views of the International Law Commission upon the subject.

6.   See *Power Authority of State of New York v Federal Power Commission* 247 F 2d 538 (1957). In 1959, the Assembly of the Inter-Governmental Maritime Consultative Organisation (IMCO), renamed with effect from May 1982 as the International Maritime Organisation (IMO), agreed that India's acceptance of the Convention of 6 March 1948, establishing the Organisation, subject to her right to adopt measures aimed solely at developing her maritime industries, was not a reservation but a declaration of policy. A similar problem arose in IMCO concerning Cuba's declaration in 1964 and 1965 in connection with Cuba's acceptance of the same Convention, that it would not consider itself bound by the Convention if IMCO made recommendations at variance with Cuban domestic law. There was a division of opinion among IMCO members whether the Cuban declaration was a statement of policy, or an impermissible reservation.

7.   Eg, some Latin American states had made claims in the 1940s and 1950s to maritime zones of 200 nautical miles under such names as 'patrimonial sea', 'epicontinental sea', or even 'territorial sea'. Article 310 allows these states to declare that, although these names may continue to appear in national laws, their practice in relation to those zones will conform to the regime of the exclusive economic zone as laid down in the Convention. For the protests of certain states against the declaration of the Philippines on signing, and again on ratifying, the Convention, with regard to the relationship between archipelagic and historic waters, claiming that the purported declaration was in reality an inadmissible reservation, and the the reply of the Philippines to these protests, see the annotations to the entry for the United Nations Convention on the Law of the Sea, 1982 in *The Status of Multilateral Conventions in Respect of Which the United Nations Secretary-General is Depositary* (1992).

Like the power of withholding ratification, the privilege of making reservations is regarded as an incident of the sovereignty and perfect equality of states. It is felt preferable that states which cannot accept certain provisions should participate in the treaty, even if only in a limited way, rather than that they should be excluded altogether from participation. Where there is agreement on the basic provisions of a convention, a certain diversity of obligation in respect of the less important provisions is regarded, subject to some limits, as permissible.

The effect of a reservation is to modify the provisions of the treaty to which the reservation relates, to the extent of that reservation, in the reserving state's relations with other parties, but leaving intact the treaty relations of non-reserving states inter se. This applies also to relations between a reserving state and a state objecting to the reservation, provided it has not opposed the entry into force of the treaty between it and the reserving state (Vienna Convention, article 21).

In principle, a state making a reservation can do so only with the consent of other contracting states; otherwise the whole object of the treaty might be impaired. Sometimes, the intention to make reservations is announced at some session or other of the Conference and the reservations are then and there agreed to by the delegates, but in principle such an 'embryo' reservation should be confirmed in the subsequent signature, ratification, acceptance, approval or accession, or at least in the formal minutes of the proceedings. If a state wishes to ratify or otherwise consent to be bound, subject to a reservation, it should inquire of the other states parties whether they assent to the reservation; and in certain circumstances the assent may be inferred.[8] The practice of making reservations has, however, become so common that states have tended to ignore the requirement of obtaining the assent of other states parties; thus reservations have frequently been made at the time of signature without being announced during the deliberations of the Conference, or at the time of ratification or accession without previous consultation or inquiry of states which have signed or ratified the treaty.

The form in which reservations have been recorded has varied; sometimes they are inserted in a Protocol of Signature annexed to the convention concerned, sometimes in the Final Act, sometimes they are specified in an exchange of notes, sometimes they are made by transcription under or above the signature for the state making them, and sometimes merely by declaration at the Conference recorded in the minutes (or *Procès-Verbal*) of the proceedings.

The Vienna Convention (see article 23) laid it down that reservations, and acceptance of, or objections to reservations, must be in writing and be duly communicated; also reservations made when signing a treaty subject to ratification, acceptance, or approval, must be confirmed in the subsequent instrument of ratification, acceptance, or approval.

Because of the special character of the Conventions of the International Labour Organisation, it is recognised that these instruments are incapable of being

8.   For the purposes of art 20 of the Vienna Convention, a contracting state is deemed to have accepted a reservation, if it has raised no objection within twelve months of notification, or by the date of its expression of consent to be bound by the treaty, whichever is later (see art 20, para 5).

ratified subject to reservations. They may, however, in certain circumstances be conditionally ratified.[9]

It is generally accepted that reservations expressly or impliedly prohibited by the terms of a treaty are inadmissible,[10] while those expressly or impliedly authorised, are effective. The Vienna Convention provides that a reservation 'expressly' authorised by a treaty does not require subsequent assent by other contracting states, unless the treaty so provides (article 20, paragraph 1).

With the increase in the number of multilateral conventions the unchecked practice of making reservations to multilateral instruments has created a disturbing problem. Obviously an excessive number of reservations tends to throw out of gear the operation of a multilateral treaty. Also, states are never sure that later, when ratifying, another state may not make a reservation which originally would have deterred them from entering into the treaty. Various solutions of the difficulty have been adopted from time to time, in order to secure a maximum number of parties to multilateral conventions. According to the solution resorted to by the Inter-American states, a signatory desiring to make reservations is not precluded from becoming a party to the convention, but the convention is deemed not to be in force between such 'reserving' state and any state objecting to the reservations.

If a limited number of negotiating states is involved, and it is clear from the object and purpose of the treaty that the application of the treaty in its entirety is an essential condition of the consent of each state to be bound by the treaty, the admissibility of the reservations will depend upon unanimous acceptance (Vienna Convention, article 20, paragraph 2).

Also, if the reservation is one to the constituent instrument of an international organisation, prima facie, acceptance by a competent organ of that institution is required, unless there is express provision to the contrary (Vienna Convention, article 20, paragraph 3).

Where these rules do not apply, a reserving state may become party to the treaty vis-à-vis a state accepting the reservation, while an objection to the reservation does not preclude the treaty coming into force between the objecting and the reserving state, unless the objecting state opposes this (Vienna Convention, article 20, paragraph 4).

In 1949–1950, the problem of maximum participation in a multilateral treaty arose in relation to objections taken to reservations of parties to the Genocide Convention 1948. The questions of: (a) the admissibility and (b) the effect of such reservations, and (c) the rights of states to object thereto, were submitted for Advisory Opinion to the International Court of Justice. The Court's views[11] (being the views of the majority) may be summarised as follows:

9. Also, a state ratifying a Labour Convention may couple its ratification with explanations of any limitations upon the manner in which it intends to execute the convention; and the provisions in the convention may be drawn so as to allow certain states some latitude in fulfilling their obligations; see *International Labour Code*, 1951 Vol I (1952), pp xcix–ci and *Conventions and Recommendations Adopted by the IL Conference 1919–1966* (1966) p viii.

10. Fg, if the treaty authorises specified reservations which do not include the reservation in question.

11. See *Advisory Opinion on Reservations to the Genocide Convention* ICJ 1951, 15 et seq.

(a)   *Admissibility of reservations.* Reservations are allowable notwithstanding the absence of a provision in the convention permitting them. There need not necessarily be an express assent by other interested states to the making of reservations; such assent may be by implication, particularly in the case of certain multilateral conventions, where clauses are adopted by majority vote of the drafting Conference. If a reservation is *compatible*,[12] objectively, with the nature and purpose of a convention, a state making it may be regarded as fully a party to the instrument; this test of compatibility is consistent with the principle that the convention should have as universal an operation as possible, and with the principle of 'integrity' of the instrument.

(b)   *Effect of reservations.* The same test of compatibility applies; therefore, if a state rightly objects that a reservation is incompatible with the convention, it may legitimately consider that the reserving state is not a party thereto.

(c)   *States entitled to object to reservations.* A state entitled to sign or accept a convention, but which has not done so, cannot validly object to reservations; nor is an objection by a signatory state, which has not ratified the instrument, effective until its ratification.

This Advisory Opinion could not be said to have solved all problems in this connection; it appeared to confer too extensive a liberty to make reservations. The objective test of compatibility also bore hardly on signatory states which might not have signed the instrument if they had subjectively realised that certain drastic reservations would be made by other states. It was significant that the International Law Commission which at the request of the General Assembly also studied the problem in 1951[13] did not follow the Court in the test of compatibility, but stressed the necessity for consent to reservations, adopting the view that it might be more important to maintain the 'integrity' of a convention than to aim at its widest possible acceptance. The Commission also suggested the insertion of express provisions in conventions dealing with the admissibility or non-admissibility of reservations, and the effect of such reservations when made.[14] However, the General Assembly in its Resolution of 12 January 1952, recommended to states that they should be guided by the Court's Advisory Opinion. Also, the general increase in the number of new states since 1952 emphasised the desirability of maximum participation by such potential parties to conventions, and therefore of greater permissibility of reservations, as against a possible risk that the integrity of a convention may be

12. According to the International Law Commission, where the treaty concerned is the constitution of an international organisation, this question of compatibility should be determined by a competent organ of that organisation; see *Report* for 1962, p 21 and cf Vienna Convention, art 20, para 3.
13. *Report* of the Commission on the work of its *3rd Session* (1951) pp 5–7.
14. As to the attitude to be adopted by the United Nations Secretariat as depositary of reservations made by states, see the General Assembly Resolution of 12 January 1952, to the effect that a depositary should in regard to future multilateral conventions maintain a neutral attitude, merely passing on documents to the interested states, leaving them to decide whether or not reservations are objectionable. This has been reaffirmed in a later Resolution of 7 December 1959, showing that the directive applies to conventions concluded before, as well as after 12 January 1952.

impaired by a more liberal admission of reservations.[15] In the Vienna Convention (see article 19), the test of compatibility with the object and purpose of the treaty was adopted, subject naturally to the principles otherwise governing admissibility of reservations, thus constituting in effect a régime of freedom to formulate reservations, with certain exceptions to such freedom.

Various expedients have been tried in order to overcome the complications caused by reservations. One method has at least the merit of stark simplicity, that is, to provide by a special clause in the Convention that no reservations at all are permissible (see, eg, article 39 of the Convention on Damage Caused by Foreign Aircraft to Third Parties on the Surface, signed at Rome on 7 October 1952 and article 309 of the United Nations Convention on the Law of the Sea, 1982), or none with regard to certain important provisions (eg no reservations were allowed as to articles 1 to 3 of the Geneva Convention on the Continental Shelf of 29 April 1958). Other formulae allow special kinds of reservations only. These methods of providing for inadmissibility of reservations are recognised by the Vienna Convention (see article 19) as valid and effective. Another method, sometimes known as the 'authorisation' method, is to specify certain admissible reservations in a clause in the convention, and to limit the choice of any parties desiring to make reservations to these.

Probably the best method in the circumstances is to insert a clause providing that the states parties to the convention are to be consulted as to all reservations intended to be made, with presumed acceptance in default of reply within a fixed period; but if objections are lodged against the reservations, the state desiring to make them should be given the alternative of ratifying or not ratifying without reservations.[16]

A practice has developed in recent years of ratifications or accessions, subject to statements by the ratifying or acceding governments of their special understandings or intepretations of the treaty concerned or particular provisions of it, or subject to some declaration as to some matter in the treaty, or as to its domestic implementation by them. There is a very thin line between such understandings, on the one hand, and reservations, on the other hand. If an understanding thus declared operates clearly to vary or to exclude an obligation under the treaty in question lying on the ratifying or acceding state, it should be considered as a reservation.[17]

It should be observed, however, that no method can be safely followed in the future by contracting states wishing to make, accept, or object to reservations, without carefully considering the impact upon the particular treaty concerned

---

15. This is a consideration which influenced the International Law Commission in 1966; see commentary on arts 16–17, Draft Arts ILC. The Commission preferred a 'flexible' system under which it is for each state individually to decide whether to accept a reservation and treat the reserving state as a party, and did not adopt the 'collegiate' system (reserving state a party only if a given proportion of other states concerned accept the reservation).

16. Note the method used in the Convention concerning Customs Facilities for Touring, of 4 June 1954 (see art 20; reservations made before signing of Final Act admissible if accepted by a majority of the Conference, and recorded in the Final Act, while reservations made after signing of Final Act not admitted if objected to by one-third of the parties to the Convention).

17. See the discussion of the United Nations Convention on the Law of the Sea, 1982, article 310, p 421, above.

of the provisions as to reservations in articles 19–23 of the Vienna Convention, referred to above.

6.   REVISION AND AMENDMENT OF TREATIES

The terms 'revision', 'amendment', and 'modification' are in current use to denote the process of altering the provisions of treaties. In the Vienna Convention (see Part IV) the words 'amendment' and 'modification' were used.

The term 'revision' frequently carries some political significance, being employed by states claiming that unjust or unequal treaties should be reviewed, and final dispositions of territory or frontiers adjusted. Such a re-examination, directed to the peaceful change of situations formerly accepted as final, may be a 'revision' in the widest sense of the term, but is not treaty revision as ordinarily understood, that is to say the alteration of treaty provisions imposing continuing obligations. For this reason, the words 'amendment' and 'modification' are perhaps preferable to denote such an alteration.

The most usual way of ensuring reconciliation of the provisions of treaties with changing conditions is through amendment clauses inserted in the treaties themselves, thus giving effect to the basic principle that a treaty may be amended by agreement of the parties (cf Vienna Convention, article 39). These clauses attempt to fix beforehand the particularities of the procedure for amendment. They generally provide that such procedure may be initiated at the request of one or a number of parties, or through some authoritative international organ. Then, usually, the move for amendment must be endorsed by the states parties to the convention and is carried out by a Conference of these states at a subsequent time. According to the clauses, the exact time at which the amendment may be made falls broadly speaking into four classes: (a) at any time; (b) after the expiration of a prescribed period dating from the entry into force of the convention; (c) periodically, at the expiration of prescribed periods; and (d) combinations of one or more of the preceding classes. Generally, unanimity is required for the adoption of the amendments, but the trend since 1945 is towards allowing amendment of multilateral conventions by a majority, if this is in the interests of the international community. The main difficulty has been in getting the parties to proceed promptly to ratification of the proposed modification. This has led to the use of certain expedients to obviate ratification. Sometimes the changes are treated as being of minor importance only, and are effected not under the procedure of the amendment clause, but by means of a *Procès-Verbal*, Protocol, or other administrative instrument opened to signature, which is regarded as sufficient.[18]

Sometimes, it is expressly provided in the convention that certain amendments may be carried out upon the recommendation of an international organ, which may or may not require endorsement—purely here an administrative act—of the contracting parties.

18. See, for example, the *Procès-Verbal* of June 1936, for amending art 5 of the Geneva Drugs Convention 1931. In some cases, non-ratifying parties have been given an option of withdrawing from the convention, or are treated as non-parties if they do not ratify within a specific time.

The Vienna Convention purports in articles 40–41 to lay down certain principles governing the procedure and effect of the amendment of multilateral treaties, such as the principles that proposals for amendment must be notified to all contracting states, that all such states are entitled to participate in the process of amendment, that every state entitled to adhere to the original treaty has a right to become party to the amending treaty, and that two or more parties may, subject to the provisions of the treaty itself and subject to giving due notice to other parties, conclude an agreement to modify the treaty as between themselves alone.

United Nations Charter and the re-examination of treaties

Article 14 of the United Nations Charter authorises the General Assembly 'to recommend measures for the peaceful adjustment of any situation . . . which it deems likely to impair the general welfare or friendly relations among nations, including situations resulting from a violation of the provisions of the present Charter setting forth the Purposes and Principles of the United Nations' (ie, the provisions of articles 1 and 2). It has been maintained that article 14 empowers the General Assembly to initiate a process of peaceful change through the readjustment of final settlements (eg, of territory or frontiers) under treaties, since the word 'situations' is capable of referring to 'situations' both under executed and under executory treaties. However, even assuming this to be the correct interpretation of article 14, the General Assembly could not take any binding action in the direction of the peaceful change of treaty settlements,[19] as its powers in this connection are recommendatory only.

7. INCONSISTENT TREATIES AND VALIDITY AND DURATION OF TREATIES

Inconsistent treaties

Some difficulty surrounds the question of the applicability of a treaty which is inconsistent with the terms of an earlier treaty.[20] The matter resolves itself essentially into one of reconciliation of the obligations of the parties to both treaties.

If one of the treaties concerned specifies that it is subject to, or that it is not to be considered as incompatible with an earlier or subsequent treaty, the provisions of this latter treaty should prevail (Vienna Convention, article 30, paragraph 2). Otherwise, as between parties to an earlier treaty who are also parties to the later treaty, the earlier treaty governs only to the extent that it is

---

19. Apart from this provision in the Charter, it is claimed that the Vienna Convention provides, to some extent, machinery of peaceful change of situations under treaties, inasmuch as it enables states, which maintain that a treaty has been invalidated by jus cogens or terminated by fundamental change of circumstances, to have disputes concerning such claims of invalidity or termination of a treaty submitted to a process of judicial settlement, arbitration, or conciliation (see pp 430, 432 below).

20. Cf for general discussion, Aufricht in 37 Cornell LQ (1952) 684 et seq, and see also commentary on art 26, Draft Arts ILC.

compatible with the later treaty (article 30, paragraph 3). Moreover, as between a state party to both treaties and a state party to only one of the treaties, the treaty to which both states are parties is to apply.

It may be also that different considerations are applicable to bilateral treaties or treaty-contracts, on the one hand, and to multilateral conventions, on the other hand. In the case of conflicting multilateral conventions, if the earlier convention does not in definite terms prohibit the later convention, and if such later instrument is in the interests of the international community,[1] or prescribes general rules of conduct, the later convention should not be held inapplicable, notwithstanding that it derogates substantially from the earlier convention and that it has not been entered into by all of the parties to the other instrument. Where the point turns on the construction of ambiguous treaty provisions, there is a presumption of non-conflict. Much may depend on whether there is or is not real incompatibility, and on the intention of the parties to both instruments; the two instruments may validly co-exist, if one may be regarded as an annex to the other, facultatively imposing wider or stricter obligations at the election of the parties concerned (as in the case of the co-existence of the Geneva Convention of 1936 for the Suppression of the Illicit Traffic in Dangerous Drugs, and the penal repression provisions of the Single Narcotic Drugs Convention signed at New York on 30 March 1961 as amended in 1975).

The United Nations Charter contains its own rule of inconsistency; under article 103, the obligations of member states under the Charter are to prevail in the event of conflict between the Charter and their obligations under other international instruments. Charter obligations are paramount.

The validity of treaties[2]
The invalidation of treaties on grounds analogous to those applicable in the domestic law of contracts, namely, contractual incapacity, absence of consent due to mistake or fraud or duress, and illegality, has been the subject of much doctrinal speculation, some of which is both inconclusive and controversial. However, a significant attempt to formulate general principles in this area, capable of obtaining general acceptance, was made in the Vienna Convention which dealt with the following six grounds of invalidity of treaties: (1) treaty-making incapacity; (2) error; (3) fraud; (4) corruption; (5) coercion; (6) conflict with a norm of jus cogens.

(1) Treaty-making incapacity
Under article 46 of the Vienna Convention states may not rely on the fact that their representatives exceeded their treaty-making powers under internal law unless such excess of authority was:

a.   'manifest', ie objectively evident to the other negotiating state acting in accordance with normal practice and in good faith; and
b.   concerned a rule of internal law of fundamental importance.

---

1.   This proviso is in accordance with the practice after the last war, as to the revision or modification of pre-war conventions, so far as this was effected without the consent of all parties to the earlier instruments.
2.   See Oppenheim *International Law* (9th edn, 1992) Vol I, pp 1284-1295, and Henkin, Pugh, Schachter and Smit *International Law; Cases and Materials* (2nd edn, 1987) pp 458–475.

Article 47 deals with the case where a representative's authority is subject to a specific limitation in point of fact; excess of authority is then not sufficient to invalidate that representative's action unless the specific restriction on the representative's authority was notified beforehand to the other negotiating states.

(2) Error

A state is entitled to rely upon error as a ground of invalidity of a treaty if the error be one as to a fact or situation assumed by the state concerned to exist at the time when the treaty was concluded, and which formed an essential basis of its consent to the treaty.[3] This ground is not open to the state if it contributed to the error by its own conduct, or the circumstances were such as to put it upon notice of a possible error, or the error related only to the wording of the text of the treaty (Vienna Convention, article 48). The last-mentioned article 48 makes no explicit reference to an error of law, although it speaks of an error relating to a 'situation', as well as a 'fact'. Nor is any distinction drawn expressly between unilateral error, on the one hand, and common or mutual error, on the other hand.

(3) Fraud

This ground of invalidity applies where the state relying upon it has been induced by the fraudulent conduct of another negotiating state to enter into the treaty (Vienna Convention, article 49). Fraud itself is not defined in the Vienna Convention, and there is a recognised lack of international precedents as to what constitutes fraudulent conduct.

(4) Corruption

If a state's consent to a treaty has been procured through the corruption of its representative, directly or indirectly by another negotiating state, the former state is entitled to claim that the treaty is invalid (Vienna Convention, article 50).

(5) Coercion

This ground is satisfied if: (a) a state's consent to a treaty has been procured by the coercion of its representatives through acts or threats directed against them; (b) the conclusion of the treaty has been procured by the threat or use of force in violation of the principles of international law embodied in the United Nations Charter[4] (see Vienna Convention, articles 51–52).[5] Quaere, whether, as claimed by some states, the word 'force' used in the United Nations Charter is capable of denoting economic or political pressure,[6] which was alleged to be characteristic

3. Almost all the recorded instances of attempts to invalidate treaties on the ground of error have concerned geographical errors, and most of them related to errors in maps. On the latter point, see (1966) 2 *Year Book of the International Law Commission* pp 243 et seq. As to error in respect to treaties generally, see T. O. Elias *The Modern Law of Treaties* (1974) pp 154–161. Cf 64 AJIL (1970) 529–530.
4. See, in particular, art 2, para 4 of the Charter.
5. In the *Fisheries Jurisdiction Cases* ICJ 1974, 3, 175, the International Court of Justice held that art 52 of the Vienna Convention could not be relied upon to show duress where the circumstances revealed that the challenged treaty had been freely negotiated by the parties on the basis of perfect equality and freedom of decision on both sides.
6. See Henkin, Pugh, Schachter and Smit *International Law; Cases and Materials* (2nd edn, 1987) pp 464–466.

of 'neo-colonialism'. By way of answer to this claim, it has been objected that it would open a wide door for the invalidation of treaties concluded at arm's length.

(6) Conflict with a norm of jus cogens

A treaty is void if at the time of its conclusion it conflicts with a norm of jus cogens.[7]

The right to invalidate a treaty on the ground of treaty-making incapacity, error, fraud, or corruption is lost if subsequently the state expressly agrees that the treaty is valid or remains in force, or its conduct is such as to lead to the inference of acquiescence in the continued validity or application of the treaty (Vienna Convention, article 45).

A state relying upon the above-mentioned grounds of invalidity must notify other parties of its claim so that the procedure laid down in articles 65–66 may be followed. This may ultimately lead to a process of judicial settlement, arbitration, or conciliation with reference to any disputed claim.

Termination of treaties

Treaties may be terminated by: (1) operation of law; or (2) act or acts of the states parties.

(1) Termination of treaties by operation of law

(i)   Extinction of either party to a bilateral treaty, or of the entire subject-matter of a treaty may discharge the instrument.[8] In connection with the former case, questions of state succession may arise where the territory of the extinguished state comes under the sovereignty of another state.[9]

(ii)   Treaties may cease to operate upon the outbreak of war between the parties. In some instances suspension of the treaty, rather than actual termination, may be the result of such a war. The matter is discussed in a later chapter.[10]

(iii)   Aside from the case of provisions for the protection of the human person contained in treaties of a humanitarian character, a material breach of a bilateral treaty by one party entitles the other to terminate the treaty or to suspend its operation, while a material breach of a multilateral treaty by one party may, according to the circumstances, result in its termination as between all parties, or as between the defaulting state and other parties, or as between the defaulting state and a party specially affected by the breach (Vienna Convention, article 60).[11]

---

7. As to jus cogens, see pp 48-50 above.
8. See Hackworth *Digest of International Law* (1940–1943) Vol V, pp 297 et seq.
9. See pp 294-299 above.
10. See Chapter 18, pp 492-494 below.
11. See Advisory Opinion of 21 June 1971, of the International Court of Justice on the *Legal Consequences for States of the Continued Presence of South Africa in Namibia (South West Africa)*, where the Court upheld the view that the failure of South Africa to comply with its obligation, as Mandatory Power in South West Africa, to submit to supervision by United Nations organs, resulted in the termination of its mandate, and therefore of its authority to administer the Territory; see ICJ 1971, 16 at 47–48.

(iv)   Impossibility of performance of the treaty due to the permanent disappearance or destruction of an object indispensable for the execution of the treaty will result in termination, but not if the impossibility is due to a breach of the treaty itself, or of any other international obligation committed by the party which seeks to terminate the treaty upon the ground of such impossibility (Vienna Convention, article 61). Case (i) above may be regarded in a sense as an instance of impossibility of performance.

(v)   Treaties may be discharged as a result of what is traditionally known as the *rebus sic stantibus* doctrine. According to this doctrine, a fundamental change in the state of facts which existed at the time the treaty was concluded may be invoked as a ground for terminating the treaty, or for withdrawing from it. It is also put that there is necessarily an implied term or clause in the treaty—the *clausula rebus sic stantibus*—to the effect that the treaty obligations subsist only so long as the essential circumstances remain unchanged. However, in its *Report on the work of its 1966 (18th) Session*, the International Law Commission rejected the theory of an implied term, preferring to base the doctrine of fundamental change upon grounds of equity and justice, and even to discard the words '*rebus sic stantibus*' as carrying undesired implications.

The matter is now dealt with in article 62 of the Vienna Convention under the heading 'fundamental change of circumstances'. The text of this article is as follows:

'*Article 62*

Fundamental change of circumstances
1.   A fundamental change of circumstances which has occurred with regard to those existing at the time of the conclusion of a treaty, and which was not foreseen by the parties, may not be invoked as a ground for terminating or withdrawing from the treaty unless:
a.   the existence of those circumstances constituted an essential basis of the consent of the parties to be bound by the treaty; and
b.   the effect of the change is radically to transform the extent of obligations still to be performed under the treaty.
2.   A fundamental change of circumstances may not be invoked as a ground for terminating or withdrawing from a treaty:
a.   if the treaty establishes a boundary; or
b.   if the fundamental change is the result of a breach by the party invoking it either of an obligation under the treaty or of any other international obligation owed to any other party to the treaty.
3.   If, under the foregoing paragraphs, a party may invoke a fundamental change of circumstances as a ground for terminating or withdrawing from a treaty it may also invoke the change as a ground for suspending the operation of the treaty.'

It will be observed that paragraph 1 of this article of the Vienna Convention involves a combination of two tests, the subjective test, on the one hand, that the parties to the treaty should have envisaged the continuance of the circumstances surrounding its conclusion as a decisive motivating factor in entering into the treaty,[12] and the objective test, on the other hand, that the change

12. A view favoured by the Permanent Court of International Justice in the *Case of the Free Zones of Upper Savoy and Gex* (1932) PCIJ Series A/B, No 46.

must be so fundamental as radically to alter the obligations of the parties.[13] The article excludes reliance on mere onerousness of treaty obligations, felt by a party at a period later than the date of the conclusion of the treaty, as of itself sufficient ground for a claim to be released from the treaty. There is no requirement that the fundamental change must occur only after a certain period of time, and this is in accordance with the current realities of international affairs, as cataclysmic changes can occur on the international scene even within months. Also the article does not preclude parties to a treaty from expressly stipulating what fundamental changes will entitle them to withdraw from the treaty.[14]

A party invoking this ground of fundamental change must give notice under articles 65–66 of the Vienna Convention to the other parties of its claim that the treaty has been terminated, stating its reasons, so as to set in motion the procedure laid down in these articles. In other words, there is no automatic termination of a treaty as a result of the doctrine of fundamental change.

(vi)   A treaty specifically concluded for a fixed period of time terminates upon the expiration of that period.

(vii)   If successive denunciations (see below as to the meaning of 'denunciation') of a multilateral treaty reduce the number of states parties to less than the number prescribed by the treaty for its entry into force, the treaty may cease to operate if this be expressly or impliedly provided; otherwise a multilateral treaty does not terminate by reason only of the fact that the number of parties falls below the number necessary for its coming into force (Vienna Convention, article 55).

(viii)   Article 64 of the Vienna Convention provides that if a new peremptory norm of jus cogens[15] emerges, any existing treaty which is in conflict with that norm becomes void and terminates. This is a controversial provision, and in the light of the opposition that it encountered at the Vienna Conference of 1968–1969 which drew up the Convention, cannot be said to contain a universally accepted rule of international law. One major objection to it is that no treaty can be safely entered into without being exposed to the hazard of subsequent invalidation by reason of some unanticipated future development in the higher governing principles of international law. Nor, it would seem, can parties by any provision now made in a treaty, agree to exclude such a hazard, for such an exclusionary provision would presumably itself be invalidated by the force of jus cogens.

13. In the *Fisheries Jurisdiction Cases* ICJ 1974, 3, the International Court of Justice recognised that article 62 of the Vienna Convention constituted a codification of existing customary international law, but held that the case did not reveal any fundamental change of circumstances within the meaning of article 62; rather the situation of controversy between the parties was exactly of the character contemplated in the relevant treaty provision.
14. See, eg, article V of the Nuclear Weapons Test Ban Treaty of 1963 referred to, p 160 above, entitling a party to withdraw if it decides that 'extraordinary events' related to the subject-matter of the Treaty have jeopardised its 'supreme interests'.
15. See pp 48-50 above.

(2) Termination of treaties by act or acts of the parties

(i) The termination of a treaty or the withdrawal of a party may take place in conformity with the provisions of the treaty, or at any time by consent of all the parties after consultation inter se (Vienna Convention, article 54). A treaty will also be considered as terminated if all the parties to it conclude a subsequent treaty relating to the same subject matter, and it appears from this later treaty or otherwise that the parties intended that the matter be governed by that treaty, or that the provisions of this later treaty are so far incompatible with those of the earlier treaty that the two instruments cannot be applied at the same time (Vienna Convention, article 59). It seems that it is also possible that, by their conduct if not by their declarations, States parties could be considered as being ad idem in regarding the treaty as being no longer in force, or as being obsolete.

(ii)   When a state party wishes to withdraw from a treaty, it usually does so by notice of termination, or by act of denunciation. The term 'denunciation' denotes the notification by a state to other states parties that it intends to withdraw from the treaty. Ordinarily, the treaty itself provides for denunciation, or the state concerned may, with the consent of other parties, have reserved a right of denunciation. In the absence of such provision, denunciation and withdrawal are not admissible, and all the other parties must as a rule consent to the denunciation or withdrawal, unless it is established that the parties intended to admit the possibility of denunciation or withdrawal, or a right of denunciation or withdrawal may be implied by the nature of the treaty (Vienna Convention, article 56). The practical difficulty with regard to denunciation or withdrawal by a state is the possibility of embarrassment to the other states parties, wishing to continue their participation in the treaty, by disturbing the general equilibrium of rights and obligations which originally made the treaty possible.

In practice, multilateral conventions contain a special clause allowing denunciation after the expiration of a certain period of time from the date of entry into force of the convention. This clause may provide that a denunciation will not take effect until a certain time (eg one year) after it is given.

Suspension of operation of treaties

The operation of a treaty may be suspended, in regard to either all parties or a particular party: (a) in conformity with the provisions of the treaty;[16] or (b) at any time by the consent of all parties after consultation (Vienna Convention, article 57); or (c) through the conclusion of a subsequent treaty, if this be the intention of the parties (Vienna Convention, article 59). Subject to the provisions of the treaty concerned, and its object and purpose, two or more parties to a multilateral treaty may suspend its operation as between themselves alone (article 58).

---

16. In regard to the suspension clauses in International Labour Conventions, see E. A. Landy *The Effectiveness of International Supervision. Thirty Years of ILO Experience* (1966) pp 147–150.

8.   INTERPRETATION OF TREATIES

Agencies of interpretation

These agencies of interpretation may be courts such as: (a) the International Court of Justice; (b) the Court of Justice of the three European Communities, which has jurisdiction to interpret the Treaties of 18 April 1951 and 25 March 1957 establishing these three Communities; and (c) the International Tribunal for the Law of the Sea, established by the United Nations Convention on the Law of the Sea, 1982, Part XV and Annex VI. Treaties are also interpreted by international technical organs, such as the International Labour Office[17] and the various organs of the United Nations,[18] and by the Executive Directors and Board of Governors of the International Monetary Fund.[19] Other expedients may be resorted to; for example, reference of the point to an ad hoc Committee of Jurists. Treaties often call for interpretation in cases before international arbitral tribunals and municipal courts; these decisions are not authoritative except as between the parties to the case but they may constitute persuasive precedents.[20]

Instruments of interpretation

Diplomatic Conferences which adopt a treaty are only too conscious themselves of drafting defects. To avoid any difficulties arising out of the construction of particular clauses or Articles, an instrument such as a Protocol, or *Procès-Verbal*, or Final Act is often annexed to the main convention containing a detailed interpretation or explanation of the doubtful provisions.

Multilingual treaties

Treaties are often drafted in two or more languages. Multilateral conventions, including conventions of the International Labour Organisation, are usually concluded in two languages—English and French—and it is provided that both texts shall be authoritative.[1] In some instances it is declared that the English or French text as the case may be shall prevail in the event of a conflict. The United Nations Charter 1945 was drawn up in five languages—Chinese, French,

---

17. For the Office's interpretations of Labour Conventions, see *The International Labour Code, 1951* (1952), and the ILO *Official Bulletin*.
18. It was recognised at the San Francisco Conference which in 1945 drew up the United Nations Charter that each organ of the United Nations would have largely to do its own interpretative work; see *Report* of the Rapporteur of Committee IV/2 of the Conference, pp 7–8.
19. Arts XVIII, XXI (d) and XXXI of the Articles of Agreement of the International Monetary Fund; see Hexner 53 AJIL (1959) 341–370; Sir Joseph Gold *Interpretation by the Fund* IMF Pamphlet Series, No 11 (1968), and the same author's *The Fund Agreement in the Courts* (1982) Vol II, pp 7–8.
20. On the interpretation of treaties in municipal law in the United Kingdom see *Fothergill v Monarch Airlines* [1981] AC 251; *Henn and Darby v DPP* [1981] AC 850. See also the Australian case *SS Pharmaceutical Co Ltd v Qantas Airways* [1991] 1 Lloyd's Rep 288, per Kirby P.
1. This means that, generally speaking, the two texts may be read in conjunction in order to ascertain the meaning of the convention. Also, in the event of discrepancies, prima facie, the least extensive interpretation should be adopted. Where the treaty is silent as to the equivalence of the two texts, possibly greater weight should be given to the language in which the instrument was first drawn up. But see now Vienna Convention, art 33.

Russian, English, and Spanish—and it was provided by article 111 that the five texts were to be 'equally authentic'.[2]

Article 33 of the Vienna Convention provides:

a. that if a treaty is authenticated in several languages, the text is equally authoritative in each language unless the treaty provides or the parties agree that one particular text is to prevail in case of divergence;
b. that the terms of the treaty are presumed to have the same meaning in each text;
c. that a construction is to be given which best reconciles the texts having regard to the object and purpose of the treaty.

General principles of treaty interpretation

Numerous rules, canons, and principles have been laid down by international tribunals, and by writers to be used as tools in the interpretation of treaties, and to serve as useful, indeed necessary, guidelines to the drafting of treaty provisions. These rules, canons, and principles, although sometimes invested with the sanctity of dogmas, are not absolute formulae, but are in every sense relative—relative to the particular text, and to the particular problem that is in question. To some extent, like presumptions in the law of evidence, their weight may depend on the cumulative application of several, rather than the application of one singly.

The following is a summary of the more general principles:[3]

(1) Grammatical interpretation, and the intention of the parties

Words and phrases are in the first instance to be construed according to their plain and natural meaning.[4] However, if the grammatical interpretation would result in an absurdity, or in marked inconsistency with other portions of the treaty, or would clearly go beyond the intention of the parties, it should not be adopted.

The related rules concerning the intention of the parties proceed from the capital principle that it is to the intention of the parties at the time the instrument

2. For rules of interpretation of multi-lingual treaties, see art 29, Draft Arts ILC, commentary, pp 108–113.
3. For references to the various authorities on which the above summary is based, see Hudson *The Permanent Court of International Justice, 1920–1942* pp 640–661; Hyde 24 AJIL (1930) 1–19; J. F. Hogg 'International Court: Rules of Treaty Interpretation' (1958–1959) 43 Minnesota LR pp 369–441, and Vol 44 (1959–1960) pp 5–73; I. Tammelo *Treaty Interpretation and Practical Reason* (1967); commentary on Draft Arts ILC, arts 27–29; and Jiménez de Aréchaga in (1978) 159 Hague Recueil des Cours pp 42–48.
4. This principle was reaffirmed by the International Court of Justice in the *Advisory Opinion on the Constitution of the Maritime Safety Committee of the Inter-Governmental Maritime Consultative Organisation* ICJ 1960, 150 (words 'largest ship-owning nations' in art 28 of the convention of 6 March 1948, establishing the Organisation, held to mean the countries with the largest figures of registered tonnage, without regard to questions of the real national ownership). Under the Vienna Convention, art 31, para 1, a treaty is to be interpreted in good faith 'in accordance with the ordinary meaning to be given' to its terms in their context and in the light of its object and purpose; this provision was relied upon by the European Court of Human Rights in February 1975, in the *Golder Case*, in reaching its conclusion that art 6(1) of the European Convention of 1950 for the Protection of Human Rights and Fundamental Freedoms, guaranteeing a right to a fair and public hearing in civil and criminal proceedings, involved a right of access to the courts, and therefore of access to legal advice.

was concluded, and in particular the meaning attached by them to words and phrases at the time, that primary regard must be paid. Hence, it is legitimate to consider what was the 'purpose' or 'plan' of the parties in negotiating the treaty.[5] Nor should a treaty be interpreted so as to restrict unduly the rights intended to be protected by it.[6] What must be ascertained is the *ostensible* intention of the parties, as disclosed within the four corners of the actual text; only in exceptional circumstances is it permissible to investigate other material to discover this intention. Moreover, a special meaning must be given to a particular term, if it is established that the parties so intended (Vienna Convention, article 31, paragraph 4).

(2) Object and context of treaty

If particular words and phrases in a treaty are doubtful, their construction should be governed by the general object of the treaty, and by the context;[7] article 31, paragraph 1, of the Vienna Convention lays down that a treaty should be interpreted by reference to its 'object' and 'purpose'. The context need not necessarily be the whole of the treaty, but the particular portion in which the doubtful word or phrase occurs. However, for the purposes of interpretation, it can include the preamble[8] and annexes to the treaty, and related agreements or instruments made in connection with the conclusion of the treaty (Vienna Convention, article 31, paragraph 2).

(3) Reasonableness and consistency

Treaties should, it is held, be given an interpretation in which the reasonable meaning of words and phrases is preferred, and in which a consistent meaning is given to different portions of the instrument. In accordance with the principle of consistency, treaties should be interpreted in the light of existing international law.[9] Also applying both reasonableness and consistency, since it is to be assumed that states entering into a treaty are as a rule unwilling to limit their sovereignty save in the most express terms, ambiguous provisions should be given a meaning

---

5. The International Court of Justice had recourse to the 'purpose' of the treaty in the *Case Concerning the Applications of the Convention of 1902 Governing the Guardianship of Infants* (Netherlands-Sweden) ICJ 1958, 55. Cf the reference by the International Court of Justice in *Nicaragua v United States* ICJ 1986, 14 at 270 et seq, to the 'whole spirit' of the Treaty of 1956 between the United States and Nicaragua of Friendship, Commerce and Navigation, as being undermined by certain United States activities. See also *James Buchanan & Co v Babco Forwarding and Shipping* (UK) [1978] AC 141 at 160 for an affirmation of the principle of the 'broad' interpretation of treaties. In the *Beagle Channel Arbitration* of 1977, 52 ILR 93 the Court of Arbitration had regard to the 'spirit and intention' of an 1881 treaty between the parties, Argentina and Chile (see para 18 of the award).
6. See *Kolovrat v Oregon* 366 US 187 (1961).
7. In its decision of 16 May 1980, in the case of *The Government of Belgium v The Government of the Federal Republic of Germany* (1980) 19 International Legal Materials 1357–1408, the Arbitral Tribunal for the London Agreement of 1953 on German External Debts had regard to the 'context' in accordance with the provisions of art 31 of the Vienna Convention.
8. In the *Beagle Channel Arbitration* of 1977, 52 ILR 93 the Court of Arbitration had regard to the preamble of an 1881 Boundary Treaty between the parties (see paras 18 et seq of the award).
9. A principle relied upon by the European Court of Human Rights in February 1975 in the *Golder Case*, in interpreting the European Convention of 1950 for the Protection of Human Rights and Fundamental Freedoms.

which is the least restrictive upon a party's sovereignty, or which casts the least onerous obligations; and in the event of a conflict between a general and a special provision in a treaty, the special provisions should control the general (cf the municipal law maxim, *lex specialis derogat generali*), unless the general stipulation is clearly intended to be overriding.

(4) The principle of effectiveness

This principle, particularly stressed by the Permanent Court of International Justice, requires that the treaty should be given an interpretation which 'on the whole' will render the treaty 'most effective and useful',[10] in other words, enabling the provisions of the treaty to work and to have their appropriate effects. This principle is of particular importance in the construction of multilateral conventions, containing the constituent rules of international organisations.[11] It does not, however, warrant an interpretation which works a revision of a convention, or any result contrary to the letter and spirit of treaties.[12]

(5) Recourse to extrinsic material

Normally, the interpreting tribunal is limited to the context of the treaty. However, the following may be resorted to, provided that clear words are not thereby contradicted:

a. Past history, and historical usages relevant to the treaty
b. Preparatory work (*travaux préparatoires*), ie preliminary drafts, records of Conference discussions, draft amendments, etc. This may be taken into account where normal interpretation leaves the meaning ambiguous or obscure, or leads to a result which is manifestly absurd or unreasonable (Vienna Convention, article 32), and more particularly to confirm a conclusion reached by normal methods of construction.[13] Abortive proposals, or secret or confidential negotiatory documents will not be so used, nor will preparatory work be given weight against a state party which

10. See commentary on art 27, Draft Arts ILC. The International Court of Justice seems to have applied this principle in the case of the *United States Diplomatic and Consular Staff in Tehran* ICJ 1980, 3, when it ruled that the fact that a dispute was before the Security Council did not prevent the Court from exercising jurisdiction (contrary to the prohibition to this effect on the General Assembly), inasmuch as under article 36, paragraph 3 of the United Nations Charter, the Security Council in making recommendations to settle disputes was to have regard to the fact that legal disputes should as a general rule be referred to the Court (see paragraph 40 of the Court's judgment). A major rationale of the principle of effectiveness is, to quote Sir Joseph Gold (*Finance and Development* September 1981, p 39), that 'the drafters of multilateral treaties, particularly if they are to regulate some new sphere of international relations, do not, and indeed cannot, foresee the issues that will arise in practice'.
11. See, eg, *Advisory Opinion on Reparation for Injuries Suffered in the Service of the United Nations* ICJ 1949, 174 for an illustration of the application of this principle, in order to enable an international organisation to function more effectively.
12. See *South West Africa Cases, 2nd Phase* ICJ 1966, 6 at 48.
13. Ibid, at 43–44. Note the speeches of members of the House of Lords in *Fothergill v Monarch Air Lines Ltd* [1981] AC 251, in which varying views were expressed about the use of *travaux préparatoires* by an English court in interpreting a treaty, eg that recourse to these should be with caution, that they should be used as an aid only, and that, in any event, they should be public and accessible. See also for the views on the subject of the Justices of the High Court of Australia, their judgments in the *Commonwealth of Australia v Tasmania* (1983) 158 CLR 1.

did not participate in the negotiations, unless the records of such preparatory work have been published.

c.   Interpretative Protocols, Resolutions, and Committee Reports, setting out agreed interpretations. Unless these form part of the treaty,[14] they will be treated as on the same level as preparatory work, subject to certain of such documents having greater weight than others, according to circumstances.

d.   A subsequent agreement between the parties regarding the interpretation of the treaty or the application of its provisions (Vienna Convention, article 31, paragraph 3).

e.   Subsequent conduct of the states parties, as evidencing the intention of the parties and their conception of the treaty, although a subsequent interpretation adopted by them is binding only if it can be regarded as a new supplementary agreement. Under the Vienna Convention (see article 31, paragraph 3), a subsequent practice in the application of the treaty, establishing agreement regarding its interpretation, may be assimilated to such a supplementary agreement.

f.   Other treaties, in pari materia, in case of doubt.

Disputes clause

It is now a general practice to insert a disputes clause in multilateral conventions providing for methods of settling disputes arising as to the interpretation or application of the convention. The alternative methods usually specified are negotiation between the parties, arbitration, conciliation, or judicial settlement.[15]

---

14.   Cf the *Ambatielos Case* ICJ 1952, 28 et seq, showing that a declaration subscribed to by parties who contemporaneously drew up a treaty, may be part of such treaty; and that the conduct of the parties may be looked to in this connection to ascertain whether the declaration was so regarded.

15.   See, eg, the United Nations Convention on the Law of the Sea, 1982, Part XV.

PART 5

Disputes and hostile relations (including war, armed conflicts and neutrality)

CHAPTER 17

International disputes

1. GENERAL

The expression 'international disputes' covers not only disputes between states as such, but also other cases that have come within the ambit of international regulation, being certain categories of disputes between states on the one hand, and individuals, bodies corporate, and non-state entities on the other.[1]

The present chapter is, however, mainly concerned with disputes between states, and these may range from minor differences scarcely causing a ripple on the international surface to the other extreme of situations of prolonged friction and tension between countries, attaining such a pitch as to menace peace and security.

To settle international disputes as early as possible, and in a manner fair and just to the parties involved, has been a long-standing aim of international law, and the rules and procedure in this connection are partly a matter of custom or practice, and partly due to a number of important law-making conventions such as the Hague Conventions of 1899 and 1907 for the Pacific Settlement of International Disputes and the United Nations Charter drawn up at San Francisco in 1945. One of the principal objects of the latter Charter in setting up the United Nations Organisation was indeed to facilitate the peaceful settlement of differences between states. This also had been the purpose of the League of Nations during the period of its activities between two world wars.

Broadly speaking, the methods of settling international disputes fall into two categories:

1. Peaceful means of settlement, that is, where the parties are agreeable to finding an amicable solution.

---

1. Eg, investment disputes between capital-receiving states and private foreign investors, the settlement of which is provided for under the Convention of 18 March 1965, for the Settlement of Investment Disputes between States and Nationals of Other States (the Convention applies to legal disputes only). Under the Convention there was established at Washington the International Centre for the Settlement of Investment Disputes (ICSID). See as to this Centre, article by P.J. O'Keefe (1980) 34 *Year Book of World Affairs* 286, Ryans and Baker (1976) 10 *J World Trade L* 65; and Boskey and Sella *Settling Investment Disputes* (1965) 3 Finance and Development 129, and, as to the Convention, Szasz (1970) 1 Journal of Law and Economic Development 23.

2.   Forcible or coercive means of settlement, that is, where a solution is found
and imposed by force.

Each class will be discussed in turn.

2.   PEACEFUL OR AMICABLE MEANS OF SETTLEMENT[2]

The peaceful or amicable methods of settling international disputes are divisible
into the following:

a.   Arbitration.
b.   Judicial settlement.
c.   Negotiation, good offices, mediation, conciliation, or inquiry.
d.   Settlement under the auspices of the United Nations Organisation.

This classification does not mean that these processes remain in rigidly separate
compartments, each appropriate for resolving one particular class of dispute.
The position is otherwise in practice. For example, the flexible machinery
established by the Convention of 18 March 1965 for the Settlement of Investment
Disputes between States and the Nationals of Other States consists of an
International Centre for the Settlement of Investment Disputes (ICSID), at
Washington, with facilities for the arbitration and conciliation of investment
disputes,[3] and provision for Panels of Arbitrators and Conciliators. The United
Nations Commission on International Trade Law adopted on 28 April 1976 a
set of arbitration rules which allow also for conciliation of disputes (the
UNCITRAL Arbitration Rules). Similarly the Permanent Court of Arbitration,
established under the Hague Convention for the Pacific Settlement of
International Disputes, 1907, provides for good offices and mediation, and for
international commissions of inquiry, as well as for arbitration (see further on
the Permanent Court of Arbitration, below).

(a)   Arbitration[4]
Ordinarily, arbitration denotes exactly the same procedure as in municipal law,
namely the reference of a dispute to certain persons called arbitrators, freely
chosen by the parties, who make an award without being bound to pay strict
regard to legal considerations. Experience of international practice has shown,
however, that many disputes involving purely legal issues are referred to
arbitrators for settlement on a legal basis.[5] Moreover, in the various treaties by

---

2.   See J. G. Merrills *International Dispute Settlement* (1984); the *Report* of a Study Group on the
Peaceful Settlement of International Disputes (David Davies Memorial Institute of International
Studies, London, 1966); Henkin, Pugh, Schachter, and Smit *International Law; Cases and
Materials* (2nd edn, 1987) pp 565 et seq; and Raman (ed) *Dispute Settlement through the United
Nations* (1977).
3.   The Convention applies to legal disputes only. See also p 441, n 1 above.
4.   For a general treatise on the subject, see J. L. Simpson and H. Fox *International Arbitration:
Law and Practice* (1959). See also J. Gillis Wetter *The International Arbitral Process; Public
and Private* (1979, 5 vols); A. M. Stuyt *Survey of International Arbitrations 1794-1989* (1990).
5.   This can be illustrated by the work of the Austrian-German Arbitral Tribunal in the period
1957–1971; see I. Seidl-Hohenveldern *The Austrian-German Arbitral Tribunal* (1972) passim.

which it has been agreed that disputes should be submitted to arbitration, frequently in addition to being directed to make their award according to justice or equity or ex aequo et bono, arbitral tribunals have been specially instructed to apply international law. A common formula in the nineteenth century was the direction to give a decision 'in accordance with the principles of international law and the practice and jurisprudence of similar tribunals of the highest authority'.

Arbitration is an institution of great antiquity (see Chapter 1, above), but its recent modern history is recognised as dating from the Jay Treaty of 1794 between the United States and Great Britain, providing for the establishment of three joint mixed commissions to settle certain differences which could not otherwise be disposed of in the course of the negotiation of the Treaty. Although these commissions were not strictly speaking organs of third party adjudication, two of the three performed successfully, and the result was to stimulate a fresh interest in the process of arbitration which had fallen into desuetude for about two centuries. A further impetus to arbitration was given by the *Alabama Claims Award* of 1872 between the United States and Great Britain. According to Judge Manley O. Hudson:[6]

> 'The success of the *Alabama Claims Arbitration* stimulated a remarkable activity in the field of international arbitration. In the three decades following 1872, arbitral tribunals functioned with considerable success in almost a hundred cases; Great Britain took part in some thirty arbitrations, and the United States in twenty; European States were parties in some sixty, and Latin American States in about fifty cases.'

Clauses providing for the submission of disputes to arbitration were also frequently inserted in treaties, particularly 'law-making' conventions, and to quote Judge Hudson again,[7] 'arbitration thus became the handmaiden of international legislation' inasmuch as disputes concerning the interpretation or application of the provisions of conventions could be submitted to it for solution. Also a number of arbitration treaties for the settlement of defined classes of disputes between the states parties were concluded.

A most important step was taken in 1899 when the Hague Conference not only codified the law as to arbitration but also laid the foundations of the Permanent Court of Arbitration. The Hague Conference of 1907 completed the work of the 1899 Conference. The Permanent Court of Arbitration is an institution of a peculiar character. It is neither 'permanent' nor is it a Court. The members of the 'Court' are appointed by states which are parties to one or both of the conventions adopted by the Hague Conferences. Each state may appoint four persons with qualifications in international law, and all the persons so appointed constitute a panel of competent lawyers from whom arbitrators are appointed as the need arises. Thus the members of the Permanent Court of Arbitration never meet as a tribunal:

Another instance is that of the Iran-United States Claims Tribunal, at the Hague, established in 1981, dealing with private claims of US citizens against Iran and of Iran citizens against the US; the Tribunal's mandate, inter alia, was to determine cases before it on the basis of respect for law, applying choice of law, rules and principles of law as thought applicable (see *Proceedings of American Society of International Law* (1984) pp 221, 227–233).

6. Hudson *International Tribunals* (1944) p 5.
7. Loc. cit, p 6.

'Their sole function . . . is to be available for service as members of tribunals which may be created when they are invited to undertake such service.'[8]

When a dispute arises which two states desire to submit to arbitration by the Permanent Court of Arbitration, the following procedure applies: Each state appoints two arbitrators, of whom one only may be its national or chosen from among the persons nominated by it as members of the Court panel. These arbitrators then choose an umpire who is the presiding member of the arbitral tribunal. The award is given by majority vote. Each tribunal so created will act pursuant to a special *compromis* or arbitration agreement, specifying the subject of the dispute and the time allowed for appointing the members of the tribunal, and defining the tribunal's jurisdiction, the procedure to be followed, and the rules of law and the principles according to which its decision is to be given. The Permanent Court of Arbitration itself has no specific jurisdiction as such. Approximately 20 arbitral tribunals have been appointed under this system since its foundation, and several important awards have been given, including those in the *Pious Fund Case* of 1902 between the United States and Mexico, the *Muscat Dhows Case* of 1905 between Great Britain and France, the *North Atlantic Coast Fisheries Case* of 1910 between the United States and Great Britain, and the *Savarkar Case* of 1911 between Great Britain and France.

Since 1932 resort to the Permanent Court of Arbitration has been infrequent, but the Bureau of the Court has been active in facilitating ad hoc arbitrations outside the formal framework of the Hague Convention. Its facilities have been used, for example, by the Iran-United States Claims Tribunal, set up in 1981. It should be noted that the national groups of members appointed under the Convention also function as the nominating bodies for periodic elections of judges to the International Court of Justice.

Notwithstanding its obvious defects—as Judge Hudson says it was hardly more than 'a method and a procedure'[9]—the Permanent Court of Arbitration was a relative success, and in the early years of this century influenced a more frequent recourse to arbitration as a method of settling international disputes, while it may be said to have moulded the modern law and practice of arbitration. This was reflected, too, in the great number of arbitration treaties, both multilateral and bilateral, and of special ad hoc submission agreements, concluded before and after the First World War. Steps have been taken to revitalise the work of the Permanent Court[10], especially by making its facilities more attractive to litigants through the adoption in 1993 of revised Optional Rules for Arbitrating Disputes Between Two Parties of Which Only One is a State.[11]

Following the First World War, several important arbitral tribunals operated. Among these may be mentioned the several Mexican Claims Commissions which adjudicated the claims of six different states against Mexico on behalf of their subjects, and the Mixed Arbitral Tribunals set up in Europe to deal with various

8. Loc. cit, p 159.
9. Loc. cit, p 8.
10. See the Report of the Working Group on Improving the Functioning of the Court *The Permanent Court of Arbitration - New Directions,* published by the Bureau in 1991.
11. Effective 6 July 1993. These rules replaced the earlier Rules adopted in 1962, and are harmonised with the UNCITRAL Rules (see above).

claims arising out of the territorial redistribution effected by the Treaty of Versailles 1919.[12]

Arbitration is essentially a consensual procedure.[13] States cannot be compelled to arbitrate unless they agree to do so, either generally and in advance, or ad hoc in regard to a specific dispute. Their consent even governs the nature of the tribunal established.

The structure of arbitral tribunals has accordingly in practice revealed anomalies. Sometimes a single arbitrator has adjudicated a dispute, at other times a joint commission of members appointed by the states in dispute, and very frequently a mixed commission has been created, composed of nominees of the respective states in dispute and of an additional member selected in some other way.[14] The nominees of a state are usually its own nationals; sometimes they are treated as representing it and being under its control—a practice which is in many ways objectionable.

Disputes submitted to arbitration are of the most varied character. Arbitral tribunals have dealt with disputes primarily involving legal issues as well as disputes turning on questions of fact and requiring some appreciation of the merits of the controversy. As a rule such tribunals have not declined to deal with a matter either on the ground that no recognised legal rules were applicable[15] or on the ground that political aspects were involved. For this reason the distinction frequently drawn by writers on international law between 'justiciable' and 'non-justiciable' disputes is a little difficult to understand and does not appear to have much practical value.[16] Inasmuch, however, as by special clauses in their arbitration treaties, states often exclude from arbitration disputes affecting their 'vital interests', or concerning only matters of 'domestic jurisdiction', such reserved disputes may in a sense be 'non-justiciable', and open only to the procedure of conciliation. An illustration is the clause in the Anglo-French Arbitration Treaty of 1903 whereby the two states bound themselves not to arbitrate disputes which 'affect the vital interests, the independence, or the honour' of the parties. A more intelligible distinction is that between legal and non-legal disputes (see, eg, article 36 of the United Nations Charter).

---

12. A number of arbitral tribunals were also established after the Second World War; among them are the Arbitral Tribunal on German External Debts set up under the Agreement on German External Debts of 27 February 1953.
13. *Advisory Opinion on the Status of Eastern Carelia* (1923) PCIJ Series B, No 5, p 27.
14. This can be a difficult process. One method that has been used successfully in practice is for each party to prepare a list of five to ten possible arbitrators from third states and to exchange these lists in sealed envelopes at a meeting. The chances are that at least one common name will apear in each list.
15. Ie, they have not in practice made a finding of non liquet; see above, p 31.
16. Writers seem generally agreed on the point, however, that a dispute in which one of the parties is in effect demanding a change in the rules of international law, is 'non-justiciable'. Other criteria of non-justiciability, which have been relied upon, include the following: (1) the dispute relates to a conflict of interests, as distinct from a conflict between parties as to their respective rights (the test of justiciability in the Locarno Treaties of 1925); (2) application of the rules of international law governing the dispute would lead to inequality or injustice; (3) the dispute, while justiciable in law, is not so in fact, because for political reasons neither of the disputant states could undertake to comply with an unfavourable adjudication, or in other words 'non-justiciability' is governed by the attitude of the parties to the dispute.

There has arisen recently a trend towards appointing current judges of the International Court of Justice as members of arbitral tribunals. This has occurred in such cases as the *Anglo-French Continental Shelf Arbitration* (1977, 1978) and the *Guinea — Guinea Bissau Arbitration* (1985). This trend may diminish as the caseload of the International Court of Justice (see below) increases, and as the alternative of using chambers of that court becomes more attractive.

There will always be a place for arbitration in the relations between states. Arbitral procedure is more appropriate than judicial settlement for technical disputes, and less expensive, while, if necessary, arbitrations can be conducted without publicity, even to the extent that parties can agree that awards be not published. Moreover, the general principles governing the practice and powers of arbitral tribunals are fairly well recognised.[17] Lastly, arbitral procedure is flexible enough to be combined with the fact-finding processes which are availed of in the case of negotiation, good offices, mediation, conciliation, and inquiry.[18]

(b) Judicial settlement

By judicial settlement is meant a settlement brought about by a properly constituted international judicial tribunal, applying rules of law.

The only general organ[19] of judicial settlement at present available in the international community is the International Court of Justice[20] at The Hague,

17. In 1953, the International Law Commission submitted a Draft Convention on Arbitral Procedure, which not only codified the law of international arbitration, but also endeavoured to overcome certain existing defects in procedure, eg disagreements between states as to whether a certain dispute was subject to arbitration, inability to establish the tribunal, failure to agree on the terms of the *compromis*, powers of the arbitral tribunal, and revision of awards. Deadlocks on the first two matters were, according to the Draft, to be broken by recourse to the International Court of Justice. For the text of the Draft and commentary thereon, see *Report* of the Commission on the Work of its *5th Session* (1953). The General Assembly did not accede to the Commission's view that a Convention should be concluded on the basis of the Draft, and in 1958, the Commission adopted a set of model Draft Articles on Arbitral Procedure, which could be used by states as they thought fit when entering into agreements for arbitration, bilateral or multilateral, or when submitting particular disputes to arbitration ad hoc by *compromis*. For the text of the model Draft Articles and commentary thereon, see *Report* of the Commission on the Work of its *10th Session* (1958), and *The Work of the International Law Commission* (3rd edn, 1980) pp 122–132. By its Resolution of 14 November 1958, the General Assembly brought the Draft Articles to the attention of member states of the United Nations for their consideration and use.
18. Eg, in the *Argentina-Chile Boundary Arbitration* (1965–6), 38 ILR 10, the arbitral tribunal caused a field mission to be sent to the disputed area for the purpose of aerial photographic surveys and mixed ground-air reconnaissance of the territory.
19. As distinct from a regional judicial tribunal, such as the Court of Justice of the European Communities under the Treaties of 18 April 1951, and of 25 March 1957. See generally H. Mosler and R. Bernhardt (eds) *Judicial Settlement of International Disputes: An International Symposium* (1974).
20. The standard authoritative treatises on the Court are S. Rosenne *The Law and Practice of the International Court* (2nd edn, 1985) and M. Dubisson *La Cour Internationale de Justice* (1964). See also the valuable manual published by the Court itself in 1976, under the title, *The International Court of Justice*, with bibliography of works etc, on the Court, at p 112, L. Gross (ed) *The Future of the International Court of Justice* (1976, 2 vols), J. G. Merrills *International Dispute Settlement* (1984) 6, pp 93 et seq, Falk *Reviving the World Court* (1986), G. Schwarzenberger *International Law as applied by International Courts and Tribunals Vol IV, International Judicial Law* (1986), C. Gray *Judicial Remedies in International Law* (1987) pp 59 et seq, and L. Damrosch (ed) *The International Court of Justice at a Crossroads* (1987).

which succeeded to and preserves continuity with the Permanent Court of International Justice. Its inaugural sitting was held on 18 April 1946, the very date on which its predecessor, the latter Court, was dissolved by the League of Nations Assembly at its final session. The essential difference between the Court, on the one hand, and an arbitral tribunal, on the other hand, can be seen by reference to the following points:

1. The Court is a permanently constituted tribunal, governed by a statute and its own body of rules of procedure, binding on all parties having recourse to the Court.
2. It possesses a permanent registry, performing all the necessary functions of receiving documents for filing, recording, and authentication, general court services, and acting as a regular channel of communication with government and other bodies.
3. Proceedings are public, while in due course the pleadings, and records of the hearings and judgments are published.
4. In principle, the Court is accessible to all states for the judicial settlement of all cases which states may be able to refer to it, and of all matters specially provided for in treaties and conventions in force.
5. Article 38[1] of its Statute specifically sets out the different forms of law which the Court is to apply in cases and matters brought before it, without prejudice to the power of the Court to decide a case ex aequo et bono[2] if the parties agree to that course. (Although not ex aequo et bono in the strict sense, equitable principles have been applied by the Court in the most recent cases before it in regard to maritime and territorial boundary delimitation.)
6. The membership of the Court is representative of the greater part of the international community, and of the principal legal systems, to an extent that is not the case with any other tribunal. (Currently six of the Court's judges come from countries in Africa and Asia, whereas initially only two judges came from these countries.)
7. In the result, it is possible for the Court to develop a consistent practice in its proceedings, and to maintain a certain continuity of outlook to a degree that is not feasible with ad hoc tribunals.

The International Court of Justice was established pursuant to Chapter XIV (articles 92–96) of the United Nations Charter drawn up at San Francisco in 1945. Article 92 of the Charter declares that the Court is 'the principal judicial organ of the United Nations', and provides that the Court is to function in accordance with a Statute, forming 'an integral part' of the Charter. By contrast, the Court's predecessor, the Permanent Court of International Justice, was not an organ of the League of Nations, although in some measure linked to the League. Inasmuch as the International Court of Justice is firmly anchored in the system of the United Nations, member states are just as much bound to the Court as to any other principal organ of the United Nations, while reciprocal duties of co-operation with each other bind the Court and United Nations organs, and

1. See pp 28-30 above, for discussion of this article.
2. 'Ex aequo et bono' means 'according to fairness and right' without necessary regard to law. Hitherto no parties have agreed to this form of proceeding before the International Court of Justice, provided for in art 38(2).

indeed in 1986 on the occasion of the Court's 40th anniversary, the President (Judge Nagendra Singh) declared that in the area of peaceful settlement of disputes the Court and UN Security Council were 'complementary organs'. Also the Court is bound by the Purposes and Principles of the United Nations as these are expressed in articles 1 and 2 of the Charter, and because the Court's Statute is annexed to the Charter and is an integral part of it, the context of the Charter is a controlling factor in the interpretation of the provisions of the Statute.

As an illustration of the fact that the Court has exercised jurisdiction over the whole range of international law, the following diverse subjects have been among those it has dealt with: maritime and territorial boundary delimitation disputes, non-use of force, non-intervention, decolonisation, treaty law and treaty interpretation, nuclear tests, diplomatic and consular law, state responsibility, treatment of aliens, the status of foreign investments, asylum, nationality and guardianship.

The Statute contains the basic rules concerning the constitution, jurisdiction, and procedure of the Court, and is supplemented by two sets of rules adopted by the Court pursuant to its rule-framing powers under article 30 of the Statute:

a.   The Rules of Court adopted on 14 April 1978 representing a major revision of prior Rules adopted on 6 May 1946, based on the corresponding Rules of 1936, applied by the Court's predecessor—the Permanent Court of International Justice, and which had been amended on 10 May 1972. They came into force on 1 July 1978, and as from that date replaced the former Rules, as thus amended, save in respect of any case submitted to the Court before 1 July 1978, or any phase of such a case, which should continue to be governed by the previous Rules.[3] The new revised Rules contain not only provisions as to procedure, but also rules governing the structure and working of the Court and of the Registry.

b.   The Resolution of 12 April 1976, concerning the Court's internal judicial practice, being a revised version of a Resolution adopted on 5 July 1968.[4] This sets out the practice to be followed by the Court with respect to exchanges of views between the judges regarding particular points, after the termination of the written proceedings, and before the commencement of the oral hearing, and with respect to the Court's deliberations in private after the conclusion of the oral hearing, with a view to reaching its decision, voting by the judges, and the preparation of the judgment, and of separate and dissenting opinions. As is recited in the preamble to the Resolution, the Court 'remains entirely free to depart from the present Resolution, or any part of it, in a given case, if it considers that the circumstances justify that course'.

3.   See S. Rosenne 'Some Reflections on the 1978 Revised Rules of the International Court of Justice' (1981) 19 Columbia Journal of Transnational Law pp 235–253.
4.   The text of this Resolution is to be found in the Court's publication of 1978, *Charter of the United Nations, Statute and Rules of Court and Other Documents* pp 165–173. Prior to 1968, the internal judicial practice of the Court was governed by the Resolution of the Permanent Court of International Justice of 20 February 1931 (as amended on 17 March 1936), by virtue of a decision of the International Court of Justice of 1946 to adopt provisionally the practice of the former Permanent Court.

It can be seen that procedural rules are to be found both in the Statute and in the Rules of Court. Broadly speaking, the difference in nature between the content of the two instruments is that the Statute is basically more important for the Court itself, while the Rules of Court are more important for the parties appearing before the Court. Moreover, the Statute is of higher legal sanctity than the Rules of Court; being an integral part of the Charter, it cannot, unlike the Rules of Court, be amended directly by the judges themselves.[5] Since the Statute is so to speak the higher law, the Rules cannot be adopted or altered in such manner as to conflict expressly or impliedly with basic provisions of the Statute.

All Members of the United Nations are ipso facto parties to the Statute, but other states may become parties to it, on conditions to be laid down in each case by the United Nations General Assembly upon the recommendation of the Security Council (article 93 of the Charter). The conditions laid down in this connection have, up to the present, been the same for each case, namely, acceptance of the provisions of the Statute, acceptance of the obligations under article 94[6] of the United Nations Charter, and an undertaking to contribute to the expenses of the Court, and were contained in the General Assembly's Resolution of 11 December 1946.

The Court consists of fifteen judges. The candidates for membership of the Court are nominated by the national groups of the panel of the Permanent Court of Arbitration.[7] From this list of nominees, the General Assembly and Security Council, voting independently, elect the members of the Court, an absolute majority in both the Assembly and the Council being required for election.[8] The procedure of concurrent election by the General Assembly and the Security Council applies also to the case of the filling of casual vacancies due to the death or retirement of a judge.[9] Not only are the highest legal qualifications (namely either capacity to be appointed to the 'highest judicial offices' in their countries, or being 'jurisconsults of recognised competence in international law'; see article 2 of the Statute) requisite under the Statute for election to the Court but also appointments are made with due regard to ensuring that the judges elected represent 'the main forms of civilisation' and the '. . . principal legal systems of the world' (article 9 of the Statute). Under a kind of 'gentlemen's agreement', currently applicable, the regional distribution of judges to be elected is: Africa, 3; Latin America, 2; Asia, 3; Western Europe and other countries, 5; and Eastern Europe, 2.[10] This regional distribution also takes into account the convention whereby a judge from each of the states Permanent Members of the United Nations Security Council (ie China, France, the Russian Federation, the United Kingdom, and the United States of America) is assured of election.

5. However, under art 70 of the Statute, the Court is entitled to propose amendments thereto. The Court exercised this power for the first time in 1969 when it proposed amendments enabling the General Assembly, upon the recommendation of the Court, to approve a place other than The Hague as the seat of the Court; see *ICJ Yearbook 1969–1970* p 113.
6. See below, p 456.
7. See above, pp 443-444.
8. Non-members of the United Nations, parties to the Statute of the Court, may participate in the elections of judges by the General Assembly in accordance with the conditions laid down in the General Assembly Resolution of 8 October 1948.
9. See art 14 of the Statute.
10. See the handbook, op cit, *The International Court of Justice* (1976) p 22.

Jurisdiction of the International Court of Justice
The Court is open:

a.   to the states (members or non-members of the United Nations) parties to the Statute; and
b.   to other states on conditions to be laid down by the United Nations Security Council, subject to the special provisions contained in treaties in force, and such conditions are not to place the parties in a position of inequality before the Court (article 35 of the Statute).[11]

The Court's jurisdiction is twofold:

a.   to decide contentious cases;
b.   to give advisory opinions.

Both functions are judicial functions.

Contentious jurisdiction
In contentious cases, in principle, the exercise of the Court's jurisdiction is conditional on the consent of the parties to the dispute. Under article 36, paragraph 1, of the Statute, the Court has jurisdiction over all cases which the parties refer to it; such reference would normally be made by the notification of a bilateral agreement known as a *compromis*. As would appear, however, from the Court's *Yearbooks* a document concluded by the parties as a 'Special Agreement', rather than a *compromis*, has become more recently the most usual form used for bringing a case before the Court. The provision in article 36, paragraph 1, is not to be taken as meaning that the Court has jurisdiction only if the proceedings are initiated through a joint reference of the dispute by the contesting parties. A unilateral reference of a dispute to the Court by one party, without a prior special agreement, will be sufficient if the other party or parties to the dispute consent to the reference, then or subsequently. It is enough if there is a voluntary submission to jurisdiction (ie the principle of *forum prorogatum*), and such assent is not required to be given before the proceedings are instituted, or to be expressed in any particular form.[12] A recommendation by the UN Security Council that the parties should settle a legal dispute by referring it to the Court (see para 3 of art 36 of the UN Charter) is not of itself sufficient to give the Court jurisdiction over the dispute. If, however, there is no consent, and no submission by the other party to the dispute, the case must be removed

---

11.   The conditions as laid down by the Security Council in a Resolution of 15 October 1946, were that such states should deposit with the Court's Registrar a declaration accepting the Court's jurisdiction in accordance with the Charter and Statute and Rules of Court, undertaking to comply in good faith with the Court's decisions, and to accept the obligations under art 94 of the Charter (see below, p 456).
12.   *Corfu Channel Case (Preliminary Objection)* ICJ, 1948, 15 et seq, and the handbook, op cit, the *International Court of Justice* (1976) p 33. Assent by conduct can scarcely be inferred where the respondent state consistently denies that the Court has jurisdiction; see *Anglo-Iranian Oil Co Case (Jurisdiction)* ICJ 1952, 93 at 114. The principle of forum prorogatum does not apply if: (a) the respondent state accepts jurisdiction only subject to a condition or conditions not assented to by the complainant state; or (b) if the complainant's claim is subsequently modified to a substantial extent.

from the Court's list.[13] Nor can the Court decide on the merits of a case in the absence of a materially interested state.[14]

Only states may be parties in cases before the Court, but the Court is empowered to obtain or request information from public international organisations relevant to these cases, or such organisations may furnish this information on their own initiative (see article 34 of the Court's Statute). Moreover, the Court has been given jurisdiction under the Statutes of the Administrative Tribunals[15] of the United Nations and of the International Labour Organisation (ILO) to determine by advisory opinion whether judgments of these tribunals have been vitiated by fundamental errors in procedure, etc, and in that connection upon requests for an advisory opinion by the international organisations concerned, may take into account written observations and information forwarded on behalf of individuals, ie, the officials as to whom the judgments have been given.[16] Such organisations cannot be parties in contentious proceedings before the Court. However, it is conceivable that under the relevant provisions of the Vienna Convention of 1986 on the Law of Treaties between States and International Organisations or between International Organisations that the Court may be called upon to adjudicate in some way in a so-called 'hybrid' dispute of treaty interpretation between a state and an international organisation. Of course, a state may in its absolute discretion espouse the case of one of its nationals, upon the ground of a breach of international law allegedly suffered by that national; but the dispute and the related proceedings will then

13. Eg, the Court made such orders for removal in 1956 in respect of the British references of disputes with Argentina and Chile concerning Antarctica, both Argentina and Chile declining jurisdiction; see ICJ 1956, 12 and 15. There have been other instances subsequent thereto, including the United States application in 1958 against the Soviet Union relative to the aerial incident of 4 September 1954; see ICJ 1958, 158.
14. See *Case of Monetary Gold removed from Rome in 1943* ICJ 1954, 19. Where parties are concerned, if one of the parties does not appear before the Court, or fails to defend its case, the other party may call upon the Court to decide in favour of its claim; before doing so, the Court must satisfy itself not only that it has jurisdiction, but also that the claim is well founded in fact and law (art 53 of the Statute). This the Court did in the *United States Diplomatic and Consular Staff in Tehran Case* ICJ 1980, 3, where Iran did not appear to answer the claim by the United States, and in *Nicaragua v United States* ICJ 1986, 14, in the merits phase of which case the United States did not participate. Jurisdiction in the latter case had been previously established to the Court's satisfaction by its judgment of 26 November 1984 (see ICJ 1984, 392), but the Court declared that it had nevertheless to find specifically that Nicaragua's claim was well-founded in fact and law, inasmuch as there was no automatic judgment in favour of a party appearing; the Court also observed that it was valuable for it to know the views of the non-appearing party, even if those views were expressed in ways not provided by the Rules of Court. Cf H. W. A. Thirlway *Non-Appearance before the International Court of Justice* (1985). For instances of judgments and orders delivered in the absence of a party, see the *Yearbook 1986–1987* (1987) of the Court, p 123, n 2.
15. These tribunals have jurisdiction to deal with complaints by officials of breaches of the terms of their appointment, etc.
16. See *Advisory Opinion on Judgments of the Administrative Tribunal of the International Labour Organisation upon Complaints made against the United Nations Educational, Scientific, and Cultural Organisation (UNESCO)* ICJ 1956, 77, *Advisory Opinion on the Application for Review of Judgment No 158 of the United Nations Administrative Tribunal* ICJ 1973, 166, *Advisory Opinion on the Review of Judgment No 273 of the United Nations Administrative Tribunal* ICJ 1982, 325, and *Advisory Opinion on the Application for Review of Judgment No 333 of the United Nations Administrative Tribunal* ICJ 1987, 18.

be between the states concerned.[17] Moreover, a request for an advisory opinion may be drawn in such a way as to enable the Court to pronounce on the rights of individuals or non-state groupings.[18] Should individuals apply to the Court with the object of obtaining a decision on questions at issue between them and their own or other governments, the practice is for the Registrar of the Court to inform such applicants that under article 34 of the Statute only states may be parties in cases before the Court; while if entities other than individuals seek to bring proceedings, the Registrar may refer the matter to the Court in private meeting, if the Registrar is uncertain as to the status of the complainant entity.[19] Suggestions have been made from time to time for altering the position under the Court's Statute so as to provide access for private individuals, corporations and non-governmental organisations. One such proposal, which seems not unreasonable, is that the Court should have jurisdiction to deal with disputes concerning the interpretation of transnational contracts between governments, on the one hand and multinational corporations, on the other hand.

The Court has compulsory jurisdiction where:

1. The parties concerned are bound by treaties or conventions in which they have agreed that the Court should have jurisdiction over certain categories of disputes. Among the instruments providing for reference of questions or disputes to the Court are numerous bilateral Air Services Agreements, Treaties of Commerce and Economic Co-operation, Consular Conventions, the Peace Treaty with Japan signed at San Francisco on 8 September 1951 (see article 22), and the European Convention for the Peaceful Settlement of Disputes concluded at Strasbourg on 29 April 1957.[20] To preserve continuity with the work of the Permanent Court of International Justice, the Statute further stipulates (see article 37) that whenever a treaty or convention in force provides for reference of a matter to the Permanent Court, the matter is to be referred to the International Court of Justice. The Court must be affirmatively satisfied that the treaty or arrangement relied upon by the complainant state for invoking the Court's jurisdiction is one which unequivocally confers jurisdiction when the Court receives the unilateral request for its exercise; thus an arrangement which contemplates a joint submission by both the complainant state and the respondent state does not amount to a commitment by the respondent state to accept the Court's compulsory jurisdiction under the arrangement.[1]

17. See handbook, *The International Court of Justice* (1976) p 31. An example is the *Barcelona Traction Case* (Belgium/Spain) ICJ 1973, 3.
18. See the Advisory Opinion of 1971 on *Legal Consequences for States of the Continued Presence of South Africa in Namibia (South West Africa)* ICJ 1971, 16 at 56, where the Court treated the *people* of the Mandated Territory of South West Africa as having rights violated by South Africa, by reason of South Africa's refusal to place the Territory under the supervision of United Nations organs.
19. This course was followed in 1966–1967 with regard to an application instituting proceedings, submitted by the Mohawk nation of the Grand River; see *ICJ Yearbook, 1966–1967* p 88, and the handbook, *The International Court of Justice* (1976) pp 31–32. According to the Court's *Yearbook 1986–1987* p 164, between 1 August 1986 and 31 July 1987 1,200 requests were received from private persons.
20. For a list of such instruments, see the Court's *Yearbook 1986–1987* pp 92–108.
1. See the *Aegean Sea Continental Shelf Case* ICJ 1978, 3.

2. The parties concerned are bound by declarations made under the so-called 'Optional Clause'—paragraph 2 of article 36 of the Statute. This clause appeared in the former Statute, in substantially the same terms as in the present Statute. It now provides that the parties to the Statute may at any time declare that they recognise as compulsory ipso facto and without special agreement 'in relation to any other State accepting the same obligation', the jurisdiction of the Court in *all* legal disputes concerning:

   a. the interpretation of a treaty;
   b. any question of international law;
   c. the existence of any fact which, if established, would constitute a breach of an international obligation;
   d. the nature or extent of the reparation to be made for the breach of an international obligation.

   These declarations may be made:

   i unconditionally; or
   ii. on condition of reciprocity on the part of several or certain states; or
   iii. for a certain time only.

   According as such declarations are made, and providing that the dispute is of a legal character and that it falls within the categories specified, the Court's jurisdiction becomes compulsory. The Court is empowered to decide whether a particular dispute is or is not one of the kind mentioned in the 'Optional Clause'.[2]

   To preserve continuity, as before, with the Permanent Court, article 36, paragraph 5 of the Statute provides that declarations made under the 'Optional Clause' in the earlier Statute are deemed, as between parties to the Statute, to be acceptances of the compulsory jurisdiction of the present Court for the period which they still have to run, and in accordance with their terms. This provision has been the subject of interpretation by the present Court. According to its decision in the *Case Concerning the Aerial Incident of July 27 1955 (Preliminary Objections)*[3] such former declarations are only transferable if made by states parties to the present Statute who were represented at the San Francisco Conference which drew up that Statute,[4] and a former declaration made by any other state party to the Statute lapsed in 1946 when the Permanent Court of International Justice ceased to exist, and on that account. However, under the Court's decision in the *Preah Vihear Temple Case (Preliminary Objections)*[5] a declaration made after 1946 by any such other state, purporting to renew a declaration under the 'Optional Clause' in the earlier Statute, is none the less

---

2. See para 6 of art 36 of the Statute, providing that in the event of a dispute as to whether the Court has jurisdiction, the matter shall be settled by the decision of the Court.
3. ICJ 1959, 127. The parties were Israel and Bulgaria.
4. There are seven such states (namely Colombia, Dominican Republic, Haiti, Luxembourg, Nicaragua, Panama, and Uruguay), who have not made new declarations, and whose declarations under the earlier Statute apply in relation to the present Court. If one of such states has continuously manifested an intent to recognise the Court's compulsory jurisdiction, it is immaterial that it did not ratify the Protocol of Signature of the Statute of the Court's predecessor, the Permanent Court of International Justice; see *Nicaragua v United States (Jurisdiction)* ICJ 1984, 392.
5. ICJ 1961, 17.

valid as a declaration under the present Statute, because owing to the dissolution of the Permanent Court, it could have no application except in relation to the present Court.

At the San Francisco Conference, some delegations had urged that the Statute should provide for some compulsory jurisdiction of the Court over legal disputes, but others hoped that this result could be practically obtained through more widespread acceptance of the 'Optional Clause'. This expectation has not been fulfilled to date.

The majority of the present declarations in force[6] are subject to a condition of reciprocity. Many of them also include reservations, excluding certain kinds of disputes from compulsory jurisdiction. The reservations as to jurisdiction are to some extent standardised, covering inter alia the exclusion of:

i   past disputes, or disputes relating to prior situations or facts;
ii.   disputes for which other methods of settlement are available;
iii. disputes as to questions within the domestic or national jurisdiction of the declaring state;
iv.   disputes arising out of war or hostilities; and
v.   disputes between member states of the British Commonwealth.

Too many of the reservations are, however, merely escape clauses or consciously designed loopholes. Such a system of 'optional' compulsory jurisdiction verges on absurdity in strict logic, but is necessary in political terms in an imperfect condition of world order.

A case of a specially contentious reservation is the so-called 'automatic' or 'self-judging' form of reservation contained in proviso b to the American declaration of 14 August 1946, reserving 'disputes with regard to matters essentially within the domestic jurisdiction of the United States of America *as determined by the United States of America*'. The validity of this reservation, more generally known as the 'Connally amendment', has been questioned.[7]

A number of points affecting the operation of the 'Optional Clause' have been settled by decisions of the present Court:

a.   Where a declaration, subject to a condition of reciprocity has been made by a state, and another state seeks to invoke compulsory jurisdiction against it, the respondent state is entitled to resist the exercise of jurisdiction by the Court by taking advantage of any wider reservation, including the 'automatic' or 'self-judging' form of reservation, made by the claimant state in its declaration.[8] Jurisdiction is conferred upon the Court only to the extent to which the two declarations coincide at their narrowest, that is to say,

---

6.   As of mid-1994 53 declarations were in force, the most recent being those of Estonia (1991), Bulgaria, Hungary, and Madagascar (all 1992). For the text of each declaration see the current issue of the Court's *Yearbook*.

7.   On the ground that it is incompatible with the power of the Court under art 36, para 6 (mentioned above) of its Statute to settle disputes as to its jurisdiction, and on the further ground that the reservation of such a discretion is inconsistent with any proper acceptance, within the meaning of art 36, para 2, of compulsory jurisdiction.

8.   See the *Norwegian Loans Case* ICJ 1957, 9, and the handbook, *The International Court of Justice* (1976) pp 38–39. Because of this decision, certain states which had made 'automatic' reservations, withdrew these.

jurisdiction is restricted to those classes of disputes that have not been excluded by any one state. But this bilateral effect does not apply in favour of a respondent state except on the basis of wider reservations actually contained in the claimant state's declaration; the fact that the claimant state would, if proceedings had been taken in the Court against it by the respondent state, have been entitled to resist jurisdiction, on the ground of a wide reservation in the respondent state's declaration, is not sufficient to bring into play the bilateral principle.[9] Nor, logically, does it apply if the respondent state elects to waive expressly any objection to jurisdiction upon the ground of this 'bilateral' effect.

b. If a dispute between states relates to matters exclusively within the domestic jurisdiction of the respondent state, it is not within the category of 'legal disputes' referred to in article 36 paragraph 2.[10]

c. A declaration made almost immediately before and for the purpose of an application to the Court is not invalid, nor an abuse of the process of the Court.[11]

d. If a matter has properly come before the Court under article 36, paragraph 2, the Court's jurisdiction is not divested by the unilateral act of the respondent state in terminating its declaration in whole or in part.[12]

Before the decision of the International Court of Justice in the *Corfu Channel Case (Preliminary Objection)*,[13] it was thought that a third category of compulsory jurisdiction existed, namely where under article 36 of the United Nations Charter, the Security Council recommended the parties to a dispute to refer their case to the Court, particularly as in paragraph 3 of that article the Council is virtually enjoined, where the dispute is of a legal character, to recommend submission to the Court. In the International Court's decision, however, seven judges expressed the view that this article did not create a new class of compulsory jurisdiction, and the same interpretation apparently applies to a decision of the Security Council under article 33 'calling upon' the parties to adjust their differences by judicial settlement.

Where the Court has compulsory jurisdiction, the normal method of initiating proceedings is by a unilateral written application addressed to the Registrar, indicating the subject of the dispute, and the other party or parties. The Registrar thereupon communicates the application to the other party or parties, and notifies all members of the United Nations and any other states entitled to appear before

9. See the *Interhandel Case (Preliminary Objections)* ICJ 1959, 6. For the purposes of the bilateral comparison in order to determine whether there is an absence of reciprocity, the *substance* of the two declarations is only to be considered, not such formal matters as duration or time limits of each state's commitment; *Nicaragua v United States (Jurisdiction)* ICJ 1984, 392.

10. See the *Right of Passage over Indian Territory Case (Preliminary Objections)* ICJ 1957, 125 at 133–134, and Briggs 53 AJIL(1959) 305–306.

11. See the *Right of Passage Case*, above, and the *Case of Certain Phosphate Lands* (Nauru v Australia) ICJ 1992, 240. This is covered by the United Kingdom reservation, excluding a dispute in which a state has so acted, or where it has deposited or ratified a declaration less than 12 months prior to the filing of its application bringing the dispute before the Court.

12. See the *Right of Passage Case*, above, n 10. See also *Nicaragua v United States (Jurisdiction)* ICJ 1984, 392 (declaration in force by reason of non-expiration of period of notice of termination under earlier declaration not affected by the lodging of a new amending declaration).

13. ICJ 1948, 15 et seq.

the Court (article 40 of the Statute). The Court cannot exercise jurisdiction of its own motion, as one party at least must elect to bring the case before it, the other party then being obliged to accept the Court's jurisdiction. There is one important element of flexibility in the system; both parties remain free at any stage to settle the dispute concerned by their own agreement, without any necessity of approval by the Court, which may then simply be notified so that the case is removed from the list (see also article 88 of the Rules of Court of 1978). Or one party only may give written notice of discontinuance of proceedings, as did Nicaragua on 12 August 1987 in the case brought by it in July 1986 against Costa Rica, whereupon the President of the Court makes orders to record the discontinuance, and for the removal of the case from the list (cf art 89 of the Rules of Court).

The effect of the exercise of compulsory jurisdiction by the Court is clarified by the provisions of article 94 of the United Nations Charter. Under this article, each member of the United Nations undertakes to comply with the decision of the Court in any case to which it is party. Further, if any party to a case fails to perform the obligations incumbent upon it under a judgment rendered by the Court, the other party may have recourse to the Security Council which may make recommendations or decide upon measures to be taken to give effect to the judgment, and these may be dictated by considerations unlike those which condition processes of execution in domestic legal systems. There are no provisions whereby the Court itself may enforce its decisions.

The procedure in contentious cases is partly written, partly oral. The written proceedings of the Court consist of communicating to it pleadings by way of memorials, counter-memorials, replies and rejoinders (replies and rejoinders may be filed only if authorised by the Court), and papers and documents in support. The oral proceedings consist of the hearing by the Court of witnesses, and experts, and of agents, counsel, or advocates who may represent the states concerned. The hearings are public unless the Court decides otherwise or the parties demand that the public be not admitted. The *South West Africa Cases* confirmed that claimants in the same interest may be joined together, that the parties can call witnesses or experts to testify personally, and that the Court itself may put questions to the parties and witnesses, but that the Court has some area of discretion in deciding whether to accede to a request for a view or inspection in loco (semble, also if the view is requested by consent of all parties).

The Court may indicate under article 41 of its Statute any interim measures necessary to preserve the respective rights of the parties, notice of which has to be given forthwith to the parties and to the Security Council.[14] It is provided in article 73 of the Rules of Court of 1978 that such provisional measures may be indicated on the *written* request 'at any time' of a party to the proceedings, while under article 75 the Court, in its turn, may 'at any time' decide to examine of its own motion whether the circumstances of the case require the indication of

---

14. Semble, such interim measures of protection may be indicated even though it is claimed that the Court has no jurisdiction in the dispute between the parties; cf, for example, the interim measures indicated by the Court on 5 July 1951, in the *Anglo-Iranian Oil Co Case* ICJ 1951, 89, on 22 June 1973, in the *Nuclear Tests Cases* ICJ 1973, 99, and 135, and more recently in *Nicaragua v United States* (order of 10 May 1984) ICJ 1984, 169 and in *Burkina Faso v Republic of Mali* (order of 10 January 1986) ICJ 1986, 3. See also articles 73–78 of the Rules of Court of 1978 under the heading *'Interim Protection.'*

provisional measures. According to the decision of the Court on 11 September 1976, in the *Aegean Sea Continental Shelf Case (Greece v Turkey)*,[15] interim measures will not be indicated where there is no risk of irreparable prejudice to the rights of the state requesting such measures, or it is not to be presumed that either party will fail to observe its obligations under the United Nations Charter, where the matter turns on the due performance of such obligations. The Court is not precluded from entertaining a request by one party for provisional measures, merely because what is sought by that party may be unilateral measures to be taken by the respondent state.[16] Provisional measures may be mandatory in nature, as well as injunctive or restraining;[17] the purpose is primarily to 'preserve the respective rights of either party' within the meaning of article 41 of the Court's Statute.

Preliminary objections may be taken, eg to the jurisdiction of the Court, or that the application is not admissible, or is non-justiciable, or by way of a plea that the matter belongs to the exclusive domestic jurisdiction of the respondent state,[18] or that the stage of a dispute between the parties has not arisen.[19] Where the preliminary objections raised matters which require fuller investigation, or which were wrapped up with the issues and evidence that might be tendered thereon, the Court did not under its pre-1972 practice decide upon them in the first instance, but joined them to the merits of the case.[20] It was the Court's majority view in the *South West Africa Cases, Second Phase (1966)*[1] that a

---

15. *Aegean Sea Continental Shelf Case; Interim Protection Order* ICJ 1976, 3. See also the *Case Concerning Passage Through the Great Belt* (Finland v Denmark) ICJ 1993, 12.
16. *United States Diplomatic and Consular Staff in Tehran Case, Provisional Measures* 15 December 1979 ICJ 1979, 7.
17. Ibid.
18. An international dispute as to the applicability of treaty provisions or of rules of customary international law, is not a matter within the domestic jurisdiction of parties to the dispute; see *Interhandel Case (Preliminary Objections)* ICJ 1959, 6. In *Nicaragua v United States (Jurisdiction)* ICJ 1984, 392, the Court appears to have accepted that there can be a preliminary objection as to the 'admissibility' of an application by a state, in respect to which objection the Court can rule whether it is admissible or inadmissible. There can, of course, be a fine line between an objection as to admissibility and an objection as to jurisdiction. Presumably, admissibility covers the possibility that the application is akin to an abuse of process, as in domestic law. As to non-justiciability, an example is perhaps that of an application regarding a dispute concerning what could hypothetically, but not with certainty, occur in the future. Semble, a dispute between two states about a question of diplomatic precedence (eg table seatings) would be both inadmissible and non-justiciable.
19. A legal dispute within the meaning of art 36, para 2 may be sufficiently inferred from diplomatic exchanges, without the necessity that it should have reached a stage of precise legal definition; see the *Right of Passage over Indian Territory Case (Preliminary Objections)* ICJ 1957, 125, and the *Aegean Sea Continental Shelf Case* ICJ 1976, 3. Diplomatic exchanges can include debates in United Nations organs as part of the normal process of diplomacy; *South West Africa Cases, (Preliminary Objections)* ICJ 1962, 319. The Court in its *Advisory Opinion* of 26 April 1988 on *the Applicability ofthe Obligation to Arbitrate under the UN Headquarters Agreement 1947* indicated that in its view, a 'dispute' existed if there were 'a disagreement on a point of law or a conflict of legal views or interests', or, even if no explicit justifications were expressed by one or other of the parties, there were 'opposing attitudes' (see paras 34–44 of the Advisory Opinion).
20. See the *Right of Passage Case* above and *South West Africa Cases, (Preliminary Objections)* ICJ 1962, 319.
1. ICJ 1966, 6 at 18, 36, 37.

decison on a preliminary objection, even of a somewhat like point, can never bind the Court where the question resolves itself into one founded on the merits, after all arguments have been presented. However, under the provisions of article 79 of the Rules of Court of 1978, corresponding to the provisions contained in the partial revision in 1972 of the formerly applicable Rules, the Court will now give its decision in the form of a judgment upholding the preliminary objection, or rejecting it, or declaring that it 'does not possess, in the circumstances of the case, an exclusively preliminary character', in which latter case the respondent state must file a defence on the merits embracing this ground if it wishes to rely thereon. In other words, it is no longer open to the Court to order in its judgment that a preliminary objection be joined to the merits, save that under paragraph 8 of article 79 of the Rules of the Court of 1978 any agreement between the parties that a preliminary objection be heard and determined within the framework of the merits is to be given effect by the Court.

All questions are decided by a majority of the judges present; and if the voting is equal, the President has a casting vote. The legal effect of the Court's judgment is set out in articles 59–61. The Court's decision has no binding force except between the parties and in respect of the particular case (article 59). The judgment is 'final and without appeal' (article 60) but a revision may be applied for on the ground of the discovery of a new 'decisive factor', provided that application is made within six months of such discovery and not later than ten years from the date of the judgment (article 61).[2] Unless otherwise decided by the Court, each party bears its own costs.

The Court has given its tacit sanction to the useful technique whereby states may, by special agreement, ask the Court to declare the principles of international law applicable to a particular dispute between them, so as to pave the way for a treaty settlement on the basis of such principles. In other words, an adversarial-type judgment or decision is not sought, but merely a preliminary elucidation of the principles or criteria to which the disputant states may have regard in reaching an arrangement to resolve particular differences. An earlier successful instance of the employment of this technique was that of the *North Sea Continental Shelf Cases*,[3] in which in 1969 the Court was requested to declare the principles applicable to the division of the common continental shelf of the German Federal Republic, the Netherlands and Denmark. In a more recent case between Tunisia and Libya, pursuant to a special agreement between these two States, the Court was asked to declare the principles and rules of international law to be applied for the delimitation of the common continental shelf of these states in the region known as the Pelagian Block or Basin, and in its decision given on 24 February 1982, the Court did formulate the applicable principles, and did clarify the practical method for implementing the principles so declared.[4]

2. In 1985 the Court rejected an application by Tunisia for the revision of its 1982 judgment in the *Continental Shelf (Tunisia-Libya) Case* ICJ 1982, 18. The Court held, inter alia, that it was not clear that the claimed new fact relied upon by Tunisia was such that it would have persuaded the Court to alter its earlier determination: see ICJ 1985, 192.
3.   ICJ 1969, 3.
4. *Continental Shelf (Tunisia/Libyan Arab Jamahiriya) Case* ICJ 1982, 18. A similar function of formulating the applicable canons of international law was performed by a five-member Special Chamber of the Court in the case concerning the *Delimitation of the Maritime Boundary in the*

According to the Court, there appear to be some essential limitations on the exercise of its judicial functions in the contentious jurisdiction, and on the rights of states to advance a claim in that jurisdiction.

First, as the *Northern Cameroons Case* shows,[5] an adjudication by the Court must deal concretely with an actual controversy involving a conflict of legal rights or interests as between the parties; it is not for the Court to give abstract rulings, inter partes, to provide some basis for political decisions, if its findings do not bear upon actual legal relationships. Otherwise, it might be acting virtually as a 'moot Court'. The correlative aspect is that the parties cannot be treated as mutually aggrieved to the extent of a 'dispute' if there is a mere difference of opinion between them, in the absence of a concrete disagreement over matters substantively affecting their legal rights or interests. In the *Nuclear Tests Cases*,[6] the Court declared that the existence of a dispute is '*a primary condition*' for the exercise by the Court of its judicial function, to the extent that the dispute must continue to exist at the time when the Court makes its decision; and where because of an undertaking given by the respondent state, the object of the claim or dispute has disappeared, the Court makes no further adjudication or determination, simply limiting itself to a finding that is 'not called upon to give a decision'.

Second and more controversially, the Court decided by a majority in the *South West Africa Cases, Second Phase*[7] that the claimant states, Ethiopia and Liberia, had failed to establish a legal right or interest appertaining to them in the subject-matter of their claims which, therefore should be rejected. This question was treated as one of an antecedent character, but nevertheless bearing upon the merits.

At the same time it is relevant to stress that the Court has expressly declared that two suggested limitiations on the exercise of its contentious jurisdiction are inapplicable in that area. First, the Court will not decline to resolve a legal question or issue, where it has otherwise jurisdiction, if that question or issue should be only one aspect of a political dispute. Second where the United Nations Security Council is exercising its function in respect of a particular dispute or situation, the Court is, unlike the United Nations General Assembly under article 12 of the United Nations Charter, not debarred from resolving any legal issue

---

Gulf of Maine (United States-Canada ICJ 1984, 24). See also the *Case Concerning Maritime Delimitation in the Area Between Greenland and Jan Mayen* (Denmark v Norway) ICJ 1993, 38.

5.   ICJ 1963, 15, esp at 33–34, 37–38; and see excellent article on the case by D. H. N. Johnson (1964) 13 ICLQ 1143–1192. The case is useful also as confirming the Court's powers to make a declaratory judgment in an appropriate case.

6.   See ICJ 1974, 253 at 270-272.

7.   ICJ 1966, 6 at 18, 51. The Court also affirmed that it could take account of moral principles only so far as manifested in legal form (ibid, p 34), and that it was not a legislative body, its duty being to apply, not to make the law (ibid, p 48). The absence of legal standing of the claimant states was attributed, inter alia, to the exclusive, institutional responsibility of League of Nations organs for supervising the fulfilment of the terms of mandates. The establishment of some concrete interest is also a condition of a state's right to intervene in a case in the Court; it is not sufficent that the state seeks to argue in favour of a decision in which the Court would refrain from adopting and applying particular criteria (see the *Continental Shelf (Tunisia/Libyan Arab Jamahiriya) Case* ICJ 1982, 18; *Application by Malta to Intervene* ICJ 1981, 3; see Leigh in 75 AJIL (1981) 949–952.

between the parties on the ground that the Security Council has, or may be entitled to take cognisance of the dispute or situation.[8]

Advisory opinions

The General Assembly and the Security Council of the United Nations may request advisory opinions from the Court. Other organs of the United Nations and the specialised agencies or other members of the United Nations 'family' may, if authorised by the General Assembly, request the Court to give advisory opinions on legal questions arising within the scope of their activities.[9] Advisory opinions can only be sought on legal questions,[10] concrete or abstract, and in giving them the Court would of course be exercising a judicial function. It seems that the Court would not give an advisory opinion on a purely academic question,[11] but so long as the advice sought may ultimately assist the international organisation concerned in discharging its functions, the questions are not to be deemed purely academic.[12] An advisory opinion is no more than it purports to be; it lacks the binding force of a judgment in contentious cases, even for the organisation or organ which has requested it, although of course such organisation or organ may choose to treat it as of the nature of a compulsory ruling. Nor does the Court have powers of judicial review or of appeal in respect of any decisions of such organisation or organ, for example by way of setting these aside, although it may incidentally in the course of an advisory opinion pronounce upon the question of the validity of a particular decision.[13] So far as states are concerned, they may by treaty or agreement undertake in advance to be bound by advisory opinions on certain questions (see, for example, section 30 of the Convention on the Privileges and Immunities of the United Nations 1946, and section 32 of the Convention on the Privileges and Immunities of the Specialised Agencies 1947). Also, in the absence of any such provisions, advisory opinions will have strong persuasive authority.

The procedure in the case of advisory opinions is that a written request must be laid before the Court containing an exact statement of the question on which an opinion is sought, while accompanying documents likely to throw light on the question are to be transmitted to the Court at the same time as the request, or as soon as possible thereafter, in the number of copies required by the Registry. This is a formal and indispensable requirement for the exercise of jurisdiction

---

8.   For the Court's rejection of these two suggested limitations, see the *United States Diplomatic and Consular Staff in Tehran Case* ICJ 1980, 3 para 37 and para 40, respectively, and also *Nicaragua v United States* (Jurisdiction) ICJ 1984, 392, paras 89–90.

9.   The Economic and Social Council, the Trusteeship Council, and the various specialised agencies have been so authorised.

10. It is no objection to the giving of an advisory opinion that the questions submitted to the Court for advice involve issues of fact, provided that the questions remain nonetheless *essentially* legal questions; *Advisory Opinion on the Western Sahara* ICJ 1975, 12. The questions put to the Court may necessarily involve identification of the factual and legal background thereof, while the legal questions really in issue, according to the Court, may not necessarily correspond precisely to the questions thus submitted to the Court; cf *Advisory Opinion on the Interpretation of the Agreement of March 25, 1981 between the WHO and Egypt*, ICJ 1987, 73.

11. Cf *Northern Cameroons Case* ICJ 1963, 15 at 33–34, 37–38, and p 437 above.

12. *Advisory Opinion on the Western Sahara* ICJ 1975, 12.

13. See *Advisory Opinion on the Legal Consequences for States of the Continued Presence of South Africa in Namibia (South West Africa)* ICJ 1971, 16 at 45.

by the Court to give an advisory opinion. The Registrar then notifies all states entitled to appear before the Court. The Registrar also notifies any state or international organisation, thought likely to be able to furnish information on the subject, that the Court will receive written or oral statements. States and international organisations presenting written or oral statements may comment on those made by other states and organisations. The advisory opinion is delivered in open court (see article 67 of the Statute). Both under article 68 of the Statute and in practice the Court's procedure has been closely assimilated to the procedure in the contentious jurisdiction. If an early answer to the request for an advisory opinion is desirable (see art 103 of the Rules of Court), the Court may accelerate its procedure by shortening time-limits, etc, as it did in the preliminary phase before the delivery on 26 April 1988 of its *Advisory Opinion on the Applicability of the Obligation to Arbitrate under the UN Headquarters Agreement 1947*.

The Court also regards itself as under a duty to observe essential judicial limitations in its advisory opinion procedure, so that it will not exercise the jurisdiction if the main point on which an opinion is requested is decisive of a controversy between certain states, and any one of these states is not before the Court.[14] For to give an advisory opinion in such circumstances would be to adjudicate without the consent of one party. The interpretation of treaty provisions is essentially a judicial task, and the Court will not reject a request for an opinion on such a question, although it be claimed that such question and such request are of a political nature.[15] In any event, the Court will not decline to give an advisory opinion, because it is maintained that in respect to such opinion the Court had been, or might be subjected to political pressure.[16]

It seems that the Court also has a discretion to refuse to give an advisory opinion upon other grounds, for example, that the question submitted involves other than legal aspects, or is embarrassing. The Court has held, however, that the circumstance that the Executive Board of the United Nations Educational, Scientific and Cultural Organisation (UNESCO) was alone entitled to seek an advisory opinion as to whether a decision of the Administrative Tribunal of the

14. See the *Advisory Opinion on the Status of Eastern Carelia* (1923) PCIJ Series B, No 5 pp 27–29. But this does not prevent the Court dealing by advisory opinion with a legal question, the solution of which may clarify a factor in a dispute between states or between a state and an international institution, without affecting the substance of the dispute, or the solution of which may provide guidance for an international organ in matters of the procedure under, or the effect to be given to a multilateral convention, notwithstanding that one of the states concerned is not before the Court or has not consented; see the Advisory Opinions of the present Court on the *Interpretation of the Peace Treaties* ICJ 1950, 65 at 221, and on *Reservations to the Genocide Convention*, ICJ 1951, 15. Similarly, the Court is not debarred from acceding to a request by a United Nations organ for legal advice on the consequences of decisions of that organ, notwithstanding that in order to give an answer, the Court may have to pronounce on legal questions upon which there is a divergence of views between a particular member state, on the one hand, and the United Nations, on the other hand; see Advisory Opinion on the *Legal Consequences for States of the Continued Presence of South Africa in Namibia (South West Africa)* ICJ 1971, 16 at 23–25, and *Advisory Opinion on the Western Sahara* ICJ 1975, 12.

15. See *Advisory Opinion on Certain Expenses of the United Nations (Article 17, paragraph 2 of the Charter)* ICJ 1962, 151.

16. *Advisory Opinion on the Legal Consequences for States of the Continued Presence of South Africa in Namibia (South West Africa)*; see ICJ 1971, 16 at 23.

International Labour Organisation (ILO) upon a staff claim was vitiated by a fundamental error in procedure, etc, and that no equivalent right of challenge was given to complainant officials, was not, because of such inequality, a reason for not complying with a request for an advisory opinion on such a question.[17]

As we have already seen above,[18] the Court applies international law, but article 38 of its Statute expressly enables it to decide a case ex aequo et bono if the parties concerned agree to this course. This means that the Court can give a decision on objective grounds of fairness and justice without being bound exclusively by rules of law. The Court will adopt this course only if so directed by the parties in the most explicit terms; so far no parties have agreed to invest the Court with this power in any case.[19] Presumably the Court could not be required to undertake, ex aequo et bono, functions which were strictly speaking of a legislative character. This consensual ex aequo et bono jurisdiction must, however, be distinguished from the Court's inherent power, as a Court of justice, to apply equitable principles.[20]

There are other points of importance concerning the Court. Nine judges form a quorum. If the parties so request, the Court may sit in Chambers. Under paragraph 2 of article 26 of its Statute the Court may at any time form a Chamber to deal with a particular case, and the number of such judges to constitute the Chambers will be determined by the Court with the approval of the parties. In January 1982, for the first time in its history, the Court constituted a Special Chamber to deal with the dispute between the United States and Canada over the delimitation of the maritime boundary in the Gulf of Maine area, and this precedent has been followed in certain later matters by the constitution of similar Special Chambers, in particular in 1985 and 1987.[1] Under art 27 of the Court's Statute, any judgement rendered by the Chamber is considered as one given by the Court. Chambers of three or more judges may be formed for dealing with

17. See *Advisory Opinion on Judgments of the Administrative Tribunal of the International Labour Organisation upon Complaints made against the United Nations Educational, Scientific and Cultural Organisation (UNESCO)* ICJ 1956, 77. In its *Advisory Opinion* of 1987 for the *Review of Judgment No 333 of the United Nations Administrative Tribunal* ICJ 1987, 18 the Court stressed also that although its power to give an advisory opinion was discretionary, the exercise of that power should not generally be refused in cases concerning the protection of UN officials.

18. See above, pp 28–30, 447.

19. See *Case of the Free Zones of Upper Savoy and Gex* (1930) PCIJ, Series A, No 24, p 10, and (1932) Series A/B No 46, 161.

20. See discussion in the *North Sea Continental Shelf Cases* ICJ 1969, 3 at 48–9. In the *Case Concerning the Barcelona Traction, Light and Power Co Ltd (Second Phase)* ICJ 1970, 3 (see paras 92–101 of the judgment), the Court declined to accept the proposition that, by virtue of equitable principles, the national state of shareholders of a company, incorporated in another state, was entitled to espouse a claim by shareholders for loss suffered through injury done to the company. On the other hand, in the *Fisheries Jurisdiction Cases* ICJ 1974, 3 at 175, the Court held that Iceland and each of the two complainant countries, the United Kingdom and the Federal Republic of Germany, were under mutual obligations to undertake negotiation in good faith for an equitable solution of their differences as to the fisheries in the disputed waters, and it indicated certain of the relevant equitable factors. In two recent cases, the Court (or a special Chamber thereof) relied on equitable criteria, not of the nature of ex aequo et bono, namely, *Libya-Malta Continental Shelf Case* ICJ 1985, 13 and *Burkina Faso v Republic of Mali* ICJ 1986, 554.

1. See Court's *Yearbook 1986–1987* p 158. Special Chambers were constituted, in addition to that for the *Gulf of Maine Case* ICJ 1982, 3, in the Cases *Burkina Faso v Republic of Mali* ICJ 1985, 6, *Elettronic Sicula SpA* ICJ 1987, 3 and *El Salvador-Honduras* ICJ 1987, 10.

particular categories of cases, for example, labour cases and cases relating to transit and communications, and annually a Chamber is formed to hear and determine cases by summary procedure, while also ad hoc Chambers may be formed at the request of parties. In July 1993 the Court announced the creation of a Chamber for Environmental Matters, to which seven judges were appointed. The principle of national judges applies under the present Statute (article 31). Judges of the nationality of parties before the Court retain their right to sit in the case; if the Court includes a judge of the nationality of one party, any other party may choose a person to sit as judge, and if the Court does not include judges of the nationality of the parties, each of the parties may proceed to appoint as judge ad hoc a person of its nationality. A judge ad hoc may also be appointed as member of a Special Chamber, as, eg, in the case of the above-mentioned Special Chamber formed in 1982 to deal with the maritime boundary in the Gulf of Maine area. If an advisory opinion is sought upon a legal question actually pending between two or more states, the Court may authorise the appointment of a judge ad hoc of one of such states; cf the appointment of a judge ad hoc by Morocco in the proceedings for an advisory opinion on the *Western Sahara* in 1975, such appointment being authorised by order of the Court on 22 May 1975.

A third state may request to be permitted to intervene if it considers that it has 'an interest of a legal nature which may be affected' by the Court's decision (art 62 of the Statute). The Court decides whether permission should be granted.[2]

It must be admitted that although both the Permanent Court of International Justice, and the International Court of Justice disposed of a substantial number of contentious matters and of requests for an advisory opinion, states generally showed marked reluctance to bring before these Courts matters of vital concern, or to accept compulsory adjudication in such matters. It is significant, also, that states have been unwilling to avail themselves of the clauses in the very large number of bilateral and multilateral treaties (see p 452, n 20 ante), providing for reference of disputes to the former, or to the present Court.

Pessimism, on this account, as to the limited scope of judicial settlement in the international community, is to some extent mitigated by the fact that both Courts adjudicated many questions raising important points of law, or difficult problems of treaty interpretation. Some of these judgments or opinions arose out of important political disputes which came before the League of Nations Council, or before the United Nations Security Council; eg the Permanent Court's Advisory Opinions on the *Frontier between Turkey and Iraq*,[3] on the *Customs Régime between Germany and Austria*,[4] and on the *Nationality Decrees in Tunis*

2. Permission is refused if the requesting state's interests are not greater than those of other non-party states, or if permission to intervene would introduce a fresh dispute; see decision on Malta's request in the *Tunisia-Libya Continental Shelf Case* ICJ 1986, 3, and on Italy's request in the *Libya-Malta Continental Shelf Case* ICJ 1984, 3. A less strict interpretation of the conditions for intervention appears to have been applied by a Chamber of the Court in the *Land, Island, and Maritime Frontier Dispute* (El Salvador/Honduras; Nicaragua intervening) ICJ 1992, 351, where for the first time in the Court's history a third state was permitted to intervene. Intervention does not constitute the intervening state a party to the proceedings, nor is that state bound by the decision in the case: ibid, and in the earlier phase of the case, ICJ 1990, 135. See generally on the subject C. Chinkin *Third States in International Law* (1993) pp vi-viii, 147-217.
3. (1925) PCIJ Series B, No 12.
4. (1931) PCIJ Series A/B, No 41.

and Morocco,[5] and the International Court's judgment in the *Corfu Channel Case (Merits)*.[6] Nor can it be denied that both Courts made substantial contributions to the development and methodology of international law.[7] So far as the present Court is concerned, reference need only be made to the Advisory Opinions on *Conditions of Membership in the United Nations*[8] and on *Reparation for Injuries Suffered in the Service of the United Nations*,[9] and to the judgments in the *Fisheries Case*,[10] the *Nottebohm Case (Second Phase)*,[11] the *Minquiers and Ecrehos Case*,[12] the *United States Diplomatic and Consular Staff in Tehran Case*,[13] and other later important cases, such as, eg, *Nicaragua v United States* (1986), referred to, in their appropriate place, in the present book. The role permitted to international adjudication may be a modest one, but it is at present indispensable, particularly for clarifying on the judicial level those issues which can be resolved according to international law.

Then there should be mentioned the possibility, as illustrated in the *Case Concerning the Arbitral Award of the King of Spain*,[14] of using the International Court of Justice for the judicial review or revision of international arbitral awards on the ground that the arbitral tribunal exceeded its jurisdiction, committed a fundamental error in procedure, etc. The International Law Commission favoured recourse to the Court for revision of an award on the ground of the discovery of some fact of such a nature as to constitute a decisive factor.[15] At present, however, any such challenge to an arbitral award is only possible by special agreement between the parties, or if the matter can be brought under the compulsory jurisdiction of the Court.

Finally not to be overlooked is the key role which the President of the Court plays in so far as he or she is called upon to appoint arbitrators, umpires, and members of Commissions, or other holders of offices[16]—to this extent, the President performs indispensable services in the field of peaceful settlement of disputes.

It is too early yet to evaluate the impact of the International Tribunal for the Prosecution of Persons Responsible for Serious Violations of International Humanitarian Law Committed in the Territory of the Former Yugoslavia Since

5. (1923) PCIJ Series B, No 4. The Court ruled that questions of nationality cease to belong to the domain of exclusive domestic jurisdiction if issues of treaty interpretation are incidentally involved, or if a state purports to exercise jurisdiction in matters of nationality in a protectorate.
6. ICJ 1949, 4.
7. See for an evaluation of the work of the International Court of Justice, Leo Gross 56 AJIL (1962) 33–62.
8. Referred to below, p 570.
9. Referred to below, p 545.
10. Referred to above, p 225.
11. Referred to above, p 310.
12. Referred to above, p 148.
13. ICJ 1980, 3.
14. See ICJ 1960, 192. In this case, the Court negatived the existence of any excess of jurisdiction, or error.
15. In art 38 of the draft model Articles on Arbitral Procedure, referred to above, p 446, n 17.
16. As to the functions of the President, see study by Sir Percy Spender (President, 1964–1967), *Australian Year Book of International Law* (1965) pp 9–22, and the Court's *Yearbook 1986–1987* pp 125–126.

1991, established by United Nations Security Council Resolution 827 (1993).[17] States are required under this resolution to co-operate with the Tribunal and will be vulnerable to sanctions imposed by the Council, if they fail to do so. The International Law Commission, at the urging of the Sixth Committee of the United Nations General Assembly, has elaborated a Draft Statute for an International Criminal Tribunal.[18] If the Statute is adopted and enters into force it will obviate the need in future to set up tribunals ad hoc to deal with violations of international humanitarian law and other international crimes, especially if the power of the Security Council to refer cases to the Tribunal, as presently proposed, is preserved as one of the ways in which the Tribunal can obtain jurisdiction.

(c) Negotiation, good offices, mediation, conciliation, or inquiry
Negotiation, good offices, mediation, conciliation, and inquiry are methods of settlement less formal than either judicial settlement or arbitration.

Little need be said concerning negotiation except that it frequently proceeds in conjunction with good offices or mediation, although reference should be made to the now growing trend of providing, by international instrument or arrangement, legal frameworks for two processes of *consultation*, both prior consultation and post-event consultation, and *communication*, without which in some circumstances negotiation cannot proceed. Illustrations of the former are the provisions for consultation in the Australia–New Zealand Free Trade Agreement of 31 August 1965, and of the latter, the United States–Soviet Memorandum of Understanding, Geneva, 20 June 1963 for a direct communication link—the so-called 'hot line'—between Washington and Moscow in case of crisis.[19] The value of continued negotiation was illustrated by the conclusion of the US–Soviet Intermediate-Range Nuclear Forces Agreement (INF) in December 1987 after the earlier unsuccessful talks between the two countries at Reykjavik, Iceland; the latter talks although abortive had nonetheless clarified some overhanging issues.

Both good offices and mediation are methods of settlement in which, usually, a friendly third state assists in bringing about an amicable solution of the dispute.[20] But the party tendering good offices or mediating may also, in certain cases, be an individual or an international organ (cf the tender of good offices by the United Nations Security Council in 1947 in the dispute between the Netherlands and the Republic of Indonesia). The distinction between good offices and mediation is to a large extent a matter of degree. In the case of good offices,

17. Text reproduced in (1993) 32 ILM 1203. The Statute of the Tribunal is reproduced in (1993) 32 ILM 1159, and the Rules of Procedure and Evidence, adopted by the Tribunal on 11 February 1994, in (1994) 33 ILM 484.
18. The Draft Statute is set out in the Report of the International Law Commission on its work at its 45th session in 1993: text also in (1994) 33 ILM 253.
19. The latter agreement was supplemented by a Modernisation Agreement of 1971 for improving the reliability of the 'hot line' link. The link has had the advantage of the addition of sophisticated technological improvements. See as to negotiation, J. G. Merrills *International Dispute Settlement* (1984) ch 1, 'Negotiation' pp 1–19, and in respect to prior consultation, Kirgis *Prior Consultation in International Law: A Study of State Practice* (1983) and Sir Joseph Gold (1984) 24 Virginia Journal of International Law pp 729–753.
20. See Part II of the Hague Convention of 1907 on the Pacific Settlement of International Disputes.

a third party tenders its services in order to bring the disputing parties together, and to suggest (in general terms) the making of a settlement, without itself actually participating in the negotiations or conducting an exhaustive inquiry into the various aspects of the dispute. Hence, once the parties have been brought together for the purpose of working out a solution of their controversies, strictly speaking the state or party tendering good offices has no further active duties to perform (see article X of the Pact of Bogotá, ie the Inter-American Treaty on Pacific Settlement of 30 April 1948). In the case of mediation, on the other hand, the mediating party has a more active role, and participates in the negotiations and directs them in such a way that a peaceful solution may be reached, although any suggestions made by it are of no binding effect upon the parties.[1] The initiative of the Soviet Government at the end of 1965 and early in 1966 in bringing representatives of India and Pakistan together at Tashkent to settle the conflict between them, and in creating a propitious atmosphere, for a settlement, seems to have lain somewhere between good offices and mediation.

It is likewise difficult to fit into the traditional third party roles in the settlement of disputes the part played by the Government of Algeria in procuring a resolution in January 1981 of the United States–Iranian dispute—perhaps better described as a 'crisis' in the relations of the United States and Iran—over the detention of American nationals (diplomatic and consular staff in particular) in Iran. In the relevant documents[2] it was stated that the Algerian Government had been 'requested' by the disputant parties 'to serve as an *intermediary* in seeking a mutually acceptable resolution', and that it had 'consulted extensively with the two governments as to the commitments which each is willing to make in order to resolve the crisis'. Moreover, the Algerian Government made two Declarations, attesting the commitments and agreements of the disputant parties, including an agreement for the establishment of an International Arbitral Tribunal, designated as the Iran–United States Arbitral Tribunal, to decide claims of American nationals against Iran, and claims of Iranian nationals against the United States. If the Algerian Government's part cannot be categorised as pertaining entirely to conciliation, or good offices, or mediation, it was nevertheless effective in achieving a settlement involving, among other points, the release of the detained American nationals.

The scope of both good offices and mediation is limited; there is a lack of any procedure in both methods for conducting a thorough investigation into the facts or the law. Hence, in the future, the greatest possibilities for both

1.   These meanings of good offices and mediation have not been strictly followed in United Nations practice. The United Nations Good Offices Committee in Indonesia appointed by the Security Council in 1947 had more extensive functions than good offices as such, eg, reporting to the Security Council on, and making recommendations as to developments in Indonesia, 1947–48; the United Nations Mediator in Palestine in 1948 was entrusted with the duties of reporting on developments, of promoting the welfare of the inhabitants of Palestine, and of assuring the protection of the Holy Places; and the Good Offices Committee for the Korean hostilities appointed by the United Nations General Assembly in 1951 was expected not merely to bring about negotiations between the contending forces, but to propose means and methods for effecting a cessation of hostilities. Cf also the case of the Good Offices Committee on South West Africa, appointed in 1957, whose duty was not only to discuss a basis of agreement with the South African Government, but to report to the General Assembly.
2.   The material documents are reproduced in 75 AJIL 418 et seq.

methods lie as steps preliminary or ancillary to the more specialised techniques of conciliation, of inquiry, and of settlement through the United Nations.

The term 'conciliation' has both a broad and a narrow meaning. In its more general sense, it covers the great variety of methods whereby a dispute is amicably settled with the aid of other states or of impartial bodies of inquiry or advisory committees. In the narrow sense, 'conciliation' signifies the reference of a dispute to a commission or committee to make a report with proposals to the parties for settlement, such proposals not being of a binding character. According to Judge Manley O. Hudson:[3]

> 'Conciliation. . . is a process of formulating proposals of settlement after an investigation of the facts and an effort to reconcile opposing contentions, the parties to the dispute being left free to accept or reject the proposals formulated.'

The fact that the parties are perfectly free to decide whether or not to adopt the proposed terms of settlement distinguishes conciliation from arbitration, and has the consequence that conciliation can be used to settle any kind of dispute or situation.

Conciliation Commissions were provided for in the Hague Conventions of 1899 and 1907 for the Pacific Settlement of International Disputes (see respectively Title III and Part III of these conventions). Such Commissions could be set up by special agreement between the parties, and were to investigate and report on situations of fact with the proviso that the report in no way bound the parties to the dispute. The actual provisions in the conventions avoid any words suggesting compulsion on the parties to accept a Commission's report. Similar Commissions were also set up under a series of treaties negotiated by the United States in 1913 and the following years, known as the 'Bryan Treaties'. Other treaties providing for conciliation are the Brussels Treaty of 17 March 1948, and the Pact of Bogotá of 1948, referred to above.

The value of Conciliation Commissions as such has been doubted by several authorities, but the procedure of conciliation itself proved most useful and important when employed by the League of Nations Council to settle international disputes. The Council's use of conciliation was extremely flexible; generally a small committee, or a person known as a rapporteur,[4] was appointed to make tactful investigations and suggest a method of composing the differences between the parties.[5] States do attach great value to the procedure of conciliation, as reflected in the provision made for it in the Convention of 18 March 1965, on the Settlement of Investment Disputes between States and Nationals of other States.

The object of an inquiry is, without making specific recommendations, to establish the facts, which may be in dispute, and thereby prepare the way for a

---

3. Hudson *International Tribunals* (1944) p 223.
4. The United Nations General Assembly also favours the flexible procedure, and has made various recommendations in the matter of the appointment of rapporteurs and conciliators; see below, p 574. Governments of a number of member states of the United Nations have designated members of a United Nations panel to serve on Commissions of conciliation and inquiry.
5. There have been several instances of the use of conciliation, outside the United Nations, since the end of the Second World War. The Bureau of the Permanent Court of Arbitration makes its facilities available for the holding of Conciliation Commissions. Cf also art 47 of the Hague Convention, 18 October 1907, on the Pacific Settlement of International Disputes.

negotiated adjustment.[6] Thus, frequently, in cases of disputed boundaries, a commission may be appointed to inquire into the historical and geographical facts which are the subject of controversy and thus clarify the issues for a boundary agreement. Also, sometimes an expert fact-finding committee is necessary to inquire into certain special facts for the purposes of preliminary elucidation.

Obviously one or more of the above methods—negotiation, good offices, mediation, conciliation, inquiry, and fact-finding—may be used in combination with the other or others.

Various endeavours have been made to improve processes of settlement, and render them even more flexible. The proposals have included the extension of fact-finding methods, and the creation of a fact-finding organ or fact-finding centre.[7] On 18 December 1967, the United Nations General Assembly adopted a Resolution, upholding the usefulness of the method of impartial fact-finding as a mode of peaceful settlement, and in which it urged member states to make more effective use of fact-finding methods, and requested the Secretary-General to prepare a register of experts whose services could be used by agreement for fact-finding in relation to a dispute. Subsequently, in accordance with the Resolution, nominations of experts were received for the purposes of the register (see Note by Secretary-General, Document A/7240), and each year the Secretary-General has transmitted to member states lists of experts so nominated. Existing facilities for fact-finding include those provided by the Panel for Inquiry and Conciliation set up by the General Assembly in April 1949. Special mention should also be made of the provisions for inquiries into alleged violations of international humanitarian law under the Geneva Conventions, 1949 (First Convention, art 52, Second Convention, art 53, Third Convention, art 132, Fourth Convention, art 149), and of the International Fact-Finding Commission established under Additional Protocol I to the Geneva Conventions (1977), art 90.

Reference should be made to the Manila Declaration on the Peaceful Settlement of International Disputes, approved by consensus by the General Assembly in 1982, and which may be regarded partly as a code of rules on the subject, partly as a manifesto of guidelines and desiderata, and partly as an elaborate hortatory instrument. In more vigorous language, many of the principles contained in that connection in the United Nations Charter are re-affirmed, states are required to have recourse to the traditional techniques of dispute-settlement already mentioned above, and their attention is drawn to all the available options for peaceful resolution of their differences. Some special points are made in the Manila Declaration, as follows:

a.   States should bear in mind that direct negotiations are a flexible and effective means of peaceful settlement of disputes, and if they choose to resort to direct negotiations, they should negotiate meaningfully.

6.   An inquiry may necessitate the lodging of written documents similar to pleadings, such as memorials and counter-memorials, and oral proceedings, with the taking of evidence, as in the *'Red Crusader' Inquiry* (Great Britain–Denmark) conducted at The Hague in 1962; see *Report* of the three-member Commission of inquiry, 23 March 1962, 35 ILR 485.
7.   See UN *Juridical Yearbook* 1964 pp 166-174.

b. States are enjoined to consider making greater use of the fact-finding capacity of the Security Council in accordance with the United Nations Charter.
c. Recourse to judicial settlement of legal disputes, particularly by way of referral to the International Court of Justice, should not be considered as an unfriendly act between states.
d. The Secretary-General of the United Nations should make full use of the provisions of the Charter concerning his special responsibilities, eg, bringing to the attention of the Security Council any matter which in his opinion may threaten the maintenance of international peace and security.

Although it may be felt that there is little that is novel in the Manila Declaration, the reaffirmation of established precepts in more elaborate and categorical language can be of value.

(d) Settlement under Auspices of United Nations Organisation
As successor to the League of Nations, the United Nations Organisation, created in 1945, has taken over the bulk of the responsibility for adjusting international disputes. One of the fundamental objects of the Organisation is the peaceful settlement of differences between states, and by article 2 of the United Nations Charter, Members of the Organisation have undertaken to settle their disputes by peaceful means and to refrain from threats of war or the use of force.

In this connection, important responsibilities devolve on the General Assembly and on the Security Council, corresponding to which wide powers are entrusted to both bodies. The General Assembly is given authority, subject to the peace enforcement powers of the Security Council, to recommend measures for the peaceful adjustment of any situation which is likely to impair general welfare or friendly relations among nations (see article 14 of the Charter).

The more extensive powers, however, have been conferred on the Security Council in order that it should execute swiftly and decisively the policy of the United Nations. The Council acts, broadly speaking, in two kinds of disputes: (i) disputes which may endanger international peace and security; (ii) cases of threats to the peace, or breaches of peace, or acts of aggression. In the former case, the Council, when necessary, may call on the parties to settle their disputes by the methods considered above, viz, arbitration, judicial settlement, negotiation, inquiry, mediation, and conciliation. Also the Council may at any stage recommend appropriate procedures or methods of adjustment for settling such disputes. In the latter case, (ii) above, the Council is empowered to make recommendations or decide what measures are to be taken to maintain or restore international peace and security, and it may call on the parties concerned to comply with certain provisional measures. There is no restriction or qualification on the recommendations which the Council may make, or on the measures, final or provisional, which it may decide are necessary. It may propose a basis of settlement, it may appoint a commission of inquiry, it may authorise a reference to the International Court of Justice, and so on. Under articles 41 to 47 of the Charter, the Security Council has also the right to give effect to its decisions not only by coercive measures such as economic sanctions, but also by the use of armed force against states which decline to be bound by these decisions.[8]

8. See further below, Chapter 20 at pp 579-584 for detailed treatment.

With the exception of disputes of an exclusively legal character which are usually submitted to arbitration or judicial settlement, it is purely a matter of policy or expediency which of the above different methods is to be adopted for composing a particular difference between states. Certain treaties have endeavoured to define the kind of dispute which should be submitted to arbitration, judicial settlement, or conciliation, or the order in which recourse should be had to these methods, but experience has shown the dubious value of any such pre-established definitions or procedure. Any one method may be appropriate, and the greater the flexibility permitted, the more chance there is of an amicable solution.

The General Act for the Pacific Settlement of International Disputes adopted by the League of Nations Assembly in 1928 was a type of instrument in which a maximum of flexibility and freedom of choice was sought to be achieved.[9] It provided separate procedures, a procedure of conciliation (before Conciliation Commissions) for all disputes (Chapter I), a procedure of judicial settlement or arbitration for disputes of a legal character (Chapter II), and a procedure of arbitration for other disputes (Chapter III). States could accede to the General Act by accepting all or some of the procedures and were also allowed to make certain defined reservations (for example, as to prior disputes, as to questions within the domestic jurisdiction, etc). The General Act was acceded to by 23 states, but accessions to it were heavily qualified by reservations. Since its machinery provisions referred to organs of the League of Nations, defunct after 1946, its utility thereafter was questioned, but the Act was successfully relied upon, as at least a prima facie basis of invoking the jurisdiction of the International Court of Justice, by Australia and New Zealand in their actions against France in the *Case Concerning Nuclear Tests*.[10] The Revised General Act, adopted by the United Nations General Assembly on 28 April 1949, has not been acceded to by a sufficient number of states to enter into force.

In this connection, there should be mentioned the problem of peaceful change or revision of treaties and the status quo which troubled publicists a good deal just before the Second World War. Many claimed that none of the above methods was suitable for settling 'revisionist' disputes, and proposed the creation of an International Equity Tribunal which would adjudicate claims for peaceful change on a basis of fairness and justice. The powers which would have been conferred on such a tribunal appear now to be vested, although not in a very specific or concrete manner, in the United Nations. Thus art 14 of the United Nations Charter already examined above in Chapter 16 on the law and practice as to treaties, empowers the UN General Assembly to recommend measures for the peaceful adjustment of any situation 'likely to impair the general welfare or friendly relations among nations', including situations resulting from a breach of the Charter.

Because of considerations of space, only brief reference can be made to the settlement of international disputes by regional agencies or groups. This is

9. The Pact of Bogotá of 30 April 1948 (Inter-American Treaty on Pacific Settlement), and the European Convention for the Peaceful Settlement of Disputes, concluded at Strasbourg on 29 April 1957, are illustrations of regional multilateral instruments with similarly detailed provisions for recourse to different procedures of settlement of disputes.
10. ICJ 1973, 99, 135 (interim measures); ICJ 1974, 253, 457 (jurisdiction and admissibility).

referred to in para 2 of art 52 of the United Nations Charter. The subject has also been dealt with in detail in the relevant literature.[11] In 1983–1988, the efforts of three regional groups in Central and South America directed to achievement of peaceful settlements in that part of the world attracted general notice. In the early 1990s the Council of Ministers of the European Communities, acting within the framework of the Conference on Security and Co-operation in Europe (CSCE) played a significant role in disputes arising in Eastern Europe, especially the former Yugoslavia (see Chapter 5, above).

3. SELF-HELP OR COERCIVE MEANS OF SETTLEMENT

When states cannot agree to solve their disputes amicably a solution may have to be found and imposed by unilateral means. The principal forcible and non-forcible modes of settlement are:

a. War and non-war armed action.
b. Retorsion.
c. Reprisals and countermeasures.
d. Pacific blockade.
e. Intervention.

(a) War and non-war armed action
The whole purpose of war is to overwhelm the opponent state, and to impose terms of settlement which that state has no alternative but to obey. Armed action, which falls short of a state of war, has also been resorted to in recent years. War and non-war armed hostilities are discussed in detail in Chapter 18, below.

(b) Retorsion
Retorsion is the technical term for retaliation by a state against discourteous or inequitable acts of another state, such retaliation taking the form of unfriendly legitimate acts within the competence of the state whose dignity has been affronted; for example, severance of diplomatic relations, revocation of diplomatic privileges, or withdrawal of fiscal or tariff concessions.[12]

So greatly has the practice as to retorsion varied that it is impossible to define precisely the conditions under which it is justified. At all events it need not be a retaliation in kind.

The legitimate use of retorsion by member states of the United Nations has probably been affected by the United Nations Charter. For example, under paragraph 3 of article 2, member states are to settle their disputes by peaceful means in such a way as not to 'endanger' international peace and security, and justice. It is possible that an otherwise legitimate act of retorsion may in certain circumstances be such as to endanger international peace and security, and justice, in which event it would seemingly be illegal under the Charter.

11. See, eg, J. G. Merrills *International Dispute Settlement* (1984) ch 9, 'Regional Organisations' pp 164 et seq, esp at pp 175–179 dealing with the limitations of regional action.
12. See Richard B. Lillich 'Forcible Self-Help under International Law' 62 *US Naval War College International Law Studies* (1980) 129, pp 130–131.

(c) Reprisals and countermeasures

Reprisals (now more often referred to in situations not involving the use of armed force as countermeasures) are methods adopted by states for securing redress from another state by taking retaliatory measures.[13] Formerly, the term was restricted to the seizure of property or persons, but in its modern acceptation connotes coercive measures adopted by one state against another for the purpose of settling some dispute brought about by the latter's illegal or unjustified conduct. The distinction between reprisals and retorsion is that reprisals consist of acts which would generally otherwise be illegal whereas retorsion consists of retaliatory conduct to which no legal objection can be taken. Reprisals and countermeasures may assume various forms, for example, a boycott of the goods of a particular state,[14] an embargo, a naval demonstration,[15] or bombardment. Few topics of international practice are more controversial, and this was well illustrated in 1973–1974 when the Arab oil producing states introduced an oil export embargo as to certain states of destination; the views expressed on the legality or illegality of this embargo were irreconcilable, and are indicative of the extent to which the law in this respect is unsettled.

It is now generally established by international practice that a reprisal or countermeasure is only justified, if at all, where the state against which it is directed has been guilty of conduct in the nature of an international delinquency. Moreover, a reprisal would not be justified if the delinquent state had not been previously requested to give satisfaction for the wrong done, or if the measures of reprisals were 'excessive' proportionately in relation to the injury suffered.[16] There have been several vivid illustrations of purported reprisal action by states, for example the expulsion of Hungarians from Yugoslavia in 1935, in retaliation for alleged Hungarian responsibility for the murder of King Alexander of Yugoslavia at Marseilles, and the shelling of the Spanish port of Almeria by German warships in 1937, as reprisal for an alleged bombardment of the battleship *Deutschland* by a Spanish aircraft belonging to the Spanish Republican forces. Perhaps the most dramatic example is the controversial case where the United States initiated aerial bombing of targets inside the borders of Libya on 15 April 1986 by way of claimed legitimate reprisal against what was said to be indiscriminate violence allegedly directed by the latter country against Americans

13. See generally O. Y. Elagab *The Legality of Non-Forcible Countermeasures in International Law* (1988). See also International Law Commission, draft art 30 on State Responsibility - 'Countermeasures in respect of an internationally wrongful act' - adopted in 1979, together with commentary: *Yearbook of the International Law Commission*, 1979-II, 115-122.
14. Unless used by way of justifiable reprisal, semble, a national boycott by one state of the goods of another may amount to an act of economic aggression in breach of international law. See Bouvé 28 AJIL (1934) 19 et seq.
15. Semble, defensive naval or military demonstrations are permissible in defence to an armed attack, but subsequent forcible self-help for purposes of redress, added precautions, etc, is not; cf *Corfu Channel (Merits) Case* ICJ 1949, 4 at 35.
16. See the *Naulilaa Case* (1928), Recueil of Decisions of the Mixed Arbitral Tribunals, Vol 8, p 409 at pp 422–425, and the *Air Services Agreement Case* (France v USA) (1978) 18 RIIA 416. The subject of the international law as to reprisals, including the question of their possible justification under certain circumstances, is thoroughly examined in a number of articles in the special Spring 1987 issue of the *Case Western Reserve Journal of International Law*. Certain of the articles also analyse the principles governing the question of the legitimacy of the American bombing of Libyan targets on 15 April 1986, considered as a reprisal.

over a period of time, including a bomb explosion on 5 April 1986 in a West German discotheque frequented byAmerican servicemen, resulting in the wounding of over 50 Americans.

Some authorities hold that reprisals are only justified if their purpose is to bring about a satisfactory settlement of a dispute. Hence the principle referred to above that reprisals should not be resorted to unless and until negotiations for the purpose of securing redress from the delinquent state fail.

Strictly speaking, retaliatory acts between belligerent states in the course of a war are a different matter altogether from reprisals, although they also are termed 'reprisals'. The object of such acts is generally to force an opponent state to stop breaking the laws of war; as, for example, in 1939–1940, when Great Britain commenced the seizure of German exports on neutral vessels in retaliation for the unlawful sinking of merchant ships by German-sown naval magnetic mines. No less than peace-time reprisals, the topic of reprisals as between belligerents is the subject of deep controversy, as reflected in the acute division of views on the matter at the Sessions in 1974–1977 of the Diplomatic Conference at Geneva on the Reaffirmation and Development of International Humanitarian Law Applicable in Armed Conflicts (see also Chapter 18, below).

As in the case of retorsion, the use of reprisals by member states of the United Nations has been affected by the Charter. Not only is there paragraph 3 of article 2 mentioned above in connection with retorsion, but there is also the provision in paragraph 4 of the same article that member states are to refrain from the threat or use of force against the territorial integrity or political independence of any state, or in any other manner inconsistent with the Purposes of the United Nations. Also, the Declaration on Principles of International Law Concerning Friendly Relations and Co-operation Among States in Accordance with the United Nations Charter, adopted by the General Assembly on 24 October 1970, expressly declares: 'States have a duty to refrain from acts of reprisal involving the use of force'. The United Nations Security Council had earlier, in 1964, by a majority, condemned reprisals as being 'incompatible with the Purposes and Principles of the United Nations'. A reprisal, therefore, being an act otherwise than for the purpose of lawful defence, under article 51 of the United Nations Charter, against armed attack, and which consisted in the threat or the exercise of military force against another state in such a way as to prejudice its territorial integrity, or political independence would presumably be illegal. Moreover under article 33 the states parties to a dispute, the continuance of which is likely to endanger peace and security are 'first of all' to seek a solution by negotiation, and other peaceful means. Thus a resort to force by way of retaliation would seemingly be excluded as illegal. The above-mentioned American bombing of targets in Libya on 15 April 1986 was justified, inter alia, on the ground that it was by way of lawful defence against alleged continuous armed attacks made by Libya.

There have also been cases of international or collective reprisals.[17]

17. By Resolution of 18 May 1951, during the course of the hostilities in Korea, the United Nations General Assembly recommended a collective embargo by states on the shipment of arms, ammunition and implements of war, items useful in their production, petroleum, and transportation materials to areas under the control of the Government of the People's Republic

(d) Pacific blockade

In the time of war, the blockade of a belligerent state's ports is a very common naval operation. The pacific blockade, however, is a measure employed in time of peace. Sometimes classed as a reprisal, it is generally designed to coerce the state whose ports are blockaded into complying with a request for satisfaction by the blockading states. Some authorities have doubted its legality. If not now obsolete, its admissibility as a unilateral measure is questionable in the light of the United Nations Charter.

The pacific blockade appears to have been first employed in 1827; since that date there have been about 20 instances of its employment[18]. It was generally used by very powerful states, with naval forces, against weak states. Although for that reason liable to abuse, in the majority of cases it was employed by the Great Powers acting in concert for objects which were perhaps in the best interests of all concerned, for example, to end some disturbance, or to ensure the proper execution of treaties, or to prevent the outbreak of war, as in the case of the blockade of Greece in 1886 to secure the disarming of the Greek troops assembled near the frontiers and thus avoid a conflict with Turkey. From this standpoint the pacific blockade may be regarded as a recognised collective procedure for facilitating the settlement of differences between states. Indeed, the blockade is expressly mentioned in article 42 of the United Nations Charter as one of the operations which the Security Council may initiate in order to 'maintain or restore international peace and security'.

There are certain obvious advantages in the employment of the pacific blockade. It is a far less violent means of action than war, and is more elastic. On the other hand, it is more than an ordinary reprisal, and against any but the weak states who are usually subjected to it, might be deemed an act of war. It is perhaps a just comment on the institution of pacific blockade that the strong maritime powers who resort to it do so in order to avoid the burdens and inconveniences of war.

Most writers agree, and on the whole the British practice supports the view, that a blockading state has no right to seize ships of third states which endeavour to break a pacific blockade.[19] It follows also that third states are not duty bound to respect such a blockade. The principle is that a blockading state can only operate against ships of other states if it has declared a belligerent blockade, that is, where actual war exists between the blockading and blockaded states and accordingly it becomes entitled to search neutral shipping. But by instituting merely a pacific blockade, the blockading state tacitly admits that the interests

---

of China, and of the North Korean authorities. A number of member states of the United Nations acted upon this recommendation. Another case was the decision of the Ministers of Foreign Affairs of the American States at Punta del Este, Uruguay, in January 1962, acting under the Inter-American Treaty of Reciprocal Assistance of 2 September 1947, to suspend trade with Cuba in arms and implements of war of every kind. It was alleged that Cuba was conducting subversive activity in America. Cuba challenged the validity of the decision on the ground that it was enforcement action taken without the authorisation of the Security Council under Chapter VII of the United Nations Charter, but this objection was denied.

18. See Walter R. Thomas 'Pacific Blockade: A Lost Opportunity of the 1930s?' in 62 *US Naval War College International Law Studies* (1980) 197 at 198.

19. The United States also consistently maintained that pacific blockades were not applicable to American vessels.

at stake were not sufficient to warrant the burdens and risks of war. On principle, therefore, in the absence of an actual war, the blockading state should not impose on third states the obligations and inconveniences of neutrality. In other words, a blockading state cannot simultaneously claim the benefits of peace and war.

The 'selective' blockade or 'quarantine' of Cuba by the United States in October 1962, although instituted in peacetime, cannot be fitted within the traditional pattern of the pacific blockades of the nineteenth century. First, it was more than a blockade of the coast of a country as such. Its express purpose was to 'interdict' the supply of certain weapons and equipment[20] to Cuba, in order to prevent the establishment or reinforcement of missile bases in Cuban territory, but not to preclude all entry or exit of goods to or from Cuba. Second, vessels of countries other than Cuba, en route to Cuba, were subject to search and, if necessary, control by force, and could be directed to follow prescribed routes or avoid prohibited zones; but it was not in terms sought to render weapon-carrying vessels or their cargoes subject to capture for breach of the 'interdiction'. Third, among other grounds, the President of the United States purported to proclaim the quarantine pursuant to a recommendation of an international organisation, namely the Organisation of American States.[1] Fourth, the quarantine was conducted in a manner unlike that characteristic of traditional pacific blockades; eg under a 'Clearcert' scheme, shippers could obtain beforehand a clearance certificate to send cargoes through the zone subject of the quarantine.[2]

Assuming that such a blockade is, in all the circumstances, permitted by the United Nations Charter, nevertheless because of the very special geographical and other conditions, no general conclusions can be drawn from it as a precedent. If not permissible under the Charter, the effect of the 'quarantine' in interfering with the freedom of the high seas raised serious issues as to its justification under customary international law.

Another special case, more recent than that of the Cuban quarantine of 1962, and likewise to be distinguished from that of a pacific blockade, was represented by the formal announcement on 28 April 1982 by the United Kingdom Government of a 200-mile Total Exclusion Zone (TEZ) around the Falkland Islands, extended on 7 May 1982 to 12 miles from the coast of Argentina; this measure preceded the steps taken by British forces to retake the territory of the islands occupied by Argentine garrisons, and was thus a warlike measure forming an integral part of a combined air, naval and military campaign. It was in point of law justified as an exercise of the right of self-defence against an armed attack under article 51 of the United Nations Charter. The terms of the formal

---

20. In the Presidential Proclamation of October 1962, instituting the blockade, these were listed as: surface-to-surface missiles; bomber aircraft; bombs, air-to-surface rockets and guided missiles; warheads of any of these weapons; mechanical or electronic equipment to support or operate these items; and other classes designated by the US Secretary of Defence.

1. Its Council, meeting as a provisional Organ of Consultation under the Inter-American Treaty of Reciprocal Assistance of 2 September 1947, adopted on 23 October 1962, a Resolution recommending member states to take measures to ensure that Cuba should not receive military supplies, etc.

2. See James J. McHugh, 'Forceable Self-Help in International Law' 62 *US Naval War College International Law Studies* (1980) 139, pp 154–156; and Henkin, Pugh, Schachter and Smit *International Law; Cases and Materials* (2nd edn, 1987) pp 702–704, 794–795.

announcement of the TEZ, so far as material, point clearly to its difference from a pacific blockade:

'... The exclusion zone will apply not only to Argentine warships and naval auxiliaries, but also to any other ship, whether naval or merchant vessel, which is operating in support of the illegal occupation of the Falkland Islands by Argentine forces. The zone will also apply to any aircraft, whether military or civil, which is operating in support of the Argentine occupation. Any ship and any aircraft, whether military or civil, which is found within this zone without authority from the Ministry of Defence in London will be regarded as operating in support of the illegal occupation and will therefore be regarded as hostile and will be liable to be attacked by British forces.'

Leaving aside the difference of this TEZ from a pacific blockade, its legality, as in the case of the Cuban quarantine, under the United Nations Charter and customary international law, has been questioned.

(e) Intervention

Examples of this measure include the incursions by Israel into Uganda in 1976 to rescue the passengers of a civil aircraft bound for Israel from France hijacked and diverted to Entebbe Airport, where the Ugandan authorities appeared to be helpless or indifferent to their safety[3]; and the failed attempt by a United States force to rescue the hostages held by Iran after the seizure of the American embassy and consulates in 1979, which was regarded by the International Court of Justice as 'calculated to undermine respect for the judicial process' then underway before the Court in respect of the matter.[4] The subject of intervention is considered in more detail in Chapter 5, above.

3. See the debates in the Security Council on this incident collected in (1976) 15 ILM 1224.
4. *United States Diplomatic and Consular Staff in Tehran Case*, ICJ 1980, 3, at para 93. At para 94 of its judgment, however, the Court refrained from pronouncing upon the legality of the incursion.

CHAPTER 18

War, armed conflicts and other hostile relations

1. GENERAL[1]

The hostilities in Korea, 1950–1953, ending with the Armistice Agreement of 27 July 1953, the fighting in Indo-China, 1947–1954, and the conflict in and around the Suez Canal Zone involving Israel, Egypt, France and Great Britain in 1956, finally confirmed a development in the practice of states which has changed the basis of those rules of international law, traditionally grouped under the title, 'the law of war'. For these were non-war armed conflicts. Further confirmation of this development was furnished by the hostilities in West New Guinea between Indonesian and Dutch units in April-July 1962, by the border fighting between India and the People's Republic of China in October-November 1962, by the hostilities in the Congo, 1960–1963, by the India-Pakistan armed conflicts of September 1965, and December 1971, and more recently by the hostilities in Lebanon in 1982–1983. None of these cases received general recognition as involving a state of war.[2]

The conflict in Vietnam was a special case. In the early stages, the Vietnam hostilities could appropriately have been fitted into the category of non-war armed conflicts. After the struggle escalated from about 1965 onwards into the

1. The literature is immense. An up-to-date review may be obtained in Y. Dinstein *War, Aggression, and Self-Defence* (1988). See also C. Greenwood, 'The concept of war in modern international law' (1987) 36 ICLQ 283, and E. Kwakwa *The International Law of Armed Conflict: Personal and Material Fields of Application* (1992). For documents and commentaries see A. Roberts and R. Guelff *Documents on the Laws of War* (2nd edn, 1989). For a concise recent manual on the law of warfare see L. C. Green *The Contemporary Law of Armed Conflict* (1993).
2. It is a moot question whether the conflict between the United Kingdom and Argentina, April-June 1982, over the occupation of territory of the Falkland Islands by Argentine garrisons, and which involved a combined military, air and naval campaign by British forces to retake the territory and expel the garrisons, could be characterised as a 'war' in the classic sense, although it was popularly referred to, or described as the 'Falklands War', notwithstanding the official attitude of the British Government that a state of war with Argentina did not exist. On the other hand, the Iraq–Iran hostilities which began in September 1980 and terminated in August 1988 when the mandatory Resolution 598 of the UN Security Council for the implementation of a cease-fire came into operation, were on such a scale as to justify description as a 'war' rather than as a non-war armed conflict.

dimensions of a major local war, this non-war characterisation was scarcely possible. Indeed some of the participants expressly referred to it as a 'war' (eg, the United States President on 30 April 1971, in an address justifying the incursion into Cambodia.[3] More decisively, the principal Agreement signed at Paris on 27 January 1973, for terminating the conflict bore the title 'Agreement on ending the *War* and Restoring Peace in Vietnam'. Opinions are divided on the point whether the Vietnam conflict can be correctly described as a large-scale civil war with heavy involvement of outside states, or an international war, or a tertium quid of an international conflict with some civil war characteristics.

The traditional rules hinged on the existence, between such states as came under the operation of the rules, of a hostile relationship known as 'war', and war in its most generally understood sense was a contest between two or more states primarily through their armed forces, the ultimate purpose of each contestant or each contestant group being to vanquish the other or others and impose its own conditions of peace. This is similar to the conception of the greatest theorist of the nature of war, Karl von Clausewitz (1780–1831), for whom war was a struggle on an extensive scale designed by one party to compel its opponent to fulfil its will. Hence we have the well-respected definition of 'war' by Hall, judicially approved in *Driefontein Consolidated Gold Mines v Janson*:[4]

> 'When differences between States reach a point at which both parties resort to force, or one of them does acts of violence, which the other chooses to look upon as a breach of the peace, the relation of war is set up, in which the combatants may use regulated violence against each other, until one of the two has been brought to accept such terms as his enemy is willing to grant.'

The Korean hostilities involved an armed conflict, at first between the North Korean armies[5] on the one hand, and the South Korean Armies and armed forces of the United Nations Command on the other hand, without any declared status of war being involved. Yet this conflict was one on the scale of war as normally understood, and made it necessary to bring into application many of the rules traditionally applicable as part of the law of war. Prior to the Korean conflict, there had been precedents of hostilities, not deemed to be of the nature of war, among which may be instanced: (a) the Sino–Japanese hostilities in Manchuria, 1931–1932, and from 1937 onwards in China; (b) the Russo–Japanese hostilities at Changkufeng in 1938; and (c) the armed operations involving (ostensibly) Outer Mongolian and Inner Mongolian forces at Nomonhan in 1939. A later example of a non-war armed conflict, the Suez Canal zone hostilities in October–November 1956, was indeed the subject of the following comment by the British Lord Privy Seal (on 1 November 1956):

> 'Her Majesty's Government do not regard their present action as constituting war . . . There is no state of war, but there is a state of conflict.'

---

3. The United States point of view, in justification of the incursion, was, inter alia, that as North Vietnam and the Vietcong had violated Cambodia's neutrality, the United States as a 'belligerent' was entitled to protect her security by way of self-preservation.
4. [1900] 2 QB 339 at 343.
5. Later including armed forces described in the Armistice Agreement as the 'Chinese People's Volunteers'.

Before the outbreak of the Korean conflict in 1950, states had already to some extent foreseen the consummation of this development of non-war hostilities.[6] In 1945, at the San Francisco Conference on the United Nations Charter, the peace enforcement powers of the United Nations Security Council were made conditional, not on the existence of a recourse to war by a covenant-breaking state as under article 16 of the League of Nations Covenant, but on the fact of some 'threat to the peace, breach of the peace, or act of aggression' (see article 39 of the Charter). In 1949, the conventions adopted by the Geneva Red Cross Conference dealing with prisoners of war, the sick and wounded in the field, and the protection of civilians were made applicable to any kind of 'armed conflict' as well as to cases of war proper.[7]

Another refinement has been introduced in the distinction between international and 'non-international' armed conflicts. The distinction was drawn in the two Protocols: Protocol I, 'relating to the Protection of Victims of International Armed Conflicts', and Protocol II, 'relating to the Protection of Victims of Non-International Armed Conflicts', adopted as additions to the Geneva Red Cross Conventions of 12 August 1949, by the Geneva Conference on the Reaffirmation and Development of International Humanitarian Law Applicable in Armed Conflicts at its final session in June 1977 (see below in this chapter). Article 1 of Protocol II virtually defines a non-international armed conflict by providing that the Protocol applies to all armed conflicts not covered by article 1 of Protocol I 'which take place in the territory of a High Contracting Party between its armed forces and dissident armed forces or other organised armed groups which, under responsible command, exercise such control over a part of its territory as to enable them to carry out sustained and concerted military operations and to implement this Protocol'. However, under the same article 1, the Protocol is not to apply to 'situations of internal disturbances and tensions such as riots, isolated and sporadic acts of violence and other acts of a similar nature, as not being armed conflicts'.

The main reasons or conditions which have dictated this development of non-war hostilities are:

a. the provisions of the United Nations Charter, especially article 2, paragraphs 3 and 4, which prohibit the resort to force by states in their international relations;
b. the desire of states to preclude any suggestion of breach of a treaty obligation not to go to war[8] (eg, the Briand-Kellogg General Treaty of 1928 for the

6. The difference between the outbreak of war and the commencement of 'non-war' hostilities was also recognised early on in the United Nations General Assembly Resolution of 17 November 1950, on 'Duties of States in the Event of the Outbreak of Hostilities' (such duties being to avoid *war*, notwithstanding the commencement of an armed conflict). See also the Resolution of the General Assembly of 16 December 1969, on respect for human rights in armed conflicts, which refers to the necessity of applying the basic humanitarian principles 'in all armed conflicts'.
7. Cf also the use of the expression 'armed conflict' in arts 44 and 45 of the Vienna Convention on Diplomatic Relations of 18 April 1961 (facilities to enable diplomatic envoys to leave, protection of legation premises, etc).
8. Cf the affirmation in Principle 2 of the United Nations Declaration of 15 December 1978, on the Preparation of Societies for Life in Peace that 'a *war* of aggression, its planning, preparation or initiation are crimes against peace, prohibited by international law'. In that connection, see

Renunciation of War, under which the signatories renounced war as an instrument of national policy);

c. to prevent non-contestant states from declaring their neutrality and hampering the conduct of hostilities by restrictive neutrality regulations;

d. to localise the conflict, and prevent it attaining the dimensions of a general war.

Hence there must now be distinguished:

1. A war proper between states.
2. Armed conflicts or breaches of the peace, which are not of the character of war, and which are not necessarily confined to hostilities involving states only, but may include a struggle in which non-state entities participate.

The distinction does not mean that the second category of hostile relations involving states and non-state entities is less in need of regulation by international law than the first.

It is significant that coincidentally with the development of the second category, as illustrated by the Korean conflict,[9] the nature of war itself has become more distinctly clarified as a formal status of armed hostility, in which the intention of the parties, the so-called animus belligerendi, may be a decisive factor. This is consistent with Clausewitz's view that war is not merely of itself a political act, but serves as a real political instrument for the achievement of certain ends. Thus a state of war may be established between two or more states by a formal declaration of war, although active hostilities may never take place between them; indeed, it appears that of the 50 or more states which declared war during the Second World War, more than half did not actively engage their military or other forces against the enemy. Moreover, the cessation of armed hostilities does not, according to modern practice, necessarily terminate a state of war.

The 'status' theory of war was reflected in the anomalous position of Germany and Japan during the years immediately following their unconditional surrender in 1945 in accordance with the formula decided upon during the War by the Big Three—Great Britain, Russia and the United States. Although both countries were deprived of all possible means of continuing war, and although their actual government was for a time carried on by the Allies, they continued to be legally at 'war' with their conquerors. In 1947, in *R v Bottrill*, a certificate by the British Foreign Secretary that the state of war continued with Germany was deemed by the Court of Appeal to be binding on the courts.[10] One object of prolonging this relationship of belligerency, if only technically, was no doubt to enable the machinery of occupation controls to be continued. The absence of immediate peace settlements with either of these ex-enemy states was a further significant circumstance.

---

also the text of the Principles of International Law Recognised in the Charter of the Nuremberg Tribunal and in the Judgment of the Tribunal, adopted in 1950 by the International Law Commission, and pp 54-55 above.

9. See L.C. Green (1951) 4 ILQ 462 et seq. for discussion on the point whether the Korean conflict amounted to a 'war', and, by same writer, 'Armed Conflict, War, and Self-Defence', *Archiv des Völkerrechts* (1957) Vol 6, pp 387–438.

10. [1947] KB 41, and cf *Re Hourigan* [1946] NZLR 1. In the American case of *Ludecke v Watkins* 335 US 160 (1948), it was pointed out in Frankfurter J's judgment that a status of war can survive hostilities. See also (1949) 2 ILQ 697.

The commercial or non-technical meaning of war is not necessarily identical with the international law meaning. Thus it was held by an English court[11] that the word 'war' in a charterparty applied to the 'non-war' hostilities in China in 1937 between Chinese and Japanese forces. The word 'peace' can similarly denote the termination of actual hostilities, notwithstanding the continuance of a formal state of war.[12]

The question whether there is a status of war, or only a condition of non-war hostilities, depends on: (a) the dimensions of the conflict; (b) the intentions of the contestants; and (c) the attitudes and reactions of the non-contestants.

As to (a), merely localised or limited acts of force fall short of war.

As to (b), the intentions of the contestants are normally decisive if the conflict concerns them only, and does not affect other states. Hence, if there is a declaration of war, or in the absence of such a declaration, the contestants treat the conflict as a war, effect must be given to such intention; if, on the other hand, they are resolved to treat the fighting as of the nature of non-war hostilities, a state of war is excluded. An insoluble difficulty arises, however, if according to the attitude of one or more of the contestants, there be a state of war, whereas according to the other or others there is no war. Recent state practice (eg, in the case of the India-Pakistan hostilities of September 1965) is inconclusive on this point. Prima facie, a unilateral attitude of one contestant that it is at war is intended as notice of a claim of belligerent rights, with the expectation that third states will observe neutrality; while a unilateral denial of war operates as notice to the contrary.

As to (c), the policies of non-contestant states enter into account when the conflict impinges on their rights and interests. Assuming the hostilities are on a sufficiently extensive scale, the decision may be made to recognise belligerency,[13] or to make a declaration of neutrality, irrespective of the intentions of the contestants. A third state, adopting this course, would be subject to the risk of the exercise against it of belligerent rights by either contestant, whose right to do so could not then be challenged. A non-war status could none the less still apply in the relations of the contestants inter se.

Rules of international law governing 'non-war' hostilities
Practice in the Korean conflict, 1950–1953, and the other conflicts mentioned above, revealed the tendency of states to apply most of the rules governing a war stricto sensu to non-war hostilities.[14] As already mentioned, the Geneva Red Cross Conventions of 1949 (for example, that relating to prisoners of war) and the Protocols I and II additional to these Conventions adopted in June 1977 by

11. *Kawasaki Kisen Kabushiki Kaisha of Kobe v Bantham SS Co Ltd (No 2)* [1938] 3 All ER 80; upheld on appeal [1939] 2 KB 544. Cf *Gugliormella v Metropolitan Life Insurance Co* 122 F Supp 246 (1954) (death in Korean hostilities 1950–1953 is the result of 'an act of war'). Also the 'war' represented by non-war hostilities ends with the termination of such hostilities; see *Shneiderman v Metropolitan Casualty Co* 220 NYS 2d 947 (1961).
12. See *Lee v Madigan* 358 US 228 (1959) (words 'in time of peace' in art 92 of the Articles of War).
13. See above, pp 138–140.
14. The United Nations Command in the Korean conflict 1950–1953 declared its intention of observing the 'laws of war', and the Geneva Red Cross Conventions of 1949. These were also observed in varying measure in the Vietnam conflict, to which of course the Geneva Conventions had application.

the Geneva Conference on the Reaffirmation and Development of International Humanitarian Law Applicable in Armed Conflicts (see above in this chapter) were in their terms expressly applicable to non-war conflicts, while the Resolution adopted by the United Nations General Assembly on 16 December 1969, with regard to respect for human rights in armed conflicts, referred to the necessity of applying the basic humanitarian principles 'in all armed conflicts'.

But every such armed conflict must vary in its special circumstances. It may be, for instance, that the states or non-state entities opposed to each other in hostilities have not made a complete severance of their diplomatic relations. Again, they may or may not seek to blockade each other's coasts.[15] It cannot therefore be predicted of any future armed conflict, not involving a state of war, that the entirety of the laws of war automatically apply to it. Which rules of war apply, and to what extent they are applicable, must depend on the circumstances.

Moreover, in the case of a non-war armed conflict, as to which the United Nations Security Council is taking enforcement action, actual decisions or recommendations adopted by the Security Council under articles 39 et seq of the United Nations Charter, for the guidance of states engaged in the hostilities, may fill the place of rules of international law. Then one has to consider also the incidence of United Nations 'peacekeeping operations', which are referred to in Chapter 20, where recommendations of the General Assembly play a primary role.

Other hostile reactions

Between a state of peace, on the one hand, and of war or non-war hostilities, on the other hand, other gradations of hostile reactions between states are possible, but have to a very limited extent only come within the ambit of international law. An example is the state of opposition—the so-called 'cold war'—which existed from 1946 until 1990 between the Western and the Communist groups of states, although from time to time there was a thaw described as a 'détente'.[16]

One of the unprecedented elements in the cold war was the so-called 'balance of terror', or its euphemism, 'Mutual Assured Destruction' (MAD), which was nothing more or less than precarious equilibrium between the United States and the Soviet Union in their possession and global deployment of nuclear and thermonuclear weapons, and missiles. Some authorities regard it as a myth that MAD represented an assurance of peace. A crucial question was to what extent this permits one of these states, purporting to act for purposes of self-defence, in the absence of an armed attack[17] on it, and without the authorisation of the United Nations Security Council, to take measures which would otherwise be a breach of international law. This issue lay behind the controversy over the legality

---

15. Cf the case of the Total Exclusion Zone (TEZ) declared by the United Kingdom on 28 April 1982, to be in force around the Falkland Islands, for the purpose of the operations to retake the territory occupied by Argentine garrisons; see Chapter 17, above, pp 475-476.
16. The 'cold war' was not a war, for the purpose of determining who are enemy aliens; see decision of Supreme Court of Alabama in *Pilcher v Dezso* (1955) 49 AJIL 417.
17. Within the meaning of art 51 of the United Nations Charter, permitting measures of self-defence against an armed attack, pending enforcement action by the Security Council to maintain international peace and security.

of: (a) the flight of the United States high-flying reconnaissance aircraft, the U-2, over Russian territory in 1960, when it was detected and shot down, and the pilot taken prisoner; and (b) the continued surveillance of Cuban territory by United States aircraft in October-November 1962, for various purposes. It is simplifying things to reduce the matter to an issue of whether or not peace-time espionage is permissible. Under normal circumstances, it is a violation of international law for the government aircraft of one state to enter the airspace of another without that state's consent. If, then, these flights were legal, the intensity of the cold war had wrought a fundamental change in the rules of international law.

A concept of a new kind made its appearance in the period 1963–1966 in the shape of Indonesia's 'confrontation' of Malaysia, after the establishment of that new state in September 1963. 'Confrontation' involved action and policies to undermine the integrity and position of Malaysia. It was short-lived, being terminated by the signature on 11 August 1966 of an agreement of peace and co-operation (drawn up at Bangkok, signed at Jakarta).

Commencement of war or hostilities

From time immemorial, state practice as to the commencement of a war has varied. Down to the sixteenth century, it was customary to notify an intended war by letters of defiance or by herald, but the practice fell into disuse. In the seventeenth century Grotius was of the opinion that a declaration of war was necessary, but subsequently several wars were commenced without formal declaration. By the nineteenth century, however, it was taken for granted that some form of preliminary warning by declaration or ultimatum was necessary.

Many instances of state practice in the twentieth century have been inconsistent with the rule. In 1904, Japan commenced hostilities against Russia by a sudden and unexpected attack on units of the Russian fleet in Port Arthur. Japan justified her action on the ground that she had broken off negotiations with Russia and had notified the Russians that she reserved her right to take independent action to safeguard her interests.

The Port Arthur incident led to the rule laid down by the Hague Convention III of 1907, relative to the Opening of Hostilities, according to which hostilities ought not to commence without previous explicit warning in the form of either: (a) a declaration of war stating the grounds on which it was based, or (b) an ultimatum containing a conditional declaration of war. It was further provided that the existence of the state of war should be notified to neutral states without delay and should not take effect as regards them until after the receipt of the notification which might, however, be given by telegraph. Neutral states were not to plead absence of such notification in cases where it was established beyond question that they were in fact aware of a state of war.

Scant respect was paid to these rules in the period 1935–1945, during which hostilities were repeatedly begun without prior declaration. So far as the post-1945 period is concerned, the parties to the majority of armed conflicts have not recognised the rules as applicable to such conflicts. This does not mean, however, that the procedure of a declaration of war, preceding the commencement of hostilities, is altogether obsolete.

Legal regulation of right to resort to war, to armed conflict, and to the use of force

In the field of international law, one of the most significant twentieth-century developments has been the legal regulation of the former unregulated privilege of states to resort to war, or to engage in non-war hostilities, or to use force, and the development of the concept of collective security.[18] The latter concept is essentially legal, as it imports the notion of a general interest of all states in the maintenance of peace, and the preservation of the territorial integrity and political independence of states, which have been the object of armed aggression. To quote Professor Bourquin:[19] 'A collective organisation of security is not directed against one particular aggression, but against war considered as a common danger'.

The League of Nations Covenant (see articles 12–15) placed primary emphasis on restricting the right of member states to resort to war, stricto sensu, in breach of certain obligations connected with accepting the arbitration or judicial settlement of certain disputes (more particularly those 'likely to lead to a rupture'), or the recommendations thereon of the League of Nations Council. But in a secondary sense, the Covenant precluded also certain kinds of recourse to non-war hostilities; for example, in imposing an obligation upon states to seek arbitration or judicial settlement of disputes which might have entered the stage of active hostilities, and an obligation to respect and preserve as against external aggression the territorial integrity and political independence of other member states (see article 10).

In 1928, under the Briand-Kellogg Pact (or, more precisely, the Paris General Treaty for the Renunciation of War), the states parties agreed generally to renounce recourse to 'war' for the solution of international controversies, and as an instrument of national policy. They also agreed not to seek the solution of disputes or conflicts between them except by 'pacific means', thus covering, no doubt, non-war hostilities.

In terms, the United Nations Charter of 1945 went much further than either of these two instruments, the primary emphasis on war stricto sensu having disappeared, while in its stead appeared the conception of 'threats to the peace', 'breaches of the peace' and 'acts of aggression', covering both war and non-war armed conflicts. In article 2, as already mentioned in Chapter 17, the member states agreed to settle their disputes by peaceful means so as not to endanger peace and security and justice, and to refrain from the threat or use of force[20] against the territorial integrity or political independence of any state. They also bound themselves to fulfil in good faith their obligations under the Charter, which include not only (a) the restriction that in the case of disputes likely to endanger peace and security, they shall seek a solution by the peaceful procedures set out in articles 33–38; but also (b) the obligation to submit to the overriding peace enforcement functions of the Security Council, including the decisions and recommendations that the Council may deem fit to make concerning their hostile activities. This conception of *peace enforcement*, not predetermined in specific

18. On the subject of the legal regulation of the use of force, see A. Cassese (ed) *Legal Restraints on the Use of Force 40 years after the UN Charter* (1986).
19. M. Bourquin (ed) *Collective Security* (1936) p 162.
20. *Meaning of 'force'*: Quaere, whether this includes political, economic, and other forms of pressure or coercion, or use of irregular forces; *UN Juridical Yearbook*, 1964 pp 79–83, 97–98. See also p 472, n 14, above, in Chapter 17.

obligations under the Charter, but to be translated ad hoc into binding decisions or recommendations of the Security Council which must be accepted by states resorting to war or to hostilities, represented the most striking innovation of the Charter.

In this connection, two aspects are of particular importance:

1. The aspect of a war or resort to hostilities, involving aggression.
2. A resort to war or to hostilities which is in self-defence.

As to (1), apart from the power of the Security Council to control 'acts of aggression' under article 39 of the Charter, the judgments of the Nuremberg and Tokyo Tribunals confirmed the view that a war of aggression, or in violation of international treaties, is illegal. The Tribunals went further in also holding that the acts of 'planning, preparation, initiation, or waging of a war of aggression or a war in violation of international treaties' are international crimes engaging the individual responsibility of those committing the acts.[1] The Tribunals' views were based on the Briand-Kellogg Pact of 1928 (mentioned above), but international lawyers have questioned the soundness of the judgments in view of state practice prior to 1941.[2]

An effective system of collective security must provide safeguards against aggression. The point of difficulty is to determine when a war is 'aggressive' for the purpose of the Nuremberg principles, or when non-war hostilities may constitute 'an act of aggression' for the purpose of the peace enforcement functions of the Security Council. If a state legitimately defends itself against attack by another (see below), it is not guilty of waging aggressive war, or of using aggressive force. But if a state attacks the territorial integrity or political independence of another state either in breach of treaty obligations, or without any justification and with the wilful purpose of destroying its victim, it is clearly guilty of aggression. In the period 1919–1939, a large number of bilateral treaties of non-aggression were concluded, and the drafters of these instruments were far from overcoming the formidable difficulties involved in the definition of aggression.[3]

The intractable difficulties involved in the definition of the concept were illustrated by the almost negative results of the labours of two Special Committees, appointed by the United Nations General Assembly in 1952 and 1954 respectively, to deal with the question of defining aggression. By Resolution adopted on 18 December 1967, the General Assembly set up a third Committee,[4]

---

1. See Principle VI of the Principles of International Law Recognised in the Charter of the International Tribunal and in the Judgment of the Tribunal, drawn up by the International Law Commission in 1950.
2. Eg, the United States Proclamation of neutrality in 1939 on the outbreak of war, professing amity with the belligerents; if the Tribunals were right, by such Proclamation the United States was in effect condoning the illegality of Germany's aggression against Poland.
3. See, eg, definition of 'aggression' in the Soviet Conventions of 1933 for the Definition of Aggression, art II; Keith *Speeches and Documents on International Affairs, 1918–1937* Vol I, pp 281–282.
4. In 1957, the General Assembly had established a Committee to study the comments of governments in order to advise the Assembly when it would be appropriate to resume consideration of the question of defining aggression. This Committee held a number of meetings, including a session in April–May 1967, some six months before the above-mentioned General Assembly Resolution of 18 December 1967.

the Special Committee on the Question of Defining Aggression, with the specific mandate of preparing 'an adequate definition of aggression', and made reference to 'a widespread conviction of the need to expedite the definition of aggression'. However, it was not until its seventh session in March–April 1974 that this Special Committee was able to adopt by consensus a definition of aggression, and to recommend that such definition be adopted by the General Assembly. By Resolution of 14 December 1974, the General Assembly approved the Special Committee's definition, the text of which was made an annexure to the Resolution, and called the attention of the Security Council to the definition, recommending that it should, as appropriate, take account of the definition as guidance in determining, in accordance with the United Nations Charter, the existence of an act of aggression for the purposes of article 39 of the Charter. During the period 1968–1974, embracing its seven sessions, the Special Committee's work and discussions had ranged over a wide field and had taken account of experience in the previous decade. Among the considerations or elements proposed for incorporation in the definition of aggression were the following:

a.   direct aggression, that is, conduct initiating or constituting the direct application of force (eg, declaration of war, invasion, bombardment, and blockade);

b.   indirect aggression, represented, inter alia, by the indirect use of force (eg, the sending of mercenaries or saboteurs to another state, the encouragement there of subversive activities by irregular or volunteer bands, and the fomenting of civil strife in other countries);

c.   priority, that is the significance to be attached to the first use of force;

d.   capacity to commit aggression, namely whether the definition should embrace aggression committed by states only or be extended to cover aggression by other entities;

e.   the legitimate use of force (eg by way of collective self-defence);

f.   aggressive intent, representing a subjective test of aggression;

g.   proportionality, involving a comparison of the degree of retaliation with the extent of force or threat of force responded to.

Some weight of opinion both in the Special Committee itself and in the United Nations General Assembly had favoured a 'mixed definition' of aggression, in which a general descriptive formula would precede and condition an enumeration of specific acts of aggression, this list being by way of illustration rather than serving to cut down the general formula, and also being without prejudice to the overriding power of the United Nations Security Council to characterise as an act of aggression some form of action not corresponding to any of the enumerated items.[5] Broadly speaking, this was the solution adopted in the Special Committee's definition of 1974 as approved by the General Assembly. Article 1 of the definition contained the following descriptive formula: 'aggression is the

5.   In the case of the Korean conflict in 1950, the Security Council determined that the action of the North Korean forces constituted a 'breach of the peace' (see Resolution of 25 June 1950). However, the United Nations Commission in Korea in its report to the General Assembly on 4 September 1950, described this as an 'act of aggression'.

use of armed force by a state against the sovereignty, territorial integrity or political independence of another state, or in any other manner inconsistent with the Charter of the United Nations as set out in this definition', the term 'state' in this article including a group of states, where appropriate, and being used without prejudice to questions of recognition or to whether the relevant state was a member of the United Nations. Under article 2, the 'first use' of armed force by a state in contravention of the Charter was to constitute prima facie evidence of an act of aggression, although it would be open to the Security Council to conclude otherwise in the light of the gravity of the conduct of that state or the consequences of such conduct. The enumeration of specific acts of aggression was made in article 3; these were, subject to the provisions of article 2, to include invasion or attack by the armed forces of a state on the territory of another state, military occupation resulting from invasion or attack, annexation by the use of force, bombardment of or the use of weapons against the territory of another state, blockade of the ports or coasts of a state, and the sending by or on behalf of a state of armed bands, groups, irregulars or mercenaries, which carry out acts of armed force against another state of such gravity as to amount to invasion, attack, bombardment, etc, or substantial 'involvement' therein by the sending state. Article 4 provides that the acts enumerated in article 3 are not exhaustive, and the Security Council is free to determine that other acts constitute aggression under the provisions of the Charter. Article 5 goes on to provide that no consideration of whatever nature, political, economic, military or otherwise, is to serve as a justification for aggression, that a war of aggression is a crime against international peace, with aggression giving rise to international responsibility, and that no territorial acquisition or special advantage resulting from aggression is or shall be recognised as lawful. Under the savings provisions of articles 6 and 7, nothing in the definition is to be construed as enlarging or diminishing the scope of the Charter, or to prejudice the right to self-determination, freedom, and independence as derived from the Charter. Finally, article 8 declares that the provisions of articles 1–7 are, in their interpretation and application, 'interrelated', and that each provision is to be construed in the context of the other provisions.

It is hardly necessary to say that this definition of aggression falls short of legal perfection.[6] The value of the Special Committee's formulations lies rather in the manner in which attention is directed to tests and criteria of the aggressive nature of conduct by a particular state, for tests and criteria can be of more value than a definition in the strict sense. Thus, one useful test of aggression is a repeated refusal to seek a settlement by peaceful means.[7]

---

6. Cf Stone 'Hopes and Loopholes in the 1974 Definition of Aggression' 71 AJIL (1977) 224–246.
7. In 1951, the International Law Commission held it undesirable to define aggression by a detailed enumeration of aggressive acts, since no enumeration could be exhaustive. It favoured the view that the threat or use of force for any reason or purpose other than individual or collective self-defence, or in pursuance of a decision or recommendation of a competent United Nations organ was aggression; see *Report* on the Work of its *3rd Session* (1951) pp 8–10. In 1954, the Commission included acts of aggression, and threats of aggression in its enumeration of acts which were 'offences against the peace and security of mankind'; see Article 2 of its Draft Code of Offences against the Peace and Security of Mankind (1954). For the best and most

As to (2)—the right of self-defence—the Charter by article 51 recognises an inherent right of individual and collective self-defence of member states against *armed attack*, pending enforcement action by the Security Council, and reserving to the Security Council full authority in the matter. It appears that consistently with article 51, the North Atlantic Powers could legitimately enter into their Regional Security Treaty of 4 April 1949, and create the machinery beforehand for collective self-defence should any one of their number be exposed to an armed attack.[8]

Qualified as it is by the reservation of ultimate authority in the Security Council, the right of self-defence conceded by article 51 of the Charter differs in scope and extent from the right of self-defence under customary international law.[9] The latter right was more restricted than the right of self-preservation, normally understood, and allowed measures of defence or protection only in the case of an 'instant, overwhelming' necessity, 'leaving no choice of means, and no moment for deliberation',[10] provided that the measures used were not unreasonable or excessive. Under article 51 of the Charter, the right of self-defence is framed as one in terms of similar rights possessed by other States,[11] and subject to conditions as to its continued exercise.[12] A matter of current controversy is whether, under article 51, nuclear and thermonuclear weapons can legitimately be used in self-defence against a non-nuclear armed attack. International lawyers are divided upon the answer to this crucial question, someholding that the use of nuclear and thermonuclear weapons is disproportionate[13] to the seriousness of the danger of a conventional attack, while others say that in some circumstances a country may be unable to defend itself adequately without recourse to its nuclear armoury. A more crucial point is the

---

comprehensive treatments of the problem of the definition of aggression, and of other aspects of aggression, see Stone *Aggression and World Order* (1958), which deals with the subject in its historical context to the end of 1957, and the same author's books, *Conflict Through Consensus: United Nations Approaches to Aggression* (1977), and *Visions of World Order— Between State Power and Human Justice* (1984).

8. For discussion of the consistency of the North Atlantic Security Pact with the Charter, see Beckett *The North Atlantic Treaty, the Brussels Treaty, and the Charter of the United Nations* (1950).
9. See Westlake *International Law* (2nd edn, 1910) Vol I, pp 309–317. for treatment of such right of self-defence.
10. A test enunciated by Secretary of State Webster in regard to the '*Caroline*' Case (1837); as to which see Oppenheim *International Law* (9th edn, 1992) Vol 1, p 420.
11. Cf Joan D. Tooke *The Just War in Aquinas and Grotius* (1965) p 234.
12. In the case of the Falklands conflict in 1982, it was claimed on behalf of the United Kingdom that the British operations to expel the Argentine garrisons from Falklands territory were conducted by way of self-defence under article 51 of the United Nations Charter, in the absence of measures concretely taken by the Security Council, notwithstanding the Council's resolution of 3 April 1983, calling, inter alia, for the withdrawal by Argentina of its forces in the garrisons.
13. *Proportionality and self-defence:* It is generally accepted that measures of self-defence should not be disproportionate to the weight and degree of an armed attack; this was seemingly recognised by the US Government at the time of the Gulf of Tonkin incident, August 1964, its armed action being officially described as a 'limited and measured response fitted precisely to the attack that produced it'. On the question whether the American bombing of targets in Libya on 15 April 1986, claimed to be self-defensive as a reaction to alleged continued Libyan attacks directed against Americans, complied with the requirement of 'proportionality', see the article by J. A. McCredie in (1987) 19 *Case Western Reserve Journal of International Law* 215 at p 233.

extent to which states involved in a nuclear 'crisis' may resort to measures of self-defence, as did the United States when it proclaimed a 'selective' blockade of Cuba during the Cuban missile crisis of 1962 (see above in Chapter 17). Obviously, such a situation was beyond the contemplation of the authors of article 51 of the Charter.

Necessity of new approach to problem of conflict regulation

The impact of these problems of nuclear weapons, the blurring of questions of responsibility by the overriding purpose of restoring or maintaining peace and security, and the range and variety of methods of pressure and coercion that may be adopted by states to secure political ends have rendered it difficult to work always with traditional concepts such as the 'threat or use of force', 'security', 'aggression', 'subversion' and 'self-defence'. For the new conditions, the United Nations Charter embodying these concepts is sometimes an imperfect tool of conflict-regulation. A new approach is necessary if this difficulty is to be overcome, and is not to be achieved merely by adopting Resolutions or instruments containing formulae or phraseology that are in effect no more than reiterative versions of United Nations Charter provisions. More radical initiatives are required in the interests of peace and security.

One of the most conspicuous fields, in this connection, where regulatory initiatives are needed, is that of civil wars.[14] It is trite law that civil wars are not prohibited by any international legal rules; this would apply a fortiori in the case of an insurgent movement designed to achieve self-determination and to eliminate colonial domination. Controversy surrounds the extent to which outside states may become legitimately involved by aid to one side or the other. Some writers are of the opinion that aid, short of the despatch of forces, may be provided to established governments against insurgents. Paragraph (5) of article 2 of the Draft Code of Offences against the Peace and Security of Mankind, adopted by the International Law Commission in 1954, treats as an offence against the peace and security of mankind: 'The undertaking or encouragement by the authorities of a state of activities calculated to foment civil strife in another state, or the toleration by the authorities of a State of organised activities calculated to foment civil strife in another State'. That there is a general consensus to the effect that such conduct is in breach of international law seems to be supported by the reiteration in Resolutions of the United Nations General Assembly of prohibitions of this or similar conduct. There is no settled rule, semble, that established governments may be assisted against outside subversion. The whole subject is overshadowed by political considerations. In recent years, mercenaries, who have no right to be treated as lawful combatants (see article 47 of Protocol I of 1977 as to international armed conflicts, above), have played an increasingly significant role in civil wars or internal armed conflicts, and here

14. The subject of civil wars has given rise to a considerable international law literature thereon; see, eg Richard Falk (ed) *The International Law of Civil War* (1971); Moore (ed) *Law and Civil War in the Modern World* (1974); J.F. Hogg 'Legal Aspects of Counterinsurgency' US Naval War College International Law Studies, Vol 62 (1980) 106. The extent to which self-defence, unilateral or collective, may be relied upon as a legal justification for involvement by one state in the struggle in a civil war in another state was thoroughly considered by the International Court of Justice in *Nicaragua v United States* ICJ 1986, 14.

again there are no settled rules determining the obligations lying upon the states of nationality of mercenaries. It has been suggested that states should accept as a basic principle that their nationals should not freely participate in conflicts as mercenaries, and that they should take appropriate action to restrict the participation and recruitment of their nationals to act as such.[15] However, the status of mercenaries is but one of a growing number of problems that require solution if peace and security are not to be imperilled by civil wars.

It is paradoxical that, notwithstanding the predominance of non-war armed conflicts in the last two decades, the subject of a just war, the jus ad bellum, and the related matter of restraints on war in its classic sense, should have attracted so much recent discussion by publicists.[16] At first sight, this seems like a return to the traditional debates of the sixteenth and seventeenth centuries, but the moral and ethical issues arise in a different context.

2.   EFFECTS OF OUTBREAK OF WAR AND OF ARMED CONFLICTS

The outbreak of war, as such, has far-reaching effects on the relations between the opponent belligerent states.

At the outset, it is necessary to know what persons or things are to be deemed of enemy character, as usually municipal legislation will prohibit trading and intercourse with the enemy, and provide for the seizure of enemy property.

The general rule of international law, as distinct from municipal law, is that states are free to enact such legislation upon the outbreak of war, and the same general rule must in principle apply in the case of non-war armed conflicts, subject to the qualification that where such a conflict comes under the peace enforcement jurisdiction of the United Nations Security Council, the states involved must abide by the Security Council's decisions or recommendations.

Under the Geneva Convention of 1949 for the Protection of Civilian Persons in Time of War, enemy nationals not under confinement or in prison may leave the territory of a state at war, unless the national interests of that state call for their detention (article 35). They are entitled to bring the matter of refusal before a court or administrative boards of the detaining Power. The Convention contains provisions forbidding measures severer than house arrest or internment, and for the proper treatment of internees.

In the following pages, the principal municipal and international effects of *war* are broadly surveyed.

Not all these effects will necessarily apply in the case of a non-war armed conflict. State practice during the Korean conflict 1950–1953, and the Suez Canal zone hostilities of 1956, revealed wide divergencies concerning state attitudes in this connection. It would seem from such practice that, in the event of a non-war armed conflict, the contesting states will not hold themselves bound to apply the same stringent rules as they would in the case of a war proper, and that, in

---

15. H.C. Burmester 'The Recruitment and Use of Mercenaries in Armed Conflicts' 72 AJIL (1978) 37 at p 56.
16. See, eg, J.T. Johnson *Just War Tradition and the Restraint of War* (1981); Walzer *Just and Unjust Wars* (1978); Michael Howard *Restraints on War* (1979); and W.V. O'Brien *Conduct of Just and Limited War* (1981).

particular, they will not necessarily to the same extent interrupt or suspend their diplomatic intercourse and their treaty relationships, but will make such adjustments as the special circumstances of the conflict require, and will—if necessary—follow the guidance of the United Nations Security Council and General Assembly through their decisions or recommendations.

Enemy character in war

As to individuals, state practice varies on the test of enemy character. British and American courts favour residence or domicile as against the Continental rule which generally determines enemy character according to nationality.[17] But as a result of exceptions grafted on these two tests, Anglo-American practice, has tended to become assimilated to the Continental practice, and there is now little practical difference between them.

Hostile combatants, and subjects of an enemy state resident in enemy territory are invariably treated as enemy persons, and residence in territory subject to effective military occupation by the enemy is assimilated for this purpose to residence in enemy territory.[18] According to Anglo-American practice even neutrals residing or carrying on business in enemy territory are also deemed to be enemy persons, while on the other hand subjects of an enemy state resident in neutral territory are not deemed to have enemy character. However, by legislation adopted in two World Wars, the United States and Great Britain have made enemy influence or associations the test of enemy character, whether persons concerned are resident in enemy or in neutral territory.

In the case of *Daimler Co Ltd v Continental Tyre and Rubber Co (Great Britain) Ltd*,[19] the House of Lords adopted the test of enemy associations or enemy control for corporations carrying on business in an enemy country but not incorporated there, or corporations neither carrying on business nor incorporated there but incorporated in Great Britain itself or a neutral country. It was ruled that enemy character may be assumed by such a corporation if 'its agents or the persons in de facto control of its affairs' are 'resident in an enemy country, or, wherever resident, are adhering to the enemy or taking instructions from or acting under the control of enemies'. This was an extremely stringent principle, and the decision has received a good deal of criticism. A company, incorporated in Great Britain, which acquires enemy character under the *Daimler* principle, is nonetheless not deemed to have its location in enemy territory; it is for all other purposes a British company, subject to British legislation, including regulations as to trading with the enemy.[20] Apart from the *Daimler* ruling, it is clear law that a corporation incorporated in an enemy country has enemy character.[1]

As regards ships, prima facie the enemy character of a ship is determined by its flag.[2] Enemy-owned vessels sailing under a neutral flag may assume enemy

---

17. See leading case of *Porter v Freudenberg* [1915] 1 KB 857, affirming the test of residence in enemy territory as determining enemy status.
18. See *Sovfracht (V/O) v Van Udens Scheepvaart* [1943] AC 203.
19. [1916] 2 AC 307.
20. See *Kuenigl v Donnersmarck* [1955] 1 QB 515.
1. See *Janson v Driefontein Consolidated Mines Ltd* [1902] AC 484.
2. On the 'conclusive' nature of the enemy flag, see *Lever Bros and Unilever NV v HM Procurator General, The Unitas* [1950] AC 536.

character and lose their neutral character if: (a) they take part in hostilities under the orders of an enemy agent or are in enemy employment for the purpose of transporting troops, transmitting intelligence, etc; or (b) they resist legitimate exercise of the right of visit and capture. All goods found on such enemy ships are presumed to be enemy goods unless and until the contrary is proved by neutral owners.

As to goods generally, if the owners are of enemy character, the goods will be treated as enemy property. This broad principle was reflected in the various wartime Acts of countries of the British Commonwealth, prohibiting trading with the enemy and providing for the custody of enemy property.

Diplomatic relations and war

On the outbreak of war, diplomatic relations between the belligerents cease. The ambassadors or ministers in the respective belligerent countries are handed their passports and they and their staff proceed home. Under article 44 of the Vienna Convention of 1961 on Diplomatic Relations, the receiving state must grant facilities enabling such persons to leave at the earliest possible moment, placing at their disposal the necessary means of transport.

Effect on treaties of war and non-war armed conflicts

The effect of war on existing treaties to which the belligerents are parties is, to quote Mr Justice Cardozo, 'one of the unsettled problems of the law'.[3] Although this judicial dictum refers to 'war' in the strict sense, it is true also of the effect on treaties of non-war armed conflicts. The Vienna Convention of 1969 on the Law of Treaties contains no provisions dealing with the consequences of the outbreak of hostilities upon treaties between the parties to the conflict. However, in 1985 the Institut de Droit International (Institute of International Law) adopted a Resolution containing a set of rules in 11 articles to govern the subject, applying both to war and non-war conflicts (hereinafter referred to as the 'Institut Resolution'). According to the older authorities, treaties were annulled ipso facto between the belligerents as soon as war came. So sweeping a view is now discounted by the modern authorities, and by the Institut Resolution (see art 2), while it is inconsistent with recent state practice according to which some treaties are considered as annulled, others are considered as remaining in force, and others are held to be merely suspended, and to be revived on the conclusion of peace.[4]

In the unsettled state of the law, it is difficult to spell out any consistent principle or uniformity of doctrine. To quote Mr Justice Cardozo again, international law 'does not preserve treaties or annul them, regardless of the effects produced. It deals with such problems pragmatically, preserving or annulling as the necessities of war exact'. Two tests are applicable in this connection. The first is a subjective test of intention—did the signatories of the

---

3.   See on the whole question his judgment in *Techt v Hughes* 229 NY 222 (1920). See also *Karnuth v United States* 279 US 231 (1929), and Henkin, Pugh, Schachter and Smit *International Law; Cases and Materials* (2nd edn, 1987) pp 498–505.
4.   Semble, belligerent states may even contract new treaties (through the auspices of neutral envoys) relevant to their belligerent relationships. The United States' practice during the Second World War was contrary to any principle of automatic abrogation of treaties by war; see McIntyre *Legal Effect of World War II on Treaties of the United States* (1958).

treaty intend that it should remain binding on the outbreak of war? The second is an objective test—is the execution of the treaty incompatible with the conduct of war?

Applying these tests, and having regard to state practice, the Institut Resolution and the views of modern authorities, we may sum up the position as follows:

1. Treaties between the belligerent states which presuppose the maintenance of common political action or good relations between them, for example, treaties of alliance, are abrogated.
2. Treaties representing completed situations or intended to set up a permanent state of things, for example, treaties of cession or treaties fixing boundaries, are unaffected by war and continue in force.
3. Treaties to which the belligerents are parties relating to the conduct of hostilities, for example, the Hague Conventions of 1899 and 1907, the Geneva Conventions of 1949 (the Red Cross Conventions), and other treaties prescribing rules of warfare, remain binding.
4. Multilateral conventions of the 'law-making' type relating to health, drugs, protection of industrial property, etc, are not annulled on the outbreak of war but are either suspended and revived on the termination of hostilities, or receive even in wartime a partial application. If the multilateral convention is one establishing an international organisation, it remains unaffected (Institut Resolution, art 6).
5. Sometimes express provisions are inserted in treaties to cover the position on the outbreak of war. For example, article 38 of the Aerial Navigation Convention 1919, provided that in case of war the Convention was not to affect the freedom of action of the contracting states either as belligerents or as neutrals, which meant that during war the obligations of the parties became suspended.[5]
6. With regard to other classes of treaties, eg, extradition treaties[6] in the absence of any clear expression of intention otherwise, prima facie these are suspended.
7. A state complying with a resolution by the UN Security Council concerning action with respect to threats to the peace, breaches of the peace or acts of aggression, must either terminate or suspend the operation of a treaty, to which it is a party, if the treaty would be incompatible with the Security Council's resolution (Institut Resolution, art 8).

Where treaties are suspended during wartime, certain authorities claim they are not automatically revived when peace comes, but resume their operation only if the treaties of peace expressly so provide.[7] Practice is not very helpful on this point, but usually clauses are inserted in treaties of peace, or terminating a state of war, to remove any doubts as to which treaties continue in force. According to art 11 of the Institut Resolution, at the end of an armed conflict and unless

---

5. Cf art 89 of the International Civil Aviation Convention 1944. It may also appear that, apart from express provision, it was the intention of the parties that the treaty should not operate in time of war, in which event effect will be given to that intention.
6. See *Argento v Horn* 241 F 2d 258 (1957). This case also shows that the parties may conduct themselves on the basis that a treaty is suspended.
7. Cf however, *Argento v Horn*, n 6, above.

otherwise agreed, the operation of a treaty which has been suspended should be resumed as soon as possible.

Prohibition of trading and intercourse in war; contracts

Trading and intercourse between the subjects of belligerent states cease on the outbreak of war, and usually special legislation is introduced to cover the matter. The details of state practice in this connection lie outside the scope of this book, but it can be said that international law gives belligerent states the very widest freedom in the enactment of municipal laws dealing with the subject.

Similarly with regard to contracts between the citizens of belligerent states, international law leaves states entirely free to annul, suspend, or permit such contracts on the outbreak of war. Consequently this is a matter primarily concerning municipal law, and will not be discussed in these pages. There is some uniformity of state practice in the matter, inasmuch as most states treat as void executory contracts which may give aid to or add to the resources of the enemy, or necessitate intercourse or communication with enemy persons, although as regards executed contracts or liquidated debts, the tendency is not to abrogate, but to suspend the enforceability of such obligations until the state of war is terminated.[8]

Enemy property in war

The effect of war on enemy property differs according to whether enemy property is of a *public* nature (ie, owned by the enemy state itself), or of a *private* nature (ie, owned by private citizens of the enemy state).

(a) Enemy public property

A belligerent state may confiscate movable property in its territory belonging to the enemy state. Where the enemy movable property is located in enemy territory under military occupation by the forces of that state, such property may be appropriated in so far as it is useful for local military purposes. Immovable property (ie, real estate) in such territory may be used (for example, occupied or used to produce food or timber) but not acquired or disposed of.[9] Ships of war and other public vessels at sea belonging to the enemy state may be seized and confiscated except those engaged in discovery and exploration, or in religious, scientific, or philanthropic missions or used for hospital duties.

(b) Enemy private property

The general practice now of belligerent states is to sequestrate such property in their territory (ie, seize it temporarily) rather than to confiscate it, leaving its subsequent disposal to be dealt with by the peace treaties. It is not certain whether there is a rule of international law prohibiting confiscation as such, and authorities are somewhat divided on the point. But private property in occupied territory must not be taken, or interfered with, unless it is of use for local military

---

8. See *Arab Bank Ltd v Barclays Bank* (*Dominion, Colonial and Overseas*) [1953] 2 QB 527, and [1954] AC 495, and *Bevan v Bevan* [1955] 2 QB 227.
9. It may also be destroyed, if it is of a military character (eg, barracks, bridges, forts), and destruction is necessary in the interests of military operations (cf art 53 of the Geneva Convention 1949, on the Protection of Civilian Persons in Time of War).

purposes,[10] for example, for goods and services necessary for the army of occupation; mere plunder is prohibited. In contrast to the substantial protection of enemy private property on land, enemy ships and enemy cargoes at sea are liable to confiscation. This does not apply to enemy goods on a neutral merchant vessel unless such goods are useful for warlike purposes, or unless they are seized as a reprisal of war for continuous breaches by the enemy of the rules of warfare.[11]

Combatants and non-combatants

Combatants are divided into two classes: (a) lawful, and (b) unlawful. Lawful combatants may be killed or wounded in battle or captured and made prisoners of war. Certain categories of lawful combatants, for example, spies as defined in article 29 of the Regulations annexed to the Hague Convention IV of 1907 on the Laws and Customs of War on Land, are subject to special risks or disabilities,[12] or specially severe repressive measures if captured. Unlawful combatants are liable to capture and detention, and in addition to trial and punishment by military tribunals for their offences.[13] Citizens of, or persons owing allegiance to one belligerent state, and who have enlisted as members of the armed forces of the opposing belligerent, cannot claim the privileges of lawful combatants if they are subsequently captured by the former belligerent state.[14] Under article 47 of Protocol I as to international armed conflicts, additional to the Geneva Red Cross Conventions of 1949 (see above in this chapter), mercenaries as defined in paragraph 2 of the article have no rights to be treated as combatants or as prisoners of war if captured.

Traditionally international law maintains a distinction between combatants and non-combatants, inasmuch as non-combatants are not in principle to be wilfully attacked or injured. Certain classes of non-combatants, for example, merchant seamen, may however be captured and made prisoners of war. Nineteenth-century official pronouncements affirmed that the only legitimate object of war was to weaken the *military* forces of the enemy. In 1863 the following passage appeared in United States Army General Orders:

> 'The principle has been more and more acknowledged that the unarmed citizen is to be spared in person, property, and honour as much as the exigencies of war will admit.'

A valiant attempt to draw a distinct line between civilians and the armed forces was also made in the Hague Convention IV of 1907 on the Laws and Customs of War on Land and its annexed Regulations. Yet under the demands of military necessity in two World Wars, the distinction came to be almost obliterated.

10. The occupant Power cannot seize property, such as stocks of petroleum, for the purposes not of the occupying army, but for its needs generally at home or abroad; see decision of Court of Appeal, Singapore, in *NV De Bataafsche Petroleum Maatschappij v The War Damage Commission* (1957) 51 AJIL 802.
11. See Chapter 19, below at pp 534–535, 538.
12. Espionage is not a breach of international law; see United States Army Field Manual on the Law of Land Warfare (1956), para 77.
13. See *Ex p Quirin* 317 US 1 (1942) at 31, and *Osman Bin Haji Mohamed Ali v Public Prosecutor* [1969] 1 AC 430 (saboteurs attired in civilian clothes, and who are members of the regular armed forces of one belligerent, are not entitled to be treated as lawful combatants by the opposing belligerent, if captured).
14. *Public Prosecutor v Koi* [1968] AC 829.

A learned author[15] who in 1945 examined the importance of the distinction under the heads of:

i   artillery bombardment;
ii. naval bombardment;
iii. sieges;
iv. blockade;
v.   contraband; and
vi. aerial bombardment,

reached the conclusion in essence that while non-combatants might not be the primary objects of these six operations of war, they were denied material protection from injury thereunder.

On the subject of aerial bombardment, the history of attempts to protect non-combatants has not been encouraging. The Hague Regulations of 1907 mentioned above (see article 25) prohibited the attack or bombardment of undefended towns,[16] villages, etc, by 'any means whatever', and this phrase was intended to cover aerial attacks. But during the First World War the rule laid down was not respected. In 1923 a Commission of Jurists at The Hague drew up a draft Code of Air Warfare, which did not come into force as a Convention, and which provided, inter alia, that bombardment was legitimate only when directed at specified military objectives such as military forces, works, and establishments, and arms factories, and was forbidden when bombardment could not take place without the indiscriminate bombardment of civilians. The Spanish Civil War of 1936–1938 showed that it was not sufficient merely to prohibit air attack on specified military objectives, and a Resolution of the League of Nations Assembly in 1938 recommended a subjective test that the intentional bombing of civilians should be illegal. But up to the stage of the outbreak of the Second World War, states had not definitely agreed on rules for the limitation of aerial bombardment.

During the War, the Axis Powers bombed civilians and civilian objectives, using explosive bombs, incendiary bombs, and directed projectiles. The Allies retaliated eventually with area and pattern bombing, and finally in 1945 with atom-bomb attacks on Nagasaki and Hiroshima, resulting in enormous civilian casualties. Whether regarded as legitimate reprisals or not, the Allied air bombardments were like the similar Axis attacks, directed at civilian morale. It would be unrealistic in the light of these events, not to consider that in modern

15. See Nurick, 39 AJIL (1945) 680 et seq.
16. '*Open cities*': Note in this connection the concept of 'open cities', which has probably become obsolete as a consequence of the provisions regarding 'non-defended localities' in article 59 of Protocol I of 1977 as to international armed conflicts, supplementing the Geneva Red Cross Conventions of 1949 (see above). An 'open city' was one so completely undefended *from within or without* that the besieging or opposing forces could enter and take possession of it without fighting or incurring casualties. In principle, a declaration was necessary by the government to which the city belonged, the purpose being to preserve it from destructive attacks or bombardment. During the Second World War a number of such declarations were made, including Paris (1940), Brussels (1940), Belgrade (1941) and Rome (1943). See as to the practice during this War, Whiteman *Digest of International Law* (1968) vol 10, pp 415, 433–435, and *Sansolini v Bentivegna* (1957) 24 Int LR 986 at 989.

total war civilian morale may, notwithstanding the prohibitions contained in international treaties or instruments,[17] become a true military objective. Indeed it is becoming more and more difficult in total war to define negatively what is *not* a military objective. Besides, the so-called civilian 'work forces', or 'quasi-combatants', that is to say those civilians employed in the manufacture of tools of war, were considered to be targets as important as the armed forces proper.

An attempt was made in the Geneva Convention of 1949 for the Protection of Civilian Persons in Time of War to shield certain classes of civilian non-combatants from the dangers and disadvantages applicable to combatants and non-combatants in a war or armed conflict. The Convention did not purport to protect all civilians,[18] but mainly aliens in the territory of a belligerent and the inhabitants of territory subject to military occupation, although other classes receive incidental protection under the provisions allowing the establishment of hospital, safety, and neutralised zones, and for insulating from the course of hostilities such persons as the sick and aged, children, expectant mothers and mothers of young children, wounded and civilians performing non-military duties. Also in the Convention are provisions that civilian hospitals properly marked should be respected and not attacked.[19]

The very necessity of such detailed provisions as the Convention contained demonstrated that, as a consequence of practices followed in the Second World War, little remained of the traditional distinction between combatants and non-combatants save the duty not to attack civilians in a wanton or unnecessary manner, or for a purpose unrelated to military operations and to abstain from terrorisation.

The necessity for the increased protection of the civilian population and of civilian objectives in time of armed conflict led to the convening of the Geneva Conference of 1974–1977 on the Reaffirmation and Development of International Humanitarian Law Applicable in Armed Conflicts which adopted, as additional to the Geneva Red Cross Conventions of 1949, Protocols I and II dealing, respectively, with international armed conflicts and non-international armed conflicts, and which are discussed below in this chapter.[1] Apart from the initial session of this Conference in 1974, the Lucerne Conference of Government Experts on the Use of Conventional Weapons, of September–October 1974, unanimously condemned the massive use of incendiary weapons against civilian centres, a conclusion approved later in the same year by the United Nations General Assembly.

The legality of the atom bomb attacks by the United States on Nagasaki and Hiroshima, referred to above, is questionable. They have been variously justified as:

a. A reprisal, although the casualties inflicted were quite out of proportion to those caused by single instances of illegal air bombardments committed by the Axis Powers.

17. Eg, Protocol I of 1977, referred to in the previous footnote.
18. For discussion of the Convention, see Draper (1965) I Hague Recueil 119–139, and the same author's book, *The Red Cross Conventions* (1958) ch 2 (pp 26–48).
19. See art 14 and following arts.
1. See pp 499-504 below.

b. As terminating the war quickly and thereby saving both Allied and enemy
    lives, which would be equivalent to relying on the doctrine of military
    necessity.

Neither ground is satisfactory as a matter of law.[2]

If there were objections to the original atom bomb, these apply with greater
force to the hydrogen bomb, and to the new highly developed nuclear and
thermonuclear weapons. The dangers and uncontrollable hazards involved in
such mass destruction weapons led to the conclusion of four treaties which are
dealt with in other chapters of this book, namely the Nuclear Weapons Test
Ban Treaty of 1963, the Outer Space Treaty of 1967 (inter alia, banning nuclear
weapons in outer space), the Nuclear Weapons Non-Proliferation Treaty of 1968,
and the Treaty of 1971 Prohibiting the Emplacement of Nuclear Weapons and
Other Weapons of Mass Destruction on the Seabed and Ocean Floor.[3] Although
only a bilateral treaty, and not one of a multilateral nature, the Intermediate-
Range Nuclear Forces Treaty (INF) concluded by the United States and the Soviet
Union in December 1987, and ratified in mid-1988, for the mutual elimination
of intermediate-range nuclear weaponry, has been hailed as an arrangement of
global significance in the realm of nuclear arms controls. Attempts since 1963
to enlarge the Test Ban Treaty into a fully comprehensive treaty banning nuclear
weapons tests in all environments (CTB) have so far failed, although by the Treaty
of Tlatelolco opened for signature on 14 February 1967, about 20 Latin
American and Caribbean states agreed to a prohibition of the presence of nuclear
weapons, and of the conduct of nuclear weapons tests in the territory of any
party to the Treaty. It may also be recalled that by a majority resolution, the
Stockholm Conference of 1972 on the Human Environment condemned all
nuclear weapons tests, especially those carried out in the atmosphere.[4]

2. Apart from the legality of the attack on civilians, the use of atom bombs could be questioned
    on the ground that they involved 'poisonous' substances, viz, radioactive fall-out (see art 23 of
    the Regulations annexed to the Hague Convention IV of 1907, mentioned above), fall-out
    propensity being a matter strongly relied upon by the complainants in 1973–1974 in the *Nuclear
    Tests Cases* before the International Court of Justice, ICJ 1974, 253, and 457, or 'uselessly'
    aggravated suffering within the meaning of the Declaration of St Petersburg, 1868. Possibly,
    also, their use is subject to the prohibitions contained in the Geneva Gas and Bacteriological
    Warfare Protocol of 1925. In *Shimoda v The Japanese State* (1963) *Japanese Annual of
    International Law* 1964, 212–252, the Tokyo District Court held that the attacks on Nagasaki
    and Hiroshima were contrary to international law. See also on the legality of nuclear weapons,
    the Ingram Memorandum (author, Mr Geoffrey Ingram) on the validity of the SALT II Treaty
    of 1979, ie the United States–Soviet Union Treaty on the Limitation of Strategic Offensive
    Weapons signed at Vienna on 18 June 1979. The text of the Ingram Memorandum, a copy of
    which was deposited with the Registry of the International Court of Justice in December 1979,
    is reproduced in (1980) 54 Aust LJ 615–620. On the legality of a 'first use' of, or 'first strike'
    with nuclear weapons (whether defensive or otherwise), see George Bunn, 'US Law of Nuclear
    Weapons' in the *Naval War College Review* July/August 1984 46 at pp 55–57 and generally on
    the subject of such weapons and the law, Miller and Feinrider (eds) *Nuclear Weapons and Law*
    (1984).
3. As to these treaties, see above p 160 (1963 Treaty), pp 163–169 (1967 Treaty), pp 283-284
    (1968 Treaty), and pp 229-230 (1971 Treaty).
4. See p 364 above.

3. THE 'LAWS OF WAR': INTERNATIONAL HUMANITARIAN LAW

The 'laws of war'[5] consist of the limits set by international law within which the force required to overpower the enemy may be used, and the principles thereunder governing the treatment of individuals in the course of war and armed conflict. In the absence of such rules, the barbarism and brutality of war would have known no bounds. These laws and customs have arisen from the long-standing practices of belligerents; their history goes back to the Middle Ages when the influence of Christianity and of the spirit of chivalry of that epoch combined to restrict the excesses of belligerents. Under present rules such acts as the killing of civilians, the ill-treatment of prisoners of war, and military use of gas, and the sinking of merchant ships without securing the safety of the crew are unlawful.

Since the nineteenth century, the majority of the rules have ceased to be customary and are to be found in treaties and conventions. Among the most important of these instruments are the Declaration of Paris 1856, the Geneva Convention 1864 for the Amelioration of the Condition of Wounded in Armies in the Field, the Declaration of St Petersburg 1868, the Hague Conventions of 1899 and 1907, the Geneva Gas and Bacteriological Warfare Protocol 1925, as supplemented by the Convention of 1972 on the Prohibition of the Development, Production, and Stockpiling of Bacteriological (Biological) and Toxin Weapons and their Destruction, the Submarine Rules Protocol 1936, the four Geneva Red Cross Conventions 1949, namely, those dealing with prisoners of war, sick and wounded personnel of armies in the field and of forces at sea, and the protection of civilians, and which effected a far-reaching revision and codification of a major portion of the 'laws of war', and Protocols I and II of 1977 on, respectively, international armed conflicts and non-international armed conflicts, adopted as instruments additional to the latter Geneva Conventions of 1949.

The essential purpose of these rules is not to provide a code governing the 'game' of war, but for humanitarian reasons to reduce or limit the suffering of individuals, and to circumscribe the area within which the savagery of armed conflict is permissible. For this reason, they were sometimes known as the 'humanitarian law of war', or the rules of 'humanitarian warfare'. Indeed, the currently recognised title for these rules is 'international humanitarian law', as illustrated by the fact that the full name of the Geneva Conference of 1974–1977 which adopted the above-mentioned Protocols I and II in 1977, for the purpose of adding to and updating the Geneva Red Cross Conventions of 1949, was 'the Diplomatic Conference on the Reaffirmation and Development of International Humanitarian Law Applicable in Armed Conflicts'. Also, the principal international institute concerned with this branch of international law is that at San Remo, Italy, known as the International Institute of Humanitarian Law. True, these rules have been frequently and extensively violated, but without

5. The International Law Commission of the United Nations favoured the discarding of this phrase; see *Report* on work of its *1st Session* (1949) p 3. Perhaps these 'laws' are more correctly termed the 'rules governing the use of armed force and the treatment of individuals in the course of war and armed conflict'. They apply to all types of armed conflicts (see above, p 479). As will appear below, the appellation 'laws of war' has been replaced by that of 'international humanitarian law'.

them the general brutality of warfare would have been completely unchecked. It would be unrealistic, in this connection, to overlook the impact of the so-called 'push-button' warfare of the future, conducted by directed missiles, nuclear weapons, etc. This tendency to the depersonalisation of war, the very antithesis of its humanisation, constitutes a grave threat to the very existence of international humanitarian law.

In practice, the military manuals of the different states contain instructions to commanders in the field embodying the principal rules and customs of war.

Inasmuch as the rules of international humanitarian law exist for the benefit of individuals, it would appear that in the case of an unlawful conflict, waged by an aggressor state, these rules nevertheless bind the state attacked and members of its armed forces in favour of the aggressor and its armed forces. However, the aggressor state may be penalised to the extent that, during the course of the conflict, neutral or non-contestant states may discriminate against it, or by reason of the fact that at the termination of hostilities it may have to bear the reparations or to restore territory illegally acquired. The rules of course must apply as well to non-war armed conflicts.

The rules of international humanitarian law are binding not only on states as such, but on individuals, including members of the armed forces, heads of states, ministers, and officials. They are also necessarily binding upon United Nations forces engaged in a military conflict, mainly because the United Nations is a subject of international law and bound by the entirety of its rules, of which the laws of war form part. There is also the consideration that if United Nations forces were not so bound, and became involved in operations against a state, the forces of the latter would be subject to the laws of war, but not United Nations forces.

Unless a treaty or customary rule of international law otherwise provides, military necessity does not justify a breach of the rules of international humanitarian law.

Impact of human rights rules and standards
One of the most remarkable developments of the last decade, and which largely explains the replacement of the former title of this branch of international law, 'laws of war', by the present name 'international humanitarian law', has been the importation of human rights rules and standards into the law of armed conflicts. As was mentioned in Chapter 12, above, a bridge has in effect been created between the doctrine of human rights and the rules of international law applicable in armed conflicts. This truly desirable change was marked by, or manifested in, inter alia,

a.   The Resolution of the International Conference on Human Rights at Teheran in 1968, recommending to the United Nations General Assembly that a study be made of existing rules for the protection of human rights in time of war.
b.   The General Assembly's Resolution of 19 December 1968, calling upon the Secretary-General to make such study.
c.   The Reports of the Secretary-General, 1969–1970, on Respect for Human Rights in Armed Conflict.
d.   The Conferences of Government Experts called under the aegis of the International Committee of the Red Cross (ICRC) in 1971–1972 on the

Reaffirmation and Development of International Humanitarian Law Applicable in Armed Conflicts.

e.   The above-mentioned Geneva Diplomatic Conference of 1974–1977 on the Reaffirmation and Development of International Humanitarian Law Applicable in Armed Conflicts by which the Protocols I and II on international and non-international armed conflicts were adopted in 1977, in order to supplement and update the Geneva Red Cross Conventions of 1949. There has been little or no dissent from this trend towards a blending of human rights principles and the rules observable in armed conflicts.

Sanctions of international humanitarian law; war crimes

While the rules of international humanitarian law are frequently violated, international law is not entirely without means of compelling states to observe them. One such method is the reprisal, although it is at best a crude and arbitrary form of redress.[6] Another sanction of the laws of war is the punishment both during and after hostilities of war criminals, following upon a proper trial.

In that connection, the trials of war criminals by Allied tribunals after the Second World War provided significant precedents.

First, there were the trials, 1945–1948, of the *major* war criminals at Nuremberg and Tokyo respectively by the International Military Tribunals. These trials have been referred to in an earlier chapter.[7] To consolidate the precedent represented by the trials, the International Law Commission acting in pursuance of a direction of the United Nations General Assembly, formulated in 1950 a set of principles under the title, 'Principles of International Law Recognised in the Charter of the Nuremberg Tribunal and in the Judgment of the Tribunal', and, as well in 1954 adopted a Draft Code of Offences against the Peace and Security of Mankind, embodying the Nuremberg principles, while the General Assembly attempted to sponsor, partly through the Commission and partly through a special Committee, the establishment of a permanent International Criminal Court to try persons guilty of such offences, and also of the offence of genocide. On 26 November 1968, the General Assembly adopted a Convention on the Non-Applicability of Statutory Limitations to War Crimes and Crimes against Humanity, obliging parties to abolish existing limitations on prosecution and punishment for such crimes, and to take measures otherwise to ensure their non-application.

Second, there were the trials by Allied courts of offenders other than the Axis major war criminals. Such accused included:

a.   persons prominently involved in war conspiracies (for example, industrialists, financiers), who were indicted for the same crimes as the major war criminals;

b.   members of the enemy forces and civilians charged with ordinary offences against the laws of war (ie ordinary war crimes); and

6.   The Geneva Conventions of 1949 prohibit reprisals against the persons protected thereby (see, eg, the prohibition of reprisals against prisoners of war in art 13 of the Prisoners of War Convention). Note also art 20 of Protocol I of 1977 on international armed conflicts which prohibit reprisals against the persons and objects protected by Part II of the Protocol, which Part bears the title 'Wounded, Sick and Shipwrecked'.

7.   See above, pp 54-55.

c.   the so-called 'quislings' or 'collaborationists' guilty of treason.

The variety and geographical range of the tribunals which tried the offenders were without precedent; these included national military tribunals, special tribunals constituted for the purpose (composed of professional judges or jurists),[8] the ordinary municipal civil courts, and even international military tribunals, while the trial venues were located in Europe, Asia, Australia, and even in the South Pacific.

Prior to the trials, it had been recognised that a belligerent was entitled to punish for war crimes those members of the armed forces of its opponent who fell into its hands, or who had committed such crimes within its territorial jurisdiction. Not every violation of the rules of warfare is a war crime, and some jurists support the view that the term should be limited to acts condemned by the common conscience of mankind, by reason of their brutality, inhumanity, or wanton disregard of rights of property unrelated to reasonable military necessity. Some such conception of a war crime emerges from the decisions of the different tribunals, referred to above, a conception which has received a flexible application, as shown in the decisions that the following persons could be guilty of war crimes:

a.   Civilians, as well as members of the forces.
b.   Persons not of enemy nationality, for example, those having enemy affiliations.
c.   Persons guilty of a gross failure to control subordinates responsible for atrocities.[9] However, it is provided in paragraph 5 of Article 85 of Protocol I of 1977 on international armed conflicts, additional to the Geneva Red Cross Conventions of 1977, that without prejudice to the application of the latter Conventions and of the Protocol, 'grave breaches' of these instruments are to be regarded as war crimes. In each of the Conventions, certain acts are enumerated as grave breaches (see eg, those specified in Article 130 of the Convention relating to the Prisoners of War), and certain additional grave breaches are set out in Articles 11 and 85 of the Protocol.

It appears clearly established also by the above-mentioned post-war trials (see, for example, the judgment of the Nuremberg Court) that orders by superiors, or obedience to national laws or regulations, do not constitute a defence, but may be urged in mitigation of punishment.[10] In 1921, in the case of the

---

8.   Eg, the special American tribunals which operated at Nuremberg under Allied Control Council Law No 10 of 20 December 1945, promulgated by the Zone Commanders of Occupied Germany.
9.   See the *Yamashita Trial* 4 War Crimes Trials Reports 1–96.
10.   To the same effect is para 627 of Pt III of the British *Manual of Military Law*. Contrast para 216(d) of the United States *Manual for Courts Martial* (1969) under which there is liability if the superior's order is one which a man of ordinary sense and understanding would, under the circumstances, know to be unlawful, or if the order in question was actually known to the person obeying it to be unlawful; this test was adopted by the majority of the United States Court of Military Appeals in *Calley v United States* (1973) 48 Court Martial Reports 19. Cf also L.C. Green *Superior Orders in National and International Law* (1976); H. W. Briggs 'The Position of Individuals in International Law' in 62 *US Naval War College International Law Studies* (1980) pp 415–425; and N. Keijzer *Military Obedience* (1978).

Llandovery Castle,[11] a German court found the accused guilty of killing defenceless persons in lifeboats in the First World War, and rejected the plea of superior orders, stating that the plea was inadmissible if the order were 'universally known to be against the law', but that such order might be an extenuating circumstance. Probably courts must take into account the state of mind of the accused; if he believed that the order was lawful, this belief might be a defence, but not if the order were obviously illegal. So, just as in ordinary criminal law, the question of mens rea is important. As the Nuremberg Court pointed out, the true test is 'whether moral choice was in fact possible' on the part of the individual ordered to commit the criminal act.[12]

The transgressions of subordinates committed under obedience to superior orders are one thing, and the responsibility of superiors for the actions of subordinates another. The post-war trials, referred to above in this chapter, suggest in principle that there must be some dereliction of duty before high command responsibility is involved. In general, a commander should take steps to prevent the commission of war crimes, and to stop the continuation of their commission once knowledge is obtained of the wrongdoing. As in the *Yamashita Trial Case*,[13] a gross failure to control subordinates responsible for atrocities, almost equivalent to tacit permission for their commission, will involve command responsibility. A fortiori, actual knowledge or grounds for possessing knowledge will import liability. Yet as has been pointed out:[14] 'The tribunals left unanswered the degree of efficiency required from the commander in preventing war crimes, in discovering information about them, and in punishing wrongdoers'.

Paragraph 2 of Article 86 of Protocol I of 1977 as to international armed conflicts, which is additional to the Geneva Red Cross Conventions of 1949, lays down the following rule:

'The fact that a breach of the Conventions [ie the Geneva Conventions of 1949] or of this Protocol was committed by a subordinate does not absolve his superiors from penal or disciplinary responsibility, as the case may be, if they knew, or had information which should have enabled them to conclude in the circumstances at the time, that he was committing or was going to commit such a breach and if they did not take all feasible measures within their power to prevent or repress the breach.'

It will be noted that responsibility is confined to 'circumstances at the time', and that a duty is imposed on the commander to take 'all feasible measures' within his power to prevent or repress the breach, committed or threatened.

The enforcement of international humanitarian law rests primarily with national authorities, who are under obligations to disseminate that law, educate

11. Annual Digest of Public International Law Cases, 1923–1924, Case No 235.
12. See *Official Record* Vol I, p 224. The International Law Commission employed this criterion of a possibility of moral choice in Principle IV of its formulation in 1950 of the Principles of International Law Recognised in the Charter of the Nuremberg Tribunal and in the Judgment of the Tribunal, but art 4 of the Draft Code of Offences against the Peace and Security of Mankind adopted by it in 1954 provided that the subordinate was not relieved from responsibility in international law if, in the circumstances at the time, it was possible for him not to comply with that order.
13. *Yamashita Trial* 4 War Crimes Trial Reports 1–96.
14. Franklin A. Hart 'Yamashita, Nuremberg and Vietnam; Command Responsibility Reappraised' 62 *US Naval War College International Law Studies* (1980) 397 at p 412.

their armed forces in it[15], and to repress breaches through prosecution before national tribunals.[16] Parties to a conflict may agree to an enquiry in relation to any alleged violation of the Geneva Conventions, 1949, and of Additional Protocol I, 1977;[17] and article 90 of Additional Protocol I provides for an International Fact-Finding Commission, but only as between states that have made the requisite declaration of acceptance of the competence of the Commission.[18] The United Nations Security Council established a precedent in 1993 in creating an International Tribunal for the Prosecution of Persons Responsible for Serious Violations of Humanitarian Law Committed in the Territory of the Former Yugoslavia Since 1991.[19] The Security Council may itself refer allegations of violations to the Tribunal and require, in the exercise of its power to pass binding resolutions, the co-operation of states in handing over offenders and evidence to the Tribunal. If proposals for the establishment of a permanent International Criminal Tribunal by the United Nations are successful[20], it may be unnecessary to establish further international war crimes tribunals ad hoc.

One further sanction of the laws of war should not be overlooked. This is contained in article 3 of the Hague Convention IV of 1907 providing that if a belligerent state violate any such laws, that state is to pay compensation, and to be responsible for all acts committed by persons forming part of its armed forces. Under this article a substantial indemnity may be exacted when the treaty of peace is concluded.

Rules of land, sea, and air warfare

The principal rules as to land warfare[1] are set out in the Hague Convention IV of 1907 on the Laws and Customs of War on Land, and its annexed Regulations. These Regulations are sometimes for the sake of convenience referred to as the 'Hague Rules' or 'Hague Regulations'. They define the status of belligerents, ie, those who will be treated as lawful combatants. Guerrilla troops and militia or volunteer corps like the British Home Guard in the Second World War are subject to the laws, rights, and duties of war if they satisfy four conditions, namely that

15. See the First Geneva Convention, 1949, art 47, and the corresponding articles in identical terms in the Second, Third and Fourth Conventions, and Additional Protocol I, 1977, arts 82, 83, 87.
16. See the First Geneva Convention, 1949, arts 49-51 and the corresponding articles in the Second, Third, and Fourth Conventions, and Additional Protocol I, 1977, arts 85-88.
17. See the First Geneva Convention, 1949, art 52, and the corresponding articles in the Second, Third and Fourth Conventions, and Additional Protocol I, 1977, art 90(2)(e).
18. As at mid-1994, 38 states had made such declarations.
19. Resolution 827 (1993), (1993) 32 ILM 1203. The Tribunal adopted its Rules of Procedure and Evidence in 1994: text in (1994) 33 ILM 484.
20. See above, pp 464-465.
1. For studies on the subject, see Greenspan *The Modern Law of Land Warfare* (1959); F. Kalshoven *The Law of Warfare* (1973); G.I.A.D. Draper 'Rules Governing the Conduct of Hostilities—The Laws of War and Their Enforcement' 62 *US Naval War College International Law Studies* (1980) 247–262; Jean Pictet *Development and Principles of International Humanitarian Law* (1983); F. de Mulinen *Handbook on the Laws of War for Armed Forces* (1987); and M. Veuthey *Guerilla Warfare and Humanitarian Law* (2nd edn, 1983); A. Cassese (ed) *The New Humanitarian Law of Armed Conflict*, 2 vols (1979-80); A.J.M. Delissen and G.J. Tanja (eds) *Humanitarian Law of Armed Conflict* (1991).

they are properly commanded, have a fixed distinctive emblem recognisable at a distance, carry arms openly, and conduct their operations in accordance with the laws and customs of war. Where there are *levées en masse*, ie, organised or spontaneous risings of the civilian population against the enemy, those called to arms by the authorities must fulfil the four conditions just mentioned in order to be respected as lawful combatants, whereas those spontaneously taking up arms on the approach of the enemy need only satisfy the two conditions of carrying arms openly, and respecting the laws and customs of war. The Geneva Prisoners of War Convention of 1949 (see article 4) provides that the troops of organised resistance movements are entitled to be treated as prisoners of war if they satisfy the above-mentioned four conditions, and even if they operate in occupied territory.[2] No such privilege as regards operations in occupied territory is conceded to *levées en masse*.

The Hague Rules of 1907 also contained provisions relative to the treatment of prisoners of war. The humane treatment of these and other captives is now dealt with in the Geneva Prisoners of War Convention of 1949, superseding a Geneva Convention of 1929, which itself replaced the Hague Rules. The 1949 Convention contains a code of provisions, more appropriate for twentieth century wars and armed conflicts than the earlier instruments,[3] but still, in the light of post-1949 experience, falling short of what is now required. Strict duties are imposed upon a Detaining Power of treating prisoners of war humanely, and there are special provisions for ensuring that they are not exposed to unnecessary brutality during the immediate aftermath of capture when their captors may attempt to procure information useful for the conduct of operations. On humanitarian grounds, it was also provided in the Convention that prisoners of war should be released and repatriated without delay after the cessation of active hostilities (see articles 118–119). These stipulations were presumably based on the assumption that prisoners would desire to return to the homeland; in the course of the negotiations for a truce in the Korean conflict, 1951–1953, a new problem[4] emerged when the United Nations Command ascertained by the so-called 'screening' of thousands of prisoners in its custody that, owing to fear of persecution, many were unwilling to be repatriated. Claims of humanity had to be weighed against the danger in the future of unscrupulous belligerents affecting to make spurious 'screenings' of captives, and the possibility that, under pretext of political objections to repatriation, prisoners of war might be guilty of treason. A compromise, giving due emphasis to grounds of humanity, was reached in the Korean Armistice Agreement of 27 July 1953 (see articles 36–58).[5]

2. Cf the 'Hostages Case' (*United States v List*, Case No 7) tried at Nuremberg in 1947–1948, *War Crimes Trials Reports* Vol 8, pp 39–92, where it was held that non-uniformed partisan troops operating in German-occupied territory in the last War were not entitled to the status of lawful combatants.
3. For discussion, see Draper (1965) 1 Hague Recueil des Cours 101–118.
4. See Mayda 47 AJIL (1953) 414 et seq, for treatment of the problem.
5. In regard to the Korean experience see the study by H.P. Ball 'Prisoner and War Negotiations: the Korean Experience and Lesson' in 62 *US Naval War College International Law Studies* (1980) 292, esp at pp 296 et seq. In the case of the India–Pakistan conflict of 1965, art VII of the Tashkent Declaration, 10 January 1966, for restoring peace, provided for repatriation of prisoners. Following hostilities again in December 1971, between India and Pakistan and the emergence of the new State of Bangladesh, India in 1972–1973 claimed to detain a number of

In the case of the Vietnam War,[6] it was provided by article 8 (a) of the Four-Party Agreement on Ending the War and Restoring the Peace in Vietnam, signed at Paris on 27 January 1973, that the return of captured military personnel and foreign civilians of the parties should be carried out simultaneously with and completed not later than the same day as the troop withdrawal provided for in article 5 of the Agreement, the parties exchanging complete lists of the persons to be returned. Articles 1 and 2 of the Protocol to the Agreement provided, in effect, for the return of captured servicemen and captured civilians to the country, authority, or party of which they were nationals or under whose command they served, such return to be controlled and supervised by an International Commission of Control and Supervision. These provisions, including the provision for return of captured civilians, reflected the unusual nature of the Vietnam conflict, and suggest the need for a convention regulating the detention and repatriation of civilians captured by contestants in future such conflicts.

The same Conference of 1949 which adopted the Prisoners of War Convention, referred to above, also adopted in place of earlier instruments:

a. A Convention on Wounded and Sick Members of the Armed Forces in the Field, containing detailed provisions requiring belligerents to protect wounded and sick personnel, and to respect the medical units and establishments normally caring for such personnel.

b. A Convention on Wounded, Sick, and Shipwrecked Members of the Armed Forces at Sea, dealing with the cognate problem of wounded, sick, and shipwrecked personnel at sea, and providing mutatis mutandis for similar duties of respect and protection.

The latter convention is notable for the important provisions relating to hospital ships, which drew upon the experience of the Second World War.[7]

Methods and means of combat and the conduct of hostilities are dealt with in Section II of the Hague Rules of 1907. Certain methods and means of war are forbidden, for example, the use of poisoned weapons, or arms or projectiles

---

Pakistani prisoners of war, without repatriating them, on grounds, inter alia, that the possibility of a renewal of hostilities could not be excluded, and that war crimes trials were contemplated; see note by H.S. Levie, 67 AJIL (1973) 512–516. The dispute was later settled for the most part by an Agreement signed by the two countries in August 1973. In May 1973, Pakistan filed an application in the International Court of Justice against India, claiming that India was proposing to hand over 195 Pakistani prisoners of war to the Government of Bangladesh, which intended to try them for acts of genocide and crimes against humanity. India denied the Court's jurisdiction. Later, in December 1973, in view of negotiations between the two countries, Pakistan requested the Court to record discontinuance of the proceedings, and the matter then was removed from the list; see ICJ 1973, 347.

6. See Ball, op cit, pp 311 et seq as to the prisoner of war situation in Vietnam during the course of the conflict. In the case of the Falklands conflict of April–June 1982, Argentine prisoners of war were speedily repatriated both before and after the cease-fire of 13/14 June 1982. See also now sub-para (b) of para 4 of art 85 of Protocol I of 1977 (p 515 below).

7. Of particular interest in both conventions are the provisions relative to the use of the Red Cross emblem, and concerning the protection of medical aircraft. For a treatise on the four conventions adopted by the Geneva Conference of 1949, see Draper *The Red Cross Conventions* (1958), and see the commentaries thereon of Jean S. Pictet, Director, International Committee of the Red Cross.

which would cause unnecessary suffering,[8] or the refusal of quarter. Ruses of war are permitted, but, according to general practice, not if tainted by treachery or perfidy, or if in breach of some agreement between the belligerents. As already mentioned, undefended towns are not subject to bombardment (article 25), and during the Second World War (1939–1945) declarations of certain undefended towns as 'open cities' were made, so as to exempt them from attack or destructive operations.[9] Military objectives in an undefended city not so open and free for entry might be bombarded from the air. Attacking officers must give warning before commencing a bombardment of defended places, except in case of an assault, and must spare distinctly marked churches, hospitals, monuments, etc. Pillage is forbidden.

The rules of naval warfare[10] are contained partly in rules of customary international law, partly in the Declaration of Paris of 1856, partly in the Hague Conventions of 1907, Nos VI, VII, VIII, IX (Naval Bombardment), X, XI, and XIII (Neutral Rights and Duties in Maritime War), and partly in the London Submarine Rules Protocol of 1936. In maritime warfare, belligerents are entitled to capture enemy vessels and enemy property. Surface ships, submarines, and aircraft engaged in sea warfare may destroy enemy merchant shipping provided that, except in the case of a persistent refusal to stop or resistance to search, the safety of the crew, passengers, and ship's papers must be definitely assured. However, as was demonstrated in the Falklands Conflict in 1982, and also in the Iraq–Iran war of 1980–1988, merchant vessels and tankers may be destroyed, wholly or partially, by missiles directed from land-based launchers or from aircraft hundreds of miles away, so that the possibility of ensuring the safety of the crew or others aboard the ship is excluded. Merchant ships are entitled to defend themselves against attacks at sight, not conforming to these rules. Privateering, ie, the commissioning of private merchant vessels, is illegal (see Declaration of Paris 1856). Merchant ships may be lawfully converted into warships, provided, according to British practice, that the conversion is effected in a home port, and not while the vessel is at sea or in a neutral port. Auxiliary vessels may be treated as being of a combatant character if they are part of the naval forces, being employed to assist naval operations.

---

8. It is difficult to reconcile with this prohibition the general practice of using flame-throwers and napalm bombs, as in the Second World War, and as in the Vietnam conflict. One generally accepted test of 'unnecessary suffering' is whether the relevant suffering is needless, superfluous, or disproportionate to the military advantage or effectiveness reasonably to be expected from the use of the particular weapon concerned; cf 69 AJIL (1975) 399–400, and *Canadian Yearbook of International Law* 1981, pp 233–234.
9. See p 496, n 16 above.
10. See as to the law of naval warfare, Tucker *The Law of War and Neutrality at Sea* (1957); O'Connell *The Influence of Law on Sea Power* (1975); G.I.A.D. Draper 'Rules Governing the Conduct of Hostilities—The Laws of War and Their Enforcement' in 62 *US Naval War College International Law Studies* (1980) 247 at pp 248–255; W.O. Miller 'Law of Naval Warfare', ibid, pp 263–270; H.S. Levie 'Mine Warfare and International Law', ibid, pp 271–279; H. Moineville *Naval Warfare Today and Tomorrow* (1983); N. Ronzitti (ed) *The Law of Naval Warfare* (1988); H. Robertson (ed), *The Law of Naval Operations*, U.S. Naval War College, International Law Studies, Vol. 64 (1991); and R. J. Grunawalt (ed) *The Law of Naval Warfare: Targeting Enemy Merchant Shipping*, U.S. Naval War College, International Law Studies, Vol. 65 (1992).

Under the Hague Convention IX (Naval Bombardment), the naval bombardment of undefended ports, towns, etc, is prohibited unless the local authorities refuse to comply with a formal requisitioning demand for provisions and supplies. Otherwise, military works, military or naval establishments, and other military objectives may be attacked.

Floating mines must not be sown indiscriminately, and it is the duty of belligerents laying such mines not merely to take all possible precautions for the safety of peaceful navigation, but to notify the precise extent of minefields as soon as military considerations permit. Unfortunately the law as to mines is uncertain because of the weakness of the text of the Hague Convention VIII (Submarine Contact Mines), and because of the development of new types of mines and new kinds of minelaying techniques and mine-launching methods (eg from submarines).

In the Second World War, the rules of naval warfare laid down in the above-mentioned instruments, in particular the Submarine Rules Protocol of 1936, were time and again disregarded. Partly this was justified on the basis of reprisals for breaches by the other side, partly this was due to conditions rendering strict compliance with the rules either dangerous or not practical for the party concerned. The new naval weapons and equipment technology, as developed in the last two decades, and the emergence of nuclear-powered vessels and submarines, capable of firing nuclear missiles, and as well the use and deployment of aircraft in naval warfare for the purpose of firing from a distance 'homing' missiles at warships (as demonstrated in the Falklands conflict of April–June, 1982), have likewise operated to render some or most of the former rules unworkable, so as further to reduce the areas of naval warfare over which regulation is possible or acceptable. Already, these technological improvements have compelled naval commands to develop the concept of 'exclusion zones' in the high seas, as was shown in the case of the Cuban 'quarantine' of 1962 and in the case of the above-mentioned Falklands conflict. Indeed, a country with an untrackable nuclear-powered submarine can virtually exclude, at their own peril, surface warships from entering a defined zone of an appropriate area in the high seas. Also, helicopters, appropriately equipped with technological capabilities, have become an integral element of naval operations, thus rendering it necessary for the rules of naval warfare to take into account the airspace as well as the high seas.

In regard to submarines, two new developments with a possible impact on the rules governing naval warfare need to be mentioned. First, intelligence and surveillance have come to be an essential component of maritime warfare, and submarines are destined to be used in such covert operations on a much larger scale. Second, the employment of overhead-based systems in outer space has become an indispensable element in the effective conduct of anti-submarine tactics, particularly detection and targeting.

As to the rules, if any, concerning aerial warfare, see above.[11]

There are no rules of international law prohibiting the use of psychological warfare, or forbidding the encouragement of defection or insurrection among the enemy civilian population.

11. Pp 548–550. Cf Hamilton De Saussure 'The Laws of Air Warfare: Are There Any?' in 62 *US Naval War College International Law Studies* (1980) 280–291.

Other special rules are contained in the above-mentioned Geneva Protocol of 1925, gas and bacteriological warfare being prohibited (see also Draft Convention of the Commission of Disarmament 1930),[12] the Protocol being supplemented by the later Convention of 1972 on the Prohibition of the Development, Production and Stockpiling of Bacteriological (Biological) and Toxin Weapons and Their Destruction, itself supplemented by a Final Declaration adopted in 1986 to strengthen verification methods, while by the International Convention for the Protection of Cultural Property in the event of Armed Conflict, signed at The Hague in May 1954, measures of protection against the ravages of war were provided for works of art, monuments, and historic buildings.[13] In 1977 there was opened for signature a Convention on the Prohibition of Military or Other Hostile Use of Environmental Modification Techniques (ENMOD Convention), to prohibit any such techniques having long-lasting or severe effects, injurious to states parties.

Apart from Protocols I and II of 1977, additional to the Geneva Red Cross Conventions of 1949, considered below in the present chapter, the latest instruments of importance to be concluded in the domain of international humanitarian law are the Convention and three annexed Protocols adopted at Geneva on October 1980 by the United Nations Conference on Prohibitions or Restrictions of Use of Certain Weapons which may be deemed to be Excessively Injurious or to have Indiscriminate Effects (more popularly known as the Conference on 'Inhumane Weapons'). When a state ratifies the Convention—the basic instrument—it must at the same time give notice of its consent to be bound by any two or more of the annexed Protocols. The first Protocol is concerned with non-detectable fragments; it prohibits the use of any weapon the primary effect of which is to injure by fragments which in the human body

12. Quaere whether this Protocol applies to the use of non-lethal tear gases or other chemical agents; the latter were employed in the Vietnam conflict. In 1966–1970, the application of the Geneva Protocol of 1925 came under close examination by the United Nations General Assembly, which in 1968 requested the Secretary-General of the United Nations to prepare a report on chemical and biological or bacteriological weapons, and the effects of their use. A report was prepared by a group of consultant experts, and issued by the Secretary-General on 1 July 1969. This contained a strong condemnation of such weapons, and led to a Resolution adopted by the General Assembly on 16 December 1969, declaring as contrary to the generally recognised rules of international law as embodied in the 1925 Protocol, the use in international armed conflicts of: (a) chemical agents of warfare with direct toxic effects on man, animals, or plants; and (b) biological agents of warfare, intended to cause death or disease in man, animals or plants, and dependent for their effects on ability to multiply. A number of important military powers, however, either voted against the Resolution or abstained from voting. Some states contested the right of the General Assembly to interpret the Protocol, claiming that this was the sole prerogative of the parties to that instrument. Since 1984 when at the Geneva Conference on Disarmament a draft text for a chemical weapons convention was put forward on behalf of the United States Government, work has been in progress for the conclusion of a convention to establish a comprehensive and verifiable system to control or ban the use or making of chemical weapons. It should be noted that the Convention of 1972 on the Prohibition of the Development, Production and Stockpiling of Bacteriological (Biological) and Toxin Weapons and Their Destruction, which supplements the Geneva Protocol of 1925, was negotiated over a period of two years at the Geneva Conference of the Committee on Disarmament (CCD).

13. *Defoliants:* As to the legality of attacks on other objectives, quaere whether jungle growth, plantations, and crops may be destroyed by defoliants or other chemical agents, even if these be used to safeguard military operations and personnel, or to prevent crops going to the enemy. From one point of view, the indiscriminate nature of the damage renders such methods of destruction objectionable.

escape detection by X-rays. The second Protocol deals with prohibitions or restrictions on the use of mines, booby traps and other like devices. The third Protocol contains restrictions with regard to the use of incendiary weapons, imposing, inter alia, obligations to record locations. The Protocols do not, however, make any listing of 'grave breach' offences as in the Geneva 1949 Conventions and the 1977 Protocols. The Conference was but a partial success; on the one hand, there was a failure to reach any agreement on certain important categories of so-called 'inhumane weapons', and, on the other hand, as in the case of other law-making conferences of the past decade, it was in effect agreed not to agree, and so three categories of weapons were set aside for future study, namely small-calibre projectiles, anti-personnel fragmentation warheads, and fuel air explosives. After a full discussion of the Convention and Protocols, an eminent expert came to the conclusion that the Conference 'has relatively minor effect on the use of effective modern conventional weapons'.[14]

A further significant step in the direction of prohibiting indiscriminate or cruel methods of warfare was the signing at Paris on 13 January 1993 of the Convention on the Prohibition of Development, Production, Stockpiling, and Use of Chemical Weapons and on their Destruction.[15]

Law of belligerent occupation of enemy territory

Belligerent occupation must be distinguished from two other stages in the conquest of enemy territory:

a. invasion, a stage of military operations which may be extended until complete control is established; and

b. the complete transfer of sovereignty, either through subjugation followed by annexation, or by means of a treaty of cession. Occupation is established only by firm possession, or as article 42 of the Hague Rules of 1907 says, only when the territory is 'actually placed under the authority of the hostile army'. As was demonstrated in practice both before and after the termination of hostilities in the Second World War (1939–45), a belligerent may also temporarily establish military government over territory of third states, liberated from enemy occupation.

The distinction from invasion is important, inasmuch as the occupant Power is subject to a number of rights and duties in respect to the population of the occupied territory. Important also is the point that belligerent occupation does not displace or transfer the sovereignty of the territory but involves the occupant Power in the exercise solely of military authority subject to international law. For this reason, occupation does not result in any change of nationality of the local citizens nor does it import any complete transfer of local allegiance from the former government. Nor can occupied territory be annexed. The occupant Power's position is that of an interim military administration, which entitles it to obedience from the inhabitants so far as concerns the maintenance of public order, the safety of the occupying forces, and such laws or regulations as are necessary to administer the territory.

14. See W.J. Fenrick 'New Developments in the Law Concerning the Use of Conventional Weapons in Armed Conflict', *Canadian Yearbook of International Law* 1981, 229 at p 255.
15. (1993) 32 ILM 804.

Lawful acts of the occupant Power will therefore normally be recognised when the occupation is terminated; but not unlawful acts (for example, the wholesale plunder of private property).

The rational basis of the international law as to belligerent occupation is that until subjugation is complete and the issue finally determined, the occupant Power's authority is of a provisional character only.

The status of Germany after the Second World War following on the unconditional surrender appears to have involved a stage intermediate between belligerent occupation and the complete transfer of sovereignty (b. above). The four Allied Powers, Great Britain, France, Russia and the United States exercised supreme authority over Germany, and in the opinions of some writers, this could not be regarded as a belligerent occupation because of the destruction of the former government, and the complete cessation of hostilities with the conquest of the country. Nor, since the occupying Powers were acting in their own interests, were they trustees in any substantive sense for the German people. At the same time, it should be pointed out that the Allied control system was expressly of a provisional character, not involving annexation, was predominantly military in form, and based on the continuance of the German State as such, and on the continuance also of a technical state of war. However, the question is now somewhat academic, except as a precedent for the future, owing to the re-establishment in 1990 of a united Germany and the formal relinquishment by the Four Powers of their rights.[16]

The rights and duties of the occupant Power are conditioned primarily by the necessity for maintaining order, and for administering the resources of the territory to meet the needs of the inhabitants and the requirements of the occupying forces, and by the principle that the inhabitants of the occupied territory are not to be exploited. The rules with regard to public and private property in the occupied territory are referred to above.[17] The inhabitants must, subject only to military necessities, be allowed to continue their lawful occupations and religious customs, and must not be deported. Requisitions for supplies or services must be reasonable, and not involve the inhabitants in military operations against their own country. Contributions are not to be exacted unless ordinary taxes and dues are insufficient for the purposes of the administration. These and other rules are set out in section III of the Hague Rules of 1907.

The provisions of the Hague Rules were supplemented by the Geneva Convention of 1949 on the Protection of Civilian Persons in Time of War (see Part III, section III, articles 47–78). In the interests of the inhabitants[18] of occupied territory, and having regard to the experience of military occupations in two world wars, numerous carefully defined duties were imposed upon occupying Powers by the Convention, duties qualified in certain particular cases by the

---

16. See below, p 520. Distinguish also: (1) The occupation of non-enemy territory in the interests of military operations; eg the Allied occupation of North Africa, 1942–3. (2) The occupation by Allies, temporarily, of the territory of another Allied state, which had been under military occupation by the enemy; eg the Allied occupation of Greece in 1944.
17. See pp 494-495.
18. Cf the reference to such persons as 'protected persons'. The rights of the inhabitants under the Convention cannot be taken away by any governmental changes, or by agreement between the local authorities and the occupying Power, or by annexation (see art 47).

requirements of internal security and order, and by the necessities of military operations; among such duties are the obligations:

a. not to take hostages,[19] or impose collective penalties against the population for breaches of security or interference with the occupying forces by individual inhabitants;

b. not to transfer by force inhabitants, individually or en masse, to other territory or to deport them;

c. not to compel the inhabitants to engage in military operations or in work connected with such operations, other than for the needs of the occupying army; and

d. not to requisition food and medical supplies, so as to impinge upon the ordinary requirements of the civilian population.

The Convention also imposes, subject to the same qualifications, a specific obligation to maintain the former courts and status of judges, and the former penal laws, and not to use coercion against judges or public officials.

Neither the Hague Rules nor the Convention purport to deal with all the problems of an occupying Power. There are noticeable deficiencies in regard to economic and financial matters. For example, what are the duties of the occupying Power in regard to banks, public finance, and the maintenance or use of the former currency or introduction of a new currency? It seems that the occupying Power must follow the principle of ensuring orderly government, which includes the proper safeguarding of the economic and financial structure, but excludes any attempt to obtain improperly any advantage at the expense of the inhabitants of the occupied territory.

Finally, as to the question of duties of obedience (if any) owed by the civilian population towards the occupying Power, it is clear that for conduct prejudicial to security and public order, for espionage, and for interference with military operations, inhabitants are subject to penalisation by the occupying Power. However, the notion of allegiance due by the inhabitants to the occupying Power was rejected by the Geneva Convention of 1949 on the Protection of Civilian Persons in Time of War (see articles 67–68). It appears that, in relation to the population, the occupying Power may prohibit certain activities by the population in the occupied territory, subject to due public notice of what is prohibited, notwithstanding that it has occupied the territory concerned following upon an act of aggression which was a crime under international law.[20]

Geneva conference on international humanitarian law in armed conflicts and the two Protocols adopted by the conference

The law as stated above is subject to such modifications and additions as were made in Protocol I on international armed conflicts and in Protocol II on non-international armed conflicts, being the Protocols adopted in June 1977 by the Geneva Diplomatic Conference on the Reaffirmation and Development of International Law Applicable in Armed Conflicts. The main purpose of this Conference, which met in sessions spread over the years 1974–1977, was to

19. Thus negativing the decision in the 'Hostages Case' (*United States v List*) p 505, n 2, above, that hostages may be executed in order to secure obedience of the local population.

20. Cf the 'Hostages Case' (*United States v List*) p 505, n 2, above.

update and revise the Geneva Red Cross Conventions of 1949, and thus to restate and reaffirm, in a new political and technological context, the laws of war, that is to say the rules of international humanitarian law applicable in armed conflicts. Protocols I and II were adopted explicitly as being in addition to the Geneva Conventions of 1949.

The necessity for such updating and revision arose, as a practical matter, from the history since 1949 of the application—and as well non-application—of the Geneva Red Cross Conventions concluded in that year, and of the Hague Rules of 1907, and from the vast political and technological changes during the post-1949 period. There had been instances of governments and entities engaged in hostilities, refusing to recognise that their armed operations were subject to the rules laid down in the Geneva Conventions of 1949. Moreover, new kinds of warfare and of armed conflicts had emerged, which did not belong to the pre-1949 stereotypes of hostilities, an illustration being the Vietnam War itself, which, as mentioned above, was partly an international conflict, and partly a major civil war, with the involvement of outside powers. Also, it was claimed that the so-called 'wars of national liberation', and anti-colonial struggles, ought to be treated as conflicts subject to the rules of international humanitarian law. This raised incidentally the problem of how guerrilla forces and mercenaries were to be treated. Besides, new weapons technology had resulted in the manufacture and use of bombs, mines, and projectiles of greater destructiveness, more unnecessary suffering, and more indiscriminate damage than previously, such as cluster and fragmentation bombs, incendiary weapons, and delayed action mines and booby traps. Moreover, as a result of world-wide moves for the protection of the environment and the conservation of natural resources, which found expression in 1972 in the Stockholm Conference for the Protection of the Human Environment (see Chapter 14 above), it was felt that the former rules required some updating and revision so as specifically to take account of this necessity for preservation of the environment. Finally, the Vietnam War had demonstrated the need for new rules in certain areas, for example with respect to the matter of speedy evacuation of wounded through the use of more highly developed means of aerial transport than existed in the year 1949, when the Geneva Red Cross Conventions were concluded.

In the progression of steps which led to the first session of the Conference in 1974, an important role was played by the International Committee of the Red Cross (ICRC), by the Secretary-General and General Assembly of the United Nations, and by the two Conferences of Government Experts of 1971–1972 which met under the aegis of the ICRC to consider the subject of reaffirming and developing international humanitarian law,[1] and in particular to examine the two draft Protocols I and II prepared by the ICRC to deal respectively with the rules in international armed conflicts, and the rules in non-international armed conflicts, these being the basic texts submitted to the first session of the Geneva Conference in 1974. The difficulties which plagued the sessions, 1974–

---

1. For an account of the steps leading to the calling of the Conference by the Swiss Government, depositary of the four Geneva Red Cross Conventions of 1949, see R.R. Baxter (later, Judge Baxter of the International Court of Justice) 'Humanitarian Law or Humanitarian Politics; The 1974 Conference on Humanitarian Law', 16 Harvard ILJ (1975) 1 at pp 4–9.

1977 of the Conference were to a large extent due to the necessity of proceeding with two draft texts, instead of a single draft, and of settling the precise scope of each.

The first session of the Geneva Conference in 1974 had to deal with a number of thorny questions, two questions in particular being the participation of National Liberation Movements in the deliberations of the Conference, and the proposal that wars of national liberation be considered international armed conflicts for the purpose of the application of the Geneva Conventions of 1949 and of the two draft Protocols. The Conference decided, as to the former question, to invite National Liberation Movements, which were recognised by the 'regional intergovernmental organisations concerned', to participate fully in the deliberations of the Conference and in its main Committees. It also decided that the statements made or the proposals and amendments submitted by delegations of such National Liberation Movements as were so participating should be circulated by the Conference Secretariat as Conference documents to all the participants in the Conference, it being understood that only delegations representing states or governments would be entitled to vote. Although National Liberation Movements had no right to vote, their views were certainly taken into consideration and influenced the attitudes of the participating states.

The subsequent sessions of the Conference in 1975–1977 were more productive of concrete results, although much ground was left uncovered and compromises were necessary to an extent that contrasted with the course of the discussions at the Geneva Conference of 1949 which drew up the four Red Cross Conventions.

Detailed consideration of the two Additional Protocols (to the Geneva Conventions) adopted by the Conference lies beyond the scope of this book, and reference can be made only to some of the principal provisions of the two texts,[2] remembering always that their effectiveness will depend more upon their practical implementation rather than upon their formal acceptance by governments.

Dealing first with Protocol I on international armed conflicts, some of the main provisions include the following:

1. The international armed conflicts covered by the Protocol include hostilities in which 'peoples are fighting against colonial domination and alien occupation and against racist régimes in the exercise of their right of self-determination' (para 4 of art 1).
2. Subject to conditions, more definite protection is assured for both service and civilian medical units and personnel, and for medical transport vehicles, ships and aircraft (articles 12–18, and 21–31).
3. Although the Protocol does not explicitly deal with specific weapons, it reiterates the prohibition or the use of weapons and methods, etc, causing superfluous injury or unnecessary suffering, and adds a prohibition on the

2. For discussion, etc, in respect to the Protocols, see Y. Dinstein 'The New Geneva Protocols: A Step Forward or Backward' (1979) Year Book of World Affairs 265; L.C. Green 'The New Law of Armed Conflict' (1977) 15 Canadian Yearbook of International Law 1; D.F.J.J. De Stoop 'New guarantees for human rights in armed conflicts—a major result of the Geneva Conference 1974–1977' (1978) 6 Australian Year Book of International Law 52; A. Cassese (ed) *The New Humanitarian Law of Armed Conflict* (1979–1981, 2 vols).

use of methods or means that are intended or may be expected to cause widespread, long-term and severe damage to the natural environment (article 35), while in the study, development, etc, of new weapons or methods of warfare, the parties are bound to determine whether these would be prohibited by the Protocol or other applicable rules of international law (article 36).

4. In situations where an armed combatant cannot distinguish himself from a civilian (for example guerrilla activities) he is only required to carry arms openly during military engagements and in visible deployment prior to the launching of attacks (article 44).

5. Articles 52–56 impose obligations for the greater protection of civilian objects and the civilian population, including prohibitions of starvation of civilians, and of destruction of foodstuffs and agricultural areas, and the protection of works and installations containing dangerous forces.

6. Provision for fundamental guarantees of human rights is made in article 75; these include criminal procedural guarantees, and protection against abusive treatment, while covering a great variety of persons. Moreover, under article 74 provision is made for ensuring the reunification of families dispersed as a consequence of armed conflicts.

7. Journalists engaged in dangerous professional missions in conflict areas are to be protected as having civilian status, and may obtain a special identity card (article 79).

8. The list of 'grave breaches' is extended in articles 11 and 85 (see above), and one such breach is 'unjustifiable delay in the repatriation of prisoners of war or civilians' (see sub-paragraph (b) of paragraph 4 of article 85); having regard to what happened in the Korean conflict 1950–1953 and the Vietnam War,[3] the latter provision is of the utmost significance.

Other provisions of Protocol I (eg, as to mercenaries) have been referred to in their appropriate place in this chapter, above. It should be added that the Protocol does not contain provisions dealing expressly with nuclear warfare, and having regard to certain reservations made upon the signature of the Protocol, it may for all practical purposes be taken that the Protocol does not extend to such warfare involving nuclear weaponry.

Protocol II is much shorter than Protocol I. It is confined to armed conflicts between non-state entities or groups. As Professor Dinstein has said,[4] its foremost aim is 'to augment the protection accorded to the victims of civil wars', and in this vein it provides a number of basic guarantees and special protection for civilians, works and installations containing dangerous forces, medical personnel, and medical transports. The main thrust of the provisions of Protocol II is to mitigate the suffering and damage that civil wars may involve, and it is hoped that, insofar as all conceivable situations are not covered in the Protocol, civil war antagonists will at least respect the spirit of humanitarianism underlying the entirety of its provisions.

---

3. See p 506.
4. (1979) Year Book of World Affairs, op cit, p 280.

Arms control—distinction from international humanitarian law
In this section of the present chapter, it remains to mention the subject of arms control, for the purpose only of distinguishing it from that of international humanitarian law, since it lies beyond the scope of the present book. The expression 'arms control' refers to accepted regulatory measures, in certain specific directions only, of the deployment, abolition, reduction or limitation, or of prohibition of the new production, of certain arms, in regard to which the primary purposes are to restore the equilibrium of deterrence, or to decrease the pitch and intensity of an arms race, or even to lessen the possible risks of escalation of armed conflicts.[5] It will be evident, then, that the predominant aim of arms control is to reduce the likelihood of armed conflicts, that is to say, to contribute to the maintenance of peace, and that it is not concerned specifically at all with reducing the suffering occasioned by the actual weaponry when used in armed conflicts. The purpose indeed is to ensure that such armed conflicts do not occur or if they do, to keep within limits the range of damage that may be caused by the weaponry used.

Arms control is to be distinguished also from disarmament. The object of disarmament is to abolish war-making capacity, while the purpose of arms control is to keep such capacity within certain bounds. So far, the subject of arms control has hardly been within the province of general international law, but has been dealt with in the main by bilateral agreements, or by multilateral agreements confined to a limited number of states.

4.   MODES OF TERMINATING WAR AND HOSTILITIES

State practice in the present century renders necessary a distinction between:

1.   Modes of termination of the status of war.
2.   Modes of termination of hostilities which are continuing in a war stricto sensu, and of the hostilities in a non-war armed conflict.[6]

(1)   Modes of termination of the status of war
The following are the principal ways of termination:

a.   Simple cessation of hostilities by the belligerents without any definite understanding being reached between them. Illustrations are the wars between Sweden and Poland (1716), between France and Spain (1720), between Russia and Persia (1801), between France and Mexico (1867), and between Spain and Chile (1867). The disadvantage of this method is that it leaves the future relations of belligerents in doubt, and is not appropriate for modern conditions under which complicated questions of property,

5.   See J. Goldblat *Agreements for Arms Control: A Critical Survey* (1982), and Julie Dahlitz *Nuclear Arms Control: With Effective International Agreements* (1983).
6.   It may also be necessary to consider a tertium quid, namely the termination of hostile or unfriendly relationships; eg, the termination of a 'confrontation', as to which, note the agreement between Indonesia and Malaysia of peace and co-operation, 11 August 1966, referred to, p 483 above.

matériel, prisoners of war, and boundaries have to be resolved usually by treaty.

b. Conquest followed by annexation. The governing principle here is that a country conquered and annexed ceases to exist at international law; hence there cannot be a state of war between it and the conqueror. It is not clear how far this principle now applies where the annexed state was vanquished in a war of aggression, illegal under international law.[7] For example, in the case of Ethiopia and Czechoslovakia, annexed in 1936 and 1939 by Italy and Germany respectively, the Allied Powers refused to recognise the territorial changes thus illegally brought about, but these were both cases where independence was restored within a reasonably short time. It may be recalled, for example, that by article 5 of the definition of aggression, adopted in 1974 by the United Nations General Assembly (see above in this chapter), no territorial acquisition or special advantage resulting from aggression is to be recognised as lawful.

c. By peace treaty. This is the more usual method. A treaty of peace generally deals in detail with all outstanding questions concerning the relations of the belligerents, for example, evacuation of territory, repatriation of prisoners of war, indemnities, etc. On all points concerning property on which the treaty is silent, the principle uti possidetis ('as you possess, you shall continue to possess') applies, namely, that each state is entitled to retain such property as was actually in its possession or control at the date of cessation of hostilities. There also applies the postliminium principle, in the absence of express provision, to the rights of the parties other than to property; that is to say, that any prior condition and prior status are to be restored; hence, legal disabilities of former alien enemies are removed, diplomatic relations are reconstituted, etc.

d. By an agreement or agreements for ending war, and restoring peace, as distinct from a peace treaty in the strict sense. This method has been adopted where one or more of the parties involved in the war was a non-state entity; an illustration is the Four-Party Agreement of 27 January 1973, for ending the war and restoring peace in Vietnam, one party to which was the Provisional Revolutionary Government of South Vietnam (Vietcong).

e. By armistice agreement, where the agreement although primarily intended to bring about a cessation of hostilities, operates subsequently as a result of its practical application by the parties de facto to terminate the status of war. This, it is believed, is largely a question of construction of the particular armistice agreement concerned.[8]

f. By unilateral declaration of one or more of the victorious Powers, terminating a status of war.[9] This seemingly anomalous procedure was adopted by certain

---

7. See above, pp 140-143.
8. Note in that connection the view adopted by Israel, and denied by Egypt that its armistice agreement of 1949 with the four Arab States, Egypt, Lebanon, the Hashemite Kingdom of Jordan, and Syria, terminated the status of war; see Rosenne *Israel's Armistice Agreement with the Arab States* (1951). But cf now the Treaty of Peace between Israel and Egypt signed at Washington on 26 March 1979, in (1979) 18 International Legal Materials 362, which expressly terminated any status of war.
9. See *Re Grotrian, Cox v Grotrian* [1955] Ch 501 at 506, [1955] 1 All ER 788 at 791.

of the Allied Powers (including Great Britain and the United States) in 1947 and 1951 respectively towards Austria and the West German Republic, principally because of irreconcilable disagreement with the Soviet Union over procedure and principle in regard to the conclusion of peace treaties.

Municipal law and the termination of war
The date of termination of a war, according to a particular state's municipal law is not necessarily the same as the date of the peace treaty, or the date of cessation of hostilities.[10] There is no rule of international law precluding the municipal law of any belligerent state from adopting a date different to that in the treaty, unless there be express contrary provision in the treaty itself.

(2) Modes of termination of hostilities
The following modes of terminating hostilities, as distinct from the status of war itself, are applicable to hostilities both in a war, and in a non-war conflict:

a.   By armistice agreement. Strictly speaking, an armistice is but a temporary suspension of hostilities, and normally signifies that hostilities are to be resumed on the expiration of the armistice period. Armistices may be, on the one hand, *general*, when all armed operations are suspended; or on the other hand, *partial* or *local*, being then restricted to portions only of the armed forces engaged, or to particular areas only of the operational zones. One modern trend in regard to general armistices, however, is that they represent no mere temporary halting of hostilities, but a kind of de facto termination of war,which is confirmed by the final treaty of peace.[11] In the case of a non-war armed conflict, as for example, the Korean conflict, 1950–1953, the armistice puts an end to the conflict, and it may also be that a final peaceful settlement is contemplated by the contending parties.[12]

b.   Unconditional surrender or other forms of general capitulation, unaccompanied by any agreement or treaty, containing terms of peace. The formula of unconditional surrender was adopted by the Allies in the Second World War for the reasons, inter alia, that it was deemed impossible to negotiate with the Axis Governments, that it was necessary to preclude any suggestion of a betrayal of the enemy armed forces by civilian governments, and to enable a process of re-education and democratisation of the enemy populations to be undertaken for a time under military controls, while a formal state of war continued.

c.   By a 'Truce' so-called. The term has been used in United Nations practice[13] (for example, the Truce established in Palestine in May–June 1948, as a result

10. See, eg, *Kotzias v Tyser* [1920] 2 KB 69, and *Ruffy-Arnell and Baumann Aviation Co v R* [1922] 1 KB 599 at 611–612.
11. As in the case of the general Armistice of 11 November 1918, in the First World War, which preceded the Treaty of Versailles 1919.
12. See, eg, the references in the Preamble to the Korea Armistice Agreement of 27 July 1953, to 'stopping the Korean conflict' and to a 'final peaceful settlement'; art 62 also refers to the eventual supersession of the Agreement by an agreement for 'a peaceful settlement at a political level'.
13. See as to the United Nations practice in respect to truces, and as well in respect to 'cease-fires' and armistices, Sydney D. Bailey 'Cease-Fires, Truces, and Armistices in the Practice of the UN Security Council' 71 AJIL (1977) 461–473, esp at p 470.

of action by the Security Council). It probably indicates a less definitive cessation of hostilities than the term 'Armistice'.[14]

d. Cease-Fire. The term more frequently used for a cessation of hostilities on the order or request of the United Nations Security Council or other international organ is 'cease-fire'; for example, the cease-fire ordered by the Security Council in December 1948, on the occasion of the renewal of hostilities in Indonesia between the Netherlands and the Indonesian Republican forces, the cease-fire of 13 October 1961, between the United Nations Force in the Congo and the armed forces of Katanga,[15] and the cease-fire in the India–Pakistan conflict 'demanded' by the Security Council in its resolution of 20 September 1965. The general effect of a cease-fire is to prohibit absolutely hostilities and operations within the area subject of the order or agreement, and during the period of time stipulated. A cease-fire subject of an order by the UN Security Council may not necessarily have immediate operation; eg, the Council's mandatory requirement for implementation of a cease-fire in the Iraq-Iran war, although made by Resolution 598 adopted in July 1987, did not obtain acceptance by the belligerents until August 1988. Cease-fire was also the term used in marking the end of the hostilities phase in the enforcement action against Iraq in respect of its unlawful occupation of Kuwait. The resolution of 2 March 1991 noting the end of hostilities was followed by the lengthy Resolution 687 of 8 April 1991 in which the Security Council laid down detailed conditions, and in which it was declared that 'upon notification by Iraq of its acceptance of the provisions above, a formal cease-fire is effective between Iraq and Kuwait and the Member States cooperating with Kuwait in accordance with resolution 678 (1990).'[16]

e. Agreement of cessation or suspension[17] of hostilities; for example, the three Geneva Agreements of 20 July 1954, on the cessation of hostilities respectively in Vietnam, Laos, and Cambodia, which ended the fighting in Indo-China between government and Viet Minh forces. The Agreement on Disengagement between Israeli and Syrian forces, in respect to the hostilities of October 1973, may be regarded as falling within this category; paragraph H of the Agreement specifically declared: 'This Agreement is not a Peace Agreement. It is a step towards a just and durable peace on the basis of Security Council resolution 338 dated 22 October 1973'.

f. By joint declaration of the restoration of normal, peaceful, and friendly relations between the contestants; eg, the Tashkent Declaration, 10 January

14. Rosenne, op cit, at pp 24–28, suggests that a truce differs from an armistice in being a more limited method, since the armistice may involve positive provisions other than the mere suspension of hostilities, and affect third parties, which a truce usually does not. See also Bailey, op cit, in 71 AJIL (1977) 462–463.

15. The termination of hostilities in Laos in 1962 was referred to as a 'cease-fire' in art 9 of the Protocol of 23 July 1962, to the Declaration on the Neutrality of Laos, of the same date. See also Bailey, op cit, at p 470 for the various categories of 'cease-fires.' The Falklands conflict of April–June 1982 was ended by surrender of Argentine garrisons and a cease-fire of 13/14 June 1982.

16. On the UN enforcement action against Iraq see further below, p 588.

17. There was a suspension in May 1965 in the case of the conflict in the Dominican Republic.

1966, as to the India–Pakistan Conflict (this included terms as to withdrawal-lines of armies, and as to prisoners).[18]

g.   De facto cessation of the fighting, as in the case of the halting of hostilities in Angola, 8–9 August 1988.

General

One unsatisfactory feature of the Second World War and its aftermath was the undue prolongation of the period between cessation of hostilities and the conclusion of a peace treaty.[19] This can leave conquered states subject to an uncertain régime, intermediate between war and peace, a possibly recurrent situation for which some solution should be found by international law. The situation in respect of Germany was complicated by the Cold War which resulted in a prolonged division of the country into two separate states, the Federal Republic of Germany and the German Democratic Republic, both established in 1949. Following the signing of the Treaty on the Establishment of German Unity between the two German States on 31 August 1990,[20] the two Germanys and the victorious powers of 1945 — France, the Soviet Union, the United Kingdom and the United States — concluded the Treaty on the Final Settlement With Respect to Germany at Moscow on 12 September 1990.[1]

18.   The terminology as to cessation of hostilities also includes a 'pause' (ie, a brief period of temporary cessation of particular kinds of operations, such as air bombardment), a 'standstill' (this can cover not only a prohibition of hostilities, ie cease-fire, but also a cessation of all movement of armaments or personnel), and 'de-escalation' (a diminution in the intensity, magnitude, and range of the hostilities).
19.   Although hostilities terminated in August 1945, the Peace Treaty with Japan was not signed until 8 September 1951.
20.   (1991) 30 ILM 457.
1.   (1990) 29 ILM 1186.

CHAPTER 19

Neutrality, quasi-neutrality, and non-belligerency

1. GENERAL

As indicated in the previous chapter, hostile relations between states comprise not only (a) war in the traditional sense, but (b) non-war armed conflicts and breaches of the peace.

Corresponding to these two categories, there are two kinds of status of the parties outside the range of such hostile relations: (a) the status of *neutrality* in a war proper; and (b) the status of non-participation or non-involvement by states or non-state entities in a non-war conflict. The latter status, (b), is sometimes (as in the case of the Korean conflict, 1950–1953) loosely referred to as neutrality,[1] but there are certain differences between it and neutrality proper. It is perhaps better to refer to it as *quasi-neutrality*, or in certain cases simply as *non-belligerency*.

Neutrality

In its popular sense, neutrality denotes the attitude of a state which is not at war with belligerents, and does not participate in the hostilities. In its technical sense, however, it is more than an attitude, and denotes a *legal status* of a special nature, involving a complex of rights, duties, and privileges at international law, which must be respected by belligerents and neutrals alike.[2] This status of neutrality has been the subject of a long and complicated development, at each stage of which the content of the status has varied with the nature of warfare, and with the conditions of political power in the international community of states.

---

1. Note, eg, the definition of states not participating in the Korean hostilities as 'neutral nations', in art 37 of the Korean Armistice Agreement of 27 July 1953, for the purposes of the appointment of a Neutral Nations Supervisory Commission. For an up-to-date treatment of the international law as to neutrality, see Yoram Dinstein 'The Laws of Neutrality' in (1984) 14 *Israel Yearbook on Human Rights* 80–110.
2. The international law status of neutrality should be distinguished from the *policy* of 'neutralism' (see Chapter 5, above at p 110). Yet to some extent neutralism or 'non-alignment' may be regarded as an ad hoc unilaterally declared status (sometimes multilaterally as under art III of the Charter of the Organisation of African Unity, May 1963) of dissociation from the 'cold war', involving neither rights nor obligations.

Neutrality gradually developed out of bilateral treaties stipulating that neither party to the treaty should assist the enemies of the other if one party were engaged in war. It was realised that it was to the general convenience of belligerent states to prevent assistance being furnished to enemies. Originally such cases of neutrality were isolated and sporadic, and stopped far short of the notion of a general status. Certainly the idea that neutral duties devolved on all non-participants in a given war was a much later development. The term 'neutrality' appeared as early as the seventeenth century, but no systematic doctrine emerged until the eighteenth century, when it was discussed by Bynkershoek and Vattel. By that date theory and practice united in acknowledging the right of independent states to hold aloof from war, and their duty in such case to be impartial as between the belligerents.

In the nineteenth century, neutrality developed much more extensively than in all its previous history. Most historians attribute this to the part played by the United States as a neutral in the Napoleonic Wars, when Great Britain was aligned against Napoleon and his continental satellites. The United States Government refused to allow the equipping or arming of vessels in American territory on behalf of the belligerents, and it prevented the recruitment of American citizens for service in the belligerent forces. At the same time Great Britain was endeavouring to block neutral commerce with France, and many rules as to neutral and belligerent rights evolved as compromise solutions of a conflict of interests between the British and United States Governments. Also, during the years of the Napoleonic Wars, Lord Stowell presided over the British Prize Court, and the newly developing law as to neutral rights and duties owed much to his intellect and genius as a judicial legislator. Later in the century the American Civil War gave rise to several disputes on questions of neutrality between the legitimate United States Government and Great Britain. Out of these arose the famous *Alabama Claims Arbitration* of 1872, concerning the construction and fitting out in England of commerce-destroying vessels for the Confederate Navy. The United States Government alleged a breach of neutrality in that the British Government had failed to exercise due care to prevent the equipping of the vessels, and their despatch to the Confederates, and a claim for damage suffered through the activities of the vessels (one of which was *The Alabama*) in the Civil War was sustained by the arbitrators.

Other important factors which favoured the development of neutrality in the nineteenth century were the permanent neutralisation of Belgium and Switzerland,[3] which supplied useful precedents for neutral rights and duties, and the general growth of great unified sovereign states. It was clearly to the interests of the latter to be able to maintain unrestricted commercial intercourse with belligerents without being drawn into war, as it was plainly to the interests of the belligerents to prevent assistance being given to their enemies by such countries. Moreover, conditions were peculiarly favourable to neutrality inasmuch as the principal wars fought in the nineteenth century were wars of limited objectives, unlikely to embroil states other than the participants, so that there was little risk of threat to neutrals as long as they observed the rules. In these circumstances the generally recognised rules of neutrality, some of them

3.   See above, pp 109-111.

embodied in instruments such as the Declaration of Paris 1856, and in the Hague Convention of 1907, commanded the support of, as they corresponded to the interests of, most states.

However, in the First World War (1914–1918)—which developed almost into 'total war'—as in the Second World War (1939–1945), most of the recognised rules of neutrality proved quite out of date, could not be applied in many instances, and instead of assisting to maintain the impartiality of states, virtually forced them into the struggle (as in the case of the United States in 1917). In its turn the Second World War was convincing proof of the archaism of the nineteenth century conceptions of neutrality. Neutral status proved to be a condition no less hazardous than that of belligerency. One neutral state after another was 'rolled up', and the two most powerful neutrals—Russia and the United States—were each attacked without warning. It is plain that in the future neutrality can only operate within a limited and quite unpredictable field, and it is questionable whether it is in the general interest to preserve an institution of so uncertain a value. At the same time, under the general approach currently of states that 'limited' wars should be 'contained' so as not to escalate into larger conflicts, the status of neutrality of non-involved states can usefully serve to influence the desired containment.

The trend towards restriction of the scope of neutrality has been confirmed by a significant post-war development, namely, the conclusion of regional security treaties, such as the North Atlantic Security Pact of 4 April 1949, in which the states parties have voluntarily renounced in futuro a right of claiming neutrality in the event of a war in which their co-parties to the treaties have been attacked, and instead will assist the states thus attacked. To this pact, the United States, formerly the most influential neutral state in past wars and the most insistent on neutral rights, is a party.

Rational basis of neutrality

Neutrality is often justified by reference to the following considerations:

1. that it serves to localise war;
2. that it discourages war;
3. that it enables states to keep out of war;
4. that it regularises international relations.

The Second World War conclusively demonstrated the fallacies of (1) and (2), inasmuch as the neutrality of states such as Norway, Denmark, Holland and Belgium proved an irresistible temptation to forcible invasion, and prevented more effective arrangements for their joint defence, with the consequence that these states were speedily overrun by superior German forces. The result was to increase Germany's power in Europe, to bring Italy into the war on Germany's side, and eventually to encourage Japan to precipitate hostilities in the Pacific. Thus, far from localising or discouraging war, the effect of neutrality was to transform a European struggle into a world conflict.

As to (3), it was virtually in defence of its neutrality that the United States entered the First World War on the side of France and Great Britain. Moreover, despite the care taken in the Second World War by Russia and the United States to preserve their neutrality, attacks by Germany and Japan, respectively, forced them into the war only two years after its outbreak in 1939.

As to (4), the experience of the League of Nations from 1920 to 1940 showed that the institution of neutrality is quite inconsistent with the maintenance in international relations of the rule of law. The unjustified reliance of states members of the League on traditional notions of neutrality contributed towards preventing the League machinery from functioning on the outbreak of the Second World War.

More convincing and more cogent are the two rationales for the institution of neutrality, according to Professor Dinstein:[4] (i) the wish of neutral states to have guarantees that they will sustain minimal injury as a consequence of the hostilities; and (ii) assurance to belligerents that neutral states will not aid or abet any adversary belligerent.

Before this war began, a fundamental change had taken place in the attitude of most states towards the status of neutrality. Far from insisting on neutral rights or belligerent duties, states were now prepared to make all possible concessions to avoid any chance of a clash with the belligerents. The First World War had shown how a neutral state like the United States could be drawn into war in defence of its neutral rights, and no state wished to repeat that experience. States were determined if possible to keep out of a general war. In 1936–1937 this attitude was reflected in the non-intervention policy of France and Great Britain towards the Spanish Civil War.

This new attitude was particularly illustrated by the attitude of the United States in 1939–1940, before Germany overran and conquered Western Europe in the summer of 1940, and by its 'Neutrality' law passed by Congress in 1937. The 'Neutrality' Act of 1937 was a misnomer; it was really a measure to ensure no contacts between the United States and belligerents which could possibly involve her in war in defence of neutral rights.

After Germany's victories in Western Europe in June 1940, the United States appeared to veer in an entirely opposite direction. Convinced that Germany's aim was world domination, the United States initiated a series of measures to aid Great Britain in the war against Germany and Italy which would have been unthinkable some twelve months previously. Whereas before she had been ready to renounce neutral rights, she paradoxically now appeared to show disregard for neutral duties, transferring destroyers to Great Britain, sending her arms, and ammunition, and patrolling dangerous sea-lanes. In addition Congress passed the Lend-Lease Act of March 1941, which made it possible to provision and equip the armed forces of Great Britain and her allies. The legality of the Lend-Lease Act and of the other measures adopted by the United States before her entry into the Second World War was justified on three grounds at least:

a.   The breach by Germany and Italy of the Briand-Kellogg Pact of 1928 for the Outlawry of War, and the fact that these Powers were guilty of gross aggression against neutral states.
b.   The principle of self-preservation as against Powers like Germany and Italy, which intended to show no respect for the rights of neutrals. There was the additional consideration here that if the United States had allowed Great Britain to be conquered, international law itself would not have survived.

4.   Dinstein, op cit, n 1, above at p 80.

c. The evidence of conspiracy on the part of the Axis Powers to launch an attack on the United States in the immediate future.

Moreover, after the United States became a belligerent, she showed little traditional regard for neutral rights. Together with Great Britain, she brought pressure to bear on European neutrals to withhold supplies from the Axis Powers. This pressure increased in measure as Allied victories removed any possibility of a threat to these neutrals from Germany, if they should cease to trade with Axis countries, until in 1944–1945 the American attitude was uncompromisingly that neutral exports of vital products to Germany would not be countenanced.

Neutrality and the United Nations Charter
Member states of the United Nations have no absolute right of neutrality. By article 41 of the United Nations Charter they may be under a duty to apply enforcement measures against a state or states engaged in war, if so called upon pursuant to a decision by the Security Council. Under paragraph 5 of article 2 they are also bound to give every assistance to the United Nations in any action under the Charter and to refrain from giving assistance to any state against which preventive or enforcement action is being taken by the Organisation.

Neutrality is not, however, completely abolished. Even where preventive or enforcement action is being taken by the United Nations Security Council, certain member states may not be called upon to apply the measures decided upon by the Council or may receive special exemptions (see articles 48 and 50). In this event their status is one of 'qualified' neutrality inasmuch as they are bound not to assist the belligerent state against which enforcement measures are directed, and must also assist the member states actually taking the measures (see article 49). It seems also that where the 'veto' is exercised by a permanent member of the Security Council so that no preventive or enforcement action is decided upon with reference to a war, in such cases member states may remain absolutely neutral towards the belligerents.[5]

Commencement of neutrality
Immediate notification of neutrality is desirable, and is regarded as necessary by most states. Although a non-belligerent state is entitled to declare itself as a neutral, it is not under any legal obligation to do so. In the Second World War, immediately after its outbreak in September 1939, almost all neutral states announced their neutrality at once and specifically communicated the fact to the belligerents. Certain of these states were then members of the League of Nations, and the declarations of neutrality were regarded as necessary statements of intention not to be bound by the obligations of the League Covenant.

Quasi-neutrality and non-belligerency
States and non-state entities, not participating in a 'non-war' armed conflict, have a status which yet remains to be defined by rules of international law.

5. On the subject of neutrality and qualified neutrality under the operation of the provisions of the United Nations Charter, see Norton in (1976) 17 Harvard ILJ 249–252, 309–311, Henkin, Pugh, Schachter and Smit *International Law; Cases and Materials* (2nd edn, 1987) pp 746–750, and Dinstein, op cit, n 1, above, at p 81.

If the events in the Korean conflict of 1950–1953 supply any guide, it is clear that there is no rigid or fixed status of quasi-neutrality or non-belligerency as in the case of neutrality in a war proper, but that the nature of the status must depend on the special circumstances of the particular conflict concerned.

Moreover, where a 'non-war' armed conflict is subject to the peace enforcement action of the Security Council of the United Nations, or to United Nations 'peacekeeping' (see Chapter 20 below), the status of a quasi-neutral, or non-belligerent, whether a member state of the United Nations or not, is governed by the provisions of the United Nations Charter,[6] and by the terms of any decision or recommendation made by the Security Council under these provisions, or of any recommendations of the General Assembly as to such 'peacekeeping'. Nevertheless, the classic terminology of neutrality may sometimes be used. Thus, during the Gulf War 1990-1991, in a desperate effort to save its aircraft from destruction through air to ground attack by forces authorised by the United Nations Security Council to expel it from Kuwait, Iraq despatched approximately one quarter of its combat aircraft to Iran, its recent enemy. The United States Government warned Iran to abide by its 'duties as a neutral' not to release these aircraft for the remainder of the period of enforcement action.

2.   RIGHTS AND DUTIES IN GENERAL OF (A) NEUTRALS, AND (B) QUASI-NEUTRALS AND NON-BELLIGERENTS

(a) Rights and duties in general of neutral states

The status of neutrality involves rights and duties inter se of neutral states on the one hand, and of belligerent states on the other. Rights and duties here are *correlative*, that is to say, a right of a neutral state corresponds to a duty of a belligerent, and a right of a belligerent state to a duty of a neutral. From the standpoint of either the neutral or the belligerent state, also, the duties of these states may be classified as:

i.   duties of abstention;
ii. duties of prevention;
iii. duties of acquiescence.

Applying this classification, the general duties of a neutral state may be described as follows:

(i) Abstention

The neutral state must give no assistance—direct or indirect—to either belligerent side; for example, it must not supply troops, or furnish or guarantee loans, or provide shelter for a belligerent's armed forces.

(ii) Prevention

The neutral state is under a duty to prevent within its territory or jurisdiction such activities as the enlistment of troops for belligerent armies, preparations

6.   See art 39-51.

for hostilities by any belligerent, or warlike measures in its territory or territorial waters.

(iii) Acquiescence
The neutral state must acquiesce in the acts of belligerent states with respect to the commerce of its nationals if they are duly warranted by the laws of war, for example, the seizure of vessels under its flag for the carriage of contraband, adjudications by Prize Courts, and so on.

Similarly, the duties of belligerent states may be summarised as:

(i) Abstention
A belligerent state must not commit warlike acts on neutral territory or enter into hostilities in neutral waters or in the airspace above neutral territory, nor may it interfere with the legitimate intercourse of neutrals with the enemy, nor may it use neutral territory or waters as a base for belligerent operations, or as a starting point for an expedition.

(ii) Prevention
A belligerent state is duty bound to prevent the ill-treatment of neutral envoys or neutral subjects or injury to neutral property on enemy territory occupied by it.

(iii) Acquiescence
A belligerent state must, for instance, acquiesce in internment by a neutral state of such members of its armed forces as take refuge in neutral territory, or in the granting of temporary asylum by neutral ports to hostile warships so that necessary repairs may be effected.

If a belligerent or a neutral state violates any one of such duties and the breach results in damage to the other, it is in general liable for the damage caused and must furnish pecuniary satisfaction to that state. In the *Alabama Claims Arbitration* (1872), the arbitrators awarded the United States a sum of 15,500,000 dollars in gold as indemnity in full satisfaction of all claims subject of the arbitration, arising out of Great Britain's failure to prevent the construction and fitting out of *The Alabama* and other commerce destroyers for arming and use by the Confederates.

As regards the above-mentioned duties of prevention a neutral state is not an insurer for the performance of these duties, or, put another way, these duties are not absolute. The neutral state is bound only to use the means at its disposal in fulfilling its obligations; for example, if unable to prevent a much stronger state from violating its neutrality, it does not become liable to the injured belligerent state for the non-performance of its duties.

With regard to the several duties of abstention of a belligerent state mentioned above, one or two important points should be mentioned. If a neutral state abstains from taking action against a belligerent violating neutral territory, etc, or if that neutral state is too weak to prevent such violation, then the opposing belligerent is entitled to intervene on the neutral territory, etc. Belligerent warships have a right of innocent passage through neutral territorial waters, but the right must not be abused. They may also, for the purpose of refuelling, repairs, etc, take refuge in neutral ports (although not more than three at the same time), and here, according to British practice, may only stay 24 hours after notice from the neutral state, subject to an extension for sufficient reasons, for example, weather or urgent repairs. If the time-limit is exceeded, the ship and crew must be interned.

Reference should also be made to certain other rights and privileges of belligerent states. Their special rights in regard to neutral trade and neutral shipping are considered in section 3 below. In addition to these, belligerents enjoy the so-called privilege of *angary*, ie, of requisitioning any neutral ships or goods physically within their jurisdiction, but not brought there voluntarily, subject to the property being useful in war and being urgently required by them, and subject to the payment of full compensation.[7] Also, according to the practice in two World Wars belligerents are, it seems, entitled to notify war zones or 'operational sea zones', on the high seas, and to designate the safe routes of passage that may be taken by neutral vessels. In the case of the Falklands conflict of April–June 1982, when on 28 April 1982 the British Government notified a 200-mile 'Total Exclusion Zone' (TEZ) around the Falkland Islands, ships and aircraft which were in the Zone without the express authority of the Ministry of Defence in London, were to be treated as hostile and liable to be attacked by British forces. Further, in the event of the enemy resorting to illegal warfare, belligerents may adopt reprisals (ie, measures otherwise illegal at international law) irrespective of the fact that injury may thereby be done to neutrals, provided only, according to British practice, that such reprisals are justified by the circumstances of the case and do not involve an unreasonable degree of inconvenience for neutrals.[8]

The situation in the Persian Gulf in 1984–1988 during the course of the Iraq-Iran War (1980–1988) must be regarded as without precedent in the history of neutrality.[9] As the Gulf coastal states and territories have become a main source of oil supplies for the rest of the world, there is a constant transit of tankers through the Gulf. During the above-mentioned period, 1984–1988, both belligerents were responsible not only for laying mines in the Gulf waters, but for hundreds of attacks on neutral tankers or merchant vessels and on the neutral warships by which these were escorted or protected. If this conduct by the belligerents was on the footing that the whole of the Gulf constituted a war zone closed to neutral shipping, it was nevertheless their obligation to assign duly regulated free lanes or channels for the necessary peaceful passage of neutral ships.[10] The United States, the United Kingdom and other concerned neutral countries were unmoved by the risks, and resolutely followed a policy of enforcing their rights of entry and transit as neutrals to the extent, on occasions,

---

7. If the goods are within the jurisdiction and have been brought there voluntarily, reasonable and not full compensation for requisitioning will be paid to the owner.
8. See *The Zamora* [1916] 2 AC 77.
9. A. de Guttry and N. Ronzitti *The Iran-Iraq War (1980-1988) and the Law of Naval Warfare* (1993).
10. See Dinstein, op cit n 1 ante, pp 101-102.

of armed action and of the operation of minesweepers to remove mines laid by the belligerents in Gulf waters.

Neutrality does not exclude sympathy between a neutral state and a belligerent, provided that this sentiment does not take the active form of concrete assistance to that belligerent. Similarly, gifts or loans of money by private citizens of the neutral state to the belligerent or other similar transactions, or individual enlistments by such private citizens in that belligerent's armed forces are not prohibited by the rules of neutrality. Such impartiality as is required of neutrals is confined to the duties of abstention, prevention, and acquiescence mentioned above. This distinction between the neutral state and its citizens has obviously been affected by the increasing range of state controls over all private transactions, and over persons. Under the impact of these controls, the duties of a neutral state must necessarily become more strict so far as liberty of action by its citizens is concerned. For example, it is probably now the duty of a neutral state not to sanction the private export of arms and ammunition.

Unneutral service[11]

Traditionally, the doctrine of *unneutral service* relates to the duties of neutral citizens in maritime warfare, and was regarded as an analogue of the doctrine of contraband. Confusion is due to this analogy, because it seemed to confine unneutral service to the *carriage* or *transport* by neutral vessels of persons and despatches, which assist one belligerent, and against which its opponent is empowered to take measures by confiscation and (if necessary) by destruction of the vessel.

It is, however, a doctrine much broader than this analogy suggests; nor in these days is it confined to ships at sea, but must include aircraft, which in time of war are commonly used for the transport of persons[12] important to a belligerent's war effort. Summing up the doctrine of unneutral service, it may be laid down that it is the duty of the owners or persons in charge of a neutral vessel or aircraft not by any acts or conduct on their part to employ the vessel or aircraft for objects or purposes (other than carriage of contraband or breach of blockade[13]) which may advance the belligerent interests of one state and injure the same interests of the opponent. For such acts or conduct, a belligerent who is or may be injuriously affected thereby, may stop the vessel or aircraft, and remove therefrom the persons[14] improperly carried, and—in more serious cases—

11. For discussions of the doctrine, see Stone *Legal Controls of International Conflict* (1954) ch XVIII, and *Supplement* 1953–1958 (1959) pp 892–893, and Dinstein, op cit, pp 105–108.
12. During the Second World War, the refusal of the British authorities to grant 'navicerts' or ship warrants (see below p 534) for particular neutral vessels, because of undesirable passengers or undesirable members of the crew, left little practical room for cases of unneutral service by the transport of persons important to the enemy's war effort; cf Medlicott *The Economic Blockade* in the series 'History of the Second World War, United Kingdom Civil Series' (ed W.K. Hancock) (1952) Vol I, pp 450–452, and (1959) Vol II pp 161 et seq.
13. See below, in section 3 of this chapter.
14. The category of persons, the carriage of whom may involve an unneutral service, includes serving members of the armed forces, reservists subject to orders of mobilisation, and semble, now, scientists important to the enemy's war effort.

capture the vessel, and condemn it or certain portions of its cargo by proceeding before a Prize Court.[15]

The more usual guilty activities of unneutral service are transport of members of the enemy armed forces, carriage of despatches to the enemy, taking a direct part in the hostilities, operating under charter to the enemy, and the transmission of intelligence in the interests of the enemy.

(b) Rights and duties in general of quasi-neutrals and non-belligerents

States and non-state entities which do not participate in 'non-war' armed conflicts are not subject, it is clear, to the same stringent duties as neutral states in a war proper, nor have they rights against the contestants as plenary as the rights of neutrals.

Practice supplies, as yet, no conclusive guide as to the extent of the rights and duties involved.

However, the contestants and quasi-neutrals or non-contestants concerned may always agree as to the extent of their respective rights and duties, inter se. As to one special point, the right of quasi-neutrals or non-contestants to protect the lives and property of nationals and to evacuate them, if necessary, seems not to be disputed by the great majority of states.[16] Where possible, due regard must be paid to the impact of principles of human rights.

In the case of an armed conflict which is subject to the peace enforcement action of the United Nations Security Council, the rights and duties of quasi-neutrals and non-belligerents whether member states of the United Nations or not may be determined by decision or recommendation of the Security Council. The matter may also be governed by recommendations of the General Assembly, eg, so far as United Nations 'peacekeeping' is concerned (see Chapter 20 below); these have permissive, although not binding force.

Mention should be made of paragraph 6 of article 2 of the United Nations Charter, under which the Organisation is to ensure that non-member states shall conform to the 'Principles' laid down in the article for the maintenance of peace and security; and one of such 'Principles' (see paragraph 5) is to give the United Nations assistance in any action under the Charter, and to refrain from giving assistance to any state against which the United Nations is taking peace enforcement action.

3. ECONOMIC WARFARE AND BLOCKADE: IMPACT UPON (A) NEUTRALS, AND (B) QUASI-NEUTRALS

During the nineteenth century and until the advent of total war in 1914, and again in 1939, neutral trading and shipping relations with belligerents, were regulated largely by the rules of *contraband* and *blockade*.

15. For the effect of Chapter III of the Declaration of London 1909, in laying down different penal consequences according to the nature of the act of unneutral service, see Stone, op cit, ch XVIII, s IV and Dinstein, op cit, pp 105–106.

16. Under article 75 of Protocol I on international armed conflicts, additional to the Geneva Red Cross Conventions of 1949, citizens of neutral or quasi-neutral states, resident in the territory of or otherwise under the power of a contestant state, are to enjoy the 'fundamental guarantees' of humane treatment provided for by that article.

These rules were, in essence, rooted in a limited conception of the economic pressure which could be applied to weaken a belligerent's capacity for war, the main concern of a contestant who resorted to contraband interception, or to blockade, being to interrupt the flow by sea of vital goods, which might help the enemy in its war effort. There was also an assumption underlying the rules that supplies from neutral states would always be channelled directly to coasts or ports of the particular enemy belligerent concerned and not by indirect routes.

However, in the course of the First World War, and again during the Second World War, Great Britain, for whom these wars were life and death struggles, was obliged to challenge the validity of so limited a conception of economic pressure and of so fallacious an assumption, and accordingly departed from the traditional nineteenth century rules of contraband and blockade (see below). Besides, the traditional system was ineffective to deal with stratagems such as the smuggling by neutral seamen of small contraband objects or articles, which might nevertheless be vital to the enemy war effort, and other forms of assistance to the enemy, for example, the transport of neutral technicians for employment in enemy war production.

Moreover, in the Second World War, Great Britain and then the United States (after its entry into the war) adopted far-reaching theories of economic warfare, which were carried into practical execution for the first time on a considerable scale. Under the new concept of economic warfare, economic pressure was not to be limited primarily to the traditional expedients of contraband interception and blockade, but was to be conducted by multifarious other methods and operations, in order effectively to weaken the enemy's economic and financial sinews, and therefore its ability to continue the struggle; for example, through such procedures as the use of 'navicerts'[17] to control 'at source' exports from overseas neutral countries to enemy and European neutral territory, the preemption or so-called 'preclusive purchase' of essential products or materials, the prevention or control of enemy exports, the withholding of credits to neutral suppliers and other forms of financial pressure, and the compulsory rationing of neutral states in essential products and materials so as not to allow an accumulation of excess commodities which might be exported to the enemy, or which might tempt the enemy to invade these states. By 1944–1945, the Allies were able to go so far as uncompromisingly to make European neutrals practically withhold all exports of essential products or materials to Germany.

Moreover, as the war progressed, the purpose was not merely to deny vital goods to the enemy and to ration neutrals, but to conserve all available supplies of scarce products for the Allies.

An almost unlimited range of techniques and expedients, not restricted to contraband and blockade controls, was adopted in the waging of this economic warfare, as is made plain in Professor Medlicott's searching survey[18] of this type of warfare during the Second World War.

---

17. See p 534 below.
18. See *The Economic Blockade* (1952) Vol I and (1959) Vol II in the series, 'History of the Second World War, United Kingdom Civil Series' (ed W.W. Hancock). Professor Medlicott makes it clear that the concept of economic warfare included attacks on the enemy's economy by sabotage behind the enemy front, and bombing of factories and communications; see Vol II at pp 630 et seq.

If any conclusion is justified by the practice of the Second World War as examined in this survey, it is that in conducting economic warfare, a belligerent is now entitled under international law to subject neutrals to any kind of pressure or restriction necessary, either on the one hand to strengthen itself, or on the other hand to weaken the enemy economically and financially, provided: (1) that the inconvenience to neutrals is, as far as possible, minimised; and (2) that the belligerent concerned stops short of causing actual grave injury to neutrals (for example, denying them the bare minimum of food and other necessaries).

The new concept of economic warfare, as thus put into practice, with its wide permissible limits, has by reflex action necessarily had the result, too, of removing a number of the qualifications upon the doctrines of contraband and blockade, which originated in the period when economic pressure in time of war was conceived in the narrowest of terms. It is perhaps not today seriously disputed that the modifications to these two doctrines, made in the course of two World Wars, will endure.

Accordingly, contraband and blockade as separate doctrines of the laws of war and neutrality, must now be treated as special topics within the larger field of economic warfare. It should not, however, be overlooked that in a special case, an operation of blockade may involve primarily naval or military aspects, rather than those of an economic character.

Although from time to time, new expedients of economic warfare were justified ostensibly on the ground of reprisals for violations of international law by the enemy,[19] practice throughout the Second World War showed that Allied belligerents did not rest the validity of economic warfare solely on this narrow basis.

Contraband

Contraband is the designation for such goods as the belligerents consider objectionable because they may assist the enemy in the conduct of war.

The importance of the conception of contraband is due to certain rules enunciated by the Declaration of Paris 1856, which are now recognised to be part of international law. The effect of these may be stated as follows: Belligerents may seize enemy contraband goods which are being carried to an enemy destination on neutral ships, or neutral contraband goods which are being carried to an enemy destination on enemy ships.[20] These rights of seizure are conceded by international law in view of the obvious necessity for belligerents, in the interests of self-preservation, to prevent the importation of articles which may strengthen the enemy.[1]

A distinction is drawn between *absolute* and *relative* contraband. Articles clearly of a warlike or military character are considered to be absolute contraband; for example, arms of all kinds, military clothing, camp equipment,

19. Note, eg, the Reprisals Order-in-Council of 31 July 1940, referred to below, p 535.
20. The same principles are presumably applicable to carriage by air in neutral or enemy *aircraft*, although there appears to be no reported Prize Court case as to the condemnation of aircraft on such grounds.
1. At common law, however, it is not illegal for citizens of the United Kingdom, as a neutral state, to trade in contraband with a belligerent country or to 'run' a blockade; accordingly contracts made with such an object are not illegal under domestic law (see the authorities cited in *Carver's Carriage By Sea* (13th edn, by R. Colinvaux, 1982) Vol I, pp 597–599).

machinery for the manufacture of munitions, and gun-mountings. Articles useful for purposes of peace as well as of war are considered to be relative contraband, for example, food, fuel, field-glasses, railway rolling stock, and if intercepted on their way to the enemy government or to the enemy forces are treated as absolute contraband and are liable to seizure by a hostile belligerent. It is doubtful if the distinction is now of any practical value.

Besides absolute and relative contraband, there is a third class of goods, known as 'free articles', which must never be declared contraband, inasmuch as they are not susceptible to use in war; for example, chinaware and glass, soap, paint and colours, and fancy goods.

So far states have not reached general agreement on what articles fall within each of the three categories mentioned, except that by universal admission instruments of war or warlike materials are absolute contraband. Even jurists and Prize Court judges have seldom been in accord on the matter, and the practice of the states shows little uniformity and many anomalies.

An attempt was made by an instrument known as the Declaration of London 1909, to draw up agreed lists of goods in the three classes, but the Declaration did not come into force for want of ratifications. Both in the First and Second World Wars, the belligerents declared goods to be absolute or relative contraband which in the nineteenth century were universally acknowledged to be non-contraband. Thus almost overnight the pedantic opinions of text-writers, the carefully drafted clauses in treaties, and the weighty judgments of Lord Stowell and other Prize Court judges were relegated to a back store-room, while the belligerents were restrained only by considerations of policy and expediency from declaring every type of article and material to be contraband. The very extensive lists of contraband drawn up by Great Britain in both wars were eloquent testimony to the desuetude of former rules and usages. By the time of the Second World War, both by practice and according to British judicial decisions, the Declaration of London was regarded as devoid of any authority. The impact of 'total war', at first in 1914, and then with much greater effect in 1939, completely revolutionised the conditions of warfare. In view of the enormous range of equipment required for modern war, of the much more advanced use of scientific weapons and instruments, and of the possible production of *ersatz* or substitute war materials, it could scarcely be predicted of any article or substance that it did not have a warlike use. For the sake of self-preservation, belligerents had necessarily to adapt themselves to these exigencies, and the old rules and usages as to contraband were disregarded by them when official lists of contraband covering every conceivable kind of article or material were drawn up.

Destination of contraband; doctrine of continuous voyage or continuous transportation

Usually the simplest case of seizure of contraband is one in which the goods are clearly of hostile destination. A number of cases invariably arise in which the purpose of supplying the enemy is sought to be achieved more indirectly, as where citizens in a neutral state adjacent to enemy territory purchase contraband for resale to the enemy in order to avoid interception at sea.

In circumstances such as these the doctrine of continuous voyage or continuous transportation becomes applicable. This consists in treating an adventure which involves the carriage or goods in the first instance to a neutral port, and then to some ulterior and hostile destination as being for certain purposes one transportation only to an enemy destination, with all the consequences that would attach were the neutral port not interposed. Accordingly, if these goods are contraband, they are liable to seizure. The doctrine was expounded in classical terms by Lord Stowell in *The Maria*.[2]

In the American Civil War, the United States Supreme Court applied the doctrine systematically to nearly all cases of breach of blockade or of contraband. Furthermore, United States courts took it upon themselves to draw presumptions as to hostile destination from all kinds of unexplained facts, for example, if the bill of lading were made out to order, or the manifest of cargo did not disclose the whole cargo, or a consignee were not named, or if the ship or cargo were consigned to a firm known to have acted as an enemy agent, or if there were a notorious trade in contraband between a neutral port and enemy territory.

Until 1909, it was nevertheless doubtful whether the doctrine was subject to general approval; at all events, it was not supported by a uniform practice. However, the Declaration of London 1909, which as mentioned above did not come into force, laid it down that the doctrine applied to absolute contraband, but did not apply to conditional contraband except in a war against an enemy possessing no seaboard.

In the First World War, the doctrine received its fullest executive and judicial application by Great Britain. British Orders-in-Council enunciated the doctrine in the widest terms, going far beyond the terms of the Declaration of London 1909. British courts also applied the doctrine systematically to a large number of cases, and in *The Kim*[3] it was declared that:

'. . . the doctrine of continuous voyage or transportation, both in relation to carriage by sea and to carriage over land, had become part of the law of nations at the commencement of the present war, in accordance with the principles of recognised legal decisions, and with the views of a great body of modern jurists, and also with the practice of nations in recent maritime warfare.'

As illustrating the wide scope of the doctrine the following principles were accepted by British courts: (1) that contraband goods might be seized on their way to a neutral country if there existed an intention to forward them to an enemy destination after their undergoing a process of manufacture; (2) that, notwithstanding that the shippers of contraband goods might be innocent of any intention of an ultimate hostile destination, yet if on the consignees' side the goods were in fact purchased for delivery to the enemy they were liable to confiscation.

The courts of other belligerents also accepted and applied the doctrine of continuous transportation.

In practice, the system of cargo and ship 'navicerts',[4] ie, certificates given by a diplomatic or consular or other representative in a neutral country to a neutral shipper, testifying, as the case might be, that the cargo on board a neutral vessel was not liable to seizure as contraband, or that the voyage of a particular ship

---

2.   (1805) 5 Ch Rob 365.
3.   [1915] P 215 at 275.
4.   'Aircerts' and 'mailcerts' for goods sent from neutral countries by air and mail, were also introduced.

was innocent, left little room for the application of the doctrine of continuous transportation. 'Navicerts' were first introduced by the Government of Queen Elizabeth in 1590, but were not used on a large scale in modern conditions of maritime warfare until 1916 when they were instituted by the Allies. 'Navicerts' were again introduced on the outbreak of the Second World War in 1939. Vessels using 'navicerts' were normally exempted from search, although there was no complete guarantee against interception or seizure, which might take place because of the discovery of fresh facts or because the destination of the cargo had become enemy occupied territory. A 'navicert' might, or course, be refused on grounds which would not be sufficient to justify belligerent seizure of a ship or its cargo, and subsequent condemnation by a Prize Court (see below). For example, at certain stages of the war, 'navicerts' were, temporarily, not granted for the consignment to neutral territory of commodities needed by the Allies, such as rubber and tin.

Originally the mere absence of a 'navicert' was not in itself a ground for seizure or condemnation. However, after the occupation of France and the Low Countries by Germany in June 1940 changed the whole circumstances of the Allied maritime blockade, Britain issued the Reprisals Order-in-Council (dated 31 July 1940), the effect of which was:

a. that goods might become liable to seizure in the absence of a 'navicert' to cover them; and
b. that there was a presumption that 'unnavicerted' goods had an enemy destination.

The Order did not make 'navicerts' compulsory in every sense for neutral shippers, but it heightened the risk of interception and seizure of cargoes by putting the onus on the shipper of establishing the innocence of the shipment. The legality of the Order was of course questioned, but it was justified as a legitimate act of reprisal[5] to simplify the blockade, and to put increased pressure on the enemy, and also possibly as a method of regulating neutral trade through a system of passes.[6]

Neutral vessels were also required to equip themselves with ship warrants, which were granted upon covenants, inter alia, not to engage in contraband trading, to search the ship for smuggled contrabands, etc. In the absence of a ship warrant, 'navicerts' might be refused, and bunkering and other facilities at Allied ports withheld.

By the system of 'navicerts' and ship warrants, British authorities were able, inter alia, to police the smuggling of small contraband objects or articles,[7] the employment of undesirable seamen, and the transport of technicians who might assist the enemy war effort.

---

5. The right of retaliation by a belligerent for a violation of international law by the enemy is a right of the belligerent, not a concession by the neutral. Cf as to reprisals, as a justification for extensions of the doctrine of contraband, Medlicott, op cit, Vol I p 9.
6. The statistics 1943–1945 show that at least 25 per cent of applications for 'navicerts' were refused.
7. 'Navicerts' were refused and ship warrants withdrawn if precautions were not taken by the shipping company and masters concerned to prevent such smuggling.

Consequences of carriage of contraband; condemnation by Prize Courts
Contraband is, in the circumstances mentioned above, liable to seizure, and under certain conditions even the vessel carrying the contraband cargo is liable to seizure. Seizure by a belligerent is admissible only in the open sea or in the belligerent's own territorial waters; seizure in neutral territorial waters would be a violation of neutrality.

According to British and continental practice, the right of a belligerent state to seize contraband cargoes or vessels carrying them is not an absolute one but requires confirmation by the adjudication of a Prize Court established by that state. The origin of Prize Courts and of Prize Law goes back to the Middle Ages when there were frequent captures of piratical vessels. In England, for example, the Court of Admiralty would inquire into the authority of the captor and into the nationality of the captured vessel and of the owners of her goods. This practice was extended to captures made in time of war and it gradually became a recognised customary rule of international law that in time of war the maritime belligerents should be obliged to set up courts to decide whether captures were lawful or not. These courts were called Prize Courts. They are not international courts but municipal courts, although they apply international law largely. Every state is bound by international law to enact only such regulations, or statutes, to govern the operation of Prize Courts, as are in conformity with international law.

The structure of Prize Courts varies in different countries. In certain states, Prize Courts are mixed bodies consisting of judges and administrative officials, but in the United Kingdom and the United States they are exclusively judicial tribunals.[8]

If the Prize Court upholds the legitimacy of the seizure, the cargo or vessel is declared to be 'good prize' and to be confiscated to the captor's state. Jurisdiction is exercised in accordance with international law, unless otherwise directed by statute. The decree of condemnation is accompanied by an order for sale under which the purchaser acquires a title internationally valid. Thenceforward, what becomes of the prize is no concern of international law, but is solely a matter for municipal law to determine.

Seized ships or goods in the custody of the Prize Court pending a decision as to their condemnation or release, may be requisitioned subject to certain limitations, one of which is that there is a real issue to be tried as to the question of condemnation.

Blockade
The law as to blockade represents a further restriction on the freedom of neutral states to trade with belligerents.

A blockade occurs when a belligerent bars access to the enemy coast or part of it for the purpose of preventing ingress or egress of vessels or aircraft of all nations. The blockade is an act of war, and if duly carried out in accordance with the rules of warfare, is effective to deny freedom of passage to the shipping or aircraft of other states. Under the Declaration of Paris 1856, which is

8.   Prize jurisdiction is exercised in the United Kingdom by the Admiralty Court of the Queen's Bench Division of the High Court.

declaratory of prior customary international law, a blockade is binding only if effective, and the effectiveness of a blockade is conditioned by the maintenance of such a force by the belligerent as is 'sufficient really to prevent access to the enemy coast'.

Ships which break a blockade by entering or leaving the blockaded area are liable to seizure by the belligerent operating the blockade in the same way as contraband cargoes, and after capture must be sent to a port for adjudication on their character as lawful prize. Generally, the cargoes carried by such ships will also suffer condemnation by a Prize Court unless those who shipped the goods prove to the court's satisfaction that the shipment was made before they knew or could have known of the blockade.

The practice of states varies greatly as to what is deemed to constitute a breach of blockade. For instance, practice is not uniform on the point whether a neutral vessel must have actual formal notice of the blockade. According to Anglo-American juristic opinion and practice, it is sufficient to establish presumptively that those in charge of the neutral vessel knew that a blockade had been established. The commander of a neutral vessel who sails for an enemy port knowing that it is blockaded at the beginning of the voyage ought to expect that it will be in the same state when he arrives in the vicinity of the port; and anything which can be proved to affect him with knowledge at the date of departure, for example, publication of a declaration of blockade, will render the vessel and its cargo liable to the penalties for breach of blockade. According to the French theory, the neutral vessel is not affected by presumptions as to continuance or cesser of blockade, but the commander of the vessel on approaching the blockaded area is entitled to individual warning from one of the blockading squadrons, the fact of the notification being entered in the vessel's log-book with specific mention of the hour, date, and place of notification. It is only for subsequent attempts to enter the blockaded area that the neutral vessel is liable to seizure.

Apart from the matter of actual or constructive notice to neutral vessels, it is an established rule of international law that a blockade must be properly declared and notified to neutral states with a specific statement as to the date when the blockade begins and the geographical limits of the coastline to which access is barred. Second, in accordance with the rule of effectiveness, the blockade must be maintained by a sufficient and properly disposed force, rendering ingress or egress by other vessels a matter of material danger. This principle is supported by authoritative British judicial pronouncements. Thus Dr Lushington declared in *The Franciska*[9] that:

'. . . (the blockaded place) must be watched by a force sufficient to render the egress or ingress dangerous; or, in other words, save under peculiar circumstances, as fogs, violent winds, and some necessary absences, the force must be sufficient to render the capture of vessels attempting to go in or come out most probable.'

Similarly, Lord Chief Justice Cockburn stated in *Geipel v Smith*:[10]

9. (1855) 2 Ecc & Ad 113 at 120.
10. (1872) LR 7 QB 404 at 410.

'In the eye of the law, a blockade is effective if the enemies' ships are in such numbers and position as to render running the blockade a matter of danger, although some vessels may succeed in getting through.'

The size of the blockading force and the distance at which it operates from the blockaded coast are alike immaterial, provided this test of danger to neutral vessels be satisfied. Thus in the Crimean War in 1854, a single British cruiser commanding the one navigable approach to the Russian port of Riga at a distance of 120 miles was deemed sufficient to constitute a blockade of the port. United States judicial decisions and practice are to the same effect as the British authorities.

In the First World War, the British Navy enforced a 'long-distance' blockade of Germany through ships and squadrons operating often more than one thousand miles from German ports. The objections raised to this type of blockade were that it extended across the approaches to the ports and coastline of neighbouring neutral countries and that it was in many respects ineffective. It was first instituted in 1915 as a reprisal for the German decision to attack British and Allied merchantmen in the waters surrounding the British Isles without regard for the personal safety of the passengers or crew. Under British Orders-in-Council, neutral vessels carrying goods of presumed enemy destination, origin, or ownership could be required to proceed to a British port to discharge their cargoes, and might be forbidden to move to a German port. If neutral vessels under colour of permission to proceed to a neutral port, sailed for a German port, they were liable to seizure and condemnation if subsequently caught. Such a blockade was probably not justified according to the rules followed in the nineteenth century, either as a retaliatory measure or as a blockade in the strict sense of that term. The British Government, however, justified the 'long-distance' blockade of Germany by reference to the changed conditions of war, stating that a modern blockade could only be effective by covering commerce with the enemy passing through neutral ports.[11] The 'long-distance' blockade was reinstituted in 1939 in the Second World War, and its rational justification[12] was likewise the necessity for waging 'total' economic warfare against the enemy. In both wars, France took action similar to that of Great Britain. Without Great Britain's predominant naval power in relation to the enemy, the blockade could not have been enforced.

Belligerent right of visit and search

Co-extensive with the right of seizing contraband or of capturing ships in breach of blockade, belligerents have by long established custom the right to visit and search neutral vessels on the high seas in order to determine the nature of the cargo and to check the destination and neutral character of the vessel. This right must be exercised so as to cause neutral vessels the least possible inconvenience. If suspicious circumstances are disclosed in the case of a

11. Medlicott, op cit, Vol I, p 4, has pointed out that the traditional blockade presupposed 'naval action close to an enemy's coasts', and had 'little relevance to a war in which modern artillery, mines, and submarines made such action impossible, and in which the enemy was so placed geographically that he could use adjacent neutral ports as a channel for supplies'.
12. Apart from the ground of reprisals for illegal enemy activities. See on the British blockade during the Second World War, Tucker 'The Law of War' in 62 *US Naval War College International Law Studies* (1980) 233 at p 243.

particular neutral vessel,[13] that vessel may be taken into port for more extensive inquiry and if necessary for adjudication before a Prize Court.

Formerly the right of visit and search was qualified by severe restrictions, designed to protect neutrals from unnecessary or burdensome interference with their commerce. In both the First and Second World Wars, the exigencies of 'total war' caused belligerents to disregard these limitations. Contrary to the rules that search should precede capture and that it should generally not go further than an examination of the ship's papers and crew and cursory inspection of the cargo, neutral vessels could be required to call at contraband-control bases,[14] or if intercepted on the high seas might be sent to port for thorough searching even in the absence of suspicious circumstances, considerable delays occurring while the vessels were so detained. On the British side, this practice of searching in port instead of on the high seas was justified on three main grounds:

a. the growth in size of modern cargo vessels, rendering concealment easier and a thorough search more lengthy and difficult;
b. the danger from submarines while the search was being conducted;
c. the need for considering the circumstances of the shipment in conjunction with civilian authorities, for example, of the Ministry of Economic Warfare.

Several international law purists criticised the British defence of the practice, but the overpowering circumstances which rendered the practice necessary could not be gainsaid.

This inconvenience to neutral vessels could, for all practical purposes, be avoided by obtaining a 'navicert'[15].

Economic warfare and quasi-neutrals or non-belligerents

Generally speaking, in the absence of a specific agreement that belligerent rights shall be applicable to a non-war armed conflict, a contestant cannot, in regard to quasi-neutrals or non-belligerents, resort to contraband interception or to blockade. Yet in the course of the India–Pakistan conflict, in September 1965, measures closely resembling a blockade were adopted, although not recognised as such by third states, save to the extent of making arrangements to overcome difficulties as to the passage of their shipping.[16] Again, in the case of the India–Pakistan hostilities of December 1971, both India and Pakistan officially announced what articles would be treated as contraband.[17]

---

13. There is a right to *detain*, in addition to visiting and searching, provided that there are reasonable grounds for suspicion, appearing in connection with the search; see *The Mim* [1947] P 115.
14. See Medlicott, op cit, Vol II, p 154. Search would also include the examination of mail, and ascertaining whether any passengers possibly useful to the enemy, eg technicians, were being transported.
15. See above p 534.
16. As to the coastal control operated by the French Government 1956–59 (of the nature of a quasi-blockade), with regard to the Algerian conflict, see R. Pinto (1965) I Hague Recueil des Cours 546–548. In the course of the 'incursion' into Cambodia (Khmer Republic) in May 1970, United States and South Vietnamese warships cut off supply routes by sea to a stretch of the Cambodian coastline in what appeared to be a partial blockade; however, the existence of a blockade was officially denied.
17. Certain non-belligerent maritime countries, eg, the United States, drew the attention of ships of their registry to these announcements; see as to the United States, 66 AJIL (1972) 386–387. For the texts of India's contraband declaration, and Pakistan's contraband proclamation, see ibid.

However, apart from matters of contraband or blockade, contestants can have recourse to any means of economic pressure, notwithstanding that this may cause damage or inconvenience to quasi-neutrals or non-belligerents, although there is possibly a duty to minimise the damage or inconvenience as far as possible.

Where the conflict is one subject to the peace enforcement jurisdiction of the United Nations Security Council, quasi-neutrals, whether member states of the United Nations or not, must submit to any measures of economic warfare[18] decided by the Security Council, although if they find themselves affected by special economic problems arising out of the action taken by the Security Council, they may consult that body regarding a solution of such problems (see article 50 of the United Nations Charter). United Nations 'peacekeeping' operations (see Chapter 20 below), raise very different considerations, as here we are in the area primarily of General Assembly recommendations, which leave room for states to opt in, or out of support for economic measures in aid of 'peacekeeping'.

18. This could include the 'complete or partial interruption of economic relations' (see art 41 of the Charter).

PART 6

International institutions

CHAPTER 20

International institutions[1]

1 THEIR STATUS AND FUNCTIONS AS SUBJECTS OF INTERNATIONAL LAW

As we have seen in a previous chapter,[2] the subjects of international law include not only states, but international institutions such as the United Nations, the International Labour Organisation, and similar bodies.[3] The word 'institution' is here used in its widest sense as the general name for the multiplicity of creations for associating states in common enterprises.

Although strictly speaking the structure and working of these bodies and associations are primarily the concern of that department of political science known as international organisation or administration, their activities nonetheless materially impinge upon the field of international law. It is important to see in what way they come within the range of international law or contribute towards its development.

In the first place, just as the functions of the modern state and the rights, duties, and powers of its instrumentalities are governed by a branch of municipal law called state consitutional law, so international institutions are similarly

1. For general works on the subject, see D. W. Bowett *The Law of International Institutions* (4th edn, 1982); R. L. Bindschedler 'International Organisations; General Aspects' *Encyclopaedia of Public International Law* Vol 5 (1983) pp 119–140; Henkin, Pugh, Schachter and Smit *International Law; Cases and Materials* (2nd edn, 1987) pp 318 et seq; H. G. Schermers *International Institutional Law* (1974, 3 vols); Kirgis *International Organisations in their Legal Setting* (1977); and Reuter *International Institutions* (1958).
2. See Chapter 3, above, pp 57-58.
3. The expansion in number, and in the scope and functions of international organisations has been remarkable during the present century. By 1950 there were, according to an official United States publication, *International Organisations in which the United States Participates* (1950), over 200 international bodies, of which about 60 could be described as major international institutions. Since 1950 the number has materially increased; see *United States Contributions to International Organisations* (1976) passim. The emergence of a very large number of regional organisations throughout the world in the post-1950 period has undoubtedly contributed to this increase. In regard to the history of the growth of international organisations since the latter part of the nineteenth century, see Bowett, op cit, pp 1–13, Potter *Introduction to the Study of International Organisation* (1948), and Mangone *A Short History of International Organisation* (1954) ch 3.

conditioned by a body of rules that may well be described as international constitutional law. These international bodies, having important duties to perform on behalf of the international community, whether of a world-wide or regional character, provide that community with its constitutional framework.

This constitutional structure does not follow precisely the same pattern as in the constitutions of modern states, but there are significant analogies. For instance international institutions perform as organs of the international society a large number of functions which can be classified as executive, legislative, and judicial in the same manner as the functions of modern states. As to international executive functions, it is true that there is no central executive organ with the same degree of authority over the international community as any government wields over a modern state, but the administrative powers that would have been vested in such a central international body if it had existed, are possessed cumulatively by, and distributed over a number of, international institutions, each with separate and different responsibilities; for example, the executive function of maintaining or enforcing world peace belongs to the United Nations, the supervision of world labour conditions is a special power of the International Labour Organisation (ILO), and the improvement of world education and learning is a particular duty of the United Nations Educational, Scientific and Cultural Organisation (UNESCO). If these individual responsibilities were discharged in toto by one instead of by several international bodies, the world would possess the organic counterpart of the executive in a modern state.

International legislative functions are performed on a limited scale by several organs, including the United Nations General Assembly, the International Labour Conference, and the World Health Assembly. To a similarly restricted extent, international judicial functions are vested in the International Court of Justice, and can be vested in other international tribunals.

However, there is no such thing as a separation of powers under the constitutions of most international institutions, which may, through their organs,[4] exercise legislative or judicial, or quasi-legislative or quasi-judicial powers, in the same way as they carry out administrative or executive functions. Nor are certain international institutions executive organs in the strict sense, being consultative and advisory only.

Varied indeed may be the legal structure of these organisations; they may be true corporate entities, collectivities of states functioning through organs taking decisions,[5] or loose unincorporated associations meeting only in periodical conferences, sometimes largely hinging on an element of continuity represented by a secretariat or secretarial bureau.[6]

Besides, there are three important general points to be noted:

4. For instance, the Commission of the European Economic Community (Common Market) under the Treaty of Rome of 25 March 1957, establishing the Community, exercises at the same time, regulatory, quasi-judicial and administrative powers.
5. See classification in *South West Africa Cases, (Second Phase)* ICJ 1966, 6 at 30.
6. Eg, the Hague Conference on Private International Law. However, even an unincorporated international organisation may have, according to its charter or by reason of its contractual or other activities, the character of a legal entity, separate from its members; see *Maclaine Watson & Co Ltd v Department of Trade and Industry* (the International Tin Council Case), [1989] Ch 72, [1988] 3 All ER 257, CA; [1990] 2 AC 418, [1989] 3 All ER 523, HL.

1. The functions of certain international institutions may be directed primarily to inspiring co-operation between states, ie, so called '*promotional*' activities, and only in a secondary degree to the carrying out directly of any necessary duties, ie, so-called '*operational*' activities. Thus the Food and Agriculture Organisation of the United Nations (FAO) and the World Health Organisation (WHO) are much more 'promotional' than 'operational' bodies.
2. Even so far as they are 'operational', international institutions are as a rule empowered only to investigate or recommend, rather than to make binding decisions.
3. In most instances, international institutions are but little removed from an international conference, in the sense that any corporate or organic decision depends ultimately on a majority decision of the member states, ie, the agreement of the corporators.[7]

Most international institutions are keyed not so much to the taking of binding executive decisions, as to the making of non-mandatory recommendations for the guidance of their organs, and of their member states.

Apart from the law and practice (based on their constitutions and on general principles of international law) of such bodies, there is another direction in which international institutions may influence the development of international law. In the past, when states were almost exclusively the subjects of the law of nations, the traditional body of international law developed through custom, treaty, and arbitral decisions as the product of the relations of states inter se. But international institutions, as subjects of international law, can have relations not only between themselves, but also with other subjects including states, so that in addition to the relations between states, we have the two following kinds of relations that can lead to the formation of new rules of international law: (1) relations between states and international institutions; and (2) relations between international institutions themselves. This was strikingly demonstrated by the conclusion of the Vienna Convention of 1986 on the law of treaties between States and International Organisations or between International Organisations. Already there have been significant instances of rules evolving from these two relations. As to (1), relations between states and international institutions, in 1948, for example, there arose the question whether in respect of injuries suffered by its agents in Palestine (including the assassination of Count Folke Bernadotte, United Nations Mediator), the United Nations could claim compensation as against a de jure or de facto government, even if not a government of a member state of the organisation, for the damage to itself through such injuries. Pursuant to a request for an advisory opinion on this point, the International Court of Justice decided in 1949 that the United Nations as an international institution was entitled to bring such a claim.[8] With regard to (2), relations of international

---

7. It is a question of construction of the relevant instruments or treaties whether the corporators (ie the member states) are entitled to exercise any powers appertaining to the institution, or whether this is a matter of organic or institutional action only; *South West Africa Cases, (Second Phase)* ICJ 1966, 6 at 29.
8. See *Advisory Opinion on Reparation for Injuries Suffered in the Service of the United Nations* ICJ 1949, 174.

institutions inter se, the practice of these bodies in concluding agreements with each other is materially affecting the rules of law and procedure concerning international transactions.

That is quite apart, too, from the relations between international institutions and individuals, which, as in the case of relations between states and individuals, already foreshadow the growth of important new principles of international law. An illustration is to be found in the Advisory Opinion, just mentioned, of the International Court of Justice, where the Court had to consider whether the United Nations, in addition to suing for compensation for the damage to itself through injuries suffered by its agents, could also recover damages for the actual loss or harm caused to such agents, or to the persons (for example, relatives) entitled through them to compensation. In effect, the question was whether the United Nations could espouse the claims of its agents in the same way as states, under the rules of state responsibility for international delinquencies, can sponsor claims by their nationals. This involved reconciling the dual position of agents of the United Nations, as servants on the one hand of the Organisation, and as nationals on the other hand entitled to the diplomatic protection of their own states. The solution adopted by the majority of the Court was that the United Nations was entitled to bring such a claim, inasmuch as its right to do so was founded on the official status of its agents irrespective of their nationality, and was therefore not inconsistent with the agents' privilege of receiving diplomatic protection from their own states.[9]

One general consideration needs to be stressed. The true nature and purpose of present-day international institutions cannot be understood unless we realise that certain of these bodies represent one kind of instrumentality whereby states are associated in a common purpose of improving human welfare.[10]

Finally, reference should be made to the regional international institutions, the purposes of which are largely integrative and functional, such as the European Union. These would require a study in themselves, to such an extent do they constitute novel precedents in the law of international organisations.[11] Nor are they necessarily limited in their scope to the region or community which is being integrated; their ramifications may extend further through 'association' conventions or Agreements as, eg, the three Lomé Conventions successively concluded in 1975, 1979 and 1984 respectively associating the European Community with certain African, Caribbean, and Pacific States.

---

9. ICJ 1949, 184-186. See also the advisory opinion of the International Court of Justice in *Applicability of Article VI, Section 22, of the Convention on the Privileges and Immunities of the United Nations*, ICJ 1989, 177.
10. Indeed, the whole field of action of many international institutions has become dominated in the last decade by the aspect of aid and technical assistance to less-developed countries.
11. On regional institutions generally, see Part Two, 'Regional Institutions' (pp 159–251) of Bowett *The Law of International Institutions* (1982), and Henkin, Pugh, Schachter, and Smit *International Law; Cases and Materials* (2nd edn, 1987) ch 19, 'Regional Economic Communities' (pp 1413–1482).

2. GENERAL LEGAL NATURE AND CONSTITUTIONAL STRUCTURE

Functions and legal capacity

International institutions are defined by reference to their legal functions and responsibilities, each such institution having its own limited field of activity. The constitutions of these bodies usually set out their purposes, objects, and powers in special clauses. For example, article 1 of the United Nations Charter defines the 'Purposes' of the United Nations under four heads, of which two in particular are the maintenance of international peace and security, and the development of friendly relations among nations based on respect for the principle of equal rights and self-determination of peoples. Similarly the constitutions of other international bodies, for example, of the International Labour Organisation (see Preamble and article 1 referring to the 'objects' of the Organisation), and of the Food and Agriculture Organisation of the United Nations (see Preamble and article 1 referring to the Organisation's 'Functions'), contain provisions defining their special objects and responsibilities.

The definition in each constitution of the international body's particular field of activity is analogous to the 'objects' clause in the memorandum of association of a limited company under British companies legislation. In both cases, the corporate powers of the international institution on the one hand and of the limited company on the other, are determined by the statement of functions or objects. The analogy can be carried further inasmuch as the recent practice in the constitutions of international organs of defining the 'objects' in as general and comprehensive a manner as possible resembles the present-day methods of company lawyers in drafting 'objects' clauses in very wide terms to preclude any doubts later arising as to the legal capacity of the company concerned.

As international institutions are defined and limited by their constitutional powers, they differ basically from states as subjects of international law. In their case, problems such as those raised by the sovereignty or jurisdiction of states cannot arise, or at least cannot arise in the same way. Almost every activity is prima facie within the competence of a state under international law, whereas practically the opposite principle applies to an international organ, namely, that any function, not within the express terms of its constitution, is prima facie outside its powers. As the International Court of Justice has said referring to the United Nations:[12]

> 'Whereas a State possesses the totality of international rights and duties recognised by international law, the rights and duties of an entity such as the Organisation must depend upon its purposes and functions as specified or implied in its constituent documents and developed in practice.'

Thus no international body can legally overstep its constitutional powers. For example, the International Labour Organisation cannot constitutionally purport to exercise the peace enforcement functions of the United Nations Security Council, and order (say) a cease-fire in the event of hostilities between certain states.

12. ICJ 1949, 180.

Besides its express powers, an international organ may have under its constitution such functions as 'are conferred upon it by necessary implication as being essential to the performance of its duties'.[13] Thus in the Advisory Opinion mentioned above on *Reparation for Injuries Suffered in the Service of the United Nations*,[14] the majority of the International Court of Justice held that by implication from its Charter, the United Nations had the power of exercising diplomatic protection over its agents, and could therefore sponsor claims on behalf of such agents against governments for injuries received in the course of their official duties. In a later Advisory Opinion,[15] the Court held that the United Nations General Assembly had implied power to create a judicial or administrative tribunal, which might give judgments binding the General Assembly itself. There is some weight of opinion to the effect that in appropriate cases, an international institution may possess impliedly not only such powers as are necessary for the performance of its duties as outlined in its constituent instrument, but also powers which may be incidental or related to such duties, or the due performance of such duties.[16]

In relation to the corporate nature of international bodies, the question arises whether they possess legal personality: (a) at international law; and (b) at municipal law.

In the case of the League of Nations, although the Covenant did not expressly confer juridical personality, the general view was that the League had both international and municipal legal personality. This was based partly on the principle that such personality was implicitly necessary for the efficient performance by the League of its functions, and partly on its practice in repeatedly acting as a corporate person, for example concluding agreements with the Swiss Government, taking over property and funds, etc.

The constitution of the League's present successor—the United Nations—likewise contained no express provision as to legal personality, the draftsmen assuming that this was more or less implicit from the context of the Charter taken as a whole, in particular, article 43 of the Charter, enabling the Security Council to enter into military agreements with member states. It was however provided in article 104 of the Charter that the United Nations should enjoy in the territory of each of its members 'such legal capacity as may be necessary for the exercise of its functions and the fulfilment of its purposes'. Subsequently, in February 1946, the United Nations General Assembly approved a Convention on the Privileges and Immunities of the United Nations which by article 1 provided that the United Nations should possess 'juridical personality' and have

13. ICJ 1949, 182, following the Permanent Court on this point.
14. ICJ 1949, 174.
15. See *Advisory Opinion on Effect of Awards made by the United Nations Administrative Tribunal* ICJ 1954, 47. The United Nations has, semble, also implied power: (1) To undertake the temporary administration of territory, as part of a peaceful settlement of a dispute between two states, and with their consent; cf the assumption of temporary administration of West New Guinea 1962–1963 by the United Nations Temporary Executive Authority (UNTEA) under the Indonesia–Netherlands Agreement of 15 August 1962. (2) To borrow money by way of bonds or other securities for its purposes under the Charter; cf the General Assembly Resolution of 20 December 1961, authorising the issue of United Nations bonds to a total of 200 million dollars.
16. Bowett, op cit, pp 337–338.

the capacity to contract, to acquire and dispose of immovable and movable property, and to institute legal proceedings. The Convention was followed by legislation in several states, but according to the municipal law of certain countries,[17] under the Convention in conjunction with article 104 of the Charter, the United Nations would probably be regarded as having legal personality even without such legislation. In this way, the municipal legal personality of the United Nations may be considered well established. As to the Organisation's international legal personality, the International Court of Justice in its Advisory Opinion mentioned above, on the right of the United Nations to claim compensation for injuries to its agents, decided that the United Nations is an international legal person, having such status even in its relations with non-member states.[18]

Apart from the United Nations Charter, the constitutions of other international institutions, both general and regional,[19] contain provisions similar to article 104 of the Charter or to article 1 of the Convention on the Privileges and Immunities of the United Nations (see, for example, article 39 of the Constitution of the International Labour Organisation, article XV (1) of the Constitution of the Food and Agriculture Organisation of the United Nations, and article IV (1) of the articles of Agreement of the International Monetary Fund). In accordance with the Advisory Opinion of the International Court of Justice, mentioned above, the majority of these institutions would be deemed to possess international legal personality. As to municipal legal personality, however, the various provisions in their constitutions reflect no coherent doctrine as to how such personality is to be recognised at municipal law. For instance, article 47 of the International Civil Aviation Convention of 1944, dealing with the legal capacity of the International Civil Aviation Organisation (ICAO), provides that:

> 'The Organisation shall enjoy in the territory of each contracting State such legal capacity as may be necessary for the performance of its functions. Full juridical personality shall be granted wherever compatible with the Constitution and laws of the State concerned.'

This formula seems to leave states parties free to grant or withhold the privilege of legal personality if their municipal law so permits, whereas the corresponding provisions in most other constitutions of international bodies bind states members fully to recognise such personality.

Classification
It is difficult to suggest a satisfactory classification of international institutions.[20]

Classification of such bodies according to functions, for example as economic, political, social, etc, or even as judicial, legislative, and administrative, leads to difficulty owing to the overlapping of their responsibilities. It is likewise unsatisfactory to classify international organisations according to whether, on

17. As to whether art 104 is 'self-executing' in the United States, see above, p 75, n 17.
18. ICJ 1949, 179–180.
19. See, as to the European Economic Community (Common Market), arts 210–211 of the Treaty of Rome of 25 March 1957, establishing the Community.
20. See Bowett, op cit, pp 10–12.

the one hand, their constituent instruments are in the form of a convention between states, or, on the other hand, these instruments are in the form of a convention between governments; as regards the major permanent international organisations now currently operating, some of which are based on inter-state constituent instruments, others on the intergovernmental form of such instruments, it is difficult to discern reasons of substance for one rather than the other form.

The possible distinction between: (a) global or world-wide bodies, for example, the United Nations and the International Civil Aviation Organisation (ICAO), and (b) regional bodies, for example, the South Pacific Commission, and the Council of Europe, will become less important in time, because of the general tendency of global bodies to establish their own regional organs or regional associations.

A suggested distinction is that of international institutions into those which are *supranational* and those which are not. A *supranational* body is generally considered to be one which has power to take decisions, directly binding upon individuals, institutions, and enterprises, as well as upon the governments of the states in which they are situated, and which they must carry out notwithstanding the wishes of such governments. The European Coal and Steel Community, created by the Treaty of 18 April 1951, is regarded as such a supranational body, inasmuch as it may exercise direct powers of this nature in regard to coal, iron and steel in the territories of its member states. So also is the European Economic Community (Common Market), established by the Treaty of Rome of 25 March 1957, now integrated within the European Union. International bodies, not of the supranational type, can only act, or execute decisions by or through member states. The defect in this classification resides in the fact that the word 'supranational' is one which lends itself so easily to misunderstandings.

Then there is also the special category of international public corporations, controlled by governments, as shareholders, or otherwise. These differ from the usual type of international organisations insofar as they are corporations governed by the municipal law of the place where their headquarters are situated, as well as by the conventions establishing them. An illustration is the European Company for the Chemical Processing of Irradiated Fuels (EUROCHEMIC) established under the Convention of 20 December 1957.

Co-ordination of international institutions

The framers of the League of Nations Covenant and of the United Nations Charter both attempted to solve the problem of integrating international institutions and co-ordinating their working. Their purpose was a highly practical one, to ensure that these bodies should function as an organic whole, instead of as a group of dispersed and isolated agencies.

Concrete and detailed provisions for the co-ordination of international bodies were included in the United Nations Charter. Their effect may be summarised as follows:

a.   The international institutions described as 'the various *specialised agencies*,[1]

---

1.   It should be noted that the language of art 57 seems somewhat narrower than the corresponding provisions of art 24 of the League of Nations Covenant, and does not cover all organs carrying on any kind of international activity.

established by intergovernmental agreement and having wide international responsibilities, as defined in their basic instruments, in economic, social, cultural, educational, health and related fields', were to be brought into relationship with the United Nations through agreements entered into between these institutions and the United Nations Economic and Social Council, such agreements to be approved by the United Nations General Assembly and by each such institution (articles 57 and 63, paragraph 1, of the Charter).

b. The United Nations Economic and Social Council was empowered to co-ordinate the activities of the international institutions entering into such agreements through consultation with and recommendations made to them, and through recommendations made to the General Assembly and member states of the United Nations (article 63, paragraph 2).

c. The United Nations, through its organs, was to make further recommendations for co-ordinating the policies and activities of these institutions (article 58).

d. Regular reports and observations thereon were to be obtained from these institutions through the Economic and Social Council in order mainly to ensure that they were giving effect to the recommendations made to them (article 64).

e. The Economic and Social Council was empowered to arrange for reciprocal representation between it and the 'specialised agencies' at their respective meetings (article 70).

Parallel provisions for co-ordination are also to be found in the constitutions of other international bodies, both of the 'specialised agencies' and of institutions not in this category, including provisions for relationship with the United Nations, for common personnel arrangements, and for common or mutual representation.[2]

Through the application in practice of these provisions the net of co-ordination has been cast not only wider, but deeper. The 'specialised agencies'—the name applied to the bodies brought or to be brought into relationship with the United Nations—have become for all practical purposes major operating arms of the United Nations, or to use a striking phrase in one official report, its 'specialised organisational tools'.[3] Further, through its Economic and Social Council (ECOSOC), the United Nations has been able to make continuous scrutiny of the activities of the 'specialised agencies' to ensure that they function with some kind of organic unity.

2. Eg, co-operative relations between the Organisation of American States (OAS) and the United Nations are provided for in the Charter of the former, and the Treaty of Rome of 25 March 1957, establishing the European Economic Community (Common Market), provides that the Community may conclude agreements with international organisations, creating an association for joint action, etc (see art 238).

3. Report of President of the United States to Congress on the United Nations 1948, p 12. Although not a specialised agency, but unofficially known as a 'related agency', the International Atomic Energy Agency (IAEA) has also been brought into working relationship with the United Nations, and with specialised agencies having a particular interest in atomic energy, by special agreements with these institutions.

Co-ordination and co-operation are also provided for by inter-organisation agreements, consisting of:

1. Relationship agreements between United Nations and the specialised agencies under article 57 and 63 of the Charter.
2. Agreements between the specialised agencies themselves.
3. Agreements between a specialised agency and a regional organisation (for example, that between the International Labour Organisation and the Organisation of American States).
4. Agreements between regional organisations.

Category (1) of the relationship agreements between the United Nations and specialised agencies contain elaborate provisions in a more or less common form for:

a. reciprocal representation at their respective meetings;
b. enabling United Nations organs and the specialised agencies to place items on each other's agenda:
c. the reciprocal exchange of information and documents;
d. uniformity of staff arrangements under common methods and procedures;
e. consideration by the specialised agencies of recommendations made to them by the United Nations and for reports by them on the action taken to give effect to these recommendations;
f. uniformity of financial and budget arrangements;
g. undertakings by each specialised agency to assist the United Nations General Assembly and Security Council in carrying out their decisions; and
h. obtaining Advisory Opinions from the International Court of Justice with regard to matters arising within the scope of the activities of each specialised agency.[4]

It is true that besides the bodies with which the United Nations has entered into relationship as specialised agencies, there are numerous other international institutions that have not been integrated into the one general system aimed at by the Charter. Where the definition of specialised agencies in article 57 is wide enough to cover them, these outside international organs will no doubt in due course become the subject of relationship agreements with the United Nations.[5] There is a committee of the Economic and Social Council known as the

4. From time to time, also, the United Nations General Assembly and the Economic and Social Council have adopted resolutions designed to make co-ordination more effective, emphasising the necessity of avoiding duplication of effort, and calling for a greater concentration of effort on programmes demanding priority of effort, with particular reference, recently, to economic, social, and human rights activities. A recent illustration was the lengthy resolution adopted by the General Assembly on 19 December 1986 for a detailed review and study of the efficiency of the administrative and financial functioning of the United Nations.

5. International, regional, and national *non-governmental* organisations (NGOs), also, may collaborate on a *consultative* basis with the Economic and Social Council under art 71 of the United Nations Charter. The Council has granted to certain such bodies 'consultative status' in categories I and II respectively. Those of category I status may propose items for inclusion in the provisional agenda of the Council and its commissions. The Council may, besides, consult ad hoc with certain non-governmental bodies, not enjoying category I or category II status, but which are on the Council's Roster. All such bodies may send observers to meetings, and may

Committee on Negotiations with Inter-Governmental Agencies which, if necessary, can act upon the specific instructions of the Council, directing it to negotiate with specific international organisations determined by the Council.

The Economic and Social Council has a primary responsibility by consultation and other action for maintaining co-ordination, particularly in the economic, social, and human rights fields.[6]

The specialised agencies are entitled to attend meetings of the Economic and Social Council and of its subsidiary organs, and to make statements at such meetings. They also may attend and make statements at meetings of the Main Committees of the General Assembly, at meetings of the subsidiary bodies thereof, and at United Nations Conferences. Similar rights are enjoyed by the 'related agencies', an expression that covers organisations for practical purposes assimilated to specialised agencies, such as the International Atomic Energy Agency (IAEA) and the General Agreement on Tariffs and Trade (GATT).

On 3 August 1962, the Economic and Social Council set up a Special Committee on Co-ordination with the following principal duties: (a) to keep under review the activities of the United Nations family in the economic, social, human rights, and development fields; (b) to study the reports of the Administrative Committee on Co-ordination, appropriate reports of the United Nations organs, the annual reports of agencies in the United Nations family, and other relevant documents, and to submit its conclusions to the Council in the form of a concise statement of the issues and problems in the domain of co-ordination arising from these documents, which should call for special attention by the Council. This Special Committee, whose name was changed in 1966 to that of the 'Committee for Programme and Co-ordination', proceeded to hold joint meetings with the Administrative Committee on Co-ordination and the Advisory Committee on Administrative and Budgetary Questions. By resolution of 13 January 1970, the Council reconstituted the Committee for Programme and Co-ordination to perform wider programming, reviewing, and co-ordinating functions as to the activities of the United Nations family in economic and social fields, and enlarged the Committee to a membership of 21 (formerly 16).

A major step was taken on 24 May 1976, when the Economic and Social Council, in the light of the fact that the economic and social sectors of the United Nations system were currently under examination by an ad hoc Committee on the Restructuring of the Economic and Social Sectors of the United Nations system, approved consolidated terms of reference for the Committee for Programme and Co-ordination. An important provision of these terms of reference was that the Committee should 'function as *the main subsidiary organ* of the Economic and Social Council and the General Assembly for planning, programming and co-ordination'.[6] Wide-ranging powers were conferred on the Committee, including powers as to programmes and priorities, and as to guidance to be given to the United Nations Secretariat in the implementation of Council

---

consult with the United Nations Secretariat. NGOs play an influential role in United Nations decision-making processes. Cf also the Council of Europe Convention of 1986 on the Recognition of the Legal Personality of International Non-Governmental Organisations.

6.   The first session of the Committee in its capacity as the main subsidiary planning, programming, and co-ordination organ of the Council and Assembly took place from 10 May to 11 June 1976.

and Assembly resolutions, while it was to assist the Council in the performance of the Council's co-ordination functions within the United Nations system. For the purpose of the due performance of its responsibilities, the Committee was to study the reports of the Administrative Committee on Co-ordination, of the Joint Inspection Unit, and of the institutions within the United Nations family, while it was to co-operate and consult jointly with the Administrative Committee on Co-ordination and the Joint Inspection Unit. Under a resolution of the UN General Assembly, adopted on 17 December 1987 on the recommendation of ECOSOC, the Committee was from 1988 onwards to be composed of 34 member states, elected for three-year terms on the basis of the following geographical distribution: 9 seats for African states, 7 for Asian states, 7 for Latin American and Caribbean states, 7 for Western European and other states, and 4 for Eastern European states.

Organic structure and composition
The organic structure and composition of the specialised agencies and other international bodies vary in the case of each institution. Nevertheless, they have some features in common:

(1) Constitutional seat or headquarters
The constitutions of international institutions usually fix the location of the headquarters, but this is sometimes left by the member states for later decision or agreement with the government of the territory of the site.

(2) Membership
The constitution usually provides that original signatories may become members upon ratification or acceptance of the instrument, while other states may become members upon admission by a special majority vote of the competent organs of the particular international body concerned. Where a clause in a constitution defines the conditions under which such other states may be admitted to membership, it is imperative, according to the International Court of Justice,[7] that such conditions be strictly adhered to. Under certain constitutions of the specialised agencies (for example, the Constitution of the United Nations Educational, Scientific and Cultural Organisation, UNESCO) the privilege of admission to membership on acceptance of the constitution is allowed to member states of the United Nations. In the case of certain specialised agencies, too, for example, the World Health Organisation (WHO) and the International Telecommunication Union (ITU), territories or groups of territories may be admitted to 'associate membership', a status which entitles them to participation in the benefits of the organisation without voting rights or the right to become a member of an executive organ. Under the Constitution of the International Labour Organisation (ILO), territories may be represented at the International Labour Conference by or through advisers appointed to the delegation of the member state responsible for the territory or territories concerned.

7.   See ICJ 1948, 61 et seq.

(3) Conditions of withdrawal by, or expulsion and suspension of, members

There is no uniform or coherent practice in this matter. For example, although the constituent instruments of the majority of international organisations contain express provisions for a right of a state to withdraw from membership, no article of the United Nations Charter confers an express right of withdrawal upon member states. Most usually members are allowed to give a twelve months' written notice of intention to withdraw; but the provisions of the constitutions vary as to the minimum period of time following admission to membership, when notice may be given; and as to whether the effectiveness of the notice depends upon the prior performance of financial or other obligations. As regards expulsion of members for failure to fulfil obligations, less value is attached to this as a disciplinary measure than before the Second World War; the modern tendency is to make no provision for expulsion, but to allow suspension of a member's privileges, including voting rights, for default in financial or other obligations, until these obligations are met.

(4) Organs[8]

Here, there is a necessary distinction between *principal organs*, and *regional* and *subsidiary organs*.

The standard *principal organs* consist of:

a. A policy-making body known usually as an 'Assembly' or 'Congress', representative of all member states, with power to supervise the working of the organisation, and to control its budget, and, more frequently, also with power to adopt conventions and other measures, and to make recommendations for national legislation (for example, the Assembly of the World Health Organisation, WHO). Variations may occur in the frequency of sessions (varying from annual to quinquennial meetings), the number of delegates, the range of this organ's supervisory powers, and the authority which may be delegated to the smaller executive body (see below).

b. A smaller executive body or council, usually elected by the policy-making organ from among the delegates to it, and representative of only a specific number of member states. Sometimes it is required that the members of this body should be selected so as to be fairly representative of the states of most importance in the specialised field (aviation, shipping and maritime transport, and industrial production) in which the organisation is active; this is so, for instance, with the Council of the International Civil Aviation Organisation (ICAO), and with the Governing Body of the International Labour Organisation (ILO). In other instances, it is required that this body should be fairly representative of all geographical areas, as, for example, with the Executive Council of the Universal Postal Union (UPU). Or, also the members may be chosen from different states, but with primary emphasis on their personal or technical qualifications, as in the case of the Executive Board of the United Nations Educational, Scientific, and Cultural Organisation (UNESCO), and the Executive Committee of the World Meteorological Organisation (WMO). The degree of executive authority of

8. See on this subject, Z. M. Klepachi *The Organs of International Organizations* (1978).

this organ may vary from the level of supreme control in regard to the member states over a particular subject matter (as in the case of the High Authority of the European Coal and Steel Community, under the Treaty of 18 April 1951), to the level of mere advice and recommendation as in the case of the Council of the International Maritime Organisation (IMO).[9]

c.   A Secretariat or international civil service staff. Most constituent instruments of international organisations stipulate that the responsibilities of their staff shall be exclusively international in character, and that they are not to receive instructions from outside authorities. To reinforce this position, such instruments generally contain undertakings by the member states to respect the international character of the responsibilities of the staff and not to seek to influence any of their nationals belonging to such staff in the discharge of their responsibilities.

As to the international position of members of Secretariats, a serious problem arose in 1952 and subsequent years with regard to the question of 'loyalty' investigations of officials by the government of the country of which they were nationals. Although such personnel should abide by the laws of their country of nationality, particularly if the headquarters of the institution be situated in that country, it is open to question whether they should be liable to dismissal or other injurious consequences for refusing legitimately on grounds of privilege to answer questions by commissions of inquiry regarding their loyalty to their country, and their alleged involvement in subversive activities previously, or while engaged upon their international responsibilities.[10] These are matters which require definition by international convention.

Regional and subsidiary organs

These have been created with relative freedom, thus accentuating the tendency towards decentralisation in modern international institutions. Instances of this flexibility of approach are:

a.   Regional conferences, for example, of the International Labour Organisation (ILO), or regional councils, for example of the Food and Agriculture Organisation of the United Nations (FAO).

9.   Formerly known as the Intergovernmental Maritime Consultative Organisation (IMCO). The new name of this body became effective as from 22 May 1982.
10. In November 1952, the Secretary-General of the United Nations sought the opinion of a special committee of jurists on this question and related aspects. The opinion given, while emphasising the necessity for independence of the staff of the Secretariat, was none the less to the effect that a refusal to answer such questions on grounds of privilege created a suspicion of guilt which, in a suitable case, ought to disentitle the employee to remain a Secretariat official. See *United Nations Bulletin* (1952) Vol 13, pp 601–603. This opinion was acted upon by the Secretary-General. The United Nations Administrative Tribunal did not, however, give full support to the committee's views; cf its judgment in *Harris v Secretary-General of the United Nations* (1953). The Administrative Tribunal of the International Labour Organisation held in several cases, that a refusal to answer loyalty interrogatories was not a sufficient ground for declining to renew the appointment of an official of the United Nations Educational Scientific and Cultural Organisation (UNESCO); see, eg, its judgment in *Duberg*'s Case (1955) ICJ 1956, 77, referred to in another connection by the International Court of Justice in its advisory opinion on the judgments of this tribunal. The subject is discussed in Bowett *The Law of International Institutions* (4th edn, 1982) pp 97–99.

b.   The appointment of advisory or consultative committees, either generally or for particular subjects (for example, the Consultative Committees of the International Telecommunication Union, ITU).

c.   The establishment of so-called *functional* commissions or committees, dealing with specialised fields of action (for example, the Functional Commissions of the United Nations Economic and Social Council, and the special technical Commissions of the World Meteorological Organisation, WMO, dealing with aerology, aeronautical meteorology, etc). The United Nations Commission on International Trade Law (UNCITRAL), in regard to which the Sixth Committee (Legal) of the United Nations General Assembly exercises largely an overseeing role may, semble, be regarded as such a functional commission.

d.   The Administrative Conferences of the International Telecommunication Union, ITU, at which the representatives of private operating agencies may attend.

e.   The delegation by Commissions of their functions to a Sub-Commission; eg, the Sub-Commission on Prevention of Discrimination and Protection of Minorities, which is a Sub-Commission of the United Nations Human Rights Commission.

f.   The creation of bodies or units with distinct appellations or titles, such as 'Agency' (eg the United Nations Relief and Works Agency for Palestine Refugees in the Near East, UNRWA), 'Conference' (eg the United Nations Conference on Trade and Development, UNCTAD), 'Fund' (eg, the United Nations Children's Emergency Fund, UNICEF, and the United Nations Fund for Population Activities, UNFPA), and 'Programme' (eg, the United Nations Environment Programme, UNEP, and the United Nations Development Programme, UNDP).

Another manifestation of this flexible devolution of powers is the formation of 'working parties', or of inner groups of states most competent collectively to deal with certain problems within the framework of the organisation.

(5) *Voting rights*

Voting by a majority of members has become the more usual requirement for the adoption of decisions, resolutions, etc, and it is seldom that unanimity is now prescribed. Special systems of 'weighted' voting rights are applied in some instances (for example, by the International Bank for Reconstruction and Development, and the International Monetary Fund), the number of votes being calculated upon a scale depending on the amount of financial contributions, or actual shares of capital. To that extent, more recent voting procedure tends 'to reflect the power and interests of the subscribing nations with particular reference to the extent to which individual nations will be affected by the organisation's activities or relied upon to execute its decisions'.[11] There is a recent tendency,

11. 61 Harvard LR (1948) 1093, reviewing Koo *Voting Procedures in International Political Organisations* (1947). For an up to date discussion of this complex subject, see Bowett *The Law of International Institutions* (4th edn, 1982) pp 401–408 where, at pp 401 et seq, the decline of the former principle of unanimity is examined.

however, that has become more common, to reach decisions by consensus.[12] For the more important decisions, for example, admission of members, or amendment of the constitution, a two-thirds majority is the more usual rule. The special voting procedure in the United Nations Security Council is discussed below in this chapter.[13]

(6) Reports by member states
The constitutions of these bodies usually provide for the supervision of reports by member states on the action taken in fulfilment of their obligations.

(7) The adoption of conventions and recommendations for action by member states
This is discussed below in the present chapter.[14]

(8) Budgetary questions
The more usual constitutional provisions are that the Secretary-General or Director-General, or other executive head of the Secretariat, formulates the estimates of future expenditure, that these are reviewed and passed by the policy-making body, subject—in some cases—to intermediate examination by a budgetary committee of that body, and by the executive organ, and that the total amount is apportioned among the member states in shares determined by the policy-making body. The control by the specialised agencies over financial and budgetary matters is subject to the supervisory and recommendatory powers of the United Nations General Assembly. These powers of the General Assembly are of the most general nature, extending not only to administrative expenses stricto sensu, but other expenditure in fulfilling the purposes of the United Nations, including costs incurred by the Secretary-General in connection with any authorised measures to maintain international peace and security,[15] and these may be apportioned among the member states.[16]

3. PRIVILEGES AND IMMUNITIES[17]

It is clear that to operate effectively and properly to discharge their functions, international institutions require certain privileges and immunities in each

12. As to decisions or resolutions by consensus, see p 46, n 6, above, in Chapter 2.
13. At pp 577-579.
14. See below, pp 562-563.
15. See *Advisory Opinion on Certain Expenses of the United Nations* (*Article 17, paragraph 2 of the Charter*) ICJ 1962, 151. Recommendations for budgeting reforms were made by a Report in 1986 of the Group of High-Level Intergovernmental Experts to Review the Efficiency of the Administrative and Financial Functioning of the United Nations.
16. *Financial Support:* The funds of international institutions are provided principally by: (a) contributions from the member states, equal, or graduated according to population or economic position; (b) the earnings or profits of the institution itself. On the budgeting of international organisations, see Bowett *The Law of International Institutions* (4th edn, 1982) pp 68, 412–421.
17. On the subject, see Henkin, Pugh, Schachter, and Smit *International Law; Cases and Materials* (2nd edn, 1987) pp 958–979; Bowett *The Law of International Institutions* (4th edn, 1982) pp

country where they may be located permanently or temporarily. Also the agents and servants, through whom such institutions must work, similarly require such privileges as are reasonably necessary for the performance of their duties. Moreover, in principle, the income and funds of such organisations should be protected from state fiscal impositions.

Obviously, this was a matter that needed to be dealt with by provisions in international conventions. It could not be left merely for separate solution by the laws and practice of the states participating in each international institution. So far as the United Nations was concerned, it was provided in general terms in article 105 of the Charter that the Organisation should enjoy in the territory of each member state such privileges and immunities as were necessary for the fulfilment of its purposes, that representatives of member states and officials of the Organisation should similarly enjoy such privileges and immunities as were necessary for the independent exercise of their functions in relation to the United Nations, and that the General Assembly might make recommendations or propose conventions for the detailed application of these general provisions. Similar stipulations on this subject were inserted in the various constitutions of the 'specialised agencies', and in treaties and agreements relative to general and regional[18] international institutions, in some instances in a more specific and more detailed form.

In February 1946 the General Assembly adopted a Convention on the Privileges and Immunities of the United Nations, providing principally for the following:

i.   immunity of the United Nations' property and assets from legal process except when waived;
ii. inviolability of the Organisation's premises and archives;[19]
iii. freedom from direct taxes and customs duties for its property and assets;
iv. equivalent treatment for its official communications to that accorded by member states to any government;
v.   special privileges, including immunity from arrest, inviolability of documents, and freedom from aliens' registration for representatives of member states on organs and conferences of the United Nations;
vi. special privileges for certain United Nations officials of high rank, including the status of diplomatic envoys for the Secretary-General and Assistant Secretaries-General, and special immunities for other officials, for example, from legal process for acts performed or words spoken in their official capacity, from taxation, and from national service obligations;
vii. a laissez-passer or special travel document for United Nations officials.

345–362; Ling 'Comparative Study of the Privileges and Immunities of UN Member Representatives and Officials with the Traditional Privileges and Immunities of Diplomatic Agents' (1976) 33 Washington & Lee LR 91.
18. See, eg, arts 5–11 of the Agreement on the Status of the North Atlantic Treaty Organisation (NATO), National Representatives, and International Staff of 20 September 1951.
19. Section 9 of the Agreement of 1947 with the United States for the Headquarters of the United Nations at New York provides for inviolability of what is known of the Headquarters District. The United States has also concluded a Headquarters Agreement with the Organisation of American States (OAS).

In November 1947, the General Assembly adopted a convention for the co-ordination of the privileges and immunities of the specialised agencies with those of the United Nations. This convention contained similar standard provisions to those mentioned above as being contained in the Convention on Privileges and Immunities of the United Nations, but it also consisted of separate draft annexes relating to each specialised agency, containing special provisions for privileges and immunities which needed to be made having regard to the particular nature of each specialised agency; for example, the draft annex as to the International Labour Organisation provided for the immunities to be extended to employers' and workers' members of the Governing Body, subject to waiver by the Governing Body itself. Each specialised agency was to be governed by the standard provisions, and was authorised to draw up, in accordance with its own constitutional procedure, a special annex of additional amended privileges based on the draft annex. Under certain of the 'protocolary' provisions of the Convention, the full details of which need not concern us, member states of each specialised agency undertook to apply the standard provisions of the Convention in conjunction with the special provisions of each annex when finally and properly drawn up. This seems a practical, if complicated, solution of a difficult problem.

The related questions of the status of the headquarters (premises and territory) of the United Nations and of the specialised agencies[1] have been regulated by special agreements (including the agreement between the United Nations and the United States of 1947). These agreements reveal the following common general features:

i.   The local laws are to apply within the headquarters district, subject to the application of staff administrative regulations relative to the Secretariat.
ii. The premises and property of the organisation are to be immune from search, requisition, confiscation, etc., and any other form of interference by the local authorities.
iii. Local officials cannot enter except with the consent of the organisation.

---

1.   The International Atomic Energy Agency (IAEA), at Vienna, which is not a specialised agency, but a 'related agency' (see p 553), entered into a Headquarters Agreement with the Austrian Government on 1 March 1958. In respect of the UN Headquarters Agreement of 1947, see Henkin, Pugh, Schachter and Smit *International Law; Cases and Materials* (2nd edn, 1987) pp 974–979. When the United States Congress passed the Anti-terrorism Act, certain sections of which directed the closure of all offices of the Palestine Liberation Organization (PLO) in the United States, the question arose of the effect of the Act on the PLO Observer Mission, accredited to the United Nations in New York. The United Nations sought to invoke the arbitration provisions of the Headquarters Agreement of 1947, governing the relations between the United States and the UN. The International Court of Justice delivered an advisory opinion that the United States was obliged to arbitrate, there being a 'dispute' within the meaning of the Agreement notwithstanding that the closure of the PLO Mission had not yet been enforced: *Applicability of the Obligation to Arbitrate Under the UN Headquarters Agreement 1947*, ICJ 1988, 12. The matter was resolved soon afterwards by a United States court which held, in enforcement proceedings against the PLO, that the Act must be read subject to the obligations of the United States under the Headquarters Agreement and therefore did not apply in the case of the PLO Observer Mission: *United States v Palestine Liberation Organization* (1988) 27 ILM 1055.

iv. The local government must use diligence to protect the premises against outside disturbance and unauthorised entry.

v. The headquarters are exempt from local taxes or impositions, except charges for public utility services (for example, water rates).

vi. The organisation enjoys freedom of communication, with immunity from censorship.

Regional and field offices of international organisations have also, in some cases, been covered by privileges and immunities agreements with the host state; cf the case of the World Health Organisation (WHO) Regional Office in Egypt which was the subject of an Agreement of 25 March 1951 between the WHO and Egypt that was considered by the International Court of Justice in 1980 in an Advisory Opinion arising out of the proposed transfer of the Office to another country.[2]

Privileges and immunities wider than those provided in the two conventions (or in municipal legislation) may, as a matter of practice, be granted by states to an international institution. Also, the constitution of an international institution may contain its own detailed code of provisions as to the privileges and immunities of the institution, and officials thereof (see, for example, the Articles of Agreement of the International Finance Corporation, of 25 May 1955, article VI, sections 2–11). The matter may, too, be regulated by bilateral agreement (as for example the Agreement of 27 November 1961, between the United Nations and the Congo Republic relating to the privileges and immunities of the United Nations Operation in the Congo and that of 27 February 1964, between the United Nations and Yugoslavia for the 1965 World Population Conference).[3]

Generally speaking, as a study of the two conventions and other instruments shows, the object in granting privileges and immunities to international institutions has been not to confer on them an exceptional rank or status of extra-territoriality, but to enable them to carry out their functions in an independent, impartial and efficient manner. The privileges and immunities are subject to waiver. It is left to the good sense of such international institutions to decide in the light of the justice of the case, and of possible prejudice to the organisation, when these should be pressed,[4] and to the practical discretion of states to determine how liberal the authorities should be in giving effect to them.

2. *Advisory Opinion on the Interpretation of the Agreement of March 25, 1981 between the WHO and Egypt* ICJ 1980, 73. The privileges and immunities of judges of the International Court of Justice and of the Registrar of the Court were, inter alia, dealt with in an exchange of correspondence between the President of the Court and the Netherlands Minister for Foreign Affairs in June 1946; see *Yearbook of the International Court of Justice, 1986–1987* pp 15, 114.

3. Such bilateral agreements may even govern the privileges and immunities of a peacekeeping force; eg, the UN-Cyprus Exchange of Letters, New York, 31 March 1964, as to the Force in Cyprus.

4. See, eg, art V, s 20, of the General Convention of 1946 on the Privileges and Immunities of the United Nations under which, in regard to officials, other than the Secretary-General, it is the latter's 'right and *duty*' to waive immunity in any case where immunity would impede the course of justice, and can be waived without prejudice to the interests of the United Nations. Cf the *Ranollo* Case 67 NYS 2d 31 (1946) (chauffeur of the Secretary-General prosecuted for speeding while the Secretary-General was riding in the car concerned—defendant's immunity not pressed). For a case in which immunity from proceedings was allowed to China's representative accredited to the United Nations, see *Tsiang v Tsiang* 86 NYS 2d 556 (1949).

4.   LEGISLATIVE AND REGULATORY FUNCTIONS OF INTERNATIONAL INSTITUTIONS[5]

There is no world legislature in being, but various kinds of legislative measures may be adopted by international institutions, and powers of promoting the preparation of conventions are vested in the General Assembly, the Economic and Social Council, the United Nations Commission on International Trade Law (UNCITRAL), and the International Law Commission of the United Nations. Six of the specialised agencies are indeed largely regulative institutions, namely, the International Labour Organisation, the World Health Organisation, the World Meteorological Organisation,[6] the International Civil Aviation Organisation, the International Telecommunication Union, and the International Maritime Organisation (formerly the Inter-Governmental Maritime Consultative Organisation, IMCO). Mention may be made of the following special legislative or quasi-legislative techniques of these bodies:

a.   The adoption of regional Regulations or operating 'Procedures' (for example, by regional meetings of the International Civil Aviation Organisation).[7]
b.   The participation of non-governmental representatives in the legislative processes (for example, workers' and employers' delegates in the International Labour Conference, and private operating agencies at Administrative Conferences of the International Telecommunication Union).
c.   Regulations (such as, eg, the smallpox vaccination certificate regulations of 1956) adopted by the World Health Assembly, which come into force for all members, except those who 'contract out', ie, give notice of rejection or reservations within a certain period.
d.   The adoption of model regulations as an annex to a Final Act or other instrument.
e.   The approval of codes or charters of guidelines for domestic implementation by the Governments of member states; eg, the International Code on the Marketing of Breastmilk Substitutes approved in 1981 by the World Health Organisation.

This development has been accompanied by the emergence, parallel to that in municipal law, of the similar phenomena of: (1) Delegated legislation; for example, the powers given to the Council of the International Civil Aviation Organisation to amend or extend the annexes to the International Civil Aviation Convention of 7 December 1944. A specially important case is that of the powers conferred upon the Council and the Commission of the European Economic

5.   See C. H. Alexandrowicz *The Law-Making Functions of the Specialised Agencies of the United Nations* (1973); Bowett *The Law of International Institutions* (4th edn, 1982) pp 140–147; Edward McWhinney *United Nations Law Making* (1984) passim. For criticism of the regulatory activities of United Nations bodies, see Jeane J. Kirkpatrick 'Regulation in the United Nations' in *Regulation* January–February 1983, pp 38–45.
6.   As to the regulatory régimes of this Organisation and of the World Health Organisation, see David M. Leive *International Regulatory Régimes: Case Studies in Health, Meteorology, and Food* (1976).
7.   The various legislative and regulatory expedients employed within the framework of this Organisation are well analysed in Thomas Buergenthal's valuable book, *Law-Making in the International Civil Aviation Organisation* (1969).

Community (Common Market) to frame and promulgate Regulations, general in their scope, and directly binding upon the citizens and enterprises of member states of the Community (see article 189 of the Treaty of 25 March 1957, establishing the Community). In addition to Regulations there are the 'directives', binding states, receiving these, with regard to the end-result, but leaving them with some initiative in the matter of ways and means. (2) The making of *subordinate* law; for example, the adoption by the United Nations General Assembly of its own Rules of Procedure, and of the so-called 'Administrative Instruments', ie, the Treaty Registration Regulations,[8] the Statute of the Administrative Tribunal, and the Staff Regulations.

Finally, reference may be made to certain organisations, apart from the United Nations and the specialised agencies, and apart from the EEC, which have been most active in recent years in the preparation of, and promoting the adoption of multilateral law-making conventions or treaties; these are the Rome International Institute for the Unification of Private Law (UNIDROIT), the Hague Conference on Private International Law, and the Council of Europe.

5. INTERNATIONAL ADMINISTRATIVE LAW

As in municipal law, not only administrative, but quasi-judicial functions have been conferred upon the organs of international institutions. In this connection, reference may be made, by way of illustration, to the number of quasi-judicial powers bestowed on the Commission of the European Economic Community (Common Market), eg, to determine whether a measure of state aid granted by a member state is incompatible with the Common Market, or is applied in an unfair manner (see article 93 of the Treaty of 25 March 1957 establishing the Community).

In turn, this has made it necessary to provide for judicial review, that is to say, the exercise of a supervisory jurisdiction to ensure that such organs do not exceed their legal powers.

Thus, the Court of Justice of the European Communities has, under the Treaties of 18 April 1951, and of 25 March 1957, establishing respectively the European Coal and Steel Community and the European Economic Community (Common Market), jurisdiction to review the legality of acts or decisions of certain organs of the Communities on the grounds, inter alia, of lack of legal competence, procedural error, infringement of the Treaties or of any rule of law relating to their application, or abuse or misapplication of powers. This supervisory jurisdiction is not to apply to the conclusions upon questions of fact considered by these bodies.[9] Another example of such judicial review is the provision in the Statute of the Administrative Tribunal of the United Nations (which deals with complaints by United Nations staff concerning alleged breaches of the terms of their employment, etc) enabling the International Court of Justice to determine by advisory opinion whether the Tribunal has exceeded its powers,

8.   See above, p 419, n 1.
9.   See generally Wall *The Court of Justice of the European Communities* (1966), Valentine *The Court of Justice of the European Communities* (1965, 2 vols), and Wyatt and Dashwood *The Substantive Law of the EEC* (1980).

or erred in law or procedure. The Administrative Tribunal of the United Nations and the similar Tribunal of the International Labour Organisation are themselves working illustrations of the vitality of international administrative law.[10]

Mention may also be made of the powers given to the organs of some international institutions to determine questions concerning the interpretation or application of the constituent instrument of the institution; for example, the Council of the International Civil Aviation Organisation under articles 84–86 of the International Civil Aviation Convention of 7 December 1944, and the Executive Directors and Board of Governors of the International Monetary Fund under article XVIII of the Articles of Agreement of the Fund.

Finally, as in the municipal administrative domain, there has developed the practice whereby an organ of an international institution delegates an inquiry to a smaller committee or other body; for example, complaints as to infringements of trade union rights come for preliminary examination before the Committee on Freedom of Association, on behalf of the Governing Body of the International Labour Organisation.[11] This committee is to some extent a quasi-judicial body.

6.   QUASI-DIPLOMATIC AND TREATY RELATIONS OF INTERNATIONAL INSTITUTIONS

Not only is the accreditation of permanent missions by member states to the United Nations and the specialised agencies well-established, but there have been some instances of quasi-diplomatic appointments by United Nations organs, for example, the appointment in 1949 of a United Nations Commissioner to assist the inhabitants of Libya in attaining independent self-government, and the appointment in 1960 of a Special Representative of the Secretary-General in the Congo.[12] The EC has set a unique precedent by accrediting permanent diplomatic missions to four countries already, viz the United States, Canada, Japan, and Australia. Apart from these cases, the United Nations, the specialised agencies, and the related agencies under the provisions of their relationship agreements and inter-agency agreements for reciprocal representation and liaison, exchange and receive representatives from each other.

10. As to the jurisdiction and activities of these Administrative Tribunals, see Bowett *The Law of International Institutions* (4th edn, 1982) pp 317–331.
11. For example, as at May 1983, there were 78 cases pending before the ILO Committee on Freedom of Association, concerning 41 countries in all regions; see *ILO Information* May 1983, p 2.
12. Note also the case early in 1962 of the United Nations 'liaison mission' which visited outposts in the Congo. It has also become commonplace in recent years for the United Nations or its specialised agencies to send missions to different countries for various purposes. Eg, in May 1983, the United Nations Secretary-General sent a mission to Iran and Iraq to visit civilian areas to determine the extent of the war damage due to the Iran-Iraq hostilities while fact-finding missions despatched to determine the extent of violations of human rights have become an established procedure of the human rights functions discharged by the United Nations (see Robert Miller in *Australian Yearbook of International Law* 1970/1973, pp 40 et seq). Then, in the case of the International Labour Organisation (ILO), there are the missions or 'direct contact missions' sent to investigate complaints of alleged infringements of the right to freedom of association (see *ILO Information* December 1982, p 2, and May 1983, p 2). All such missions are despatched with the consent of the receiving states.

Treaty relations

The constitutions of certain international institutions expressly contemplate the exercise of a treaty-making power; for example, the United Nations Charter provides for the conclusion of trusteeship agreements, of relationship agreements with the specialised agencies, and of military agreements between the Security Council and member states (see article 43). Besides, international institutions must, as a matter of implication from their constitutions, have such treaty-making power as is necessary for the performance of their functions. It seems that such treaty-making power may be delegated; cf for example, the Agreement signed at the end of 1982 between the United Nations High Commissioner for Refugees and the Government of Pakistan with regard to Afghan refugees. Wide treaty-making power has, in some instances, been conferred upon regional international institutions, eg, the European Community (Common Market), under article 238 of the Treaty of Rome of 25 March 1957, establishing the Community. Lastly, and conclusively, on 21 March 1986 there was concluded the Vienna Convention on the Law of Treaties between States and International Organisations and between International Organisations; this represented definitive international recognition of the treaty-making power of international organisations.

At all events, a large number of international bodies have de facto entered into treaties, both inter se and with states and other entities. These instruments reveal a significant flexibility and simplicity, with but limited deference to Chancery traditions. In passing, reference may also be made to the absence from these agreements of the usual formal or 'protocolary' clauses,[13] and to the analogy to ratification in the usual requirement in these instruments that the agreement concerned is to come into force only when 'approved' by the policy-making body of the institution.

7. DISSOLUTION OF INTERNATIONAL INSTITUTIONS; AND SUCCESSION TO RIGHTS, DUTIES AND FUNCTIONS

Dissolution

International institutions become dissolved: (a) if created for a limited period only, upon the expiration of that period; (b) if of a transitional nature, upon the passing of the situation or the fulfilment of the purpose for which they were created; (c) by decision of the members, express or implied. It would seem that such decision need not necessarily be unanimous, but that it is sufficient as a practical matter if it be by a substantial majority, including the votes of the greater Powers. Thus, the League of Nations and the Permanent Court of International Justice were declared to be dissolved by Resolutions of the League of Nations Assembly in plenary session on 18 April 1946, without the individual assent of all member states or of all parties to the Statute of the Court.[14] In the absence of any express contrary provision in the constituent instrument, there is implied power in the members or corporators of an international institution to dissolve it.

13. See p 560, above.
14. Note, also, that it was by a Protocol signed by delegates to the World Health Conference at New York on 22 July 1946, that the *Office International d'Hygiène Publique* was dissolved.

The *liquidation* of the assets and affairs of the dissolved organisation is another matter. Practice here supplies no guide. In the case of the League of Nations, there were special circumstances, inasmuch as all parties concerned desired to vest as much as possible of the assets upon dissolution in the United Nations and the specialised agencies.[15]

Succession and international institutions

Where problems arise of the succession of one international institution to the rights, duties, etc, of another,[16] the question of the transmission of constitutional *functions*, in addition to the passing of rights and duties, is involved.[17]

First, it is essential that the successor institution should expressly or impliedly have constitutional competence to take over the rights and functions of the predecessor. For example, article 72 of the Constitution of the World Health Organisation enabled the Organisation to take over resources and obligations from bodies of cognate competence, and in virtue of that constitutional authority, the functions and assets of the Health Organisation of the League of Nations duly passed to the World Health Organisation.

Second, the successor institution cannot take over a function which does not lie within its constitutional competence, a principle which explains the non-passing, as a rule, of political functions. Thus in 1946 the Executive Committee of the Preparatory Commission of the United Nations advised against the transfer of the League's political functions to the United Nations, the political responsibilities of the two bodies being markedly dissimilar.[18] It may be mentioned, however, that the United Nations did take over from the League certain functions which it was desirable in the interests of the international community that it should possess, namely, the custody of treaties, the international control of narcotic drugs, the suppression of the traffic in women and children, and inquiries concerning the status of women.

A novel question of implied succession came before the International Court of Justice in 1950, and was dealt with in its *Advisory Opinion on the International Status of South West Africa*.[19] From that Advisory Opinion, the principle emerges that where an international organ such as the League of Nations Permanent Mandates Commission, which is discharging certain functions in the international sphere, is dissolved, and the continued execution of those functions has not been provided for by treaty or otherwise, those functions may then automatically devolve upon an international organ, such as the Trusteeship Council of the United Nations, which is discharging cognate functions in regard

---

15. See Myers 'Liquidation of League of Nations Functions', 42 AJIL (1948) 320 et seq, and Bowett *The Law of International Institutions* (4th edn, 1982) pp 377 et seq.
16. According to Bowett, op cit, p 382, there is no rule of automatic succession between a predecessor international institution and its successor.
17. The succession of an institution to the powers of another which has ceased to be, involves different considerations from the case of a reconstituted organisation. Quaere, whether the Organisation for Economic Co-operation and Development (OECD), which replaced the Organisation for European Economic Co-operation (OEEC), with wider geographical and other powers, was a case of 'reconstitution'.
18. See Myers, loc cit, pp 325–326.
19. ICJ 1950, 128.

to a similar field of activity.[20] The Court's view was, in fact, that in respect of the Mandated Territory of South West Africa, although South Africa had not, as she was so entitled, accepted the supervision of the United Nations General Assembly and Trusteeship Council, these bodies could none the less discharge the similar functions of supervision of the extinct Mandates Commission.[1]

If the constituent instrument of the successor institution sets out the precise terms and conditions under which the functions of the predecessor devolve upon the new body, the question of succession is governed by these express provisions. No better illustration of this principle can be given than certain provisions contained in the present Statute of the International Court of Justice, successor to the Permanent Court of International Justice (see, eg, articles 36–37).

8. THE UNITED NATIONS

The United Nations is a pivotal organ of world government, and the most important of all international institutions. As we have seen earlier in this chapter[2] through it are integrated those international bodies known as the 'specialised agencies', but this function of co-ordinating international organs by no means exhausts its responsibilities. At the date of writing, it has a membership of more than 180 states, making it for all practical purposes a universal organisation.

The true name of the Organisation is the 'United Nations', although it is often referred to as the 'United Nations Organisation' or 'UNO' or 'UN'.

The United Nations may be defined in a simplistic way as an organisation of independent states which have accepted the obligations contained in the United Nations Charter signed at San Francisco on 26 June 1945. On the one hand, however, this definition needs to be amplified by considering the origins of the Charter and the nature of the machinery created under it. On the other hand, such consideration serves to give only an incomplete picture. It must be stressed that it would be perhaps more correct to describe the United Nations, in the light of its present structure, as distinct from its form as contemplated in the Charter, as a system rather than as an organisation, stricto sensu, for it operates through a multiplicity of related or associated organs and units—some with a certain degree of autonomy—which are interconnected and integrated into one complex. The body or main stem of the United Nations is represented by the organs expressly named in the Charter, but from this initial basis there have evolved ramifications on a scale unprecedented for any other international institution; these are not mere offshoots, but organs and units, and as well Special and Ad Hoc Committees designed to play a significant role in international affairs. Leaving aside the specialised and 'related' agencies, these ramifications

20. But this organ would not necessarily be bound by the *procedure* followed by its predecessor; see *Advisory Opinion on the Admissibility of Hearings of Petitioners by the Committee on South West Africa* ICJ 1956, 23 (General Assembly could authorise oral hearings of petitioners, notwithstanding contrary practice of Permanent Mandates Commission).
1. There can be no succession of rights from an international institution to individual member states where they did not possess previously the rights claimed to pass; *South West Africa Cases, (Second Phase)* ICJ 1966, 6 at 35.
2. See above, pp 550 et seq.

include such entities as the UN Relief and Works Agency for Palestine Refugees in the Near East (UNRWA), the UN Conference on Trade and Development (UNCTAD), the UN Environment Programme (UNEP), the UN Capital Development Fund, the UN Development Programme (UNDP), the Special Committee against Apartheid, the Ad Hoc Committee on the Indian Ocean, and the Special Committee on the Charter of the United Nations and on the Strengthening of the Role of the Organisation.

Origins

The principles stated in the Charter were derived from the conceptions and plans of the wartime Allies, which first found expression in:

a.   The Atlantic Charter subscribed to by the President of the United States and the Prime Minister of Great Britain in August 1941.[3]
b.   The United Nations Declaration signed by 26 nations on New Year's Day 1942 after Japan had opened hostilities in the Pacific.
c.   The Moscow Declaration of October 1943, issued by the Governments of the United States, Great Britain, the Soviet Union and China, recognising the need for establishing a general international organisation based on the principle of the sovereign equality of all peace-loving states, and open to membership of all states large or small, in order to maintain international peace and security.

In the late summer and early autumn of 1944, draft proposals for such an organisation were worked out at Dumbarton Oaks by representatives of these four Powers. Then at the Yalta Conference in February 1945, of leaders of the Big Three—the United States, Great Britain, and the Soviet Union—the decision was taken, at a time when final victory against Germany was imminent, to call a general conference of about 50 nations to consider a constitution based on the Dumbarton Oaks proposals. At Yalta, agreement was also reached on voting procedure and arrangements in the proposed Security Council of the new Organisation. Two months later, a Committee of Jurists representing 44 countries met at Washington and drafted a Statute for the proposed International Court of Justice, which was to be an integral part of the proposed Organisation.

The Conference to consider the Dumbarton Oaks proposals held its discussions at San Francisco from 25 April to 26 June 1945, and succeeded in drawing up the present United Nations Charter, containing also the Statute of the International Court of Justice. The debates were by no means free of disagreements, particularly between the Four Sponsoring Powers—the United States, Great Britain, the Soviet Union and China—and the delegates of the so-called 'middle' and 'small' Powers over such matters as the 'veto' in the Security Council, and the functions of the General Assembly. In the circumstances, it is remarkable that in the short space of two calendar months there should have emerged an instrument so detailed and comprehensive as the Charter.

The United Nations came into being on 24 October 1945 ('United Nations Day'), on the Charter receiving the ratifications necessary to bring it into force, being those of China, the Soviet Union, Great Britain and the United States, and

---

3.   For discussion of the Atlantic Charter, see Stone *The Atlantic Charter* (1943).

of a majority of the other signatories. The first meeting of the General Assembly was held in London on 10 January 1946, while only three months later there took place the last session of the League of Nations Assembly for winding up the League as a going concern.

'Purposes' and 'Principles'

The 'Purposes' of the United Nations are stated in article 1 of the Charter from which it appears that the United Nations is primarily an organisation for maintaining peace and security, with the additional functions of developing friendly relations among nations, of achieving international co-operation in economic, social, cultural, and humanitarian matters, of developing respect for human rights and fundamental freedoms, and of providing a means for harmonising international action to attain these aims. It is questionable whether these general objectives, constituting the raison d'être of the Organisation, can be regarded as embodying rules of law, authorising its organs and member states to take action not specifically provided for in the operative articles of the Charter.

Article 2 of the Charter also sets out certain 'Principles'. Two of these 'Principles' are laid down for organic observance by the United Nations itself, namely, that the basis of the United Nations shall be the sovereign equality of all its members and that it shall not intervene (except where 'enforcement action' is called for) in matters 'essentially' within the domestic jurisdiction of any state (paragraph 7 of article 2 of the Charter).[4] Four other 'Principles' are set down for observance by member states, namely, that they should fulfil their obligations under the Charter, settle their disputes by peaceful means, not threaten or use force against the territorial integrity or political independence of any state, and give assistance to the United Nations while denying such assistance to any state against which preventive or enforcement action is being taken.

Membership

The members of the United Nations consist of: (a) original members; and (b) members admitted in accordance with article 4 of the Charter.

The original members are those states which having participated in the San Francisco Conference of 1945 or having signed the United Nations Declaration on New Year's Day 1942, sign and ratify the Charter.

As to members other than the original members, article 4 of the Charter provides that membership is open to 'all other peace-loving states which accept the obligations contained in the present Charter and, in the judgment of the Organisation, are able and willing to carry out these obligations', and that such admission will be effected by a decision of the General Assembly upon the recommendation of the Security Council (this in effect means by at least a two-

---

4. For comment, see Bowett, op cit, pp 24–25. The corresponding provision in the League of Nations Covenant, dealing with the powers of the Council of the League, namely paragraph 8 of article 15, was in these terms: 'If the dispute between the parties is claimed by one of them, and is found by the Council, to arise out of a matter *which by international law is solely* within the domestic jurisdiction of that party, the Council shall so report, and shall make no recommendation as to its settlement'. The italicised words should be contrasted with the expression 'essentially' used in paragraph 7 of article 2 of the Charter.

thirds vote of the General Assembly on the recommendation of at least nine members of the Security Council including the five permanent members).

In its Advisory Opinion on *Conditions of Membership in the United Nations* (1948),[5] the International Court of Justice by a majority held that article 4 lays down five conditions by way of exhaustive enumeration, and not merely by way of illustration, namely, that any new applicant must: (a) be a state; (b) be peace-loving; (c) accept the obligations of the Charter; (d) be able to carry out these obligations; and (e) be willing to do so. The Court also ruled that a state member voting on the admission of a new state (whether on the Security Council recommendation or on the General Assembly decision) is not entitled to make its consent to the admission of an applicant dependent on the fulfilment of conditions other than those prescribed in article 4, and in particular is not entitled to make such consent dependent on the admission of other applicants. In the Court's view a state member must in voting have regard only to the qualifications of a candidate for admission as set out in article 4, and not take into account extraneous political considerations.

Under present usage and procedure (see, for example, rule 60 of the Rules of Procedure of the Security Council) the Security Council practically decides in the first instance on the application of a state for admission as a new member, and by reason of the 'veto' may fail to make an effective recommendation. The International Court of Justice has, however, ruled that the General Assembly cannot by its own decision admit a new member state, where the Security Council has failed to make any recommendation as to admission to membership, favourable or otherwise.[6] The General Assembly remains, of course, always free to reject a candidate recommended by the Security Council.

In December 1955, a remarkable expedient was adopted to overcome admission blockages in the Security Council. Sixteen states were admitted as new members of the United Nations as the result of a so-called 'package deal', whereby one group of voting states made its affirmative vote for certain candidates conditional on an affirmative vote by another group for the remaining candidates. By a strained, if not utterly elastic construction of the Advisory Opinion, above, on *Conditions of Membership in the United Nations* (1948), this 'deal' was considered not to be inconsistent with the Court's opinion that a conditional consent to admission is not permitted by the Charter.

Articles 5–6 of the Charter deal with the suspension or expulsion of member states, which is effected by a decision of the General Assembly on the recommendation of the Security Council. Members may be suspended from exercising the rights and privileges of membership if preventive or enforcement action is taken against them by the Security Council, or be expelled if they persistently violate the principles of the Charter.

It is to be noted that there are no express provisions in the Charter permitting a member state to withdraw unilaterally from the United Nations, whereas in the case of the League of Nations Covenant, it was provided in paragraph 3 of article 1 that any member state might, after two years' notice of its intention to do so, withdraw from the League, provided that all its international obligations

5. See ICJ 1948, 61 et seq.
6. See ICJ 1950, 4.

and all its obligations under the Covenant had been fulfilled at the time of such withdrawal. Commission I of the San Francisco Conference of 1945 adopted the view that the Charter should not make express provision either to permit or to prohibit withdrawal from the United Nations; the highest duty of member states should be to continue their co-operation within the Organisation for the preservation of peace and security. This view was approved by the Conference in plenary session. However, it was recognised that member states could not be compelled to remain if the Organisation proved ineffective as a peace-maintaining body, or if amendments to the Charter, not concurred in by them, should change their rights and obligations. No member state has been expelled from the United Nations. Indonesia withdrew in 1965 but resumed participation a year later. South Africa was excluded from participation in the debates and work of the General Assembly, but not from membership as such, from 1974 until 1993 on the ruling of the President of the General Assembly following a finding of the Credentials Committee of the Assembly that the ruling government of South Africa, committed to the practice of *apartheid*, did not represent all its people. The legality of this action has been questioned[7]. Moreover, it may be observed that many states members of the United Nations are represented by undemocratic governments. It should be remembered that the United Nations is an organisation of states, not of governments.[8] The background to the ambiguous status of the Federal Republic of Yugoslavia after 1991 has been noted in Chapter 5, above. By Resolution 47/1 of 1992 the General Assembly considered that the Federal Republic of Yugoslavia (Serbia and Montenegro) could not continue automatically the membership of the former Socialist Federal Republic of Yugoslavia. It decided that the Federal Republic of Yugoslavia should apply for membership anew and that, in the meantime, it should not participate in the work of the General Assembly. This Resolution appears to recognise a temporary and shadowy status of a state subject to continuing obligations of membership, such as amenability to the decisions of the Security Council and to the jurisdiction of the International Court of Justice,[9] but unable to exercise the normal rights of membership.

Organs of the United Nations

The United Nations differs from the League of Nations in its *decentralised* character, the powers and functions under the Charter being distributed among six '*principal*' organs: (1) The General Assembly. (2) The Security Council. (3) The Economic and Social Council. (4) The Trusteeship Council. (5) The International Court of Justice. (6) The Secretariat. Each organ has sharply defined

7. See references in J. Dugard *International Law: A South African Perspective* (1994), 298.
8. The converse of the South African situation occurred in 1971 when the General Assembly resolved 'to restore all its rights to the People's Republic of China and to recognize the representatives of its government as the only legitimate representatives of China in the UN'. This brought to an end the representation of China by the representatives of the Nationalist Government exiled since 1949 in Taiwan (the Republic of China). The notion of a 'two Chinas' policy was rejected.
9. Cf the action brought before the Court by Bosnia-Herzegovina against the Federal Republic of Yugoslavia (Serbia and Montenegro) in the *Case Concerning Application of the Convention on the Prevention and Punishment of the Crime of Genocide*, ICJ 1993, 3 (request for provisional measures).

spheres of action, and although in a sense the residue of authority is vested in the General Assembly, the latter's powers are mainly supervisory and recommendatory, so that possibly some particular field of international action may be outside the operational competence of the United Nations. As distinct from the principal organs, there are the '*subsidiary*' organs of the United Nations, as to which there is a considerable degree of flexibility, since paragraph 2 of article 7 of the Charter provides that 'such subsidiary organs as may be found necessary may be established in accordance with the present Charter', and articles 22 and 29 empower the General Assembly and the Security Council respectively to establish subsidiary organs deemed necessary for the performance of their functions. Instances of the exercise of these powers are referred to below.

The General Assembly[10]

The General Assembly is the only principal organ of the United Nations consisting of all members, each member having only one vote, though allowed five representatives. It meets regularly once a year, but can meet in special session if summoned by the Secretary-General at the request of the Security Council or of a majority of the members of the United Nations, or at the request of one member concurred in by a majority of the members.

It is essentially a deliberative body, with powers of discussion, investigation, review, supervision and criticism in relation to the work of the United Nations as a whole (see article 10 of the Charter), and of the various other organs of world government provided for in the Charter including the specialised agencies. Generally speaking, its powers are limited to making recommendations and not binding decisions, although it is empowered to take certain final decisions, for example, as to the budget or as to the admission, suspension or expulsion of members. However, its recommendations, while not creating legal obligations, may operate with permissive force to *authorise* action by member states.[11] Votes on 'important' questions such as the election of the non-permanent members of the Security Council and other questions specifically enumerated in article 18, paragraph 2, of the Charter are to be taken by a two-thirds majority; other questions, including the determination of additional 'important' questions requiring a two-thirds majority vote, are to be dealt with by a simple majority vote. The five Great Powers, who are permanent members of the Security Council, have no right of 'veto' as they do when voting in the Council.

The General Assembly's powers and functions consist of the following:

i.   powers of discussion and recommendation in relation to the maintenance of international peace and security;
ii.   the direction and supervision of international economic and social co-operation;
iii. the supervision of the international trusteeship system;
iv.   the consideration of information as to non-self-governing territories;

10. As to the General Assembly, its structure and powers, see Bowett, op cit, pp 42–58, and Finley *The Structure of the United Nations General Assembly* (1977).
11. It is, however, doubtful whether such recommendations could authorise independent international institutions, eg, the International Bank for Reconstruction and Development (World Bank) to take action, which their competent organs had not duly decided upon.

v. budgetary and financial powers whereby it has exclusive control over the finances of the United Nations;

vi. powers of admitting, suspending and expelling states members (see above);

vii. powers in relation to the adoption of amendments to the Charter (see articles 108–109);

viii. the election of members of other organs;

ix. the receipt and consideration of reports on the work of the United Nations; and

x. the adoption of international conventions.

But, as article 10 of the Charter shows, its powers of discussion and recommendation are not limited to these matters.

Although the primary responsibility for the maintenance of peace and security belongs to the Security Council, the General Assembly is given in this connection certain facultative or permissive powers of consideration and recommendation. It 'may consider' the general principles of co-operation in the maintenance of peace and security including the principles as to disarmament and armament regulation, and may make recommendations on the subject to the member states or to the Security Council (article 11, paragraph 1); it 'may discuss' any specific questions relative to the maintenance of peace and security brought before it by a member state or by the Security Council or by a non-member and make recommendations thereon (article 11, paragraph 2); it 'may recommend' measures for the peaceful adjustment of any situation likely to impair the general welfare or friendly relations among nations (article 14); and it 'may call the attention' of the Security Council, as the body primarily responsible for enforcing peace to any situation likely to endanger peace and security (article 11, paragraph 3). There is one general restriction on these powers of recommendation, namely, that while, in the exercise of its functions under the Charter, the Security Council is actively dealing with any dispute or situation, the General Assembly—although it is not precluded from discussion—is not to make a recommendation in regard thereto unless the Security Council so requests (article 12, paragraph 1). But to prevent important matters relating to peace and security from being 'frozen' on the Security Council agenda and therefore from coming under the searchlight of General Assembly procedures, it is provided that the Secretary-General is with the Security Council's consent to notify the General Assembly when such matters are being dealt with, and immediately the Security Council ceases to deal with them.

Within these limits, it is remarkable that in practice the General Assembly has been able to take a leading role in questions of international peace and security. It has discussed some of the leading political problems brought before the United Nations such as those relating to Palestine, Greece, Spain, Korea, Suez, the Congo, and the Middle East, and also taken concrete action with reference to them. For instance, in regard to Palestine, it appointed a Special Committee in 1947 to investigate the facts, and subsequently in 1948 appointed a Mediator to secure peace between the parties in strife, and later a Conciliation Commission. As mentioned below, it materially contributed to the settlement of the Suez Canal zone conflict in October–November 1956, and in September 1960, it authorised the continued maintenance in the Congo of a United Nations Force.

The stultifying result of the 'veto' upon the work of the Security Council brought about a further significant development, under which the General Assembly impinged more and more upon the broad field of peace and security, to the extent of making general, and even specific, recommendations in this domain, although it could not of course compel compliance with these recommendations. Moreover, it came to be accepted that a matter might be removed from the agenda of the Security Council by a procedural vote, thus eliminating the use of the 'veto' to preclude a matter from being brought before the General Assembly.

Illustrations of the General Assembly's achievements in the domain of peace and security are the following:

a. The recommendations made by the General Assembly in April 1949 for setting up a panel of individuals to serve on commissions of inquiry and conciliation, and that the Security Council examine the desirability of using the procedure of rapporteurs or conciliators for disputes or situations brought before the Council for action.[12]

b. The so-called 'Uniting for Peace' General Assembly Resolution of 3 November 1950, providing for emergency special sessions at 24 hours' notice on the vote of any seven members of the Security Council, or a majority of member states, if the Security Council failed to act because of the 'veto', and pursuant to which there were set up a Peace Observation Commission, to observe and report on the situation in any area where international tension threatened international peace and security, and a Collective Measures Committee, to consider methods which might be used collectively to maintain and strengthen international peace and security.

c. The General Assembly recommendations on 17 November 1950, as to the appointment of a Permanent Commission of Good Offices.

d. The several General Assembly Resolutions relative to the situation in Korea, 1950–1953, including the Resolution of 1 February 1951 pursuant to which there was set up an Additional Measures Committee, composed of members of the Collective Measures Committee, which reported on measures of economic enforcement action to be taken.

e. The General Assembly's labours in the field of disarmament,[13] leading initially in 1961 to the establishment of an Eighteen-Nations Disarmament Committee, which was the predecessor body for the Committee on Disarmament (CD), composed of representatives of 40 member states, with the mandate of conducting negotiations for general and complete disarmament under international control and for arms control agreements, which Commission was re-christened at the 1984 session as the 'Conference on Disarmament', and leading as well to the reinstitution by it of the United Nations Disarmament Commission (UNDC), while it also held in 1978 and 1982 two Special Sessions on Disarmament and proclaimed in 1969 and 1980, respectively, successive Disarmament Decades.

The part played by the General Assembly in November 1956 in effecting a cease-fire in the Suez Canal zone conflict, involving Israel, Egypt, France, and

---

12. Approved, in effect, by the Security Council in May 1950.
13. Partly, it is true, in pursuance of art 11, para 1, referred to, p 573 above.

Great Britain, represented perhaps the high water mark of its work on peace and security. After Security Council action had proved impossible because of the 'veto', a special emergency session of the Assembly was convened for 1 November 1956, by a vote of seven members of the Security Council, in pursuance of the 'Uniting for Peace' Resolution, mentioned above. At this session, the Assembly adopted Resolutions for a cease-fire by all contestants, and for the creation of a United Nations Emergency Force[14] to guarantee peaceful conditions in the Suez area, with the ultimate consequence that peace and order were restored.

Another instance of significant General Assembly action, pursuant to the 'Uniting for Peace' Resolution, occurred on 19 September 1960, when the General Assembly authorised the Secretary-General to continue to take vigorous action pursuant to the earlier Resolutions of the Security Council for United Nations military assistance to maintain law and order in the Congo.[15]

The General Assembly's continued interest in the field of peace and security was also illustrated by its resolution, adopted on 4 November 1982, calling upon the United Kingdom and Argentina to resume negotiations, under United Nations auspices, to find as soon as possible a peaceful solution to the sovereignty dispute over the Falkland Islands which had led to the conflict of April–June 1982. It was true that the Resolution was unacceptable to the United Kingdom which, apart from other considerations, opposed it for not making provision for the principle of self-determination to be applied to the Falkland Islanders.

Reference may also be made to the creation by the General Assembly, in 1947, of an Interim Committee (the so-called 'Little Assembly') to assist it in its duties in relation to maintaining peace and security.[16] This Committee was made necessary by the fact that the General Assembly is under continual pressure at its annual sessions to dispose of a heavy agenda, and needs to make its own arrangements for keeping in touch with questions of peace and security. It was thought that through such a body as the Interim Committee, with a watching brief over all matters of peace and security and with the power to carry out special studies or inquiries, the General Assembly could effectively discharge its functions in relation to peace and security without detracting from the authority of the Security Council or intervening in the Council's work.

The Interim Committee reported in 1947–1948 to the General Assembly on two important matters which it investigated:

14. *United Nations Forces:* The respective powers of the Security Council and of the General Assembly to establish United Nations field forces are discussed by Sohn 52 AJIL 229–240. Clearly, the Security Council may authorise the creation of an observer group force (as in Lebanon in 1958), eg, to supervise a truce. It is, however, a matter of controversy whether either organ may establish forces in order to restore or maintain peace and security, in the absence of a valid decision of the Security Council to institute enforcement action under Chapter VII of the Charter; see below, p 586 as to the Security Council and the Congo situation. See also Bowett *United Nations Forces* (1964), and pp 590-592 below as to United Nations peacekeeping. Reference should be made also to the use of the Swedish Stand-by Disaster Relief Unit, made available through the United Nations pursuant to a tripartite agreement between that body, Peru and Sweden, for rehabilitation work in Peru following the earthquake in May 1970. What has been called 'disaster preparedness' presumably falls within the international humanitarian powers of the United Nations (cf art 1, para 3 of the Charter).
15. See also below, p 586, n 18.
16. Cf L. C. Green 'The Little Assembly', in *The Year Book of World Affairs*, 1949 pp 169 et seq.

a.   The adoption of practices and procedures designed to reduce difficulties due to the 'veto' in the Security Council.[17]

b.   Methods for promoting international co-operation in the political field.[18]

This Interim Committee is but one example of the decentralisation that the General Assembly did effect internally, to cope with its work. It has established Procedural Committees, Main Committees[19] which meet in connection with plenary sessions, Standing Committees (such as the Committee on Contributions, the Advisory Committee on Administrative and Budgetary Questions, and the Joint Panel of External Auditors), and subsidiary bodies for important political and security matters, such as the Disarmament Commission,[20] subject to a duty of reporting to the Security Council.

The General Assembly is in addition given the mandatory power, as distinct from the facultative or permissive powers set out above, of initiating studies and making recommendations for the purpose of promoting international co-operation in the political field and of encouraging the progressive development of international law and its codification (see article 13, paragraph 1, a).[1]

As to (ii), the direction and supervision of international economic and social co-operation, the General Assembly exercises the powers and functions of the United Nations in this sphere (articles 13 and 60), the Economic and Social Council being under its authority. As referred to above,[2] it also approves the 'relationship agreements' negotiated by the Economic and Social Council with the 'specialised agencies', and is authorised to make recommendations for co-ordinating the work and policies of these agencies.

One of the General Assembly's most important functions is to elect members of other organs (see (viii)); thus it elects the ten non-permanent members of the Security Council (article 23), the members of the Economic and Social Council (article 61), and by a system of parallel voting in conjunction with the Security Council, the fifteen judges of the International Court of Justice. It also appoints the Secretary-General.

Finally, mention should be made of its international legislative functions (see (x)). Already it has approved and adopted the texts of several international conventions, including the Conventions on the Privileges and Immunities of the United Nations, and of the Specialised Agencies of 1946 and 1947 respectively, and the Genocide Convention of 1948, while it took the final decision to summon

17. This report formed the basis of a General Assembly recommendation in April 1949, that permanent members of the Security Council confer on the use of the 'veto', that they refrain from using it in certain specific cases, and that they treat certain questions as procedural.

18. Including recommendations as to rapporteurs or conciliators in Security Council matters, and a panel of persons to serve on commissions of inquiry and conciliation, adopted by the Assembly; see above, p 574. As to the Interim Committee, see Bowett, op cit, p 49.

19. These are the First (Political and Security Questions), Special Political Committee (sharing the work of the First (Committee), Second (Economic and Financial Questions), Third (Social, Humanitarian, and Cultural Questions), Fourth (Trusteeship and Non-Self-Governing Territories), Fifth (Administrative and Budgetary Questions), and Sixth (Legal Questions).

20. Established on 11 January 1952, in replacement of the two former Commissions, the Atomic Energy Commission and the Commission for Conventional Armaments.

1.   In execution of this power, the General Assembly in 1947 established the International Law Commission.

2.   See pp 552–553.

such law-making Conferences as the Geneva Conference of 1958 on the Law of the Sea, the Vienna Conferences of 1961, 1963, and 1968–9 on Diplomatic Relations, Consular Relations, and the Law of Treaties, and the Third United Nations Conference on the Law of the Sea (see Chapter 9, above), resulting in conventions on these subjects. It also served as the main forum for the conclusion of the conventions and other instruments governing state activities in outer space (see Chapter 7, above).

The Security Council[3]
The Security Council is a continuously functioning body, consisting of fifteen member states; five are permanent and are named in the Charter, being China, France, the Russian Federation,[4] Great Britain and the United States. Ten[5] non-permanent members are elected by the General Assembly for a term of two years, and in their election due regard is to be specially paid in the first instance to the contribution of member states to the maintenance of peace and security, to the other purposes of the United Nations, and to equitable geographical distribution (article 23). There are provisions for participation in the Security Council's discussions by states other than permanent and non-permanent members: (a) any member state of the United Nations may participate without vote in a discussion of any question brought before the Security Council if the Council considers the interests of that member state are specially affected (article 31); (b) any such member state or any non-member state, if it is a party to a dispute being considered by the Security Council, is to be invited to participate without vote in the discussions concerning the dispute (article 32). There have been proposals since 1985 to enlarge the membership of the Security Council on the ground of ensuring a claimed more equitable geographical distribution of seats on the Council. This might also involve increasing the number of permanent members.

Voting procedure in the Security Council
The voting procedure in the Security Council requires special consideration. Each member of the Council has one vote. Decisions on procedural matters are to be made by an affirmative vote of nine members (the former affirmative vote required was of seven members). Decisions on all other matters (ie, non-procedural matters) are to be made by an affirmative vote of nine members, including the concurring votes of the five permanent members, provided that in decisions under Chapter VI (pacific settlement of disputes) and under paragraph 3 of article 52 (pacific settlement under regional arrangements) a party to a dispute shall abstain from voting. It is here that the so-called 'veto' operates, as if a permanent member does not affirmatively vote in favour of a particular

3. On the Security Council, see Bowett, op cit, pp 26–42; S. D. Bailey *The Procedure of the United Nations Security Council* (1975); and Kerley 'The Powers of Investigation of the United Nations Security Council' 55 AJIL (1961) 892.
4. The Russian Federation replaced the Soviet Union in its UN seat, including permanent membership of the Security Council, in 1991. It did so with the general acquiescence of UN members and with the express concurrence of the other successor states to the Soviet Union.
5. Formerly, the number was six, but this was increased to ten under amendments to the Charter which came into force in 1965.

decision, that decision is blocked or 'vetoed', and fails legally to come into existence.[6]

There are certain exceptions to the rigidity of the 'veto' provisions, both under the Charter and in practice. Under the Charter, as mentioned above, in connection with decisions concerning the pacific settlement of disputes, whether under Chapter VI or under article 52, paragraph 3 (reference of a dispute to regional settlement), any permanent or non-permanent member, if a party to the particular dispute under consideration, must abstain from voting (article 27, paragraph 3). The exception in practice is that the voluntary abstention of a permanent member from voting has consistently been interpreted as not constituting a bar to the validity of a Security Council decision;[7] the legality of the practice was upheld by the International Court of Justice in the Advisory Opinion of 21 June 1971, on the *Legal Consequences for States of the Continued Presence of South Africa in Namibia (South West Africa)*, in which it ruled that a Security Council Resolution of 1970 declaring illegal the continued presence of South Africa in South West Africa (Namibia) was not invalid by reason of the abstention from voting of two permanent members.[8] A more difficult question is whether the absence of a permanent member from proceedings in which a vote has been taken (eg, the absence of the Soviet Union when the decisions as to Korea were taken on 25 and 27 June 1950) should be taken as equivalent to an abstention, as did happen. The theory of 'implied concurrence' applicable to abstentions, according to some writers, seems to be legally irrelevant.[9]

Since the inception of the Security Council, the permanent members' right of veto has been the subject of questionings. Such questionings were foreshadowed at the San Francisco Conference, and publicists and writers claimed that the original doubts have been justified inasmuch as the power of veto has been abused.[10] The central theory behind the right of veto is that since the permanent members as Great Powers naturally bear the main burden of responsibility for maintaining peace and security, no one permanent member should be compelled by a vote of the Security Council to follow a course of action with which it disagrees. In other words, the possibility of division among the Great Powers on particular questions of collective security was foreseen. At the San Francisco Conference, the Four Sponsoring Powers (Great Britain, the United States, Russia and China) issued a Joint Interpretative Statement pointing out that the veto should be retained, as any steps going beyond mere discussion or procedural

6. Before the amendments which raised the number of non-permanent members from six to ten, and the required affirmative vote from seven to nine, the five permanent members could, in effect produce a block 'veto' by all abstaining from voting; this is no longer possible. Although a Security Council resolution may be vetoed, even though there is a majority in favour, quaere whether a member state may rely on the majority view as justifying *unilateral* domestic action by it; see note by W. M. Reisman 'The Legal Effect of Vetoed Resolutons' in 74 AJIL (1980) 904–907.
7. See Bowett, op cit, pp 31–32. As to Portugal's claim that the Security Council Resolution of 9 April 1965, authorising the United Kingdom to take steps to prevent the arrival at Beira of vessels taking oil to the Rhodesian régime, was invalid because of the abstention from voting of two permanent members, see Cryer *Australian Year Book of International Law*, 1966 pp 95–96.
8. See ICJ 1971, 16 at 22.
9. Cf Bowett, op cit, p 32.
10. See Evatt *The United Nations* (1948) pp 55 et seq.

preliminaries might initiate a 'chain of events' which in the end could or should require the Security Council to take enforcement action, and that such action must naturally attract the right of veto.[11] The same Statement added that the Great Powers would not use their powers 'wilfully' to obstruct the operations of the Security Council. Undoubtedly, as the veto has been used, Security Council procedure has been stultified, and attempts have been made to find ways to liberalise the voting practice, while keeping within the limits of the principles justifying the veto. It is clear that the following are subject to the right of exercise of the veto: (a) the actual decision whether a question to be put to the vote is one of procedure or of substance;[12] (b) any executive action; (c) a decision to carry out any wide investigation of a dispute. But the mere preliminary discussion of a subject, decisions on purely preliminary points, and the hearing of statements by a state party to a dispute would not be within the scope of the veto.[13] Questions concerning the admission of new member states, or concerning the suspension of existing member states are deemed to be of a non-procedural character, whereas a question of acceptance or non-acceptance of the credentials of a government is treated as one of a procedural kind. Perhaps it is well to remember also that the veto is not the main obstacle to the Security Council reaching its full stature as an organ for maintaining peace and security. One learned writer has said: '. . . . In a curious way it [the veto] may have preserved the United Nations by allowing or forcing it to yield to reality.'[14] Even if there were no veto, it is probable that some alternative methods of obstructing the Security Council's work would have been resorted to, leading to equal abuses and absurdities, or that, as occurred in the League of Nations, certain Powers might have quitted the Organisation.

Powers and functions of the Security Council[15]

The Security Council has been given primary responsibility under the Charter for maintaining peace and security, in order that as a smaller executive body with a permanent core of membership of the Great Powers, it can take effective decisions to ensure prompt action by the United Nations. Under article 25 of the Charter, the member states agree to abide by and to carry out the Security Council's decisions. Although the Security Council has primary responsibility for maintaining peace and security, this responsibility is not exclusive. The General Assembly has powers of discussion and recommendation in regard to

11. See *United Nations Documents*, 1941–45 (pub 1946, by Royal Institute of International Affairs) pp 268–271, for text of the Statement.
12. The so-called 'double veto' arises if a permanent member should veto such a decision. However, on at least one occasion, the 'double veto' was ousted, the President of the Security Council ruling the matter to be procedural; see Stone *Legal Controls of International Conflict* (1954) pp 224–225 and *Supplement* 1953–1958 (1959) p 870. As to the use of the veto, see also Edward McWhinney *United Nations Law Making* (1984) pp 87 et seq.
13. On 8 September 1959, the President of the Security Council ruled (against protest by the representative of the Soviet Union) that the appointment of a sub-committee to examine statements concerning Laos, etc, being for the establishment of a subsidiary organ under art 29 of the Charter, was a procedural matter. He also ruled that the draft Resolution to determine whether the question of this appointment was procedural, was not subject to the veto (thereby excluding the 'double veto').
14. See W. M. Reisman in 74 AJIL (1980) 907.
15. See generally S. D. Bailey *The Procedure of the United Nations Security Council* (1975).

the subject, and action may be taken under regional arrangements or by regional agencies (see articles 52–53 of the Charter). Nor should it be forgotten that, generally speaking, action by the Security Council must be brought within the four corners of a particular article or particular articles in Chapters VI or VII of the Charter, and even then because of the 'veto' or other voting disagreement no action may be decided upon. On the other hand, on one view, the Security Council has general overriding powers for maintaining peace and security, not limited to the specific express powers in Chapters VI or VII, as like other international organs, it has such implied powers as are necessary and requisite for the proper fulfilment of its functions.[16] If this view be correct, the Security Council could take action on a matter which did not come within the express terms of Chapters VI or VII.[17]

The principal powers and functions of the Security Council relate to the following matters:

i.   the pacific settlement of international disputes;
ii.   preventive or enforcement action to maintain peace and security;
iii.   regional agencies and regional agreements;
iv.   the control and supervision of trust territories classified as 'strategic areas' (see Chapter 5 above);
v.   the admission, suspension, and expulsion of members (see above);
vi.   amendments to the Charter (see articles 108–9);
vii.   the election in conjunction with the General Assembly, of the fifteen judges of the International Court of Justice.

In relation to (i) above, the pacific settlement of disputes, the powers of the Security Council as provided for in Chapter VI of the Charter are as follows:

a.   The Security Council 'shall, when it deems necessary' call on the parties to a dispute, the continuance of which is likely to endanger peace and security, to settle that dispute by negotiation, inquiry, mediation, conciliation, arbitration, judicial settlement, action by regional agencies or under regional arrangements, or other peaceful means (article 33).[18] An example of the exercise of this power was that in regard to the complaint by Chad to the Security Council against Libya, when in April 1983 the Council called on both states to settle their differences 'without undue delay and by peaceful means' on the basis of the Charters of the United Nations and of the Organisation of African Unity (OAU).[19] In the case of the Argentine occupation of the Falkland Islands in 1982, the Council initially (on 1 April) called on Argentina and the United Kingdom to refrain from the use or threat of force, and then (on 3 April) called for an immediate withdrawal of Argentine forces from the Islands and an immediate cessation of hostilities,

16. Cf *Advisory Opinion on Reparation for Injuries Suffered in the Service of the United Nations* ICJ 1949, 182.
17. See also below p 586, as to the Security Council and the Congo situation.
18. Under art 33, it is the duty of parties to such a dispute to seek a peaceful solution by these means.
19. This dispute was decided later by the International Court of Justice in the *Case Concerning the Territorial Dispute* (Libya v Chad), ICJ 1994, 6.

and in addition called on both parties to 'seek a diplomatic solution to their differences and to respect fully the purposes and principles of the United Nations Charter'. But if the parties fail to settle it by these means—no time limit for such failure is indicated—whether at the request of the Security Council or otherwise, they must refer the dispute to the Security Council. Thereupon, if the Security Council deems that the continuance of the dispute is in fact likely to endanger peace and security it shall decide: (1) whether to recommend 'appropriate procedures or methods' of settlement, or (2) whether to recommend actual terms of settlement (Article 37).

b. The Security Council may investigate not only any kind of dispute, but also 'situations'[20] which are such that they may lead to international friction or give rise to a dispute, in order to determine whether the dispute or 'situation' is likely to endanger peace and security (article 34). This investigation is a preliminary to further action by the Security Council. Such disputes or 'situations' may be investigated by the Security Council of its own motion, or be brought to its attention by member states of the United Nations (whether parties or not to the dispute), or by non-member states which are parties to the dispute (article 35), or by the General Assembly (article 11, paragraph 3), or by the Secretary-General under his power to bring to the Security Council's notice any 'matter' which in his opinion threatens the maintenance of peace and security (article 99).

c. During the course of any dispute or situation, the continuance of which is likely to endanger peace and security, the Security Council may recommend 'appropriate procedures or methods' of settlement. In general, legal disputes are to be referred to the International Court of Justice (article 36).[1]

d. If all the parties to any such dispute so request, the Security Council may recommend terms of peaceful settlement (article 38).

There are several points in connection with the Security Council's powers of settling disputes that call for comment. First, its powers of calling upon the parties to settle disputes by peaceful means (article 33) or of recommending procedures or methods of adjustment (article 36) or of recommending terms of settlement (articles 37 and 38) are recommendatory only, and limited to disputes which are likely to endanger peace and security. It has no such powers with regard to all disputes, although it may investigate any dispute to see if it is likely to endanger peace and security (article 34). Whether, apart from Chapter VI of the Charter, it has any powers at all with regard to disputes in general is an open question. Second, a not very clear or happy distinction is drawn between 'disputes' and 'situations' (note that a situation' is not mentioned in article 27, paragraph 3, as to voting). The Security Council can under article 34 investigate 'situations' which may lead to international friction or give rise to a dispute to see if they are likely to endanger peace and security, but its only other express power with

---

20. The words 'which might lead to international friction or give rise to a dispute' in art 34 qualify the word 'situation', and not the word 'dispute'; see Hasluck *Workshop of Security* (1948) pp 43–44.

1. The significance of this provision in art 36 was stressed by the International Court of Justice in the case of the *United States Diplomatic and Consular Staff in Tehran* ICJ 1980, 3 at para 40. See also *Nicaragua v United States (Jurisdiction)* ICJ 1984, 392, paras 89–90.

regard to a 'situation' is the power under article 36 of recommending procedures or methods of adjustment for a 'situation' likely to endanger peace and security. Who determines whether the circumstances amount to a 'dispute' or a 'situation'? Sometimes 'disputes' and 'situations' overlap, and a 'situation' may itself be in the nature of a 'dispute'. Is this a matter for the Security Council to decide? On several occasions rulings as to the question have been given by the Chairman of the Security Council, although it has been suggested that whether a matter is a 'dispute' or a 'situation' depends on the terms of the complaint bringing it to the Security Council's notice.[2] Third, what are the circumstances which constitute a 'dispute'? Certain of the cases that have come before the Security Council are quite unlike text book disputes, ie, clear differences between states over a contested issue, being rather complaints over situations seemingly of remote concern to the complainant state (for example, the Ukrainian complaint in 1946 as to conditions in Greece). Generally speaking, the Security Council has determined what specific acts in regard to the settlement of disputes come within its powers under the Charter, as, for example, in the case of Trieste in 1946–7 when it accepted the responsibility of appointing a Governor.[3] It also undertakes its own investigations of the relevant aspects of the dispute, not necessarily being bound by any statements of the parties in conflict.[4]

The more important responsibilities of the Security Council arise with reference to (ii), preventive or enforcement action under Chapter VII. The Security Council is empowered to determine the existence of any threat to the peace, breach of the peace, or act of aggression and to make recommendations or decide what enforcement measures are to be taken to maintain or restore peace and security (article 39). It may call on the parties involved to comply with provisional measures,[5] and take account of any failure to comply therewith (article 40).

Attention should be drawn to one difference as to the dispute-settling powers of the Council, on the one hand, and its enforcement powers, on the other hand. In the context of paragraph 1 of article 1 of the Charter the former power is to be exercised 'by peaceful means, and in conformity with the principles of justice and international law'. These criteria, in particular that of conformity with international law, are not expressed in terms as governing the suppression of threats to the peace, breaches of the peace, and acts of aggression.[6]

2. Art 32 of the Charter, under which a non-member of the Security Council, party to a *dispute* under consideration by the Council, may be invited to participate in the discussion, does not apply to a 'situation'; see *Advisory Opinion* of the International Court of Justice *on the Legal Consequences for States of the Continued Presence of South Africa in Namibia (South West Africa)* 21 June 1971 (South Africa not invited to the discussion by the Council in 1970 of the 'situation' in South West Africa; decision by Council that South Africa's continued presence there was illegal); see ICJ 1971, 16 at 22–23.
3. See Hasluck, op cit, pp 44-45.
4. See Kerley, 'The Powers of Investigation of the United Nations Security Council' 55 AJIL (1961) 892. As regards fact-finding, see Henkin, Pugh, Schachter and Smit *International Law; Cases and Materials* (2nd edn, 1987) pp 583–585.
5. Eg, in the case of the Falklands affair of 1982, the Security Council by resolution of 3 April 1982, called, inter alia, for the immediate withdrawal of the Argentine forces from the Falkland (Malvinas) Islands.
6. This appears to have been accepted by the majority of the International Court of Justice in the provisional measures phase of the *Aerial Incident at Lockerbie Case* (USA/UK v Libya), ICJ 1992, 3, but remains to be considered more fully at the merits phase of the case.

There are two kinds of enforcement action which can be decided by the Security Council: (1) Measures not involving the use of armed force. The Security Council may call upon member states to apply complete or partial interruption of economic relations, and of all means of communication, and to sever diplomatic relations. (2) Action by air, sea, or land forces where the measures under (1) are inadequate. This may involve a blockade of one of the parties concerned. The Security Council may decide whether the action necessary to carry out its enforcement decisions is to be taken by all or some member states only, and to mitigate any possible hardships, member states are to co-operate in carrying out the Security Council decisions (articles 48–49). Also, if any member or non-member is faced with special economic problems arising from carrying out the preventive or enforcement action decided upon, it has the right to consult the Council on these (article 50).[7]

These far-reaching powers of the Security Council have to be considered in conjunction with other provisions in Chapter VII of the Charter, namely, those providing for a Military Staff Committee composed of the Chiefs of Staff of the five permanent members, to advise and assist the Security Council on the military aspects of enforcement action (as well as on disarmament and armament regulation). In addition, article 43 provides for agreements between the Security Council and member states as to the armed forces and other assistance they can make available for enforcement action; this provision so far as concerns the armed assistance, etc, to be furnished to the Security Council has not yet been carried into execution although the Military Staff Committee has been considering principles and methods in this connection. The result is that the Security Council has not yet the necessary concrete basis for acting in a decisive manner through the Military Staff Committee, as intended by the provisions of Chapter VII of the Charter. However, as shown below, this was deemed not to preclude it, in the case of the Korean conflict and of the Congo situation, from validly authorising measures, with a view to restoring or maintaining international peace and security.[8]

Although member states of the United Nations are entitled to defend themselves individually or collectively against an armed attack, this right of self-defence is not to impair the primary authority and responsibility of the Security Council for enforcement action to maintain or restore peace (article 51).[9]

In its Advisory Opinion of 21 June 1971, on the *Legal Consequences for States of the Continued Presence of South Africa in Namibia (South West Africa)*, the International Court of Justice ruled that the Security Council's primary authority and responsibility for maintaining peace entitled the Council to make a binding determination (as it did in a Resolution in 1970) that the continued presence of South Africa in the Territory of South West Africa was illegal because its mandate

7. Eg Jordan in relation to the sanctions imposed on Iraq in 1990-1991.
8. See also *Advisory Opinion on Certain Expenses of the United Nations (Article 17, paragraph 2 of the Charter)* ICJ 1962, 151.
9. It was contended by Russia and certain other States that the North Atlantic Pact of 1949 was a violation of the Charter in that it permitted joint military action without the authority of the Security Council. In answer to this the signatories of the Pact stated that it was an agreement enabling the parties to co-ordinate beforehand plans for self-defence under art 51. See also Beckett *The North Atlantic Treaty, the Brussels Treaty, and the Charter of the United Nations* (1950).

for the Territory had terminated through failure to comply with its obligation to submit to the supervision of United Nations organs; see ICJ 1971, 16 at 54.

The question may be asked—are there any legal or practical limitations on the Security Council's far-reaching powers under the Charter? Legal limitations are those in articles 1 and 2 of the Charter concerning the 'Purposes' and 'Principles' of the United Nations; for example, the adjustment or settlement of international disputes that may lead to a breach of the peace is to be brought about by 'peaceful means, and in conformity with the principles of justice and international law' (paragraph 1 of article 1), and apart from enforcement action, the United Nations is not to intervene in matters 'essentially within the domestic jurisdiction of any state' (article 2). But even such legal limitations have to be adjusted to the circumstances; for instance the Security Council has in practice adopted the view that questions will cease to be 'essentially' matters of domestic jurisdiction if in its opinion they raise issues of international concern transcending state boundaries.[10] As to practical limitations on its powers, in addition to the 'veto', there is the limitation that every decison depends on receiving the agreement of a proportion of the members.[11]

Other important duties fall upon the Security Council under Chapter VIII of the Charter in connection with regional agencies and regional arrangements (see (iii) above).[12] It is to encourage the pacific settlement of local disputes by such means (article 52), and where appropriate may use these means for enforcement action under its authority. Generally speaking no enforcement action is to be taken by regional agencies or under regional arrangements without the authority of the Security Council except in regard to ex-enemy states. To preserve its primary authority, all action taken or intended to be taken under regional arrangements or by regional agencies to maintain peace and security is to be reported to the Security Council.

United Nations peace enforcement and similar operations

The distinction between peace enforcement and peace-keeping, hitherto observed in United Nations practice, has been found inadequate in the experience gained in many situations since the action against Iraq in 1990-1991, and having regard to the greater degree of flexibility shown by the permanent members of the

10. Hasluck, op cit, pp 56–57. This involves essentially a political judgment on the part of the Security Council; cf Bowett, op cit, p 25.
11. In his 1982 Report to the General Assembly, the United Nations Secretary-General made some significant suggestions designed to enable the Security Council to play a more active role in preventing conflicts rather than examining faits accomplis; these included: (a) more effective action through conciliation and compromise; (b) a more forthright role allowable to the Secretary-General under art 99 of the Charter (bringing peace and security threats to the Council's attention); (c) a diplomatic 'early warning' system, based on systematic fact-finding in potential conflict areas; and (d) effective follow-up action and support for Council resolutions, and getting Governments to give due effect to such resolutions.
12. The Soviet Union maintained that the North Atlantic Pact of 1949 was not a true regional agreement under Chapter VIII inasmuch as: (a) it comprised states located in two continents, America and Europe; and (b) it did not relate to true regional questions. The United States Government declared that the Pact was no different from the inter-American Security Arrangements of 1945 (Mexico City), 1947 (Rio de Janeiro), and 1948 (Bogotá) which are consistent with Chapter VIII.

Security Council following the collapse of the Soviet Union. New reflections on the powers of the Security Council have identified:

a. peace building (international regimes and in-country peace building);
b. maintaining peace (preventive diplomacy and preventive deployment);
c. restoring peace (peace making and peace keeping);
d. enforcing peace (sanctions and peace enforcement).[13]

It will be seen in what follows that some recent actions decided by the Security Council have a novel or mixed character.

The Korean conflict 1950–1953 provided a significant testing-ground of the Security Council's effectiveness as a peace enforcement body. At the time of the crossing by North Korean troops into South Korean territory in June 1950, the Soviet Union was absent from the Security Council, and the Nationalist Chinese Government, to whose credentials the Soviet Union objected, was represented on the Security Council. Hence the subsequent Security Council Resolutions, finding that a 'breach of the peace' had been committed, recommending assistance to the South Korean authorities, and providing for a Unified United Nations Command under United States direction, were taken without the Soviet Union's concurrence. The Resolutions did, however, receive the supporting vote of Nationalist China.

The Soviet Union challenged the validity of the Resolutions on the ground that any such vote thereon required her positive concurrence under the voting provisions of the Charter, and also the concurrence of the Government of the People's Republic of China, which was in its view the true legal government. In reply to the Soviet Union's contention, it was maintained that for purposes of determining whether the Soviet Union had or had not concurred, an absence had necessarily to be disregarded in the same way as, in practice, an abstention from voting,[14] and that the Chinese Nationalist Government rightly represented China.

The subsequent reappearance of the Soviet Union in the Security Council proved that United Nations intervention in the Korean hostilities had been made possible only by an unusual conjunction of circumstances—a situation favouring the non-exercise of the 'veto', the presence of American troops in Japan, and the possibility of appointing an American Staff in command of United Nations forces. Moreover, upon a close analysis of their terms, the Security Council Resolutions actually adopted were difficult to support as being a valid exercise of the powers conferred by articles 39–43 of the Charter (quaere, eg, whether the Security Council could make a 'recommendation',[15] as distinct from a decision, that member states furnish armed assistance). For this reason some writers have inclined to view that the 'United Nations' action in Korea was such in name only, but not in substance, and was nothing more than a voluntary,

13. See further the response of the Australian Foreign Minister to the Report of the United Nations Secretary-General Dr Boutros Boutros-Ghali *An Agenda for Peace*, June 1992: G. Evans *Cooperating for Peace: The Global Agenda for the 1990s and Beyond* (1993).
14. See also above, p 578.
15. See Stone *Legal Controls of International Conflict* (1954) pp 228 et seq, and *Supplement 1953–1958* (1959) pp 870–871.

collective effort under United Nations licence to restore and maintain peace and security in that area.

In the case of the Congo situation, 1960–1964, the Security Council's action[16] was without precedent. It resulted in the despatch of a United Nations Force to the newly independent Congo, not by way specifically of enforcement action against a state under Chapter VII of the Charter, but as military assistance for the purpose of preserving law and order pending the withdrawal of Belgium troops, as called for by the Security Council's Resolutions. After the Belgian troops had been withdrawn, the United Nations Force was maintained in the Congo for the same purpose, and more particularly in order to prevent the occurrence of civil war and to reduce inter-tribal fighting. Primary responsibility for carrying out the Security Council's mandate fell upon the Secretary-General. The basis of the Security Council's action was primarily that the internal strife in the Congo might, in the absence of such action, deteriorate into a threat to international peace.[17] Thus, it would seem, although this is not undisputed, that the Security Council (as also the General Assembly[18]) may *authorise* measures with a view to maintaining international peace and security, notwithstanding that these measures do not strictly fall within the pattern of enforcement action under Chapter VII,[19] and without the necessity of explicit adherence to the procedural requirements of the provisions in the Chapter.

However, in 1962–1963, the operations of the United Nations units in the Congo, involving the clearing of road blocks and the establishment of effective control in the Katanga area, assumed the character of veritable military enforcement measures; this action has been regarded by some commentators[20] as going beyond the scope of the role merely of 'peacekeeping' and/or 'policing', which was thought to be envisaged by the earlier Security Council Resolutions. The Congo cannot be regarded as a very clear case of the interpretation and application of the provisions of Chapter VII of the Charter, and remains controversial.

In the case of the Rhodesian situation, in 1965 and following years, there were initially three important Security Council Resolutions directed against the Rhodesian régime, established by unilateral declaration of independence from the United Kingdom. There were two Resolutions, to begin with, for so-called 'voluntary' sanctions of enforcement action, namely those Resolutions adopted in November 1965 (of a general nature) and April 1966 (more specific in character, and, inter alia, empowering the British Government to take steps 'by the use of force if necessary' to prevent ships taking oil to ports from which it

16. By Resolutions of 14 July, 22 July and 9 August 1960 (initial action).
17. Although this became controversial; some states objected that certain operations of the United Nations Force amounted to intervention in internal conflicts.
18. In an emergency special session called under the 'Uniting for Peace' Resolution, the General Assembly by a Resolution of 19 September 1960 in effect authorised the continuance of action under the Security Council's Resolutions.
19. The expenses incurred by the Secretary-General in taking such measures are expenses of the United Nations which may be apportioned among the member states by the General Assembly under art 17, para 2 of the Charter; see *Advisory Opinion on Certain Expenses of the United Nations (Article 17, paragraph 2 of the Charter)* ICJ 1962, 151.
20. See article by Professor Leo Gross 'Domestic Jurisdiction, Enforcement Measures and the Congo', *Australian Year Book of International Law*, 1965, 137 at pp 155–157.

could be supplied or distributed to Rhodesia).[1] The third Resolution was that adopted in December 1966 for selective 'mandatory' sanctions[2] (although there was no specific provision for enforcement if a state failed to apply them); this was indeed the first time that mandatory enforcement action had been decided by the Security Council. There was an additional Resolution in 1968, followed by subsequent related Resolutions on the Rhodesian situation. The situation constituted by the self-declared independent régime was declared to be a threat to international peace and security;[3] there appears to be little doubt about the legitimacy of this determination, which was one that was within the province of the Security Council to make, although there can be arguments, as in the Korean case, with regard to the applicability of the terms of articles 39–43 of the Charter. The vital point remains whether a situation, in a large sense within the domestic sphere, since it turned so much on the relationship of the new régime with the United Kingdom, is stricto sensu one within the ambit of Chapter VII of the Charter. There persists the uneasy thought that the gates are being opened wider than contemplated by those who originally drafted Chapter VII of the Charter; eg, quaere whether parent governments can activate the Security Council to take enforcement action against insurgents, or whether a federal government could similarly approach the Council for measures to be taken against a unilaterally seceding state, where, of course, there are circumstances somewhat similar to the situation in Rhodesia.[4]

These measures against Southern Rhodesia now belong to past history, although constituting a precedent for future Security Council action. On 21 December 1979, having regard to the decision that there should be created a new state, Zimbabwe, with majority rule, the Council decided to call upon member states to terminate the measures. Sanctions were dissolved, and the inalienable right of the people of Zimbabwe to self-determination was reaffirmed.

It is relevant to mention another instance of a mandatory embargo decided upon by the Security Council. By two Resolutions of August and December 1963, the Council had called for a ban on the sale and shipment of arms and related materials to South Africa. By Resolution adopted in November 1977, this ban was made mandatory. The Council also set up a Committee to supervise the

---

1. This was indeed the first time that the Security Council had made such a grant of authority to a single United Nations member to take forcible action, which would otherwise be unlawful. See generally Cryer 'Legal Aspects of the *Joanna V* and *Manuela* Incidents, April 1966', *Australian Year Book of International Law*, 1966 pp 97–98.
2. These included prohibition of the import of certain products and commodities from Rhodesia, and action to prevent certain exports and transfers of funds to Rhodesia, and as well as the supply of armaments, aircraft, and motor vehicles. The Resolution made specific reference to arts 39 and 41 of the Charter. On 6 April 1976, the Security Council, acting upon a recommendation from its Sanctions Committee, reaffirmed its earlier Resolutions as to mandatory and other sanctions against the Rhodesian régime, declared again that the situation in Southern Rhodesia constituted a threat to international peace and security, stated that it was acting under Chapter VII of the Charter (arts 39–51), and expanded the mandatory sanctions to include other items.
3. According to one view, this threat lay in the possibility of violent action by African States against Rhodesia, because of the treatment by the Rhodesian régime of the majority African population.
4. Sanctions came to an end with the political settlement in Rhodesia, the advent of majority rule, and the emergence of the new state of Zimbabwe in 1979.

implementation of the embargo,which Committee has since periodically reported to the Council on its work.

The enforcement action against Iraq in 1990-91, after Iraq attacked, and purported to annex, the neighbouring state of Kuwait, was doubly significant in the history of the United Nations. In the first place, the shadow of the automatic use of the veto by the Soviet Union against any perceived Western interest had been removed by the great political changes that had occurred in that country. The attitude of China, however, remained uncertain. In the second place, the enforcement action itself contained novel features, not least in its aftermath.[5]

On the day that Iraq invaded Kuwait, 2 August 1990, the Security Council in Resolution 660 (1990) voted 14-0 (Yemen abstaining) to condemn it and to demand Iraq's immediate withdrawal. In a close succession of ten further resolutions, passed between 6 August and 28 November 1990 the Security Council, acting under chapter VII of the Charter, decided on a range of sanctions against Iraq, including an embargo on trade and financial dealings (except for medical or humanitarian purposes), declared Iraq's annexation of Kuwait null and void, demanded the release of third-country nationals held in Kuwait and Iraq, established a maritime cordon to inspect shipping to and from Iraq, directed the freezing of Iraqi assets abroad, and condemned Iraq's taking of hostages, its deportation of Kuwaitis, and its destruction of Kuwaiti property and records. By Resolution 678, passed on 29 November 1990 (China abstaining, Cuba and Yemen voting against) the Security Council gave Iraq 'one final opportunity, as a pause of goodwill', to comply fully with all previous resolutions, and authorised 'Member States cooperating with the Government of Kuwait, unless Iraq on or before 15 January 1991 fully implements ... the foregoing resolutions, to use all necessary means to uphold and implement resolution 660 (199) and all subsequent relevant resolutions and to restore international peace and security in the area'. Iraq failed to comply, and 'Operation Desert Storm' began on 15 January 1991.

The legal basis for Resolution 678 (1990) was not entirely clear. Resolution 660 (1990) had expressly invoked articles 39 and 40 of the Charter, but in all subsequent resolutions the Security Council prefaced the dispositive paragraphs with the phrase 'acting under chapter VII of the Charter'. Chapter VII, of course, includes article 51, which confirms the right of individual and collective self-defence against armed attack. The notion that the Security Council might not be acting under article 42, which refers to enforcement by air, sea and land forces and which implies that the Security Council itself will take direct responsibility for those forces placed at its disposal under article 43, was strengthened by its reference to 'Member States cooperating with the Government of Kuwait', ie in the collective defence of Kuwait against armed attack. These states were principally the United States, the United Kingdom, and France. If this were the correct interpretation, those states might be thought to have had a freer hand in the conduct of hostilities, since self-defence is an inherent right and can be relied on to justify measures to respond to a rapidly changing situation until such time

5.   See M. Weller (ed) *Iraq and Kuwait: The Hostilities and Their Aftermath* (1993) (documents and commentary); E. Pisani *The Gulf Crisis* (1991); J.N. Moore *Crisis in the Gulf: Enforcing the Rule of Law* (1992).

as the Security Council can order effective measures to meet these changed circumstances. Yet another possible interpretation of the Resolution is that the Security Council was relying on the totality of its powers under chapter VII, express and implied. In the event, nothing occurred to require the legal basis of the action to be clarified.

Active hostilities ceased with the surrender of Iraqi forces on 2 March 1991. By the lengthy and detailed Resolution 687 (1991) of 3 April 1991,[6] the Security Council, again acting under Chapter VII of the Charter, laid down the conditions to be met by Iraq for a formal cease-fire to be effective. These conditions included: (a) the agreement of Iraq to the establishment of a boundary commission to demarcate the boundary between Iraq and Kuwait and to the institution of a border demilitarised zone; (b) Iraq's unconditional acceptance of the destruction and removal, under international supervision, of all chemical and biological weapons, and of all ballistic missiles with a range greater than 150 kilometres (as to which the Security Council established a Special Commission — UNSCOM — to monitor compliance); (c) Iraq's unconditional agreement not to acquire or develop nuclear weapons (as to which UNSCOM was also assigned monitoring responsibilities); and (d) the liability of Iraq to pay compensation for any direct loss or damage, including environmental damage, as a result of its invasion and occupation of Kuwait (the Security Council deciding also to create a compensation fund, a Commission to administer the fund and to decide on claims, and measures to enforce Iraq's contributions to the fund from its future export revenues). The Resolution maintained existing trade and other sanctions against Iraq with a view to their progressive relaxation dependent on the extent to which Iraq complied with these and the other demands made of it.

Almost immediately after the cease-fire Iraq began turning its forces against its own Kurdish population, which had long been restive. Villagers fled in great numbers to the mountains bordering Turkey. In resolving to act to protect the Kurds the Security Council had to seek a different legal basis for intervention. The preambular wording of Resolution 688 (1991) reflected the delicacy of appearing to intervene in matters 'essentially within the domestic jurisdiction of any state' (forbidden by article 2(7) of the Charter). Yet the scale of the human suffering involved was great. While reciting both these considerations, the Resolution referred to 'the massive flow of refugees towards and across international frontiers and to cross-border incursions, which threaten international peace and security in the region', thus bringing the matter within chapter VII, although that chapter was not expressly invoked.[7] Similar considerations underlay the institution of 'no-fly zones' in the south of Iraq in support of the 'marsh Arabs' threatened by punitive action by Iraq.

The experience of the aftermath of the enforcement action against Iraq served to widen the view taken of its powers by the Security Council, and encouraged it to include situations not previously regarded as coming within Chapter VII of

6. Text reproduced in (1991) 30 ILM 846. This Resolution was popularly dubbed 'the mother of all resolutions' in ironical allusion to the earlier boast of President Saddam Hussein that any attempt to expel Iraq from Kuwait would lead to 'the mother of all battles'.

7. Text in (1991) 30 ILM 858. See generally P. Alston, 'The Security Council and human rights: lessons to be learned from the Iraq-Kuwait crisis and its aftermath', (1992) 13 Aust YBIL 107-176.

the Charter. The situation in the former Yugoslavia after 1991 was essentially a series of civil wars in the various successor states, but with evidence of some external support. Hence, sanctions were imposed on the Federal Republic of Yugoslavia (Serbia and Montenegro), but the United Nations Protection Force (UNPROFOR), established in February 1992 in the territory of Bosnia-Herzegovina, was a more traditional peace-keeping force (see below) charged with creating conditions of peace and security, facilitating a settlement of the conflict, and ensuring the delivery of humanitarian relief.[8] But the situation in Somalia in 1992 had no external aspects other than the international resonance of concern at the massive sufferings of people, conveyed in the modern age primarily through television pictures. The Unified Task Force (UNITAF), which landed in Somalia in December 1992, was directed by the Security Council to protect deliveries of relief aid to the victims of the famine against warring bands, all effective government having collapsed. What began as a humanitarian mission underwent a transformation into a species of enforcement action, pursuant to Security Council resolution 814 (1993), under the name of the United Nations Operation in Somalia (UNOSOM), charged with the responsibility to work for peace, stability, law and order in Somalia.

Other actions of the Security Council have had differing or ambiguous legal justifications. An embargo on arms, and on all air traffic to and from Libya, was imposed by Resolution 748 (1992) in response to Libya's refusal to hand over two of its nationals, accused of responsibility for, or complicity in, the sabotage of an American passenger aircraft over Lockerbie, Scotland, to either the United Kingdom or the United States. The arms and oil embargo placed on Haiti by Resolution 841 (1993), however, was in response to the continued refusal of the military rulers of Haiti to allow the return of its democratically elected president.

The conclusion may be drawn that, in the practice of the Security Council since 1991, the breakdown of internal order in a state, humanitarian needs in cases of grave emergency, gross oppression of minority groups, and perhaps now grave abuses of human rights, including the right to democratic governance,[9] may be the occasion for the exercise of the powers of the Security Council.

United Nations 'peacekeeping'[10]

The word 'peacekeeping' is not used in the United Nations Charter, yet in the last fifteen years the 'peacekeeping' concept has emerged to receive as much attention as any other current or projected programme of United Nations action. Broadly speaking, United Nations peacekeeping has served as an anti-escalation device.

The use of the word 'peacekeeping' seems somewhat unfortunate. To be more precise, the issues involved are in what circumstances, in the absence of Security Council enforcement action, interposition forces, groups, or missions can be sent by the United Nations to areas of conflict, with functions related to the restoration or maintenance of peace, or the mitigation of deteriorating situations (eg, for

8. For documentation see D. Bethlehem and M. Weller (eds) *The Yugoslav Crisis in International Law* (1993).
9. T.M. Franck, 'The emerging right to democratic governance', (1992) 86 AJIL 46.
10. On the subject of such 'peacekeeping', see Cassese (ed) *United Nations Peace-Keeping* (1978).

observation, truce supervision purposes, cease-fire monitoring, negotiation, restoring freedom of movement).[11] Clearly any such interposition, where the Security Council has made no determination, is dependent upon the consent of the states concerned, as to the locality where the force, etc, is to function, as to the importation of supplies, and as to contacts with the conflicting entities or forces. Thus peacekeeping by the United Nations is essentially consensual, and in theory of a defensive or protective nature only. The Security Council has alone, under the Charter, executive responsibility to establish and operate a force compulsorily in the territory of a member state. According to the Secretary-General of the United Nations no peacekeeping operation 'could function or even exist without the continuing consent and co-operation of the host country' (see document S/7906, 26 May 1967). This was the principal justification for the withdrawal of the United Nations Emergency Force (UNEF) from Egyptian territory, prior to the Israeli-Arab hostilities of 5–10 June 1967, although for other reasons (eg, the applicability of a 'good faith' accord for the continued presence of UNEF), the withdrawal has been the subject of controversy.

There continues to be a deep division of opinion among member states, resulting in two independent impasses, one legal, and the other practical. Some countries are adamant that peacekeeping must be confined within the scope of Security Council action under Chapter VII; others hold that the consensual character of peacekeeping enables authorisation by the General Assembly or by the Secretary-General, within the ambit of the wider purposes of the Charter; while others object altogether to the principle of United Nations peacekeeping forces. In any event, the practical aspect of reliable financing of peacekeeping, in the absence of readiness by all states to accept mandatory assessments of contributions, is one that must be solved, even if the controversy over the legal issue could be settled. The system of voluntary contributions, eg, in relation to the funding of the United Nations peacekeeping operation in Cyprus (UNFICYP), has proved to be one fraught with difficulties.

In the case of the peacekeeping forces in the Congo (ONUC) and in Cyprus (UNFICYP), entrusted with functions of maintaining law and order, difficulties were revealed with reference to the observance of two necessary restraints upon a peacekeeping force, namely, not to intervene in internal strife, and as far as possible not to apply force beyond the necessities of self-defence.

For the reasons given above with regard to peace-enforcement, the United nations is now facing traditional and new situations requiring the interposition of forces with a new sense of the legal possibilities of action, but as yet with an unclear sense of the extent to which such action may be possible in practical

11. Illustrations have been the UN Emergency Forces in the Suez and Sinai areas, the UN Truce Supervision Organisation in Palestine, the UN Force in Cyprus, the UN Mission in the Dominican Republic (established in May 1965), and the UN Military Observer Group in India and Pakistan. The peacekeeping forces have been designated under various titles, eg, 'Truce Supervision Organisation', 'Disengagement Observer Force', and 'United Nations Force'. These would not exhaust the variety of the tasks which are contemplated by the protagonists of UN peacekeeping. According to L. L. Fabian *Soldiers Without Enemies, Preparing the United Nations for Peacekeeping* (1971) p 17, through United Nations peacekeeping 'cease-fires have been monitored, borders patrolled, troop disengagements supervised, truces guaranteed, hostile armies insulated at safe distances, internal security maintained, and essential governmental functions preserved'.

and political terms. The discussion provoked by Secretary-General Boutros-Ghali's report *An Agenda for Peace* in 1992 will continue.

The following are just some of the many UN operations of a peace-keeping or mixed character currently in progress. The United Nations Iraq-Kuwait Observation Mission (UNIKOM) was established in April 1991 to observe the border between the two countries after the cessation of hostilities. In February 1993 it was given additional powers by the Security Council to act as an armed force to prevent small-scale violations of the demilitarised zone established under Resolution 687 (1991) (see above). Earlier, at the conclusion of the Iran-Iraq conflict in 1988, the Iran-Iraq Military Observer Group (UNIIMOG) was established to supervise the cease-fire and to monitor the withdrawal of troops from the frontier. The United Nations Transitional Authority in Cambodia (UNTAC) was a large and ambitious operation established in March 1992 to bring about conditions in which it would be possible to hold free elections. Those elections were held in April 1993. The United Nations Operation in Mozambique (ONUMOZ) was established by the Security Council in December 1992 to assist in electoral processes and in humanitarian relief. Humanitarian relief was also the basis for the initial operations of the United Nations in Rwanda in 1994, but the situation at the time of writing was turning into one more resembling Somalia, and even more immense in the scale of suffering. Purely observer missions have been sent in such cases as the Angola Verification Mission (UNAVEM), the Mission for the Verification of the Referendum in Western Sahara (MINURSO), the Mission to Verify the Referendum in Eritrea (UNOVER), and the Observer Mission to monitor the border between Rwanda and Uganda (UNOMUR)

The Economic and Social Council[12]

This organ, operating under the authority of the General Assembly, is concerned with promoting economic and social progress and better standards of human welfare as well as the observance of human rights and fundamental freedoms. The United Nations Charter recognises that progress in these fields is essential to maintain peaceful and friendly relations between nations. The members of the Economic and Social Council are elected by the General Assembly for three years, and retiring members are eligible for re-election.[13] Representatives of any member state or of the 'specialised agencies' can participate in its discussions without vote.

Its particular role with respect to the co-ordination of the activities of the 'specialised agencies' has already been discussed in this chapter. Besides this part of its activities, it initiates studies, surveys, and reports on various economic, social, health, and related matters, and prepares draft conventions for submission to the General Assembly on matters within the scope of its powers, and is empowered to call international conferences on these matters (article 62 of the Charter). It has also played a primary part in the organisation of the programme of technical assistance for undeveloped countries. All decisions are taken by a majority of the members present and voting.

12. See as to the Economic and Social Council, Bowett, op cit, pp 58-72.
13. See para 2 of art 61 of the United Nations Charter.

The Economic and Social Council's work is 'sectionalised' through special Commissions of which four are regional economic commissions concerned with special problems in particular areas—Europe, Asia and the Far East, Africa, and Latin America; the others, the so-called 'Functional Commissions', deal with particular subjects such as Human Rights, Transport and Communications, Narcotic Drugs, Population, and Status of Women. There seems to be no limit on the number of functional or ad hoc committees, commissions, etc, which may be established under the aegis of the Council to deal with special subjects within its competence. In pursuance of decisions of 1982 the Council has taken steps towards streamlining its work, including the rationalisation of its processes of regional co-operation.

Of the three other principal organs of the United Nations, the Trusteeship Council and the International Court of Justice have been discussed above, in Chapters 5[14] and 17[15] respectively, and the Secretariat may now be referred to. The Secretariat consists of the administrative staff of the United Nations, and really represents an international civil service. Its chief administrative officer is the Secretary-General, who is appointed by the General Assembly on the recommendation of the Security Council.[16] The independent, international character of the Secretariat is specially safeguarded by the provisions of articles 100–101 of the Charter, which are expressed to bind both member states and officials of the Secretariat.[17]

9. THE INTERNATIONAL LABOUR ORGANISATION AND OTHER 'SPECIALISED AGENCIES' AND 'RELATED AGENCIES'

The International Labour Organisation (ILO) was originally created under Part XIII of the Treaty of Versailles 1919, but subsequently, to dissociate the Organisation as far as possible from the League of Nations and from the Treaty itself, this section of the Treaty was detached, and its clauses renumbered, and it emerged with the new title of the 'Constitution of the International Labour Organisation'.[18] This Constitution was amended in 1945, 1946, 1953, 1962, and 1964. Formerly the International Labour Organisation had some organic connection with the League of Nations but that was altered by the constitutional amendments of 1945 and 1946, and in the latter years it became a specialised agency linked with the United Nations by a special relationship agreement.

14. See above, pp 106-108.
15. See above, pp 446-464.
16. For discussion of the role of the Secretary-General in carrying out the provisions of the Charter, and in giving effect to decisions of United Nations organs, see Stein 'Mr. Hammarskjold, the Charter Law and the Future Role of the United Nations Secretary General' 56 AJIL (1962) 9–32. See also Meron *The United Nations Secretariat* (1977), and Schwebel *The Secretary-General of the United Nations; His Political Powers and Practice* (1952). On the question of the Secretary-General taking a more forthright role under section 99 of the UN Charter, in addition to 'quiet diplomacy' (eg, fact-finding, problem-monitoring, taking advice from military advisers), see Edward McWhinney *United Nations Law Making* (1984) p 223, and Henkin, Pugh, Schachter and Smit *International Law; Cases and Materials* (2nd edn, 1987) pp 583–586.
17. See above, p 556, for a reference to the 'loyalty' investigations of Secretariat officials.
18. On the history of the ILO, see Alcock *The History of the ILO* (1971); Sir Harold Butler *Confident Morning* (1950) ch IX (pp 155 et seq), entitled 'Birth of the ILO'.

From the outset, the main object of the Organisation has been to promote international co-operation in the sphere of industry and labour so that economic competition between states or other like conditions shall not militate against the realisation of minimum as well as uniform labour standards throughout the world. The Organisation's efforts are principally directed to bringing the legislation and practice of each state into line with the most enlightened modern conceptions as to the treatment of labour, and with changing economic and social conditions in each such country. The idea of social justice underlying its work has been made more manifest in the amendments to the Constitution of 1945 and 1946, and was given particular solemn expression in the Declaration of Philadelphia adopted by the International Labour Conference in 1944 and annexed to the Constitution. That Declaration reaffirms the principles that labour is not a commodity, that freedom of expression and association are essential to international progress, and that poverty is a danger to prosperity, and it also recognises that the obligation of the Organisation is to further among nations world programmes designed to achieve full employment, higher standards of living, the provision of facilities for the training and transfer of labour, and the extension of social security measures.

The outstanding feature of the International Labour Organisation is its tripartite character, as it is representative in its organs of governments, employers, and employees.

The three main organs of the Organisation are: (1) the International Labour Conference; (2) the Governing Body; (3) the International Labour Office.

The International Labour Conference is a policy-making and legislative body, being in effect a 'world industrial Parliament'. It consists of four representatives in respect of each member state, two representing the government and one each labour and management respectively in that country. Delegates speak and vote independently. Voting is by a two-thirds majority. The Conference promotes labour legislation in each state, by adopting: (a) Recommendations; and (b) Conventions. A Recommendation enunciates principles to guide a state in drafting labour legislation or labour regulations, and for this reason has been termed a 'standard-defining instrument'.[19] States, however, are under no binding obligation to give effect to a Recommendation, although they are duty bound to bring it before the appropriate national legislative authority. A convention is in the nature of a treaty, although it is adopted by the Conference and not signed by delegates of the member states. Primarily, it is conceived as a model for domestic legislation. Member states are under an obligation to bring the Convention before the competent authorities for the enactment of legislation or other action (article 19 of the Constitution). If a member state obtains approval for a convention, it is bound to ratify it, and thereupon assumes the obligation of applying its provisions. Also that member state is bound to report annually on the measures it has taken to bring its legislation into accord with the Convention.

19. See *The International Labour Code* (edn of 1939), published by the International Labour Office, p xii, and *The Impact of International Labour Conventions and Recommendations* (ILO publication, 1976) passim.

The Governing Body, which meets several times a year, is more or less the executive organ of the Organisation. It has a similar tripartite character to that of the Conference, being composed of 56 members, 28 representing governments, 14 representing management and elected by the employers' delegates to the Conference, and 14 representing labour and elected by the workers' delegates to the Conference. The Governing Body appoints the Director-General of the International Labour Office, proposes the Budget of the Organisation and supervises the work of the Office and of the various Committees and Commissions.

The amendments of 1945 and 1946 to the Constitution were made principally with a view to strengthening the provisions for the application of conventions adopted by the Conference, to make the Organisation completely independent of League of Nations machinery, and to enable it to co-operate more fully with the United Nations and other international institutions. This involved a thorough redrafting of article 19 of the Constitution concerning the obligations of member states with reference to conventions and Recommendations, including the addition of an obligation for member states to report from time to time on their relevant law and practice even where the competent authorities had not approved of the instruments submitted to them for approval and other action, and including also more specific provisions as to the application of these instruments within federal states. Further by article 19 of the Constitution, the term 'Convention' was substituted for the former misleading term 'Draft Convention', and in article 13 provision was made for the independent financing of the Organisation.

Besides conventions and Recommendations (so far more than 160 conventions and more than 170 Recommendations have been adopted) the Organisation has through its organs adopted less formal instruments to express its policies; for example, resolutions, conclusions, observations, codes of guidelines, and reports. Collectively all these instruments form an International Labour Code embodying world standards of labour policy. At the date of writing, there have been more than 5,000 ratifications of ILO Conventions. Other important features of the Organisation's machinery are the provisions in articles 24–25 of the Constitution conferring on industrial associations of employers and workers the right to make a representation to the Governing Body that a member state has failed to observe effectively a convention binding it; several such representations have been made. Then there is the procedure of complaint by member states set out in articles 26 to 34; this may lead to the appointment of a Commission of Inquiry and action against the state not fulfilling its obligations, to induce it to comply therewith. Supervision of the implementation of ILO instruments is carried out by a Committee of Experts on the Application of Conventions and Recommendations.

The third organ of the International Labour Organisation, the International Labour Office, represents the administrative or civil service staff of the Organisation, discharging very similar functions to those of the United Nations Secretariat and acting as a publishing house.

In the last two decades the International Labour Organisation has moved strongly into the field of expert advice and technical assistance, manpower organisation, productivity and management, education and development, the working environment, occupational health and safety, social security, and workers' education.

The 'specialised agencies' and 'related agencies'[20]
Besides the International Labour Organisation, there are the various 'specialised agencies' and 'related agencies', each corresponding to certain aspects of world affairs demanding organic direction by a specialised international administrative body. Thus the Food and Agriculture Organisation of the United Nations (FAO) is concerned with improving living standards and the nutrition of peoples, and with promoting the increased production and more efficient distribution of food and agricultural products.[1] The field of education, culture, knowledge, and science is covered by the United Nations Educational Scientific and Cultural Organisation (UNESCO), the sphere of international air navigation and air transport by the International Civil Aviation Organisation (ICAO), international banking and economic and monetary matters by the International Bank for Reconstruction and Development, the International Monetary Fund, and the affiliated International Finance Corporation, international cooperation in matters of shipping, navigation, and maritime safety by the International Maritime Organisation (IMO) (formerly the Inter-Governmental Maritime Consultative Organisation), the organisation and improvement of postal services throughout the world by the Universal Postal Union (UPU), whose origins as an institution date back to 1874–5, and the peaceful uses of atomic energy by the International Atomic Energy Agency (IAEA), established in 1956. Other bodies are the International Telecommunications Union (ITU), the World Health Organisation (WHO), the World Meteorological Organisation (WMO), the World Intellectual Property Organisation (WIPO), the United Nations Industrial Development Organisation (UNIDO), the International Fund for Agricultural Development, the International Development Association (IDA), and the World Tourism Organisation (WTO), whose titles indicate the particular functions they perform.

As to such agencies, it may be said in conclusion that they have so far fulfilled two objects, implicit in their establishment:

20. The term 'related agencies' is used to cover an institution such as the International Atomic Energy Agency (IAEA) which is not a specialised agency, but which has a working relationship with the United Nations, and the General Agreement on Tariffs and Trade (GATT).
1. Considerations of space have precluded a detailed treatment of each of the related agencies. However: (a) The sections in the present chapter dealing with the organic structure and composition of international institutions, their integration and co-ordination, etc, have been expanded in order to supply more detail as to the related agencies. (b) Much of the ground that would have been covered in separate detailed analyses of each body has already been included in the preceding portions of the chapter. (c) There is contained in the readily available and inexpensive publication in its latest edition, *Everyman's United Nations*, a concise treatment of each specialised agency, of the International Atomic Energy Agency (IAEA), and of the system of meetings of the contracting parties under the General Agreement on Tariffs and Trade (GATT) of 30 October 1947 to which a new Part IV (encouragement of development of the less-developed countries) was added in February 1965. For more detailed information, the reader is referred to the latest current edition of the *Yearbook of the United Nations*, and to the constitutions of the agencies related to the United Nations (see the *United Nations Treaty Series*). See also Oppenheim *International Law* (8th edn, 1955) Vol 1, pp 977–1029, C. H. Alexandrowicz *World Economic Agencies: Law and Practice* (1962) and Bowett *The Law of International Institutions* (4th edn, 1982) passim.

1. That, not only should they buttress and give vitality to the United Nations, but that they should draw strength from their association with the United Nations.
2. The involvement of the national authorities of different states into more direct and continuous association with the work of international institutions.

Note on bibliography

Treatises
Lists of the principal international law treatises are given in the following works:

a. Ingrid Delupis *Bibliography of International Law* (1975) pp 25–48.
b. J. Robinson *International Law and Organisation. General Sources of Information* (1967) pp 37–130.
c. Oppenheim *International Law* (8th edn, 1955) Vol 1, pp 99–105.
d. J. G. Merrills *A Current Bibliography of International Law* (1978).
e. S.M. Kleckner *Public International Law and International Organization: International Law Bibliography* (1988).
f. E. Beyerly *Public International Law: A Guide to Information Sources* (1991).

State practice and the practice of international institutions
The most authoritative compilation as to British practice (although a number of volumes remain to be published) is the *British Digest of International Law*, edited by the late Clive Parry, with the late Judge Sir Gerald Fitzmaurice as Consulting Editor. See also *British and Foreign State Papers*, covering the period from 1812 to 1970.

With regard to United States practice, there are the following important compilations:

Moore *Digest of International Law* (1906) 8 vols.
Hackworth *Digest of International Law* (1940–1944) 8 vols.
Marjorie M. Whiteman *Digest of International Law* (1963–1973) 15 vols, the successor Digest to *Moore* and *Hackworth*, and the *Annual Digests of United States Practice in International Law* (covering United States practice since 1973, and published by the Department of State).

See apart from these, *Foreign Relations of the United States, Diplomatic Papers* (formerly published under the earlier titles of *Papers Relating to Foreign Affairs,* and *Papers Relating to the Foreign Relations of the United States*) covering the period since 1861.

Two important collections of basic documents on United States foreign relations, embracing the period 1941–1955, are *A Decade of American Foreign Policy: Basic Documents*, 1941–1949, and *American Foreign Policy*, 1950–1955: *Basic Documents* (published by the Department of State). Volumes in this series for the year 1956 and following years have been issued under the title *American Foreign Policy: Current Documents*. See also the American Law Institute *Restatement of the Foreign Relations Law of the United States* (3rd edn, 1987).

On French practice, there is the important compilation, Kiss *Répertoire de la Pratique Française en Matière de Droit International Public* (1962-1972).

Schiffer *Répertoire des Questions du Droit International Général posées devant la Société des Nations* (1942), is a compilation devoted to the practice of the League of Nations. As to the practice of the United Nations, see *Repertory of Practice of United Nations Organs*, in 5 vols, with Supplements, and *Répertoire of Practice of the Security Council, 1946-1951* (1954), with Supplements to 1971.

Treaties and conventions

For the texts of modern or recent treaties and conventions, reference should be made to the following official compilations: (i) the United Kingdom Treaty Series (from 1892 onwards); (ii) the League of Nations Treaty Series; (iii) the United Nations Treaty Series (published in pursuance of article 102 of the Charter).[1]

Hudson *International Legislation*, published by the Carnegie Endowment for International Peace in 9 volumes, 1931-1950, and covering the period as from 1919, is an unofficial compilation of the more important multilateral treaties and conventions concluded in this time. The texts of the older instruments are printed in such collections as those of Martens, Dumont, Hertslet, Malloy, and other compilers of treaties listed in Oppenheim, above, Vol I, pp 108-111, and are now reprinted in *The Consolidated Treaty Series, 1648-1918* (annotated), edited by Clive Parry. See also Professor Parry's *Index of British Treaties, 1101-1958*. For the texts of International Labour Conventions, see *International Labour Conventions and Recommendations adopted by the I.L. Conference, 1919-1981* (1982).

For a useful guide to compilations of treaties, for purposes of research, see Ervin H. Pollack *Fundamentals of Legal Research* (1967) pp 421-450. For materials on the environment, see B. Ruster and B. Simma *International Protection of the Environment: Treaties and Related Documents* 30 vols (1975-1983).

An invaluable reference work to the current status of parties to multilateral treaties is M.J. Bowman and D.J. Harris *Multilateral Treaties: Index and Current Status* (Butterworths, London, 1984), with regular cumulative supplements published by the University of Nottingham Treaty Centre.

Judicial and arbitral Decisions

The decisions and opinions of the Permanent Court of International Justice and of the International Court of Justice are published in the official reports of these two Courts.

Hudson *World Court Reports* 4 vols, 1934-1943, published also by the Carnegie Endowment for International Peace, is an unofficial collection in convenient form of the decisions and opinions of the Permanent Court.

See also generally as to the case law of both courts, E. Hambro and A. W. Rovine *The Case Law of the International Court* 12 vols, 1952-1974, and J. H. W. Verzijl *The Jurisprudence of the World Court* Vol I (1922-1940), published 1965, and Vol II (1947-1965), published 1966.

For the municipal judicial decisions of all countries on points of international law, from 1919 onwards, see the *Annual Digest of Public International Law Cases*, the title of which was changed in the 1933-1934 volume to the *Annual Digest and Reports of Public International Law Cases*, and which as from 1950 has been published annually under the title, *International Law Reports*. Decisions of British Courts are to be found in the collection, Clive Parry (ed) *British International Law Cases* (first vol. published 1964). See also Clive Parry and J. A. Hopkins *Commonwealth International Law Cases*.

1. Treaties and international agreements entered into by the United States, 1895-1949, are published in the *Statutes at Large*; from 1950 onwards in the compilation, *United States Treaties and Other International Agreements* (TIAS).

The principal awards and adjudications of the Permanent Court of Arbitration are reprinted in Scott *Hague Court Reports* (1916), a second series of which was published in 1932. Other collections of arbitral decisions are the *United Nations Reports of International Arbitral Awards* (RIAA), Moore *History and Digest of International Arbitrations to which the United States has been a party* (1898) 6 vols, the same author's *International Adjudications Ancient and Modern* (1929–1936), A.M. Stuyt *Survey of International Arbitrations 1794-1989* (1990) and De la Pradelle and Politis *Recueil des Arbitrages Internationaux*.

Schwarzenberger *International Law as Applied by International Courts and Tribunals* Vol I, *General Principles* (3rd edn, 1957), Vol II, *Law of Armed Conflict* (1968), Vol III, *International Constitutional Law* (1976) and Vol IV, *International Judicial Law* (1986) are valuable major accounts of international law based mainly on international judicial and arbitral decisions.

Other outstanding works, rich in citation of the sources of international law, are J.H.W. Verzijl *International Law in Historical Perspective*, 9 vols (1968-1978), and Ch. Rousseau *Droit International Public*, 5 vols (1971-1983).

General

A most useful first port of call in researching any topic of public international law is R. Bernhardt (ed) *Encyclopedia of Public International Law*, prepared under the auspices of the Max Planck Institute for Comparative Public Law and International Law, Heidelberg. It was published in 12 instalments, 1981-1990. The first of the projected four volume library edition, updating and regrouping alphabetically the earlier entries, was published in 1992.

Throughout this book, there are references in the footnotes to certain articles, treatises, and textbooks, most of which are readily accessible, and may be consulted for wider reading on each of the different branches of the subject.

The leading periodicals in English in international law are the *American Journal of International Law* (AJIL) (quarterly) and the *British Yearbook of International Law* (BYIL). Mention may also be made of the *Canadian Yearbook of International Law* (*Annuaire Canadien de Droit international*), the *Australian Year Book of International Law*, and of the *International and Comparative Law Quarterly* (British Institute of International and Comparative Law). An important annual publication in India is the *Indian Year Book of International Affairs*, the 1964 issue of which contained a number of historical studies.

Leading and important foreign periodical publications include the *Annuaire Français de Droit International* and *Revue Générale de Droit International Public* (French), the *Netherlands International Law Review*, the *Soviet Year-book of International Law* (Soviet Association of International Law), the Zeitschrift für ausländisches öffentliches Recht und Völkerrecht (German), and the *Japanese Annual of International Law*.

Current, continuing compilations of legal documentary materials include *International Legal Materials* (ILM)(American Society of International Law), and the *United Nations Juridical Yearbook* (United Nations).

For bibliographies on international law, see Ingrid Delupis, op cit, J. Robinson, op cit, and Clive Parry *The Sources and Evidences of International Law* (1965).

A select bibliography on the law and practice of treaties is contained in the United Nations publication, *Laws and Practices concerning the Conclusion of Treaties* (1953) pp 141–189.

In the *Yearbooks* of the International Court of Justice there is much useful information concerning the Court, its adjudications, and its functions generally. Prior to the *Yearbook*, 1964–1965, these annual volumes contained an extensive bibliography of books, articles, and studies published concerning the Court, but the bibliographies are now being published separately in annual issues.

Index